FOR REFERENCE

Do Not Take From This Room

A

FINANCIAL
HISTORY

of the

UNITED STATES

From

*Enron-Era Scandals to
the Subprime Crisis
(2004-2006)*

Works by Jerry W. Markham

A Financial History of the United States
From Christopher Columbus to the Robber Barons (1492–1900)

A Financial History of the United States
From J.P. Morgan to the Institutional Investor (1900–1970)

A Financial History of the United States
From the Age of Derivatives into the New Millennium (1970–2001)

A Financial History of Modern U.S. Corporate Scandals
From Enron to Reform

A Financial History of the United States
From Enron-Era Scandals to the Subprime Crisis (2004–2006)

A Financial History of the United States
From the Subprime Crisis to the Great Recession (2006–2009)

A

FINANCIAL HISTORY

of the

UNITED STATES

From

Enron-Era Scandals to the Subprime Crisis (2004-2006)

JERRY W. MARKHAM

M.E.Sharpe
Armonk, New York
London, England

Library of Congress Cataloging-in-Publication Data

Markham, Jerry W.
A financial history of the United States : from Enron-era scandals to the subprime crisis (2004–
2006) : from the subprime crisis to the Great Recession (2006–2009) / Jerry W. Markham.
    v. ; cm.
    Includes bibliographical references and index.
    Contents: Enron and its aftermath — Other Enron era scandals — Corporate governance
reforms — Securities, banking, and insurance — Commodity markets — The rise of the hedge
funds and private equity — The mortgage market — A critical look at the reformers.
    ISBN 978-0-7656-2431-4 (cloth : alk. paper)
    1. Financial crises—United States—History—21st century. 2. Corporations—Corrupt
practices—United States—History—21st century. 3. Enron Corp—Corrupt practices—History.
4. Investment banking—United States—21st century. 5. United States—Economic policy—21st
century. I. Title.

HB3722.M375 2010
332.0973'090511—dc22   2010007754

Printed in the United States of America

The paper used in this publication meets the minimum requirements of
American National Standard for Information Sciences
Permanence of Paper for Printed Library Materials,
ANSI Z 39.48-1984.

EB (c)   10   9   8   7   6   5   4   3   2   1

For the Markhams

I am opposed to millionaires,
but it would be dangerous to offer me the position.

—Mark Twain

Contents

FROM THE SUBPRIME CRISIS
TO THE GREAT RECESSION (2006–2009)

Photographs follow page 622.

List of Abbreviations

ABCP	asset-backed commercial paper
ACORN	Association of Community Organizations for Reform Now
AMLF	Asset-Backed Commercial Paper Money Market Fund Liquidity Facility
AFSCME	American Federation of State, County and Municipal Employees
ARMs	adjustable-rate mortgages
ARS	auction rate security
B&Ls	building and loan societies
BIF	Bank Insurance Fund
BIS	Bank for International Settlements
CalPERS	California Public Employees' Retirement System
CARS	car allowance rebate systems or "Cash for Clunkers"
CBOE	Chicago Board Options Exchange
CBOT	Chicago Board of Trade
CDs	certificates of deposit
CDOs	collateralized debt obligations
CDOROM	Moody's risk model
CDS	credit-default swaps
CEA	Commodity Exchange Act of 1936
CFMA	Commodity Futures Modernization Act of 2000
CFPB	Consumer Financial Protection Bureau
CFTC	Commodity Futures Trading Commission
CIBC	Canadian Imperial Bank of Commerce
CME	Chicago Mercantile Exchange
CMOs	collateralized mortgage obligations
CoCos	contingent convertible bonds
CPDO	constant proportion debt obligation
CPFF	Commercial Paper Funding Facility
CRA	Community Reinvestment Act (1977)
CSEs	consolidated supervised entities

CTAs	commodity trading advisers
DCMs	designated contract markets
DCO	derivatives clearing organization
DOE	Department of Education
DTCC	Depository Trust & Clearing Corporation
DTEFs	derivatives transaction execution facilities
ECB	European Central Bank
ECMs	exempt commercial markets
ECNs	electronic communication networks
ERISA	Employee Retirement Income Security Act of 1979
ETFs	exchange traded funds
FASB	Financial Accounting Standards Board
FCIC	Financial Crisis Inquiry Commission
FCM	futures commission merchant
FDIC	Federal Deposit Insurance Corporation
FERC	Federal Energy Regulatory Commission
FFEL	Federal Family Education Loan
FHA	Federal Housing Administration
FHLBB	Federal Home Loan Bank Board
FHLBs	federal home loan banks
FinCEN	Financial Crimes Enforcement Network
FINRA	Financial Industry Regulatory Authority
FIO	Federal Insurance Office
FIRREA	Financial Institutions Reform, Recovery and Enforcement Act
FRBNY	Federal Reserve Bank of New York
Freddie Mac	Federal Home Loan Mortgage Corporation
FSA	Financial Services Authority (UK)
FSB	Financial Stability Board
FSLIC	Federal Savings and Loan Insurance Corporation
FSOC	Financial Stability Oversight Council
FTC	Federal Trade Commission
GAO	Government Accountability Office
GDP	gross domestic product
Ginnie Mae	Government National Mortgage Association (GNMA)
GSEs	government-sponsored enterprises
HAMP	Home Affordability Modification Program
HMDA	Home Mortgage Disclosure Act (1975)
HOEPA	Home Ownership and Equity Protection Act (1994)
HOLC	Home Owner's Loan Corporation
HUD	U.S. Department of Housing and Urban Development
IASB	International Accounting Standards Board
ICE	InternationalExchange
IMF	International Monetary Fund

IOSCO	International Organization of Securities Commissions
IPO	initial public offering
ISDA	International Swaps and Derivatives Association
ITIN	individual taxpayer identification number
JGBs	Japanese government bonds
KKR	Kohlberg Kravis Roberts
LBOs	leveraged buyouts
LGIP	Local Government Investment Pool (Florida)
LIBOR	London interbank offered rate
LTCM	Long Term Capital Management
M&A	mergers and acquisition
MERS	Mortgage Electronic Registration Systems
MGIC	Mortgage Guaranty Insurance Corporation
MLEC	Master Liquidity Enhancement Conduit
MMIFF	Money Market Investor Funding Facility
MOC	Mortgage Origination Commission
MRBs	mortgage revenue bonds
MSRB	Municipal Securities Rulemaking Board
NAIC	National Association of Insurance Commissioners
NAMA	National Asset Management Agency
NASAA	North American Securities Administrators Association
NASD	National Association of Securities Dealers
NASDAQ	originally National Association of Securities Dealers Automated Quotations
NAV	net asset value
NBER	National Bureau of Economic Research
NCUA	National Credit Union Administration
NFA	National Futures Association
NOW	negotiable order of withdrawal
NRSROs	national recognized statistical ratings organizations
NSMIA	National Securities Markets Improvement Act of 1996
NYBOT	New York Board of Trade
NYMEX	New York Mercantile Exchange
NYSE	New York Stock Exchange
OCC	Options Clearing Corporation
OCC	Office of the Comptroller of the Currency
OFAC	Office of Foreign Asset Control
OFHEO	Office of Federal Housing Enterprise Oversight
OPEC	Organization of Petroleum Exporting Countries
OSHA	Occupational Safety & Health Agency
OTC	over-the-counter
OTS	Office of Thrift Supervision
PennyMac	Private National Mortgage Acceptance Company
PIPEs	private investments in public equities

PPIP   Public-Private Investment Program
PWG   President's Working Group on Financial Markets
RBS   Royal Bank of Scotland
REIT   real estate investment trust
REMICs   real estate mortgage investment conduits
RESPA   Real Estate Settlement Procedures Act (1974)
RFC   Reconstruction Finance Corporation
RPF   Reserve Primary Fund
RTC   Resolution Trust Corporation
S&L   savings and loan
SAIF   Savings Association Insurance Fund
Sallie Mae   Student Loan Marketing Association
SBICs   small business investment companies
SEC   Securities and Exchange Commission
SEIU   Service Employees International Union
SILF   Student Loan Insurance Fund
SIMEX   Singapore International Monetary Exchange
SIPC   Securities Investor Protection Corp.
SIVs   structured investment vehicles
SPACs   special-acquisition companies
SPAN   Standard Portfolio Analysis of Risk
SPVs   special-purpose vehicle
SWFs   sovereign wealth funds
TAF   term auction facility
TALF   Term Asset-Backed Securities Loan Facility
TARP   Troubled Asset Relief Program
TIPS   Treasury inflation protected securities
TLGP   the FDIC Temporary Liquidity Guarantee Program
TSLF   Term Securities Lending Facility
UAW   United Auto Workers
USDA   United States Department of Agriculture
USFE   United States Futures Exchange
VaR   value-at-risk models
VCs   venture capitalists
YSP   yield spread premium

Preface

This is the fifth volume in a series on the history of finance in America. The first three volumes trace the development of finance in America from the colonial period to the beginning of this century. They are entitled *A Financial History of the United States: From Christopher Columbus to the Robber Barons (1492–1900)*; *A Financial History of the United States: From J.P. Morgan to the Institutional Investor (1900–1970)*; *A Financial History of the United States: From the Age of Derivatives into the New Millennium (1970–2001)*. The fourth volume describes the Enron era financial scandals and other developments in finance during the period 2001 to 2005 and is entitled *A Financial History of Modern U.S. Corporate Scandals: From Enron to Reform.*

This volume starts with the aftermath of those scandals, particularly the prosecution of the executives caught up in them. It also addresses the considerable concerns that have been raised by the Enron-era reforms and prosecutions, describing how the Justice Department and the then–New York attorney general, Eliot Spitzer, resorted to unseemly practices in order to gain convictions. In addition, this volume discusses the debate over executive pay and corporate governance practices that arose from the Enron-era scandals.

The history then turns to developments in the securities and derivative markets, covering hedge funds, venture capital, private equity, and sovereign wealth funds. It considers the development of the mortgage market in the United States, addressing the government housing policies that promoted subprime lending and describing predatory lending practices in the subprime market. A sixth volume in this series will address the events that preceded the subprime crisis and elaborates on that crisis in detail.

Acknowledgments

The author thanks Beth Peiffer for research assistance, reading, correction of the manuscript, and preparation of the index. He also acknowledges support from the Florida International University College of Law.

Introduction

The ten-year bull market that preceded the stock market crash in 2000 was an era of high expectations, as stock market indexes exploded in value, reaching heights undreamed of in earlier years. The Dow Jones Industrial Average doubled and then doubled again during that bull market, reaching a height of 11,722 on January 14, 2000. Spurred by the growth of the high-tech "dot.com" companies that had exploited the Internet in numerous innovative ways, the stock market bubble in the 1990s was described in 1996 by Alan Greenspan, the then–Federal Reserve chairman, as the result of "irrational exuberance."

Greenspan single-handedly burst the dot.com bubble through a series of punitive interest rate increases. More than $8 trillion in stock value evaporated in the ensuing downturn. The Federal Reserve's (henceforth, the Fed's) actions also helped push the country into the near-recession that greeted the newly inaugurated forty-third president of the United States, George W. Bush. Although the Fed reversed course and started cutting interest rates in January 2001, that action was too little and too late to prevent a downturn.

The economy encountered another setback as a result of the terrorist attacks on September 11, 2001. Those attacks not only brought down the World Trade Center and nearly emptied the financial district in New York, but also dealt a blow to the economy that sent stock market prices plunging. That catastrophic event was followed by a succession of accounting scandals of unprecedented proportions involving Enron, WorldCom, Tyco, HealthSouth, Global Crossing, Adelphia, and many others. The federal government prosecuted large numbers of executives ensnared in those accounting scandals. An "Enron Task Force" created by the Justice Department became noted for its zealous prosecutorial tactics, which were encouraged at the highest levels of the department. Despite its unseemly and often-vicious prosecutorial practices, the government suffered some embarrassing losses in several of the Enron-era prosecutions.

The Enron-era accounting debacles were joined by a series of scandals related to Wall Street, one of which involved several well-known financial analysts who were privately disparaging stocks that they were touting to the public for investment. That scandal was uncovered by the crusading New York attorney general, Eliot Spitzer, who would go on to launch numerous other attacks on financial services firms. One such campaign began after Spitzer discovered that mutual funds were allowing hedge funds to trade improperly in their shares. That trading resulted in large profits for hedge funds at the expense of retail investors. Spitzer again made headlines by attacking two giant insurance companies, Marsh & McLennan and American International Group (AIG), over their accounting and business practices. Spitzer then turned his attentions to the $187 million retirement package given by the New York Stock Exchange (NYSE) to its CEO, Richard Grasso. This led to Grasso's dismissal and to the transformation of NYSE into an electronic exchange. It also set off a war of words in both the press and the courts between Spitzer, on the one hand, and Grasso and his supporters, on the other. Grasso won that fight, but only after a long and costly court battle.

Spitzer used the notoriety gained from his attacks on financial services firms and their executives to launch a successful bid for the governorship of New York State. Spitzer won by a convincingly large majority, but soon learned that the hardball tactics he had employed as attorney general were not so well received in Albany. A hue and cry arose after revelations that Spitzer's staff in Albany had conducted a clandestine investigation of a senior leader in the state legislature who was resisting Spitzer's programs. Spitzer then shook the nation when he was forced to resign as governor after confessing that he was the subject of a federal investigation involving possible money laundering used to conceal his payments to a prostitution ring that he frequented.

The Enron-era scandals touched off a wave of populist anger over the enormous sums paid in compensation to executives at public companies. Numerous corporate governance reforms were sought to curb pay perceived as excessive and to put a rein on management. Those efforts all failed, as they have in the past. Another reaction was the passage of the Sarbanes-Oxley Corporate Reform Act of 2002 in response to the Enron and WorldCom scandals. This book describes how that legislation proved costly, how it failed to curb accounting misstatements, financial fraud, or bad business judgments at publicly owned companies, and how it caused significant erosion in America's once-dominant position in worldwide financial services.

This book examines the role played by hedge funds and other collective asset managers in the economy in the aftermath of the Enron-era scandals. It addresses the transformation of the securities and derivatives markets from open-outcry exchanges to electronic platforms, the role of clearinghouses, and regulatory concerns such as capital requirements. The transformation of the mortgage market into an "originate and distribute" model is described, as is the growth of subprime lending, which laid the groundwork for the subprime crisis—the subject of the next volume in this series.

A

FINANCIAL
HISTORY

of the

UNITED STATES

From

*Enron-Era Scandals to
the Subprime Crisis
(2004-2006)*

Part I

Enron and Corporate Reforms

1. Enron and Its Aftermath

The Enron Scandal

Background

At the height of its glory, the now-legendary Enron Corporation billed it-self as the "world's leading energy company." Enron owned pipelines and electrical generation facilities and even branched out into water production facilities around the world. The company was also noted for its innovative trading operations, which included a "gas bank" for natural gas purchases, an electronic trading platform called EnronOnline, the delivery of high-speed Internet transmissions through Enron Broadband Services, and a broad array of merchant investments.

Enron was picked by *Fortune* magazine as the most innovative company in America for five years running, and it was also ranked "No. 1 in quality of management." Enron's chief executive officer (CEO), Ken Lay, was called a "master strategist" in the press, and the Enron board of directors was ranked by *CEO* magazine as one of the five best in America. Enron's chief financial officer, Andrew Fastow, was given a CFO Excellence Award by *CFO* magazine. Those accolades were preceded by rapid growth in Enron's reported profits, and its stock price tripled during a two-year period. However, these glowing reports masked some serious problems encountered by the company as the new century began. Enron's disastrous investment in a massive power plant program in Dabhol, India, had been well publicized, but it was also facing huge losses in its Azurix water business, and elsewhere abroad, which was withheld from investors.

Enron's "mark-to-market" accounting for its trading programs and inven-tory made its balance sheet volatile and earnings uncertain as market condi-tions worsened and the value of those assets declined. In order to conceal its deteriorating financial position, Enron began moving assets off its balance sheet into various special-purpose entities called LJM1, LJM2, and Raptors. In the midst of these operations, Jeffrey Skilling replaced Ken Lay as Enron's

CEO in an orderly transition. However, Skilling unexpectedly resigned a few months later. That resignation touched off a crisis at the company, and Ken Lay was brought back to replace him.

Lay tried to restore confidence by assuring the press and investors that the company was sound and profitable. However, Enron continued its decline, and its accounting practices were being openly questioned in the press and internally. An Enron accountant, Sherron Watkins, assumed the role of a whistle-blower by objecting to Enron's accounting practices in a letter to Ken Lay after he returned to replace Skilling. An internal investigation concluded that there was no basis for her claims that Enron was engaged in improper accounting activities, but, unrelated to Watkins' claims, the company subsequently reported a $618 million loss in the third quarter of 2001, and it wrote down $1.01 billion in assets. Reporters for the *Wall Street Journal* began an investigation into Enron's accounting practices after that announcement. Their questioning led to the revelation that Enron's chief financial officer (CFO), Andrew Fastow, had engaged in some "related party" transactions with Enron while moving assets off its balance sheet. Related party transactions are suspect because they involve insiders at the company who are in a position to take improper advantage in the transaction. Fastow had profited handsomely from those transactions, and he was fired after the revelation of personal profits, which totaled over $75 million, touched off a firestorm in the press. Enron's stock then plunged, and it faced difficulty in selling its commercial paper on money markets. Lay tried to save Enron through a merger with Dynegy, a smaller competing energy company. In the midst of those negotiations, however, Enron announced that it was restating its financial statements for the period from 1997 to 2001, reducing profits by $586 million and shrinking shareholder equity by over $2 billion. Debt was thereby increased by $2.5 billion.

These problems lowered Enron's credit rating, which in turn triggered cash repayment obligations in several of Enron's off-balance-sheet subsidiaries. The effect was similar to a run on a bank. Enron soon exhausted all its credit lines, and its declining position effectively shut it out of the capital markets. Banks refused further lending after Enron announced that it had additional, previously undisclosed liabilities totaling $25 billion. Dynegy withdrew from the planned merger, and desperate efforts to obtain a rescue from the federal government failed. Enron declared bankruptcy on December 2, 2001. It was at that point the largest bankruptcy in American history, an honor it would not hold for long, as it was pushed aside a few months later by the bankruptcy of WorldCom, following another accounting scandal.

Government Response

The accounting scandal at Enron touched off a media and political storm that President George W. Bush responded to with a speech on Wall Street promising tough action. That action came in the form of aggressive Justice Department prosecutions of executives at Enron and other corporations involved in accounting scandals that were blossoming as the economy slowed and the stock market crashed. This prosecutorial assignment was carried out through a Corporate Fraud Task Force—a "financial crimes SWAT team" that was headed by Michael Chertoff, assistant U.S. attorney general and later secretary of homeland security. Chertoff acted with zeal, indicting hundreds of executives caught up in these scandals. A centerpiece of Chertoff's prosecutorial effort was the creation of an "Enron Task Force" in the Justice Department.

Justice Department prosecutors employed a number of techniques in the Enron-era scandals that were designed to break the will of the executives targeted for prosecution and to coerce them into guilty pleas. Such coerced pleas allowed prosecutors to avoid having to try a case that, given the complexity of the accounting manipulations employed at Enron and elsewhere, might be difficult to win. Hundreds of executives were arrested, and many were subjected to what became a ritual in the Enron-era scandals—the "perp walk"—in which executives were paraded in handcuffs in front of the waiting press. Ken Lay's staged, but memorable, perp walk featured his being shackled and led into the courthouse by an attractive female FBI agent.

This practice reached its nadir with the apprehension of an executive at another company caught up in an accounting scandal. John Rigas, the eighty-year-old head of Adelphia Communications, who was suffering from cancer, was arrested in a dawn raid on his apartment in New York and shackled for his perp walk. Rigas would have voluntarily surrendered at the location of the government's choice, but there was no drama in that. The cynicism of these theatrics was made clear when the domestic diva Martha Stewart, who was indicted on charges of obstruction of justice in an insider-trading scandal, was allowed to surrender at her leisure by the same U.S. attorney's office that had its minions seize Rigas in his home. Stewart was allowed to surrender and enter a plea of "not guilty" without handcuffs or any other restraints.

After the arrest of an executive, the work for prosecutors really began. They immediately started coercing lower-level employees to "flip" by offering lenient sentences in exchange for testimony against senior executives. If that tactic did not work, more charges were added so that the employee faced the possibility of a long prison term unless he or she "cooperated." If that coercion failed, the government approached family members in an effort to pressure the targeted employee. For example, as discussed below, Andrew Fastow, the Enron CFO, pleaded guilty and turned on Lay and Skilling after his wife was indicted, and prosecutors threatened to imprison them both so they could not care for their small children.

The next phase of the government's prosecution plan was stacking the deck against any executive demanding a trial. This included sending target letters to potential defense witnesses advising them that they might be subjects of a possible criminal prosecution in order to intimidate them so that they would be afraid to testify, lest they too be indicted. That tactic was employed against

Skilling, Lay, and Bernie Ebbers, the convicted former head of WorldCom. Then came the now-infamous "Thompson Memorandum," named after its author, Deputy Attorney General Larry D. Thompson. It stated that the policy of the Justice Department was that, in order to avoid indictment for the accounting misdeeds of their employees, public companies would have to "cooperate" with the Justice Department in its investigations. Because an indictment would generally destroy or cripple a public company, cooperation was virtually mandatory. According to the Justice Department, cooperation meant waiving attorney–client privilege, firing any executive targeted by prosecutors before trial or even indictment, and then cutting off their attorney fees, even if those fees were required to be paid by contract or state law.

The Justice Department seemed to have sought convictions at any cost. Where there was no crime, the Justice Department prosecutors simply made one up and forged onward to trial. Skilling and Lay were among those so targeted. It took prosecutors two years to invent a crime for which they could be charged. Enron's auditor, Arthur Andersen, was indicted on one theory but convicted on another, after the first theory imploded at trial. Although the Supreme Court eventually set aside that conviction, Arthur Andersen's business was destroyed, and some 28,000 of its employees lost their jobs. Some Merrill Lynch executives caught up in the Enron scandal were tried under a nebulous theory and jailed for a year before their convictions were thrown out. That did not deter the prosecutors, who merely made up another theory and continued their relentless pursuit of those defendants, demonstrating a zeal that would have made Inspector Javert proud. As the basis for many of these charges, prosecutor used the federal "honest services" fraud statute, a twenty-eight-word law that critics called vague and unfair because of its nebulous prohibition against corporate executives engaging in a scheme or artifice that would deprive shareholders of "the intangible right of honest services." In 2010, the Supreme Court ruled that the Justice Department had improperly applied that honest services charge to prosecute Skilling.

Sentencing abuses were next on the agenda. Prosecutors asked for a 215-year sentence for Rigas at Adelphia, but the judge only gave him a term of fifteen years, later reduced to twelve after an appeal. Ebbers, the WorldCom CEO, who was sixty-three and suffering from heart problems, was sentenced to twenty-five years in prison by Judge Barbara Jones. That sentence was upheld on appeal, even though it exceeded by many years sentences commonly meted out to those convicted of second-degree murder and child abuse. Indeed, life sentences are now the standard for senior corporate executives convicted in financial scandals. California, which for years banned the execution of murderers, sentenced the mastermind of a Ponzi scheme to 127 years in prison. Judge Denny Chin, of the Manhattan federal court, found such a sentence too short for seventy-one-year-old Bernard Madoff, who perpetrated the world's largest Ponzi scheme. Madoff was sentenced to 150 years in prison.

In the end, the Justice Department's harsh tactics gained guilty pleas from more than 300 executives and employees caught up in the Enron-era scandals. However, prosecutors suffered some embarrassing setbacks in the Enron cases that actually went to trial. Several of those convictions were set aside on appeal because of the flawed legal theories employed by the Enron Task Force. The Justice Department was also forced to revise the "cooperation" standards in the Thompson Memorandum, after being rebuked by a federal judge for using it to deny defendants their constitutional rights, but by then the damage had been done. The Justice Department had already run roughshod over anyone it targeted in the Enron-era scandals, and the effects of that misconduct could not be reversed, as evidenced in the Arthur Andersen case.

The Trials

The Arthur Andersen Fiasco

Enron's auditor, Arthur Andersen, was widely attacked in the press for not discovering Enron's accounting manipulations. That criticism turned into rage after the accounting firm reported that its Enron audit partner had ordered the wholesale shredding of Enron work papers. Because of that action Arthur Andersen became the first target of Chertoff's Enron Task Force. Instead of indicting only the audit partner that had ordered the shredding, Chertoff decided that Arthur Andersen itself had to be dismantled because he did not believe the firm was cooperative enough. Chertoff was unmoved by Arthur Andersen's offer of a massive settlement and the proposal of a restructuring of its operations, which would focus on preventing accounting manipulations in the future.

Chertoff's task of destroying Arthur Andersen was made easier by the fact that it was already staggering from a split with its consulting partners. The consulting partners had spun off their business into Accenture, which became a very successful consulting firm. Arthur Andersen was also embroiled in litigation over other large audit failures and was paying huge sums to settle suits related to Sunbeam and the Baptist Foundation of Arizona.

One of the worst of Arthur Andersen's problems involved the audit of Waste Management, a large trash removal company that had been forced to restate $3.5 billion in earnings in 1998. Arthur Andersen had failed to detect those manipulations and certified the accuracy of the financial statements containing those bogus earnings. Four Arthur Andersen partners were sanctioned by the Securities and Exchange Commission (SEC) for that audit failure. The firm agreed to pay the SEC a $7 million penalty, which was then the largest such sanction ever imposed on an accounting firm. Arthur Andersen also paid $220 million to settle class-action shareholder lawsuits stemming from the failed Waste Management audit engagement.[1]

Arthur Andersen was regrouping and dealing with those problems before the Enron scandal broke. That effort fell apart after Arthur Andersen reported to the Justice Department that its Houston office had shredded large amounts of Enron documents and had deleted computer files and e-mails concerning Enron. David Duncan, the Arthur Andersen partner in charge of the Enron account, supervised that destruction. Duncan was indicted and agreed to plead guilty to charges of obstruction of justice. As a part of that plea bargain, Duncan also agreed to testify against his employer, Arthur Andersen.

Arthur Andersen's negotiations with the Justice Department to avoid indictment as a result of Duncan's actions were to no avail. Department officials were concerned with failed audits by Arthur Andersen, including WorldCom, which imploded after the Enron scandal. Chertoff was also angered by a protest rally of Arthur Andersen employees urging the Justice Department not to indict Arthur Andersen. That rally made the news and even attracted the support of the Reverend Jesse Jackson. Chertoff knew that no financial services firm had ever survived an indictment, but went forward with the prosecution of Arthur Andersen anyway. The result of the indictment was the immediate destruction of that accounting firm and the loss of 28,000 jobs by those it employed. Adding insult to injury, the IRS later challenged the tax returns of Arthur Andersen partners who had written off the value of their capital accounts as a result of the closing of the firm.

Innocent bystanders were also harmed by the indictment. Arthur Andersen had proposed a settlement of $750 million for its Enron-related liabilities that was to be paid out of the accounting firm's future revenues. That offer was taken off the table after the indictment, which meant that investors received only a fraction of the offered amount after Arthur Andersen declared bankruptcy. Because of the indictment, Arthur Andersen was also unable to comply with an agreement to pay $217 million to the mostly elderly investors who lost their investments in the Baptist Foundation of Arizona, which had been running a Ponzi scheme that had gone undetected by Arthur Andersen auditors. Investors in companies audited by Arthur Andersen that were involved in other Enron-era scandals, such as WorldCom, were also denied any recovery from Arthur Andersen.

The Arthur Andersen criminal trial in Houston turned into a circus. The jury concluded that Duncan had not obstructed justice despite his guilty plea in which he had admitted that he had done exactly that. This was because Duncan was forced to admit on cross-examination that he did not have any intention to commit a crime when he ordered the destruction of the Enron documents and data. That should have finished the case, but the prosecutors also claimed that a lawyer at Arthur Andersen, Nancy Temple, obstructed justice, and the jury bought the prosecutors' claims with regard to some of that activity.

Temple had advised Duncan and other Arthur Andersen employees to make sure that they were complying with the firm's document retention policies. That advice triggered the shredding ordered by Duncan. The prosecutors claimed that Temple further obstructed justice when she directed Duncan to remove some wording from a memorandum to the file, which stated that a proposed Enron press release could be misleading.

Temple offered what seemed to be legitimate reasons for her conduct when she testified about her actions and Arthur Andersen's role in the scandal before Congress. However, the Enron Task Force prosecutors were able to keep her off the witness stand during the Arthur Andersen criminal trial by sending her a "target letter." No lawyer worth his salt would allow a client to testify under such circumstances, so Temple was not able to provide her explanation to the jury.

After some strong-arming and one-sided instructions from the trial judge, Melinda Harmon, the jury concluded that Temple's actions constituted obstruction of justice. Interestingly, no indictment was ever brought against Temple, and class-action claims against her were later dismissed. The prosecutors' hardball tactics succeeded at trial with a jury of people who generally trust the honesty and integrity of prosecutors. However, the Arthur Andersen conviction was overturned by unanimous decision of the U.S. Supreme Court, which found that the government had employed a legal theory that was unsupportable by the law it had relied on in the prosecution.[2]

The Supreme Court held that there was nothing inherently wrong with a corporation's ordering employees to destroy documents, noting that such "document retention" policies are common among corporations. The Court also pointed out the obvious: Those policies are designed to prevent information from falling into the hands of the government as well as others. The Supreme Court also faulted the trial judge for handing out one-sided instructions to the jury. Among other things, Judge Harmon had instructed members of the jury that they could find Arthur Andersen guilty of obstruction even if it "honestly and sincerely believed that its conduct was lawful."

Duncan was allowed to withdraw his guilty plea after the Supreme Court reversed the Arthur Andersen conviction. Duncan later settled civil charges brought by the SEC by agreeing not to appear before that agency as an accountant in the future. Three other Arthur Andersen accountants also settled with the SEC on account of their role in the Enron audits. They agreed to be barred from SEC accounting audits, if they could seek reinstatement after two or three years.

Six years after Enron fell, the SEC also suspended two other former Arthur Andersen audit partners because of their work on the Enron account. The SEC noted that Arthur Andersen had identified Enron as a maximum risk audit client, and the SEC asserted that the audit partners should have realized that many risk factors for fraud were present that they should have considered in their audit activities. Of course, no one suspected any fraud at Enron until after its failure, but the SEC's 20/20 hindsight was, as usual, perfect, even though with all its resources that agency was caught unawares by the Enron scandal, just as the auditors had been.

The reversal of the Arthur Andersen conviction was a stunning setback for the Enron Task Force, but it came too late to save that firm and the jobs of its employees. Aside from the impact on Arthur Andersen employees, a study by the London School of Economics determined in April 2008 that the remaining Big Four accounting firms were able to increase their fees because of their dominance of the market.

The Nigerian Barge Fiasco

The Enron Task Force next turned its attention to what became known as the Nigerian barge case. That prosecution related to the purported $28 million sale by Enron in 1999 of some barges to a special-purpose entity called Ebarge, which had been created by Merrill Lynch, the giant brokerage firm that would spectacularly fail during the subprime crisis. The barges, anchored off the coast of Nigeria, were used as a platform for electricity generators. The government charged that there was no true sale of the barges to Merrill Lynch because Enron CFO Fastow had assured Merrill that Enron would repurchase the barges six months later, at a profit to Merrill Lynch of 15 percent. The government claimed that the transaction between Merrill Lynch and Enron was a sham used to allow Enron to book improperly $12 million in earnings that should have been reported as debt. In light of the billions of dollars in losses by Enron, and the massive accounting schemes used to inflate Enron's earnings by billions of dollars, $12 million seemed like pocket change. The transaction, nevertheless, for some reason enraged the Enron Task Force, and it prosecuted the case with zeal far beyond its monetary value.

The Enron Task Force indicted four employees at Merrill Lynch, as well as three at Enron, including Fastow. The defendants included Dan Boyle, an Enron vice president of finance; Sheila Kahanek, an Enron accountant; Daniel Bayly, chairman of Merrill Lynch's investment banking group; and James Brown, Robert Furst, and William Fuhs, who worked for Merrill Lynch's investment banking group. Jeff McMahon, who replaced Fastow as Enron's CFO and also served as the company's president, had proposed the Nigerian Barge deal to Merrill Lynch. For unknown reasons, McMahon was not indicted, but he did agree late in 2007 to settle SEC charges concerning his involvement in that transaction by paying a civil penalty of $300,000. McMahon was also barred from serving as an officer or director of a publicly traded company for five years.

Merrill Lynch settled with the prosecutors under a deferred prosecution agreement in which it agreed to cooperate with the Enron Task Force to ensure the conviction of the indicted Merrill executives and to create an internal compliance committee that would report to a lawyer approved by the Enron Task Force. Merrill Lynch was forced to agree to those requirements because, as Arthur Andersen and Drexel Burnham Lambert, a brokerage firm caught up in the Michael Milken scandal in the 1980s, had discovered, an indictment of a financial services firm could prove fatal. That knowledge gives prosecutors great leverage and allows them to intrude deeply into the operations of financial services firms whenever there is employee misconduct. Merrill Lynch did have one success in the affair. A shareholder derivative action seeking damages because of the participation of Merrill Lynch executives in the Nigerian barge deal was dismissed.

Ben F. Glisan, Jr., a former Enron treasurer who had pleaded guilty to criminal charges for his role in the Enron affair (see below), was the government's principal witness at the Nigerian barge trial, which lasted six weeks. Glisan, dressed in prison attire, testified that the transaction was a sham designed to move the barges off Enron's books temporarily by treating it as a sale to Merrill Lynch. This "risk-free" transaction was needed to boost earnings at year-end in order to help Enron meet analysts' expectations and thus keep Enron's stock price rising.

Other evidence showed that James Brown, one of the indicted Merrill Lynch employees, had raised internal concerns at his company regarding the "reputational risk" of "aid[ing]/abetting Enron Income stmt. manipulation."[3] A Merrill Lynch lawyer had also raised concerns with the year-end nature of the deal. A Merrill Lynch financial analyst, Tina Trinkle, testified that she had participated in a conference call with Bayly in which Enron employees had told him that the repurchase agreement could not be put in writing because the creation of such a record might come to the attention of the auditors, and would impair the favorable accounting treatment that Enron was seeking through the deal.

By the time of the Nigerian barge trial, Fastow had pleaded guilty and agreed to cooperate with the government, but he did not appear to testify. That seemed strange since he was the one who had allegedly promised to repurchase the barges from Merrill Lynch at a guaranteed profit. Observers thought the government was saving Fastow for the Lay and Skilling trial on charges of fraud and other misconduct stemming from their roles as CEOs at Enron. Actually, the reason Fastow was not called by the government to testify was that he had told the FBI that no such promise had been made. Rather, it was discovered after the Nigerian barge trial that Fastow had advised the FBI that he had made that statement to other Enron employees in order to "light a fire" under them to find a buyer to take the barges permanently.[4]

That information was not provided to the defendants as required by law, and the jury convicted all but Sheila Kahanek, the Enron in-house accountant. The government then asked for a fourteen-year sentence for Bayly on the grounds that his conduct had caused the failure of Enron. That claim was, of course, completely absurd. The transaction was minor in relation to Enron's other problems. Moreover, Bayly did not profit from the transaction and did not structure it or sign off on it. He had merely discussed it with Fastow and internally at Merrill Lynch. Such a draconian sentence for such minor involvement was deemed excessive by many in the business community. Bayly was also an unlikely criminal. He was known as a low-key, amiable, and very cautious investment banker, who was preparing to retire before the Enron case exploded after having worked at Merrill Lynch for thirty years without a blemish on his record.

The trial judge, Ewing Werlein, Jr., imposed a sentence on Bayly less severe than that sought by prosecutors, but it was still stiff. Bayly was sentenced to thirty months in prison, and similar sentences were imposed on the other defendants. In addition, the judge denied the defendants bail pending their appeals; an unusual punishment for what even Judge Werlein called a relatively benign crime. However, the hysteria engendered by the Enron scandal bent all rules. As if that were not enough, Bayly was sent to a maximum-security prison, where he was housed with hardened criminals some 700 miles from his family.

Bayly's appeal was argued before the Court of Appeals for the Fifth Circuit several months later. After listening to his lawyer's arguments, the court ordered Bayly and two other Merrill Lynch executives, with the exception of Brown, to be released on bail pending its decision on the appeal. Bayly had been in jail almost a year before that release. On August 1, 2006, the appeals court ruled on the defendants' appeals. Brown's perjury and obstruction conviction was upheld because he had falsely testified before the grand jury that there was no agreement with Enron for the repurchase of the barges. However, the court reversed all the defendants' convictions on mail and wire fraud charges. The court held that the defendants were not guilty of "honest services" mail and wire fraud, as charged in the government indictment. (That statute prohibits any scheme or artifice that would deprive a person of "the intangible right of honest services.") Such a charge requires the government to show that defendants defrauded their employer by some dishonest act, usually bribery or kickbacks. In this case, the court found that the defendants' actions and consequent enhanced compensation were consistent with the goals set by their corporations and both mutually benefited.[5]

This was a stunning setback for the Enron Task Force because it had claimed that the case was essentially a slam dunk. However, that reversal did not stop the government's crusade against Merrill Lynch executives. Although the Enron Task Force had been disbanded, prosecutors announced early in 2007 that they planned to retry three of the Merrill Lynch defendants whose convictions had been overturned by the appeals court—notwithstanding the constitutional bar against double jeopardy. The appeals court had stated in its decision setting aside the convictions that it was not ruling that no fraud had occurred, only that the prosecutors had not proved their theory of a transgression of "honest services." The prosecutors claimed that this gave them leave to adopt a new theory of the crime, which they did in an amended indictment.

Judge Werlein initially allowed the prosecutors to proceed, but directed that Brown be tried separately. The retrial of Bayly and Furst was scheduled to begin in January 2008, but was postponed to allow another appeal on the issue of double jeopardy. In its decision on June 16, 2009, the court held that double jeopardy was not involved.[6] However, just two days later, the Supreme Court held that double jeopardy did bar a retrial in another Enron-related case. Bayly and Furst's retrial was set for May 2010, but the government dropped the charges against Bayly in January 2010, after he settled a related civil case brought by the SEC by agreeing to pay $300,000 into an Enron investor recovery fund. The government continued to insist on a retrial for Furst, but a settlement was reached when the prosecutors agreed to drop all charges after Furst successfully served one year of probation.

The Court of Appeals for the Fifth Circuit had earlier ruled that there was insufficient evidence to support the conviction of William Fuhs, the other convicted Merrill Lynch employee, so he could not be retried. Dan Boyle, the Enron vice president, did not appeal and served out his sentence. Government prosecutors wanted James Brown to serve out the remainder of his original nearly four-year prison sentence even though the appeals court had overturned three of the five counts on which he had been convicted. Brown had served sufficient time under sentencing guidelines to satisfy the counts on which he was convicted. However, the government wanted him to be retried on the counts reversed by the appeals court. Defense lawyers had complained that the government prosecutors were trying to coerce Brown into testifying against his fellow executives through these hardball tactics. Brown's retrial was delayed to allow the court to consider defense claims that government prosecutors improperly withheld evidence. Prosecutors dropped those charges just before trial. Brown continued to fight his prior conviction.

The government spent untold sums to prosecute the Nigerian barge case, which dragged on for years, and it imposed undue hardship on the defendants for a relatively minor matter that turned into a complete fiasco. The matter could have been easily handled in civil court by the SEC and appropriate sanctions negotiated with the parties. Instead, the Department of Justice chose to bend the criminal laws and use its massive resources to beat the defendants into submission, all for the purpose of making the Justice Department look tough in the Enron affair.

Broadband Services Prosecutions

Another Enron Task Force prosecution was underway before the appeals court's reversal of the Nigerian barge convictions. That case arose after Enron unsuccessfully tried to enter the Internet market as a provider through Enron Broadband Services, an Enron unit headed by Kenneth Rice. This business unit sought to construct and manage a nationwide fiber-optic network that would provide expanded bandwidth transmission of data in greater amounts and at higher speeds than was possible with other technology. Enron also created a market in bandwidth capacity.

Enron Broadband Services grabbed media attention with the announcement of a joint venture with Blockbuster Video that would provide videos on demand by streaming them to consumers over the Internet. Enron widely touted these operations as successful and claimed that they would earn billions of dollars in profits. In fact, the joint venture with Blockbuster was a disaster for Enron and caused large losses because it failed to overcome several technical problems that made it impractical, at the time, to stream video into consumers' homes and demand for the product was, in any event, very low.

The prosecutors charged that those problems were covered up by false press releases claiming that technical problems had been overcome and that the business would be wildly profitable. Prosecutors also charged that losses at Enron Broadband Services were concealed through various accounting manipulations that boosted Enron's earnings from what prosecutors charged was a sham sale of future earnings at inflated prices that were unlikely. Despite those losses, in 2000, Kenneth Rice was paid $47 million, more than Skilling and Lay earned that year.

The Enron Task Force indicted the entire senior management at Enron Broadband Services. Rice was charged with selling 1.2 million Enron shares for $76 million at a time when he knew that Enron Broadband Services was in trouble. The Rice indictment contained forty counts related to his promotion of the failing entity. If found guilty on all counts, Rice would have faced decades in prison. The alternative was a guilty plea with a much-reduced sentence. Rice chose the latter option, pleading guilty to a single count, and agreed to forfeit $13.7 million.

Rice's guilty plea also required him to testify against his fellow Enron Broadband Services executives and then to testify against Skilling and Lay in their trial. This posed no problem to Rice. Enron Broadband Services was originally based in Portland, Oregon, as a part of Portland General Electric, which Enron had acquired to expand its access to electricity markets, particularly California. However, in a power play over its management, Rice tried to have the unit moved to Houston, which created much animosity toward Rice among executives wishing to stay in Portland. He would reciprocate with his testimony at the Broadband trial.

The five defendants were charged with making $160 million in profits from their Enron stock by helping to boost its price through a series of false statements made over a two-year period concerning Broadband Services' capabilities. The Broadband Services trial lasted three months, starting in April 2005. Rice was the government's principal witness, but he made a serious misstep when he wrongly testified that a film of Skilling talking up Enron had been shown to financial analysts. Skilling appeared at the trial to observe its proceedings before his own trial, but Vanessa Gilmore, the federal district court judge hearing the case, had him removed from the courtroom.

In response to Rice's testimony, the defendants testified that he was out of touch with Broadband's business and that he did not understand the technology. The defendants also testified that their claims as to the capabilities of Broadband Services were accurate. They were able to stream video over the Internet; the Broadband division even streamed the Country Music Awards live. The defendants further testified that the press releases they prepared were vetted by technology experts and were true to the best of their knowledge.

Despite Rice's testimony, the jury hung on several charges and acquitted the defendants on others. Three of the five defendants in that action—F. Scott Yeager,

Joseph Hirko, and Rex Shelby—were re-indicted on the charges on which the jury could not reach a decision. This was the government's eighth superseding indictment of these defendants. They appealed that action, but the appeals court held that they could be tried again on those charges. The U.S. Supreme Court agreed to review the appeals court's decision to determine whether a retrial was permissible. The Supreme Court ruled on June 18, 2009, that a retrial would constitute double jeopardy, but left open some issues on money laundering and insider trading for the appeals court to reconsider.[7] The prosecutors used that opening to continue their relentless pursuit of these individuals. Hirko finally threw in the towel in September 2009 and agreed to a plea bargain. He was sentenced to sixteen months in prison and ordered to pay $8.7 million in restitution.

Meanwhile, the remaining two of the original five defendants, Michael W. Krautz and Kevin A. Howard, were retried in a proceeding that took place at the same time as Skilling and Lay's trial, in another part of the same courthouse in Houston. That proximity concerned the Broadband defendants when the Lay and Skilling convictions were announced just before the Broadband Services jury began its deliberations. The Broadband Services lawyers requested that Judge Gilmore question the Broadband jurors on whether they were prejudiced by those verdicts, but she refused to do so.

Surprisingly, in view of the ongoing Enron hysteria in Houston, the jury acquitted Krautz. Howard was convicted, but that conviction was later set aside by Judge Gilmore because it was based on the same "honest services" theory that had been thrown out by the appeals court in the Nigerian barge case following the Broadband trial. The prosecutors appealed a portion of that decision, which also overturned a conviction for falsifying Enron's books and records. The appeals court rejected that appeal on February 12, 2008, and affirmed the district court's dismissal of the charges. Among other things, the appeals court found that the government never proved who actually falsified Enron's books and records and that its conspiracy charge against Howard was "tainted" by the prosecution's improper "honest services" claim.[8] The prosecution, nevertheless, sought and was allowed a retrial on whether Howard had caused Enron's SEC filings to be false. Howard then agreed to a guilty plea in exchange for the prosecution's commitment not to seek a sentence exceeding twelve months of home detention. Judge Gilmore thereafter sentenced Howard to nine months of home confinement and a $25,000 fine.

In the meantime, Rice began serving his two-year sentence in July 2007. Another Broadband executive, Kevin Hannon, pleaded guilty and was also serving a two-year sentence. However, the government had little else to show for this misguided prosecution.

The NatWest Three

The excessive zeal of the task force prosecutors turned another Enron prosecution into an international incident, which did nothing to help repair America's already tattered image abroad. That case involved three bankers working at the London offices of the NatWest Bank (now the Royal Bank of Scotland, which was nationalized by the UK government during the subprime crisis). Those bankers, David Bermingham, Gary Mulgrew, and Giles Darby, participated in a transaction with Fastow in which he purported to hedge the price of a stock position held by Enron in a company called Rhythms NetConnections. This hedge was implemented through a special-purpose entity (SPE) called LJM Swap Sub, which required outside funding to meet accounting requirements for such transactions. Credit Swiss First Boston and NatWest supplied that "independent" ownership capital.

The Rhythms NetConnections stock subsequently rose in value, and Fastow arranged with the three NatWest bankers to sell NatWest's now-profitable position in that SPE to another entity at a price well below its actual value. The NatWest bankers were then able to make a profit of $7.3 million when the Rhythms NetConnections stock was resold. Fastow skimmed off an additional $4.5 million in that sale for his private foundation. His assistant, Michael Kopper, received a like amount, and Fastow doled out another $3.3 million to other Enron employees participating in the transaction.

The three NatWest bankers were charged by the Enron Task Force in Houston with defrauding NatWest, despite the absence of a complaining witness in the form of the bank or any of its officers. Prosecutors claimed that the $7.3 million profit kept by the three individual bankers belonged to NatWest and should have been turned over to the bank. Equally bizarre was the fact that the prosecution was brought in Houston, even though the crime was alleged to have occurred in London, where the purported victim resided, as did the three bankers who purportedly committed the crime.

The NatWest bankers fought their extradition with vigor, even hiring a public relations firm to fight their cause. They battled unsuccessfully through the British courts and then appealed to the British home secretary, Charles Clarke. Clarke denied their petition and ordered their extradition under a newly passed treaty with the United States, which had been adopted in order to make it easier to extradite terrorists. That treaty allowed U.S. prosecutors to demand extradition of British citizens from the UK without any showing of a *prima facie* case that a crime has occurred. Ironically, the United States had not yet even signed the treaty.

The extraterritorial actions of the Enron Task Force in prosecuting and extraditing the three NatWest bankers caused outrage in England. The NatWest bankers became a cause célèbre in that country, where they were called the "NatWest Three," an appellation reminiscent of famous cases in which defendants were unfairly prosecuted because of their race or political views. The supporters of the NatWest Three included several politicians and human rights activists. The House of Lords voted to overturn the extradition treaty with the United States, but a vote on the issue failed in Parliament. Adding intrigue to the affair, Neil Coulbeck, a fellow NatWest employee and possible informant against the NatWest Three, was found dead in a London park, an apparent suicide. The NatWest bankers were nonetheless arrested and flown to the United States, where they arrived in court unshaven and disheveled.

The NatWest Three were released on bail by a federal magistrate, but were restricted in their movements to the Houston area and were prohibited from visiting their families in London. That was no small hardship. One of the defendants had five children living in London, one with a learning disability. Another of the NatWest Three had sole custody of his ten-year-old son in London, and the third defendant had a wife and three children there. The NatWest Three were also required to maintain separate residences in Houston, so their expenses, while awaiting trial, were tripled. One of the defendants called these restrictions "psychological torture." A correspondent for the *Financial Times* in London called it "judicial torture."[9]

The NatWest Three claimed in court papers that the Enron Task Force was withholding exculpatory information from them and that they were being prevented from obtaining testimony and evidence from employees at their old employer. The NatWest Three also protested the prosecutors' "honest services" charge in the indictment for wire fraud. The prosecutors dropped that charge after it was rejected by the Fifth Circuit in the Nigerian barge case, but then amended the indictment on the basis of a new theory, simple theft.

After awaiting trial in Houston for more than two years, the NatWest Three had had enough and each pleaded guilty to one count of wire fraud. The prosecutor agreed to recommend a sentence of thirty-seven months in prison for the defendants, which is what they received. They were also required to repay the Royal Bank of Scotland the $7.3 million in profit that they obtained from their Enron transaction. The defendants asked to be allowed to serve their sentence in England, so that they could be closer to their families, and the federal prosecutors agreed not to oppose that request as a part of the plea bargain. In the meantime, the Houston court rejected a request by Gary Mulgrew to return briefly to London to contest the abduction of one of his children by his former wife, who took the child to Tunisia in order to be with a boyfriend. The NatWest Three were initially sent to a federal prison in Pennsylvania and were subsequently transferred to an English prison under the Department of Justice's International Prisoner Transfer Program, which allows foreign prisoners to serve their time in a prison in their own country.

After this experience England was not as accommodating in extraditing those accused of business crimes in the United States. The British House of Lords refused to extradite Ian Norris, the CEO of Morgan Crucible, to the United States to face price-fixing charges. Their lordships ruled that such conduct was not illegal in Great Britain at the time it occurred. Norris still faced the possibility of extradition on charges of obstruction of justice in the United States, and his appeal of extradition on that charge was dismissed in February 2010.

The Lay and Skilling Criminal Trial

The Enron Task Force claimed that more than a hundred co-conspirators at Enron had participated in a criminal scheme to defraud public investors, thirty-two of whom were indicted and about half of whom pleaded guilty. However, the principal targets of the Enron Task Force, Ken Lay, the Enron CEO and chairman, and Jeffrey Skilling, Enron's CEO before his resignation, vowed to fight and refused to plead to any charges. Skilling and Lay were hard targets with sufficient wealth to defend themselves fully, but for pressing political reasons they had to be brought down by the Enron Task Force. The Enron scandal had grown to monumental proportions as a result of the hysteria being whipped up by the press. That publicity engendered bitterness toward Skilling and Lay from Enron employees, shareholders, and even the general public, which the Justice Department believed was sufficient justification for their prosecution, whatever the legality of their conduct.

Skilling and Lay were unlikely felons. Lay was a self-made man who had put himself through the University of Missouri and earned a Ph.D. in economics. He had served in the Navy and was for a time undersecretary for energy policy in the Department of the Interior. Lay had worked for several oil companies as an executive and had managed the merger of Houston Natural Gas and InterNorth, which became Enron. Skilling had an equally stellar resume. He had earned his MBA at Harvard Business School. After graduation, Skilling had risen through the ranks and become a partner at the renowned McKinsey consulting firm before joining Enron. Both executives were well paid. Lay received more than $230 million in compensation from Enron, while Skilling received about half that amount.

Skilling and Lay's personalities differed. Lay was warm, understated, and unassuming. In contrast, Skilling was aggressive, mercurial, and sometimes arrogant, famously publicly replying to an analyst's comment that Enron was being slow in publishing a quarterly report with the words: "Thank you very much, asshole." Skilling also suffered from bouts of depression. As the government focused on him following Enron's collapse, he even contemplated suicide and was drinking heavily. After being indicted, Skilling was taken to a hospital by officers in the New York Police Department when he was reported as being intoxicated and behaving bizarrely on Park Avenue at 4:00 A.M. The Enron Task Force then demanded that Skilling be restricted in his activities as a condition of his continued bail. The court imposed a midnight curfew and ordered Skilling to stop drinking and to seek counseling.

As in the Arthur Andersen prosecution, the Enron Task Force found it necessary to invent a crime where none existed. In an article published in the *New York Times* after the trial, the prosecutors even boasted that they had had no real case against Skilling and Lay when their investigation began. However, after two years of intensive efforts, the Enron Task Force was able to invent what it called the "Dorian Gray" theory on which to indict Skilling and Lay.[10]

The Dorian Gray theory was based on the Oscar Wilde story about a man whose portrait showed him as aged and corrupt, while he himself outwardly retained his youthful appearance. This new crime from the literary world was apparently a serious one; the Enron Task Force was seeking maximum prison terms of 175 years for Lay and 325 years for Skilling.

The task force likened Skilling and Lay to Dorian Gray on the grounds that those executives were presenting a vibrant face for Enron to the public while they watched it crumble internally. However, Skilling and Lay's real crime in the eyes of the Enron Task Force was that they had been talking up the Enron stock right up until its ultimate demise, all the while selling off chunks of Enron stock that they held personally.

In any event, the task force needed to find some evidence to support this colorful theory. It simply extorted testimony from witnesses by employing tactics that were even more coercive than those used in its Arthur Andersen and other Enron-related prosecutions and was well staffed for that effort. Leslie Caldwell, a prosecutor noted for her hardball tactics, which included prosecuting the elderly mothers of two drug dealers in order to bring them to justice, initially headed the Enron Task Force. Those same tactics would be employed to win a guilty plea from Fastow, requiring him to inculpate Skilling and Lay into his own wrongdoing.

Fastow had been indicted by the Enron Task Force, but he claimed he was innocent and initially refused to plead guilty and to testify against Skilling and Lay. The Enron Task Force then doubled up the charges against him, increasing his maximum jail time, if convicted, from a mere 90 years to 140 years. Fastow still refused to plead guilty to lesser charges and to testify against Skilling and Lay. The prosecutors then indicted Fastow's wife, Lea, on income tax evasion charges in order to force her husband to submit to a guilty plea and "cooperation" agreement for testimony against Skilling and Lay.[11]

Initially, it looked like the Fastows were going to stand firm in the face of this intimidation and coercion, and they had reason to do so. The charges brought against Lea were bogus. The Enron Task Force charged that the joint tax return she filed with her husband did not report some $67,000 that Andrew had treated as a gift rather than income. Normally, payment of the taxes and a small penalty would resolve such a problem, especially since the Fastows had paid taxes on more than $60 million in income that year, which suggests that, whatever else he did, Fastow was not a tax cheat. However, the prosecutors were counting on the Enron hysteria's prevailing at the time to convince the Fastows that a conviction on any and all charges was assured, whatever the substance of the evidence. However, Fastow still refused to plead guilty to any charges or to testify against Skilling and Lay.

The Enron Task Force then upped the ante and declared that Lea Fastow would be tried first, before her husband or any other Enron executive. It might seem strange to some that the task force would focus on Lea Fastow, since she had left her position at Enron before the accounting manipulations had begun, and since she was not otherwise involved in the wrongdoing at Enron. However, to the Enron Task Force prosecuting Fastow's wife was the key to the success of its case against Skilling and Lay because it would persuade Fastow to testify against them.

The Fastows tried to have Lea's trial delayed until after Andrew's trial, so that he could testify in her favor without waiving his Fifth Amendment rights against self-incrimination in his own trial. Federal district court judge David Hittner rejected that request. The Fastows continued to resist the prosecutors' tactics for some time, but eventually their resolve broke down. The Enron Task Force made it clear to them the prospect that both would end up serving lengthy prison sentences at the same time, leaving them unable to care for their two children, one of whom, ironically, was named after Jeffrey Skilling.

This prospect was enough for the Fastows, who then pleaded guilty to reduced charges. It was agreed with prosecutors that they would be given sequential jail terms to allow one parent to care for the children while the other was behind bars. Still, the arrangement nearly came unglued after Judge Hittner demanded more jail time for Lea Fastow than had been agreed to by the Enron Task Force. Judge Hittner had good reason for his disdain for the Fastows, having personally lost some $40,000 from his investment in Enron's stock. For reasons unknown, the Fastows did not seek to recuse Judge Hittner.

The Enron Task Force was eventually able to patch together another agreement that satisfied Judge Hittner. He then sentenced Lea to a maximum-security prison, where she was assigned to an overcrowded cell and kept under bright lights for a year. That harsh action was needed to warn Andrew Fastow what was in store for him if he did not bring down Skilling and Lay. Fastow did deliver at their trial, but he also tearfully testified that Lea did not know anything about the Enron transactions or the tax issues that were the subject of her indictment. He testified that he had lied to her about the nature of the payments that were reported as gifts on their tax return. That lack of knowledge had no effect on the Enron Task Force, which was pleased that its tactics had worked as planned. Surprisingly, the Court of Appeals for the Fifth Circuit ruled in another case that such coercion by the government was permissible.[12]

With Fastow in the bag, the Enron Task Force was prepared to go to trial, but first obtained a guilty plea from another Enron executive, Richard Causey, Enron's chief accounting officer. Causey was indicted with Lay and Skilling and was to be tried with them. Causey had vowed to fight the charges, but later agreed to plead guilty to one count of securities fraud, and he further agreed to testify against Lay and Skilling. In exchange, Causey was sentenced to five and a half years in prison. That plea bargain was announced on December 28, 2005, just one week before the trial was to commence. The judge hearing the case, Simeon T. Lake III, granted a three-week delay to allow defense lawyers to deal with that setback, but that was about the only relief that Judge Lake would give the defendants throughout the trial. Among other things, the judge had twice rejected requests by the defendants for a change of venue because of juror prejudice against Enron in the Houston area, which had become apparent from surveys conducted by the defendants' lawyers. In the end, the government decided not to call Causey as a witness, and the long-awaited trial of Skilling and Lay finally began at the end of January 2006. At the insistence of Judge Lake, a jury was impaneled in one day.

Daniel Petrocelli, a California attorney who had never previously tried a criminal case, headed Skilling's legal team. Petrocelli, a skilled lawyer, was known for the large civil judgment he had obtained against O.J. Simpson after that former football and movie star had been acquitted of murdering his former wife and her boyfriend in a sensational murder trial. Michael Ramsey, who represented Lay, was a local Texan and an experienced criminal lawyer. Ramsey was a low-key individual, but was also a self-described hard-drinking, chain-smoking, legal warhorse.

The first government witness at the trial was Mark Koenig, the former Enron head of investor relations, who pleaded guilty to criminal charge. Koenig also agreed to pay the SEC a fine to settle charges that he had helped prepare false press releases on Enron's financial condition and misled analysts. He agreed as a part of his plea bargain to testify against other Enron executives. In fulfilling that bargain, Koenig testified that Lay and Skilling had participated in misleading the public concerning Enron's businesses. He stated that a reorganization of Enron's retail energy operations was conducted in order to conceal a loss of $220 million in that unit by moving it to the more-profitable wholesale business. On cross-examination, the defense lawyers attacked Koenig's lack of knowledge of accounting practices used to justify the reorganization. They also attacked Koenig's credibility because his jail sentence, which could be as much as ten years, would be determined by the effectiveness of his testimony against Lay and Skilling. After giving his testimony, Koenig was rewarded with a relatively light eighteen-month sentence.

The second witness presented by the government was Kenneth Rice, the former head of Enron Broadband Services. He had previously pleaded guilty to criminal charges in connection with his stewardship of that unit, and he agreed in his plea bargain to cooperate with prosecutors by testifying against other Enron executives. Rice, who had been a close friend of Skilling's while at Enron, testified that Skilling had told him not to increase a projected $65 million loss in that faltering broadband unit because he was under a lot of pressure from analysts "and we don't need any more bad news." However, on cross-examination, Rice appeared to be out of touch with his job at Enron, not even knowing how many employees worked for him at Enron Broadband Services. Rice was rewarded for his testimony with only a twenty-seven-month sentence, far less than the sentence sought for Skilling and Lay, and a $15 million fine, which was only a fraction of Rice's earnings at Enron.

Rice was followed on the stand by Paula H. Rieker, Enron's investment relations manager and corporate secretary. She testified that Skilling and Lay had misled investors about Enron's finances. Her testimony was especially damaging, but she conceded on cross-examination that she did not consider their conduct criminal at the time. Instead, Rieker asserted that she had been brainwashed. When confronted with the fact that Enron made some of the disclosures in SEC filings that she claimed Skilling and Lay had omitted in their remarks to analysts, Rieker stated that most analysts did not read SEC filings. That seemed to be more of an indictment of the SEC and the analysts than of Skilling or Lay, because most of the investing public believed that those SEC filings were the primary basis for the analysts' reports. Indeed, the massive expense incurred by public companies in making those filings has been justified on the grounds that they create "transparency" that financial analysts analyze.

The defense attorneys also noted that Rieker had "overstretched" her performance evaluation in order to obtain a bonus at Enron. The defense further pointed out that, in order to induce her to testify against Lay and Skilling, prosecutors had allowed Rieker to plead guilty to an insider-trading charge for a day when her trading profits were minimal so that she would receive a reduced sentence. Rieker was subsequently sentenced to only two years probation in exchange for her testimony.

In the midst of the trial, the *New York Times* reported in a front-page article that Ken Lay was nearly bankrupt; his net worth had fallen from $400 million to $650,000, with more legal bills looming. The article also reported that William Lerach, the lead counsel in the Enron class-action suits, did not expect any recovery from Lay because the Justice Department and federal regulators were bent on engineering Lay's financial ruin. To its credit, the coverage of the trial by the *New York Times* was relatively balanced, pointing to several instances where the defense scored points. In contrast, the *Wall Street Journal*'s coverage focused on evidence supporting the government's case and downplaying instances where the defense rebutted a government claim. This difference in reporting styles may have been due to the fact that the *Wall Street Journal* had a dog in the fight. As a part of his defense, Jeffrey Skilling was blaming Enron's failure on a series of articles in the *Wall Street Journal* that he claimed had undermined market confidence in the company and created the equivalent of a run on a bank.

The government continued its case with a stream of witnesses who had pleaded guilty to criminal charges or who had settled SEC claims. The picture that emerged was that Enron management was indeed focused on meeting and exceeding analysts' projections. Clearly, Enron management had used various accounting gimmicks to achieve the desired results, including dipping into reserves. One witness testified that Enron used "backward engineering," in which it first set what its earnings per share would be for a particular quarter and then subordinates would be told to find revenues even after the books were closed for the quarter. Another witness said that the Enron retail division found a box under a trader's desk with millions of dollars in uncashed checks from electricity consumers in California. This did not seem to have much relevance to the charges against Skilling and Lay, but it did suggest that Enron was being sloppily managed.

Fastow was then called to the stand. He admitted he had been "very greedy," that he had lost his "moral compass," and that he had misled his wife into signing a false tax return that led to her imprisonment, even crying to emphasize the point. Fastow testified that Skilling and Lay had been informed of his accounting manipulations. Fastow stated that Skilling liked the idea of using the special-purpose entities called LJM1 and LJM2 to manipulate Enron's accounts by selling underperforming assets and taking them off the Enron balance sheet. Fastow quoted Skilling as saying, "give me all the juice you can." Fastow also testified that, when Ken Lay returned to Enron after Skilling's resignation, Fastow told Lay that there were $5 billion to $7 billion in "embedded problems" that would take years to correct. Despite having that knowledge, Lay then told the press that Enron was in the "strongest and best shape that it has ever been in."

Fastow claimed that Skilling had approved millions of dollars in undisclosed compensation for Fastow as a result of these off-balance-sheet activities, which Fastow called "bear hugs." However, Fastow had no proof of any such approval except for a document that he called the "Global Galactic" agreement. Fastow testified that he and Enron's chief accounting officer, Rick Causey, agreed in that document that any losses to an LJM entity purchasing Enron assets would be made up in subsequent deals. He admitted that he had destroyed the original of that agreement and lost the only other copy, but claimed he found another copy in a safe deposit box after he began negotiations with the government over his plea bargain. Fastow admitted that he had never shown the agreement to Lay or Skilling, but claimed Skilling was orally informed of its existence by Causey, who did not testify.

Fastow was harshly attacked on cross-examination for sacrificing his wife to reach a plea deal and for his fraud in looting Enron assets. The defense lawyers presented him with a "booty sheet" of $120 million in Enron assets that Fastow had siphoned off for personal use through his off-balance-sheet transactions. Fastow conceded that none of the money went to Lay or Skilling. Fastow's notes showed that as the company unraveled Skilling had stated in a telephone call that Enron should make full disclosure of any problems. Skilling had also defended the company's accounting practices as correct.

At the conclusion of his cross-examination of Fastow, Ken Lay's lawyer, Michael Ramsey, remarked to his daughter, who was sitting at the defense table, that he thought that he had just suffered a heart attack. Ramsey decided to ignore the symptoms. Sherron Watkins then took the stand to retell her story about how she warned Lay of an impending implosion from the LJM structures. She complained that Lay should have investigated her claims by hiring a new accounting firm, and she was not satisfied even though the LJM transactions she complained about were later settled without loss.

Watkins had become a celebrity in the press for voicing her complaints to Ken Lay. She was even named a "Person of the Year" by *Time m*agazine. However, Watkins never actually blew the whistle on anybody to any government regulator. Max Hendrick II, a partner in the law firm of Vinson & Elkins, who conducted the internal investigation of the allegations Watkins expressed to Lay, testified for the defense that he found her claims to be based only on office gossip and some footnotes in an Enron filing with the SEC. Watkins also could not explain on cross-examination why she had not been criminally prosecuted for her stock sales that were made at a time when she was complaining that Enron was manipulating its accounts. That was the same misconduct that the Enron Task Force was charging that Lay and Skilling had engaged in at the very same time Watkins was making her sales.

The whole Enron whistle-blowing saga became even more complicated after *USA Today* reported that Lynn Brewer, another Enron whistle-blower, was a fraud. Emulating Watkins, Brewer claimed to be a former Enron "executive" in a book that she wrote about her exploits as a whistle-blower at the company. She was charging $13,000 a speech to preach ethics to corporate executives around the world on the basis of her Enron experiences. The Nobel Peace Center in Norway even mounted an exhibition in her honor as a corporate whistle-blower. However, an investigative reporter for *USA Today* found out that Brewer had never reached the executive ranks at Enron. She was actually a clerk who did research and trained others how to access publicly available databases, such as Factiva. It also appeared that Brewer had never blown any whistles at Enron. Rather, she was let go from her position at Enron after she was sent to London for a training session but never went to the office. Instead, Brewer spent her time in England, at Enron's expense, with her fiancé, and then claimed there was some unspecified terrorist threat that prevented her from going to Enron's London offices where the training session was to be held.[13]

Two Arthur Andersen accountants followed Watkins to the stand. One of the accountants testified that Enron had wrongly released loss reserves in order to boost earnings. John R. Sult, another Arthur Andersen accountant, testified that Enron had tried to avoid a $700 million write-down of its Azurix water business by falsely claiming that it was implementing a $1 billion growth strategy for that unit—which would have triggered a disastrous downgrade in Enron's credit rating. The accountant said that Lay had told him such strategy was under way, but he was unable to tie him to any accounting discussions over the issue.

Ronald Barone, a managing director at Standard & Poor's, took the stand for the prosecution and testified that Lay had assured him on October 12, 2001, that there would be no further write-downs, so Barone did not seek a reduction in Enron's credit rating. Another government witness, Christopher Loehr, testified that documents were backdated for the LJM transactions, but that someone other than Lay and Skilling had done that. The government also called a retired Enron employee to testify about the disastrous losses in his retirement account from Enron stock that he bought and held because of Ken Lay's assurances that the company was in strong shape.

Ben F. Glisan, Jr., appeared from his jail cell to testify for the government. Formerly Enron's treasurer, he was one of Fastow's "field marshals." Glisan had initially refused to cooperate with the prosecutors. Instead, he pleaded guilty to criminal charges and asked for immediate sentencing so that he could put his jail time behind him. That request was granted, and Glisan was sentenced to five years in prison. He then learned the value of testifying against his fellow executives.

As his cross-examination revealed at the Skilling and Lay trial, Glisan had been "hot boxed" in prison by being placed in solitary confinement and then lodged with some dangerous prisoners in order to convince him to cooperate with the Enron Task Force. That coercion worked, and Glisan agreed to testify. He was then given better accommodations and furloughs home so that he could work with prosecutors in preparing his testimony against Skilling and Lay. Glisan performed other chores for the prosecution. On one occasion, he was brought from his jail cell in manacles and placed in an elevator with Skilling, who had just been arrested and handcuffed for his "perp walk." The prosecutors wanted to intimidate Skilling with that little staged drama.

Judge Lake jumped in to help Glisan with his testimony. He granted Glisan immunity from prosecution of other crimes that might be revealed during his testimony. Such requests had been denied by Judge Lake when made by defense lawyers seeking cooperating witnesses for their case.[14] Glisan was even allowed to take off the prison attire he wore in the Nigerian barge case and don a suit for his testimony. The prosecutors wanted to provide Glisan with an executive persona to offset that of Skilling and Lay. It seemed to work because the jury was reported to have been impressed with Glisan's testimony. It also paid off for Glisan. He was released from prison after serving only three years of his five-year sentence.

Glisan testified that Skilling had agreed to the use of the LJM Raptors as a way to "circumvent" accounting requirements, but he backed off that claim in cross-examination. Glisan also claimed that Lay knew that various Enron assets were overvalued, including its Azurix water business, but conceded that he had left an October 22, 2001, meeting before Richard Causey advised Lay that Arthur Andersen had concluded that no write-downs were necessary. Glisan admitted that his claims of overvaluation were "economic" issues and that relevant financial accounting standards might not require a write-down on the company's financial statements. Glisan claimed that he had warned Lay that bankruptcy was "inevitable" because of a liquidity crisis just before Lay publicly stated that there were no liquidity problems. However, the defense showed that Glisan was providing Lay and the Enron board of directors with reports that showed a high degree of liquidity and even that liquidity was increasing. Glisan also claimed that Skilling was making adjustments to assets for accounting manipulations, but admitted on cross-examination that Skilling's statements addressed the need to account for mark-to-market requirements, which required company assets to be accounted for at their current market value.

Michael Ramsey, the lead attorney for Ken Lay, called Glisan a "performing monkey" for the government and was blasted in the press for that remark. In the midst of Glisan's testimony, Ramsey's coronary problems worsened, and he had to have emergency surgery to place a stent in his coronary artery to relieve the effects of a blockage. That procedure occurred over a weekend. Ramsey selflessly returned to work the next day to continue his defense of Lay, but he had to be hospitalized again soon thereafter for an operation to remove the blockage. Lay decided, for financial reasons, not to seek a delay or continuance of the trial while Ramsey was recuperating.

Glenn Ray, a stockbroker for Jeffrey Skilling, testified that Skilling wanted him to avoid telling Enron that he was selling his shares after the September 11 terrorist attack, but the broker admitted that most of his clients wanted their sales kept confidential. The defense also established that Enron was notified of the sales before their consummation. Although Lay was not charged with insider trading, the government's last witness was Joanne Cortez, an Enron employee who handled Ken Lay's drawdowns on his Enron credit line. Cortez testified that she was shocked when the Enron compensation committee increased Lay's credit line from $4 million to $7.5 million after Enron reported large losses in October 2001. Lay then began making recurring drawdowns on the credit line that he repaid with Enron shares. Cortez admitted on cross-examination that she was unaware of the fact that Lay was using the line of credit to meet margin calls or that Enron's accountants and lawyers had vetted the program. That concluded the government's case. The prosecutors then dropped four counts in the Skilling indictment and one count against Ken Lay.

The defense put on its case, which was designed to show that Enron was destroyed by bad publicity and extraneous market events, rather than any fraud committed by Lay or Skilling. The defendants' lawyers complained, however, that they were being hampered in their ability to prove their case because witnesses were too frightened by government intimidation to come forward and testify. According to the defense lawyers, the witnesses were concerned that the government would indict them if they testified on behalf of Skilling and Lay. The government did nothing to disabuse them of that notion, refusing to grant immunity to any witnesses other than its own.

In order to lay a groundwork for their defense, Lay and Skilling's lawyers introduced a film of those two executives during their tenure at Enron, which showed them boasting that Enron had reached its goal of becoming the "World's Leading Energy Company" and that the new goal would be to make it the "World's Leading Company." The tape also showed Skilling admitting that Enron's accounting was a "black box," but he asserted that it was a "good black box" because Enron's businesses were growing. The defense lawyers argued that this film proved that Lay and Skilling believed passionately in the future of Enron. The lawyers also introduced their principal theme—that Enron was brought down by a panic in the market that was touched off by *Wall Street Journal* articles questioning the Fastow-related party transactions.

The defense called several former Enron employees who testified that the Enron retail services unit was not combined with the wholesale unit in order to cover up losses in the retail unit. One of those witnesses testified that the combination reduced duplication and saved the company money. An earlier government witness had claimed Ken Lay had vetoed a write-off in order to avoid taking a loss. However, a defense witness testified that a write-off was not required because a California tariff that would have cut profitability and required a write-off could not be computed until several more months after Enron's demise.

Another Enron executive, J. Mark Metts, who was in charge of asset sales testified that Skilling had been "extremely supportive" of his position that Fastow and the LJM entities should not be given any preference in asset sales. Skilling had stated that everyone must play by the same rules. Other former Enron employees testified that Enron's accounting for a controversial Dabhol power project was proper and that no further write-off was required. Other defense witnesses asserted that the company was seeking to deal with its Broadband Services business in a responsible manner.

Enron's former general counsel, James V. Derrick, Jr., defended the investigation of Watkins's complaints. Derrick testified that Enron executives had relied heavily on advice from outside counsel and accountants in making their decisions on the appropriateness of write-offs or other accounting or legal issues. He further testified that the Enron board of directors had not required Skilling to sign off on the deals with the LJMs. Rather, that authority was delegated to two other executives. Derrick also testified that Lay focused on broad policy at Enron and not day-to-day accounting or legal issues.

Jeffrey Skilling took the stand on April 11, 2006. He admitted that he was nervous and that "in some ways my life is on the line." Skilling declared his innocence and blamed the company's downfall on the *Wall Street Journal* articles that had questioned the LJM partnerships. Skilling claimed that the articles were an organized effort to destroy Enron. Skilling testified that he had urged Ken Lay to respond to those charges, that Lay should "open the kimono" and make expanded disclosures regarding Enron's finances. Skilling defended his leadership at Enron. He asserted that he resigned because he was depressed by family matters, burned out on the job, and was frustrated by his inability to stabilize Enron's stock price.

Skilling stumbled over a conversation that he had had with a broker in which Skilling stated that he wanted to sell several hundred thousand shares of Enron stock after he left Enron. He was unable to do so before the September 11 terrorist attacks temporarily closed the New York Stock Exchange (NYSE), on which Enron was listed. After the exchange reopened, Skilling increased the size of his sell order and stated in an SEC deposition that he sold his stock because of the September 11 attack. The government contended this was a lie because he had planned to sell before the attack. Skilling testified in the criminal trial that he did not recall that conversation with his broker.

Skilling testified that he had attempted to assemble a consortium of investors to save Enron by a $700 million infusion of cash. He offered to invest $70 million of his own money in that effort, but the company came unglued before completion of the deal. Skilling asserted that he had no "bear hug" deal with Fastow that would protect Fastow against loss and that he had never heard the term before. Skilling testified that he had given Fastow an ultimatum, in which he had to choose to continue as Enron's CFO or resign and become LJM's general partner. Fastow chose to remain at Enron.

Skilling rejected the claim that he had manipulated results in the second quarter of 2000. He pointed to the fact that he was in Africa during the period in question and was unreachable. Skilling also expressed indignation at the government's charges and accused the prosecutors of rewriting history and of intimidating witnesses.

Skilling was then cross-examined by Sean Berkowitz, the head of the Enron Task Force. Berkowitz aggressively challenged Skilling on his stock sales. Berkowitz also focused on a comparatively nominal $180,000 investment by Skilling and a smaller amount by Lay in a company doing business with Enron. Those investments were made by Skilling and Lay without first obtaining a conflict of interest waiver from Enron's board of directors. That waiver seemed unnecessary because to Skilling the amount was pocket change, and the Enron board normally only considered issues with a minimum floor value of millions of dollars. However, the company in question was owned by a girlfriend of Skilling's, which the jury viewed as problematic. Berkowitz also claimed that Skilling had backdated a check to her for an unexplained reason. That, too, was embarrassing to Skilling, but it had nothing to do with the charges in the case, as Skilling pointed out to the prosecutor. The defense also called the Enron employee handling that business to testify. She stated that she was unaware of Lay and Skilling's investment in the firm.

Ken Lay followed Skilling on the stand, but Ramsey was still ailing and was replaced by George McCall Secrest, Jr., who sometimes fumbled in his examination. Like Skilling, Lay compared Enron's demise to a run on a bank set off by the *Wall Street Journal* articles on the LJMs. He claimed that a group of hedge funds that he called "vultures" had driven down the Enron stock through short sales, a claim similar to one that would be made by investment banking firms that failed during the subprime crisis.

Lay called Fastow a liar and a thief, and he testified that he refused Fastow's request for a $5 million severance package. Lay, normally noncombative, was unexpectedly feisty on cross-examination. He asserted that the prosecutors were trying to misconstrue and criminalize routine business practices. When asked if he had repaid loans to himself from Enron, Lay said no, because the prosecutors had frozen his assets. Lay testified that he had a negative net worth and owed his lawyers money. The cross-examination also focused on Lay's stock sales, even though he had not been charged with inside trading. Lay asserted that he did not disclose his Enron stock sales to the public because they were forced by margin calls and were not optional.

In response to Lay's claim that Enron was the victim of short sellers, the government embarrassed him by showing that Lay's son had sold Enron stock short. This was effective with the jury in impugning Lay's credibility, but his son's sales had nothing to do with the charges. Lay's attorney also showed on re-direct that those sales were marked as short sales by the brokers in error, but the damage could not be undone by mere facts.

The prosecution also embarrassed Lay by showing that he spent $200,000 on a birthday party for his wife and made expensive purchases while selling Enron stock. Again, this character assassination was effective but had nothing to do with the allegations in the indictment. With respect to what was actually charged in the indictment, Walter Rush, an accounting expert, and Jerry Arnold, an accounting professor at the University of Southern California, both testified that Lay and Skilling had properly relied on advice received on the accounting requirements for reserve accounts at Enron and that the company's assets had been properly valued.

The government established that Lay had other assets that could have been used to meet margin calls on his stock, rather than sell it back to Enron through his credit line in order to meet those calls. However, because he had used the stock as security for the margin loans and Lay had ready access to the Enron credit line, that claim really did not make practical sense. In that regard, Christopher Barry, a professor of finance at Texas Christian University, confirmed that Lay's stock sales were indeed forced sales. To the government's charge that Lay could have borrowed money elsewhere, Barry stated that it would be like using your MasterCard to pay off your Visa bill. He also noted that Lay had been given $10 million by the Enron board to induce him to return after Skilling's resignation. Lay used that money to pay off debt instead of selling Enron stock. Barry supported Skilling and Lay's claim that Enron's demise was the result of a classic bank run.

The government's only witness on rebuttal was an employee of Portland General Electric who testified that she believed Lay's assurances that Enron was in good shape and was shocked when its large losses were announced. However, on cross-examination she admitted that she was unaware of what information Lay was relying on in making his statements.

The defense renewed its motion asking for Enron executives who would not otherwise testify for the defense to be granted immunity. Judge Lake refused that request. In the end, only Ben Glisen, who turned state's evidence, was given immunity. After fifteen weeks of trial the defense rested on May 9, 2006. Michael Ramsey was able to return to make brief closing arguments on Lay's behalf. Judge Lake then gave the jury an "ostrich" instruction, which would allow them to convict if they found that Lay or Skilling consciously avoided or deliberately ignored evidence of fraud at Enron.

As the jury began its deliberations, a second trial began for Ken Lay, on charges that he had violated federal margin requirements in Federal Reserve Regulation U. The government charged that Lay had used more than 50 percent of the proceeds of a bank loan to make investments in publicly traded stocks. Lay waived a jury trail in that criminal case, also heard by Judge Lake. Lay admitted that he failed to comply with the Regulation U, but asserted that he was unfamiliar with those complex margin requirements, as were most people.

Bettors on a Dublin-based gambling Web site were betting heavily in favor of a guilty verdict for both Lay and Skilling, and they proved to be right. The jury found both guilty on May 25, 2006. Judge Lake then announced that he had also found Lay guilty of the margin and bank fraud charges.

The government's hardball tactics in convicting Skilling and Lay were lauded in a front-page *New York Times* article,[15] but the trial may have had a fatal effect on Ken Lay. About six weeks after the trial and while he was awaiting sentencing, he died of a sudden heart attack at a vacation rental home in Aspen, on July 5, 2006. An autopsy determined that he had severe blockages in his three main coronary arteries and that he had suffered two prior heart attacks. That condition was certainly not aided by the stress of the trial and the conviction.

Ironically, Lay's death turned him into an innocent man because his conviction was still subject to appeal at the time of his death. The Court of Appeals for the Fifth Circuit had ruled in an earlier case that convictions must be set aside under such circumstances and that the government's forfeiture proceedings must cease. Many leaders of the community, including a former mayor and a former Texas governor, attended Lay's memorial service in Houston. Also attending were George H.W. Bush and his wife, Barbara, and former secretary of state James A. Baker III. Some mourners at Ken Lay's funeral, including civil rights advocate Reverend Bill Lawson, claimed that Lay was the victim of a lynching.

Skilling was also crumbling under the pressure of his conviction. Shortly before his sentencing, Skilling was arrested for public intoxication after leaving a restaurant in Dallas as a part of a controversial Dallas police force program to observe local restaurants for departing guests who may have had too much to drink. Skilling was briefly jailed and paid a fine of $385.

Judge Lake imposed a much stiffer sentence on Skilling for his Enron conviction. Lake ordered Skilling to pay $24 million in restitution and sentenced him to twenty-four years in prison. In contrast, Fastow was sentenced to only six years. His testimony against Skilling and Lay did, indeed, pay off for him personally.

Skilling was denied bail pending his appeal and was kept under house arrest in his 9,000-square-foot mansion in Houston while awaiting assignment to a prison. He began serving his sentence in December 2006 at a minimum-security prison in Minnesota located on what was once a college campus. Skilling was assigned a former dorm room, which he shared with three other convicts. He was later moved to a prison in Colorado.

There appeared to be some hope for Skilling on appeal. In denying Skilling bail, the appeals court asserted that there appeared to be some "serious frailties" involving fourteen of the nineteen counts on which Skilling had been convicted. Reversal of those fourteen counts would not release Skilling from prison, hence the denial of bail, but would probably reduce his sentence.

Skilling's lawyers were forceful in their appeal brief, not mincing words. They stated: "Profound, inherent weaknesses in the government's case—not just gaps in its evidentiary proof, but doubts about its basic theories of criminality—motivated the government to resort to novel and incorrect legal theories, demand truncated and unfair trial procedures, and use coercive and abusive tactics."[16] The defendants' appeal pointedly attacked the Enron Task Force, charging:

> The [Enron] Task Force crossed the line in skewing the evidence in this case. It obstructed Skilling's access to witnesses and documents. It withheld crucial exculpatory evidence. It coerced and threatened witnesses. It secured unlawful plea agreements. It destroyed documents that would have revealed the varied and conflicting statements of its principal witness, Andrew Fastow. It affirmatively misled the jury about Fastow's motive to give false testimony against Skilling. These are not perfunctory complaints. This was a systematic suppression of evidence, sanctioned by the highest officers of the Task Force, revealed by their own documents. It was an indispensable part of the prosecution of this case, and it prevented Skilling from mounting a full and fair defense.[17]

Skilling contended in his appeal that the government had withheld from him FBI notes of interviews with Andrew Fastow that conflicted with Fastow's testimony at trial, in which he stated that he had discussed the "global galactic" agreement with Skilling at a particular meeting. Those notes were also claimed to have included other exculpatory information. The trial judge, Simeon T. Lake III, denied access to the FBI notes that had been sought by Skilling's lawyers. Judge Lake had reviewed the notes and concluded that they were innocuous. However, when they were subsequently produced, upon the order of the court, Skilling's lawyers charged that those documents did corroborate their claim that Fastow had made inconsistent statements.

On January 6, 2009, the Court of Appeals for the Fifth Circuit issued its ruling, upholding Skilling's convictions, but vacating his sentence and remanding it for resentencing because of an error in the way that sentence was computed. The appeals court held that Skilling was entitled to a presumption that the jury pool was prejudiced against him because of the massive publicity surrounding the Enron affair. However, it found that through careful questioning the district court judge had assured that the jury was not prejudiced.

The appeals court also upheld the district court's ruling that the government had not intimidated witnesses. It left open the slim possibility of a new trial on whether the government had improperly failed to disclose a side deal with Fastow while rejecting most of Skilling's claims with respect to the FBI notes, but asserted that the withholding of some of those notes was "troubling." However, any motion on what action should be taken had to be made first before the Judge Lake, so it was unlikely that Skilling would receive any relief there. Nevertheless, on October 13, 2009, the Supreme Court granted Skilling's petition for a writ of certiorari seeking review of his conviction. The court was concerned with the application of the "honest services" prohibition against corporate executives. During oral argument, the justices noted that under the government's theory an employee calling in sick in order to attend a ball game would be guilty of a felony.

The Supreme Court ruled on June 25, 2010. The Court was divided, but the majority rejected Skilling's claim that the jury pool was biased against him and that a change of venue should have been ordered. The Court held that the "honest services" requirement would apply only to bribery or kickbacks and there had been none in the case of Skilling. However, the Supreme Court remanded the case to the Fifth Circuit for a determination of whether the jury would have convicted Skilling anyway for mail fraud on other grounds. The majority suggested that there were grounds for believing that to be the case.

Lou Pai

There seems to have been some disconnect when it came to dealing with Lou Pai, a senior Enron executive who married a stripper and fortuitously left Enron before the company collapsed. Pai sold $270 million worth of Enron stock, using some of the proceeds to buy a 77,000-acre ranch in Colorado that included its own mountain. It was unclear why Pai had been so highly compensated at Enron. The businesses he ran there suffered large losses.

In a class-action lawsuit Pai was charged with aiding other Enron officers in running a Ponzi scheme with Enron by inflating profits and inducing a continuous stream of new investors as the stock price rose from those manipulations. This allowed Pai, it was claimed, to accumulate large holdings in Enron stock as bonuses and to sell those stocks at inflated prices.

> Moreover, as is typical in a Ponzi scheme, the monster created required increasing funds to sustain it. [Enron] EES had to attract more and more clients by more and more such fraudulent deals to keep up its artificially inflated financial reports and to make the business appear successful so that investors would continue to believe the contracts were making money and pour their money into Enron stock.[18]

Surprisingly, Pai was never indicted, despite his massive compensation and claimed wrongdoing. The SEC did bring a civil suit against him in 2008, long after the Enron scandal had passed. The SEC charged that, shortly before he left Enron, Pai had engaged in insider trading when he sold 338,897 shares of Enron stock and exercised stock options that resulted in the sale of 572,818 shares, yielding unspecified millions of dollars in proceeds. The SEC asserted that, before making these sales, Pai learned that the unit in which he worked, Retail Energy Services, should have shown a quarterly loss of $60 million, rather than the profit of $40 million reported in Enron's Form 10-Q for the first quarter of 2001.

The SEC noted that, by selling his shares in May and June 2001, before the collapse of Enron's share price, Pai avoided millions of dollars in losses. Pai settled the SEC lawsuit, without admitting or denying the SEC's allegations, and agreed to pay what was, in the context of his massive profits, a nominal $31.5 million in fines and disgorgement. He was also barred from serving as an officer of a public company for five years, as if anyone would want him in such a position.

Summing Up the Enron Litigation

The Prosecution's Scorecard

The Justice Department's scorecard for its nationwide Corporate Fraud Task Force, of which the Enron Task Force was a subset, comprised convictions of 214 CEOs and presidents, 53 chief financial officers, 23 corporate attorneys, and 129 corporate vice presidents. However, the vast majority of the convictions by the Justice Department's Corporate Fraud Task Force came from guilty pleas, many of which were suspect because of the coercion employed by the Justice Department to obtain those pleas.

The SEC also used its powers to coerce fines and restitution from companies involved in the Enron-era scandals. By February 2008, the SEC had distributed over $3.5 billion to investors from collections and enforcement actions, most of which was obtained through settlements in which the defendants neither admitted nor denied the charges. The distribution of those funds to investors became ensnarled in the government bureaucracy, requiring the SEC to create a special office in February 2008 to handle future distributions.

There was a troubling problem with the SEC fines. The largest of those civil penalties were imposed against the corporation itself and were paid from the funds of the shareholders, rather than the individual wrongdoers. This gave rise to criticism that the SEC was actually punishing the innocent shareholders of the company for the actions of its officers. In response to that criticism, the SEC issued guidelines on appropriate penalties for corporations. Those guidelines weigh whether the conduct was widespread, whether the company benefited from the misconduct, and whether the company cooperated in the investigation. The SEC illustrated how the guidelines worked in two cases. McAfee was fined $50 million for inflating its earnings by $622 million between 1998 and 2000. The company benefited because this bolstered its stock price, which was important because it was using its stock for acquisitions. In contrast, Applix was not fined at all because the company did not benefit from the fraud at issue.

Enron Bankruptcy Proceedings

Plaintiffs in civil litigation against Enron and its banks fared better than the criminal defendants, but they did face some setbacks. Enron's creditors had received about 52 cents on the dollar for their claims by October 2008, far exceeding initial expectations, and more was distributed in 2009. The Enron Creditors Recovery Corporation (ECRC), the entity pursuing Enron's creditors in bankruptcy, distributed $21.4 billion to creditors between 2004 and 2008 and was holding an additional $4.5 billion as a reserve against unresolved claims. By October 2009, ECRC had recovered $21.5 billion for the Enron estate.

One of the Enron assets that continued to perform after its bankruptcy was Northern Natural Gas (NNG). NNG was the successor to InterNorth, the Omaha company that merged with Houston Natural Gas to form Enron. NNG was a pipeline company with hard assets, and Dynegy used it as collateral for a $2.5 billion capital infusion when it was planning to buy Enron. Ken Lay had moved its headquarters to Houston after the Enron merger, but it was sold by Dynegy after Enron went bankrupt. NNG moved back to Omaha and is now a part of Warren Buffett's Mid-American Energy Holdings.

One settlement in the ECRC litigation involved the Houston Astros baseball club, which paid the Enron estate $2.1 million to regain the right to name its ballpark in Houston. Enron had paid $100 million for the right to name that stadium "Enron Field." Enron's outside lawyers, Vinson & Elkins, paid $30 million and dropped claims of $4 million in the bankruptcy proceeding.

ECRC's biggest recoveries were from the investment banks.[19] Those settlements included $1.7 billion from nine banks that had participated in Enron's off-balance-sheet activities, which allowed Enron to conceal its declining position. JPMorgan Chase agreed to pay $350 million in that "MegaClaims" litigation. JPMorgan Chase also agreed to "subordinate" its own claims as a creditor to those of other creditors. Since the claims of those other creditors were expected to consume the entire estate, this meant that JPMorgan Chase was dropping its claims, which totaled $660 million.

The Canadian Imperial Bank of Commerce paid $250 million and agreed to subordinate its claims as a creditor. Barclays paid $144 million and dropped claims totaling $310 million. Credit Suisse First Boston paid $90 million to settle creditors' claims and dropped its own claims against the Enron estate totaling $337 million. Deutsche Bank paid $25 million and agreed to drop $416 million of its own claims. Toronto-Dominion Bank paid $70 million; the Royal Bank of Scotland paid $41.8 million; Lehman Brothers paid $70 million; UBS paid $115 million; and Merrill Lynch paid $29.5 million. Those institutions also agreed to drop their own creditor claims against the Enron estate.

ECRC was seeking an additional $21 billion from Citigroup, and a trial on that issue was set to commence in April 2008. However, Citigroup agreed to settle the claim by paying $1.66 billion and forgoing claims of its own in the bankruptcy. Citigroup also agreed to assume liability, in an unspecified amount, for the claims of creditors on some credit-linked notes that were related to the bankruptcy claims.

Class-Action Suits

Citigroup's reluctance to settle with ECRC may have stemmed from its experience in the class-action lawsuits brought on behalf of Enron shareholders. Citigroup paid $2 billion to settle those claims before the Court of Appeals for the Fifth Circuit dismissed the case. Citigroup was not allowed to recover the funds it had paid in settlement before that decision. In total, settlements of $7.3 billion were obtained in that class-action litigation before its dismissal. This was the largest amount of settlements ever obtained in securities-related litigation, surpassing the $6.1 billion obtained in the WorldCom litigation.

Most of the settlements obtained in the Enron class-action litigation were contributed by the banks that had participated in structuring the off-balance-sheet special-purpose entities that had allowed Enron to conceal its declining financial condition. Those settling defendants included Citigroup, JPMorgan Chase, and the Canadian Imperial Bank of Commerce, which settled for a combined $6.6 billion. The Canadian Imperial Bank of Commerce paid $2.4 billion in the Enron settlement, and JPMorgan Chase paid $2.2 billion. A separate class-action brought against JPMorgan Chase, concerning its creation of special-purpose entities designed to facilitate disguised loan transactions with Enron, was dismissed by a federal district court in New York, and that dismissal was affirmed in January 2005 by the Court of Appeals for the Second Circuit because there was no showing of an intent to defraud.

Other settling defendants in the Enron shareholder litigation were Bank of America ($69 million); Lehman Brothers ($222.5 million); Kirkland & Ellis, one of Enron's outside law firms ($13.5 million); and several Enron board members ($168 million). Arthur Andersen agreed to pay $72.5 million in settlement, down from the $750 million it had offered before its indictment. Arthur Andersen's international umbrella organization, Andersen Worldwide, chipped in another $40 million.

Several of the principal defendants refused to settle, including Merrill Lynch, Barclays, and Credit Suisse First Boston, and an April 2007 trial date was set for them. However, the Court of Appeals for the Fifth Circuit dismissed the case in March, just before the trial began, ruling that the banks were not primary players in the fraud that caused Enron's bankruptcy.[20] The plaintiffs were proceeding under a "scheme liability" theory that would have made Enron's bankers liable for participating in its fraudulent activity.

The plaintiffs' lawyers asked the Supreme Court to overturn that ruling. The Supreme Court deferred ruling on that request until it considered that issue in another Enron-era accounting scandal involving Charter Communications, a company that was also audited by Arthur Andersen. The Supreme Court ruled in that case in January 2008, declining to find such liability. The Court held that investors must show some reliance on the defendants' activities, which could not be done, of course, because they were concealed from the public.[21] Shortly after rendering that decision, the Supreme Court rejected the Enron class-action petition to overturn the appeals court ruling that dismissed the case.

The lead lawyers for the class-action plaintiffs was the San Diego firm Coughlin Stoia Geller Rudman & Robbins, which was founded by William Lerach, the dean of the class-action bar, who would, shortly after these settlements, plead guilty to felony violations for paying kickbacks to class-action plaintiffs. His firm was awarded $668 million in fees for its success in obtaining the prior Enron-related settlements that totaled over $7.2 billion and which did not have to be returned notwithstanding the appeals court's ruling.[22] The class-action plaintiffs tried to amend their complaint to add a new charge against Merrill Lynch, Barclays, and Credit Suisse First Boston, but that effort was rebuffed by the district court in March 2009.

Dynegy

Dynegy agreed to pay the Enron estate $25 million to settle claims arising from its decision to walk away from its merger with Enron—Ken Lay's eleventh-hour attempt to save Enron from bankruptcy. Dynegy also paid $468 million to settle class-action litigation over its own accounting manipulations and paid the SEC another $3 million.

A Dynegy employee, Jamie Olis, was arrested in a dawn raid on his home by FBI agents, who drew their guns on Olis and his pregnant wife. Olis, a Dynegy finance executive, was charged with, and subsequently convicted of, manipulating Dynegy's books in order to deceive its auditor, Arthur Andersen, into believing certain borrowings were actually cash flow. District Court Judge Simeon T. Lake III, the same judge who had sentenced Jeffrey Skilling at Enron to a lengthy imprisonment, gave Olis a twenty-four-year prison term that was almost universally viewed to be excessively harsh and was set aside by the appeals court.[23] Lake then sentenced Olis to six years, but he was released after five years. Dynegy cut off paying Olis's legal fees after it was threatened with prosecution by the government. A jury subsequently found that Dynegy had acted improperly in taking that action and awarded Olis's attorney $2.5 million in damages.

This harsh treatment and the lack of success in the Enron criminal trials suggest that the government was overly zealous in its prosecutions. As will be described in the next chapter, that zeal would also be exhibited in other Enron-era prosecutions.

2. Other Enron-Era Scandals

The Telecom Scandals—The Aftermath

Background

The telecommunications industry was experiencing a meltdown as Enron was imploding. That industry had once been limited to telephones using landlines, a business that was completely dominated by AT&T. Commonly dubbed "Ma Bell," a reference to its lineage from Alexander Graham Bell, that colossus was broken up in 1982 by an antitrust suit brought by the Justice Department that lasted nearly ten years. Under the settlement decree resolving that case, AT&T spun off its operations into seven regional operating companies, which were required to operate independently of one another. The regional companies were dubbed the "Baby Bells."

Ironically, the AT&T empire was being reassembled in 2005 and 2006 as four of the seven Baby Bells merged, including BellSouth, which was brought into the fold in March 2006 at a purchase price of $67 billion. Those mergers made AT&T the largest telecom firm in the United States, once again. The reborn AT&T was given a boost when the Apple iPhone was introduced in 2007, with AT&T as exclusive carrier. However, in 2009 Congress and the Obama administration began investigating such exclusive arrangements and other wireless arrangements to determine whether they were in violation of antitrust laws.

The Telecommunications Act of 1996 had sought to enhance competition in the industry by, among other things, requiring competition among local and long distance carriers. Actually, it was advances in technology that drove the growth of telecoms as the twentieth century ended. The development of cell phones, cable companies, satellite TV, and the growth and success of the Internet led to explosive growth in the industry. Fiber-optic cables were being laid everywhere in the 1990s, including under the oceans, in order to increase bandwidth. The American landscape became dotted with cell phone towers, and profit available to the telecoms appeared limitless.

New telecom companies sprang up everywhere to exploit this market. However, the market became quickly saturated, and profits began to suffer as the economy slowed. Because the telecom firms were public companies, their share prices were subject to the whims of financial analysts. A failure to meet analysts' expectations for even one quarter would result in a sharp drop in the price of the company's stock. This meant that executive compensation in the form of stock options would be lost, in amounts that often totaled hundreds of millions of dollars.

Telecom executives had few options but to cook the books in order to please the analysts and to keep the money machine running. Nevertheless, the problems that the firms were facing eventually surfaced because their accounting manipulations were effective for only a limited time. That time ran out as overcapacity in the industry and a slowing of the economy proved longer and deeper than expected.

AT&T had to restate its accounts and earnings for 2001 and 2002. Lucent Technologies, one of the Baby Bells, had even greater problems. Lucent was among the high-flying telecom companies that cashed in on advances in telecommunications equipment, sending its stock price soaring. However, Lucent was slow to enter the field of electronic data transmission because of accounting issues related to its spinoff from AT&T. It then tried to play catch-up through some costly acquisitions that turned out to be disasters when overcapacity led telecom earnings to plunge.

Lucent's stock plummeted in 2000 after the announcement that the company would not meet analysts' expectations. Lucent subsequently disclosed that it had engaged in some massive accounting manipulations, which were designed to conceal its declining earnings. Like Enron and other icons of the era, Lucent eventually ran out of manipulation schemes and had to face the music. Lucent was forced to disclose that it concealed more than $20 billion in losses through various accounting manipulations. The value of Lucent stock dropped by $250 billion between 1999 and 2001, and the company was forced to lay off over 70,000 employees.

Lucent settled the resulting class-action lawsuits for $653 million and paid $25 million to settle charges brought by the Securities and Exchange Commission (SEC), a sum that was increased by the SEC's view that Lucent had not cooperated in the agency's investigation. However, in May 2009, a federal district court dismissed SEC claims against the Lucent executives who, the SEC charged, were primarily responsible for the manipulations. The court held that they had played no such role, but allowed claims of aiding and abetting to proceed. PricewaterhouseCoopers was the auditor for Lucent and for other companies caught up in the Enron-era scandals, but unlike the hapless Arthur Andersen, it suffered no real damage from this scandal.

Lucent entered into another settlement with the SEC and the Justice Department in 2007, after it was discovered that the company had violated the Foreign Corrupt Practices Act. Lucent had spent millions of dollars on 315 sightseeing trips taken by Chinese government officials between 2000 and 2003 that were ostensibly related to sales. In fact, those trips were actually for entertainment and tourist travel. Although not for business, the trips were designed to develop goodwill among Chinese government officials. Lucent paid the SEC and the Justice Department $25 million to settle those charges.

Despite its many problems, Alcatel, a French company, acquired Lucent for a whopping $13.4 billion in 2006. However, that acquisition proved a poor bargain for Alcatel. For the fourth quarter of 2007, the combined Alcatel-Lucent reported a $3.65 billion write-down, which was due to further losses at Lucent.

Qwest Communications International was another giant telecom firm that had grown through acquisitions, including that of one of the Baby Bells, U.S. West. Like Lucent, Qwest began massively manipulating its accounts in 2000 and 2001 as overcapacity and a market downturn bit into earnings. Arthur Andersen audited Qwest during the period that those accounting manipulations took place. Qwest settled SEC charges over those manipulations by paying $250 million. In the meantime, its stock fell from a high of $50 to $2.79. However, the company returned to profitability in 2006 and resumed paying dividends in 2007. Qwest's stock traded above $7 per share as 2007 ended, but by 2009 when the subprime crisis peaked, that price had dropped by 50 percent.

Seven Qwest executives were indicted for insider trading and accounting manipulations. Two of those indicted were acquitted after a trial. Four others pleaded guilty but received no jail time. The seventh, Joseph Nacchio, the Qwest CEO, was indicted for insider trading, after it was discovered that he had sold $100 million of his Qwest stock before the price collapsed in the accounting scandal at that company. Nacchio's defense was that he had favorable classified inside information about secret government contracts that would offset other areas of the business that were in trouble. That defense did not work. Nacchio was convicted on nineteen counts, sentenced to six years in prison, fined $19 million, and ordered to reimburse investors $52 million in insider-trading profits.

Nacchio appealed his conviction, asserting that the adverse information the government claimed he had acted on was not material and that the trial judge wrongly excluded an expert witness on that issue. That witness was the former dean of the University of Chicago Law School, Daniel Fischel. He was prepared to testify that Nacchio's sales were not consistent with the use of inside information. Fischel did not fit the mold of a stereotypical left-wing law professor. Rather, he was quite conservative, at least, on financial matters. Fischel had previously written a book that fiercely denounced the then–U.S. attorney Rudolph Giuliani's prosecution of Michael Milken, the junk bond king. Fischel accused Giuliani of engaging in a "reign of terror" that employed "the same anti-capitalist greed-bashing rhetoric used so successfully in communist countries."[1]

This was not the first time that someone had tried to sideline Fischel as an expert witness. Noted class action lawyer William Lerach had sued Lexecon, a firm owned in part by Fischel that provided expert witness testimony. Lerach claimed that the firm had prepared expert reports used as a basis for allowing a savings and loan association to continue in business until it ultimately failed, spectacularly. Lexecon settled the suit by paying $700,000, but Fischel thought that the lawsuit was simply an effort to undercut his credibility as an expert witness. Lawyers from the Lerach firm were also disparaging Fischel in other litigation. One was reported to have said that "that little shit is dead, and he'll never testify again." Fischel sued for defamation, but suffered several setbacks in that litigation before the U.S. Supreme Court ordered the case to be tried in Chicago, Fischel's hometown. The jury came back with a guilty verdict asking for payment of $45 million in actual damages before it began deliberating on punitive damages. Lerach settled the case by paying $50 million to Fischel, who insisted that the money be wire-transferred before he allowed the jury to be released from the case.

A three-judge panel from the Court of Appeals for the Tenth Circuit in Colorado granted Nacchio bail pending appeal of his conviction, suggesting that the judges thought the appeal might have merit. Nacchio's conviction was reversed on appeal (in a 2–1 decision) because of the exclusion of Fischel's testimony. The trial judge had excluded that testimony because he did not believe that its methodology had been sufficiently established. However, the majority on appeal noted that the judge could have allowed Fischel to testify on his methodology before the jury. Prosecutors could then point out any flaws on cross-examination.

The appellate panel also took the unusual step of removing the trial judge from further participation in the case—a sanction normally levied only in cases where a trial judge badly overstepped his authority. However, in a highly unusual action, the entire Tenth Circuit group of judges, sitting *en banc,* reversed the decision of the majority of the three-judge panel by a vote of 5 to 4, and Nacchio was jailed on April 14, 2009. The Supreme Court declined to consider an appeal of that decision.

Nacchio had only a little better luck in the appeal of his sentence. The Court of Appeals for the Tenth Circuit ruled that it was improperly calculated and returned the case to the lower court for resentencing. However, the district court reduced his six-year sentence by only two months. He was represented in that proceeding by Sean Berkowitz, the former Enron Task Force prosecutor in the case against Ken Lay and Jeffrey Skilling. Nacchio received better treatment with respect to his objection to Qwest's $400 million settlement of a class-action shareholder lawsuit brought by a union pension fund over the Qwest accounting manipulations. Nacchio was excluded from the settlement, even though Qwest was obligated to indemnify Nacchio from such liabilities. An appeals court ruled that the lower court had acted wrongly in allowing Nacchio to be excluded from the settlement.[2]

Nortel

A serial accounting manipulator was Nortel Network, which was forced to lay off over 60,000 employees when the company's executives could no longer cover up its declining finances. Nortel's stock price plunged 90 percent after the company disclosed that it had lost $19 billion in the fourth quarter of 2000. That loss tied with the one by General Motors for the largest-ever quarterly loss, a record that had been set in 1992. Both records would fall during the subprime crisis when the American International Group (AIG) posted a quarterly loss of over $60 billion. Meanwhile, executives at Nortel were paid $2.5 billion in stock options as compensation. Accounting problems continued at Nortel for several years. The company was not even able to file financial reports in 2003 or 2004. It reported a $2.58 billion loss for 2005, and in 2006 it restated $866 million in revenue in prior years. That was the third restatement in three years.

Nortel agreed to pay $2.4 billion to settle various class-action suits over its accounting practices in February 2006. The lead plaintiffs in the class actions were the Ontario Public Service Employees Union Pension Fund and the Ontario Teachers' Pension Plan Board. The Court of Appeals for the Second Circuit upheld a fee award to the Milberg Weiss & Bershad law firm in August 2008 equal to 3 percent of its recovery in the Nortel litigation. That settlement was for $438 million in cash plus Nortel common shares valued at more than $700 million. An 8 percent award of attorney fees was given in another action by another class of plaintiffs for a settlement of a similar amount.

Nortel also agreed late in 2007 to pay the SEC $35 million to settle charges over its accounting manipulations between 2000 and 2003. The SEC agreed to distribute those funds to shareholders, which meant that it was taking funds from existing shareholders and giving them to shareholders who held the stock while the wrongdoing was under way. That redistribution of wealth was ordered even though the existing shareholders had done nothing wrong. Moreover, the prior shareholders were the ones who were supposed to be monitoring the company while the wrongdoing was occurring. Nortel also agreed to report periodically to the SEC on its efforts to improve its accounting practices.

This was a highly favorable settlement for Nortel, but it was obtained at the expense of its officers, who had also been sued by the SEC. One of those employees, MaryAnne Pahapill, an assistant controller, complained that Nortel had stopped paying her legal fees because of pressure from the SEC that required the company to "cooperate" in order to reach a favorable settlement with the agency. After Pahapill lost her right to counsel, she represented herself. She agreed with the SEC to suspend the statute of limitations without understanding what that waiver meant for her liability.

Frank A. Dunn, Nortel's former CEO, made the same complaint over the decision by Nortel to cut off legal fees for employees involved in the accounting scandals. His troubles only increased. The Royal Canadian Mounted Police, which acts as Canada's policing body for financial as well as other crimes, obtained criminal charges against three former executives of Nortel in June 2008, including Dunn. The charges related to their role in the accounting manipulations that occurred in 2002 and 2003.

Nortel continued to struggle. In the first quarter of 2008, it lost $138 million, $35 million more than it reported to have lost in the first quarter of the prior year. In the third quarter of 2008, Nortel had a $3.41 billion loss and announced the layoff of 1,300 workers. It finally declared bankruptcy in January 2009, after it was unable to meet its debt obligations. The company also announced plans to cut another 3,200 employees.

Adelphia

An even bigger scandal unfolded at Adelphia Communications. The Rigas family of Coudersport, Pennsylvania, built that cable company into a giant in the industry and maintained control of the company after it went public in 1986. Using that control, the family entered into a "co-borrowing" arrangement with Adelphia under which Adelphia and the Rigas family could draw from the same credit line. The Rigas family withdrew $2.3 billion for personal use without publicly disclosing the amount of the loan. An internal investigation by the company also discovered that members of the Rigas family had helped themselves liberally to the company's corporate jet and used company assets to fund a rich lifestyle.

The accounting firm Deloitte & Touche agreed in 2006 to pay $210 million to settle claims over its failed audits of Adelphia Communications. Three Rigas family members were indicted, including the eighty-year-old John Rigas, the company's founder then suffering from cancer, and his two sons. They were arrested in a dawn raid on their New York apartment. John Rigas was handcuffed for his perp walk before the press, a bit of dark theater that drew a harsh rebuke from the New York Civil Liberties Union.

The Rigas family members went on trial, which lasted for months. John Rigas and his son Timothy were convicted on some, but not all, charges. The jury was deadlocked over the charges brought against the other son, Michael, so a mistrial was declared for Michael. Prosecutors requested sentences of up to 215 years for John and Timothy Rigas, but the judge sentenced Timothy Rigas to a term of twenty years and John Rigas to fifteen years. Such a sentence probably meant the elderly Rigas would die in prison, but the judge provided a rather obscure formula for Rigas's release in the event it appeared that he was in extremis after two years of imprisonment. In order to avoid a second trial, Michael Rigas pleaded guilty to a single count of altering business records and was given a sentence of ten months of home confinement. The Court of Appeals for the Second Circuit ordered John and Timothy Rigas to be resentenced after it overturned on appeal one of the eighteen counts on which they were convicted. They were given twelve and seventeen years, respectively, a three-year reduction.

Other Telecom Firms

The list of telecom companies embroiled in accounting scandals was long. They included Global Crossing, headed by Gary Winnick and audited by Arthur Andersen, in the fourth-largest bankruptcy in U.S. history. The company had massively manipulated its accounts, but Winnick escaped prosecution by both the SEC and the Justice Department. He also kept the fortune that he had reaped from the company, estimated at more than $1 billion, which was held in a controversial tax shelter. Winnick spent $94 million of those profits to purchase an estate in Bel Air, California, and with the rest had thoughtfully, and liberally, contributed to politicians of both political parties, so politicians did not have much interest in pursuing him.

Winnick agreed to pay a paltry $30 million to settle class-action claims for his role at Global Crossing. That class action garnered some $450 million in total settlements, mostly from the company's investment bankers and commercial banks. That was little recompense for the $45 billion in shareholder value that was lost after the company revealed its accounting manipulations. The lead plaintiffs in that class action were the Public Employees Retirement System of Ohio and the State Teachers Retirement System of Ohio. They lost more than $110 million on their Global Crossing stock. Global Crossing was reorganized and emerged from bankruptcy in 2003.

WorldCom

Perhaps the WorldCom scandal was the most explosive scandal of all. Its bankruptcy surpassed even that of Enron's as the largest ever, until the fall of Lehman Brothers during the subprime crisis. At the time it failed, WorldCom had revenue of $30 billion and more than 60,000 employees. The firm was an amalgamation of companies put together by Bernie Ebbers, who had been a teacher-coach, a warehouse manager, and the operator of a string of motels before investing in Long Distance Discount Services (LDDS), a small long-distance telephone company in Mississippi. LDDS was failing before Ebbers reorganized it, and under his leadership it began a string of acquisitions that culminated in the formation of WorldCom. His largest acquisition was MCI Communications, a company two and a half times the size of WorldCom. That merger was the largest in history at the time.

Then in 2000 Ebbers attempted to acquire Sprint for $129 billion, but the Justice Department and the European Union blocked that deal on antitrust grounds. That was a very poor decision. The acquisition would have helped reduce growing overcapacity problems in the industry. Consolidation would have allowed the combined company to reduce expenses and cut operations, something those two as competitors were loathe to do. When the dot.com bubble burst later in 2000, both WorldCom and Sprint found themselves crippled.

WorldCom started unraveling after announcing on October 26, 2000, that it was writing off $685 million in receivables. That bad news was followed by a profit warning of lower than expected profits for the fourth quarter of that year. The company's stock went into free fall, plunging by 75 percent from its high in 1999. WorldCom tried to support its stock by claiming large profits for 2001 and for the first quarter of 2002. However, the company was actually losing money, and the claimed profits were coming from accounting manipulations that were concealed from its unseeing auditor, Arthur Andersen.

By the first quarter of 2002, WorldCom had run out of accounting manipulations, and it was clear that the company was suffering. The SEC began an investigation of WorldCom's accounting practices and, shortly afterward, the WorldCom board asked for Ebbers's resignation. Before that action was taken by the board, Ebbers had borrowed $408 million from WorldCom, which he used to meet margin calls on loans secured by his declining WorldCom stock— loans not disclosed to the public.

WorldCom continued its downward spiral and declared bankruptcy on July 21, 2002, wiping out what had once been $180 billion in shareholder equity. Subsequent investigations of WorldCom's claimed profit in 2000 of $4.6 billion showed that the company was actually experiencing a loss of $48.9 billion. The reported profit in 2001 of $2.1 billion was found in reality to be a loss of $15.6 billion.

Following closely in the wake of the Enron collapse, the WorldCom bankruptcy set off a media and prosecutorial frenzy. Internal reports commissioned by WorldCom resulted in the trashing of Ebbers and his management team. A "corporate monitor," appointed by a court in an action brought by the SEC, was given authority to oversee the management of WorldCom. This became a favorite prosecutorial demand in the Enron-era scandals. These corporate monitors were often former prosecutors with little or no practical business experience. In the case of WorldCom, the corporate monitor was Richard Breeden, a former SEC chairman turned corporate gadfly.

Ebbers was indicted for fraud after the revelation of the size of the loans made to him by WorldCom, a disclosure that set off a storm of adverse publicity. Several other WorldCom executives were also indicted for fraud and pleaded guilty, including WorldCom's chief financial officer, Scott Sullivan. Although Sullivan had initially claimed that Ebbers had had no knowledge of the accounting manipulations, he changed that story in order to reach a favorable plea bargain with prosecutors. As part of his "cooperation" agreement with federal prosecutors, Sullivan became the lead witness against Ebbers at his trial.

Sullivan testified that Ebbers had refused to issue a profit warning after it became clear in the third quarter of 2000 that WorldCom would not meet analysts' expectations. Sullivan stated that he had told Ebbers that it would be necessary to make an improper adjustment to revenue figures, in the amount of $133 million, in order to cover up the declining revenues. Sullivan testified that Ebbers responded by stating "we have to hit our numbers."

Sullivan also discovered that WorldCom's "line cost expenses" were almost $1 billion greater than anticipated. Sullivan claimed that he had reported this discovery to Ebbers, who demanded that Sullivan continue to meet the numbers. Sullivan came up with a plan to capitalize the line costs, which took them out of the expense category and reduced their effect on earnings. Some $717 million of line costs were then capitalized. Sullivan testified that he had told Ebbers that what he was doing "wasn't right," but Ebbers did not object to the adjustment and later approved it. Sullivan testified that Ebbers had said "we have to grow our revenue and we have to cut our expenses, but we have to hit the numbers this quarter." Ebbers did not tell financial analysts about this adjustment when he spoke to them. Instead, Ebbers stated that "there were no storms on the horizon" and that investors should "go out and buy stock."

Two WorldCom employees objected to those adjustments, saying that "we shouldn't be making adjustments; we've got to get the operations of this company going; we shouldn't be putting people in this position." Sullivan testified that Ebbers apologized to one of the objecting employees. Thereafter, WorldCom lowered its earnings estimates. However, WorldCom was not able to meet even the revised expectations of analysts and made more improper accounting adjustments to reduce line costs in order to reduce the damage.

The situation continued to deteriorate, so Sullivan created a program he called "Close the Gap," which involved massive accounting manipulations needed to raise WorldCom's revenues enough to meet its market guidance claims. Sullivan testified that he had described these adjustments to Ebbers. In a voice mail to Ebbers, Sullivan called these adjustments "accounting fluff," "one-time stuff," and "junk." Ron Beaumont, WorldCom's chief operating officer, briefed the WorldCom board of directors on the "Close the Gap" exercise. One board member questioned Sullivan on the appropriateness of such a program. When informed of that fact, Ebbers told Sullivan and Beaumont that the next board presentation should be on a higher level and should omit the "Close the Gap" briefing.

Trial testimony also established that Ebbers had sent a memorandum to Beaumont, asking him where they stood "on those one-time events that had to happen in order for us to have a chance to make our numbers." During one meeting on line costs, Ebbers stated that his "life blood was in the stock of a company" and that if the share price fell below $12 he would be destroyed financially. WorldCom employees, thereafter, capitalized an additional $610 million in line costs in order to meet WorldCom's 12 percent growth rate target.

More manipulations were implemented in the fourth quarter of 2001 in order to meet growth targets. In an analysts' conference call discussing those fourth-quarter results (such conference calls were a ritual carried out by executives at public companies to expound upon their quarterly results and explain away any problems), Ebbers stated, "we stand by our accounting" and, later in a TV interview, declared that "we've been very conservative on our accounting." However, the wheels soon came off WorldCom, and it fell into bankruptcy.

Ebbers testified at his criminal trial that he was financially unsophisticated and that he had little knowledge about technology, which seemed inconsistent with his position as the head of one of the world's most sophisticated technology companies. Ebbers claimed that his business success was due to his ability to supervise salespeople and put together acquisitions. He denied Sullivan's accusations that he had been made aware of the fraudulent accounting programs constructed by Sullivan. However, the federal judge hearing the case, Barbara S. Jones, instructed jurors that they could find Ebbers guilty if he deliberately closed his eyes to fraud and that no "direct proof" was needed to establish guilt. That helped assure a conviction, and prosecutors then demanded and received what amounted to a life sentence for Ebbers from Judge Jones.

Ebbers, age sixty-three and suffering from heart problems, was given a twenty-five-year sentence. In contrast, Sullivan, who was twenty years younger than Ebbers, was sentenced to only five years even though he was, as the district court concluded, the "architect" of the accounting fraud at WorldCom. Unlike Ebbers, Sullivan had no basis for claiming a lack of knowledge concerning accounting practices. Sullivan was a certified public accountant who was fully aware of the effects of the accounting manipulations that he designed and implemented. The Court of Appeals for the Second Circuit affirmed Ebbers's conviction on appeal.

Ebbers contended in his appeal that government prosecutors acted improperly when they granted immunity to six of their own witnesses but refused to do the same for potential defense witnesses who were refusing to testify. Those defense witnesses were concerned that the government might prosecute them if they cooperated with the defense. The appeals court conceded that the ability to grant immunity to government witnesses while denying immunity to defense witnesses was a potentially powerful tool for a prosecutor. This was especially true because prosecutors can create incentives for defense witnesses to invoke their right against self-incrimination, such as having received a "target letter." However, the court concluded that there was not a sufficient showing by Ebbers's lawyers that the witnesses they sought immunity for would have provided enough exculpatory evidence to convince a jury of his innocence.

The court also concluded that Ebbers's sentence was not unreasonable. Ebbers had argued that his sentence should be no greater than that of Sullivan. The company's controller, David Myers, and the accounting director, Buford Yates, received sentences of only a year and a day. The director of management reporting, Betty Vinson, was given only five months, and the director of legal entity accounting, Troy Norman, was sentenced to three years on probation. That contrasted sharply with the sentence meted out to Ebbers.

The court acknowledged that "twenty-five years is a long sentence for a white-collar crime, longer than the sentences routinely imposed by many states for violent crimes, including murder, or other serious crimes such as serial child molestation." It noted, however, that under federal sentencing guidelines "it may well be that all but the most trivial fraud in publicly traded companies may trigger sentences amounting to life imprisonment." The court conceded the danger of such sentences. "Even the threat of indictment on wafer-thin evidence of fraud may therefore compel a plea" of guilty from corporate executives. Instead, it washed its hands of the matter by asserting that it was up to Congress, not the courts, to change sentencing guidelines.

The court also deemed that Ebbers's conduct went beyond "puffery or cheerleading or even a misguided effort to protect the company, its employees, and its shareholders" from a temporary downturn in business. Rather, it found that Ebbers was seeking to create a false picture of profitability in order to protect his own personal finances. In view of those circumstances and federal sentencing guidelines, the court concluded that Ebbers's sentence was "harsh but not unreasonable."[3]

The two lead partners at Arthur Andersen assigned to the WorldCom account reached a settlement with the SEC. Melvin Dick agreed not to practice as an accountant for a public company for four years. Kenneth Avery, Dick's partner, agreed to a bar of three years in April 2008. Proving once again that human cupidity has no limits, and that the SEC's insider trading rules pose no deterrent to those possessing inside information, Van D. Greenfield agreed to settle charges that he had traded on inside information obtained while serving on bankruptcy committees at WorldCom and Adelphia.

Other Scandals

HealthSouth

HealthSouth in Alabama hosted another Enron-era accounting scandal. Richard Scrushy, the company's founder and chairman, was paid over $260 million between 1996 and 2002. That compensation was mostly in the form of stock options, which had been inflated in value as a result of massive accounting manipulations at HealthSouth that overstated assets and earnings by $2.7 billion—dodges that later cost HealthSouth $445 million to settle a class-action suit. The company also paid $3 million as a part of a deferred prosecution agreement with the Justice Department and another $100 million to the SEC. HealthSouth's auditor, Ernst & Young, agreed to pay $109 million to settle class-action claims over its audits of the company.

Fifteen HealthSouth executives pleaded guilty to criminal charges, including all five chief financial officers who served over a fifteen-year period. The district court meted out only lenient sanctions to the defendants. However, the Court of Appeals for the Eleventh Circuit ruled that the district court had erred in awarding no jail time to Malcolm McVay, a former chief financial officer at HealthSouth. McVay was then sentenced to six months' home detention. Another CFO, Mike Martin, had to be resentenced three times. The first sentence mandated no jail time; the second required only one week of imprisonment; and the third was a more hefty three years.

One of the stiffest sentences went to a whistle-blower in the case, Weston Smith, who was given twenty-seven months. Two HealthSouth executives were acquitted after a jury trial. Hannibal Crumpler, a HealthSouth vice president, was the only person convicted by a jury of a crime in connection with HealthSouth's accounting manipulations. He was sentenced to eight years in prison.

Scrushy was indicted, but fought the charges vigorously in and out of court, launching a publicity campaign to portray himself as a friend of the underprivileged. After a month of deliberations, the jury acquitted Scrushy of all charges despite tape recordings of a HealthSouth CFO-turned-government informant, who had unsuccessfully tried to entice Scrushy into making admissions of his knowledge of the fraud. The government also tried to prejudice the jury by showing Scrushy's rich lifestyle, but that effort failed. The prosecutors tried to bring up the Enron scandal, but the trial judge ruled out mention of it because Scrushy had nothing to do with Enron. Scrushy walked away from that trial a free man, but he later agreed to pay the SEC $81 million to settle claims concerning his involvement in the accounting manipulations at HealthSouth.

Scrushy successfully turned the tables on the prosecutors by actively seeking to prejudice the jury pool by creating favorable publicity about himself while awaiting trial. He did so through a talk show that he hosted, on which he interviewed individuals being pilloried in the press. One show featured Judge R.M. Moore, who had been removed from the Alabama bench for keeping a sculpture on display in the courthouse on which the Ten Commandments were written. Scrushy also joined a local black church in Birmingham in an area from which the jury would be selected. After his acquittal, Scrushy made a point of appearing at the trial of Enron executives Ken Lay and Jeffrey Skilling in Houston during the testimony of Andrew Fastow. Scrushy likened Fastow to the executives who had testified against him without success. That appearance and other statements by Scrushy appeared to be throwing sand in the face of the government prosecutors.

The prosecutors dropped their initial plans to appeal Scrushy's acquittal after his lawyers reminded them that the Constitution bars double jeopardy. Instead, the prosecutors relentlessly continued their pursuit of Scrushy on other fronts and eventually indicted him, and former Alabama governor Don Siegelman, on bribery-related charges. This turned into a donnybrook for all involved. The new charges against Scrushy and Siegelman were a convenient "two for one" retaliatory prosecution for prior government setbacks against both Scrushy and Siegelman.

Previously, in 2004, the Justice Department had charged Siegelman with fraud in connection with an alleged bid-rigging scheme. Those charges were dropped by the U.S. Attorney's Office in the Northern District of Alabama, after the jury was seated and after the judge excluded much of the testimony that the government was planning to offer. The judge harshly rebuked the prosecutors for bringing that case. Siegelman, a Democrat, called this whole effort "Republican politics at its worst." Again, defiance served only to enrage the prosecutors and spur them on to bring more charges.

The new charges against Scrushy and Siegelman were somewhat murky and not a little absurd. They involved a claim that Scrushy had been appointed to the Alabama Certificate of Need Board, which licensed hospitals in the state, in exchange for campaign contributions totaling $500,000. Those contributions were used to pay off debts of the Siegelman campaign to the Alabama Lottery Foundation and the Alabama Education Foundation. Those debts were the result of Siegelman's efforts to create a lottery in Alabama in order to raise funds for improving the quality of education in that state, which, on its face, seemed to be a worthy cause that has been adopted in many states.

Siegelman's lawyers pointed out that every candidate for a high-profile elective office was guilty of the same conduct—the making of political contributions followed by appointment to office. Indeed, if it were otherwise, appointees to embassies in attractive locations would be especially ripe for prosecution. After all, Joseph P. Kennedy's geopolitical skills were not the basis for his appointment to the Court of St. James by Franklin Roosevelt, and Kennedy's business ethics certainly were not the reason for his appointment to be the first chairman of the SEC. Normally, such conduct is considered politics as usual, but not in the Enron era, particularly after two high-profile losses by the government at the trials of Scrushy and Siegelman.

The Scrushy case suffered from a number of other weaknesses, not least of which was the fact that Scrushy had served on the licensing board under three prior administrations, which suggests that he had the experience for the position. The prosecution also claimed that Siegelman would have been personally liable for the debts if they were not paid off, but that was a most unlikely scenario.

After Scrushy and Siegelman refused to plead guilty, the government then issued a superseding indictment, adding on more charges and including two of Siegelman's aides in the governor's office. The prosecutors apparently hoped those aides would turn on Siegelman, but they remained loyal, went to trial, and were acquitted on all counts. Scrushy and Siegelman did not fare so well. The jury convicted them, but only after the trial judge twice ordered the jury to continue deliberations after they had reported that they were deadlocked. That "Allen charge" tends to influence jurors into believing that the judge thinks that a conviction is appropriate. The convictions were also sullied by the fact that the indictment included a charge that Scrushy and Siegelman had deprived the state of Alabama of the "honest" services of its governor. That was the very same theory relied upon by the Enron Task Force.

The trial judge sentenced Scrushy and Siegelman to over six years in prison and denied both bail pending appeal. The defendants appealed the denial of bail, and the Court of Appeals for the Eleventh Circuit directed the district court to explain the reason for that denial. The trial judge subsequently set forth his reasons, concluding that there was no substantial question on appeal that would justify overturning their convictions. The appeals court disagreed, holding that "substantial questions" had been raised in Siegelman's appeal, and it ordered his release, pending his appeal, on March 27, 2008, after he had spent nine months in jail.

Siegelman's conviction on the bribery charge was subsequently upheld on appeal, but the "honest services" charges were dismissed, and an order was issued for him to be resentenced. Despite the fact that Siegelman had earlier been sentenced to only six years and that some of the charges were dismissed on appeal, prosecutors asked for a sentence of twenty years for the reduced charges.

Siegelman's prosecution became the center of a political controversy of no small moment. The Democratic Party was claiming that his prosecution by the Justice Department was as politically motivated as the firing of several U.S. attorneys had been. Forty-four state attorneys general signed a petition, a list that even included a few Republicans, asking Congress to investigate the prosecution of Siegelman. The House Judiciary Committee requested that Siegelman be brought to Washington, DC to testify on his claim that he was being prosecuted because he was a popular Democratic candidate in Alabama. A Judiciary Committee spokesperson said his testimony was necessary because the Justice Department had refused to cooperate with the committee's inquiries of his claims.

A letter from the Judiciary Committee to the then–attorney general Alberto R. Gonzales noted:

> In May, 2007, Jill Simpson, a Republican attorney in Alabama who had worked for Mr. Siegelman's 2002 Republican opponent, swore in an affidavit that in 2002, a former protégée of Karl Rove [President George W. Bush's political adviser] told a small group of Republican political operatives that Karl Rove and two U.S. Attorneys in Alabama were working to "take care of" Mr. Siegelman. The Rove protégé, Bill Canary, is married to Leura Canary, who[m] President Bush appointed in 2001 to be the U.S. Attorney in the Middle District of Alabama. In 2005, the U.S. Attorney's Office in the Middle District of Alabama indicted Mr. Siegelman (Ms. Canary recused herself from participating in the Siegelman case in 2002). In her affidavit, Ms. Simpson said that Bill Canary told her and two colleagues that "Karl [Rove] had spoken with the Department of Justice and the Department was already pursuing Don Siegelman." The phone call that Ms. Simpson was referring to occurred in November, 2002, when Mr. Siegelman was seeking a recount of the vote he had just lost, and when Republican operatives were concerned that Mr. Siegelman could be a significant political threat in future elections.[4]

Gonzales and Rove left the government as this controversy expanded. The fire was fueled further in February 2008 after *60 Minutes* featured a segment on the Siegelman prosecution. A few months later, Rove was subpoenaed to appear before the House Judiciary Committee to testify on the role he played in the prosecution of Siegelman. He initially refused to testify, but later did so and denied any substantial involvement in the U.S. attorney scandals. Harriet E. Miers, a one-time Supreme Court nominee and White House aide to President Bush, also agreed to testify.

More controversy arose in November 2008, after it was disclosed that Leura Canary, the U.S. attorney in Alabama, had continued to participate in the Siegelman prosecution after the date that she claimed to have recused herself from the case. Some jurors were also said to have sent text messages to one another during the trial and passed notes to the prosecution during the trial asking about the marital status of an FBI agent. However, the appellate court rejected claims of jury tampering.

The convictions of Scrushy and Siegelman were upheld by the Court of Appeals for the Eleventh Circuit. However, in June 2010, the Supreme Court ordered the Eleventh Circuit to reexamine those convictions in light of the Supreme Court's decision in the case against Enron's Jeffrey Skilling, which held that the honest services prohibition in the mail and wire fraud statute applies only to bribes and kickbacks. Although the appeals court had dismissed the honest services charge against Siegelman, it was also required to consider whether the jury instructions on that charge tainted other charges or confused the jury.

Scrushy refused to testify in his HealthSouth criminal trial, but he was compelled to testify in a case brought on behalf of HealthSouth shareholders. Scrushy denied any knowledge of the accounting manipulation, but the jury found otherwise and levied a $2.88 billion judgment against him.

Tyco

One of the most famous Enron-era scandals involved Dennis Kozlowski, the CEO of Tyco International. Kozlowski, who began his career as an auditor, built Tyco into a diversified conglomerate in the 1990s through hundreds of acquisitions, many of which were multibillion-dollar deals. By 2001, Tyco had over 270,000 employees and reported revenues of $36 billion for the year. Kozlowski was likened to a corporate "Babe Ruth" due to the success of those transactions. However, questions began to be raised concerning Tyco's accounting procedures and as the twenty-first century opened the stock began to suffer.

Scandal emerged in June 2002, after it was announced that Kozlowski was being indicted on charges that he had evaded New York state sales taxes on artwork valued at $13 million. That artwork was bought for a Fifth Avenue apartment, which Tyco had purchased for Kozlowski's personal use. The indictment was a bit abnormal in that normally it is the seller who is responsible for assuring that sales taxes are paid, rather than the buyer. Kozlowski resigned from Tyco after his indictment and after an internal investigation disclosed a number of his abuses of Tyco funds. In particular, furnishings for the apartment were lavish, including a $6,000 shower curtain. Kozlowski also spent $2.1 million in Tyco funds on a birthday party for his wife that was held in Sardinia.

Kozlowski's indictment was expanded, after he refused to plead guilty, to include charges that he and Mark Swartz, another Tyco executive, had stolen $170 million from the firm through bonuses that were not approved by the board of directors. Tyco's general counsel, Mark Belnick, was also indicted for not properly disclosing loans made to him by Tyco on an internal document called an officers and directors questionnaire, which asked for disclosure of nonroutine transactions.

The trial of Kozlowski and Swartz lasted six months, and a single juror ("Juror No. 4," later identified as Ruth Jordan) refused to vote in favor of conviction, thus a mistrial was declared. Jordan was pilloried in the press. Kozlowski and Swartz were convicted in a retrial, but only after another lone juror holdout finally succumbed to pressure for a conviction. Kozlowski, age fifty-eight, received a sentence that required him to serve a minimum of just over eight years in prison and up to as much as twenty-five years. Kozlowski, thereafter, settled his sales-tax charges by agreeing to pay $21.2 million. This was in addition to the $167 million he had been ordered to pay in fines and restitution relating to his convictions for looting Tyco. Adding insult to injury, Kozlowski's wife, Karen, sued him for divorce after he began his prison sentence and sought most of what was left of his assets. Kozlowski reached a settlement with her that required the sale of their $19 million mansion in Boca Raton, Florida. She had been living there pending the divorce proceedings.

Kozlowski returned to the public eye in a lengthy television interview conducted from prison by Neil Cavuto, a host at the new FOX Business News channel, in November 2007. Kozlowski described how, instead of managing a Fortune 500 company like Tyco, his job in prison was to "run the laundry room." Appearing contrite, he conceded that the party on Sardinia had been "over the top," but claimed that he was surprised to see the models who had been hired to circulate at the party dressed in skimpy Roman togas.

Kozlowski returned to the airwaves on March 19, 2008, in a CNBC program on his leadership at Tyco. Called "American Greed," the show repeated scenes from the toga party on Sardinia as well as photos of the infamous shower curtain. Juror No. 4, a former law school graduate and a schoolteacher, was interviewed at length, and she appeared to be anything but the unstable person previously portrayed in the press. Kozlowski was also interviewed and appeared to be somewhat crestfallen, which may have been due to the fact that an appeal of his conviction had just been denied. That decision was affirmed by New York's highest court on October 16, 2008, and in June 2009 the U.S. Supreme Court declined to review that decision.

A jury acquitted Mark Belnick. He later agreed to settle a SEC case by

returning the $14 million in loans he had been accused of wrongfully conceal-
ing, and he was barred for five years from acting as an officer or director of
a public company. A federal court refused to dismiss a case brought by the
SEC against another former Tyco executive, Richard Power, for his role in
the financial fraud at that company. The court rejected a claim that the SEC's
case had exceeded the five-year federal statute of limitations. The actions that
were the subject of the SEC complaint took place in 1999, and the SEC did
not file its complaint until 2006.

   In 2007, PricewaterhouseCoopers paid $225 million to settle claims over its
audit work for Tyco. Tyco settled SEC claims over its accounting manipulations under Kozlowski in April 2006 by paying $50 million. Tyco also paid
$3.2 billion to settle a class-action lawsuit over its accounting misstatements.
The class-action law firm in that case, Milberg Weiss, was paid $120 million
for services rendered in collecting that sum.

   A class action filed against Merrill Lynch claimed that one of its analysts,
Phua Young, had filed false and misleading financial analyst reports on Tyco
because of his close relationship with Kozlowski, who had befriended Young.
They had exchanged gifts of wine and champagne. Young was also allowed
to fly on the Tyco jet, and Kozlowski, somewhat bizarrely, used Tyco funds
to hire a private investigative firm, Kroll Associates, to investigate Young's
fiancée. Kozlowski rewarded Merrill Lynch with lead underwriter status in
a $2.1 billion Tyco bond offering after it hired Young. There was a potential
class of over 600,000 investors in this lawsuit, but it was settled by Merrill
Lynch for a mere $4.9 million, the judge noting that the case was extremely
weak. That settlement payment would have about covered Young's salary
at Merrill Lynch for one year. Young did not escape sanctions entirely. The
National Association of Securities Dealers (NASD) suspended him from the
securities industry for a year after the Tyco scandal broke.

Cendant and AOL

More than five years after the Enron fiasco, other contemporaneous accounting scandals were still winding up. One pre-Enron scandal was also lingering
at Cendant, where revenues had been inflated by more than $500 million and
assets were also grossly inflated. Walter Forbes, former chairman of Cendant,
was charged with insider trading for selling $11 million in Cendant stock
before the disclosure of its accounting problems. Forbes claimed that he had
been unaware of the accounting manipulations, revelation of which caused a
$14 billion drop in the value of the company's stock.

   Forbes was tried three times. The first two juries were hung, suggesting that
it was a difficult case. Nevertheless, federal prosecutors tried him for a third
time, a trial in which he was convicted. Forbes was sentenced to over twelve
years in prison and ordered to pay $3 billion in restitution. At age sixty-four,
Forbes seemed to have gotten off lightly in comparison to others convicted of

Enron-era crimes. Forbes's conviction and sentence were upheld by the Court of Appeals for the Second Circuit, which rejected his claim that the trial court had erred in refusing to grant immunity to a witness the defense wanted to call at trial, a former chief financial officer. In rejecting that claim, the appeals court cited its prior decision in the Ebbers case.[5]

The criminal conviction of Cendant vice chairman E. Kirk Shelton for his role in the accounting manipulations at the firm was upheld on appeal. He was sentenced to ten years in prison and ordered, like Forbes, to pay more than $3 billion in restitution. Ernst & Young agreed to pay Cendant $300 million to settle claims over its audit work for the company. The accounting firm had previously paid $335 million to settle shareholder claims over that audit work. Cendant itself paid $3.5 billion to settle shareholder claims.

Cendant was the largest shareholder in Homestore, a company that was assisted by AOL Time Warner in manipulating its accounting records through circular transactions that allowed both companies to inflate their revenue. The Court of Appeals for the Ninth Circuit set aside the conviction of Stuart Wolff, the former CEO of Homestore, finding that the district court judge should have recused himself from the case because he owned stock in America Online. Ten other Homestore executives pleaded guilty to criminal charges. However, their sentences were relatively light, at most a year in prison and an additional six months of home detention. AOL Time Warner agreed to pay $6.5 million to settle a lawsuit brought by Homestore over those accounting practices.

AOL Time Warner engaged in similar conduct at PurchasePro.Com, where three executives pleaded guilty to criminal charges. Three other PurchasePro executives were acquitted at trial, and charges against a fourth executive were dismissed. Two former AOL employees were also acquitted of charges related to that conduct. Federal prosecutors then focused their attention on Charles E. Johnson Jr., CEO and founder of PurchasePro. A mistrial was declared after three weeks of testimony in his case because it was discovered that e-mails Johnson had produced to the government were forged by Johnson to undercut the government's case. Johnson's lawyer, who had previously represented Monica Lewinsky, withdrew from the case, and a new lawyer was hired, someone who had been one of the many lawyers representing O.J. Simpson.

Further charges were brought against Johnson in connection with those forgeries. He claimed that he had created the e-mails as a joke for his lawyer and that they had mistakenly found their way into the documents given to the government. Johnson was, thereafter, convicted on the charges brought against him and given a nine-year sentence. The district court also enjoined Johnson in an SEC action against him and barred him permanently from serving as an officer of a public company, as well as fining him $3 million.

It was claimed by some of the PurchasePro defendants that federal prosecutors had engaged in a little misconduct of their own. The SEC sought to double-team the PurchasePro defendants by bringing both a civil case and a criminal case. However, the federal district court judge in that case chastised the SEC for its "extremely questionable" treatment of witnesses who had entered into cooperation agreements with the commission. The judge found that the SEC had prevented the cooperating executives from being deposed by Johnson's lawyers, so he could not shape his defense based on an examination of their testimony before his criminal trial. The SEC did this by intentionally delaying seeking immunity for those witnesses or requiring them to be deposed as a part of their agreement to cooperate. The judge stated that neither the SEC nor the Justice Department had "dealt straightforwardly, candidly and in good faith" in carrying out those actions.[6]

The district court rejected a SEC request that a permanent injunction, and a permanent bar from serving as an officer of a public company, be imposed on one of those executives, Christopher Benyo. He had been found guilty at trial on one of the four counts brought against him by the SEC, but the court stated that the sanctions sought by the SEC were inappropriate and so disproportionate to the conduct at issue as to be "foolish."

AOL Time Warner paid $300 million to the SEC in 2005 to settle charges that it had inflated its revenue. The SEC continued its pursuit of AOL executives involved in that accounting manipulation. In May 2008 the commission charged eight former AOL executives with fraud in inflating online advertising revenue by more than $1 billion in 2000. That inflation occurred just about the time that AOL was planning to merge with Time Warner. Four defendants settled the SEC charges without admitting or denying its allegations. They agreed to pay fines ranging from $750,000 to $4 million. Two of the defendants were barred from serving as directors of public companies for periods of seven and ten years, respectively. Four defendants, including Joseph A. Ripp, the former AOL chief financial officer, vowed to contest the SEC's charges. Ironically, Ripp had been billed by the Justice Department as a whistle-blower who discovered and moved to stop the fraud at PurchasePro and Homestore.

In another case, a federal district court dismissed criminal charges against three executives of FLIR Systems because of misconduct by the SEC and the FBI. The defendants were charged with inflating FLIR's revenues through a series of fraudulent revenue recognition and accounting practices. In dismissing the charges, the district court found that the FBI had improperly used an SEC civil investigation to gather information for criminal charges. Prosecutors suspected that the targets would not cooperate if they became aware that a criminal investigation was under way.[7] The Court of Appeals for the Ninth Circuit reversed the dismissal of the indictment, concluding that such conduct was permissible.[8]

Computer Associates

Computer Associates International (subsequently renamed CA and later CA Technologies) was at the center of still another massive accounting fraud. It booked more than $2 billion in unearned revenue between 2000 and 2001. Charles Wang, its CEO, was paid $700 million and retired before those problems surfaced. His successor, Sanjay Kumar, was left with the blame for the accounting fraud. Kumar pleaded guilty to criminal charges and was sentenced to twelve years in prison. He was initially required to pay $1.02 billion in restitution, but he negotiated that amount down to $52 million, which he paid off early. Wang was not subjected to criminal charges and was protected from shareholder lawsuits as a result of a settlement of such claims by the company. However, CA was having second thoughts about that settlement and threatened to bring its own lawsuit against Wang.

The company was still trying to get its accounting right long after this scandal came to light. In June 2006, CA announced that its annual report would be delayed and that it would be restating its third-quarter results for the prior year. Nevertheless, the company did have several profitable quarters in 2007.

Grocery Store Accounting

Several grocery store chains and wholesale grocery distributors ran into problems with their accounting during the Enron era. Those companies included Kroger, ConAgra Foods, and A&P. In October 2008, Penn Traffic, a supermarket operator on the East Coast, agreed to settle SEC charges that it had inflated its operating income by prematurely recognizing promotional allowances. The activity occurred from mid-2001 until 2004. One of the larger grocery company scandals involved Royal Ahold, a Dutch company that owned grocery stores around the world, including Bi-Lo, Stop & Shop and Tops in the United States. It manipulated its accounts and was forced to acknowledge a previously undisclosed loss of $1.41 billion for 2002. A court subsequently approved a $1.1 billion settlement by Royal Ahold of a class-action suit over its accounting manipulations. Cees van der Hoeven and Michel Meurs, two senior executives at Royal Ahold, were found guilty by a Dutch court of fraud in connection with that company's accounting manipulations. They were each fined $290,000, but were given no jail time. The company returned to profitability in 2007, and even declared a dividend as 2008 began.

The largest grocery store scandal of all involved Parmalat Finanziaria, an Italian company that was looted by its founders. It was eventually determined that some $20 billion was missing from the company's treasury. Charges were brought in the Italian courts against fifty-five defendants. Their trial began in March 2008 and was expected to last at least three years. Citigroup, Morgan Stanley, Bank of America, UBS, and Deutsche Bank were charged in separate actions with manipulating the share price of Parmalat's stock. Other litigation involved the company's auditors and lawyers.

A New Jersey state court judge threw out many of the claims brought by Parmalat against Citigroup. After a jury trial in New Jersey, Citigroup was found not liable for the remaining claims brought against it by Parmalat, and the jury ordered Parmalat to pay Citigroup $364 million in damages. The federal district court in New York dismissed securities fraud suits against Bank of America and Citigroup by Parmalat in August 2008. A class-action suit against Bank of America was dismissed in September 2009, as was a suit against Parmalat's auditor, Grant Thornton. Parmalat settled claims brought by its own shareholders by agreeing to pay the comparatively small sum of $40 million. Several other settlements were reached, including one with Unicredit for $475 million.

Pharmaceutical Companies

Frederick S. Schiff, the CFO of Bristol-Myers-Squibb, was indicted for his role in the inflating of that company's revenue by over $500 million through "channel stuffing." That practice involved providing incentives to distributors to stock up on unneeded drugs so that the company could meet analysts' projections. The prosecutors in that case encountered a setback when the trial judge entered an order limiting the government's proof, after prosecutors repeatedly changed their theory of liability. The government vowed to appeal that ruling and did, but lost before the Third Circuit Court of Appeals.

Bristol-Myers-Squibb had previously entered into a deferred prosecution agreement and paid $300 million in penalties. It also paid some $500 million to class-action claims. In another case, GlaxoSmithKline, the giant pharmaceutical company, agreed to pay $3.4 billion to settle a tax claim brought by the IRS. The IRS charged that the company had improperly accounted for transactions with related entities that allowed it to reduce tax liabilities. Such "transfer pricing" schemes were common, but this was the largest-ever settlement of a tax dispute with the IRS.

Conrad Black

Still another Enron-era scandal involved Conrad Black, the English Lord and conservative publisher of several newspapers, including the *Chicago Sun-Times,* the *Daily Telegraph* of London, and the *Jerusalem Post.* The SEC accused Black of looting the holding company for his newspapers, Hollinger International. Richard Breeden, who had been appointed by the SEC as Hollinger's "corporate monitor," published a report on an "internal investigation" that he had conducted for Hollinger concerning Black's extravagant use of corporate funds. Those disclosures featured an expensive dinner party to celebrate his wife's birthday at New York's La Grenouille restaurant, where eighty celebrity guests were treated to Beluga caviar and sixty-nine bottles of expensive wine. Lord Black also spent $28,000 on dinner parties for Henry Kissinger, the former secretary of state. Those amounts were mere pocket change for Hollinger, but the stories made sensational headlines. Breeden also accused Black and his sidekick, F. David Radler, of looting $400 million from Hollinger enterprises. The SEC claimed a much smaller, but still respectable, $85 million in looting. In April 2008 Hollinger agreed to pay the SEC $21 million to settle claims concerning its prior accounting problems.

Lord Black was the target of a "documentary" titled *Citizen Black*. It was more of a parody than a documentary. Predictably, Black became the target of a criminal investigation and was indicted in Chicago by the U.S. Attorney's Office. Black was charged with looting Hollinger through payments from purchasers of Hollinger newspapers. Those payments were purportedly given in exchange for what the prosecutors claimed was a worthless agreement not to compete with the new owners.

The prosecutors were able to "flip" Radler, and he agreed to testify against Black. The trial judge, Amy St. Eve, tried to help the prosecutors by giving an "ostrich" jury instruction, allowing the jury to convict if they found that Black had consciously avoided or deliberately ignored evidence of fraud. In other words, Black did not have to commit fraud to be convicted; he only had to know of it or to have closed his eyes to it. That strategy proved only partially successful. After a four-month trial, Black was acquitted by the jury of the most serious charges brought against him. He was convicted, however, of mail and wire fraud for denying the company his "honest services" by looting some $6 million from it, an amount considerably smaller than that claimed by the prosecution.

Black was also convicted of obstruction of justice in seeking to destroy some Hollinger files, after the jury was shown a film of him removing boxes of documents from his office and loading them in his car. Black's lawyers claimed that it was not an act of obstruction because the documents were being removed after he was ousted from his position at Hollinger and because this had occurred in full view of Hollinger personnel and security cameras.

Radler, who was at the very center of the looting, was rewarded for his testimony in Black's conviction with a relatively light prison sentence of twenty-nine months and a fine of $250,000. Radler was also ordered to pay restitution amounting to several million dollars. Three other Hollinger executives were convicted with Black. Hollinger's former general counsel, Mark Kipnis, was given only six months of home confinement. The trial judge treated Black much more harshly, sentencing him to six and a half years in prison and denying him bail pending his appeal.

On March 3, 2008, at age sixty-three, Black reported to prison in Coleman, Florida, to serve his sentence, accompanied by his wife, Barbara Amiel. In the meantime, Black's notoriety had spread to his family. His son's arrest on a minor hit-and-run charge made headlines throughout the world. Conrad Black seemed unfazed by it all. He managed to write and publish a lengthy biography of Richard Nixon while awaiting trial.[9] In reviewing Nixon's legal problems during the Watergate inquiry, and the methods that were used to break Nixon's associates through the criminal process, Black gave a rather accurate description of how the process works:

> The American prosecutorial system encourages a system of suborned or intimidated perjury, or at least spontaneous clarity of recollection, to move upwards in inculpation of officials in any organization where wrongdoing is alleged. Plea bargains are negotiated by threat and financial strangulation and reduction of penalties, as lower echelons rollover in sequence blaming higher-ups. . . . This process is topped out with the "allocution," as the plea-bargainer denounces himself like the tortured victim of Stalin's show trials.[10]

Sun-Times Media, which at the time published the *Chicago Sun-Times,* declared bankruptcy in March 2009, as a result of a $510 million tax claim by the government that was a part of its vendetta against Conrad Black. The newspaper had spent about $118 million to defend Black and other executives from claims brought by class action and other defendants.

The U.S. Supreme Court agreed to review Lord Black's mail and wire fraud conviction, along with that of Enron's former CEO, Jeffrey Skilling. The issue decided by the Supreme Court was the government's expansive application of the "honest services" prohibition in the mail and wire fraud statutes. The Supreme Court ruled in June 2010 that such honest services charges were limited to cases of bribery and kickbacks and remanded the matter to consider whether Black's convictions were supportable on other grounds. The court of appeals subsequently struck two of Black's fraud count convictions, but upheld two other counts.

Kmart

Kmart filed for bankruptcy on January 22, 2002, in the middle of the Enron crisis—the largest retail bankruptcy in American history. Two Kmart vice presidents were indicted, but those charges were later dropped. A federal judge also dismissed claims against Kmart's auditor, PriceWaterhouseCoopers. The SEC brought charges against Kmart CEO Charles Conaway and CFO John McDonald. They were charged with making false statements about Kmart's liquidity and financial condition. McDonald settled the charges just before his trial started by agreeing to pay $120,000 as a civil penalty and to be barred from appearing as an accountant before the SEC for three years. A jury found Conaway guilty in June 2009. A federal magistrate ordered him to pay $10 million for that conduct, but declined to bar him from serving as an officer of a public company.

Tax Shelters: Another Enron-Era Scandal

The large accounting firms all had lucrative tax advisory practices that focused on wealthy clients. The accounting firms developed a number of complex tax shelters that allowed wealthy clients to shelter billions of dollars of income from federal tax. These tax shelters were given imaginative acronyms such as BLIPS, COBRA, BOSS, and Son of BOSS. The Justice Department began attacking those shelters in the wake of the Enron scandal. Normally, challenges to tax shelters are handled through additional legislation, administratively by the IRS, or through a civil action in federal court. After Enron, however, any matter in finance deemed objectionable by the Justice Department was subject to criminal prosecution.

KPMG entered into a deferred prosecution program with the Justice Department because of its tax shelter programs, in order to avoid the fate of Arthur Andersen. A deferred prosecution agreement avoids an indictment provided that the company does not violate the law again within a specified period, usually a year. The subject of the deferred prosecution agreement is forced to admit to having committed crimes. Heavy fines are imposed under these agreements. KPMG made its *mea culpa* and paid the federal government $456 million in order to avoid prosecution. It also paid $225 million to settle class-action lawsuits arising from that investigation.

Nineteen senior partners at KPMG were indicted for their roles in the tax shelters deemed abusive by the Justice Department. Two of those KPMG defendants pleaded guilty. Four others went quickly to trial. Three of them were convicted, and one was acquitted. Another defendant who was convicted was R.J. Ruble, an outside tax lawyer at Sidley Austin Brown & Wood, who had provided legal opinions to KPMG that concluded the shelters were legal. Normally, lawyers are free to express their legal opinions without fear of criminal prosecution, even if they are wrong, but Enron changed all the rules in financial services. Ruble was given a sentence exceeding six years. The two KPMG accountants were given sentences of eight and ten years, respectively.

The KPMG deferred prosecution agreement required it to "cooperate" with the Justice Department, which meant that it had to cut off attorney fees to partners targeted by the Justice Department. The prosecutors wanted a slam-dunk in their prosecutions, which could be obtained more easily if the defendants were unable to afford counsel in what would inevitably be a prolonged and expensive trial. The Justice Department did not want to have to face competent counsel in a financial services–related crime, since its cases were often overturned when experienced defense lawyers were on hand for the trial. In addition, cutting off attorney fees was another way for the Justice Department to force plea agreements, because individual defendants would be bankrupted or unable to hire a capable attorney.

The Justice Department enforced this fee cutoff by claiming that paying attorney fees for employees under investigation or indictment evidenced a lack of cooperation by the company. This meant that the company would be indicted and destroyed if those fees were not cut off. Faced with no other choice if they were to survive, companies entering into deferred prosecution agreements agreed to this demand, even when state law and contracts with executives required indemnification for their attorney fees.

The Justice Department was widely criticized for this questionable, unethical, and perhaps illegal conduct.[11] Denial of counsel also contravened the spirit if not the letter of the U.S. Constitution. Indeed, the Bill of Rights has been read by the Supreme Court to require the right to competent counsel even for indigent defendants, and even if the government must pay for that counsel.

Executives at Enterasys Networks accused the government of misconduct in their trial for requiring a fee cutoff. That trial was delayed for three months to investigate those allegations, after which the company agreed to pay the legal fees. Similar hardball tactics were employed against the defendants in the KPMG tax shelter cases. U.S. district court judge Lewis Kaplan concluded that such conduct by the government was "shameful and may be worse than that." Judge Kaplan ruled that the Justice Department had violated the rights of defendants by pressuring KPMG to cut off their attorney fees. He found that the government had been "economical with the truth" in claiming that it had not pressured KPMG to take that action. Judge Kaplan also faulted the government for failing to produce required document discovery to the defense in a timely manner. In July 2007, Judge Kaplan dismissed charges against thirteen of the KPMG tax shelter defendants.[12] The Court of Appeals for the Second Circuit affirmed Judge Kaplan's decision, and the Justice Department declined to seek review by the Supreme Court. In still another case, the Tenth Circuit Court of Appeals ruled that the Justice Department acted improperly in sharing information with the IRS that the department had obtained under a confidentiality order in an SEC action brought against Merrill Scott & Associates, an investment adviser that was selling tax shelters.

As a result of the Justice Department abuses, the House of Representatives passed a bill that would have prohibited the federal government from pressuring companies to waive attorney–client privilege or to take punitive action against employees in order to receive credit for cooperation. The Justice Department subsequently backed off some of the worst of the "cooperation" requirements in the Thompson Memorandum, named after Deputy Attorney General Larry D. Thompson who issued it. Among other things, the Justice Department now requires a special review for any waiver of attorney–client privilege demands, and prosecutors are prohibited from demanding that companies cut off attorney fees for employees as grounds for cooperation. Still, prosecutors continued to try to use deferred prosecution agreements as leverage to force companies to waive attorney–client privileges. For example, in a deferred prosecution agreement entered into by BP America in October 2007, the Justice Department reserved the right in future investigations of BP to demand production of attorney–client privilege materials and to view a refusal to supply such documents as a failure to cooperate, which would mean indictment and destruction of the company. Those reservations became important after BP came under the scrutiny of federal prosecutors for its failure to prevent and contain the massive oil spill in the Gulf of Mexico in 2010.

The setbacks dealt by the Thompson Memorandum did not reduce the zeal of the Justice Department prosecutors. They brought another indictment against

Robert Pfaff, one of the KPMG partners who insisted on his constitutional right to trial. The additional indictment was designed to make the defendant forgo that right and to force him to enter a guilty plea because, if convicted, the defendant would face decades in prison. Pfaff was charged with hiding $3.7 million in fees that he earned from the tax shelters. In order to prejudice the jury, and to smear Pfaff, the government announced that he had used the monies for various extravagances, including the purchase of a Steinway piano and a Mercedes-Benz for his sister.

In another setback for the government, a federal judge in Texas ruled that the IRS had improperly applied its rules retroactively to disallow deductions taken for BLIPS tax shelters. The IRS had collected $3.7 billion in settlements from investors in BLIPS before that ruling. However, the U.S. Court of Federal Claims ruled in December 2007 that the "Son of BOSS" transaction was an abusive tax shelter without economic substance. In that case, two brothers had sheltered $30 million through an investment of only $300,000, plus about $1 million in fees paid to AIG and to a hedge fund, Sentinel Advisors. The money being sheltered was from attorney fees for representing the state of Texas in the massive tobacco litigation. That decision was upheld on appeal.

The IRS adopted an amnesty program that allowed taxpayers using the Son of BOSS shelters to avoid prosecution by paying the taxes that they owed. However, 27 percent of the investors who agreed to this program failed to pay their taxes on time. That failure rate was much higher than for other IRS settlement programs. In any event, by mid-2009, the IRS was being inundated with settlement proposals from those participating in questionable tax shelters. It also created a new unit called the Global High Wealth Industry group for the purpose of targeting wealthy taxpayers for possible prosecutions.

The Senate Permanent Subcommittee on Investigations sought to have corporations incriminate themselves by requiring them to disclose the amounts that they had set aside to cover potential challenges to their tax strategies, so that the IRS could uncover and challenge those strategies. New accounting rules required the amount of such reserves to be disclosed to investors, and Senate investigators were using that as a fulcrum to try to uncover more scandal. President Barack Obama declared war on offshore tax havens on May 4, 2009, in an effort to raise $210 billion from taxes from offshore earnings and shelters.

The Justice Department continued its attacks on tax shelters, indicting Denis Field, the CEO of BDO Seidman, a large accounting firm, for promoting fraudulent tax shelters. Also indicted was a prominent tax attorney, Paul M. Daugerdas, and five others, including two other lawyers and two employees of Deutsche Bank. Another tax shelter scandal emerged in May 2008 after a Dutch bank, Rabobank Group, was accused by a whistle-blowing former employee of having structured tax avoidance transactions for U.S. corporations, including General Electric and Merck. That tax shelter scandal widened with a plea bargain from the HVB Group, the second-largest bank in Germany, which agreed to pay $30 million and to admit to criminal wrongdoing. Deutsche Bank was also under investigation for promoting abusive tax shelters. German authorities raided the offices of Credit Suisse in Frankfurt after it purchased stolen data that indicated the bank was arranging tax evasion by German citizens.

UBS was the target of another U.S. government investigation concerning its involvement in a tax evasion scheme in which funds from Americans were diverted to UBS operations in Liechtenstein and Switzerland. That business was lucrative, generating large revenues for UBS annually. Bradley Birkenfeld, a banker at UBS, was indicted on charges of having assisted Igor Olenicoff, a billionaire U.S. real estate developer, in evading taxes on $200 million in income. Olenicoff pleaded guilty to criminal charges but was given no jail time. Instead, he was placed on two years of probation and ordered to perform 120 hours of community service, plus a $52 million payment to settle his tax problems. Birkenfeld pleaded guilty to a felony charge and became a whistle-blower. Despite his cooperation, Birkenfeld was given a rather stiff forty-month sentence, drawing protests from his lawyers that he was being punished more severely than noncooperating defendants.

Raul Weil, the chairman of UBS's Global Wealth division, was also indicted in the United States for his role in the tax shelter program for wealthy Americans. Weil became a fugitive from justice in January 2009 after he failed to come to the United States to plead to the indictment. Steven M. Rubinstein, a UBS tax shelter client, pleaded guilty to criminal charges for evading taxes through a UBS offshore account.

A former UBS executive agreed to cooperate with the Justice Department in its probe of UBS. The bank then advised several of its executives not to leave Switzerland, lest they be arrested or ensnared by the Justice Department. Federal U.S. authorities detained UBS executive Martin Liechti, who was in charge of private banking for UBS in the United States. He was suspected of promoting abusive tax shelters. Liechti was subsequently discharged by the bank in an effort to appease U.S. prosecutors.

The Justice Department expanded its probe to include accountants and lawyers in Switzerland. Several Swiss banks warned employees against traveling outside Switzerland. The expanded investigation set off shock waves at UBS, which was already staggering from massive subprime-related losses. After pressure from the Justice Department, and the issuance of a congressional report critical of the UBS tax evasion schemes for U.S. citizens, UBS announced that it would curb the use of offshore accounts by Americans. In order to avoid prosecution some clients in the UBS tax evasion program turned themselves in to the IRS, which demanded that UBS give up the names of other American clients involved in the program. A federal judge authorized prosecutors to obtain American client names from UBS, which would place the bank in a difficult position because Swiss law requires that information be kept confidential.

According to initial newspaper reports, the Justice Department was seeking to determine whether UBS had allowed 20,000 wealthy American clients to hide over $20 billion in secret offshore accounts, allowing them to evade more than $300 million a year in federal income taxes. However, an internal review by UBS concluded that only a few U.S. clients were engaging in tax fraud through the bank. In order to settle the matter, UBS agreed in February 2009 to give up the names of 250 American clients and to pay a fine of $580 million to the Justice Department under a deferred prosecution agreement. It also agreed to pay the SEC $200 million to settle charges that it was illegally operating as an unregistered broker-dealer and investment adviser in marketing the tax shelter programs. In a bizarre twist, the day after this settlement the government announced that it would seek a court order to compel UBS to disclose the names of 52,000 additional Americans who might be involved in tax evasion schemes. That action drew a protest from the Swiss government. Bowing to U.S. pressure, however, Switzerland, Austria, Luxembourg, and Monaco announced in March 2009 that they would relax their bank secrecy laws in order to cooperate with U.S. tax investigations. The Swiss government asked the Obama administration to drop its case against UBS in exchange for a new tax treaty.

Switzerland reported on June 19, 2009, that it was entering into a new tax treaty with the United States under which it would share information on individuals using abusive tax shelters, but it would decline to name existing bank clients who were involved in shelters. The Swiss government also stated that it would block the disclosure of the 52,000 names sought by the Justice Department, even if a U.S. court ordered their production. However, UBS reached another agreement with the Justice Department in August 2009, pursuant to which it agreed to disclose 5,000 to 10,000 names and pay a fine. The Justice Department then immediately began demanding that UBS give up names of Americans engaging in tax shelters in UBS's Hong Kong operations.

The Swiss government threw in the towel on the bank secrecy issue in November 2009, agreeing to provide the Justice Department with the names of all American account holders with over $1 million in funds on deposit as well as those with lower amounts that appeared to be suspicious. However, a Swiss court ruled in January 2010 that the Swiss government had violated Swiss law in turning over client information to the U.S. Justice Department. In June 2010, the lower house of the Swiss parliament initially rejected a government effort to amend the country's bank secrecy laws to allow disclosure. That body reversed itself a few days later.

The effort by the Swiss to close the holes in its bank secrecy requirements was dealt another setback when it was reported that Herve Falciani, an employee of HSBC Holdings PLC, had stolen account information on 24,000 accounts held in the HSBC private Swiss bank. Falciani tried to sell that information to various governments before French investigators seized the data, which they planned to use and share with other governments in pursuing tax evaders.

Thousands of tax cheats rushed to seek settlements with the IRS before disclosure of their names by UBS. Almost 15,000 Americans submitted to an IRS amnesty program for foreign account holders. But not all pursued settlements. Finn M.W. Caspersen, the long-time head of Beneficial, and heir to a fortune from that business, was being targeted by the Justice Department for evading some $100 million in taxes through secret offshore accounts. Well known as a philanthropist, giving millions to Harvard and Princeton and numerous charities, he committed suicide over the Labor Day weekend in 2009.

Other Accounting Scandals

Xerox agreed in March 2008 to pay $670 million to settle a class-action suit over accounting manipulations that occurred between 1998 and 2002. Xerox had inflated its revenues during that period by $6.4 billion. Its auditor, KPMG, agreed to pay an additional $80 million in settlement to private litigants and $22 million to settle SEC charges for its role in auditing the company. Four KPMG partners agreed to settle SEC charges concerning their audits of Xerox. Two of those partners paid record penalties for individual auditors of $150,000 each. KPMG also agreed to pay $22.5 million to Targus Group International to settle claims over an audit that failed to discover a large embezzlement by a company employee. The judge had previously sanctioned KPMG in that case for obstructing pretrial discovery.

Deloitte & Touche paid $100 million in January 2006 to settle charges for its audit work on Fortress Re, the world's largest aviation reinsurer at the time of its failure after the September 11 attacks. Insurance companies that reinsured through Fortress Re claimed that Deloitte had improperly allowed liabilities to be kept off the books.

Two Deloitte partners agreed to permanent bars from practicing before the SEC as a result of their work in connection with audits of Delphi between 2000 and 2001. The SEC charged that Delphi had not followed generally accepted accounting principles for certain transactions, resulting in improper classification of various accounts. Deloitte agreed to pay $38 million to settle class-action claims that arose from audits of Delphi.

The SEC settled charges brought against Robert A. Fish, a former PricewaterhouseCoopers partner, for his work on the failed audits of Take-Two Interactive Software. That company had been inflating its revenues through various parking transactions involving its video games, in which the company sold games to distributors with an agreement to buy them back. Fish was suspended from practice before the SEC for one year.

Bally Total Fitness Holdings agreed in February 2008 to settle SEC charges that its accounting statements had fraudulently overstated earnings between 1997 and 2003. The company had declared bankruptcy but had emerged and was operating again in 2008. It was then under private, rather than public, ownership.

Daniel P. Burnham, the former chief executive officer of Raytheon, agreed to pay $1.75 million to settle SEC charges over the company's accounting manipulations between 1997 and 2001. General Electric agreed in August 2009 to pay $50 million to settle SEC charges that it manipulated its earnings between 2002 and 2003. Boeing agreed in May 2006 to pay $615 million to settle Justice Department charges over its contracting abuses in order to avoid indictment and destruction from the attendant publicity.

The Wall Street Scandals

The Financial Analyst Scandals

The Enron-era accounting scandals were joined by a series of scandals on Wall Street, which were exposed in many instances by New York attorney general Eliot Spitzer. Spitzer gained fame through these scandals, paving his way to the governorship in New York. Indeed, Spitzer became a national figure as a result of his crusade against Wall Street. He had prospects for a future presidential run until his own scandal derailed his meteoric rise to power. One of Spitzer's more famous crusades against Wall Street began after he discovered that Jack Grubman, a leading telecom financial analyst for Salomon Smith Barney, a unit of Citigroup, had been privately disparaging stocks that he was recommending to the public as buys, calling one such company a "pig."

More spectacular was the charge that Grubman had changed his negative recommendation on AT&T at the request of Sandy Weill, the head of Citigroup. According to e-mails from Grubman to a girlfriend, Weill needed the support of an AT&T executive serving on the Citigroup board in order to win control of Citigroup from John Reed—who was then serving along with Reed as a co-CEO. Weill also wanted AT&T's investment banking business. In exchange for altering his recommendation, Grubman sought Weill's assistance in gaining admission for his two children to an exclusive preschool program conducted by the 92d Street Y—accomplished by a $1 million donation from Citigroup to the school.

Weill and Grubman denied that there was any *quid pro quo* for the revised AT&T analysis, but the press and Spitzer did not accept that claim. This was, of course, spectacular news, and Spitzer played it for all it was worth in the press. Weill survived the scandal but retired not long afterward, leaving inadequate leadership in place to deal with the forthcoming subprime crisis at Citigroup. Grubman was barred from the securities industry for life. However, in December 2005, an arbitration panel dismissed a $900 million claim by an investor who asserted that Grubman's recommendations had misled him into buying overvalued stocks. The investor was Donald Strum, who at one point was on the Forbes list of the wealthiest people in the United States.

Henry Blodget was another financial analyst who came into Eliot Spitzer's crosshairs. Blodget was a financial analyst for Merrill Lynch, leading its Internet research group. He became famous for predicting that Amazon's stock would reach $400 per share, which seemed impossible at the time, but it did so even more rapidly than Blodget had predicted. Blodget was also recommending stocks to the public that he was privately disparaging as "crap," "a dog," and a "piece of junk." Spitzer fined Merrill Lynch $100 million after those revelations. However, a federal district court later dismissed a complaint charging that an investor had been misled by one of Blodget's reports. The court could not link his losses to those reports.

Spitzer and other state officials, as well as the SEC, which had largely been marginalized as Wall Street's regulator by Spitzer, broadened their investigations into the activities of financial analysts associated with other investment banking firms. That eventually led to a global settlement with those investment banks. Spitzer engaged in some heavy-handed tactics in order to force the firms into settling. He summoned representatives from ten of the largest investment banking firms to a meeting in his office, where he berated them with a lengthy lecture on their ethics, and then gave them the option of being indicted under New York's Martin Act, which allows for a criminal conviction without need for criminal intent.[13]

The investment bankers knew that an indictment would spell the end of their franchises. So, they quickly caved in and agreed to pay a collective $1.4 billion. The size of that payment was certainly not based on the extent of actual harm to customers. That was proved in June 2009, when a federal judge concluded that the settlement had considerably overstated customer losses and found that the amount of settlement funds set aside for investor losses far exceeded the amount of actual claims.

More than 150 class actions were filed against Merrill Lynch after the exposure of its financial analysts' reporting scandal. However, the Supreme Court reversed the state class-action suits against the firm, finding that federal law preempted them. The class actions brought in federal courts were consolidated, and the federal district court dismissed two test cases. The Court of Appeals for the Second Circuit upheld their dismissal, which led to a settlement of the remaining claims. The district court subsequently approved a class-action settlement by Merrill Lynch with purchasers of its own stock, who claimed that they had been harmed by the Merrill Lynch analysts' scandal in January 2008. The settlement was for a nominal $15 million.

That was the third such settlement reached by Merrill Lynch with various groups of stockholders claiming injury from those scandals. Two broader classes of litigants settled for a total of about $165 million, which was sizable but certainly not of the magnitude that one might expect, given the widespread publicity Spitzer gave this affair. Litigation continued. A federal district court certified a class-action lawsuit in October 2008 that had been brought against Goldman Sachs. The lawsuit claimed that the firm had failed to disclose conflicts of interest between its investment banking operations and its purportedly independent financial research reports during the period 1999 to 2001. A class action brought against more than a dozen large investment banks for alleged analyst misconduct involving more than 300 stocks was settled in October

2009 for $586 million. The plaintiff's lawyers demanded over $170 million in fees from that settlement.

Other Financial Analyst Issues

Spitzer had threatened Morgan Stanley with criminal prosecution if it did not agree to join the giant financial analyst settlement. Morgan Stanley resisted but finally caved in and agreed to pay, but only $50 million as its contribution to the massive settlement. The SEC chairman, William Donaldson, chastised Morgan Stanley's CEO, Philip Purcell, after Purcell had stated in the press that, despite the settlement, Morgan Stanley had not done anything wrong. This broke a basic requirement of SEC settlements. The SEC could crow its victory to the press in forcing a settlement, but settling defendants were not permitted to deny the truth of SEC allegations, which effectively muzzled them.

Morgan Stanley announced in March 2006 that it was eliminating some fifty research jobs, as that business had lost its luster as a result of Spitzer's charges. The SEC continued its attacks on Morgan Stanley. The firm agreed in May 2006 to pay $15 million to the SEC to settle charges over its failure to retain e-mail messages that had been sought by the SEC during the analysts' investigation. Morgan Stanley faced further embarrassment after it was reported in the press that it had fired a financial analyst and three other employees for accompanying an institutional client to a strip club.

The role of the financial analyst diminished at other firms as well after the settlement with Spitzer. Between September 2008 and May 2009, coverage on over 2,200 securities—about a quarter of all coverage—was dropped by financial analysts. The settlement with Spitzer raised other issues. It required investment banks to provide their clients with independent research for five years, dedicating $460 million of the settlement to that program, but it turned out that investors had little interest in such research. Several of the settling firms announced that they would not renew the program after it expired in the summer of 2009. Indeed, Credit Suisse did not even wait for the five-year period to end, agreeing to pay $275,000 to settle charges that it failed to post independent research properly on its Web site as required by the settlement.

Liability concerns were constricting information flows. More companies were declining to provide financial analysts with earnings forecasts, including Pfizer, Citigroup, Intel, Motorola, General Motors, and Ford. Independent researchers, who were supposed to be the saviors for investors under the Spitzer settlement, were under assault from lawsuits initiated by the companies they covered and began to leave the business in droves.

The SEC staff joined in one of those battles by issuing subpoenas to analysts and reporters covering Overstock.com, which claimed that the analysts were joining with hedge funds to drive down its stock price. Among those subpoenaed in the SEC probe was a reporter for Dow Jones, whose notes and e-mails were requested by the SEC. Those subpoenas caused a stir in the press, and

SEC chairman Christopher Cox rebuked the staff and had them withdrawn. However, the SEC staff later subpoenaed Gradient Analytics, an independent research firm, for e-mails and notes of any communications that its employees had with journalists concerning Overstock.com. An article in the *Wall Street Journal* asserted that the SEC's siding with Overstock.com was intimidating independent analysts.

Financial analysts were often criticized for not filing negative reports on companies that they covered. Merrill Lynch responded to the criticism by announcing in May 2008 that it was requiring its analysts to report "underperforming" on at least one out of every five stocks that they cover. The playing field remained uneven. The *Wall Street Journal* reported on August 24, 2009, in a front-page story that Goldman Sachs's analysts were having periodic "huddles" on market developments. They then tipped favored clients in advance of publication of changes in outlook that were mentioned during the huddles.[14] The SEC began an investigation.

Frank Quattrone

The Spitzer-inspired investigations had found conflicts of interest between the analysts and their investment banking associates. The analysts were supposed to be independently assessing stocks, but the investment bankers wanted them to forgo that independence and to tout stocks that the investment bankers were underwriting. Spitzer's global settlement on the financial analysts required almost complete separation between the financial analysts and the investment bankers.

If discussions did occur between an analyst and an investment banker, a lawyer (a "chaperone") was required to be present to assure that nothing improper was discussed. The investment banking firms entering into the global settlement were also required to appoint independent "monitors" to ensure that they complied with the terms of the settlement. However, it was disclosed in August 2008 that Citigroup was developing a plan that would reverse its agreement with Spitzer to separate its financial analysts from its investment bankers. That agreement was the centerpiece of Spitzer's massive settlement. The remerging of those two operations was said to be a cost-cutting measure needed by Citigroup, which was then in the midst of the subprime crisis. In March 2010, the SEC and twelve large Wall Street firms petitioned a federal judge to modify the settlement to allow investment bankers to meet with financial analysts outside the presence of a chaperoning lawyer. However, Judge William H. Pauley III rejected that petition, asserting that it would undermine a key goal of the settlement—separating the functions of analysts and investment bankers.

The investment bankers engaged in other questionable practices. One highly visible investment banker was Frank Quattrone, who worked at Credit Suisse First Boston (CSFB). Quattrone earned more than $200 million between 1998 and 2001, which made him instantly suspect in the eyes of prosecutors. He headed CSFB's technology development group, which prospered during the dot.com era, with clients including Amazon and Cisco Systems, two of the hottest Internet stocks. Quattrone used CSFB analysts to pump up the stock of his clients. He also kept his corporate clients happy by allocating "hot issue" initial public offering (IPO) shares to those clients, who were referred to internally as "friends of Frank." Hot issues during the dot.com era had a tendency to increase in value quickly, creating large profits for the purchasers of the stock in the IPO. The investment bankers knew this and tried to cultivate clients by allocating shares in those IPOs to them, a practice called "spinning."

Spinning was common on Wall Street, but it was condemned in the wake of the Enron-era scandals. A New York State court judge ruled that Clark E. McLeod, the CEO of McLeod-USA, acted illegally in receiving shares in hot-issue IPOs from Salomon Smith Barney. Those allocations were given in exchange for McLeod-USA's investment banking business. The judge concluded that this practice was "a sophisticated form of bribery." However, the SEC lost a case against Kenneth Langone's firm, Invemed Associates, which charged that the firm had improperly shared in customer profits from hot-issue IPOs. A cofounder of Home Depot, Langone was also a member of the New York Stock Exchange (NYSE) board of directors who was involved in another imbroglio with Spitzer over a controversial retirement package for Richard Grasso, the CEO of NYSE. (See Chapter 3.)

JPMorgan Chase paid $425 million to settle class-action charges that it had been "laddering" IPO shares during the dot.com boom, in which an investment banker required investors receiving IPO shares to make additional purchases at increasingly higher prices. Another settlement was reached on these practices in April 2009 with several investment banks, including Morgan Stanley and Goldman Sachs. They collectively agreed to pay $586 million. Morgan Stanley and Goldman Sachs also each paid $40 million in SEC settlements. CSFB paid $100 million to settle SEC and NASD charges that its brokers had received kickbacks in the form of higher commission charges from investors receiving hot-issue IPO allocations.

Quattrone's high profile made him a natural target of criminal prosecution. He was indicted on a dubious charge of obstruction of justice, based on his forwarding an email from CFSB counsel requesting his investment banking team to clean up its files because of anticipated litigation. Quattrone's e-mail, one of twenty he sent in less than an hour before he left the office that day, "strongly" advised that members of his department should follow the advice of the firm's lawyer, who e-mailed employees with instructions on the firm's record retention and destruction policies. Quattrone was not himself a lawyer, and the charge against him was based on the same misguided charges that had been brought against Arthur Andersen and that were rejected by the Supreme Court.

The principal witness against Quattronne was CSFB's general counsel, David Brodsky. CFSB waived its attorney–client privilege to permit Brodsky to testify as a part of its cooperation agreement that allowed the firm to escape criminal prosecution by throwing Quattrone to the wolves. Brodsky related a conversation in which he warned Quattrone of a grand jury investigation into CSFB's commission practices for IPO allocations. Quattrone testified that he did not relate that probe to documents kept by his group.

Quattrone's first jury was unable to reach a verdict despite some heavy-handed efforts by the trial judge, Richard Owen, to force a conviction. Among other things, Judge Owen instructed the jury in essence to ignore Quattrone's testimony because he had an interest in the case. However, Quattrone was convicted in the retrial, largely due to the one-sided rulings of Judge Owen. Indeed, Quattrone's conviction was called a "judicial mugging" by the National Association of Criminal Defense Lawyers. Judge Owen sentenced Quattrone to sixteen months in jail, which was five months more than recommended by the Probation Department. He also denied Quattrone bail pending appeal, but that ruling was reversed on appeal.

The Court of Appeals for the Second Circuit subsequently overturned Quattrone's conviction, finding that Judge Owen had given improper jury instructions. The appeals court further found that Judge Owen had improperly required Quattrone to respond to cross-examination questions only with "yes" or "no" answers, denying him any opportunity to provide an explanation. That, and other misconduct, resulted in an assignment of the case to a new judge.[15]

A few days after that decision, the SEC ruled that the NASD (now the Financial Industry Regulatory Authority, or FINRA) had acted improperly in imposing a lifetime ban on Quattrone's working in the securities industry. The ban had been imposed because Quattrone, who was facing criminal charges, had asserted his Fifth Amendment privilege not to testify in the NASD investigations.

Prosecutors announced that they would not pursue Quattrone further. He then began exploring private equity opportunities, but had limited success because of the credit crunch in 2007. Instead, in March 2008 Quattrone announced that he was returning to his roots and creating a new merchant banker, the Qatalyst Group, which would focus on technology companies. The Qatalyst Group appeared to be an instant success, receiving support from Eric Schmidt, Google's CEO, Bill Campbell, chairman of Intuit, and from executives at YouTube and Yahoo!. Quattrone advised Google, which had an interest in a high-profile takeover fight between Yahoo! and Microsoft because Google was considering a joint advertising venture with Yahoo!. Yahoo! was resisting a Microsoft bid, looking to AOL and News Corp. as alternatives. Yahoo! and Microsoft eventually agreed to a joint venture, as an alternative to a merger. Quattrone was back in the news in June 2009 as an adviser to Data Domain, which also became the subject of an intense bidding war.

Spitzer's Downfall

Eliot Spitzer continued his bullying in other investigations, including a dispute with Grasso at NYSE and another with Hank Greenberg, the chairman and

CEO of the American International Group (AIG). Both scandals, and their disastrous results, are discussed elsewhere. Suffice it to say that Spitzer did not cover himself with glory in either episode. Grasso prevailed in the fight over his pay despite misconduct by Spitzer. AIG's settlement with Spitzer wrecked the company's management and was a centerpiece of AIG's spectacular failure during the subprime crisis, requiring a monumental government bailout. Still another Spitzer-inspired scandal over "late trading" and "market timing" of mutual funds, which is discussed in Chapter 6, resulted in settlements in which massive amounts of funds were collected, but when put to test in court, Spitzer, once again, did not prevail.

There were other Spitzer contretemps. H&R Block restated its financial reports for 2004 and 2005 because of errors in its own tax returns. That announcement was followed by a lawsuit filed by Eliot Spitzer, who claimed that the company had defrauded customers by steering them to retirement accounts that charged more in fees than the clients earned as a return on their funds. Mark Ernst, CEO for H&R Block, defended that retirement plan in an op-ed piece in the *Wall Street Journal.* Spitzer responded by threatening to destroy the company with a criminal prosecution if it did not settle the case. However, a New York state court subsequently dismissed Spitzer's lawsuit against the H&R Block parent company because of a lack of jurisdiction. Another suit filed by Spitzer against the H&R Block unit selling the retirement plans also ran into trouble. A New York state court dismissed six of the seven counts listed in the indictment. A class-action lawsuit was also dismissed.

Spitzer successfully used his Wall Street crusades to win the New York governorship with a majority of 69 percent of the vote. Indeed, his campaign was more like a victory lap than a contest. At times, it appeared that Spitzer was running against the *Wall Street Journal,* which continued to criticize his overly zealous prosecutorial tactics while he served as New York attorney general, and Spitzer could not resist responding.

Spitzer had to deal with a scandal during his election campaign that involved another New York corporate reformer, Alan Hevesi, the New York State comptroller, who was also running for reelection. Hevesi was caught using state employees to drive for his wife, who had a variety of health problems, a practice that Hevesi had engaged in for three years. One employee served as Hevesi's wife's personal assistant, providing such services as watering plants, taking out the trash, hanging curtains and pictures, dropping off dry cleaning, taking her shopping, and picking up her purchases.

Hevesi's opponent in the election exposed these practices, and, to quell criticism, Hevesi agreed to repay the state over $200,000. That appeared to satisfy the electorate, and Hevesi was reelected by a wide margin. However, the scandal did not die, and New York attorney general and governor-elect Eliot Spitzer vowed to pursue the case. Hevesi then agreed to plead guilty to a single felony count, allowing him to avoid multiple charges of fraud. Unlike the Enron-era corporate executives, Hevesi served no jail time and was fined only a nominal $5,000.

Spitzer's role in forcing a guilty plea from Hevesi was certainly not carried out with the same enthusiasm as he had demonstrated against executives working for financial services firms. There was also more to the story. Spitzer's successor as New York attorney general, Andrew Cuomo, indicted David Loglisci, the New York deputy comptroller under Hevesi, for selling access by investment firms to the billions of dollars in the New York public employee retirement plan. Also indicted was Henry Morris, a political fund-raiser for Hevesi. On April 30, 2009, Cuomo indicted Saul Meyer for assisting Hevesi's son in a transaction in Mexico in exchange for a $200 million investment from the New York pension fund. That investment was managed by Meyer through Aldus Equity, which was based in Dallas. Raymond B. Harding, a prominent New York politician who headed the state's Liberal Party, pleaded guilty to charges that he had received $800,000 from the New York State pension fund in exchange for doing Hevesi favors, including procuring a state assembly seat for Hevesi's son. Elliott Broidy, a California money manager, pleaded guilty to charges that he had provided Hevesi and his staff with some $1 million in gifts, travel and entertainment, including $75,000 worth of first-class airfares.

Spitzer was thwarted in his role as governor after the New York State Assembly refused to approve his choice of replacement for Hevesi. The legislative leaders had previously stated that they would approve nominees recommended by an independent group, but those leaders then decided to appoint one of their own choices instead. Spitzer charged that the legislative leaders had displayed a "stunning lack of integrity" and that they had let "politics and cronyism" triumph over sound judgment. Spitzer further charged that we "have just witnessed an insider's game of self-dealing that unfortunately confirms every New Yorker's worst fears and image of all that goes on in the Legislature of this state." Spitzer was also reported by the *New York Post* to have threatened one legislator, declaring himself a "fucking steamroller, and I'll roll over you and anybody else." In a fit of megalomania, Spitzer also stated, "I've done more in three weeks than any governor has done in the history of the state."

After a short time in office, Spitzer became involved in another scandal called "troopergate," which involved the use by Spitzer's staff of the New York State Police to investigate New York State Senate majority leader Joseph Bruno, a Republican. Spitzer was widely reported to have described Bruno as "an old, senile piece of shit." This Spitzer investigation started after questions were raised about the propriety of Spitzer's use of state airplanes for fund-raisers. Spitzer tried to deflect that inquiry by having his staff focus attention on Bruno's own use of state aircraft. Spitzer's staff had the state police obtain Bruno's travel records, which were then leaked to the press.

After word of Spitzer's investigation of Bruno appeared in the press, Cuomo chastised Spitzer's staff for this unauthorized investigation. It was uncertain what role Spitzer had played in this investigation. Denying any involvement, he was able to block investigators from looking into his personal role. However, a former staff member claimed that Spitzer had been deeply involved in the effort to embarrass Bruno. Spitzer was accused of encouraging the leaking of Bruno's travel records and was reported to have told an aide to "shove it" to Bruno with a "red hot poker."

Further scandal followed the revelation that the chairman of the New York State Ethics Commission, Herbert Teitelbaum, had leaked information to an aide of Spitzer's on the commission's investigation of Spitzer's role in the troopergate scandal. The whole affair proved more of an embarrassment to Spitzer than to Bruno. After the governor's downfall, Bruno was indicted by federal authorities for accepting $3.2 million between 1993 and 2006 as inducements for him to push legislation through the New York State Senate. Bruno was convicted of two counts but these "honest services" charges were called into question by the Supreme Court's Enron decision.

Spitzer had other problems that could not be dealt with using threats and intimidation, which proved to be his undoing and put an end to his quest to become president of the United States, an office that, immediately after his election to the governorship, had appeared to be within reach. One serious misstep was Spitzer's effort to enter the national debate on immigration by floating a proposal that would have allowed illegal immigrants to obtain a New York State driver's license. That proposal raised a storm of controversy, and Spitzer was forced to drop it.

Spitzer was also facing a $4.4 billion deficit in the New York State budget as 2008 began. His response was to propose a spending increase of 5 percent and to expand the state workforce to more than 200,000 employees. Spitzer also sought to cut back on proposals to extend property tax relief to homeowners who were suffering from some of the highest property tax rates in the country. He sought tax increases on gasoline even though its price was already surging and wanted to increase taxes on alcohol and introduce taxes on illegal drugs, although it was not clear how the latter tax would be collected.

In retrospect, those problems showed a lack of leadership ability and bad temper but were not in themselves fatal to a political career of a populist crusader. Despite his lack of success in court, Spitzer's attacks on financial services firms had endeared him to the electorate in New York. Spitzer also painted himself as a paragon of moral virtue and political correctness. Among other things, he forced the withdrawal of an advertisement for Camel cigarettes that extolled the virtues of partying and drinking. He also attacked prostitution rings and pursued environmental causes by, unsuccessfully, attacking, among other things, pollution drifting into New York from other states. Consequently, it came as a shock to Wall Street, and, for that matter, much of the nation, when newspapers reported on March 10, 2008, that Spitzer was the target of a federal investigation involving his participation, as a client, in a prostitution ring.

This scandal was touched off by the *New York Times* after it was tipped off that senior prosecutors from the Justice Department's government integrity section had appeared in court at the arraignment of employees of a prostitution ring called Emperor's Club VIP, which charged between $1,000 and $5,500 for services rendered. Their appearance alerted the newspaper to the fact that there had to be a high-level government official involved with the prostitution ring. The reporters were then able to ferret out Spitzer's name. Identified only as "Client-9" in government court filings, Spitzer was recorded on government wiretaps while negotiating the terms of a liaison. It was also reported that Spitzer had paid $4,300 for "unsafe" sex in his room at the Mayflower Hotel in Washington, DC, with a "pretty brunette" named "Kristen" (which turned out not to be her real name) on February 13, 2008. Spitzer was in Washington on that date to testify on how the subprime crisis was affecting New York.

The court papers filed by the government also indicated that Spitzer, who was married and had three daughters, used the Emperor's Club VIP on other occasions, with some reports claiming that he had spent as much as $80,000 on prostitutes. Apparently, Spitzer's involvement with the prostitution ring had come to light as a result of Suspicious Activity Reports that banks are required to file under money-laundering statutes. Two banks that he had used, HSBC and North Fork, filed reports with federal authorities concerning payments that Spitzer was making to the prostitution ring. Both banks were targets of prosecution while he was attorney general. It appeared to the banks that he was trying to "structure" his payments to the prostitution ring to stay below the $10,000 reporting level in the Bank Secrecy Act. The payments were made by Spitzer to two shell corporations controlled by the prostitution ring, which is what caused concern at the two banks.

Spitzer was facing possible charges of money laundering, which carries heavy sentences, and Mann Act violations for transporting a woman across state lines for immoral purposes. Spitzer began negotiating desperately with federal prosecutors in an effort to avoid criminal indictment and imprisonment. No charges were brought against him, a decision that contrasted markedly with the treatment of financial services executives. Spitzer initially apologized for his conduct, but he offered no explanations and refused to answer any questions on the subject. However, the disclosure of Spitzer's involvement with the prostitution ring touched off a firestorm in the press, and he was forced to resign as governor of New York on March 12, 2008, after only sixteen months in office. Unbowed, Spitzer soon began a comeback with newspaper editorials criticizing financial services firms and appearing on talk shows. In June 2010, CNN hired him as a co-host for a prime time program on current events.

3. Corporate Governance Reforms[1]

Sarbanes-Oxley

The Enron Reforms

After the Enron scandal, Congress began looking for a way for regulators to gain control over public companies. The corporate reformers then took a grab bag of previously rejected corporate governance reforms and repackaged them for presentation to Congress. The resulting legislation, the Sarbanes-Oxley Corporate Reform Act of 2002,[2] sought to restore integrity to the accounting statements of public companies that were filed with the SEC. That effort failed, as the following elaborates.

Sarbanes-Oxley had little effect on the integrity of the financial reporting system created by the SEC. Indeed, in 2003 a new record was set in the United States for the number of restatements of quarterly and annual reports filed with the commission. One study found 2,319 restatements between 2003 and 2005, a year in which the number of restatements nearly doubled. The number of restatements was lower in the first half of 2006, but still totaled 424. That slowdown was not long-lived. A new annual record for restatements was set in 2006, when1,876 restatements were filed with the SEC by public companies (compared to 90 in 1997).[3] The SEC then complained that many restatements are unnecessary. However, executives were facing the possibility of criminal charges and life in prison if they did not restate for errors uncovered by a government official. Therefore, they took the most cautious approach by restating. In the process, they wasted a lot of time, incurring unnecessary expenses and undermining the SEC's full disclosure system.

The number of restatements rose again in the first half of 2007. That occasioned an inquiry by Treasury Secretary Henry Paulson as to what was causing the increase. His study was part of a report being prepared by the Treasury Department on its review of the competitiveness of U.S. capital markets. It found that the number of restatements accelerated in the year before the adoption of Sarbanes-Oxley and continued thereafter. The study also concluded that adverse market reaction from restatements had decreased because the public was now accustomed to such events. In other words, the market assumed that accounting errors and manipulations were a normal part of the SEC's full disclosure system.

Interestingly, the number of restatements fell to 1,235 for 2007 and to 869 in 2008, but those numbers derive from the fact that during that period many major financial companies collapsed, after announcing massive write-downs on the subprime investments held on their SEC-regulated balance sheets. The write-downs nearly cratered the world's economy, required a massive, unprecedented government bailout and proved, once again (if proof were needed), that SEC financial reports are highly unreliable and often mask the true condition of public companies. Still another study in February 2010 found that many companies were improperly rounding up their earnings reports in order to meet analysts' expectations.

Sarbanes-Oxley posed other problems. The now-infamous Section 404 of that statute required management to certify that the company's internal controls were adequate to ensure the integrity of its financial statements. The Public Company Accounting Oversight Board (PCAOB), created by Sarbanes-Oxley to oversee audit standards, narrowly averted a constitutional challenge to its operations. The Supreme Court ruled in June 2010 that provisions in the Sarbanes-Oxley Act that did not allow the SEC to remove PCAOB members for other than cause were unconstitutional. However, the Court held that PCAOB could continue its operations with that provision excised. PCAOB had sought to soften this most expensive and controversial provision in Sarbanes-Oxley concerning the adequacy of internal accounting controls. PCAOB reduced its regulations for accountants, shortening that assessment from 180 to 65 pages. Although the cost of complying with Section 404 declined a bit in 2007, larger public firms still spent almost $900,000, on average, annually for auditor's internal control reviews, which constituted almost 25 percent of total audit fees for those companies. The average audit fees for those large firms was about $3.6 million. Smaller companies' audit fees averaged about $500,000 in 2007.

Policing SEC accounting requirements remained problematic. The government was dealt another high-profile setback in a case brought against David Stockman, who had served as head of the Office of Management and Budget under President Ronald Reagan. After leaving government, Stockman became a private equity investor and from 2003 to 2005 was the chief executive officer (CEO) of Collins & Aikman, a supplier of plastic parts for the major automakers. Stockman had struggled to keep Collins & Aikman out of bankruptcy after automakers demanded steep price cuts from their parts supplier. Stockman was charged in March 2007 with manipulating Collins & Aikman's financial accounts in order to obtain bank loans and capital. He claimed that the indictment was due solely to overreaching by prosecutors, and in a startling volte-face the government later dropped all charges against him, and others indicted with him, after a further review of the evidence. This raised the question as to why such a review had not been conducted before the indictments were filed.

Other Sarbanes-Oxley Reforms

Sarbanes-Oxley prohibits loans by public companies to management. This provision was added after the disclosure of the "co-borrowing" arrangement between Adelphia Communications and its controlling stockholders, the Rigas family. Other big-time borrowers from their corporations were Ken Lay at Enron and Bernie Ebbers at WorldCom. Another provision in Sarbanes-Oxley required executives to forfeit their bonuses if their company subsequently restated its financial statements. This "clawback" provision was largely ignored until the subprime crisis renewed interest in excessive executive compensation. The SEC brought a case in July 2009 seeking to claw back the $4 million bonus of Maynard Jenkins, CEO of CSK Auto. That bonus was the result of inflated profits from an accounting manipulation, but the SEC seemed to be overreaching in view of the fact that Jenkins was not involved in that misconduct. The SEC also brought a clawback action against Ian J. McCarthy, CEO of Beazer Homes USA, after that company restated its earnings for 2000 to 2007. The company had understated earnings by $63 million between 2000 and 2005 and overstated earnings by $47 million between 2006 and 2007, which suggested a competency problem rather than cupidity since the company was understating earnings that would have pushed its stock price up.

The SEC was authorized to freeze "extraordinary" compensation payments at companies involved in accounting manipulations. This, too, seems to have been inspired by Bernie Ebbers's generous compensation package after his termination from WorldCom. The commission sued Jean-Marie Messier, the former chairman of Vivendi Universal, under this provision and forced him to give up a $25 million termination package. In another case, a Ninth Circuit panel held that a payment of $37.6 million in cash and 6.7 million shares of stock to two executives at Gemstar-TV Guide was not extraordinary, which meant that those payments could not be frozen pending an SEC action charging the executives with inflating accounts. However, that decision was reversed in an *en banc* decision of the circuit court.[4] The Ninth Circuit also upheld an order requiring Henry Yuen, CEO of Gemstar-TV Guide, to pay $22.3 million in an SEC action over accounting manipulations at that company.

A group of law professors scored a coup by persuading Congress, through a round-robin petition, to include a provision in the Sarbanes-Oxley Act governing the responsibility of lawyers for client misconduct. That provision requires corporate lawyers to report "up the chain" of management and ultimately to the board of directors of public companies, if they observe any violation of federal securities laws. This changed the role of lawyers from confidential advisers to government informants.

The law professors had expressed outrage that lawyers for Enron and WorldCom had not stopped the violations of the federal securities laws occurring at those companies. However, these professors seem to have forgotten some basic concepts of American law, namely the presumption of innocence. Indeed, not a single outside lawyer for either of those companies was ever indicted or convicted. The law professors expressed particular outrage at the fact that Vinson & Elkins, Enron's Houston-based law firm, had failed to stop the activities of Andrew Fastow. No Vinson & Elkins lawyer was ever charged with participating in any misconduct, and that firm paid only a modest settlement to rid itself of the massive class-action and other lawsuits that followed the Enron scandal.

The SEC reached a settlement with two Enron in-house lawyers. One of whom, Rex Rogers, was the Enron associate general counsel and former SEC enforcement attorney. They were charged with advising Ken Lay not to disclose his own sales of Enron stock at a time when Lay was urging employees to buy it. It was hardly an impressive settlement. The two lawyers agreed to pay $1 in disgorgement, and each agreed to pay a $25,000 civil penalty and to be barred from practicing before the SEC for two years, mild sanctions compared to the sentence meted out to Jeff Skilling.

The number of SEC actions brought against lawyers increased "dramatically" after adoption of its Sarbanes-Oxley rules. This raised criticism that "the SEC has changed from a pre-Sarbanes orientation of presumptively not initiating actions against lawyers to a post-Sarbanes orientation of aggressively targeting lawyers for disciplinary action, often for some vague, SEC conceived role as 'gatekeepers.'" Lawyers were thus added to CEOs and CFOs as presumptive targets of prosecutors when there is a problem at a public company.[5]

Small Companies

An SEC advisory committee recommended that 70 percent of public companies—the smaller public companies, which were particularly hard hit by Sarbanes-Oxley compliance costs—be exempted from some of the more-onerous provisions of the Sarbanes-Oxley Act. The SEC took some minor steps toward easing the Sarbanes-Oxley burdens on small businesses by creating a category of "small reporting company," a group with less stringent obligations. A small reporting company was defined as one with a stock float of less than $75 million. These companies were also excluded from the SEC's rules on disclosure of executive compensation.

Arthur Levitt, a former SEC chairman turned corporate gadfly, was leading an effort to pressure the SEC not to exempt smaller companies from the staggering costs of the Sarbanes-Oxley internal controls requirements. Paul Volcker, a former chairman of the Federal Reserve, John Bogle, the chairman of the Vanguard mutual fund complex, and John Biggs, the former CEO of TIAA-CREF, joined that appeal.

SEC regulations were imposing compliance costs totaling an estimated $25 billion each year, and underwriting costs abroad were less than half of those in the United States. The effects of those costs on the market in the United States were soon evident. The *Wall Street Journal* noted in 2006 that venture capital funds traditionally "used the IPO market as their exit strategy. Today, however, nearly 90 percent of those venture-capital-backed startups are sold to strategic buyers in private transactions."[6] In 2006, the total capital raised from private placements, which did not have to be registered with the SEC, exceeded the total amounts raised through registered securities sold on NYSE, NASDAQ, and the American Stock Exchange. Private placements in the first half of 2007 were 43 percent higher than during the same period the previous year.[7]

Loss of Competitive Advantage

Competition from Abroad

Financial services were migrating abroad as the costs of regulatory compliance mounted in the United States. Only one of the top twenty (5 percent) of global initial public offerings in 2006 was listed in the United States, compared with 60 percent of the top twenty offerings five years earlier. The United States was responsible for only 28 percent of global equity raised in leading markets in 2006, compared with 41 percent in 1995. The Sarbanes-Oxley legislation also forced many foreign companies out of U.S. markets. Its onerous burdens reduced the cachet that once existed for the listing of foreign firms on U.S. markets.

As one Sarbanes-Oxley critic has noted:

> Between 1996 and 2001, the New York Stock Exchange averaged 50 new non-U.S. listings annually; in 2005, it was 19. In the same year, the London Stock Exchange, including its small company affiliate, the Alternative Investment Market, gained 139 new listings while Nasdaq attracted 19. Since the end of 2004, 30 foreign companies have left the NYSE and Nasdaq. Financial capital—the kind that finances mergers, acquisitions and new business formation—is also increasingly finding a more comfortable home abroad. Large offerings by Chinese, Korean and Russian companies—involving billions of dollars—have occurred in Hong Kong and London; meanwhile, large new foreign offerings this year by Russian aluminum producers and Kazakhstan oil and copper companies are planning to list in London.[8]

The costs associated with the Sarbanes-Oxley Act were blamed for this shift.

Blue Ribbon Reviews

The effort to reform the reforms continued with a report of a blue ribbon Committee on Capital Markets Regulation (CCMR), which found that excessive regulation was hurting the securities markets and making foreign markets more competitive. The CCMR concluded that the competitive position of the United States in financial services was "seriously eroding" and had "deteriorated significantly" in recent years.[9] The CCMR noted that the U.S. share equity raised in global public markets had dropped sharply after 2002, when Sarbanes-Oxley was passed.

The U.S. share of global initial public offerings (IPOs) by foreign companies had also declined significantly. In 2007, only about 10 percent of such foreign-based IPOs were listed on a U.S. exchange, in contrast to 44.5 percent in 1996. In 1996, eight of the twenty largest global IPOs were listed on a U.S. exchange, compared to 2006, when only one such offering was listed here. Many foreign firms were delisting from U.S. exchanges, a process that hit a peak in 2006. Statistics also showed that when seeking to raise funds in the United States, foreign firms were turning to unregulated private offerings. Moreover, the number of IPOs by U.S. companies abroad significantly increased.

The CCMR recommended that Congress decrease the burden of regulation and litigation in order to increase U.S. competitiveness. The committee predicted that, within ten years, unless changes were made, the United States would no longer be the financial capital of the world. However, before his downfall, New York's governor-elect Eliot Spitzer called the committee's proposals absurd because, among other things, they would limit state prosecutions of financial crimes.

The U.S. Chamber of Commerce appointed a bipartisan, independent commission that issued a report expressing concern over unnecessary regulation. The commission stated: "In recent years, the U.S. has experienced a steady decline in its share of the global capital markets activity as international financial centers have grown to challenge this historical dominance."[10] Among other things, the commission urged Congress to grant limited liability to accounting firms in order to avoid their failure from jackpot class-action litigation. That report also urged public companies to stop providing earnings guidance on a quarterly basis and, instead, provide it annually. The Aspen Institute declared in September 2009 that the focus on short-term objectives had eroded faith in corporations as the foundation of the free-enterprise system. That statement was signed by several prominent businessmen, including Warren Buffett.

Another report by the Financial Services Roundtable noted:

> Effective regulation and the competitiveness of U.S. financial markets and firms are vital to consumers, capital formation, job creation, and sustained economic growth. Consumers of all kinds—small savers, first-time homebuyers, college students, small businesses and medium-sized enterprises, large corporations, issuers, investors, pension funds, and even governments—benefit when markets are safe, stable, and secure as well as when they are vibrant and innovative, and financial services

firms actively compete for their business. Today, financial services firms directly account for 5% of total US employment, and 8% of US gross domestic product (GDP).[11]

The Roundtable's report urged the adoption of principles-based regulation that would be risk-oriented and cost-effective and would become the standard across financial markets. The authors of the report included James Dimon, CEO of JPMorgan Chase, and Richard Kovacevich, chairman of Wells Fargo, two banks that would be deeply involved in the subprime crisis and that would perform as leaders for the industry in dealing with that crisis.

A report by a blue ribbon Committee on Capital Markets concluded that excessive regulation in the United States was making foreign markets more competitive.[12] That shift was largely due to the fact that most large financial service firms could elect to operate in London, where regulation was, at least until the subprime crisis, much less intense and much less expensive. With that location as a base, services could be offered throughout the European Union (EU) under the "passport" provisions of the EU Market in Financial Instruments Directive, which took effect November 1, 2007. Deutsche Bank announced in April 2008 that it was moving the management of its global merger and acquisitions department from New York to London. This appeared to be further evidence that financial services were fleeing the United States because of the high cost of regulation.

Even the Bush administration, which approved Sarbanes-Oxley, appeared to recognize that regulation of financial services in the United States had gone awry after the Enron-era scandals. Treasury Secretary Henry Paulson, a former Goldman Sachs CEO, warned in 2006 that the country was "creating a thicket of regulation that impedes competitiveness."[13] By then, politicians normally in favor of every form of regulation had also realized that things had gone too far. Senator Charles Schumer (D-NY) co-authored an op-ed piece in the *Wall Street Journal* with the mayor of New York City, Michael Bloomberg, that called for a study to determine whether New York was losing its position as the world's leading financial center because of overregulation and abusive shareholder litigation.[14] The resulting study stated that its findings were

> quite clear: First, our regulatory framework is a thicket of complicated rules, rather than a streamlined set of commonly understood principles, as is the case in the United Kingdom and elsewhere. The flawed implementation of the 2002 Sarbanes-Oxley Act (SOX), which produced far heavier costs than expected, has only aggravated the situation, as has the continued requirement that foreign companies conform to U.S. accounting standards rather than the widely accepted—many would say superior—international standards. The time has come not only to re-examine implementation of SOX, but also to undertake broader reforms, using a principles based approach to eliminate duplication and inefficiencies in our regulatory system. And we must do both while

ensuring that we maintain our strong protections for investors and consumers.

Second, the legal environments in other nations, including Great Britain, far more effectively discourage frivolous litigation. While nobody should attempt to discourage suits with merit, the prevalence of meritless securities lawsuits and settlements in the U.S. has driven up the apparent and actual cost of business—and driven away potential investors. In addition, the highly complex and fragmented nature of our legal system has led to a perception that penalties are arbitrary and unfair, a reputation that may be overblown, but nonetheless diminishes our attractiveness to international companies. To address this, we must consider legal reforms that will reduce spurious and meritless litigation and eliminate the perception of arbitrary justice, without eliminating meritorious actions.[15]

New York's governor, Eliot Spitzer, despite being the person most responsible for the excessive regulation of financial service firms, also supported this proposal. The *New York Times,* which normally favors regulation, also signaled that a rollback of the post-Enron regulations might be in order. This sudden concern over excessive regulation had some basis: The securities industry accounted for 20.7 percent of total wages in New York City and 18.7 percent of total tax receipts in New York State.

Government Concerns

The accounting firm Grant Thornton published a study in November 2009 that found that the number of public companies in the United States had decreased 39 percent in eleven years. Contributing to that decline were privatizations, mergers, and failures, but most troubling was a decline in the number of IPOs. The report attributed this reduction to the lack of coverage by research analysts for small-cap companies. That coverage had been a victim of the financial analysts' settlement forced by Eliot Spitzer. Even the government noticed the loss of primacy by the United States in financial services, a concern that would dissipate after the subprime crisis. An SEC official conceded in May 2008 that the number of foreign companies registered with the commission was declining because they preferred to raise money in markets with less regulation. A study by the Federal Reserve Bank of New York released at the end of July 2007 noted a shift to foreign listings and a decline in listings on U.S. securities exchanges. The New York Fed also concluded that the U.S. bond market was losing out to European markets and that the United States was no longer the first choice for many U.S. debt issuers.

The number of foreign delistings increased to fifty-six in 2007, almost double that of the year before and nearly twelve times the number in 1997. Foreign issuers seeking capital were increasingly turning to private offerings under

SEC Rule 144A. More alarming, almost 10 percent of public offerings by U.S. firms in 2007 were done through a foreign listing; only three such listings occurred between 1996 and 2001. The London Stock Exchange claimed the title of world leader in international share offerings in 2007, with eighty-six IPOs from twenty-two countries, double the amount of such offerings in the United States on NYSE and NASDAQ.

The SEC announced in November 2007 that it would allow foreign companies listing their stock in the United States to use International Financial Reporting Standards (IFRS) in lieu of Generally Accepted Accounting Principles (GAAP) without reconciliation between the two standards. The SEC had long resisted such an approach, but GAAP accounting had proved to be less than a success and was widely criticized as inferior to IFRS. This would make foreign listings easier in the United States and was expected to lead to a push for replacing GAAPs with IFRS, even for domestic companies.

In November 2008, in an almost complete switch from its long-held, sometimes almost fanatical, support of GAAPs, the SEC announced that it was proposing the mandatory use of IFRS. In the meantime, the largest U.S. companies were allowed to adopt such standards voluntarily. However, the subprime crisis upended this program. Mary Schapiro, the SEC chairman appointed by President Barack Obama after he took office, expressed the view that the adoption of those international standards should proceed cautiously. This appeared to be a signal that she was considering retaining the complex and outmoded GAAP rule formulations.[16] However, a senior SEC staff member later stated that the agency remained committed to adopting IFRS.

The Executive Compensation Controversy

Background

Concerns were raised after the Enron-era scandals after it was discovered that executives (like those at Enron and WorldCom) had received hundreds of millions of dollars in compensation before their accounting manipulations were exposed and their companies bankrupted. The subprime crisis gave rise to more anger and much populist rhetoric over the outsize bonuses given to executives at financial services firms that were bailed out by the government. A bailout of the automakers caused even more anger, after it was learned that their executives had flown on corporate jets to the congressional hearing considering their bailout requests. The Sarbanes-Oxley Act had tried to address such excesses, but it had no effect on the massive bonuses paid to Wall Street executives from subprime-related investments that would later devastate those firms.

Actually, the decrying of executive compensation did not begin with Enron or peak with the subprime crisis. The robber barons of the nineteenth century had inspired the same concerns. The reformers of that era, then called "muckrakers," were mostly journalists like Ida Tarbell, who attacked John D. Rockefeller after he put her father out of business. The muckrakers exposed the fantastic wealth of the robber barons as well as some of their industrial abuses. The "conspicuous consumption" of some members of that genre included such things as a "palatial chateaux on New York's Fifth Avenue, their ornamental 'cottages' in Newport, their extravagant parties, their ocean going yachts, their retinues of servants, and their arranged marriages."[17]

Parties thrown by these moguls were regularly highlighted in the press. One such soirée involved a formal dinner served indoors with the tuxedo-clad diners seated on their favorite horses and attended by liveried servants. A party thrown at Sherry's restaurant in New York at the beginning of the twentieth century was reported to have cost $200,000, a sum so extravagant that the sponsor was assumed to be looting funds from an insurance company that he controlled. The actual cost of the party was $13,000, but that did not lessen the scandal. Indeed, that party led to a massive investigation by New York of the entire insurance industry, resulting in state legislation that restructured that industry and, ironically, shielded it from federal regulation by keeping insurance companies out of the stock market during the 1920s.

Some of the compensation received by those earlier magnates was unimaginable at the time. In 1863, Alexander Stewart, the owner of a popular department store in New York, made $1,843,637, exclusive of dividends, in a single year while his clerks were paid $300 for the year. The wealth of New York was also then concentrated among a small group of 1,600 families that earned about 60 percent of all taxable income, which again excluded the dividends that were often the bulk of their income. Andrew Carnegie was paid $10.52 million in 1898, although much of that river of cash was from interest and dividends. A few years later Carnegie would become the richest man in the world, but only for a short time. John D. Rockefeller, of Standard Oil fame, shoved Carnegie aside for that title. Rockefeller was also in the $10 million–a-year club. Indeed, he was said to have made $55 million in just nine months.

Interestingly, those "captains of industry" were not always profligate, in contrast to some of today's corporate pirates. Andrew Carnegie, J.P. Morgan, John D. Rockefeller, and Andrew Mellon, while living well beyond the means of the rest of the world, were not ostentatious spenders, often focusing their wealth on the purchase of art works and philanthropy. Perhaps to assuage their consciences, or just because they believed it was the right thing to do, many of the robber barons became the great benefactors of universities (Vanderbilt, Stanford, Duke, and the University of Chicago, to name a few), art galleries (for example, the National Gallery in Washington, DC, and the Metropolitan Museum of Art in New York), libraries (like the New York Public Library, the Morgan Library, and the Carnegie libraries), as well as many other symbols of progressivism, which today dominate the cultural lives of elitist America, such as dance companies, orchestras, concert halls, and even the Nobel Peace Prize.

These robber barons and financiers, nevertheless, became the touchstone for the measurement of excessive compensation by corporate reformers. The names of John D. Rockefeller and J.P. Morgan need only be mentioned by modern reformers in order to seal their arguments that current executive compensation packages are a sign of evil that must be stopped by public exposure and government intervention. These corporate reformers give no credit to those industrialists and financiers for transforming the U.S. economy from a set of localized markets to a national system of production and distribution. They receive no credit for creating an economic system in which opportunities and the quality of life are unequaled in the world on many levels.

Fiduciary Duties

The corporate reform movement grew to include several leftist law professors who sought to curb excesses of corporate executives at public companies through punitive legislation. These professors dominated the business side of the law faculties of most universities for many years, and they still hold sway despite the introduction of a competing philosophy from the so-called Chicago school of law and economics. The theoretical basis for these leftist corporate reformers is found in the landmark work of Adolf Berle, whose "name rhymed with 'surly' (*Time's* apt touch)",[18] a Columbia University law professor who thought the Soviet system was a great alternative to capitalism, and Gardiner Means, a Harvard economist in the 1930s.[19]

In their still-famous book, *The Modern Corporation and Private Property,* Berle and Means observed that public companies with dispersed shareholders were experiencing a separation of ownership and control, with control vested in managers.[20] Berle and Means were concerned that the managers would be tempted to manage in favor of their own interests, rather than protecting the interests of the owner-shareholders. A principal concern was that those managers would compensate themselves excessively, whatever their performance as managers. That division of management and ownership remains a concern of corporate reformers today, who inevitably point to the large pay packets of executives at public companies to decry the abuse of their role as managers.

The corporate law reformers, led by Berle, initially sought to force managers to forgo their own interests in favor of those of shareholders through the creation of "fiduciary" duties that, if not met, would vest the manager with personal liability. Economists of the Berle era further contended that express limits should be placed on executive compensation, asserting that no man could be worth $1 million a year, a cry that would be repeated during the subprime crisis. That pronouncement came after the stock market excesses of the 1920s, which witnessed a steep increase in executive compensation. Cornell law professor George T. Washington noted in his article "The Corporation Executive's Living Wage," published in the *Harvard Law Review,* "By 1928, the executives of some of our largest companies were receiving compensation running as high as $1,000,000 or $1,500,000 annually."[21]

The fiduciary-duty concept, which posits that such duties should seek to prevent the waste of corporate assets, was used to challenge one particularly large compensation scheme during the 1930s at American Tobacco. That incentive arrangement, which had been approved by shareholders, provided executives with a bonus of 10 percent of earnings increases over a benchmark amount. The president of American Tobacco received $842,000 in 1930 as a bonus under that compensation scheme, plus his salary of $168,000. That windfall was the result of an unexpected explosion in cigarette consumption that began during World War I. However, this payout came just as the Great Depression was settling on the country, and it aroused much ire.

A minority shareholder challenged the bonus scheme through a lawsuit claiming a breach of fiduciary duty. The case eventually wound its way to the Supreme Court, which ruled that compensation could, at some point, become so excessive as to amount to waste but set no formula for that determination. Instead, the Supreme Court remanded the case for the district court to consider.[22] The claim was then settled with few changes in the scheme, and a subsequent challenge to that compensation scheme led a New York court to simply throw up its hands on the issue. That judge did not believe himself capable of assessing the appropriate level of executive compensation in such a large enterprise.[23]

Another high-profile challenge to executive pay was directed at Bethlehem Steel in 1931. That company was led by Charles M. Schwab, who had become famous for helping Andrew Carnegie with the sale of his steel mills to U.S. Steel as the twentieth century began. U.S. Steel then became the first $1 billion company and the largest business enterprise in the world. As a reward for his efforts, Schwab was made the head of that giant enterprise, at the then-astonishing annual salary of $1 million. Schwab was a big spender, notorious for his appearances at casinos in Monte Carlo, where he was a high-stakes gambler. Schwab built a house on New York's Riverside Drive at a cost of nearly $4 million, including a swimming pool, gym, and power plant.

After quarrelling with his board at U.S. Steel, Schwab took control of Bethlehem Steel and turned it into an industrial giant. Schwab created a bonus system at Bethlehem Steel that paid its executives over $6 million between 1911 and 1929. Those payments were challenged by shareholders as excessive and in breach of the board's fiduciary duty. That effort achieved notoriety but met with limited success in court through a settlement.

Still another highly visible attack on excess executive pay was aimed at the compensation paid to the CEO at the National City Bank, Charles Mitchell, who had been given a bonus of $1.4 million in 1928. By the time of this challenge in 1934, Mitchell was somewhat infamous, having been charged with income tax fraud involving a stock buyback scheme with his wife. That bit of legerdemain allowed him to evade paying taxes on over $1 million in income in 1929. That tax case went to the Supreme Court. Mitchell avoided jail but did have to pay taxes on the sales.

Mitchell carried other baggage. Before being promoted to lead National City Bank, he headed that bank's broker-dealer subsidiary, which became infamous for high-pressure sales programs promoting worthless securities. Those operations led to the passage of the Glass-Steagall Act, which required the separation of commercial and investment banking until its repeal in 1999. Mitchell was also responsible for legislation strengthening the Federal Reserve Board in Washington, after he defied its efforts to raise interest rates to restrain the stock market bubble in the 1920s. Yet, despite his reputation, the challenge to Mitchell's pay at the bank was successful only in establishing that certain incentive compensation had been wrongly computed.

In the wake of these cases, Professor Washington noted that, while it was being said that no man could be worth $1 million a year: "Perhaps this is true. Perhaps not. In any event, it is hardly a matter for courts and lawyers to settle." The professor also noted that, by 1941, the courts had declined to determine what level of compensation was appropriate.

> In effect, they put aside the problem of "reasonableness" and simply ask: "Is this corporation being honestly and fairly run by its directors, with observance of the formal requirements of the law?" If the answer is in the affirmative, the judgment of the directors as to the amount of compensation which should be paid to the executives will be allowed to control.[24]

Ovitz's Compensation

After the publication of Professor Washington's article in 1941, the use of fiduciary duties to challenge corporate compensation in court was largely abandoned in favor of other reforms. However, another challenge using that theory was mounted in the twenty-first century after the Walt Disney Company gave Michael Ovitz a $130 million severance package. Ovitz received that package even though he was terminated after only fourteen ineffective months on the job, resulting in a salary of $9.2 million per month.

Despite the staggering size of that payment, the Delaware state supreme court could find no breach of fiduciary duties by the Walt Disney directors in negotiating an employment contract that provided for such a massive severance package for so little work. The court held that the payment to Ovitz was protected by the business judgment rule, which posits that courts will not second-guess the business judgment of corporate officers and directors, absent a breach of fiduciary duties.[25] This case demonstrated that the courts simply do not have the ability, or desire, to review executive compensation levels to determine whether they are excessive, and courts will generally defer to the board of directors' discretion on such matters.

Nonetheless, Ovitz did not retire quietly from the scene. He was among those testifying in the criminal trial of Anthony Pellicano, a private investigator, who was charged with using illegal wiretaps and intimidation on behalf of his celebrity clients. Ovitz hired Pellicano to investigate a reporter who was writing articles that were detrimental to his new business, Creative Artists Agency. That business had been created by Ovitz to stage a comeback in Hollywood, but it did not take off because, he claimed, newspaper articles were undermining confidence in him among his clients. According to the newspaper reporter, her phone was tapped and she was physically threatened by some thugs, who had tried to run her over in a Mercedes-Benz.

In any event, broad application of the business judgment rule forced the corporate reformers to look elsewhere for tools to curb excessive executive compensation. They have not entirely given up, as demonstrated by the unsuccessful attack by Spitzer, while attorney general, on the $187 million compensation package given to Richard Grasso, the CEO of NYSE, an event discussed below.[26]

Confiscation Through Taxes

Another method used to attack excessive compensation was federal tax laws that, after the adoption of the Sixteenth Amendment, allowed the use of "progressive" income taxes or, more accurately, "soak the rich" taxes. The first tax under that amendment was levied in 1913 at a rate of 7 percent on those few Americans with incomes over $500,000. That rate was later increased to 65 percent for investment income. However, in the 1920s, Andrew Mellon, as treasury secretary, contended that lower tax rates would encourage economic growth and reduce tax avoidance by the wealthy, who were then investing heavily in tax-exempt municipal bonds.

After some initial setbacks, Mellon was able to convince Congress to lower the top rate to 25 percent in 1926. Exempt entirely from taxation were married filers with incomes of less than $4,000, which included most of the population. After the passage of that tax, Mellon asserted that the income tax had "become a class rather than a national tax," and he was able to reduce the national debt substantially after those changes generated more income for the government because wealthy taxpayers had a reduced incentive to avoid or evade income taxes.[27]

Mellon's "supply-side" economics proved to be decades ahead of their time, and, as a result, they were short-lived. Tax rates on the wealthy were raised during the Great Depression until they were virtually confiscatory. The top tax rate was raised to 63 percent by President Herbert Hoover in 1932, as a "temporary" measure to deal with declining government revenues. A tax bill introduced in 1935 by President Franklin Roosevelt that was widely viewed as a "soak-the-rich" bill, raised the top rate to 79 percent.

None of those tax increases helped the economy. If anything, they inhibited recovery and assured that capital would remain in hiding. As one executive testified before Congress in 1936, "If an investment proves successful, most of the profit goes to the government. If unsuccessful, the individual bears all the loss; the investor hesitates to wager several to one on a venture attended with such risk."[28] Those taxes, and other attacks on business by the Roosevelt administration in 1936, sent the country's economy into a deeper depression, just as it seemed to be recovering from the horrors of prior years.

One author noted that the New Deal leaders

> made far-reaching changes in the use of the taxing power. They envisioned individual income taxation as both a financing device and a means of redistributing the wealth. . . . Reflecting this sentiment, in the spring of 1935 President Roosevelt complained that the revenue laws "have done little to prevent an unjust concentration of wealth and economic power." . . . Critics assailed the president's program as class legislation and confiscatory taxation. Congress warily responded by increasing the tax rates for a relative handful of very rich persons but declined to enlarge the income tax base to encompass middle-class families. Despite the fear of confiscatory taxes, the redistributive effect of the New Deal tax laws was modest. There was very little change during the 1930s in the share of income received by the wealthy.[29]

The top tax rate reached 91 percent during World War II, but was lowered to 70 percent in 1963. That reduction was part of a "reform" effort by President John F. Kennedy, who thought that lower rates would reduce incentives for tax avoidance and evasion and would cause the closing of loopholes used by the wealthy to reduce their taxes. Ironically, Republicans, including former president Dwight D. Eisenhower, were opposed to the Kennedy tax cuts, claiming that they were irresponsible in light of large budget deficits.

Even after the Kennedy reductions, executives had little incentive to take risks to increase their wealth, since they would retain only 30 percent of any increases. Where risks were taken successfully, the resulting high tax rates were avoided or evaded by many wealthy individuals through tax shelters, foundations, and other means. For example, the oil depletion allowance could be used legally to reduce taxable income from $100,000 to $10,000.[30]

The "death" tax or "estate" tax, as it is respectively called by its opponents and proponents, was another effort to grab much of the wealth accumulated by executives during their careers. The death tax seized another 50 percent of the decedent's estate in excess of specified amounts. However, it, too, could be avoided or evaded by various schemes. The residences of many wealthy families looked like the scene of a home invasion after the death of a surviving parent, as the children grabbed everything movable in order to avoid the taxman. Trusts and foundations were set up to shield wealth from the estate tax. This had the effect of preserving wealth rather than redistributing it. Those trusts and foundations also undercut the most successful wealth redistribution scheme of all—the American success story of from rags to riches and back to rags again in three generations, as the succeeding generations often squandered their successful parent's estate. Instead, the foundations and trusts assured that the children were saved from themselves and that wealth remained concentrated. The Kennedy and Rockefeller families are two such examples.

Still another tax, the alternate minimum tax (AMT), was designed to assure that executives paid a minimum amount of tax, no matter which tax shelters they might employ. That tax was passed after it was revealed that twenty-one millionaires had paid no taxes in 1967. Of course, like many financial "reforms," these had unintended consequences. The AMT was not indexed for inflation, and it began increasing the tax burden on many middle-class households as their incomes reached the level liable to the AMT, even as the tax burden was being reduced for the wealthy. Congress "patched" this legislation at the end of 2007 in order to provide relief to some of the middle-class taxpayers that were falling under its provisions, but a great many of them still found their income subject to it. This tax became a target of Senator John McCain's presidential bid in 2008. He vowed to eliminate it, but lost the election.

The Reagan and Bush Tax Cuts

The high rate of income tax set by the Roosevelt and succeeding administrations was deeply opposed by Ronald Reagan. When he came into office as president, he reduced the top marginal tax rates, as tax reduction became a pillar of the Republican Party. Reagan believed in the supply-side economics advocated by Mellon in the 1920s. The supply-siders argued that "high marginal tax rates created a perverse incentive for American workers and businesses to slow down, work less, and invest in tax shelters, not productive enterprises. Cut the confiscatory rates, they said, and people will work harder and invest more."[31]

Reagan and like-minded theorists pointed to the Laffer curve (famously posited by economist Arthur Laffer on a napkin) to support the argument that lower taxes can even result in more tax revenues through increased economic growth. They further asserted that, with lower tax rates, there was less incentive to avoid or evade taxes.

Under Reagan, legislation enacted in 1983 cut personal income tax rates by 25 percent and capital gains taxes fell from 28 percent to 20 percent. In 1986, corporate tax rates were reduced from 46 percent to 34 percent. James A. Baker III, who served as White House chief of staff and later as treasury secretary under the Reagan administration, boasted (before the subprime crisis) that "our tax cuts triggered what has now turned out to be more than twenty-four years of sustained, non-inflationary growth, punctuated only by two modest slowdowns."[32]

George H.W. Bush, who succeeded Reagan, lost his bid to be re-elected as president after he failed to keep his pledge not to raise taxes ("read my lips, no new taxes") and after the country experienced a brief economic slowdown that further tax cuts might have mitigated. Although Reagan's views on taxes had many adherents, large spending deficits in the federal budget led to a successful effort by the Clinton administration to raise taxes. That increase appeared to have little effect on a booming economy and stock market until both crashed in 2000. Learning from his father's experience, George W. Bush twice ran for president by promising tax cuts. He was opposed by Democratic candidates who waged class warfare by seeking wealth redistribution through taxes on the wealthy. Bush was particularly successful in pushing back tax rates on individuals with higher incomes. He even achieved a gradual phaseout, albeit a temporary one, of the death tax. Under this phase-out schedule, the estate tax was completely eliminated in 2010 but was to return in full force in 2011 unless Congress acted to continue the repeal, which is unlikely. Dan L. Duncan, a Texas billionaire worth $9 billion, paid no estate taxes after he died in 2010, saving him 55 percent of his fortune. The estate of Yankee owner George Steinbrenner also benefitted.

Despite some rocky times, including a near recession inherited from the Clinton administration, the 9/11 terrorist attacks, and corporate scandals, the economy remained strong under the Bush administration until the subprime crisis sent the economy into a steep recession. Projected budget deficits due to the War on Terror were also cut sharply before the subprime crisis. In support of its tax cuts, the Bush administration argued that wealthy individuals pay more than their proportionate share of taxes. The top 1 percent of taxpayers (those making over $313,000 annually) paid 37.4 percent of federal income taxes in 2000, but collectively they received only about 21 percent of the nation's adjusted gross income. The top 5 percent of income earners were paying 55 percent of personal federal income taxes while receiving 34 percent of adjusted gross income. The trend continued even after the Bush tax cuts came into effect. In 2004, the top 1 percent of those filing income tax returns paid 35 percent of all individual income tax payments. Those earning more than $1 million in adjusted gross income paid a total of $178 billion in taxes.

Those statistics should provide evidence that wealthy executives are being punished enough under the tax code. However, plenty of statistical ammunition remains available to wage class war against the wealthy. For example, the top 0.1 percent of taxpayers earned more than the bottom 40 percent of taxpayers in 2004. The continual announcements of large executive pay packets also stir class envy that the Democratic Party seeks to exploit by attacks against the rich. In his presidential campaign, Barack Obama promised an increase in capital gains taxes, even after it was pointed out to him that lowering those taxes had, in the past, resulted in increased tax revenues and that raising capital gain taxes would likely reduce revenue. Both Obama and McCain called for limits on executive compensation. McCain said, "there is a backlash in America today against corporate greed." Of course, money talks, even in politics. Obama spent $745 million to defeat McCain, who raised only half that amount.

McCain's defeat and Democratic control of Congress probably meant that the Bush tax cuts would be left to expire, and that the death tax would be reinstated. Shortly after taking office, President Obama announced that he intended to raise the highest income tax bracket from 35 percent to 39.6 percent and to limit deductions by the wealthy. It was projected that this increase would raise $300 billion from taxpayers earning over $250,000.

Among the items included in the Obama budget was $630 billion for national health insurance. However, the projected cost for that program soon soared to over $1 trillion over the next ten years, and the overall deficit was revised later to reach an expected $9 trillion over the next decade. That cost was proposed to be paid for by raising taxes through a surcharge on small businesses and the wealthy—those making over $250,000. When that proposal raised protests, including the objection that taxes on those two groups were already being disproportionately increased by the termination of the Bush tax cuts, the president stated he would apply the surcharge only to those making over $1 million. That revision was accompanied by a nationwide protest in the form of "tea parties" that was held on tax day (April 15) in 2009, in order to protest the Obama administration's spending programs. Hundreds of thousands attended those events. This grassroots Tea Party movement blossomed into a general protest of the Obama administration

Compensation Arrangements

Golden Parachutes

Another target of corporate governance reformers were "golden parachutes": employment contracts that provide for large payouts to corporate executives in the event that their company is taken over by a hostile raider. The theory in support of these payments is that the threat of a potentially hostile takeover will make the executive too worried about his future to concentrate on business. Presumably, the golden parachute would remove that concern. In actual practice, these payments acted as a deterrent to hostile takeovers because, if they occurred, the executives would leave the company with their golden parachutes, robbing the business of needed management and draining the corporate treasury in the process.

The golden parachute was given a bad name in 1983, when William Agee was awarded a $3.9 million payout after losing a fight over control of his company, Bendix. Bowing to the cries of outrage over that payment, Congress amended the Internal Revenue Code in 1984 to prohibit the deduction of golden parachutes when the payments totaled more than three times the executive's average annual compensation. A 20 percent excise tax was also imposed on such payments. Ironically, this tax served only to legitimize the use of golden parachutes. Such compensation arrangements were rare before that tax was enacted, but spread to more than half of large companies surveyed in 1991 and to more than two-thirds of large public companies in the twenty-first century.

To ease the pain of the excise tax, executives receiving a golden parachute were given additional amounts (called a "gross-up") to cover payment of the tax. Some two-thirds of all S&P 500 companies provided such gross-up payments in 2008. Those gross-ups were not small. For example, John Kanas, erstwhile CEO of North Fork Bancorp, was paid $107.6 million to cover his taxes for the payout he received after that bank was acquired by Capital One in 2006.

During the subprime crisis a backlash emerged against gross-ups for taxes on executive compensation and perks. Several companies announced in 2009 that they were limiting such payments. Hewlett-Packard, for example, dropped gross-ups for personal use of the company's jets, which is taxed as compensation. Golden parachutes still continue to be awarded. James Kilts received $180 million after the merger of Gillette and Proctor & Gamble, a payout that inspired howls of outrage in the press. Wallace Barr, CEO of Caesars Entertainment, was paid $20 million after his company was taken over by Harrah's. That amount seemed paltry when compared to other such payments, but was criticized anyway in the press.

More ways were found to milk the cow. Executives were allowed to make huge profits from their stock holdings in negotiated mergers, which they proceeded to do after adopting poison pills to ward off unwanted suitors. Steve Ross at Warner Brothers pocketed almost $200 million in its merger with Time in 1989. Ross was also the first executive of a public company to be paid over $10 million in compensation for a single year's work. That occurred in 1981, when he was paid $22 million.

Another form of compensation was a large "sign-on" bonus for a newly hired executive. Some executives were given guaranteed multiyear bonuses, a practice that was attacked harshly during the subprime crisis. Retirement packages for executives were also sometimes huge, for example, the package awarded to Grasso at NYSE. Even executives given the boot by their company were being richly rewarded. Carly Fiorina received a $42 million severance package after it appeared, prematurely, that the merger she had engineered between Hewlett-Packard and Compaq Computer was faltering. Fiorina went on to win the Republican nomination for a California Senate seat in 2010.

The $200 million retirement package given to Henry McKinnell, CEO of Pfizer, was not greeted kindly either. That company's stock had fallen by 37 percent on his watch. Jay Sidhu was ejected from his role as chairman and CEO of Sovereign Bancorp, for poor stock performance, but was nonetheless handed a $40 million retirement package. Even the subprime crisis could not halt the growth in executive compensation. Overall executive pensions increased by 19 percent in 2008, when the subprime crisis was at its peak.

Another compensation arrangement growing in popularity was the "golden coffin," or payments made to the estate of an executive who died in office. Some of the amounts could be dizzyingly high. The estate of Brian L. Roberts, CEO of Comcast, would receive nearly $300 million, if he died while employed by the company. The estate of Eugene M. Eisenberg, the seventy-eight-year-old executive at Nabors Industries, would receive $288 million, and James C. Flores, CEO of Plains Exploration & Production, would gain his estate $165 million in the event of his demise while in office. Boeing would pay the estate of its CEO, W. James McNerney Jr., a comparatively paltry $42.2 million if he expired at his desk, on the corporate jet, or elsewhere, before his retirement. The death of Lazard CEO Bruce Wasserstein led to a payout to his estate of $188 million, showing that he was one of the world's great dealmakers both in life and death.

Golden coffin arrangements also included postmortem salaries, allowing family members to collect unvested stock positions, and severance payments. Critics argued that these payouts were not performance based and should be curbed. The American Federation of State, County, and Municipal Employees (AFSCME) targeted Walt Disney and sought a shareholder vote on whether such payments should be stopped. That effort was supported by the giant California Public Employees' Retirement System (CalPERS) and RiskMetrics, a corporate reform organization that advises institutional investors on how to vote in a politically correct manner on corporate-proxy proposals.

Another compensation tactic involved insurance policies on the lives of executives, with the employer as beneficiary. Bank of America bought $17.3 billion in life insurance on its executives in 2009. Congress tried to limit this practice in 2006 because it was being extended even to low-level employees in order to obtain tax-free benefits, earning it the name "janitors' insurance." The 2006 legislation restricted such insurance to the highest-paid one-third of employees.

Class Warfare and the Criminalization of Executive Pay

Damning the wealthy was a political tactic adroitly used by Franklin Roosevelt to conduct class warfare through populist attacks on wealthy executives. Among other things, Roosevelt asserted that businessmen were a "stupid class,"[33] and that the "day of the great promoter or the financial Titan, to whom we granted everything if only he would build, or develop, is over." Roosevelt also promised to give the people "their fair share in the distribution of the national wealth."[34] Of course, class warfare and attacks on the wealthy were not new to American politics. In reference to his war against the second Bank of the United States, President Andrew Jackson memorably charged: "The mass of the people have more to fear from the combinations of the wealthy and professional classes—from an aristocracy which through the influence of riches and talents, insidiously employed, sometimes succeed in preventing political institutions, however well adjusted, from securing the freedom of the citizen."

Roosevelt took this class warfare farther than any of his predecessors. In support of Roosevelt's attacks, Congress ordered the Federal Trade Commission and the Internal Revenue Service to collect data on executive compensation, which it then published annually. Companies paying executives more than $17,500 were denied certain government contracts, and the Reconstruction Finance Corporation (RFC) was prohibited from making loans to companies that were deemed to be overpaying their executives, a practice that would be adopted for government bailouts during the subprime crisis. Of course, the financiers of that earlier era did not help themselves with their tax-avoidance schemes. Particularly troubling to the public was the fact that not a single one of the wealthy partners at J.P. Morgan paid any income taxes in 1931 or 1932. However, they had a good reason for not doing so—the partnership did not make any profits in those years.

Franklin Roosevelt's attacks on business during the Great Depression expanded to include "a campaign of terrorism, with the tax laws as a weapon" against those who opposed his policies.[35] One target was Moses Annenberg, a newspaper publisher who had been critical of Roosevelt's economic programs. Roosevelt wanted Annenberg "for dinner," and his administration threatened, *à la* the Enron Task Force, to bring criminal charges that would result in a prison sentence of 147 years. Annenberg, who was dying from a brain tumor, responded that, like Nathan Hale, he regretted that he did not "have enough years to give to my country." Annenberg did plead guilty after the government threatened, as did the Enron Task Force many years later for others, to indict his son, Walter, who went on to become a popular publisher, philanthropist, and socialite.

Roosevelt failed in his efforts to jail Andrew Mellon. A grand jury refused to indict Mellon on tax fraud, possibly because the Treasury Department thought he was owed a refund after reviewing his income sources and tax payments. A civil suit brought by the Roosevelt administration on its tax claim against Mellon resulted in the "notorious 'Mellon Tax Trial' of 1935–1936" that was prosecuted by future Supreme Court Justice and Nuremberg War Crimes prosecutor Robert J. Jackson, but it ended in failure.

The Mellon Tax Trial largely ended the prosecution of business executives as a political tool until the 1980s, when it became a blood sport for a politically ambitious prosecutor by the name of Rudolph Giuliani, who was then the U.S. attorney in New York. Giuliani attacked a number of Wall Street operators, but his most famous case was the jailing of Michael Milken (the "junk bond king"), a prosecution that began after it was reported that his employer, Drexel Burnham Lambert, had paid Milken over $550 million in a single year. Using its now-customary strong-arm tactics, including indicting Milken's brother and sending FBI agents to question Milken's ninety-two-year-old grandfather, the government forced Milken to plead guilty to some convoluted violations of complex SEC regulations.

Milken was initially sentenced to ten years in prison, a staggering term at the time, but that sentence was later substantially reduced. That, and other convictions of financial figures, many of which were later reversed on appeal because of abusive practices and lack of evidence, made Giuliani a national figure. Those prosecutions assured his election as the mayor of New York, a job for which he was well suited, but Giuliani's political career ran out of steam in 2007; his quest to become president ended after he was soundly defeated in the 2008 primaries. Interestingly, Giuliani became an investment banker at Giuliani Capital Advisors (which he later sold) when he returned to private life from public office, as well as a partner in a large law firm and head of Giuliani Partners, a security consulting firm.

Giuliani's jailing of Milken would become the template for the prosecution of celebrity financiers after the Enron and WorldCom scandals. It also crippled Milken's firm, Drexel Burnham, the fifth-largest investment banking firm in the United States and one of the most successful, posting a profit of $545 million in 1986. In December 1989 Giuliani charged that firm with multiple criminal counts, to which it pleaded no contest and settled by paying the government $650 million. The criminal charges and fine crippled Drexel Burnham, and it was forced to lay off 5,300 employees, about the same number of jobs lost when Enron collapsed. Drexel was unable to recover and declared bankruptcy in February 1990.

Giuliani became noted for his hardball prosecution tactics in prosecuting white-collar criminals, including threatening relatives of targeted executives and demanding that corporate targets waive their attorney–client privilege in order to avoid indictment. Those tactics became standard operating procedure in the Justice Department and were employed with a vengeance by the Enron Task Force. Giuliani's successor as New York attorney general, Eliot Spitzer, also closely copied these hardball tactics, but Spitzer was even more ruthless and zealous in his campaigns.

Richard Grasso's Retirement Package

Eliot Spitzer, while New York attorney general, made headlines with a high-profile attack on the $187 million retirement package of Richard Grasso, the CEO of NYSE. The news of this giant payout hit the press just at the peak of controversy over large pay packets given by Enron to its executives and by other public companies, some of which were involved in accounting manipulations that were designed to boost the company's share price and increase the value of executive stock options.

Because NYSE was essentially a private club, whatever payments Grasso received would not ordinarily have raised much interest. However, the Enron-era scandals had touched off a whole new wave of populist morality, and envy, that Spitzer was quick to exploit. As in the case of most of Spitzer's prosecutions, this turned into a food fight that splattered everyone involved and proved nothing. In fact, Grasso could claim some justification for this outsize retirement payout. Grasso had accumulated about $140 million of this payout over the more than thirty-five years that he had worked at the exchange. The remaining amount was to be paid for future work and to keep him from carrying out his threat to retire.

Grasso did not grow up as a member of a privileged class. He dropped out of college and started his NYSE career as a clerk, working his way up through the ranks even though he lacked a college degree. After reaching the top, Grasso kept NYSE competitive in the face of severe competitive threats from NASDAQ, electronic communication networks, and international trading. Despite that competition, NYSE market share in the stocks it listed for trading was 85 percent in 2001. NASDAQ lost 30 percent of its volume to electronic communication networks, while NYSE lost only 7 percent. Under Grasso NYSE provided its specialist members with profits of $2.12 billion between 1995 and 2000. The price of NYSE membership nearly doubled during Grasso's tenure, and average daily trading volume increased from 179 million shares in 1991 to about 1.4 billion shares in 2000. Grasso had also acted forcefully in reopening the exchange after the September 11 attacks.

None of that was of any interest to Eliot Spitzer. He brought suit to recover Grasso's pay as an unlikely champion of NYSE's powerful and wealthy members. Spitzer did so on the somewhat tenuous ground that, because NYSE was a not-for-profit corporation, Grasso's compensation package violated the New York not-for-profit statute because it was excessive. Normally, any such action by a state attorney general would be brought against a charitable organization being exploited by its executives through the diversion of charitable contributions via unwarranted and unjustified compensation to officers of the charity. Here, while the highly profitable NYSE was a not-for-profit organization, its members were some of the wealthiest individuals and financial institutions in the world that hardly needed Spitzer's help in protecting their own interests.

Spitzer tried to undercut Grasso's successes as a manager by filing the report of an "expert" who was a finance professor at the University of Utah. That report noted that new U.S. listings on NYSE had dramatically decreased during Grasso's tenure, that market share declined slightly, and that volume increases were comparable to those on NASDAQ and the London Stock Exchange. That, of course, omitted the fact that Grasso kept NYSE competitive in the face of harsh assaults from the rapidly growing electronic communication networks (ECNs) and competition abroad as well as keeping the antiquated specialist system operational to the considerable benefit of those NYSE members. Indeed, Grasso's successors at NYSE folded their hands as it confronted ECN competition, merging with Archipelago Holdings, an electronic exchange. NYSE then went public and acquired Euronext, a European electronic exchange. In order to close that deal, NYSE had to surrender half its board seats to Europeans, thus giving up control by Americans of one of the oldest, most venerated of the country's financial institutions. NYSE then transformed into an electronic exchange that was rapidly shutting down its trading floor.

Another problem with Spitzer's suit against Grasso was that NYSE incorporated as a for-profit corporation after its merger with Archipelago Holdings.

This raised the question of who would receive the proceeds of any recovery in the Spitzer suit—the incredibly wealthy former NYSE members or the new shareholders who bought into the institution that Grasso had managed with such success? Aside from that issue, some of Spitzer's claims were simply silly. For example, he claimed that Grasso had been able to trick NYSE board members into approving his pay by not fully disclosing its amount. That must have been a shock to those sophisticated individuals, who included the heads of major brokerage firms and other financial institutions. Those individuals fully understood large compensation packages, themselves being on the receiving end of many.

More controversy was caused when Spitzer included Kenneth Langone, the then-current head of the NYSE compensation committee, in the suit brought against Grasso. That action raised issues because Spitzer did not sue that committee member's predecessor, Carl McCall, a former New York State comptroller and powerful New York Democrat, who had actually approved the payments to Grasso. The omission of McCall as a defendant was necessary because McCall was a powerful figure in New York politics, and his support was needed for Spitzer's gubernatorial campaign, which was just getting under way.

Like Grasso, Langone refused to roll over when he was subjected to Spitzer's charges. He mounted a vigorous defense that enraged Spitzer. Jack Welch, the former head of General Electric, reported that Spitzer had told him that he (Spitzer) was going to "drive a stake" into Langone's heart. Bizarrely, at least in light of the charges brought against Grasso, Spitzer also bragged to Welsh that he (Spitzer) was worth $20 million, which was a lot for someone who had never engaged in business and spent most of his career in government. The populist Spitzer was the beneficiary of family wealth, which was estimated to total over $500 million. Spitzer's family wealth allowed him to enjoy an annual income of over $1 million and to be given access to such perquisites as a luxurious rent-free apartment overlooking Central Park. That wealth also attracted attention after Spitzer was caught circumventing election laws in his first race for attorney general by funding his campaign with millions of dollars obtained through his father, who ran the family's real estate empire.

Spitzer did not intimidate Langone. Langone prophetically told the *New York* magazine in 2005, "One way or another, Spitzer is going to pay for what he's done to me and the havoc he's caused in the New York business climate," a prediction fulfilled when Spitzer was forced to resign as governor after revelations that he had patronized a prostitution ring. Langone less than graciously stated after that disclosure, "I had no doubt about his lack of character and integrity. It would only be a matter of time, I didn't think he would do it this soon or the way he did it." He added, "We all have our own private hells, I hope his private hell is hotter than anybody else's." The SEC could not resist piling on the Spitzer bandwagon. The SEC sued Langone's investment firm, Invemed Associates, charging that it had improperly shared in customer profits from hot-issue IPOs. Langone prevailed in that litigation and continued his war with Spitzer.

Grasso's lawyers put up stiff resistance in the cases pending against him in the New York courts. Discovery was voluminous, and many rulings were appealed. A trial judge ruled favorably for Spitzer on two counts, holding that Grasso had to return at least $100 million because he had not sufficiently informed the NYSE board of the size of the package. The judge apparently concluded that the incredibly sophisticated financers sitting on the NYSE board were either too stupid or too lazy to figure it out themselves. Grasso appealed the decision.

In the meantime, an intermediate appeals court dismissed the four remaining counts in Spitzer's complaint. That decision was upheld by the New York Court of Appeals, that state's highest appellate court. The court held that the case could no longer be prosecuted under New York's not-for-profit statute because NYSE was now a for-profit corporation. A few days later, the appellate division dismissed the remaining counts, reversing the decision of the trial judge that had favored Spitzer. It also threw out the case against Langone. By that time Spitzer had moved on, and his successor as attorney general, Andrew Cuomo, who was conducting his own compensation crusades, threw in the towel. It was estimated that the involved parties had spent some $70 million pursuing this litigation. Langone commented, "The previous attorney general's waste of taxpayer resources on this matter ranks as one of the most misguided and irresponsible efforts in the history of that office." Yet, the saga continued with the announcement that the Internal Revenue Service was challenging the $161 million tax deduction taken by the NYSE Euronext for the payout to Grasso.

SEC Full Disclosure

Background

The theory of "full disclosure" under the federal securities laws has long been used to attack excessive executive compensation. This theory posits that disclosure not only will allow an informed investment decision but also will deter abusive practices by corporate managers. In the famous words of Louis Brandeis, "sunlight is said to be the best of disinfectants, electric light the most efficient policeman."[36] Brandeis was a leading corporate reformist and critic of financial service providers, like banks and insurance companies. Brandeis's full disclosure theory found a welcome home in the federal securities laws.

One of the principal targets of reform through full disclosure was excess executive compensation. Corporate executives who increased their salaries to compensate for reduction in profit-based bonuses after the stock market crash of 1929 spurred that effort. Those increases came while thousands of employees were being laid off and made destitute. As part of an effort to curb those excesses, the Securities Act of 1933[37] required public disclosure of all material information about companies offering their stock to the public, including executive salaries. A schedule to the registration statement filed with the SEC before a public offering could be made required disclosure of the compensation of officers and directors for the prior year and the year following the offering, if such compensation exceeded $25,000. That schedule also required the identification of any options on the company's stock and the identity of the holders.

The Securities Exchange Act of 1934[38] additionally required companies traded on stock exchanges to disclose the compensation of officers and directors and persons other than directors and officers exceeding $20,000 per year. Bonus and profit-sharing arrangements had to be disclosed as well as options issued on the registrant's stock. In 1938, the SEC went further and adopted executive compensation disclosure requirements for proxy statements. The SEC, thereafter, periodically adjusted its various compensation disclosure requirements. In 1978, for example, it required disclosure of all direct and indirect compensation in tabular form, including options. In 1980, the agency amended its rules to require disclosure of the amounts of unexercised options. In 1983, the SEC acted again on executive compensation, adopting a narrative approach to such disclosures. However, those amendments required disclosure of only the net value realized from the exercise of options.

In 1992, the SEC adopted significant revisions to its disclosure requirements that moved from a narrative disclosure approach to formatted tabular disclosures. The SEC joined the then-ongoing executive compensation reform crusade and tried to discourage excessive compensation through disclosures that would presumably shame executives into avoiding large payouts. The rules adopted by the SEC, among other things, required disclosure of the compensation of the CEO and the other four-highest paid managers. The compensation committee was required to describe the performance factors that it used in setting the compensation of the CEO and to discuss its policies with respect to other executive officer compensation. The company also had to disclose the hypothetical value of option grants using the Black-Scholes model or some other recognized valuation method. In addition, the performance of the company's stock had to be compared to that of an index of stocks, such as the S&P 500 Composite Price Stock Index.

Disclosure Fails

The SEC's disclosure regulations did not curb executive compensation packages. Rather, as is often the case for government regulation, the doctrine of unintended consequences intervened. Those disclosure requirements only encouraged competition for ever-larger pay packages, and disclosure actually made legitimate even the most excessive payments—because if it was disclosed, then there was no wrongdoing. This competition for ever-increasing payouts to executives became institutionalized through "peer group" reviews, which compared the CEO's compensation package with those of other CEOs in his peer group. That meant that each executive in the peer group was competing against the other to push packages upward, and the peer-group selection could be manipulated to assure the highest possible package. Among those claimed to have abused this practice was Grasso.[39]

The disclosures mandated by the SEC gave rise to an industry of compensation consultants who scoured those reports for information that would boost their client's case for increased compensation. Those consultants were also seeking to create ever more innovative compensation increases for their clients, methods that were quickly mimicked by others. Efforts were soon under way to challenge the use of such consultants through class-action lawsuits that claimed conflicts of interest and breach of fiduciary duties. However, that only added more expense to be absorbed by the shareholders or passed onto consumers. Indeed, pay consultants were soon demanding indemnification from their corporate clients for claims arising from their advice. Once indemnified, they could redouble their efforts for the justification of ever-higher compensation levels.

One study noted that between 1993 and 2003,

> Executive pay has grown much beyond the increase that could be explained by changes in firm size, performance and industry classification. Had the relationship of compensation to size, performance and industry classification remained the same in 2003 as it was in 1993, mean compensation in 2003 would have been only about half of its actual size.[40]

Another study showed that between 1992, when the SEC's regulations were adopted, and 2006, CEO compensation quadrupled, while the real wages of average workers declined.[41] The SEC's full disclosure system was also corrupted by a large portion of corporate America, as executives sought to meet the expectations of financial analysts and to boost stock prices so that those executives could reap large profits from incentive programs.

The SEC Tries Again

The SEC broadened its efforts to curb executive compensation in 2006 by, once again, attacking excess compensation through more disclosures. The topic was a hot one, as evidenced by the fact that more than 20,000 comment letters were received by the agency on its proposed changes. The amendments, as adopted, expanded the number of executives whose compensation had to be disclosed to include the principal executive officers, the principal financial officers, other highly paid executives, and members of the board of directors. An entire book was soon published to explain the operation of these rules.[42]

The SEC ran into controversy after it was noted that, as originally proposed, the rules would have required disclosure of the salaries of highly paid anchors at the television networks and sport stars. The SEC quickly backed off and amended its rule proposals to require only disclosure of those employees with executive responsibilities. This was quickly dubbed the "Katie Couric amendment" after the well-paid CBS news anchor, who would not have to disclose her pay under the amended rules. No adequate explanation has ever been given as to why the disclosure of the stratospheric compensation given to news anchors is somehow improper, but corporate executive pay packages must be exposed to public scrutiny. In any event, *TV Guide* had no qualms about disclosing her pay, reporting in 2009 that she was earning $15 million per year, even though her career was in decline.[43]

The SEC, in a "Christmas surprise," changed its new rules only a few months after their adoption to allow executives to report less compensation from their options. That change prompted a front-page editorial rebuke in the *New York Times* and a follow-up piece condemning that action.[44] The amendments, in the end, did nothing to slow executive compensation and only added confusion. A front-page article in the *Wall Street Journal* on March 21, 2008, noted that the SEC's new executive compensation disclosure rules had only resulted in greater verbosity and more tables and confusion to the point that the disclosures were "unfathomable."

Some of the compensation paid to executives was truly outsize. Reuben Mark at Colgate-Palmolive received $141 million in 2003. Steven Jobs at Apple Computer was paid $74 million, and George David at United Technologies earned $70 million. John F. Antioco at Blockbuster was paid almost $20 million in salary between 1999 and 2004, in addition to uncounted millions in stock options. Blockbuster lost $3 billion during the period that he was receiving that remuneration. Gross examples continued. Barry Diller, CEO of IAC/Interactive, earned $470 million in 2005. According to the *Wall Street Journal,* Diller was also the leading jet-set executive in 2004, running up an impressive $832,000 tab on the corporate jet. Wallace D. Malone Jr., was given a $135 million retirement package after Wachovia bank acquired the bank that he headed, SouthTrust Bank.

Compensation Concerns Grow

Compensation as Politics

Excessive executive compensation for CEOs became a popular political issue as the new century dawned. Reports surfaced daily in major newspapers, often on the front page, on some excess in executive compensation. Excessive executive compensation even found its way into the 2004 congressional elections as a campaign issue. Those attacks drove President George W. Bush to deliver a Wall Street address in which he charged that action was needed by board directors to curb executive compensation by tying it to performance, a goal that had already proved disastrous with the stock option reforms of the 1990s. The president did eschew government intervention, and his hectoring had little practical effect.

On April 9, 2006, the *New York Times* devoted its Sunday business section to excessive compensation issues. The paper set forth a chart of the compensation paid by some 200 companies to their chief executive officers in 2005. Average compensation had risen 27 percent over one year to $11,304,000, with median income of $8,431,691. An example of the sensationalism in the press over executive compensation was the coverage of the $245 million payout to Robert Nardelli, the CEO at Home Depot. A front-page story in the *New York Times* in May 2006 showcased that payout, noting that, under his tenure, the company's stock price stagnated. Some Home Depot shareholders were up in arms over its poor performance. To quell that opposition, Home Depot announced a $3 billion buyback of its own stock in order to boost its price. However, that effort failed, and as 2007 began Nardelli, a former star executive at General Electric, abruptly resigned. Home Depot's stock had dropped 15 percent during his tenure, while the stock of its chief competitor, Lowe's, nearly tripled. Nardelli's successor was paid a more modest $8.9 million for his first year on the job. Of course, the average worker might think that even that amount is excessive.

Nardelli's forced resignation made the front pages of both the *New York Times* and the *Wall Street Journal* and consumed much of the *New York Times* Business Section. Both newspapers published additional follow-up stories. Corporate governance reformers were calling Nardelli's resignation a victory, but he left with an exit package valued at $210 million, which included a $20 million bonus for being a good sport about his dismissal. That was in addition to the $63.5 million Nardelli had been paid while in office. Even the *New York Times* was forced to concede that executive compensation had continued to spiral up despite all the efforts of reformers.[45]

Incentive Compensation

Options

Perhaps the height of folly was reached in the 1980s, when corporate reformers began advocating another mechanism for aligning shareholder interests with those of management through options grants. Led by Michael Jensen at Harvard Business School and Kevin Murphy at the University of Rochester, these theorists posited that stock options would provide management with an incentive to work harder in order to increase the price of the company's stock, thereby benefiting shareholders as well as increasing the value of their stock options. This theory was premised on the belief that managers being paid only a large salary would have no incentive to work hard and would merely spend their days on the golf course or in other leisurely pursuits.

Congress sought to aid the corporate governance options movement through the Omnibus Revenue Reconciliation Act of 1993.[46] That legislation prohibited corporations from deducting more than $1 million for the salary of a CEO and for the salaries of the other four most highly compensated employees without shareholder approval. Performance-based compensation was excluded from the $1 million ceiling on deductions. This tax was intended to push executives toward options as compensation in order to align their interests with those of their shareholders.

Incentive stock options granted to executives had some advantages. They could be used to obtain tax-advantaged capital gains instead of the higher marginal income tax rates when held for specified periods. Options, at least until recently, had another advantage for executives. Unlike a salary, these awards were not treated as an expense on the company's books. This meant that option grants had no effect on earnings, no matter how large the profits received by the executive from the options upon their exercise. This was significant because earnings drive stock prices. If paid in cash, those earnings would be reduced by the associated expense if they had to be accounted for on the company's ledger.

After the enactment of the Omnibus Revenue Reconciliation Act of 1993, compensation schemes at public companies were restructured to cap salaries at $1 million. Actually, this cap on deductible salary became the "minimum wage" for CEOs.[47] As sought by Congress, options became popular in executive compensation schemes. The SEC noted in 1992 that options were one of the "most rapidly growing areas of executive compensation."[48] More than 90 percent of the leading 200 American industrial and service corporations began to compensate executives using stock options. By 2000, about 80 percent of executive compensation was paid in options.

This corporate governance reform turned into a disaster. As an SEC chairman ruefully noted: "This tax law change deserves pride of place in the Museum of Unintended Consequences."[49] That change in taxation had the predictable effect of steering executives into options because they were performance based and exempt from the $1 million salary limitation on deductibility. However, it had the unexpected effect of inducing the massive accounting manipulations exposed in the Enron-era scandals, which were designed to push stock prices ever upward and increase the profits realized from option exercises.

The employment of options as the primary basis for compensation, in all events, did not curb the amount of compensation being paid to executives. Indeed, overall executive compensation increased by 450 percent in the 1990s. At the CEO level, compensation witnessed an even more startling increase of 2,500 percent during that period. Another study, just before the turn of the century, found that the gap between CEO compensation and that of other officers at the same company had doubled since the 1960s. CEOs were increasingly given "megagrants" of options (an option on one million shares), and when those ran out they were replaced by "reload" options (options that grant additional options upon exercise of the original option grant and which have the same expiration date as the originals, and after stock prices fell, their exercise price was "reset" to a lower level).

To name a few benefiting from megagrants, Larry Ellison, the head of Oracle, made $706 million on his options in a single year. Michael Dell of Dell Computer was paid $233 million for a single year of labor. Sanford Weill at Citigroup was paid a total of almost $1 billion while head of that institution. Michael Eisner at Walt Disney was paid $575 million in 1998 and received over $900 million in total compensation from that company. William McGuire at UnitedHealth Group was paid a whopping $2.2 billion. Another executive at UnitedHealth received $853 million. Richard D. Fairbanks at Capital One Financial was paid $250 million in 2005.

In order to limit this money grab, corporate reformers sought to require public companies to expense option grants. This would have had the effect of reducing earnings and would have adversely affected stock prices, making it harder for executives to profit from large option grants. In the 1990s, this idea attracted the attention of the Financial Accounting Standards Board (FASB), which floated a proposal that would have required options to be expensed. However, opponents asserted that it would be difficult to value options for purposes of expensing. The options-expensing idea also met stiff resistance from the so-called dot.com companies of that era that were using option awards to attract and retain talented employees. In May 1994 the Senate, by an overwhelming majority, passed a resolution condemning the proposal to expense options, which led the FASB to retreat from the proposal.

Option Effects

Executives at public companies focus on short-term management of quarterly earnings reports in order to meet analysts' expectations. Those quarterly reports were introduced by the SEC in 1970 and became the barometer for valuing the stock of public companies. Stock price increases were largely dependent on the views of financial analysts. A failure to meet even one quarter's "consensus" earnings estimates from analysts caused a sharp decline in a company's stock, which undercut the profit on executive stock options.

This constant demand for quarterly increases in earnings had the undesirable effect of focusing management's attention on short-term goals. This meant that executives had a disincentive to focus on long-range initiatives that might be a drag on earnings for a considerable period of time before becoming profitable. This flaw in option-based compensation, while seemingly obvious, was not widely recognized until July 2006, when the Business Roundtable Institute for Corporate Ethics called for the end of quarterly guidance given by executives to analysts. That body stated that quarterly earnings goals had become an obsession and were diverting attention from long-range goals and planning at public companies. This focus was widely in evidence at Enron, which advised its shareholders in 2000, the year before its sensational collapse, that the company was "laser focused on earnings per share." There was good reason for that focus. In 2000, over 200 executives at Enron were paid more than $1 million in compensation. In total, the Enron executives received $1.4 billion that year.

Large businesses cannot be run on the premise of continually growing quarterly earnings. As the business grows and matures over the years, some quarters will be down and others will be up. Yet financial analysts demanded constant quarterly growth. "Momentum" investors will dump a company's stock on the first occasion that analysts' quarterly consensus estimates are not met. This places excessive pressure on management to manipulate quarterly earnings with accounting gimmicks in order to keep their stock price up. When management runs out of accounting gimmicks, the stock price inevitably crashes, causing unsuspecting shareholders great losses. This phenomenon was at work in the Enron, WorldCom, and other accounting scandals of that era.

Options did not align shareholder values with those of management. Rather, options produced unimaginable profits for management in the short term and massive losses to investors in the long run. Even General Electric's former CEO, Jack Welch, who was regarded as the father of the "shareholder value" movement that has dominated the corporate world for more than twenty years, concluded that it was "a dumb idea for executives to focus so heavily on quarterly profits and share price gains." Welch also said that boosting a company's share price should not be the main goal of executives. "The idea that shareholder value is a strategy is insane. It is the product of your combined efforts—from the management to the employees."[50]

The Enron-era accounting scandals resulted in a new wave of reform in executive compensation. The FASB jumped in by revisiting the options-expensing proposal after the Enron-era scandals, and it was able to adopt such a requirement after opposition was weakened by the corporate scandals. That, too, did little to stem the growth of executive compensation. Although a number of firms did stop granting options, a study at the University of Michigan concluded that this requirement did not reduce the overall number of firms granting options to executives, and grants increased about 24 percent. That reform also did not stop abuses.

More Scandals

Option Backdating

The SEC's 2006 amendments to its executive compensation disclosure rules arrived just in time to greet a new wave of options scandals. Those scandals were touched off by a study of the Center for Financial Research and Analysis, which concluded that options were being backdated on a massive scale in order to increase executive profits when exercised. Executives at numerous public companies were caught up in scandals involving the backdating of their option grants.

More than 130 companies were under investigation for options backdating. Those companies were in a broad range of industries spread across the economy. One study concluded that some 850 CEOs had increased their compensation through backdated options. Another study estimated that some 2,200 companies had engaged in this practice. Even outside directors, who were supposed to act as watchdogs over management, received backdated options as compensation. Top executives and directors were forced to resign at Apple Computer, Brocade Communications, Brooks Automation, CNET, Monster Worldwide, Power Integrations, Rambus, Vitesse, BCGi, and Sanmina-SCI.

Corinthian Colleges admitted that it had backdated options to take advantage of the rebound in its price after the September 11 terrorist attacks. Even Chuck E. Cheese, the restaurant chain for children, was backdating, requiring its parent company, CEC Entertainment, to make a $30 million restatement to reflect options associated expenses. Computer Associates admitted to backdating options for as long as two years. Broadcom announced that it had underreported $1.5 billion in expenses between 1998 and 2003 as a result of backdated options, and it was restating its accounts in that amount. Mercury Interactive issued a $525 million restatement because of such practices. However, a district court dismissed several of the charges brought by the SEC against four Mercury Interactive executives for backdating options.

The SEC charged Analog Devices with options backdating, and the company agreed to settle the charges by paying a fine of $3 million. Executives at Research in Motion, the maker of the Blackberry communication device, agreed to pay $75 million to settle options backdating claims in February 2009. Cablevision was found to have awarded options posthumously to a vice president through a backdating scheme.

William McGuire, the CEO at UnitedHealth Group, was forced to resign after an internal report found that options had been backdated. However, it was not exactly a brutal sacking. McGuire had been paid over $2.2 billion by the company, including a retirement package worth more than $1 billion from his stock options (even after they were recomputed to reflect actual values at the time of their granting). McGuire was also entitled to a pension of $5 million per year, continued use of the corporate jet, and a wide range of other perks. If the payments to McGuire were treated as a golden parachute for tax purposes, McGuire was also entitled to a gross-up to cover that expense.

UnitedHealth executives agreed to give up $390 million in compensation from backdated options. The company also agreed to pay $900 million to settle shareholder class-action lawsuits brought over the backdating issue. McGuire kicked in an additional $30 million and returned options on more than 3 million UnitedHealth shares worth over $600 million. The UnitedHealth general counsel, David Lubben, agreed to pay $900,000 and gave up $1.4 million in compensation. He was also barred from serving as an officer or director of a public company for five years. This did not discourage UnitedHealth from granting big pay packages. McGuire's successor made almost $100 million in 2009 from the exercise of stock options.

Private lawsuits over options backdating otherwise produced only meager results in settlements because it was difficult to show that shareholders had suffered damages. The Court of Appeals for the Eleventh Circuit dismissed a backdating class action brought against Witness Systems because there was no showing of intent to defraud. A New York court dismissed a derivative lawsuit against Bed Bath & Beyond brought on behalf of shareholders to recover profits from improper option backdating. A federal court also dismissed a class-action lawsuit against ePlus that involved backdated options.

One study found that between 2000 and 2004 backdated options increased the average executive's pay at forty-eight companies by 1.25 percent, translating, on average, to $600,000. The market price of those companies' stock dropped by an average of 8 percent, or $500 million, after disclosure of those practices. That overreaction probably was a result of a shareholder base that was still spooked by the Enron-era scandals. This reflects that the politics surrounding executive compensation are driven more by negative public opinion than by the actual effect of questionable practices on company earnings. Its value to the press is evident from the fact that the *Wall Street Journal* was awarded a Pulitzer Prize for its coverage of options backdating.

Prosecutions

The SEC and the Justice Department began investigating backdated options. Steve Jobs at Apple Computer was found to have selected dates for backdating, but was forgiven by his company and the SEC. Apple general counsel Nancy R. Heinen agreed to settle an SEC case concerning her role in stock options backdating at that company. She paid $2.2 million, a figure that included her profits from the backdating and interest, plus a $200,000 civil penalty. Another Apple executive, Fred Anderson, settled similar charges by paying $3.5 million.

A district court dismissed SEC backdating charges brought against two executives at Engineered Support Systems. That dismissal came at the end of the presentation of the SEC's case. The SEC had failed to prove that the company's stock option plan prohibited looking back to assign a grant date. Quest Software and three of its executives agreed in March 2009 to pay $300,000 to settle charges that they had backdated options for three years, beginning in 1999. The CEO of Maxim Integrated Products, John Gifford, agreed to pay $800,000 to the SEC to settle charges that he had improperly backdated stock option grants. The SEC was targeting members of the compensation committee at Mercury Interactive, who had approved backdating options for an executive at that company. Some thirteen senior lawyers at public companies were also forced to resign because of their role in backdating options. Apparently, the Sarbanes-Oxley requirement that lawyers police their clients' conduct backfired. The lawyers simply joined management in their misdeeds

Surprisingly, government prosecutors brought very few criminal cases against executives involved in the backdating. Among those few was Nancy Tullos, a vice president at Broadcom. She pleaded guilty to a charge of obstruction of justice that involved her instructions to another employee to delete an e-mail that discussed an options backdating scheme. Tullos was fined $1.36 million in a related SEC action. The SEC charged additional Broadcom executives in May 2008 with improper activity in backdating options between 1998 and 2003. Broadcom agreed to pay $12 million to settle an SEC action over its options backdating practices and took a $750 million charge against earnings over the previous five years as a result of options backdating.

Broadcom's CEO, Henry T. Nicholas III, was indicted in June 2008 for his role in backdating options. Nicholas was also indicted for distributing and dropping drugs in the drinks of other executives. In another blow to the heavy-handed tactics of government prosecutors, however, federal district court judge Cormac J. Carney dismissed all criminal charges against two Broadcom executives and dismissed the SEC action against them as well. The judge found that the government had intimidated and improperly influenced three defense witnesses and leaked grand jury testimony to the press. The judge also vacated a guilty plea by Broadcom's co-founder, Henry Samueli, because it had been coerced and ordered the government to show cause why the indictments against Nicholas should not be dismissed, including the drug charges. Shortly after that decision, Broadcom settled its options backdating class-action suits for $160 million.

KB Home was suffering badly from the subprime crisis, and its troubles only multiplied after Bruce Karatz, its CEO, was indicted in connection with an options backdating scheme at that company. Karatz was convicted of those charges in 2010. He had previously agreed to settle SEC charges over this conduct by paying $7 million. Karatz had received backdated options between 1999 and 2005 that resulted in $6 million in gains. His total compensation was $43 million in 2005, and his income at the company between 2002 and 2005 was over $230 million.

Gregory L. Reyes, CEO of Brocade Communications Systems, was convicted in August 2007 for his role in backdating options compensation in the first such case to go to trial and sentenced to twenty-one months in prison and fined $15 million. Reyes had concealed hundreds of backdated stock options from auditors from 2001 to 2002. However, his conviction was set aside on appeal by the Court of Appeals for the Ninth Circuit because of prosecutorial misconduct. The prosecutors had falsely claimed that Reyes had concealed the options backdating from his own employees, but the prosecutors knew that Brocade employees were aware of the process. Reyes was convicted once again after a retrial in March 2010.

Another Brocade executive, head of human resources Stephanie Jensen, was convicted because of her efforts in concealing the backdating at that company. Jensen was given a prison sentence of four months and fined $1.25 million, a conviction only partially affirmed on appeal. Her obstruction of justice conviction was overturned, and resentencing was ordered. Her prison sentence was thereafter reduced to two months. Brocade agreed to settle a class-action lawsuit over this backdating for $160 million, although it was unclear why the company should be paying its own shareholders such an amount.

Kent Roberts, general counsel for McAfee, was acquitted of criminal charges involving options backdating after a three-week trial. The SEC then agreed to drop civil charges it had brought against Roberts for the same conduct. Ryan Brant, the founder of Take-Two Interactive Software, which created the Grand Theft Auto video game, pleaded guilty to falsifying documents in order to backdate options. He paid a $1 million fine and agreed to pay the SEC $6.3 million to settle its charges over the backdating. Take-Two agreed to pay $3 million to the SEC and paid $300,000 to settle charges brought by a New York County district attorney.

Three executives at Comverse Technology were indicted for backdating options. One of those executives, Jacob "Kobi" Alexander, made $138 million over a fourteen-year period from his options, of which about $6.4 million was from backdating. Alexander fled the country and was arrested in Namibia, where he had transferred his funds. He was released on bail pending extradition proceedings. Extradition, however, was uncertain, because Namibia has no extradition treaty with the United States. Alexander then became a celebrity fugitive, joining the ranks of Robert Vesco and Eddie Gilbert of years past. He remained in the news, as the subject of a front-page *Wall Street Journal* article that described a four-day bar mitzvah for his son in Namibia including a band imported from Israel and two hundred guests flown in from New York and Israel at Alexander's expense.

Carole Argo, CEO of SafeNet, pleaded guilty to charges that she backdated millions of dollars of employee stock options. She was given a six-month prison sentence and fined $1 million as well as agreeing to return $236,000 in profits that she had received from backdated options. The president of Monster Worldwide, James J. Treacy, was indicted and convicted for his role in backdating options and sentenced to twenty-four months in prison. That backdating allowed him to make a profit of $13.5 million. Another executive at Monster, Andrew McKelvey, had been given a deferred-prosecution agreement due to a terminal medical condition. By that point, twenty individuals had been indicted for options backdating.

Other Abuses

Executives at public companies used corporate funds to engage in massive buybacks of their own company's stock in order to boost its price. That price boost gave them more compensation as a result of the increased value of their options. The SEC adopted a safe-harbor rule to govern such repurchases and to prevent obvious manipulations, but that rule did not prevent repurchases. More options problems surfaced after it was discovered that options exercise prices were being changed by executives in order to obtain more favorable tax treatment.

Some companies repriced the backdated options granted to executives but also compensated executives for the loss in value of those options. A mini-scandal arose with the discovery that "spring-loaded" options were granted to executives shortly before announcements of good news by their companies. This practice was apparently widespread. Among those spring-loading was Cyberonics, which paid its executives $50 million in stock-related bonus compensation at a time when the company was losing money. The company also gave a former member of Congress below-market options three years before he joined its board, when he became a member of the company's compensation committee. The chairman and CFO at Power Integrations resigned after being found to have engaged in such practices.

Another popular practice to boost option profits was called "bullet-dodging," which involves granting options directly after an unexpected event has driven down stock prices. The *Wall Street Journal* reported that some ninety public companies made large options grants to their executives just after the 9/11 terrorist attacks, when stock prices were reduced by the highest percentage since the outbreak of World War II. The market recovered, generating huge profits for those executives. Of course, that action would appear to reflect a commendable amount of confidence in the company and the economy, which the more timid did not share.

Executives at some public companies used prepaid variable-forward contracts to sell their stock holdings, locking in their profits and gaining tax advantages. In one such transaction, Don Ackerman, chairman of WCI Communities, received $14 million from an investment banker for a base amount of 500,000 shares of his company's stock to be delivered three years later. The number of shares to be delivered would be reduced if their share price rose but would not have to be increased if share prices fell.[51] That seemed to be a fortuitous investment in light of the fact that WCI Communities declared bankruptcy in 2008.

The subprime crisis also raised some concerns over options. It was estimated that over 90 percent of options held by Fortune 500 CEOs had no current value in December 2008 because of the market plunge during the subprime crisis. In 2009, some companies, such as Intel, Google, and eBay, allowed employees to exchange options rendered worthless by the freefall in the market for lower-priced options. The companies claimed that these swaps were necessary in order to boost employee morale.

The War on Perks

Another area of concern for corporate reformers has been the perquisites given to executives, which range from the free use of the corporate jet to tickets to sporting events. This concern first arose in the 1970s, when Henry Ford II was lambasted in the press for using Ford Motor Company aircraft to ferry his wine and the family's cats and dogs to various exotic destinations. On one jaunt,

Ford diverted a jet to pick up a package of cigarettes for a guest at a total cost to the company of $6,000. Ford also spent $300,000 in corporate funds on a party he hosted at a national governors conference. Such extravagant entertainment would be criticized again during the subprime crisis.

Even more entertaining is the case the SEC brought in 1980 against Playboy Enterprises, the publisher of the once-popular skin magazine and one-time proprietor of nightclubs featuring scantily clad hostesses called "bunnies." The SEC charged that Playboy had failed to disclose in its public filings with the agency that Hugh Hefner, its founder and majority shareholder, was living in the company's mansions in Chicago and Los Angles while paying only nominal rent. In addition, the company was picking up most of Hefner's living expenses. The SEC's complaint against Playboy described those luxurious accommodations in detail, including the fact that the Chicago mansion had a dormitory that housed as many as thirty bunnies. Hefner was also charged with having used the corporate jet, named the "Big Bunny," for personal trips. Playboy settled the case with the SEC without admitting or denying the charges. However, the merits of the case were a bit doubtful. In fact, the SEC must have been the only male-dominated organization in the country that was unaware of the fact that Playboy was subsidizing Hefner's hedonistic lifestyle at the mansions and that the company was using that lifestyle as a giant publicity machine for its magazine and nightclubs.

The subsequent Enron-era scandals exposed even greater perk abuses, led, of course, by the excesses of Dennis Kozlowski at Tyco International. Even Jack Welch, the venerated head of General Electric (GE), was given a drubbing in the newspapers over his perks. Welch was paid $400 million over a ten-year period. In light of his managerial success, that figure met general acceptance. However, Welch was embarrassed after it was revealed in his divorce proceedings that he had been given many perks as a part of his retirement package, including tickets to sporting events, use of a corporate jet, and a car and driver. The SEC sued GE for failing to disclose those perks in its financial reports, even though their total value was only some $2.5 million, a sum immaterial to GE's income. Such actions will, of course, only inspire retiring executives to demand higher payouts so that they can pay for their own perks. Divorce proceedings of United Technologies CEO and chairman George David revealed that he had used corporate aircraft for some 900 flights for personal travel and that, in 2006, his personal use of corporate aircraft cost over $600,000.

Fidelity Investments, the world's largest mutual fund complex, was fined $8 million by the SEC because its employees had accepted gifts of tickets and flights to popular concerts and sporting events, such as the Ryder Cup, which had been provided by brokerage firms. Fidelity had a policy of limiting gifts to its employees to $100, which was far below the amount that employees actually received. One of the recipients of those gifts was the legendary Peter Lynch, who had managed the Magellan Fund for many years before stepping down to an executive position. The SEC charged that the sixty-four-year-old

Lynch received sixty-one tickets to twelve events, including a U2 rock concert, which totaled $16,000 in value. In view of the token amount of these tickets in the context of a multibillion-dollar mutual fund, it all seemed rather a waste of time, but the charges did make good press for the SEC.

Todd Thomson, head of wealth management at Citigroup and a potential successor to CEO Charles Prince, was fond of perks. His extravagant office overlooking Central Park, which included a lavish aquarium and a wood-burning fireplace, was nicknamed the "Todd Mahal." Thomson's undoing came after rumors began flying over his use of the Citigroup corporate jet to squire CNBC's "Money Honey" Maria Bartiromo across the Pacific. Thomson flew with a group of Citigroup employees to China, but left them there to return alone with Bartiromo. Those executives complained, and the issue touched off a media blitz over the ethics of reporters' receiving such treatment. He was also in the process of obtaining financing for a series on the environment that Bartiromo was to co-host on the Sundance Channel, which raised more ethical issues. Prince fired Thomson in order to quiet the scandal.

Corporate jet use became the subject of two front-page articles in the *Wall Street Journal* in 2005, one of which carefully charted the use of such aircraft for executive golf outings in Florida. Corporate perks remained front-page news, as evidenced by another *Wall Street Journal* report that News Corporation was paying $50,000 a month to rent an apartment for Rupert Murdoch, its chairman. However, Murdoch was also paid $25.7 million a year, and no doubt he could have demanded more in lieu of this $600,000 annual perk.

Tom Coughlin pleaded guilty to charges that he had improperly used about $500,000 in corporate funds for personal gift cards and other expenses while serving as vice chairman of Wal-Mart. He was sentenced to twenty-seven months of home detention and agreed to pay $450,000 in fines and restitution.

Then there is David Wittig, who was CEO of Westar Energy. Wittig made the cover of *Fortune* magazine for the $200,000 in compensation that he had received as a young trader at Salomon Brothers. That was only the beginning. Wittig was paid millions by Westar in relocation expenses, but never moved. He spent $6.5 million on the renovation of his office and $110,000 on window treatments on Alf Landon's old house, which Wittig purchased and then renovated, including the addition of a $1,200 bronze alligator. The scandal over his misuse of company funds at Westar was dubbed the "Enron of Kansas" affair.

Wittig made profligate personal use of the Westar corporate jet, including a family trip to Europe. He was indicted for failing to disclose his personal use of the corporate jet in a questionnaire used by the company to compile executive perks for disclosure under SEC rules. Wittig's first trial resulted in a mistrial. The retrial resulted in conviction and an eighteen-year sentence. That verdict was reversed on appeal, except on a few counts that were dismissed after the Supreme Court's "honest services" decision.

The Court of Appeals for the Tenth Circuit doubted the government's claims that Wittig's personal executive travel robbed the company of a large sum. Government witnesses claimed that Wittig's total personal travel on the jet was worth $1 million, based on the cost of comparable charter flights. However, the appeals court rejected that valuation method, concluding instead the proper measurement was the incremental additional cost of personal travel over what the company would have spent on the jet if it had been sitting in the hangar. The court stated, "Even when the trip is solely for pleasure, the cost to the corporation may be modest. If the pilot is on a salary and is not working overtime, the extra cost might be limited to fuel and maintenance."[52]

After that victory, a special master ruled that Westar pay $2.46 million to cover Wittig's attorney fees. The government announced that it would retry Wittig for a third time, but that trial was delayed pending another appeal, this time on double-jeopardy grounds. The appeals court ruled in August 2009 that the trial could proceed. In the meantime, Wittig was given a four-year sentence after conviction in another case, in which he was found to have lent $1.5 million to Topeka bank president Clinton Odell Weidner II and to have helped Weidner conceal the loan from the bank and its regulators. The scheme involved the approval by Weidner of a $1.5 million line of credit to Wittig, which Wittig then transferred to Weidner so that he could make an investment. Wittig's retrial on the Westar looting charges was set for September 20, 2010, but those charges were dropped after the Supreme Court ruled in the government's case against Enron CEO Jeffrey Skilling that "honest services" mail and fraud charges must be limited to bribes and kickbacks.

The IRS and Congress have tried to make it more difficult to deduct the use of a corporate jet for personal use. In 2004, Congress limited the deductibility of corporate jet travel to the equivalent of a first-class commercial ticket, but that effort did not slow executive travel. One study found that the median value of executive corporate jet perks increased by 29 percent in 2008, although that increase was driven in part by increased fuel costs. Executives demanding the luxury of a corporate jet willingly have their company absorb those costs, so shareholders only end up paying more in the long run, as taxes are increased and deductions reduced.

Even Warren Buffett, America's most popular entrepreneur, travels on a corporate jet and named it with a bit of realism: *The Indefensible*. Oprah Winfrey has her own private jet and was unrepentant about this fact, even during the furor over executive perks that arose during the subprime crisis. As a commencement speaker at Duke University in May 2009, she said to the graduates: "Anyone who tells you that having your own private jet isn't great is lying to you."[53]

The costs associated with corporate jets are considerable, about $1.3 million per year for the maintenance and operation of an upper-end plane. That is in addition to their cost, which starts at about $7 million for a Lear jet and could be as high as $60 million for a Gulfstream G650. Yet, at least before the subprime crisis, airports were running out of hangers for corporate jets, and hanger space for a single jet cost more than $18,000 per month per jet at one airport. In early 2008, companies that specialized in upgrading corporate jets had backlogs of several years for their expensive projects, which included the installation of luxurious bathrooms and bedrooms. However, that was the peak for the corporate jet market. By November 2008, orders were down for new jets, and more than 2,500 pre-owned business jets were put up for sale, an increase of more than 50 percent over the previous year. Corporate jets sold in droves, even as criticism mounted of bailouts for companies that were ferrying their executives around in expensive private jets.

Auto industry executives embarrassed themselves when they appeared before Congress in 2008 to seek a massive bailout of their industry. When asked how they had reached Washington, each of the executives admitted that he had flown on a corporate jet, which did much to derail their bailout plea for several months. As 2008 ended, Citigroup, which also received massive funds in the bailout, sent its former CEO, Sandy Weill, to a Mexican resort on a New Year's holiday aboard a company jet. Having received billions in bailout money, the corporation was even more embarrassed after its purchase of a $42 million Dassault Falcon 7X. Citigroup was forced to cancel the order at the direction of the federal government and was blasted by President Obama in a speech in which he declared, "they should know better."

A front-page article in the *Wall Street Journal* on June 19, 2009, reported that the newspaper had accessed FAA records and was able to determine that executives of firms receiving bailout money from the federal government had been using company aircraft to fly to vacation destinations. Among others, Kenneth Lewis, the embattled CEO of Bank of America, which had received $45 billion in bailout funds, flew to resorts and numerous times to his vacation home during the height of the subprime crisis. Lewis faced other compensation issues. He was forced to resign as CEO because of large bonuses paid to some Merrill Lynch employees after it was rescued by Bank of America with the backing of federal government funds. John Mack, the beleaguered head of Morgan Stanley, which had been bailed out by the government, used a corporate jet to fly to his vacation home in North Carolina during the subprime crisis, as well as to other destinations.[54] Mack wisely decided to forgo any bonuses during the subprime crisis and announced that he was leaving Morgan Stanley in 2009.

Unlike business executives, government officials, who are also addicted to corporate jets, are free to move about the country with little more than mild criticism. Eliot Spitzer, the New York attorney general, was a high-profile critic of the misuse of corporate funds. However, he conducted his campaign for governor on a corporate jet that was owned by a lobbyist with interests in New York thoroughbred racing and who was seeking a gambling license in New York for an Indian tribe. Spitzer was charged only a nominal cost for use of the jet.

The use of corporate jets by members of Congress became a centerpiece of the Democratic Party's platform, which brought them back into control of both the House and Senate in 2006. The new House Speaker, Nancy Pelosi, then passed changes in House rules that prohibit its members from hitching rides on corporate jets. However, after enacting those "reforms," Pelosi demanded that the Defense Department provide her with a jumbo jet for her own personal use so that she could fly herself, her staff, and her family and friends around the country. One conservative group found in 2009 that Pelosi's requests for special aircraft to ferry her around the country had been so numerous after assuming the Speaker's office that it appeared that she was using the military as her own private airline.

More scandalous was the disclosure in August 2009 that the House had approved appropriations of $550 million for eight new jets in the Air Force executive fleet, which is used by Pelosi and other members of Congress for their transportation needs. That appropriation came in the midst of an increasingly ugly fight in Congress over concerns that the Obama health-care plan and other programs would increase the ballooning budget deficit.

Corporate Reforms—Shareholder Voting

Proxy Votes

One long-held corporate reform dream has been to give shareholders more power through the proxy voting machinery to curb excessive executive compensation. At least until the subprime crisis, that dream had been completely unrealistic because management controlled the proxy process. The expenses associated with a proxy challenge involving hundreds of thousands of shareholders in a public company have made such challenges extremely rare.

The pitfalls of proxy fights to control executive compensation were well illustrated early on by a proxy fight in the 1950s at the Fairchild Engine and Airplane Corporation. In that case, the founder of the company challenged a large payout to the chairman who had succeeded him. However, that challenge was not cheap. It required an expensive campaign, which included the hiring of proxy solicitors and legal counsel, with costs that would be beyond the capabilities of most shareholders. Another famous challenge to management was in the battle initiated by Walter B. Hewlett, who was seeking to stop a merger between Hewlett-Packard (HP) and Compaq Computer in 2002. Hewlett, who was the son of one of the founders of HP, lost that expensive proxy fight and was removed from the HP board.

Small shareholders could not afford the massive costs required to wage a successful proxy fight against management. Even large institutional investors have no interest in challenging management. Instead, most investors, with the exception of union pension funds and a few hedge funds, follow the "Wall Street rule" of voting with their feet. In other words, investors who are dissatisfied with management because of concerns over their compensation or management abilities simply sell their stock. The Wall Street rule assures that bad management is disciplined by such selling, which will place downward pressure on the company's stock price.

Corporate reformers are harsh critics of the Wall Street rule and have sought to avoid the costs of a proxy battle by proceeding through the free access to the ballot required by the SEC under its Rule 14a-8. That rule requires management to include in its proxy materials, at company expense, shareholder proposals, which may also include a supporting statement of fewer than 500 words. The SEC allows management to exclude shareholder proposals if they fall within any one of a dozen or so categories, such as those pertaining to the ordinary business operations of the corporation, matters that involve a personal griev-ance, or a matter that is beyond the power of the company to effectuate.

Corporate gadflies initially used this SEC rule to push their sometimes-eccentric agendas. Lewis and John Gilbert, for example, owned small amounts of stock in over 800 corporations and attended more than 2,000 annual meet-ings of those companies, where they would berate management. The Gilberts did have some success on occasion in obtaining access to the proxy ballot through the SEC rule. However, they rarely prevailed in the subsequent votes because most voters cast their ballot in favor of management with respect to such proposals. The Gilberts were followed by the "corporate responsibility" reformers who were pushing various social agendas, such as opposition to the Vietnam War, smoking, employment discrimination, cruelty to animals, and, most recently, executive compensation and nomination and election of directors. The green movement also sought numerous proxy votes on global warming concerns in 2009.

The corporate responsibility movement has segued into investment pro-grams that invest only in companies that are considered socially responsible. The amount of assets in such socially responsible investments grew by 18 percent between 2005 and 2006. However, one socially responsible mutual fund, Pax World, was charged with fraud by the SEC, after it was discovered that the mutual fund had been making investments in companies involved with alcohol, gambling, and defense work, all of which were in contravention of its prospectus. The adviser to the fund agreed to pay a penalty to the SEC of $500,000.

Investment programs based on religion also became popular. The Timothy Plan, a faith-based mutual fund supporting Christian values, provided the best performance for such funds in 2007, and it even outperformed many secular mutual funds. Such faith-based funds managed more than $17 billion in 2007. However, a growing countermovement of vice funds emerged that invest in "sin" stocks of companies involved in gambling, tobacco, alcohol, and other vices. Evidently, forces beyond mere profit, namely ideology, were motivating some investors. A particularly popular corporate governance reform effort in recent years has been a campaign to curb executive compensation through proxy proposals under SEC Rule 14a-8. Indeed, the number of shareholder resolutions on executive compensation tripled between 2006 and 2007. Shareholders at more than ninety public companies sought to include proposals in proxy materials in 2007 seeking to limit executive compensation. However, the effort to curb excessive compensation through the SEC rule had to be made indirectly because the rule allows exclusion of proposals that violate law. The SEC previously interpreted that provision to exclude proposals requiring an executive compensation package to be revoked because they would violate contract law.

One indirect method for attacking executive pay under Rule 14a-8 was to submit a proposal demanding that the company's compensation committee (which approves executive compensation arrangements) prepare a report to shareholders explaining executive compensation packages or to take other action that would supposedly embarrass the compensation committee into reducing executive compensation. In that regard, the SEC staff required Wal-Mart to include a proxy proposal that would require its compensation committee to prepare a report comparing the total compensation of Wal-Mart executives with that of its lowest-paid workers.

Another ploy is to seek an advisory shareholder vote on executive compensation, commonly referred to in corporate governance vernacular as "say-on-pay." Rarely will the vote carry the day. Aflac, the Georgia insurance company that features an eccentric duck in its advertisements, allowed its shareholders to vote at its 2008 annual meeting through a nonbinding advisory motion on the compensation paid to the company's chief officers. Aflac was the first public company to agree to such a vote. The vote on the proposal was hardly reflective of a shareholder revolt. About 93 percent of shareholders approved the $12 million compensation package for CEO Daniel P. Amos for 2007. Only 2.5 percent of the shareholders voted against it.

Efforts were also undertaken by the managers of union pension funds to use their political influence to persuade Congress to require a say-on-pay vote by shareholders. After the subprime-crisis furor over executive pay at bailed-out firms, the House of Representatives passed a bill in 2007 that would require public companies to hold shareholder advisory votes on executive compensation. The Senate did not immediately approve a similar measure, but political pressure for its passage remained strong, and the Obama administration supported it, but passage was delayed by extended debate over other aspects of financial reform legislation in 2010. Congress did require companies receiving bailout money during the subprime crisis to adopt say-on-pay proxy votes.

The SEC later adopted a similar requirement in a rule change that did not lead to an outpouring of shareholder sentiment against management payouts. A survey by the *Wall Street Journal* found that the approval rate for pay by shareholders, at fifteen of the largest companies having such votes, ranged from 63.5 percent at Motorola to 98 percent at Goldman Sachs.[55] Interestingly, in Great Britain, which adopted a say-on-pay requirement in 2003, shareholders voted against the compensation scheme at GlaxoSmith Kline. After the subprime crisis, UK shareholders also voted against pay packets at the Royal Bank of Scotland Group, Bellway, Provident Financial, and Royal Dutch Shell.

One corporate governance proposal adopted by several companies is a requirement that the company claw back compensation paid to executives that was inflated by accounting misstatements. Some 300 companies adopted such provisions between 2004 and 2008. The American Federation of State, County, and Municipal Employees (AFSCME) also promoted proposals that would require bonuses to be held in escrow for a period, in order to determine whether achievement of the benchmark upon which they were based had been manipulated, so that claw back would be easier.

A survey conducted in August 2009 showed that say-on-pay proposals were supported on average by 45.8 percent of respondents, compared with 41.5 percent in 2008. However, support for proposals limiting golden parachutes fell from 56.2 percent of respondents in 2008 to 35.4 percent in 2009. Two proposals against gross-ups received majority support, but barely—50.5 percent.

Election Proposals

Corporate reformers were seeking to use proxy proposals to gain some say in the selection of members of the board of directors. Traditionally, management at public companies selects a committee that nominates members of the board of directors for election at the annual shareholders' meeting. This assured that management would have friendly representatives on the board. Corporate reformers have also sought to have their own nominees on the board so that they could pursue their efforts to control management. This movement has been led largely by union pension funds, most notably, the California Public Employees' Retirement System (CalPERS), which held $244 billion in assets as 2008 began and was the largest public pension fund. It was aided by a sister union pension fund, the California State Teachers Retirement System (CalSTRS), which held $165 billion in assets.

Board nomination proposals sought by corporate reformers faced some legal obstacles, the most formidable being the fact that SEC Rule 14a-8 allowed companies to exclude proposals that relate to board elections. After the Enron-era scandals, however, the SEC proposed a rule that would have allowed shareholders holding 5 percent or more of a company's stock to nominate directors under certain conditions. The SEC rejected such a proposal in 1942, after members of Congress claimed that it was communist in nature. Such a proposal was rejected again in 1992, and even in the midst of the post-Enron hysteria, its more recent iteration met widespread opposition. The SEC received more than 16,000 comment letters on this issue. Even longtime corporate governance gadfly Evelyn Davis opposed turning control of corporate America over to labor unions, which were about the only ones with sufficient stock and interest to make such nominations.

The SEC backed off its nomination proposal in the face of this onslaught, allowing its staff to advise registrants that they could exclude such proposals under Rule 14a-8. However, a union pension fund challenged that approach and was given a boost by the Court of Appeals for the Second Circuit.[56] The appeals court held that the SEC rule excluding shareholder proposals that "relate to an election" did not apply to a proposal to amend corporate by-laws to establish a procedure to allow shareholder-nominated candidates to be included on the corporate ballot. The court noted that the exclusionary language of the rule was ambiguous and that the SEC had changed its initial interpretation of the rule without adequate explanation.

The SEC then went back to the drawing board and sought public comment on two competing proposals, one that would have allowed proxy access, and the other that would not. SEC chairman Christopher Cox voted in favor of both proposals in order to break an impasse between the Democratic and Republican commissioners. The SEC received more than 39,000 comment letters on these proxy-access proposals, but resignations from the SEC made it impolitic for the commission to proceed until the Obama administration appointed a new SEC chair, Mary Schapiro.

Schapiro hired Kayla Gillan, former general counsel to CalPERS, to spearhead that effort. The result was a proposal to allow shareholders to nominate directors for election, a clear victory for the union pension funds. The SEC approved the rule but split on party lines, 3–2. Schapiro also appointed Gregg Berman, a former executive at the corporate governance firm RiskMetrics, to act as a senior policy adviser in the SEC's newly created Division of Risk, Strategy, and Financial Innovation. This division was headed by former University of Texas law professor Henry Hu, a longtime opponent of derivative instruments and other financial innovations.

The subprime crisis gave the labor unions and other reformers additional leverage to pursue their dreams of taking over corporate America. Perhaps the most startling reform effort was taken by the Delaware General Assembly, which had pledged to make Delaware the most corporate-friendly state in the union. Instead, the General Assembly passed legislation in 2008 that allowed shareholders to adopt proposals requiring their company to allow a shareholder to make board nominations and to demand reimbursement of a shareholder's costs in conducting a proxy contest. Management could still resist such proposals, but the existence of the legislation provides the labor unions with leverage to demand adoption of such requirements. As Charles Elson, the chairman of the University of Delaware's corporate law center, concluded, this law may well change "the balance in the election process."[57] HealthSouth announced in October 2009 that it would be the first public company to adopt a bylaw under this new legislation. Its bylaw provided for payment of reasonable expenses to successful dissident board candidates and a portion of expenses for unsuccessful candidates receiving at least 40 percent of votes cast. CalPERS was gearing up for a major push to add its directors to corporate boards. Among other things, CalPERS created a database of candidates it would slate in future elections.

Majority Votes

The pension fund of the United Brotherhood of Carpenters and Joiners of America has led a movement of its fellow union pension funds to impose "simple majority voting." This reform effort seeks to displace the traditional "plurality" voting requirement adopted by most state laws. Under those statutes, directors are elected if they receive a plurality of votes, which might be less than 50 percent of the votes cast. In attacking management, the pension funds withhold their votes and ask other shareholders to withhold votes on candidates nominated by management. For example, CalPERS went after the head of Walt Disney, Michael Eisner, when he failed to obtain the approval of 43 percent of shareholders in a vote of confidence on his stewardship, an amount far higher than normally expected in corporate elections. CalPERS and others claimed that this meant that Eisner should resign. Eisner refused that demand, but did agree to retire in two years, after his handpicked successor, Robert A. Iger, took over.

In another such action, CalSTRS, which held 5 million shares of Morgan Stanley stock, tried to use its leverage to persuade other Morgan Stanley shareholders in 2008 to withhold votes for eight directors because of the firm's compensation practices. However, all the directors were elected with overwhelming majorities. In light of what happened to Morgan Stanley during the subprime crisis, CalSTRS would have been much better served by following the Wall Street rule. Indeed, the largest state and municipal pension funds, which lead the corporate governance movement, lost 30 percent of their value in 2008 and lost another 9 percent in the first two months of 2009, totaling more than $1 trillion in losses.

A survey conducted in 2009 found that proposals on requiring majority vote for the election of a director had gained traction. The corporate reformers seem to be selling their claim that, without a majority-approval requirement, corporate board elections are no better than those held in the Soviet Union in the days of Stalin. Actually, the lack of a majority-voting requirement has not impaired our own democracy. Four presidents were elected with less than a majority of the popular vote. Abraham Lincoln received only 39 percent of the popular vote when he was elected; John F. Kennedy received 49.7 percent of the popular vote; Bill Clinton won 43 percent of the popular vote in his first presidential election; and George W. Bush was elected despite the fact that he actually lost the popular vote. Ironically, Zimbabwe, where a majority vote is required to elect the president, is the paradigm of a failed state and a state that is anything but democratic.

The reasoning behind the claim that majority voting is Stalinist is uncertain on other grounds, given that voters in the Soviet Union had no choice, while investors in America can mount a proxy fight if they wish. Of course, shareholders have to pay for the large expenses associated with such an effort, but union pension funds have enough capital on hand to pay those expenses, if they think the effort is truly worthwhile. More important, corporate shareholders in public companies, unlike the citizens of the Soviet Union, can vote with their feet by selling their stock and reinvesting in the millions of alternate investments available to Americans. That is the most effective vote of all in signaling unhappiness with management. It is, indeed, the Wall Street rule.

Staggered Boards

Another populist reform effort has been to eliminate staggered boards of directors, or boards in which only a portion of the directors are elected each year; for example, three of nine directors are elected each year, instead of the whole board. The theory behind the use of such staggered boards is that it assures continuity of management. Actually, staggered boards are popular because they can be used by management to fend off hostile takeovers because the acquiring company would have to wait many years before it could replace the complete board with its own nominees. That would be a highly undesirable situation for the acquirer.

A leader in the movement against staggered boards was the Union for Textile and Hospitality Industry Workers. However, Amalgamated Bank, which was owned by the union, was asking its shareholders to approve a staggered board and to adopt a poison pill, a by-law provision that works to discourage hostile takeovers.

Political Correctness

The attack through the ballot box by corporate reformers took other forms. Institutional investors, like mutual funds, were sometimes required to vote the shares held in their portfolios for clients. Because these institutions were mostly passive investors, and not active managers of the companies in which they invest, they had neither the time nor inclination nor ability to tell management how to run their companies. In order to meet what they perceived as their fiduciary duties in deciding how to vote, these institutional investors turned to various groups that advise on how votes should be made on particular proxy ballot issues. This led to the creation of a cottage industry of firms that provide politically correct advice on how shares should be voted.

Where those groups acquired the expertise to tell management how to run their companies is unknown. Indeed, the proxy advisory firms telling shareholders how to vote were themselves criticized for their own corporate governance procedures. Critics also claimed that these proxy advisory firms were often uninformed about the issues on which they were advising.[58]

In 2008, the U.S. Chamber of Commerce began challenging proxy advisory firms on their lack of transparency regarding how they reached decisions to recommend that shareholders vote one way or another. The Chamber of Commerce was particularly concerned about the activities of RiskMetrics Group, one of the largest of these entities. The chamber charged that RiskMetrics had achieved the status of a government agency or self-regulatory organization because many institutional investors followed its recommendations, yet it was completely unaccountable to anyone.

Broker Votes

Another fight over proxy voting involved a NYSE rule that, since 1937, had allowed broker-dealers to vote proxies on behalf of their shareholder customers who failed to give voting instructions on routine matters at least ten days before a scheduled stockholder meeting. In 2006 NYSE proposed making the election of directors a nonroutine matter, which would mean that broker-dealers could not vote for shareholders in such elections. This raised a number of issues for mutual funds that would be forced to vote in these elections, so they were granted an exemption from the proposed rule. The rule also raised concerns as to whether some companies would be able to obtain a quorum if the rule were adopted, and the expense of proxy voting would be increased substantially.

This proposal was supported by corporate activists and opposed by many public companies. It was stalled at the SEC until the Obama administration selected its SEC chairman, who used the pretext of the subprime crisis to adopt this proposal and Congress confirmed that authority in 2010. The SEC's approval of that requirement raised a storm of controversy over a board election at the Bank of America (BOA) in May 2009. CalPERS and a coalition of other unions attacked BOA management, and those dissidents did not want broker votes to be counted, even though the election occurred before the effective date of the SEC rule. In the end, Kenneth Lewis, BOA's CEO and the center of much criticism over his stewardship of the bank during the subprime crisis, and all the directors were reelected to the board.

Separation of Chairman and CEO

The BOA board election involved another reformist goal—that of splitting the role of CEO and board chairman. In May 2009, BOA shareholders approved a proposal recommending the splitting of Lewis's roles, which the bank did after the vote. This vote was unusual for the normally passive shareholders of public companies. Of course, the BOA had other problems that might have disturbed shareholders and encouraged their demand for an independent chairman. The federal government had lent BOA $45 billion during the subprime crisis, and it threatened to oust the entire board after the bank tried to pull out of a merger with Merrill Lynch, which the government had funded in its bailout of both firms. The government later sought to shake up the bank's board after it concluded that BOA needed to raise an additional $33.9 billion in capital. The government also wanted the bank to bring in individuals with more bank experience to serve as board members, and the board makeup was changed in response to that request. New York attorney general Andrew Cuomo eventually hounded Lewis out of the bank over compensation issues involving bonuses paid to executives of Merrill Lynch after it was rescued by BOA.

A failed effort to create an independent chairman occurred at ExxonMobil. That proposal was rejected despite the support of the Rockefeller family, which had founded Standard Oil, Exxon's predecessor. The proposal was supported by 39.5 percent of the votes at the company's annual meeting in May 2008. On average, unless supported by management, such resolutions received only 34 percent of votes cast. Only 15 percent of voters supported such a proposal at Chevron in May 2008.

Nevertheless, the vote at BOA showed that corporate governance reformers were making some headway in their efforts to separate the roles of chairman and CEO at public companies. By 2008, more than a third of the companies listed in the S&P 500 index had separated those roles, albeit usually with management approval. This was an increase of more than 14 percent since 2002. The United States was still behind Great Britain in this effort. There, most public companies split those roles.

Interestingly, no evidence indicates that splitting the roles of chairman and CEO improves the efficiency of management or prevents fraud. It is notable that those roles were both split at WorldCom and Enron. Most cynically, the leading "independent" firm that advises investors on how to vote on corporate governance proposals, RiskMetrics Group, had long advocated that investors vote to split the role of chairman and CEO. However, that company refused to split those roles for its own CEO and chairman, Ethan Berman, despite a pledge to do so when the company went public. RiskMetrics was also taking other positions on corporate governance and executive compensation for its own operations that were inconsistent with the advice being tendered to its clients.

Shareholder Bill of Rights

The subprime round of corporate reforms seemed to have reached its zenith with the introduction of legislation in May 2009 by Senator from New York Charles Schumer called the Shareholder Bill of Rights Act. That bill sought to prohibit staggered boards of directors, to require board members to be elected by a majority shareholder vote, to require the splitting of the role of chairman and CEO, to require say-on-pay votes, to allow long-term investors holding 1 percent or more of the company's stock to nominate directors, and to require creation of a risk committee to assess the appropriateness of risks incurred by management. It was a reformist dream package highly praised by CalPERS and other unions and much of it was passed in 2010.

Other Reforms

Class-Action Lawsuits

The class-action lawsuit was another reform measure that turned into a corporate nightmare. These class actions are filed on behalf of shareholders of public corporations whenever there is any setback at a company. Corporations are afraid to face a jury because of a perceived bias among most jurors against large corporations. Rather than face the possibility of massive judgments and staggering punitive damages, corporations almost inevitably settle class-action lawsuits, whatever their merits, if they cannot convince a judge to dismiss the case before trial. Between 1995 and 2010 only nine securities class-action lawsuits went to a verdict before a jury. The other several thousand such suits were either settled or dismissed. One class-action lawsuit from the Enron era that went to verdict in January 2010 was brought against Vivendi Universal, S.A., a French conglomerate that had transformed itself from an obscure water utility to an international entertainment firm. In the process, Vivendi massively manipulated its accounts. Damages could total $9 billion. Interesting was the fact that the jury found Jean-Marie Messier, the Vivendi CEO, not guilty. The Vivendi CFO was also adjudged innocent. Messier had been sued by the SEC for those accounting manipulations and was forced to give up his $25 million retirement package, plus another $25 million, to settle that case.

Class-action lawsuits are driven by the contingency-fee system for lawyers and have became a cottage industry for a relatively small segment of the bar. Under a contingency-fee arrangement, the lawyer receives nothing if he loses the case, but receives a substantial percentage of the award when successful. Such contingency-fee arrangements are unique to the United States. Individual shareholders cannot afford to finance a lawsuit against a large corporation, but the lawyers do have the financial wherewithal, and they are happy to make such an investment in order to garner billions of dollars in fees.

Rarely do the plaintiffs on whose behalf the suit is brought actually receive any material benefit from the settlements. Many class-action lawsuits are settled by giving the plaintiffs coupons or discounts that might attract more business for the defendant. In the case of securities class actions, small shareholders receive only minute benefits, if any. Large shareholders, most notably, the union pension funds, because of their large stock holdings, do receive substantial rewards from settlements and thereby increase the return on their investments. The bringing of such lawsuits by union pension funds is now a standard part of their investment practices. However, critics charge that the pension funds are trying to have their cake and eat it, too. The pension funds pursue a modern portfolio strategy of diversification that assumes some stocks will suffer losses from fraud or misadventure, but that these will be offset by fortuitous events at other companies. By bringing class-action lawsuits, whenever a company's stock drops in value, the pension funds can improve on that diversification strategy. Large diversified investors like CalPERS were being overcompensated for their losses in such litigation because they did not have to pay back gains from stocks inflated by securities fraud, while small investors were being undercompensated.

Class-action lawsuits have a history of abuse. Newt Gingrich's "Contract with America," which gained the Republican Party popularity in the 1980s, contained, as a part of its platform, a proposal that would have applied the "English rule" for lawyer fees in class-action litigation. This would mean that the loser pays. Under the American system, the defendants in class-action lawsuits must bear their own costs, so class-action lawyers do not have to worry about paying for the other side's attorney fees if they lose a case. Under the English rule, the plaintiff would have to pay the corporation's attorney fees if the plaintiff lost, which, of course, would put an end to frivolous class-action litigation. However, the trial lawyer associations in the United States are a powerful lobbying force, and they joined with the usual gaggle of corporate law professors in blocking the Gingrich proposal.

Instead, Congress adopted the Private Securities Litigation Reform Act of 1995 (PSLRA), which was the only legislation passed by Congress over a veto by President Bill Clinton. That legislation required more specific pleading of the facts upon which claims of fraud were based and fraudulent intent had to be shown. The trial lawyers initially tried to evade that statute by moving their class actions to state courts, which were unaffected by the statute. Congress responded with more legislation in 1998 that allowed removal of such claims to federal court, where they were to subject to the PSLRA pleading requirements. Undaunted, the trial lawyers simply inflated their complaints by hundreds of pages designed to overwhelm the courts with unproven allegations and details often taken from newspaper articles.

In another effort to curb class-action abuses, Congress passed the Class Action Fairness Act of 2005, which sought to prevent class-action plaintiff lawyers from shopping for the most favorable state for large class-action awards by allowing those actions to be removed to federal court. Greater judicial scrutiny of class-action settlements was also required. "Coupon" settlements were of particular concern because they were of little value to the class-action members, but large cash sums were paid to the class-action plaintiff lawyers. The legislation required that such settlements and attorney fees be based either on the value of the coupons actually redeemed or on the amount of time spent on the case by lawyers, rather than on the overall value of the coupons issued.

The judiciary in the United States, which is already a battleground between conservative and liberal politics, was being further politicized by fights between the trial lawyers and business interests that were seeking to place elected judges on state court appellate benches that would favor their respective causes. A John Grisham novel published in 2008, called *The Appeal,* was a fictional portrayal of such a fight in Mississippi. However, a real-life episode was soon to follow. A divisive battle occurred in Wisconsin over election for a seat on that state's supreme court, in March 2008. Louis Butler, the incumbent who had been appointed by the governor, was an ultraliberal who led the majority of the court in expanding tort suits in that state. Butler lost the election narrowly to Michael Gableman, a conservative candidate. The election campaign was funded by labor unions and trial lawyers, on the side of Butler, and by business interests, on the part of Gableman.

The U.S. Supreme Court had initially broadly construed the federal securities laws in order to encourage class-action claims in the federal courts. But soon the federal courts were inundated with complex and time-consuming securities-related litigation. The Supreme Court then began to backtrack and in recent years has sought to make it harder to bring such lawsuits. Among other things, the court has required a showing of scienter, that is, fraudulent intent; it has required plaintiffs to show reliance on any claimed misstatements or omissions; it has rejected aiding and abetting liability; and it has required a showing of all loss causation and economic loss. The Supreme Court has also set aside some extraordinarily exorbitant punitive damage awards. For example, the court held in June 2008 that a $2.8 billion punitive damage award against Exxon as a result of the 1989 *Valdez* oil spill was excessive, and it reduced that award to $507.5 million.

Plaintiff's lawyers sought to avoid loss causation requirements by a new theory of "scheme liability," which would have made anyone liable who participated in any way in transactions that resulted in the inflation of public company accounts. However, the Supreme Court rejected that theory in an Enron-era scandal involving Charter Communications. The plaintiffs there sought to hold customers and suppliers of Charter liable for agreeing to arrangements that allowed the company to inflate its revenues and to issue misleading financial statements to the public. The Supreme Court held that there could be no liability because those customers and suppliers had themselves made no misrepresentations to plaintiffs.[59] However, legislation passed in 2010 required reports on whether that ruling should be changed by statute.

Surprisingly, the SEC has, in recent years, expressed concern over abusive class-action lawsuits and sought to limit the liability of accounting firms for failed audits. However, there was some question as to how heartfelt that concern really was at the agency, and the subprime crisis resulted in renewed hostility by the SEC toward the companies that it regulates. In any event, the number of class-action lawsuits continued to grow. About 60 percent of the companies comprising the Dow Jones Industrial Index have been the subjects of class-action litigation since 1999. The number of class-action lawsuits doubled between 2000 and 2001, reaching almost 500 in 2001. Settlement costs increased by 20 percent during that period.

The number of class-action lawsuits increased by another 16 percent in 2004, but fell 17 percent in 2005, after the government indicted a prominent member of the class-action bar and targeted two of the nation's largest class-action law firms on the same charges. Still, settlements in securities-related class-action lawsuits that year climbed to $9.6 billion, a new record (including $6.1 billion from the WorldCom litigation), compared with $150 million in 1995.

The number of class-action suit filings dropped again in 2006. The *Wall Street Journal* attributed that decline to the fact that the stock market was stable through the year. It also noted most of the class-action suits were Sarbanes-Oxley-type claims of accounting misstatements. However, that decline was only temporary. In 2007, 111 class actions were settled, including the third-largest securities settlement in history, $3.2 billion in settlement paid by Tyco International. It was second only to the record-breaking WorldCom settlement of $6.1 billion and the Enron class-action settlements from the banks and other service providers that totaled $7.2 billion.

In the first four months of 2008, about two lawsuits were brought every day on charges in connection with subprime problems. After a two-year decline, 163 cases were filed in 2007, compared with 109 in 2006, a 43 percent increase. That increase was attributed principally to subprime mortgage cases. Some ninety lawsuits were filed in the last quarter of 2007, and 188 lawsuits were filed in 2008, charging securities laws violations in connection with subprime losses.

The number of securities class actions increased by 19 percent in 2008 compared with 2007 and more than 80 percent compared with 2006. The actions filed in 2008 sought more than $800 billion in damages. Many of those lawsuits claimed that financial services firms had overvalued their subprime investments. After its failure, Merrill Lynch settled one such lawsuit in January 2009 by agreeing to pay investors and employees $550 million. It settled another such action for $150 million. The lead plaintiff in that case was the Louisiana Sheriffs' Pension and Relief Fund. In a class-action suit against American Express over subprime disclosure issues, a federal judge appointed Local No. 38 International Brotherhood of Electrical Workers Pension Fund as lead plaintiff despite the fact that a Swedish money manager had a larger stake in the litigation. Pension funds and other institutional investors were able to gain higher settlements as joint lead plaintiffs than they would have as individual lead plaintiffs. (See below.)

The class-action bar seemed to have exhausted itself in 2008 because the number of class-action lawsuits dropped by 24 percent in 2009. The number of lawsuits concerning subprime credit-related issues was down sharply as the market began its recovery in the last three quarters of that year. However, the widely publicized problem of stuck gas pedals on Toyota automobiles led to a frenzy in the class-action bar to gain lead status in the class actions brought against the Toyota Motor Co. Abuses continued. Class-action law firms were reported by the *Wall Street Journal* to have made over $20 million in campaign donations to elect state officials over the last ten years and over 60 percent of that amount went to races outside the law firms' home states. The small Norfolk County pension fund in Massachusetts had brought twelve class-action lawsuits for stocks that declined in its portfolio. The county treasurer who chaired the pension board was given $34,000 in campaign donations by the New York law firm he hired to bring those suits.

Some Corporate Pushback

A circuit court in April 2008 dismissed a class action against cigarette companies claiming that smokers were misled by the purported safety of "light" cigarettes. That was a reversal of the days when any cigarette litigation was a sure ticket for billions of dollars in settlement. Another victory appeared as a result of a unique litigation strategy taken by one pharmaceutical company. Most companies in the United States seek to avoid a jury trial at all costs. However, Merck decided that it would not succumb to blackmail from lawyers representing clients who used the drug Vioxx, an arthritis drug that was withdrawn from the market after it was claimed that the drug more than doubled the risk of heart attack and stroke. The plaintiffs' lawyers claimed that the drug had killed more than 50,000 people and caused 138,000 others to have heart attacks. Merck was hit with thousands of lawsuits seeking tens of billions of dollars in damages.

In a controversial and daring litigation move, Merck vowed to fight each lawsuit individually. That strategy was called into question after a Texas jury awarded a plaintiff $254 million, including $229 million in punitive damages. However, Texas law caps punitive damages at $1.6 million, reducing the verdict to $26 million. A Texas appeals court later set aside even that verdict. Merck prevailed in other cases. A New Jersey judge tried to strong-arm verdicts against Merck, but a New Jersey appeals court struck down the award in one of the cases tried in that court.

After years of litigation, plaintiffs prevailed only in four of the sixteen cases that were tried, making it clear to the plaintiffs' lawyers that there was no guarantee of a giant payday from these cases. The result was that Merck was able to negotiate a global settlement for more than 44,000 eligible cases, in which it would pay $4.85 billion. That was a lot of money, but the amount was small in comparison to what the plaintiffs' lawyers were seeking, and thought they would surely reap, before Merck decided to stand and fight. Merck also settled Vioxx advertising claims brought by twenty-nine state attorney generals and the District of Columbia for a relatively paltry $58 million.

Other pharmaceutical companies also had some success in litigation. A federal district court dismissed a class-action suit against Pfizer. That suit claimed that the company had misled investors on the safeness and efficacy of a drug to be used for the treatment of heart disease. Pfizer was settling claims involving its Bextra and Celebrex drugs. Reportedly, Bextra cases were settled for less than $50,000 per client, and Celebrex cases were settled for as much as $200,000 per client. The Court of Appeals for the Second Circuit affirmed the dismissal of a class-action lawsuit against GlaxoSmithKline, which contended that the company had made false representations concerning the antidepressant drug Paxil.

Nevertheless, Merck and other pharmaceutical companies continue to be punching bags for massive litigation. Merck agreed in February 2008 to pay $650 million to settle litigation over some of its sales and marketing practices. The Justice Department and forty-nine states, as well as the District of Colombia, joined that litigation as plaintiffs. The suit, the result of a whistle-blower claim, charged that Merck had given discounts on its drugs to some distributors but not to Medicaid recipients. In another action initiated by whistle-blowers, Pfizer agreed to pay a record $2.3 billion in September 2009 to settle a criminal case brought by the Justice Department over the use of Bextra and other Pfizer drugs for unapproved uses. The payment included a $1.2 billion criminal fine.

There may still be hope. Representative Jeb Hensarling (R-TX) introduced legislation in February 2008 requiring plaintiffs' lawyers in class-action lawsuits to pay the legal fees and costs of the defendants who prevail in such litigation. This was sort of a modified "English rule" for attorney fees that would attack the problem at its heart. It would impose an obligation on class-action lawyers to ensure that their claims were properly brought. However, the class-action bar and its supporters were too powerful to permit passage of this reform legislation.

Class-Action Lawyer Scandals

Before enactment of the PSLRA, members of the class-action plaintiff bar competed with one another for the spoils from cases brought against public companies. Dozens, and sometimes hundreds, of lawsuits were filed whenever a scandal broke out or bad news was announced by a public company. There was a race to the courthouse by the class-action lawyers in order to gain lead plaintiff status. Such status was desirable because the attorneys for the lead plaintiff would control the litigation and could then claim the lion's share of the contingency fees.

Some of the larger class-action firms kept clients holding small amounts of stock in a large number of public companies on standby, to serve as an instant plaintiff upon the announcement of any adverse news by a public company. This caused some inconvenience to the client because he would have to be deposed at length by the defendants' lawyers, which could be time-consuming. In exchange, the plaintiff would receive only an aliquot portion of the damages obtained by the lawyer, which was typically a minuscule amount for each share of stock held. In order to more fully compensate those clients, some law firms began giving clients under-the-table payments in substantially larger amounts than they would have received under the class-action settlement agreement. However, this required the titular clients to lie in their depositions and to the court hearing the case because they had to represent that they were not receiving any such special compensation.

The PSLRA tried to curb these and other abuses by directing the courts to appoint a plaintiff with the greatest interest in the litigation. This inevitably turned out to be a union pension plan because those plans are diversified and hold large amounts of stock. That change in the law did not prove a problem for the class-action lawyers. They simply made themselves available for hire by the pension funds, which were happy to retain them because of their expertise and prior successes. The pension funds were also happy to achieve lead counsel status so that they could boast of their successes to their pension fund beneficiaries.

Unfortunately for the class-action bar, the Justice Department began investigating the pre-PSLRA under-the-table payments made by some prominent class-action lawyers to individual clients. The probe centered on the Milberg Weiss law firm. The case broke after Seymour M. Lazar, one of its pet plaintiffs, entered a guilty plea for lying about under-the-table payments that he had received from Milberg Weiss. Lazar was given six months of home detention, was fined $600,000, and forfeited $1.5 million. Prosecutors charged that the payments made to Lazar and other plaintiffs by Milberg Weiss had allowed that law firm to collect more than $250 million in legal fees from the settlement of class-action lawsuits. This scheme had been carried out over a thirty-year period.

Three Milberg Weiss partners and two of their professional plaintiffs pleaded guilty to charges in connection with the scheme. Richard Purtich pleaded guilty to using his law firm as a conduit to allow Milberg Weiss to conceal payments to plaintiffs. Milberg Weiss and two of its partners, David Bershad and Steven Schulman, were indicted in May 2006 for their role in paying kickbacks to professional plaintiffs, like Lazar, in class-action lawsuits brought by their firm. Bershad pleaded guilty to making payoffs from money stashed in a safe in his office. He was sentenced to six months in prison. Schulman also pleaded guilty, and he received the same sentence. The Milberg Weiss law firm paid at least $11 million in kickbacks to its professional plaintiffs. The law firm settled the charges brought against it by agreeing to pay $75 million over a five-year period. The law firm had also been paying stockbrokers to refer clients for class-action lawsuits.

This was stunning news in view of the prominence of the Milberg Weiss law firm in exacting massive payments from large companies in order to settle class-action lawsuits. The real shocker came when William Lerach, who was considered the dean of class-action lawyers, pleaded guilty to charges of paying kickbacks to professional plaintiffs. Lerach had, at one point, boasted that he read as many as six newspapers a day in order to glean information about companies having problems, which he would utilize to provide a basis for a class-action lawsuit. Venture capitalist John Doerr called Lerach a "cunning economic terrorist" for his class-action lawsuits against public companies.[60] Lerach earned more than $200 million in legal fees from the class actions that he had paid $11 million in kickbacks to obtain. He defended those payments as being due to his zeal in fighting corporate greed, and he asserted that they were a standard industry practice. Lerach was represented by John W. Keker, the same lawyer who had represented Andrew Fastow of Enron fame and Frank Quattrone, the investment banker who was charged with criminal misconduct.

Lerach was sentenced to only two years in prison and was ordered to pay a mere $8 million in restitution and fines. He was released from custody in March 2010 and was summarily disbarred from practice by the California bar association a few days later. Still, his punishment seemed rather lenient in view of the decades-long sentences of corporate executives such as Jeffrey Skilling and Bernie Ebbers and the vast amounts of money that Lerach made from the strike suits brought against public companies. Lerach obtained this sweetheart deal even though he had refused to cooperate with federal prosecutors in the prosecution of other Milberg Weiss lawyers.

On March 20, 2008, Melvyn Weiss, age seventy-two and a founding partner of Milberg Weiss, agreed to plead guilty for his role in this scandal. Like Lerach, Weiss was considered a leading figure in the prosecution of securities class-action lawsuits. The two men had once been partners at Milberg Weiss, where they made the payoffs, but they later quarreled and formed separate firms. They then commenced an intense rivalry to gain lead counsel status in class-action lawsuits. Weiss was sentenced to thirty months in prison for his crimes and agreed to pay a comparatively paltry $10 million in fines and penalties. He sparked outrage after it was disclosed that his former law firm agreed to pay him about 15 percent of fees awarded in settlements still pending at his firm. Those settlements were some of the largest in history, including those of Tyco and Enron. This meant that Weiss would receive tens of millions of dollars from those payments while sitting in prison. The law firm also agreed to pay the legal fees stemming from his indictment, a practice that the Justice Department had sought to deny to other business executives caught in its crosshairs. Perhaps there was some justice because Weiss was one of the victims of Bernie Madoff's giant Ponzi scheme. Weiss lost an estimated $20 million in that affair.

John Torkelsen, an expert witness employed by the Milberg law firm, pleaded guilty to charges that he had given false testimony in class-action litigation brought by the firm. That witness was given a share of the attorney's fees in exchange for his testimony, payments that were concealed from the courts and from lawyers for the corporate defendants. Torkelsen was already in prison, having been convicted on unrelated charges.

The Milberg Weiss law firm was also accused of inflating its expenses in class-action suits submitted to the courts for approval for payment from corporate defendants and their officers. This included inflated costs for expert witnesses, like Torkelsen, who were paid a fee contingent on the success of the litigation. This allowed the law firm to avoid having to pay for experts in cases in which they were not successful. However, in order to make it up to the expert witnesses, the lawyers would inflate the expert fees in subsequent cases. Torkelsen alone billed the law firm for more than $60 million between 1993 and 1996. He also accused Lerach's law firm of engaging in the same practices. That firm, Coughlin Stoia Geller Rudman & Robbins, led in amounts recovered from settlements in class actions in 2006 and filed a number of class actions related to subprime problems in 2008.

In another stunning revelation, Gene Cauley, a Lerach protégé, who formed his own securities class-action law firm in Arkansas with Lerach's help, in May 2009 agreed to plead guilty to two felony counts. Cauley had stolen $9.3 million in client settlement funds in a suit brought against BISYS Group, an insurance firm that was later acquired by Citigroup. In 2005 Cauley had been named one of the nation's foremost young attorneys by the *National Law Journal*. He was sentenced to seven years in prison.

Scandals also broke out in class-action lawsuits brought outside securities law. The King of Torts, Richard ("Dickie") Scruggs, was involved in a particularly shocking scandal. Scruggs rose to fame through the asbestos litigation that dragged on for years and bankrupted several companies. He was also a leader in the tobacco litigation that led to the largest settlement in history. Scruggs's battle with the tobacco companies was the subject of a popular movie called *The Insider.* He was reported to have earned a $1.4 billion fee from that litigation, or an hourly billing rate of $22,500.[61]

Scruggs's most recent venture was to sue the insurance companies for their refusal to cover damages from Hurricane Katrina. However, his fortunes changed in 2007, after he was accused of attempting to bribe a state court judge to persuade him to sign a court order approving Scruggs's request for fees in a case that was heard before the judge. Scruggs's co-conspirator was caught in the act of bribing the judge and agreed to secretly tape-record his conversations with Scruggs about the bribes. On March 14, 2008, Scruggs pleaded guilty to criminal charges and was sentenced to five years in prison, later increased to seven after a guilty plea on other charges. He was fined $200,000 and ordered to pay the cost of his imprisonment. Scruggs's son, David (Zack), also pleaded guilty to participating in this conduct. This scandal widened after Bobby DeLaughter, a Mississippi judge and celebrated prosecutor of the killer of Medgar Evers, was indicted by federal prosecutors for giving favored treatment to Scruggs. DeLaughter was allegedly offered a federal judgeship by Senator Trent Lott (R-MI), Scruggs's brother-in-law, as an inducement for the favored treatment of Scruggs in proceedings in DeLaughter's court.

Another class-action lawyer abuse scandal arose in Kentucky. There, a group of lawyers was accused in a private lawsuit of defrauding 400 class-action plaintiffs of more than half of a $200 million settlement involving a drug manufacturer that was selling a diet drug called Fen-phen. Three of the class-action lawyers were indicted for the conduct. One was acquitted and two were convicted after a retrial. The two convicted lawyers were given sentences of 25 and 20 years. The lawyer receiving the 20-year sentence, Shirley Cunningham Jr., had used $1 million of the stolen money to fund a chair at Florida A&M University's law school in Orlando, Florida, which resulted in a $750,000 matching grant from another source. Cunningham filled the chair himself. He was paid $125,000 per year, but never showed up to teach. Another lawyer in that action, Paul J. Napoli, was standing trial in New York in a case in which his clients accused him of manipulating the distribution of a settlement funds in another case to favor some clients over others. The total settlement was said to be $1 billion. In the meantime, Napoli was one of the lead lawyers for the 9,000 ground-zero workers who were suing New York City, claiming injury to their health from contaminants in the air after the collapse of the World Trade Center.

In California, class-action lawyers were found to have falsified evidence in suits brought there against Dole Food on behalf of banana plantation workers in Nicaragua. The lawsuit claimed that Dole had used a pesticide that caused sterility. However, Dole discovered that the plaintiff lawyers had submitted evidence from individuals who had never worked on a Dole plantation and from individuals who were not sterile. One such worker had fathered three children.[62] In Florida, attorney Scott Rothstein was charged with running a $1.2 billion Ponzi scheme in which, among other things, he sold interests in large non-existent settlements in sex discrimination and whistle-blower suits to unwitting investors.

A few states tried to limit abuses by the lawyers in tort claims. In Texas, the state constitution was amended to limit noneconomic damages (pain and suffering) in tort cases to $750,000. Mississippi limited noneconomic damages to $500,000 in medical malpractice cases and $1 million in other cases. West Virginia went further, limiting such damages to $250,000. These states were reporting increased business activity and were attracting an influx of medical doctors, who were receiving the benefit of reduced insurance premiums.

Part II

Financial Market Developments

4. Securities, Banking, and Insurance

Securities Market Developments

Some History

The securities markets were experiencing some revolutionary changes even as the Enron scandals were unfolding. The attack by Eliot Spitzer on Richard Grasso's retirement package would also have a dramatic effect on one of the nation's most venerable institutions, the New York Stock Exchange (NYSE). That exchange traces back to March 1792, when a meeting was held at Corre's Hotel in New York City that resulted in the "Buttonwood Agreement." Still in existence, that document reflected an agreement by a group of brokers to fix their commissions on sales of public stock and to give each other preference in their dealings. At the time only five "stocks" were traded in New York. Three were U.S. government securities, and the other two were bank stocks.

NYSE, then called the New York Stock & Exchange Board, was formally organized in 1817. It sought to monopolize trading in the stocks it "listed" by allowing only members to access its trading floor. Some competition arrived from brokers who stood in the street to trade NYSE and other stocks, but it was limited because the curb brokers lacked immediate access to NYSE prices. Trading volume peaked in 1824 on NYSE and declined by 85 percent over the remainder of the decade. However, the arrival of railroad stocks in 1830 led to renewed interest in stock trading. Indeed, railroad stocks would dominate NYSE trading for the rest of the century.

In 1836, NYSE prohibited its members from trading in the curb market. Actually, the curb market posed no substantial threat to the exchange until the Civil War touched off a frenzy of speculation. Numerous exchanges appeared in New York during that conflict as speculation became popular, particularly in gold, which fluctuated wildly in value as Union prospects waxed and waned. NYSE prohibited its members from communicating with anyone connected to a notorious bucket shop operation that was NYSE's largest competitor, the

Consolidated Exchange.[1] "The president of the New York Stock Exchange admitted that the purpose of the rule is to drive the Consolidated out of business."[2] Nevertheless, competition from these alternative markets, which were also trading NYSE stocks, caused the value of NYSE seats to fall to $500 in 1861, down from a high of $4,000.

Later in the century, competitors sought to use NYSE's price quotes as the basis for conducting their own markets in those stocks. However, NYSE was able to restrict access to its price quotations through court actions. The courts recognized the proprietary rights of NYSE in protecting and distributing that information, thereby enhancing its growing monopoly status in the stocks it traded.[3] Another significant development on exchange was the introduction of the continuous trading system in 1871. Previously, NYSE was a "call" market, in which stocks were called from a list in sequence and sold by auction. This rotation was conducted twice daily in two sessions, one in the morning, and one in the afternoon. Changing to continuous trading made NYSE stocks more liquid because they could be bought and sold at any time during the trading day. This continuous trading system gave rise to "specialists" who remained at one location on the NYSE floor. The specialists concentrated on trading only a few securities. The specialists at first competed with one another in particular stocks, but eventually a single specialist was given a monopoly over market making in each listed stock.

Their monopoly position allowed specialists to reap vast benefits, at least until electronic trading arrived in the twenty-first century. This is because the specialist enjoyed a time and place advantage over all other traders. No one could react to market-moving events more quickly than the specialist because all NYSE orders first had to go through him. The specialist stood ready to both buy and sell the stocks in which he specialized. However, those prices were quoted at a "spread" in which the bid was lower than the offer. This meant that, if stock prices did not change, a person who purchased a stock from a specialist and then resold it would sustain a loss equal to that spread. Consequently, anyone entering orders on NYSE had to pay the specialist his spread. The specialists justified this charge on the grounds that they were providing liquidity to traders, a service for which they demanded compensation.

The specialist enjoyed still another advantage. He kept, and was the only person who had access to, the customer's book of limit orders. These limit orders instructed the specialist to buy or sell a particular amount of securities in the event of a market move. For example, a customer might want to keep a "stop loss" order with the specialist that would instruct the specialist to sell the customer's securities in the event that the price of that stock dropped, say by $5. Information gleaned from limit orders told the specialist what to expect in the event the market moved in either direction. Specifically, he would know the amount and level of limit orders that would be touched off in the event the market in a stock encountered a price change. This was valuable inside information to the specialist that allowed him to set his quotations accordingly.

Regulation

NYSE went unregulated for almost 150 years, but the stock market crash of 1929 ended that freedom. As a result of the passage of the Securities Exchange Act of 1934, NYSE was required to register with the Securities and Exchange Commission (SEC) as a "national securities exchange," and it became subject to SEC oversight of its operations. The SEC required a reorganization of NYSE after a scandal involving one of its more prominent members, Richard Whitney. Otherwise, the SEC generally left NYSE to its own devices, except for the notable exception of forcing the exchange to ban floor traders in 1964. Those floor traders were NYSE members who traded for their own accounts on the exchange floor. The SEC thought that the time and place advantage gained by the floor traders on the floor was unfair to other traders.

The SEC allowed the specialists to remain on the NYSE floor. However, the agency exacted a price for the monopoly they enjoyed. The SEC required the specialists to maintain a continuous two-sided market, and the specialists were further required to maintain a "fair and orderly" market in their stocks. The continuous market obligation was intended to promote liquidity. The fair and orderly market obligation sought price stability because it required the specialist to buy in the face of a declining market and to sell in a rising market. This all seems strange, in that it suggested that the SEC viewed a monopoly to be more efficient than a competitive market, and that price stability, rather than price efficiency, was a more desirable goal.

The SEC also allowed NYSE to continue to enforce the exchange's prohibition on the trading of its stocks in any location other than the NYSE floor. That rule was a critical factor in maintaining the specialists' monopoly. There was some evasion of this rule through the "third" and "fourth markets." The former involved transactions in NYSE stock executed by broker-dealers who were not NYSE members and, therefore, not subject to NYSE rules. The fourth market involved transactions between nonmember institutional investors directly, without exchange or broker-dealer intermediation.

Another source of competition to the NYSE specialist was "block trades." These were large transactions in NYSE stocks that were arranged "upstairs" by a NYSE member broker-dealer and "crossed" (matched against each other) on the NYSE floor. Institutions liked this service because the specialist often could not make a competitive market in such large transactions. Goldman Sachs made a specialty of this business for its large institutional customers. NYSE was executing almost 70 percent of total orders and 80 percent of volume for its listed stocks in the 1990s. However, about half that volume came through block trades, evidencing the rise of a new force in the market, the institutional trader.

Institutional traders, such as mutual funds and union pension funds (and now hedge funds, private equity, and sovereign wealth funds), began supplanting the individual retail investor in the securities markets after World

War II. By 1992 institutions accounted for more than 80 percent of trading volume on stock markets. At that time, institutions owned over 50 percent of all U.S. equities, compared with 30 percent in 1975. This growth had several implications, but of critical importance was the fact that the SEC and the federal securities laws were structured to protect only the small investor, not institutions and sophisticated investors who could look out for themselves. This allowed institutions and wealthy individuals to operate outside much of the SEC regulatory framework.

National Market System

The SEC conducted a study in 1971 on the growth of institutional trading because of its concern that the growth of such trading might create separately tiered markets for institutions and retail investors. The concern was that a three-tiered market was developing that was composed of (1) large institutions; (2) medium-sized institutions and wealthy individuals; and (3) small retail customers. The SEC was also concerned with market "fragmentation" that might result in disparate pricing for the same securities in different markets.

The SEC sought to counter these concerns with a vague concept it dubbed the "Central Market" System, later renamed the "National Market System" (NMS), through amendments that were added in 1975 to the Securities Exchange Act of 1934. Those amendments gave statutory recognition to the development of a central market system, but failed to specify what such a market would look like. This entire effort turned out to be an exercise in futility. The high water mark of the SEC's central market program appears to have been the consolidated tape of last sale reports by exchanges, which now seems quaint in light of other technological advances.

An electronic link among the specialists trading the same stock on different exchanges was also created. This Intermarket Trading System (ITS), as it was dubbed, had little effect on NYSE's domination of its listed stocks because specialists on the regional exchanges simply traded off the NYSE specialist quotes, not wanting to compete with the more powerful NYSE market maker. ITS adopted a requirement in 1981 "that changed the essential nature of the ITS system from a voluntary execution system, in which a market-maker in one market could choose to execute trades in other markets, to a mandatory execution system, in which a market marker in one market center, under some circumstances, was forced to execute trades in other markets."[4]

A link was also created between NYSE specialists and NASDAQ market makers, but significant volume flows from one to the other had to await the repeal of NYSE Rule 390, which prohibited NYSE members from executing transactions in NYSE securities other than through the exchange floor. The SEC eventually required NYSE to limit its Rule 390 to only those NYSE stocks listed before April 26, 1979. NASDAQ market makers were then allowed to access the ITS for NYSE stocks listed after that date. However, the stocks still grandfathered in under Rule 390 were some of the bluest of the blue chips and were responsible for a substantial percentage of NYSE trading volume. It was not until December 1999 that NYSE agreed to drop Rule 390 entirely, and only after it received much pressure from the SEC to do so.

Sticking to its Central Market concept, the SEC, in 1997, adopted a "trade-through" rule that required NASDAQ market makers to inform customers of matchable limit orders from other customers at a price more favorable than the market maker's quote and to disclose whether the market maker had traded at better prices on an electronic trading platform. Later, in 2005, the SEC expanded the trade-through rule in its Regulation NMS, which included an "Order Protection Rule." That rule required "trading centers" to create written procedures to prevent the execution of "trade throughs," which were orders executed at prices inferior to quotations displayed in other trading centers.[5] Trading centers included national securities exchanges, exchange specialists, electronic communication networks, over-the-counter (OTC) market makers, and block positioners.

The SEC also adopted an "Access Rule" that required nondiscriminatory access to quotations at trading centers and prohibited market participants from displaying quotations that locked or crossed automated quotations, which were bids and offers with no spreads or inverted spreads. Regulation NMS further contained a "Sub-Penny Rule," which prohibited market participants from accepting, ranking, or displaying orders, quotations, or indications of interest in a pricing increment smaller than a penny, except for orders, quotations, or indications of interest that are priced at less than $1.00 per share.

Specialists' Problems

The specialists and floor brokers on NYSE have been the center of a number of scandals in recent years. In one instance, prosecutors charged that floor brokers were improperly positioning themselves between customer orders, but those cases fell apart. Two NYSE specialists had their convictions reversed on appeal by the Court of Appeals for the Second Circuit. The appeals court held that there was insufficient evidence to prove deception with respect to the interpositioning claim. The conviction of another specialist had been set aside earlier on the same grounds. The government dropped criminal cases against seven of the fifteen specialists previously indicted, and two other cases resulted in acquittals. One specialist was a fugitive from justice. Two others pleaded guilty, but the district court judge vacated the guilty pleas in light of the ruling by the appeals court.

The SEC was more successful in its charges against several specialist firms that agreed to pay $241 million to settle charges that they were trading ahead of customer orders. The specialists were also charged with improperly taking customer orders into their accounts that could have been matched with other customer orders. In March 2007, the SEC struck again and charged fourteen specialist firms with engaging in improper trading practices, including trading ahead of customer orders on the Chicago Board Options Exchange (CBOE), American Stock Exchange (AMEX), Philadelphia Stock Exchange (PHLX), and the Chicago Stock Exchange. The firms included units of Goldman Sachs and Citigroup. They agreed to pay $70 million collectively to settle these charges.

Information Technology

In 1957, NYSE commissioned a study by Ebasco Services, which recommended automation of transaction reporting and improved clearing and quotation services. However, it was not until 1966 that transmission of trading data from the floor was fully automated. The paperwork crisis at the end of the 1960s demonstrated that the exchange's clearing and settlement system had to be more fully automated if the exchange was to grow or even survive high-volume trading. A study commissioned by NYSE in 1971, which was conducted by former Federal Reserve Chairman William McChesney Martin, Jr., concluded that computers were changing the securities markets and "because of the communications systems they make possible, [they] offer the means to improve radically the way markets operate."[6] That prediction was prophetic. Information technology created an almost complete revolution in the securities industry over the next thirty-five years.[7]

NYSE introduced its Designated Order Turnaround (DOT) system in 1976, followed by the Super-DOT system in 1984. These systems allowed the electronic transmission of customer orders to the specialist. The Super-DOT system was handling about 90 percent of NYSE volume in 2000. NYSE made a major upgrade to its trading floor technology in 1979, allowing it to handle its first 100-million-share trading day in 1982. NYSE spent over $1 billion on technology between 1982 and 1995, allowing it to handle average daily trading volume in excess of 200 million shares and to cut order execution times dramatically.

The exchange began another effort to upgrade floor technology in 1995 through the addition of handheld terminals, fiber optics, cell phones, and high-definition flat screens for information displays. In 1997, NYSE introduced a wireless data system that allowed its floor brokers to receive orders, report executions, and access market information, wherever they might be at any given time on the floor. Two years later, the exchange introduced a 3D Trading Floor Operations Center.

Those improvements allowed the exchange to handle daily order flows in excess of 1.4 billion shares as the market surged at the end of the twentieth century. That was in stark contrast to the 10-million-share trading days that almost destroyed NYSE during the paperwork crisis in the 1960s. The billion-plus trading days so easily handled on the exchange during the market run up at the end of the 1990s also contrasted sharply with the 600-million-share days that the NYSE trading floor was unable to deal with during the stock market crash in October 1987. However, these improvements did not create an electronic exchange; rather, it was called computer assisted trading (CAT), to signify that the specialist was merely being aided, not replaced, by technology.

NYSE was losing pieces of its monopoly, the repeal of Rule 390 being the most distressing. In 2002, the exchange allowed some access to the specialists' book of limit orders, allowing off-floor participants to see buying and selling interest beyond the best bid on an offer. In 2004, NYSE increased the size of orders that could be executed entirely electronically through the specialist. In 2005, the exchange created a "hybrid" trading environment, in which trading was conducted entirely by electronic trading without specialist intervention or, if preferred, through the specialist's book.

The NYSE created a new market model in October 2008 to meet the increased competition from electronic trading platforms. The NYSE then dropped its historical specialists system of trading and substituted "Designated Market Makers" to play that role in the new electronic trading environment. These entities retained their monopoly on individual stocks and continued to maintain a position on the exchange floor, but now do most of their trading electronically off the floor. The Designated Market Makers continued to have the obligation to quote a two-sided market in an orderly fashion.

In March 2010, the NYSE invited Getco to take over Barclays Capital as a designated market maker for 350 stocks. Getco was already acting as a NYSE "Supplemental Liquidity Provider," another new element added in October 2008. These were upstairs electronic trading firms using their own proprietary capital to trade. Supplemental Liquidity Providers were intended to "complement" the Designated Market Makers, and they assumed certain quoting obligations in making a market. The NYSE was also redesigning its trading floor to unify upstairs and the remaining floor trading that was being conducted by some 100 floor broker operations. The floor brokers were also evolving. They were conducting "upstairs" trading on the NYSE floor by routing orders to different markets.

More Automation

Automation increased elsewhere. NASDAQ, where OTC stocks are traded, utilized an electronic "quotation" system that was developed in the 1960s, after a Special Study of the Securities Markets by the SEC staff. That report suggested the desirability of such an automated system to replace the manual printing of quotes circulated to broker-dealers through the "pink sheets." NASDAQ supplanted the pink sheets, but did not entirely replace them. Incredibly, the pink sheets survived the computer age. They were bought in the 1990s by Cromwell Coulson from the National Quotations Bureau and became a sort of Wild West of small-cap trading as this century began.

NASDAQ employed competing market makers, rather than the specialist auction system used by NYSE and other exchanges. NASDAQ was divided into tiers: the NMS for larger companies, a small-cap market for small and medium-sized companies, and a bulletin board for illiquid securities. The NASDAQ market became successful. By 1992, its volume accounted for some 42 percent of total share volume on all U.S. markets. By 2000 NASDAQ volume sometimes exceeded 2.5 billion shares a day, which was a billion more shares than were traded on NYSE.

NASDAQ did not initially provide for the automated execution of orders. Rather, a broker observing a quote on a computer screen for a stock posted on NASDAQ would contact the posting market maker and negotiate the trade. NASDAQ developed a small order execution system (SOES) for the automatic execution of small customer orders, but large trades were still negotiated orally with the market makers. The SOES system was abandoned after a number of abuses by market makers who were being attacked by "day traders" using SOES, in favor of its SuperMontage electronic trading system. Another improvement was SelectNet, a screen-based trading system that allowed NASDAQ members to enter and negotiate the terms of trades by computer.

Electronic improvements in the securities industry included automated systems for broker-dealer back-office processing of securities transactions. Improved screen-based information and services were also provided to broker-dealers by private vendors such as Reuters, Quotron Systems, Telerate, Automatic Data Processing, Knight-Ridder, and Bloomberg. A congressional staff study in 1990 noted that "financial information vendors may move toward offering transactional services using automated execution systems."[8] One such effort, GEMCO, had failed, but the Instinet was more successful. Created in 1969 as the Institutional Network Corporation, Instinet was later acquired by Reuters, and it began offering an electronic securities trading system that, by the early 1990s, was executing an average of 13 million shares a day in NYSE and NASDAQ stocks. Instinet allowed broker-dealers and institutional traders to indicate their interest in purchasing or selling NYSE or NASDAQ securities. Participants could respond to those indications of interest by making bids or offers, and Instinet would then process and report executions. Orders were not publicly disclosed, protecting the identity of the institution in the trade. By the end of the twentieth century, Instinet was processing 170 million shares per day, of which 20 million were executed after traditional trading hours.

The ECNs Compete

Electronic trading facilitates the execution of orders electronically by algorithms. The exchanges were unwilling to use algorithms to replace their trading-floor functions because that would have undermined the specialists. However, private companies had no such qualms. Participants in these new ventures soon learned the benefits of electronic trading systems, which included reductions in cost, fewer trading errors, enhancement of operational efficiencies, and benefits associated with risk management. The SEC initially called these electronic trading platforms electronic communication networks (ECNs) and later "alternative trading systems" (ATS). The ECNs were screen-based and were initially regulated by the SEC as broker-dealers. The SEC did not require the ECNs to register as a national securities exchange, as was required for NYSE. Registration as an exchange would have imposed self-regulatory and other requirements that those electronic trading systems could not have met without incurring great expense. The SEC concluded that the ATS need not register as a national securities exchange because, unlike NYSE specialists, the ATS were not making a continuous market in securities. Rather, they were only matching orders for third parties.

The ECNs arrived in force in the financial markets at the end of the twentieth century and provided a wide variety of automated trading systems for institutional traders. By 1994, those proprietary systems executed about 13 percent of NASDAQ volume. The ECNs, however, were then capturing only about 1.4 percent of NYSE volume because of the then-continuing effects of Rule 390. Broker-dealers also operated automated systems that matched customer orders internally, but NYSE Rule 390 required orders for stocks subject to that rule to be executed on NYSE, until that rule was repealed.

In preserving market share through Rule 390, NYSE also reported record profits. However, the battle with the ECNs was already joined at NASDAQ, where market share was greatly eroded by their trading. Instinet partnered with several online brokers who permitted their customers to enter orders on the Internet. In August 1999, Instinet also joined with several large brokerage firms, including Merrill Lynch, Goldman Sachs, and Morgan Stanley, to form Primex Trading, an electronic platform for institutional traders in NYSE stocks, a project that NASDAQ also joined.

Other ECNs included Wit Capital, OptiMark, Easdaq, POSIT, the TONTO System (which became Archipelago), Bloomberg Tradebook, the Attain System, MarketXT, the GFINet System, Bridge Trader, the Strike System, and the Trading System. Bloomberg's TradeBook system was an ECN that represented its customers on NASDAQ. The BRASS Utility System was an ECN that provided automatic execution, clearance and settlement of trades in NASDAQ national market system and small-cap stocks. The BRUT System was a computer-based proprietary system that allowed participants to match orders in NASDAQ national market and small-cap securities on an anonymous basis. Turquoise was an electronic trading system created by nine large investment banks for equity trading to compete with the European exchanges. The London Stock Exchange purchased a majority of Turquoise in 2009.

Some ECNs grew so big that they sought registration as an exchange in order to compete directly with the traditional markets through their electronic facilities. Archipelago Holdings became a stock exchange through an arrangement with the Pacific Exchange. Island ECN, a leading ECN, also applied to the SEC to become a stock exchange. In response to this competition, some regional exchanges in the United States adopted electronic trading in whole or in part. A pioneer in developing that exchange-based electronic trading was Bernard Madoff, who became infamous during the subprime crisis after he confessed to running a Ponzi scheme in the world's largest-ever investment fraud. Madoff spent over $250,000 in the 1970s to convert the Cincinnati Stock Exchange into an all-electronic exchange. That exchange opened in 1885 as a call market, where local stocks were orally called in rotation for trading in morning and afternoon sessions. Madoff correctly believed that most stock trading would eventually become entirely electronic. In order to induce firms to trade with him electronically, Madoff also pioneered the concept of "payment for order flow," wherein brokerage firms were paid for directing their customer order flow to his firm. This did not endear him to market makers in the more traditional markets. By the 1990s, Madoff executed some 10 percent of NASDAQ share volume.

The Cincinnati Stock Exchange moved to Chicago in 1995 and became the National Stock Exchange. By then it was facing severe competition from other electronic trading platforms. It entered into a linkage agreement with Island, a popular ECN. Reuters, the owner of the Instinet Group, bought Island. Those two firms accounted for about 22 percent of NASDAQ listed stocks before NASDAQ acquired Island. The Midwest Stock Exchange changed its name to the Chicago Stock Exchange and became an all-electronic exchange trading NASDAQ, NYSE, and AMEX stocks on the Internet.

SEC chairman Arthur Levitt noted in 2000 that ECNs "have provided investors with greater choices, and have driven execution costs down to a fraction of a penny. As a result, these networks present serious competitive challenges to the established market centers."[9] Electronic trading was also adding some new dynamics in the market. In 2005, an execution on the NYSE floor took approximately fourteen seconds. In 2008, orders were matched in three to seven milliseconds. The speed of light was becoming a problem for some traders located away from an execution center.[10]

This is not to suggest that electronic trading is without challenges. The "fat finger" syndrome involving order-entry errors caused some large losses. Computers were known to break down, occasionally at critical times, which can prevent orders from being executed in a timely manner. The London Stock Exchange suffered a breakdown in its computer operations on September 8, 2008, and traders on that exchange were frozen out of a rallying market for more than seven hours. The Toronto Stock Exchange was closed on December 17, 2008, because of data transmission problems, and the electronic Globex futures market on the Chicago Mercantile Exchange (CME) was down for over three hours on December 24, 2008, due to technical problems. Regulatory problems can affect execution quality, as occurred in September 2008, after the SEC imposed short-sale restrictions at the height of the subprime crisis.

Concerns with electronic trading grew on May 6, 2010, after the Dow Jones Industrial Average dropped by almost 1000 points in just a few minutes, the "flash crash." The sell-off was variously attributed to high frequency algorithmic orders, trading errors, uncertainty in Europe over economic conditions, a Procter & Gamble sell order, a large trade on the CME by Waddell & Reed, a mutual fund, and a large options trade by a hedge fund advised by Nassim Taleb, an author of popular books on random events. Mary Schapiro, the SEC chair, summoned the leaders of the exchanges to Washington, and they agreed to adopt circuit breakers to interrupt trading when such a downturn begins. Schapiro also demanded that the exchanges build a multi-billion dollar repository for trading data so that future events could be more easily traced. Another concern was "stub quotes," which were quotes placed well off the market by market makers who did not want to trade but were required to maintain a two-sided market.

Electronic trading systems can also be used for fraud. A citizen of Slovakia was found to have fraudulently solicited the account of a client in an Internet chatroom. The defendant then misappropriated the customer's funds by trading against the customer's account in illiquid contracts that he could manipulate, and which were traded on eCBOT, an electronic trading system operated by the Chicago Board of Trade (CBOT).[11]

NASDAQ

NASDAQ was reeling from ECN competition. By 2002, ECNs accounted for some 70 percent of volume in NASDAQ-listed securities. NASDAQ demutualized by converting to publicly owned corporations from privately owned membership organizations in order to gain access to a larger capital base. NASDAQ sold off a portion of itself in private placements and then made a public offering. After those offerings, NASDAQ owned only about 26 percent of itself, but retained control through a special voting structure that would expire after its holding company conversion was complete. NASDAQ also became a national securities exchange in 2006, in order to compete with NYSE on all levels.

NASDAQ competed with the ECNs through its SuperMontage electronic trading program, which was developed at a cost of over $100 million. NASDAQ subsequently went a step further into all-electronic trading by acquiring Instinet's ECN operations for about $1.9 billion in April 2005. It also tried to stem its loss of market share by mergers. However, a merger with AMEX proved unsuccessful and had to be undone. NYSE acquired AMEX in 2008. A merger by NASDAQ and PHLX, the nation's oldest exchange, also initially fell through, but NASDAQ acquired PHLX in November 2007, for $652 million. NASDAQ also acquired the Boston Stock Exchange. NASDAQ was operating a corporate bond trade reporting system called TRACE, which was proposed as a credit-default reporting center in order to deal with problems in that market that arose from the subprime crisis.

More competition was added when the SEC allowed a London ECN to operate in the United States without requiring it to register as a national securities exchange under the Securities Exchange Act of 1934. This led NYSE and NASDAQ to seek linkages to markets in London, Paris, Tokyo, Mexico, São Paulo, Amsterdam, and elsewhere. Globalization was ripe for exploitation by foreign ECNs because they had the ability to overcome the "home bias" that had caused American investors to favor domestic exchanges. ECNs were simply mathematical models that were largely unaffected by local favoritism or uncertain rule interpretations.

The exchanges in Montreal, Vancouver, Toronto, and Alberta reorganized into a pan-Canadian exchange. The European exchanges also combined to become Euronext. The London Stock Exchange became increasingly popular for companies that did not want to submit to intrusive SEC regulations. That competition was enhanced after the London and Frankfurt Stock Exchanges merged. They entered into a linkage with the Paris Bourse and with NASDAQ, which had failed in its efforts to gain control of the London Stock Exchange. NASDAQ sold its 28 percent ownership interest in that exchange to Dubai World, a sovereign investment fund in that country, as well as a 20 percent stake in NASDAQ itself. NASDAQ acquired control of OMX, a Nordic market operator, in a joint venture with Borse Dubai for almost $5 billion.

Transformation of NYSE

NYSE successfully resisted competition from the ECNs until 2003, when a scandal arose concerning the $187 million retirement package given to its chief executive officer, Richard Grasso. Volume exploded on NYSE during Grasso's tenure; the exchange still executed 85 percent of transactions in its listed stocks; and the price of NYSE seats doubled on his watch. Although NYSE was a not-for-profit corporation, it had total profits of over $2 billion between 1995 and 2000. Grasso kept NYSE competitive by constantly updating its technology to speed up execution times. During the 1990s NYSE spent over $2 billion on technology. Its information technology (IT) budget was $350 million per year as the new century began.

Grasso finally gave into pressure and allowed the remaining vestiges of Rule 390 to be repealed in 1999. Still, NYSE held its own in the twenty-first century, with nearly an 80 percent market share of trading in its listings. However, Grasso made a mistake in judgment when he insisted on a payout of his accrued retirement package of $187 million as a condition for remaining at NYSE. Never mind that the money was owed to him, and that he had already earned most of it, the Enron-era scandals made all large executive payouts the subject of opprobrium. Grasso's outsized package led to howls of outrage in the press. As described in Chapter 3, the firestorm of criticism in the press over Grasso's payout quickly caught the eye of New York attorney general Eliot Spitzer. Spitzer brought suit against Grasso claiming that the retirement package was excessive and in violation of New York statutes that govern not-for-profit corporations.

The NYSE governing board gave in to pressure and fired Grasso. That deci-sion had an enormous impact on NYSE. He had kept it strong by holding off competition from the ECNs that were savaging the NASDAQ market. With Grasso's finger removed from the dike, it was not long before the new NYSE management began dismantling the NYSE trading floor and transforming it into an electronic exchange. Henry J. Paulson, a senior partner at Goldman Sachs (and, later, treasury secretary who reigned during the subprime crisis), spearheaded that effort. Paulson was aided by Grasso's replacement, John Thain, who was also a partner at Goldman Sachs. Thain, too, would be a leading figure during the subprime crisis, when he was brought in to rescue Merrill Lynch, and would be embarrassed by his own somewhat outlandish demand for $10 million after only a few months of work at Merrill Lynch, which failed on his watch.

Goldman Sachs actually had a dog in the fight over Grasso and NYSE's future. Institutionally, brokerage firms like Goldman Sachs preferred to execute their orders internally ("upstairs"), rather than run them through an exchange, where the specialists reaped the spread. Goldman had sought to obtain the best of both worlds by acquiring Spear, Leeds, & Kellogg, a leading NYSE specialist firm in 2000, through a transaction valued at $6.5 billion. Both parties boasted that this merger ensured their position at the center of order flow, both upstairs and down on the floor. It actually turned out to be a bad investment for Goldman Sachs, after ATS competition started taking market share from NYSE.[12]

Although Spear, Leeds's role as a specialist firm gave Goldman Sachs a vested interest in preserving the NYSE, Paulson, Thain, and their colleagues at Goldman Sachs came to believe that electronic trading would become the method of choice for order execution. They were willing to undercut their investment in Spear, Leeds to accomplish that goal and to further another Goldman investment. Goldman Sachs held a 15 percent ownership interest in Archipelago Holdings, a Chicago-based ECN that executed about 500 million shares a day, mostly in NASDAQ stocks. Thain and Paulson wanted NYSE to merge with Archipelago, but Grasso blocked that move.

Paulson was instrumental in having Grasso removed as the scandal over his compensation emerged. With Grasso gone, and with Thain named as his replacement as NYSE head, Paulson and Thain were able to arrange a merger of NYSE with Archipelago. This created a robust electronic trading platform for NYSE, which was named Arca. This coup did not go unchallenged by some NYSE members, but a New York State appeals court dismissed a claim brought by objecting NYSE members, who claimed that Thain had misled them because he did not adequately disclose the possibility of a merger with Archipelago. The plaintiffs sold their seats before the announcement of that merger, which caused a sharp rise in the value of NYSE memberships.

As a part of its merger with Archipelago, NYSE gave up its not-for-profit status, demutualized, and became a public company, changing its name to

NYSE Group. Thain then turned to globalizing NYSE. He was right to do so. Since 2000, the number of foreign customers trading on U.S. exchanges has more than tripled, while the number of U.S. customers trading on foreign exchanges has more than quintupled. U.S. investors held some $7.2 trillion in foreign securities at the end of 2007. To compete in a global market, Thain concluded, a foreign partner was needed, but such a relationship would erode NYSE's domineering role in equities trading. NYSE "was a brand that had taken two hundred years to build, one that every man and woman on Main Street equated with Wall Street and American finance."[13] However, American control of that institution was lost in 2006, after NYSE merged with Euronext, an amalgamation of European exchanges that traded electronically.

A bidding war broke out when NYSE announced its intention to acquire Euronext. The competing bidder was the Deutsche Börse, but NYSE prevailed. As a condition of that merger, NYSE agreed to split management and board control of the new entity evenly with the European exchanges, thus giving up domestic control of one of America's oldest financial institutions. Euronext was also given the right to withdraw from the combined operation, in the event that the SEC tried to regulate its European operations, which is a testament to how the rest of the world values SEC-style regulation.

NYSE Euronext continued its global expansion by entering into an alliance with other foreign exchanges. These ventures included a linkage with the Tokyo Stock Exchange and a joint venture with the Abu Dhabi Securities Market to develop trading technology and new investment instruments. NYSE Euronext also agreed to buy 25 percent of the Qatar stock market. However, a proposal to form a strategic global alliance or merger with the Deutsche Börse fell through in December 2008.

In 2000 NYSE created a new trading facility that featured the latest in market data display technology, but still retained a floor-based auction market. That facility was closed in 2007, as NYSE Euronext began converting to electronic executions. The exchange also announced in 2006 that it would begin electronic trading in 4,000 bond issues. NYSE Euronext bought AMEX for $260 million in January 2008, and over half of that exchange's staff was slotted for layoffs. The NYSE-Euronext merger had some other wide-ranging effects. In 2007, National Association of Securities Dealers (NASD) Regulation merged with NYSE Regulation to become the Financial Industry Regulatory Authority (FINRA), thereby creating a single self-regulator and eliminating much overlap and redundancy. In addition, NYSE and the NASD merged their arbitration programs.

Between 2005 and August 2008, after the Euronext merger, NYSE market share in NYSE-listed stocks declined from 78.9 percent to 25.1 percent. NASDAQ increased its matched market share of NYSE stocks from just over 10 percent in 2006 to about 25 percent in 2008. That competition increased to the point that, on July 11, 2008, NASDAQ traded more shares listed on the NYSE than did NYSE itself. However, this competition was a two-way street. In 2006, NYSE processed 21.3 percent of NASDAQ volume. Additional competition arrived from Kansas City–based BATS Trading, which became a regulated national securities exchange in August 2008. Previously, BATS had been responsible for about 10 percent of the trading activity on NASDAQ and NYSE. A national securities exchange, it was open to any broker-dealer, unlike the typical exchange, which had restricted membership.

The NYSE Euronext merger was followed by the dismantling of a considerable portion of the NYSE floor and resulted in the layoff of hundreds of NYSE employees. In 2003 there were about 3,000 floor brokers, specialists, and their employees on the floor; by the end of 2007 that number had been reduced to 1,200. The number of employees employed by specialists on the NYSE floor was cut in half, and the number of specialist firms was reduced to seven, compared with forty in the 1990s. The specialist also lost its icon status. NYSE was even considering a name change for them to "market maker" or "liquidity provider," a change that was subsequently implemented

Those were all blows to NYSE's historical role, but the exchange's demutualization appeared to be a success. NYSE's own stock price increased 355 percent as revenues and earnings soared in the first months after the merger. However, NYSE Euronext experienced a fourth-quarter loss in 2008 and announced that it was commencing a program to regain market share in 2009. Ironically, trading volume on what remained of the NYSE floor increased a bit during the subprime crisis. According to the *Financial Times,* that order flow reflected a desire for personal contact in an uncertain time. There was also some repopulation of the floor after the acquisition of AMEX, whose option floor traders were moved onto the NYSE floor. However, this rally appeared to be only temporary. NYSE's market share in its own listed stocks dropped from 75 percent to 36 percent between 2005 and 2009. As the *New York Times* pointed out in a front-page story on October 15, 2009, that loss in market share was aided by some new forces at work in the market, including "dark pools" (unregulated exchanges), in which institutions could trade anonymously, away from regulatory scrutiny. However, the SEC announced in October 2009 that it was proposing rules to make the dark pools more transparent.

Another element in the market was the growing popularity of a new force at work called "high-frequency trading." This algorithmic trading is conducted in rapid and continuing bursts to take advantage of even minute market disparities. High-frequency trading accounted for about 50 percent of stock trading volume by mid-2009 and was approaching 70 percent a year later. Nanoseconds mattered to these traders, and some even moved closer to exchange servers to cut down transmission times. This trading occurred at a speed of 400 microseconds. NYSE began building a massive facility in New Jersey to accommodate this trading, which was planned for opening in 2010. A European "liquidity data center" was opened in 2010 and a migration of forty high frequency trading platforms to a combination of the main matching engines of NYSE, Euronext, NYSELiffe, NYSE Arca Europe, and Smartpool markets was planned for later in the year. A leading high-frequency trader was Getco, a private trader that in August 2009 accounted for 10 to 20 percent of daily trading volume of several popular stocks.

As always, new market developments are attended by fraud. A former Goldman Sachs employee was arrested for stealing the firm's computer code for its high-frequency trading. High-frequency trading was also raising regulatory concerns, particularly the practice of "flash orders," which involve high-speed, brief postings of quotes by high-frequency traders. Those postings were being encouraged by commodity exchanges as a way of creating a high-speed market-making function. The commodity exchanges encouraged flash orders through rebates to the posting party from exchange fees paid by traders accepting the posted bid or offer. The SEC was also concerned with high-speed trades and "naked-access" trading, which in December 2009 accounted for 40 percent of equity volume. Naked-access traders were being given direct access to exchanges without the direct oversight and supervision of a regulated broker-dealer. The SEC believed that naked-access trading posed the potential for disrupting or causing market problems because the exchanges did not know the identity of the traders. It was also concerned that computer glitches or other problems at naked-access firms could disrupt the entire market. Anything new in the market was suspect and the SEC subsequently proposed a ban on naked-access trading and flash orders.

The SEC and Senator Charles Schumer from New York aimed to stop flash orders because of their concern that retail traders were excluded from this trading. NASDAQ then announced that it was banning the use of such orders. However, the Direct Edge trading system continued to execute flash orders and defended the practice, claiming that it provided access to dark pools that would otherwise be unavailable to some traders. As of August 2009, Direct Edge executed about 12 percent of U.S. listed stock volume.

NYSE Euronext began expanding its trading programs. It bought Powernext, a Paris-based spot market for carbon dioxide allowances, which were to be used by companies subject to reduction targets specified in the Kyoto protocols. There was competition in this area. UBS announced in January 2008 that it planned to create a derivatives index for climate change to be based on a global warming index. The Chicago Climate Exchange traded derivatives on greenhouse gases. NYSE Euronext also created a subsidiary, NYSE Liffe, that purchased the Chicago Board of Trade (CBOT) precious metals futures operations after the merger of the New York Mercantile Exchange (NYMEX), CBOT, and the Chicago Mercantile Exchange into a single exchange, which had competing precious metals futures business.

Broadening Markets

The stock market had become global, as could be seen from the NYSE and Euronext merger and the NASDAQ linkages. The SEC was seeking to advance a "mutual recognition" program that would provide for reciprocal recognition of exchanges and securities firms by the SEC and a foreign country with a regulatory system deemed adequate by the SEC. This arrangement would allow American investors to have direct access to foreign markets.

The Financial Services Authority in London announced that it planned to authorize different levels of listings, a proposal being pushed by the SEC, which was criticizing the quality of the listings on London markets. A similar approach was employed by NASDAQ, which has a separate listing for the larger companies and a small-cap market listing for the smaller ones. AMEX was also seeking to allow tiered listings. This seems to be a throwback to the "unlisted" trading of speculative stocks that was stopped on NYSE after the Panic of 1907 caused much criticism of the speculative unlisted securities.

Another innovation was the dark pool, private markets for large block trades by institutional investors, such as mutual funds and pension funds. These dark pools matched orders anonymously and reported only after completion, so that the market would not become unbalanced by the entry of a large order. The largest dark pool was Sigma X, which was operated by Goldman Sachs. The dark pools provided ultrahigh-speed order processing. NYFIX acknowledged receipt of orders in three milliseconds. CrossFinder, a dark pool created by Credit Suisse Group, also offered ultrahigh speed, which it called ultralow latency.

The London Stock Exchange and Lehman Brothers agreed in June 2008 to form a pan-European trading system for dark liquidity pool trading. This new trading system, called Baikal, was to be an off-market trading network that would allow the anonymous execution of large orders by institutions. However, the development of this market was interrupted by Lehman Brothers' bankruptcy during the subprime crisis. SecondMarket provided an alternative nonpublic market that electronically traded shares of private companies, and it created a market for banks to sell troubled subprime mortgage products.

Overlapping Regulation

The Treasury Department in March 2008 expressed concern over the inefficiencies caused by overlapping regulation under the present regulatory system. As an example, it pointed to a dispute between the SEC and the Financial Planning Association, a trade group representing financial planners, that arose after the SEC approved the use of fee-based accounts by broker-dealers. Those accounts provided a package of services, including trade executions, incidental investment advice, and custody services, for a single annual fee that was based on a percentage of the assets under management.

The creation of such fee-based brokerage accounts had been encouraged as the result of a 1995 study by the Committee on Compensation Practices, which was created by the SEC to consider alternatives to traditional, transaction-based commissions. The SEC was concerned that such transaction-based compensation created the appearance of a conflict of interest among broker-dealers and their account executives. The very prominent and well-regarded members of that blue ribbon committee concluded that asset-based fees would alleviate such concerns. However, the Financial Planning Association and others raised questions as to whether those fees would subject the accounts to the Investment Advisers Act of 1940. Such treatment would have precluded their operation.

In order to alleviate such concerns, the SEC adopted a rule exempting such accounts from the reach of the Investment Advisers Act. However, the District of Columbia Circuit Court of Appeals struck down that rule. The court held that the provisions relied upon by the SEC to exempt those accounts from the Investment Advisers Act did not authorize such action.[14] Actually, it appeared that the court was angry over the SEC's cavalier rejection of its prior decision to set aside an SEC regulation requiring mutual funds to have a supermajority of outside directors. Further retaliation came after that court struck down the SEC's rule requiring hedge funds to register as investment advisers.[15] This little tit-for-tat between the SEC and the DC circuit court established the court's primacy, but did nothing for investor protection. The fee-based brokerage sought to reduce conflicts of interest by broker-dealers accounts. That proved a popular program. More than a million fee-based brokerage accounts, totaling $300 billion in customer assets, were affected by the court's ruling.

The SEC tried to salvage the situation by promulgating a temporary rule that provided a means for broker-dealers to continue their fee-based accounts by treating them as nondiscretionary advisory accounts. The temporary rule allowed broker-dealers dually registered as investment advisers to comply in a practical manner with the requirements of the Investment Advisers Act. However, only dually registered broker-dealers could use this rule, and its terms were still inhibiting and costly. The SEC continued to study this issue and commissioned a study by the RAND Corporation to assess the respective roles of investment advisers and broker-dealers. That study found no basis for concluding that overlapping regulation under the Investment Advisers Act of 1940 and the Securities Exchange Act of 1934 was, in any way, needed.

The Obama administration proposed legislation to allow the SEC to authorize fee-based brokerage account arrangements and to set fiduciary standards for brokers providing investment advice. As enacted, the SEC was directed to prepare a report and adopt rules on broker-dealer standards of care. It was not allowed to ban commission-based products by brokers acting as investment advisers, which is what the Financial Services Authority did in London.

The Options Exchanges

Some History

The very first options equity exchange was the Chicago Board Options Exchange (CBOE), created by the Chicago Board of Trade (CBOT) in 1973 as a means of applying commodity futures–style trading to securities. Prior to the creation of the CBOE, stock option trading was conducted over the counter by a small group of broker-dealers specializing in that business. The CBOE applied a mixture of stock and commodity futures trading principles and operations to options trading on its floor.

Like the futures exchanges, CBOE floor operations involved open-outcry trading. However, unlike futures exchanges, the CBOE imposed market-making obligations on floor traders like those imposed on the stock exchanges. CBOE floor traders competed with one another for orders on the floor, while the book of customer limit orders was maintained by an exchange employee, rather than by a specialist. In 1999, however, the CBOE adopted a designated primary market-maker system, which had aspects of the specialist system.

The stock exchanges began trading stock options after witnessing the CBOE's success, but they continued to employ the specialist system for market making. For many years, however, the CBOE's only real competition was the Philadelphia Stock Exchange. NYSE was slow to enter the market, and it was crippled by concerns over side-by-side trading of stock and options. It exited that market but reentered it again through NYSE Arca, which was able to gain almost 10 percent of options trading volume by 2007. NASDAQ also began trading options, using its competing market-maker system. The equity options exchanges reacted to electronic trading competition in much the same way as the stock exchanges. The CBOE was even a little ahead of the stock exchanges, opening a high-tech trading floor in 1984 in order to deal with increased trading volumes. The CBOE also mimicked NYSE by beginning an after-hours electronic trading program in 2001. In 2003, the CBOE began a "hybrid" program of side-by-side trading of electronic executions and open-outcry executions, again reflecting events that were occurring at NYSE. The CBOE was additionally seeking to demutualize, an effort that was slowed by CBOT because it believed it had some equity interest in the CBOE as its creator. However, a settlement on those issues was reached in 2009, and the demutualization process resumed with the announcement of a public offering valued at $300 million. That offering was completed on June 15, 2010.

Competition

The option equity exchanges did not actively compete against one another for individual listings of equity options until 2000. If one exchange traded options on a given underlying stock, the other exchanges would generally abstain from listing those options. This system created a single market for each stock option contract and insulated the exchanges from competition with one another. That situation paralleled the market-sharing arrangements of the futures exchanges and Rule 390 on NYSE.

Initially, the stock option exchanges used a NFL-style draft to select contracts so that there would be no competition in options trading on the stocks of the companies selected in this draft. Later, a form of lottery was used to allocate trading and options on particular securities among exchanges, until the SEC ordered the exchanges to stop that practice and to permit multiple listings.

The stock option exchanges ignored that SEC order. Any exchange that proposed a competitive listing was met with threats of retaliatory listings, and adverse action was threatened against market makers. However, in 2000, the Justice Department attacked the agreement of the stock options exchanges not to compete with one another in an antitrust suit. A consent decree in that action was entered into by the stock option exchanges. It required them to stop those anticompetitive practices.[16]

This action by the Justice Department opened up the stock option exchanges to competition. The International Stock Exchange (ISE), an electronic exchange initiated in 2000, was then able to compete head-to-head with the floor trading operations of the stock options exchanges. ISE's business plan was to trade equity options on a broad range of stocks already listed on other option exchanges. ISE announced that it would list options accounting for 90 percent of existing trading volume.

The result of ISE's market entry was the introduction of broad-based competition in stock option exchange products. ISE became the world's largest equity options exchange, supplanting the CBOE in that role. The effects of the competition on the equity options exchanges from the ISE competition can be seen from the following breakdown of market share in October 2006:

- ISE   31.74%
- CBOE   28.01%
- PHLX (Philadelphia Stock Exchange)   15.17%
- AMEX   10.46%
- NYSE Arca   9.96%
- BOX (Boston Options Exchange)   4.66%

The ISE competition had some salutary effects on the market. The SEC found that, in addition to narrowing spreads, the expansion of multiple trading led to "market structure innovations that were designed to attract more order flow by enhancing the efficiency, transparency and liquidity of their markets."[17] Soon a global player, ISE was acquired by Eurex in 2007. No merger is complete without an insider-trading scandal, and the acquisition of ISE did not disappoint. John Marshall, an executive at ISE, pleaded guilty to criminal charges that he had traded on inside information about the acquisition. He was sentenced to eighteen months in prison plus one year of home confinement.

More competition was added from the NASDAQ OMX Group, and the BATS Exchange Inc. announced in February 2010 that its electronic trading platform would be offering lower rates than other exchanges. The CBOE was also facing lawsuits from competing exchanges that challenged the exclusive rights of CBOE to trade on its three most popular products, the Dow Jones

Industrial Average, the S&P 500, and Volatility Index (VIX). An Illinois court ruled in favor of the CBOE in July 2010. Traders on the CBOE were noted for the complexity of some of their trades, which were given exotic names such as the "jelly roll," "condor," "mombo-combo," "surf and turf," "vertical," "horizontal" and "diagonal" trades, and the "butterfly spread."

Subprime Crisis

The options markets benefited from heavy trading during the subprime crisis. Volume had been increasing for several years at double-digit rates, and a record was set in 2008. The CBOE Volatility Index had become popular as the markets gyrated up and down. That index was widely used as a barometer of market stability and investor sentiment, particularly during the incredible volatility in the stock market during the third and fourth quarters of 2008.

Clearing and Settlement

Securities Industry

Clearing and settlement are key elements in the financial services infrastructure. The term "clearing" refers to the confirmation of the identity and quantity of securities that are bought and sold in a transaction, the transaction price, the date of the transaction, and the identity of the buyer and seller. "Settlement" is a reference to the fulfillment, by the parties of their respective obligations, to deliver the securities and to pay for that delivery.[18] Payment and settlement system daily process transactions in the United States were valued at $13 trillion in 2010, a sum that was about equal to the country's annual gross domestic product.

Clearing and settlement operations have existed in the United States for well over a century. Those operations attracted little attention until the SEC's *Special Study of the Securities Markets* concluded in 1963 that there was a danger that securities handling, clearing, and settlement methods could prove inadequate in the event of a sustained increase in securities trading volume.[19] That warning went unheeded, and the stock markets nearly foundered in the late 1960s because of the "paperwork" crisis that resulted from unexpected increases in trading volume. Clearance and settlement systems were simply incapable of dealing with the paperwork generated by that volume increase. "Fails to deliver" and "DK" (don't know) trading reports became common. In 1969, there were over $4.4 billion in fails to deliver, and some $4.7 billion in fails to receive, among NYSE members during the paperwork crisis. Broker-dealers not only lost control of their records, they also lost large amounts of securities that were supposed to be in their safe custody. Millions of dollars in securities were simply lost or stolen.

In light of today's multibillion-share trading days, it boggles the mind to think that the clearing and settlement systems of the 1960s were incapable of dealing with daily share volumes of 16 million shares. To deal with the paperwork crisis NYSE reduced its trading hours, and some broker-dealers computerized their operations and increased the number of back-office personnel. However, those efforts could not keep up with the increasing volume and even exacerbated the problem when expensive computer programs malfunctioned and the firms failed to maintain hard-copy backups. The addition of new employees created further problems because they were often inadequately trained.

In the wake of the paperwork crisis, Congress required the SEC to report on unsafe and unsound practices in the securities industry. The resulting SEC report found that a significant portion of the "functions performed by broker-dealers for customers are directed to the effectuating of the delivery and transfer of securities."[20] The report noted that during the paperwork crisis the "back offices of many a broker-dealer resembled a trackless forest" and that, as a result of unexpected large-volume increases in securities transactions, "[t]he entire machinery for the delivery and transfer of securities and the concomitant remittance of funds became clogged." The clearing, settling, delivering, and transferring of securities "nearly drowned the financial community in a tidal wave of uncontrolled paper."[21]

In order to explore the various problems in the delivery and transfer process and to consider alternatives, on June 29, 1971, the SEC convened a conference of representatives of the securities industry and of companies and organizations that had engaged in studies of delivery and transfer problems. The SEC concluded from that conference that there was a need for it to develop a single nationwide integrated system for clearing and settlement. The SEC sought legislation to assist in that effort, but it was delayed for several years by a dispute with the banking regulators over whether the SEC should be given exclusive jurisdiction to regulate clearing and settlement by banks as well as broker-dealers. Finally, in 1975, a compromise was reached that allocated jurisdiction between the SEC and banking authorities over clearinghouses and transfer agents.

In the meantime, the securities industry had been working to develop its own procedures for dealing with clearing and settlement. A principal concern was the paperwork created upon the purchase and sale of stock. A new stock certificate had to be issued to each stockholder by the transfer agent upon the purchase of a security. At the same time, the certificate held by the seller had to be canceled. This created much paperwork and confusion when stocks were actively traded. The industry concluded that it was not possible under many state laws, and politically, to eliminate the stock certificate, but that a processing system could be developed that would make the clearing and settlement process much less burdensome.

One of the first steps was to create more modern clearinghouses for stocks. NYSE established the New York Clearing Corporation, AMEX created its counterpart, the American Clearing Corporation, and the National Over-the-

Counter Clearing Corporation was developed for trading in that market. In addition, the New York Clearing Corporation created the Central Certificate Service (CCS), which was to serve as a depository for stock certificates.

The Banking and Securities Industry Committee (BASIC), which was created by the banking and securities industries to address securities processing problems, proposed immobilizing stock certificates by keeping them in a bank vault and using computer book entries to record the identity of their owners and transfer instructions. BASIC sought to create a national depository system that would broaden the role of the CCS. Using CCS, a selling broker could, in order to execute a delivery, simply instruct CCS to debit its account for the amount of the sale and credit the buying broker's account. Title to the shares would be transferred by computer entries, which eliminated the need for physical transfer of the certificate. Previously, brokerage firms executing a sale had to obtain a certificate from the customer, and verify that it was signed, stamped, and then physically delivered. The buying broker would have to engage in a similar procedure upon receipt of a stock certificate.

Another development came from the Committee for Uniform Security Procedures (CUSIP) of the American Banking Association. It proposed the creation of uniform identification codes that would allow automated processing of securities transfers. That recommendation was adopted, and a CUSIP number is now assigned to each security. Like the automobile license plate, this has proved a useful tool for dealing with lost or stolen securities. Legislation passed in 1975 further directed the SEC to develop a program to prevent trafficking in lost, stolen, or counterfeit securities. The Securities Information Center now operates a computerized database for lost, stolen, missing, or counterfeit securities for the SEC. Financial institutions are required to report lost, stolen, or counterfeit securities to the database. Financial institutions must also query the securities information center whenever they receive security certificates for more than $10,000, in order to determine whether they are lost, stolen, missing, or counterfeit.

Another concern arising during the paperwork crisis was trade comparison, a process in which broker-dealers agree on the terms of their securities transactions and confirm to the clearinghouse that a contract is scheduled for settlement and clearing. The New York Clearing Corporation used a "daily balance order system" for such settlement, while other exchanges used a "continuous net settlement system." Under the latter system, trades were compared and each participant's trades in every security were netted each day. The duty to deliver the net sales or receive the net purchases was added to the outstanding delivery or receives obligations of each participant. Deliveries were made to the clearing corporation under the continuous net settlement system, rather than from one broker to another, as was done in the daily balance order system. Net obligations with the clearing corporation were settled on a daily basis by certified check under the continuous net settlement system. The clearing corporation guaranteed the settlement obligations of each of the opposite parties for the transactions being cleared. This reduced concerns of counterparty risk in the event of a default. The clearing agencies maintained safety funds to provide a cushion in the event of a failure of a member. Fees assessed on clearing members supported those funds.

The NASD retained a consulting firm, Arthur D. Little, to address the problem of fails to receive and deliver that arose during the paperwork crisis. It concluded that there was a need to establish a nationwide clearing system that would use the continuous net settlement system. The NASD then agreed to fund a national OTC clearing system. NYSE and AMEX agreed to convert their daily order balance system into a continuous net settlement system. They also agreed to form the Securities Industry Automation Corporation (SIAC) to jointly operate their clearing facilities. In 1975, NYSE, AMEX, the NASD, and other exchanges agreed to establish a jointly owned clearing agency for all their securities transactions. The National Securities Clearing Corporation (NSCC), created for that purpose, was registered with the SEC as a clearing agency.

As the 1990s began, the NSCC processed about 95 percent of all equity trades in the United States and provided clearing services to over 2,000 broker-dealers and financial institutions. It also serviced regional exchanges. Today, the NSCC provides centralized clearance and settlement services for virtually all broker-to-broker equity, corporate bond and municipal bond, exchange-traded funds, and unit investment trusts traded in the United States.

AMEX and the NASD created the Depository Trust Company in the wake of the paperwork crisis as a way to immobilize stock certificates. Eventually, that depository was able to transfer securities among broker-dealers by computer book entry, substantially immobilizing most stock certificates. The National Institutional Delivery System handled settlements between broker-dealers and institutional customers, with the Depository Trust Company as its central processor.[22]

The new clearing and settlement systems were able to deal with the large volume increases that occurred in the 1980s and continued thereafter. Under this system, most securities are held in "street name," which means that instead of being held in the name of the beneficial owner/customer, the securities were registered with the customer's broker-dealer as the owner of the securities of its customers. The broker-dealer would then report to the customers the securities positions for which they were beneficial owners and which were held at the Depository Trust Company in the name of the broker-dealer. Customers could still demand stock certificates, and often did in earlier times, but rarely do so today.

Additional Developments

The stock market crash of 1987 raised some additional systemic concerns with clearing and settlement. Systemic risks are those that cause a loss of confidence in the financial system and can in turn have serious adverse effects on the economy as a whole. The Presidential Task Force on Market Mechanisms (Brady Commission), which was created by presidential order to study that crisis, noted that the unprecedented volume during that event resulted in a large number of questioned trades in the securities markets. Its report stated that, during the crisis in 1987, "the massive volume, violent price volatility and staggering demands on clearing and credit raised the possibility of a full-scale financial system breakdown."

The Brady Commission, whose work is further discussed in Chapter 5, recommended that clearing systems be unified "across all markets" in order to reduce financial risk."[23] That recommendation was never implemented. The stock exchanges have a unified clearing structure, which is separate from the options exchanges, which is separate from the commodity markets.

The Uniform Commercial Code was amended in 1994 to allow book-entry securities issuances rather than certificates. Delaware, a leader in corporate law and the preferred state of incorporation by many large public companies, amended its laws in 2005 to allow book-entry-only stocks. That change allowed securities with no certificate that were recorded only by electronic entry, further streamlining the clearing and settlement process.

Another advance was the reduction in settlement time. Historically, it was customary to use a five-business-day settlement cycle period for the settlement of securities transactions. However, a review of the settlement process conducted in 1992 by the Group of Thirty Clearance and Settlement Project concluded that the settlement period could be reduced to three business days, finding that 80 percent of funds due from customers were already available within that period. Thereafter, an industry task force headed by John W. Bachmann, the managing principal of Edward D. Jones, was created to review the settlement process. It recommended that, in order to increase the safety and soundness of the securities markets, the settlement cycle should be reduced from five business days to three (T+3). That recommendation was subsequently adopted by the SEC, which asserted that a substantial portion of risk in clearance and settlement was directly related to the length of time it takes for trades to settle.

The Municipal Securities Rulemaking Board also sought to improve and automate clearance and settlement in municipal securities transactions. It had some success in that effort. By 1987, $400 billion in municipal securities, about half the existing outstanding municipal securities, was held in book-entry form at four depositories. Clearance and settlement of municipal securities were linked with the NSCC and the Depository Trust Company.

A Government Securities Clearing Corporation was created to handle the clearing of U.S. government securities. In 1994, the Depository Trust Company created the CMO Trade Adjustment System, which allowed it to clear private-label mortgage-backed securities as well as credit-default swaps. The MBS Clearing Corporation was created to clear mortgage-backed securities. The Participants Trust Company acted as a depository and book-entry system for securities guaranteed by Government National Mortgage Association (Ginnie Mae) and other government-sponsored enterprises.

The NSCC created a Collateral Management Service that provided automated access to margin and other deposits at several clearing organizations. Further centralization occurred when the NSCC and the Depository Trust Company merged in 1999. At that point the Depository Trust Company held $19 trillion in securities and processed $77 trillion in transactions annually, while the NSCC settled over $40 trillion in transactions annually.

Transfer Agents

The 1975 amendments to the federal securities laws required transfer agents to register. These firms maintain a list of shareholders for public companies, continually updating them as purchases and sales occur. The SEC adopted regulations to govern these entities. Among other things, transfer agents were required to turn around at least 90 percent of all routine items received for transfer within three business days. They were required to respond to inquiries on transfers within five business days, but the jobs of the transfer agents were made easier by the use of the Depository Trust Company and street name securities. By 1999, over 70 percent of all outstanding stock shares were held in street name.

Transfer agents were required to establish written procedures for the cancellation, storage, transportation, destruction, or other disposition of securities certificates. Canceled securities had to be marked with the word "canceled" and maintained in a secure storage facility. There was a reason for this requirement. In 1992, canceled bond certificates with a face value of over $110 billion disappeared after being delivered from a transfer agent to a certificate destruction vendor. The certificates then circulated worldwide and were used to defraud several institutions. In 1994, canceled bonds with a face value of $6 billion were stolen after being delivered by a transfer agent to two certificate destruction vendors.

Treasury Report

In March 2008, the Treasury Department issued recommendations concerning the regulation of clearance and payment settlement systems. The department sought the creation of a federal charter for systemically important payment and settlement systems. It further recommended that the Federal Reserve should have primary oversight responsibility for such systems and that state law should be superseded for entities operating under the federal charter. The Treasury Department noted that poorly designed payment and settlement systems could contribute to financial crises.

The Treasury report recommended that the Fed be given authority to set standards governing settlement, segregation of funds, permissible investments for such funds, and operational safeguards. Treasury also thought that the Fed should be authorized to conduct examinations and impose sanctions. It wanted the Fed to regulate the U.S. operations of payment and settlement systems located abroad and that legislation was enacted in 2010.

International Clearing

By 1992, about 20 percent of equity trading, measured in dollar terms, involved an international security, and traders increasingly invested in foreign securities. Each foreign exchange has its own clearing and settlement facilities. Eurex Clearing, for example, provided a broad range of clearing and settlement services that spanned several asset classes, including bonds, repurchase agreements (repos), and derivatives traded on Eurex, equities traded on the Irish Stock Exchange and the Frankfurt Stock Exchange, and emission rights traded on the European Energy Exchange.

Clearstream, a subsidiary of the Deutsche Börse that was the result of the 2000 merger between Deutsche Börse Clearing and Cedel International, provided international settlement services for the exchange of cash and securities after a trade. As of 2008 it serviced some 2,500 customers in over 110 countries and 45 markets, settled more than 250,000 transactions per day, and provided custody services for more than 300,000 traded bonds, equities, and investment funds. Cedel was formed in 1970 to provide international settlements and clearance of securities transactions. It created settlement links in a wide range of countries in order to provide customers with foreign currency settlement capabilities.

Another international clearance and settlement facility is the Euroclear System, created in 1968 by the Morgan Guaranty Trust Company in New York for settling U.S.-dollar-denominated eurobonds. Incorporated in Belgium, Euroclear operated an international central securities depository. It used its depository facility to immobilize security transfers through simultaneous book-entry exchange of cash and securities in advance of a similar effort in the United States. Initially, all processing was done manually but later was performed electronically.

Several years after its creation, Morgan Guaranty sold Euroclear to Euroclear Clearance System but continued to operate its facilities. Banks, brokers, and investment institutions that utilized the system owned the new entity. By 1988, Euroclear held almost two-thirds of all internationally traded debt securities.

The London Stock Exchange spent some $600 million for an unsuccessful clearing and settlement system called Taurus in the 1990s. It was scrapped and replaced by a system called Crest, which later merged with Euroclear. In 2007, Euroclear settled securities transactions valued at €561.8 trillion, an increase of 24 percent over the previous year. It was also acting as custodian for customer assets valued at €19.2 trillion.

In 1980, Cedel and Euroclear entered into an agreement that allowed them to settle transactions without requiring the physical delivery of securities. This was done through an electronic bridge that allowed securities transactions between the two systems to occur through book-entry transfers. This system was upgraded in 1993 through the introduction of a nighttime processing cycle, in addition to the existing daytime processing cycle, which allowed transactions to be processed several times overnight as well as during the day.[24] The European Central Securities Depositories Association, whose members included all central depositories in the European Union and Switzerland, was created in 1997 to develop links between its members and enhance trade settlements within Europe.

Concerns over Cross-Border Settlement

In September 1992 the Bank for International Settlements (BIS) published a report titled *Delivery Versus Payment in Securities Settlement Systems,* written by the Committee on Payment and Settlement Systems of the central banks of the Group of Ten countries.[25] That report analyzed the risks associated with securities settlements and their implications for the stability of payment systems and financial markets, as well as the containment of systemic risk. The same committee published a report in March 1995 that addressed the risks associated with cross-border settlement systems. It concluded that central banks should be concerned about systematic risk that derived from the manner in which foreign intermediaries in cross-border settlements managed their risks.[26]

A white paper published by Clearstream International in 2002 found that the cost of clearing an international transaction was significantly higher than that of a domestic transaction. The disparity in cost was estimated at about €4.3 billion per year. Much of this disparity was due to a UK stamp duty and a need for "regulatory translation" as a result of different laws, taxes, and rules for corporate actions. About 20 percent of the disparity was due to inefficiencies among intermediaries, exchanges, clearinghouses, and central securities depositories. About 40 percent of these incremental costs were the result of different languages and cultures, and lower cross-border trading volumes for behavioral reasons, such as investors' home bias. The result was that cross-border wholesale trades cost 30 percent, and retail trades 150 percent, more than a corresponding domestic trade to clear and settle.[27]

The failure of a clearinghouse could have systemic, even catastrophic, effects worldwide. In order to deal with such concerns, in 2001 the central banks of the Group of Ten countries developed a set of core principles for systemically important payment systems. The European Association of Central Counterparty Clearing Houses (EACH) developed risk management standards, and CCP-12, a group that included clearinghouses from Asia, the Americas, and Europe, sought to broaden the acceptance of those standards.

A Task Force on Securities Settlement Systems was commissioned in 2004 by the BIS Committee on Payment and Settlement Systems. The Technical Committee of the International Organization of Securities Commissions

(IOSCO) also developed risk standards for central clearinghouses that included the development of transparent and recognized legal standards for clearing, the securing of collateral, and counterparty risk assessment procedures.[28]

The European Union (EU) also addressed concerns over clearing systems in its constituent countries. The Giovannini Group was formed in 1996 to advise the European Commission on issues relating to EU financial integration and the efficiency of euro-denominated financial markets. Under the chairmanship of Dr. Alberto Giovannini, the group consisted of financial-market participants and published a report in 2001 that addressed concerns over clearing and settlement. The report concluded that clearing and settlement are complex operations and that cross-border securities transactions normally involve more participants than domestic transactions do, which presents increased risks of default throughout the system. The Giovannini Group Report also set forth a country-by-country analysis of clearing systems in each of the member countries of the EU.[29]

The EU sought to establish policy guidelines for clearing and settlement that would prevent barriers to competition and that would monitor industry consolidation for competition concerns. It also desired the development of a common regulatory and supervisory framework for clearing and settlement as well as government oversight for clearing and settlement systems. The EU issued a directive on May 19, 1998, on settlement finality in payment and securities settlement systems both domestic and cross-border. Among other things, that directive required that transfer orders and netting be legally enforceable in bankruptcy proceedings.[30]

Equity Options Clearing

Exchange-traded equity options in the United States use a single clearinghouse, the Options Clearing Corporation (OCC). The OCC clears and settles all options traded on national security exchanges and NASDAQ. OCC's participant exchanges include AMEX, CBOE, ISE, NASDAQ OMX, PHLX, NYSE Arca, and the Boston Options Exchange (BOX). The OCC also clears futures contracts for the CBOE Futures Exchange, the Philadelphia Board of Trade, and single stock futures for OneChicago. The OCC uses a book-entry method for the transfer and settlement of options. The lack of stock certificates makes the OCC's job much easier than that of the stock exchanges and allows overnight settlement.

Custody and Payment Systems

Free Credit Balances

Prior to the passage of the SEC's Customer Protection Rule in the 1970s, broker-dealers used free credit balances of customers as overnight investments for the broker-dealer's own account. That was a source of large profits for those broker-dealers. It was estimated in 1969 that NYSE member firms earned over $230 million on customer free credit balances. At that time, such income accounted for about 50 percent of Merrill Lynch's earnings. The SEC sought legislation in 1941, 1956, and 1959 that would have required broker-dealers to forgo such profits by requiring them to maintain customer free credit balances in segregated accounts that could not be used by the broker-dealers in their own operations. Industry lobbying defeated those efforts. The SEC did require that broker-dealers give their customers notice that the funds were being used in the broker-dealer's operations, but placed no restrictions on their use.

The paperwork crisis at the end of the 1960s renewed concern over this practice. It was harshly criticized in a book by a former SEC staff member, Hurd Baruch, called *Wall Street Security Risk*. He believed that free credit balances and their profits belonged to the customers and that they should not be used in, and endangered by, the broker-dealer's operations.[31] The result of such concerns was the passage of the SEC's Customer Protection Rule, which required customer securities to be maintained separately from those of the broker-dealer.[32] This requirement was intended to protect customer funds in the event of a broker-dealer insolvency. That need was heightened by the creation of the Securities Investor Protection Corporation (SIPC) insurance fund in 1970, which required customers to be compensated for the loss of their free credit balances in the event of a broker-dealer insolvency.

Under the SEC Customer Protection Rule, customer funds were required to be kept in special bank accounts identified as accounts holding customer funds. The amount of customer funds to be kept segregated was determined using a formula established by the SEC, the "Reserve Formula," which was to be computed at least weekly. Broker-dealers were required to segregate customer securities from those of the broker-dealer and to conduct a "box count" on a daily basis to ensure that those securities were on hand and not lost or stolen. This meant that broker-dealers could no longer lend or hypothecate customer securities. Instead, those securities had to be in the possession and control of the broker-dealer and held by the broker-dealer in a secure ("good") "control location." In the event of any shortfall, the broker-dealer had to buy the securities at its own expense.

Some broker-dealers quickly found a way to continue using customer funds by paying down loans that were secured by customer securities just before their weekly Reserve Formula computation. The secured loans would be replaced that day with unsecured loans, and the customer secured loans would be re-instated the day after the computation. The SEC acted to stop those practices. They were replaced by "seg-offset" arrangements in which the broker-dealer was, in effect, given credit by its banks for funds held in the reserve accounts, in the form of an unsecured loan. The SEC permitted this as long as the bank agreed that it had no claim against the reserve bank accounts.

Banks also perform custodial services including the safekeeping of as-sets, collecting dividends and interest, and performing a variety of associated services, such as currency translations and private wealth management. Bank custody services can also involve holding securities and international transactions for the purpose of clearance and settlement. This provides customers with a single access point to clearinghouses in other countries through a network of subcustodians in those countries. These subcustodians are often local branches or subsidiaries of the global custodian or local agents. The use of global custodians became popular with nonresident traders in securities because of reduced cost and provided efficiencies.[33]

Collateral Arrangements

Another large business operation is the management of collateral required for trading operations. For example, in a repo transaction, the security purchaser demands collateral to secure repayment. Repo and reverse-repo transactions involve the sale of a security with an agreement to buy it back at a future date at a higher price, in effect creating a secured loan. These transactions are collateralized by the sale of the security. The failure to maintain that collateral properly created a crisis in the repo market in the 1980s. The repo market was then regulated, after the failure of a number of repo dealers, including Drysdale Securities. The Federal Reserve also took steps to assure better collateral maintenance procedures.

In its report "Collateral in Wholesale Financial Markets: Recent Trends, Risk Management and Market Dynamics," the BIS stated:

> The use of collateral has become one of the most important and widespread risk mitigation techniques in wholesale financial markets. Financial institutions extensively employ collateral in lending, in securities trading and derivatives markets and in payment and settlement systems. Central banks generally require collateral in their credit operations. Over the last decade, the use of collateral in wholesale financial markets has grown rapidly. The collateral most commonly used and apparently preferred by market participants are instruments with inherently low credit and liquidity risks, namely government securities and cash. With the growth of collateral use so rapid, concern has been expressed that it could outstrip the growth of the effective supply of these preferred assets. Scarcity of collateral could increase the cost of financial transactions, slow or inhibit financial activity and potentially encourage greater reliance on more inefficient non-price rationing mechanisms, such as restricting access to markets. These developments suggest two questions for exploration. The first is to what extent trends in the use of collateral and its supply have created or have the potential to create a relative scarcity of low-risk, liquid collateral and, if such scarcity emerges, how markets could adjust. The second is how such adjustment mechanisms and other changes in collateral usage might alter market dynamics and the risk management demands on financial institutions, particularly in stress periods.[34]

This report also prophetically noted that securitization techniques could be applied to develop instruments with high credit quality and liquidity, which is exactly what occurred with respect to subprime mortgages. The subprime crisis also exposed a danger from collateral arrangements in trading operations. Bear Stearns, Lehman Brothers, and American International Group (AIG) were brought down by collateral calls in their trading operations and withdrawal of funds in custody when concerns were raised over their liquidity and market exposure. The result was that they were effectively shut out of the money market.

Payment Systems and Central Banks

Bank payment systems have historically focused on the clearing of checks and settlement of interbank balances. Initially, settlements were carried out through messengers, but in the nineteenth century most large cities had bank clearinghouses. The leading clearinghouse was the New York Clearing House, which was formed by an association of sixty-two banks in 1853. The Clearing House Association of the Banks of Philadelphia, which was formed by thirty-eight national banks, required each bank to send representatives to a daily meeting in a room maintained by the clearinghouse in order to settle their balances. Rather than having each representative carry cash to each meeting, funds were kept on deposit with a clearinghouse committee. That committee issued certificates against those deposits to banks that were owed funds by the bank against which the certificate was issued.

Before the creation of the Federal Reserve, clearinghouse certificates were used in New York and elsewhere to supply liquidity in times of crisis, and they basically acted as loans and as a substitute for cash. Such certificates were issued during the panics of 1873, 1884, 1890, 1893, and 1907.[35] Banks that were illiquid could post collateral with the clearinghouse in exchange for a clearinghouse certificate that gave them liquidity. The Federal Reserve and Treasury Department would use a remarkably similar method for rescuing financial service firms during the subprime crisis when financial institutions were allowed to post illiquid subprime securities in exchange for loans from the Federal Reserve.

The creation of the Federal Reserve in 1913, after the Panic of 1907, evidenced a need for a central bank that could supply liquidity in a time of financial crisis. The Federal Reserve's responsibilities included the development of a more efficient national system of clearing checks. This created some friction because country banks had been able to charge fees for clearing out-of-town checks. The Federal Reserve charged no fees and was much quicker and efficient than the country banks in settling out-of-town checks. A bank in Atlanta sued the Federal Reserve in an effort to stop that competition, but the Supreme Court rejected that challenge.[36]

Despite the introduction of the Federal Reserve, check clearing and settlement remained a labor-intensive enterprise, especially since the actual check had to be routed through the system until payment was made, and the canceled check then returned to the customer. The Check Clearing for the 21st Century Act (Check 21), which was enacted in 2003, sought to speed the check collection process by creating a new instrument called a "substitute check" that allowed banks to process check information electronically. Under this system, the original check was "truncated" and a substitute check was treated as the legal equivalent of the original check and included all the information contained on the original check. Such remote deposit captures, however, present risks to banks that multiple images of the same check could be presented for payment.

Earlier, the Electronic Funds Transfer Act of 1978 recognized the use of electronic payments by consumers and provided regulatory protection to them by requiring that electronic transfers be properly documented. Limitations were also placed on the customer's liability in the event of a breach in security. Notable is the fact that cash and checks were becoming a smaller and smaller part of the payment system. Electronic transfers through credit cards, debit cards, and automatic payments substituted for checks in many instances. As a result of such alternative payments, the number of checks written in the United States decreased by 37 percent between 1997 and 2003. In 2007, the number of debit card payments exceeded the number of check payments. The amount of check writing had declined so much that the Federal Reserve reduced its number of locations for processing paper checks to one by 2009, compared with forty-five in 2003.

CHIPS

The banking system also relies on electronic payment mechanisms. The Clearing House Interbank Payments System (CHIPS), an electronic payment system created by the New York bank clearinghouse, is widely used. CHIPS is a real-time, final payment system that uses bilateral and multilateral netting. As of 2008 it processed more than 350,000 payments a day, with a gross value of $2 trillion, as well as more than 95 percent of U.S. dollar cross-border payments.

The Bankhaus Herstatt created a crisis in CHIPS in 1974 after it suffered large losses in the foreign currency market. The bank declared bankruptcy at the end of its business day in Europe, but trading continued in the United States. An issue arose as to whether the closed positions in Germany could be netted against offsetting contracts in the United States that were still open. The Herstatt accounts in the United States were frozen, and wire transfers on CHIPS were stopped for its account. Concern arose that there could be other failures, and CHIPS became gridlocked as banks each waited for the other to be the first to pay. That impasse was finally broken after First National City Bank began making payments. Settlement procedures were, thereafter, changed to prevent the recurrence of such a gridlock. That affair led to the creation of the Basel Committee on Banking Supervision within the framework of the BIS.

To further reduce concerns over foreign currency settlements, a CLS Bank International was launched in 2002. By 2008, 55 percent, or $2.1 trillion, in foreign currency settlement was completed through that bank, which had become the dominant settlement method for foreign currency. It used a payment-versus-payment (PVP) system that appears to have virtually eliminated the principal risk associated with settling foreign currency trades.[37]

Fedwire

The Federal Reserve Bank of San Francisco began exchanging electronic payments with its Los Angeles branch in 1972. That system, now called Fedwire, was expanded to all Federal Reserve banks in 1978. A real-time payment system operated by the Fed for banks that have reserve or clearing accounts with a regional Federal Reserve bank, Fedwire was used for 135 million transactions in 2007, with an average daily value totaling $2.6 trillion. At that time, approximately $36 trillion in securities was held in custody through the Fedwire Securities Service. Fedwire is also used for the clearance and settlement of securities issued by the Department of the Treasury, federal agencies, government-sponsored enterprises, and certain international organizations.

Fixed Income Clearing Corporation

Also involved in that settlement process is the Fixed Income Clearing Corporation (FICC) and two clearing banks, the Bank of New York Mellon and JPMorgan Chase. The FICC, which provides trade comparison, trade netting, and risk management services, acts as a central counterparty, interposing itself between seller and buyer, for trades of members. It uses a netting system that establishes a single deliver or receive obligation for the trading activity of a member in each security. In 2009, FICC processed more than $1.4 trillion a day in U.S. government and mortgage-backed securities.

Disruptions in the money markets caused serious problems for repo dealers during the subprime crisis. Firms borrowing Treasury securities delayed their return. Because of the flight to safety by panicked investors, those Treasury securities were needed to fund the borrowers' operations. The Fed considered the creation of a central clearing facility for the repo market. JPMorgan Chase and Bank of New York Mellon had handled most of that business, but there was a concern that this critical market could be exposed to systemic risk if either of those institutions failed. The size of the repo market was estimated at $4.5 trillion in January 2009.

SWIFT

The Society for Worldwide Interbank Financial Telecommunications (SWIFT), an international communications system headquartered in Brussels, provides a messaging system that facilitates interbank transfers and communications worldwide, serving banks in more than 200 countries. SWIFT was used by over 8,300 institutions in 2008. But it is only a message carrier and does not hold bonds or store financial information. It merely transports messages between financial institutions, assuring confidentiality and message integrity. In 2008 SWIFT transmitted an average of 15 million such messages a day.

SWIFT found itself at the center of an international controversy after it was disclosed that the U.S. government had used its facilities to monitor terrorist financial activities. Critics claimed that this surveillance was an unwarranted invasion of privacy, while others claimed that the disclosure of the program by the *New York Times* and other newspapers in June 2006 endangered American security. The Bush administration asserted that the program had led to the capture of terrorists, including the mastermind of the 2002 Bali resort bombing. The EU was initially critical of this intrusion, but an agreement was reached that allowed the surveillance program to continue in 2010.

Payment System Concerns

In 1990, a Committee on Interbank Netting Schemes submitted a report to the Group of Ten countries (the Lamfalussy Report) that analyzed issues affecting cross-border and multicurrency netting schemes. The report sought to establish minimum standards and general goals for the operation of such systems. Concerns over payment systems thereafter broadened. To address such concerns, in 1998 the Committee on Payment and Settlement Systems (CPSS) of the central banks of the Group of Ten countries established a Task Force on Payment System Principles and Practices. That committee sought to develop consensus on principles for the operation of payment systems.

The BIS also led an effort to develop sound practices for the operation and central bank oversight of payment systems. In December 1999, the BIS published a set of "core principles" that identified the key characteristics that payment systems should contain. Those core principles were thought necessary in light of concerns that payment systems are systemically important and are a major channel for transmitting shocks across domestic and international financial systems and markets.

The core principles were somewhat vague, but they generally advocated that payment systems have clearly defined procedures for the management of credit and liquidity risks. This means that assets used for settlement should be a claim on the central bank or instruments that carry little or no credit risk and little or no liquidity risk. In addition, the system should permit fair and open access.[38] The Basel Committee also developed a set of fourteen principles for best practices in managing liquidity in banking organizations.

Large-value payment systems (LVPS) play a key role in the financial infrastructure by discharging payment obligations between banks. Before the 1990s, deferred net settlement was used with settlement only at the end of the day for these payments. That method was changed in the 1990s to real-time gross settlement, with settlement on a continuous basis. This change was made possible by advances in information and communication technology and was motivated by the desire of central banks to reduce systemic risks in the payment systems.[39]

In 1993 the Federal Reserve Bank of New York created the Payments Risk Committee, which was a private sector group comprising senior managers from several major banks, such as Bank of America, Bank of New York Mellon, Bank of Tokyo-Mitsubishi, Citibank, Deutsche Bank, HSBC Bank USA, JPMorgan Chase, State Street Bank and Trust Company, UBS, and Wachovia. The committee's meetings were also attended by Federal Reserve staff members. Members of the committee were asked to analyze and identify issues concerning payment systems. Among other things, this committee recommended that the banking industry develop cross-currency intraday swaps, cross-border intraday collateral swaps, and cross-currency intraday repos in order to enhance banks' daily liquidity needs.[40]

In November 2001, the CPSS and the Technical Committee of the International Organization of Securities Commissions (IOSCO) published a report on securities settlement systems. That report identified nineteen minimum standards for such settlement systems to assure financial stability, reduce risk, and increase efficiency of the settlement process globally. Those recommendations were incorporated into the Federal Reserve Policy on Payments System Risk for risk management in U.S. payment and settlement systems.

In 2004, the Group of Ten requested an analysis of liquidity concerns during times of stress and its implications for central banks. The BIS through its CPSS responded with a report on the acceptance of foreign collateral by central banks to secure loans to their member banks in order to further the liquidity of commercial banks on an intraday basis. The Group of Ten's central banks had agreed on an à la carte approach to this issue, leaving it to each central bank to decide whether and when it would accept foreign collateral to secure loans to its member banks. Timothy F. Geithner, then president of the Federal Reserve Bank of New York and a key player during the subprime crisis, chaired the CPSS before and after he became treasury secretary in 2009. The CPSS concluded in 2006 that routine cross-border collateral arrangements could act as natural shock absorbers in an emergency.[41]

In the United States, regulation of payment and settlement systems was scattered among various agencies, including the SEC under the federal securities laws, the Commodity Futures Trading Commission (CFTC) under the Commodity Exchange Act of (1936), and bank regulators under the Bank Service Company Act. The Treasury Department noted in 2008 that regulation needed for payment and settlement systems was institutionally different from that required for financial institutions. Payment and settlement systems are concerned with processing transactions and not trading, investing, or other activities typically associated with a financial institution regulated under systems dealing with capital adequacy and consumer business practices.

Stock Lending

Securities lending arrangements form an important part of financial markets. Securities are frequently lent to parties or used as collateral to raise short-term funds. Such transactions include repos, securities loans, and sale buy-back agreements. By the turn of the twenty-first century, the daily volume of securities transactions used for financing purposes considerably exceeded that of ordinary purchase and sale transactions. Securities lending was structured to give the borrower legal title to the securities for the life of the loan, and the lender was given contractual rights similar to those of the beneficial owner of the securities, which included the right to all interest payments or dividends and to have equivalent securities returned upon termination of the loan. A borrowing fee was generally agreed to in advance of the loan.

The Bond Market Association developed a set of standards for securities lending that included specified collateral margins and collateralization of accrued interest. Banks also lent stocks to broker-dealers on behalf of their clients, such as insurance companies, university endowment funds, and other institutional investors. Such lending activities allowed the institutional investor to earn incremental income that could be used to offset custodial fees. Legislation was enacted to allow corporate pension funds to lend securities to broker-dealers. Such lending activities were spurred by convertible bond arbitrage and tax arbitrage strategies. Because of regulatory restrictions, U.S. and UK lenders developed an offshore securities lending market.

Stock lending was associated with some abuses. Several traders were indicted for taking kickbacks for their activities in connection with stock-lending practices. Stock lending also supported short-sale activities that became controversial during the subprime crisis because investment banks claimed that short sellers undermined the confidence of their customers and counterparties. A short sale in this context is the sale of a security that the seller does not own. In order to deliver the security to the purchaser, the short seller borrows the security, typically from a broker-dealer or an institutional investor. The short seller later closes out the position by purchasing the security in the market and returning the security to the lender. Short sales may be used for many reasons, but speculators use short sales to profit from downward price movements.

"Naked" short sales occur where the short seller makes a sale without arranging to borrow the stock for delivery. This was a much-criticized practice during the subprime crisis because it increased the ability of the short sellers to drive down market prices. Utah even passed a statute that allowed its corporations to collect a $10,000–a-day fee from broker-dealers who failed to notify the Utah Securities Commission within twenty-four hours of short sales that would not be delivered on time. As Daniel Drew famously stated in the nineteenth century, "he who sells what isn't his'n, must buy it back or go to prison."

Short selling was the subject of another scandal. Thirty individuals were indicted for charging bogus fees to finders of stock needed for loans to short sellers. Twenty-nine of those defendants pleaded guilty and were given sentences of up to three years. The remaining defendant, Darin DeMizio, an employee of Morgan Stanley, went on trial in March 2009 and was convicted and sentenced to three years in prison.

The SEC also went on a losing campaign against hedge funds that shorted stock in connection with PIPE (private investments in public equities) transactions, which were a convenient way for companies to privately place their stock, especially where the public market for the stock is unattractive. Conversely, such transactions allowed purchasers a convenient way to acquire a large position in a public company, often at a discount. PIPEs were especially attractive during the subprime crisis. PIPE purchasers were frequently given downside protection by the issuer through the issuance of additional stock, which are sometimes called "death spiral" arrangements. They have, in all events, not been popular with the SEC.

A federal district court dismissed an SEC action against a hedge fund in which the commission claimed that the hedge fund was improperly shorting the issuing company's stocks. The SEC lost three other cases in which it charged that hedge funds had improperly covered their short sales with restricted stock.[42] It did obtain an injunction, by consent, against GLG Partners, a London-based hedge fund that was engaged in illegal short selling in connection with fourteen public offerings. A consent judgment was also entered against Hazan Capital Management for improper and complicated short-selling operations called "reverse conversions" and "resets."

Capital Requirements

Bank Capital Requirements

Financial services regulators are concerned with the financial solvency of the firms that they regulate as a customer protection measure and in order to protect government insurance funds. Bank solvency and liquidity are governed by reserve and capital requirements. Reserve requirements seek to assure that banks will have adequate liquid assets on hand to meet customer withdrawal demands. Bank capital requirements seek to ensure that, in the event of a bank failure, shareholders, rather than creditors, will bear the loss and that the insurance fund administered by the Federal Deposit Insurance Corporation (FDIC) will be protected. The bank's capital, which is provided by its shareholders, and its retained earnings serve as a cushion to absorb losses from highly leveraged bank operations. Banks have highly leveraged balance sheets because the funds used for lending are largely borrowed, rather than sourced from shareholders or retained earnings.

Initially, bank regulators tried to regulate bank capital by declaring that it was an "unsafe and unsound practice" to be undercapitalized. However, no precise formula existed for making that determination. The OCC tried to use peer group comparisons as a basis for determining capital adequacy, but ran into trouble with that formula in the courts. A federal appellate court held that peer group review by itself was insufficient evidence of capital adequacy.[43]

In response to that decision, Congress passed legislation that gave federal bank regulators discretionary authority to issue capital directives setting minimum levels of capital for banks subject to such directives.[44] This ad hoc approach was not particularly effective. To provide some uniformity, bank regulators subsequently adopted a "leverage ratio" that divided a bank's capital by its assets. That ratio then became an important part of the bank's Capital, Assets, Management, Earnings, Liquidity, and Sensitivity (CAMELS) rating during regulatory bank examinations. The CAMELS rating formula is used by bank regulators to assess the condition and viability of banks under regulation. Depending on the leverage ratio, banks were classified into one of five categories that ranged from "well capitalized," with at least a 5 percent leverage ratio, to "critically undercapitalized," with a leverage ratio of under 2 percent.

As part of computing the leverage ratio, assets on the balance sheet were typically based on historical cost, unless the assets were used for trading and held for less than one year, in which case those assets were required to be reported at market value (marked-to-market).[45] Marking-to-market was not particularly a problem for banks before the subprime crisis when subprime mortgages, which were being traded and warehoused in portfolios by banks or their affiliates, had to be marked down drastically in value. The mark-to-market requirement for those securities would prove to be nearly the undoing of the nation's financial system during the subprime crime crisis.

Globalization of banking services resulted in a demand for a uniform and more workable capital requirement for banks throughout the world. The creation of an international capital standard for banks was carried out through the BIS. The Basel Accord of 1988 (Basel I) resulted from their deliberations.[46] Basel I sought to improve on the leverage ratio by risk-weighting assets. In other words, some assets were less risky than others and needed less capital to support them in the event of financial problems, and thus they were less likely to decline in value. Therefore, the risk to creditors from such assets was minimal. Other assets, however, were more risky and required a greater capital cushion.

Basel I created five categories of weighted risk that ranged from assets requiring no capital support, such as U.S. government securities, to 50 percent risk-weighting for first mortgages on residential real estate. Some off-balance-sheet exposures were also included in the Basel I computation, such as standby letters of credit, unused portions of loan commitments, and documentary letters of credit.

Basel I employed two different capital ratios, a Tier 1 leverage ratio of at least 4 percent and a total capital ratio of at least 8 percent. Tier 1 capital was composed of stockholders' equity, certain types of preferred stock, and retained earnings. That figure was adjusted by deductions for goodwill and other intangible assets. In addition, as much as 25 percent of Tier 1 capital could be composed of "trust-preferred securities," or hybrid instruments that have characteristics of both equity and debt. They are created by the issuance of subordinated debt by the bank to a subsidiary that is organized as a trust. The trust then sells preferred stock in itself to investors. The bank deducts the interest payments on the subordinated debt for tax purposes and is able to treat the proceeds from the offering as equity capital for Basel I purposes, giving the bank the best of both worlds of stock and bonds.

Basel I was adopted by regulators in the United States and in over a hundred countries. However, criticism soon arose over its "one size fits all" approach to bank capital requirements. For example, all commercial loans carried the same risk-weighting, no matter how creditworthy the counter-party. This meant that a commercial loan to a large Fortune 500 company carried the same risk-weighting as a loan to a new, untested start-up company. Basel I also did not consider operational risks and did not account for portfolio risks. These criticisms convinced the regulators, who turned to risk-based measures for determining capital adequacy. That effort, which was first announced in 1999, was controversial and took several years, but finally resulted in Basel II. Basel II was not finalized until 2004, and it was not until July 2007 that bank regulators in the United States required its implementation, just in time for it to be tested during the subprime crisis, an examination that it failed.

Basel II is based on three "pillars": (1) a specified minimum capital re-quirement, (2) supervisory review, and (3) market discipline. With respect to the first pillar, banks were generally required to hold 6 percent of their assets as Tier 1 capital and 10 percent as "core" capital. Risk-weighting for assets became more flexible. For example, commercial loans could receive risk-weightings that ranged from 0 to 150 percent, depending upon the credit rating of the company taking out the loan. This created a dependency on credit rating agencies, such as Standard & Poor's and Moody's. Critics contended that those ratings were not always reliable and that the rating agencies had a tendency, during economic downturns, to downgrade commercial loans out of panic. This requires the banks to obtain more capital and, thereby, exacerbates a downturn, which is exactly what happened in the subprime crisis.

Basel II also allowed an alternative to the traditional risk-weighting of loans made by banks. Large banks (those with more than $250 billion in assets) were allowed to use their own internal risk assessment systems for weighting risks for capital purposes. Critics charged that this was like asking the fox to watch the henhouse, but a greater concern was whether these risk models were truly predictive of risk. Internal "value at risk" (VaR) assessment systems had been in use for a number of years at many large financial institutions. VaR was a risk-modeling concept that was developed at JPMorgan in the early 1990s. It sought to measure risk in a portfolio mathematically. The VaR model was touted as having the ability to predict with 99 percent certainty the maximum amount of money that a portfolio could lose over a specified short period of time.

In 1994, when the VaR model was created, the chairman of JPMorgan was Dennis Weatherstone. He wanted to know more about the risks embedded in JPMorgan's operations and how positions in one class of assets might affect the firm's risk from other classes.[47] The creation of sometimes-exotic derivative instruments also created a demand for a more sophisticated valuation system. The JPMorgan VaR system proved highly predictive, so the firm freely provided the system to other financial services firms. It was published and became a software product in 1996.

JPMorgan also created a firm called RiskMetrics, in 1998, to develop VaR systems for clients. RiskMetrics was later spun off from JPMorgan and became a consulting company that was expanded to become a part of a group that included Institutional Shareholder Services (ISS). ISS was founded in 1985 with a goal of promoting good corporate governance and guiding institutional investors in fulfilling their fiduciary duties by responsibly voting proxies on issues presented to public company shareholders. The corporate governance reform movement had thus not only sought to undermine management in public companies but also laid the groundwork for the risk modeling failures in the subprime crisis. As its Web site noted, as of 2008 RiskMetrics served more than 3,300 of the most important institutions and corporations in the world.

When these VaR analyses were first introduced in the 1990s, critics charged that they were not reliable and failed to account for the hundred-year storm or the possibility of outliers. That criticism proved prescient during the subprime crisis, a true catastrophic event that the risk models did not take into account. However, rather strong warning signals had been given before that event. In 1998, large losses were sustained by financial institutions as a result of market disruptions caused by a financial crisis that had suddenly appeared and spread rapidly from Asia to Russia. A number of sophisticated hedge funds, with equally sophisticated risk modeling systems, lost large sums of money during that event. Tiger Management lost $2.1 billion in September 1998 and $3.4 billion in October. It lost $2 billion from currency trading in a single day in October of that year. George Soros's Quantum Group (which had $20 billion in assets) also sustained massive losses.

The highest-profile meltdown occurred at Long-Term Capital Management (LTCM). It lost $4.8 billion in September 1998, 90 percent of its capital. That firm had several academic superstars, including some Nobel Prize winners, who were thought to have mastered risk assessment before LTCM melted down. The LTCM VaR was modeling for risks that had occurred only within the previous five years, which omitted the damage from the stock market crash of 1987 and other catastrophic events. Those events were viewed as anomalies at the time, although, in fact, they signaled that the perfect storm could, indeed, arrive unexpectedly. In the event, the warning was ignored and the use of VaR models spread widely. They continued to be based on risk projections for limited time periods that did not contain unexpected events.

The risks ignored by the models were not known, so the possibility of their occurrence was ignored. Nassim Taleb, a former options trader, crusaded against the false security of VaR models for over a decade before the subprime crisis, pointing out that unusual events do occur, even if they are random. His book, *The Black Swan*, criticizing these flaws became a best seller. Another flaw in the VaR risk models used in mortgage valuations, which were at the center of the subprime crisis, was that they were based on historical data from a rising housing market that was being artificially inflated by government programs designed to increase homeownership and by artificially low interest rates. "When the VaR models looked back, they wrongly modeled a low risk of default."[48]

In 2002, bank regulators allowed banks to risk-weight recourse obligations, residual interest, and asset securitizations on the basis of their credit ratings. This made the rating agencies the arbiter of bank capital standards. Unfortunately, the models used by the rating agencies in formulating their ratings proved to be seriously flawed, as evidenced by the subprime crisis, when thousands of mortgage-backed securities were sharply downgraded. Another gap in risk modeling involved off-balance-sheet mortgage-backed securities that, in some instances, concealed exposures of banks to those offerings.

The Financial Accounting Standards Board (FASB) required mortgage-backed securities used to fund commercial paper programs to be kept on the balance sheet of the sponsoring banks. Nevertheless, bank regulators allowed the banks to exclude those assets from their risk-weighted asset base for capital computation purposes (with the exception of a 10 percent conversion factor on liquidity facilities with an original maturity of one year or less).

Subprime Reaction

In light of the massive losses sustained by large international banks during the subprime crisis, critics charged that Basel II was a failure because it did not account for off-balance-sheet exposures and appropriate treatment for trading book securities. Critics also charged that Basel II was pro-cyclical, in that it required more capital when there is an economic downturn, which reduces the ability of banks to lend at a time when such activity is most needed. Regulators around the world sought increases in capital requirements for banks that would be very costly. However, the Group of Twenty, which is composed of finance ministers from industrialized and leading emerging market countries, agreed not to implement such increased requirements until 2012.

SEC Net Capital Requirements

Background

The SEC has its own net capital rule, which varies from the approach taken by bank regulators in that the SEC prescribes a rigid formula for computing the minimum net capital deemed necessary for customer protection. The SEC rule was designed to assure that broker-dealers had sufficient liquid capital to meet customer demand, as well as to protect investors in the event of insolvency. This rule has its origin in a program introduced by NYSE in the 1920s that established a maximum permissible ratio between a broker-dealer's capital and its customer debit balances.

Based on that model, the Securities Exchange Act of 1934 included a provision that allowed the SEC to adopt rules establishing a permissible ratio of aggregate indebtedness of broker-dealers to their net capital that could not exceed 200 percent.[49] However, the SEC did not adopt a net capital rule until October 29, 1942. Further, in deference to NYSE, which had its own capital rule, the SEC rule applied its rule only to broker-dealers who were not NYSE members. The SEC net capital rule contained definitions of the terms "aggregate indebtedness" and "net capital." Excluded from net capital (in addition to fixed assets and exchange memberships) was a percentage of the market value of securities held by broker-dealers. This reduction, called a "haircut," was intended to provide a cushion for market fluctuations in portfolio values and difficulties in liquidating securities that might result in the realization of less-than-current market prices through a distress sale.

A Special Study of the Securities Markets commissioned by the SEC in 1963 found, as might be expected, that thinly capitalized broker-dealers were the most likely to fail and were also the most likely to violate SEC rules.[50] The Special Study concluded that broker-dealers with significant capital were more responsible in carrying out their business activities. Nevertheless, some larger firms faced a net capital crisis during the "paperwork crisis" that occurred at the end of the 1960s. More than 100 NYSE member firms went out of business during the paperwork crisis, even though the exchange suspended enforcement of its net capital rule. NYSE chairman Robert Haack stated that if the exchange had strictly enforced its net capital rule during the crisis, another 100 NYSE member firms would have failed.

Another concern with shortfalls in broker-dealer capital was the account insurance fund. In response to the paperwork crisis, Congress created the SIPC to provide account insurance for customers of insolvent broker-dealers. Initially, that insurance covered up to $50,000 per account, but in 1980 the amount was increased to $500,000. Like the FDIC, the SIPC created a moral hazard because customers of broker-dealers had a reduced incentive to monitor the financial condition of their broker-dealer.

To deal with that risk, Congress passed legislation in 1975 that required the SEC to establish minimum financial responsibility requirements for all brokers-dealers. The SEC did so with its Uniform Net Capital Rule, which continued the "basic" method of computing net capital but limited the permissible amount of aggregate indebtedness to 1,500 percent of the broker-dealer's net capital. The minimum amount of excess net capital required under this rule, which ranged from $2,500 to $100,000, depended on the nature of the

broker-dealer's business. The new rule also contained an "alternative" computation that could be elected by a broker-dealer. Under the alternative method,
the broker-dealer was required to maintain net capital in an amount equal to
$100,000 or 4 percent (later reduced to 2 percent), whichever was greater, of
"aggregate debit items."

Aggregate indebtedness included the amount of funds held by the broker-
dealer for customers, certain other items, and the value of items borrowed from
customers. The amounts of funds owed by customers to the broker-dealer were
deducted from that figure to reach aggregate indebtedness. Since aggregate
indebtedness included most of the unsecured borrowings of the broker-dealer,
this test limited the broker-dealer's leverage.

The SEC net capital rule required broker-dealers to cease business when
they fell below the minimum net capital requirement. The rule further required
broker-dealers to give the SEC and self-regulatory bodies an early warning
notice whenever their net capital fell to a level above the minimum but at
a threshold low enough to indicate that the firm's financial condition was
deteriorating. Broker-dealers were also required periodically to report their
financial condition to regulators.

The stock market crash of 1987 posed a major test of the SEC net capital
requirement. That event caused the failure of a few broker-dealers and threatened the viability of a number of others. About fifty introducing brokers (firms
that did not clear securities) had to cease operations because of an inability to
comply with the SEC net capital requirement, which was a very low standard
for such firms given that they did not carry customer positions. The firms that
suffered the most were those with large proprietary trading operations or those
that were acting as market makers.

An SEC staff study of that event also expressed concern over the fact that
affiliates of many broker-dealers were engaging in unrelated securities or
banking activities that imposed risks that regulated broker-dealers could not
themselves incur. The SEC subsequently increased its net capital requirement
for broker-dealers carrying customer accounts, increasing that requirement
from $100,000 to $250,000 for firms using the alternative method.

Drexel Burnham

The Market Reform Act of 1990 addressed concerns raised by activities of
affiliates of broker-dealers and their interrelated demands for capital. That
legislation was enacted in the wake of the stock market crash of 1987 and
after the failure of Drexel Burnham Lambert, the employer of the junk-bond
king Michael Milken, an investment banker responsible for Drexel's massive
junk bond underwritings. Drexel Burnham employed a holding company
structure, and the parent company moved a great deal of capital out of its
broker-dealer affiliate before the company became bankrupt as a result of its
criminal prosecution for Milken's junk-bond activities (see Chapter 6). The

liquidation of Drexel Burnham required the joint efforts of the Federal Reserve Bank of New York, the Treasury Department, the Federal Reserve, NYSE, the CFTC, and the SEC.

Although Drexel's customer accounts at its broker-dealer affiliate were transferred or liquidated without loss, the collapse of that firm led to much concern as to the capital adequacy of broker-dealers operating in a holding company structure. It was found that Drexel's parent company, over which the SEC did not have regulatory control, had siphoned off excess capital from the regulated broker-dealer affiliate. The holding company was having difficulty obtaining short-term financing as a result of its regulatory troubles and market conditions.

Drexel had issued over $1 billion in commercial paper, but encountered difficulty in rolling over that paper as its troubles mounted. By the time the SEC learned of Drexel's financial plight, the firm had more than $400 million in short-term liabilities coming due within two weeks and an additional $330 million scheduled to mature in the following month. The holding company was then forced to look to the liquid sources of capital in its broker-dealer affiliate. Drexel transferred $200 million to the holding company without the knowledge of NYSE or the SEC.

The Market Reform Act of 1990 directed the SEC to monitor financial services firms to ensure that affiliate activities did not endanger the broker-dealer part of the business. The SEC and bank regulators were directed to notify each other in the event that an entity under their regulation posed a danger to an affiliate overseen by another regulator. The SEC also amended its net capital rule to prohibit broker-dealers from withdrawing capital to benefit affiliates or parent companies in cases in which such withdrawals would be detrimental to the integrity of the broker-dealer.

Consolidated Supervised Entities

The SEC made a radical change in its capital requirements for large broker-dealers in 2004. That rule change allowed large, highly capitalized broker-dealers to use mathematical models to calculate net capital requirements for market and derivative-related credit risk. In order to take advantage of that rule, those broker-dealers were required to elect consolidated supervision for their ultimate holding company and affiliates. Such firms were called "consolidated supervised entities" (CSEs).

The SEC's change in approach for large broker-dealer holding company systems came in response to an EU directive issued in 2002. This directive required foreign financial services firms with operations in the EU to demonstrate that they were subject to holding company supervision in their home country equivalent to EU consolidated supervision. This requirement was applicable to many large broker-dealer operations in the United States, including Bear Stearns, Lehman Brothers, Merrill Lynch, Goldman Sachs, and Morgan Stanley.

A "broker-dealer could use this 'alternative/CSE' method only if its ultimate holding company agreed to compute group-wide allowable capital and allowances for market, credit, and operational risk in accordance with the standards adopted by the Basel Committee on Banking Supervision. The holding company also had to consent to group-wide SEC supervision."[51] The broker-dealer's ultimate holding company and affiliates (the CSE) were also required to consent to groupwide SEC supervision. Special provisions were made for the supervision of bank holding companies and holding companies regulated in the EU. This effectively treated these large broker-dealer holding companies as banks, at least for net capital purposes.

The mathematical models that could be used by a CSE for risk assessment included VaR models and scenario analysis, which were already a part of these entities' internal risk management control systems. Those risk management systems could be used to calculate the market risk and derivative-related credit risk components of the CSE's net capital requirement, replacing the traditional "haircut" approach. The SEC also proposed allowing broker-dealers to use a theoretical pricing model when they calculated net capital charges for listed options and related positions. This was designed to be a "risk capital" approach to net capital, which was a significant variation from the liquidity test otherwise employed in the SEC's net capital rule. The proposed theoretical methodology was based on the Cox-Ross-Rubinstein binomial model, which determined theoretical gains and losses based on a repricing of an option in relation to assumed changes in the value underlying the instrument.

In adopting the Basel II approach, the SEC was leveling the playing field for capital requirements among the large broker-dealers and the commercial banks that were all competing with each other. Even so, Vikram Pandit, who became the Citigroup CEO during the subprime crisis, complained in an op-ed piece in the *Wall Street Journal* in June 2008 that capital requirements should be uniform for all large financial institutions. Pandit also sought greater transparency and systemic oversight for large financial institutions, but by then it was too late to save some of the most famous Wall Street firms.[52] All but two of the firms opting for CSE status failed during the subprime crisis, and the remaining two, Goldman Sachs and Morgan Stanley, converted to bank holding company status.

Insurance Capital Requirements

The insurance industry, unlike other financial service sectors in the United States, is regulated only at the state level. This development can be traced back to the beginning of the twentieth century, when the growing reserves of insurance companies provided them with a great deal of economic power. That concentration of assets engendered criticism from corporate reformers. Louis D. Brandeis, a future Justice on the U.S. Supreme Court, stated in 1905 that insurance companies were "the greatest economic menace of today" and that as "creditors of [the] great industries," they used their power "selfishly, dishonestly [and] inefficiently."[53]

Brandeis's criticism appeared to be given credence by events unfolding at the Equitable Life Assurance Company, where twenty-three-year-old James Hyde had succeeded his father. Hyde was given to ostentatious displays of his wealth that marked him as a less-than-serious businessman. His excesses and other industry problems sparked so much criticism that the New York superintendent of insurance initiated an investigation of the insurance industry. That investigation led the New York State legislature to appoint its own investigating committee, headed by Senator William W. Armstrong. The committee was charged with undertaking a broad review of the activities of New York insurance companies. Charles Evan Hughes, a future Chief Justice of the U.S. Supreme Court, acted as the Armstrong Committee's counsel, and his performance in that role as a tough inquisitor made him a national figure.

The Armstrong investigation led to more stringent regulation of the insurance industry. One of those "reforms" was to require disclosure of the names of any employee making over $5,000 ($120,000 in today's dollars). That statute was amended to increase the disclosure level to $60,000 in 1985, but it was still considered so intrusive that the New York State legislature amended it in 2008 (in the midst of the subprime crisis) to apply its disclosure requirements to only ten of the most highly paid executives and employees.[54] The Armstrong Committee also concluded that insurance companies were a part of the trend toward the accumulation of great capital by a few individuals and enterprises. The committee stated, "No tendency in modern financial conditions has created more widespread apprehension than the tendency to vast combinations of capital and assets."[55]

Another matter of concern for the Armstrong Committee was that the large reserves held by the insurance companies were increasingly invested in the stock market. The committee recommended that insurance companies be prohibited from investing their reserves in stocks because such investments endangered the companies' ability to pay claims. The New York State legislature, thereafter, restricted the ability of insurance companies to invest in common stocks. Another reform required insurance companies to divest themselves of bank stocks. Insurance companies were prohibited from acting as underwriters for securities or engaging in securities syndications.

After the Armstrong investigation, insurance companies initially engaged in some lobbying for federal regulation in order to avoid multiple-state regulation. The industry soon took the view, however, that state regulation was preferable to federal regulation. The insurance industry was able to escape federal regulation after the stock market crash of 1929 because they were not invested in stocks and thereby avoided most of the excesses of that period. However, a federal regulatory threat did arise after the Roosevelt administration created the Temporary National Economic Committee (TNEC) to investigate the concentration of economic power in the United States. The TNEC was chaired by Senator Joseph O'Mahoney and was composed of representatives from the SEC, the Federal Trade Commission, and the Justice Department. One of its targets was the insurance industry, but federal regulation was not imposed despite the discovery of some abuses.

Another regulatory threat arose after it was discovered that, from March 1933 to October 1938, the major U.S. and Canadian insurance companies held conferences at the offices of Arthur Hunter, chief actuary and vice president of the New York Life Insurance Company, where they set annuity rates and policy terms. This raised antitrust concerns, and in 1944 the Supreme Court held that some two hundred insurance companies were subject to the federal antitrust laws.[56] Those insurance companies were charged with violating the Sherman Antitrust Act by joining the South-Eastern Underwriters Association. The government contended that the purpose of this association was to control the fire insurance business and to discriminate and to retaliate against insurance companies that were not members of the association.

After the Supreme Court's decision, insurance companies became concerned that they would not be able to pool their loss statistics or jointly compute actuarially sound premiums. States were concerned that federal antitrust laws would preempt state regulation. Some insurance companies refused to comply with state insurance laws on those grounds. Congress responded to those concerns by passing the McCarran-Ferguson Act in 1945.[57] That statute granted insurance companies immunity from federal antitrust laws to the extent they were regulated by state law. That legislation largely exempted the insurance industry from federal regulation, an approach diametrically opposed to the regulatory structure for the securities industry. However, the Obama administration was threatening to seek a repeal of the McCarran-Ferguson Act in October 2009, if the insurance industry did not tone down its criticism of the president's universal health-care proposals.

Another effort at federal regulation was undertaken in 1988, when Congress held hearings on the need for such regulation. After forty multistate insurance companies failed in 1992, the Federal Insurance Solvency Act (FISA) was proposed, which sought to create a Federal Insurance Solvency Commission (FISC) that would have established national standards for financial soundness and solvency of insurance companies. That legislation was beaten back by the industry. The Treasury Department also proposed in March 2008 that Congress create an optional federal charter for insurance companies. State regulation would continue for those insurance companies that did not elect a federal charter, but state jurisdiction would be preempted for companies that did. That proposal was watered down and only a Federal Insurance Office was created to monitor the industry.

In lieu of a federal regulator, the National Association of Insurance Commissioners (NAIC) coordinates state insurance regulation and registration examinations. NAIC drafts model laws, but, as a voluntary organization, it cannot compel state legislatures to adopt model acts or regulations.[58] Like banking and securities, capital requirements were used by the states as a regulatory tool under the guidance of NAIC. Before 1992, most states had capital require- ments for insurance companies that were based on static minimum amounts of capital and surplus. Risk-based capital standards changed this structure to require capital levels premised on the risk of the investments in an insurance company's portfolio, a change made in response to a number of insurance company failures. This new approach brought risk-based capital requirements full circle, to include banks, broker-dealers, and insurance companies.

The adoption of risk-based capital requirements had a dramatic effect on the corporate structure of many large insurance companies. It placed pressure on them to increase their capital, a task that was difficult for many of these companies because they operated as mutual companies that were owned by their policyholders. In order to alleviate that problem, New York adopted legislation permitting mutual life insurance companies to convert to stock companies, which could raise capital through public offerings. This idea quickly spread, and many large mutual insurance companies became conventional shareholder-owned corporations. For example, the Equitable Life Assurance Society demutualized in 1992. The Mutual Life Insurance Company of New York, a company that had operated in a mutual form for 150 years, joined it five years later. Prudential, the largest insurance company in the country, which was founded as a mutual company some 130 years earlier, demutualized, as did the Metropolitan Life Insurance Company (MetLife), and many others.

Insurance companies, with a few notable exceptions, such as American International Group (AIG), were able to weather the subprime crisis with damages less than those suffered by the investment and commercial banks. Damage in the insurance industry was limited by state restrictions on insur- ance reserve investments that restricted the ability of insurance companies to make risky investments. For example, New York allowed a maximum of 20 percent of reserve assets to be invested in equities. Insurance companies had traditionally invested in mortgages, but the amount of real estate in- vestments was limited to specified percentages of the insurance company's reserves. Real estate mortgage investments were also limited by specified minimum loan to property value ratios. Nevertheless, the insurance compa- nies were being stressed by precipitous market declines that occurred across nearly all asset classes. NAIC rejected a proposal that would have reduced capital requirements for insurance companies by over $22 billion in order to relieve that stress. Hartford Financial, which suffered large losses and whose rating was downgraded during the crisis, sought and obtained relief from insurance officials to allow it to reduce its capital requirements by $1 billion. Regulators also granted capital relief to Lincoln National, which was suffering from losses.

The situation worsened in 2009. Some two dozen insurance companies experienced ratings downgrades in the first quarter of 2009. Insurance company stocks were down 59 percent for the year on March 12, 2009, a market low point. Several insurance companies sought bailout money from the federal government. The Treasury Department approved such funding for six insurance companies on May 15, 2009, but the then-ongoing attacks on executive pay, and government interference with management of firms receiving bailout money, had made such relief untenable. Among those declining government bailout money was Allstate and MetLife. Only two of the six qualifying insurance companies expressed continuing interest in receiving bailout money: Hartford Financial Services, which was given $3.4 billion, and Lincoln National, which received $2.5 billion. The stock of both of those companies had fallen by more than 70 percent over the previous fifteen months.

Enron CEO Ken Lay died before his Enron conviction became final. (*James Nielsen/AFP, photographer, Getty Images* ©)

Former Enron CEO Jeffrey Skilling walks to the federal courthouse for his sentencing hearing. (*Johnny Hanson, photographer, Getty Images ©*)

The NatWest three, Giles Darby (L), Gary Mulgrew (3L), and David Bermingham (R), listens as their attorney, Reid Figel (2L), makes a statement on their guilty plea. (*Dave Einsel, photographer, Getty Images ©*)

New York governor Eliot Spitzer—the former crusading attorney general—
resigns in disgrace. (*Timothy A. Clary/AFP, photographer, Getty Images* ©)

California Public Employees' Retirement System building in Sacramento, California. CalPERS has led the attacks on corporate governance in America. (*Max Whittaker, photographer, Getty Images* ©)

Traders on the floor of the New York Stock Exchange, which rapidly transformed into an electronic exchange. (*Mario Tama, photographer, Getty Images* ©)

Chicago Mercantile Exchange, the nation's largest futures exchange, embraces electronic trading. (*Scott Olson, photographer, Getty Images* ©)

Financier Henry Kravis led the revolution in private equity. (*Scott Wintrow, photographer, Getty Images ©*)

Laurence Fink, chairman, CEO, and founder of BlackRock, who on more than one occasion was called on to sort out financial disasters during the subprime crisis. (*Andrew Harrer, photographer, Bloomberg via Getty Images* ©)

5. Commodity Markets

Market Developments

Some History

Derivative markets were another portion of the financial markets that came under scrutiny during the subprime meltdown and became a target for added regulation.[1] Those instruments trace their history to the development of futures trading on the Chicago Board of Trade (CBOT). Trading occurred there before the Civil War in standardized contracts that called for the delivery of grain in Chicago-area warehouses. Standardizing contract terms allowed grain merchants to offset buy and sell obligations, giving rise to a trading market in those contracts. As in the New York Stock Exchange (NYSE), an important aspect of the history of the futures markets was the desire of their members to limit trading to recognized exchanges, eschewing any form of over-the-counter (OTC) trading. In 1873, CBOT adopted regular trading hours for futures transactions and declared that all transactions executed by its members after hours were unenforceable. This was an effort to confine futures trading to the trading floor. However, the Chicago Open Board of Trade, a competing exchange, allowed trading after hours, and a curb market was operating in the streets of Chicago.

These alternative markets were often little more than gambling dens ("bucket shops") that allowed speculators to bet on price changes reported by CBOT. Like NYSE, CBOT sought to stop the bucket shops by cutting off access price reports emanating from the trading floor. CBOT used the courts to enforce that prohibition and was supported in its efforts by the Supreme Court.[2] That campaign formed the foundation for the monopoly in futures exercised by the commodity exchanges, which lasted until the end of the twentieth century, when the Commodity Futures Modernization Act of 2000 was passed to allow off-exchange trading of a broad range of derivative instruments by institutional investors. The commodity exchanges also failed in the twenty-first century to curb the growth of electronic communication networks by cutting off access to their quotes. In 2007, the Court of Appeals for the Second Circuit held that settlement prices on the New York Mercantile Exchange (NYMEX) were not protected by copyright.[3]

Additional commodity exchanges sprang up in Chicago and elsewhere in the nineteenth century. The Chicago Butter and Egg Board, which was founded in 1898, evolved into the Chicago Mercantile Exchange (CME) after World War I. Another of the larger commodity exchanges was NYMEX, which traces its history back to a butter and cheese exchange that was operating in 1872. NYMEX became an amalgamation of several New York commodity exchanges, including the Commodity Exchange (COMEX), which was itself a consolidation of several other exchanges. NYMEX was acquired by the CME in 2008. The CME had earlier acquired CBOT and, today, is the medium for virtually all exchange-traded futures contracts.

Significantly, the futures exchanges were not in serious competition with the stock exchanges until the last quarter of the twentieth century. Until then, the commodity exchanges were mostly just that—they traded only agricultural commodities—while the securities markets traded only securities. However, in 1973, CBOT decided to apply commodity futures trading practices to securities when it created the Chicago Board Options Exchange (CBOE). Around that time, the CME also began trading commodity futures on precious metals and currencies. CBOT and the CME then segued into trading futures on a number of financial instruments (including government securities and stock indexes). Futures and options trading on financial instruments soon dominated their trading floors.

Regulation

The commodity exchanges were largely untouched by federal regulation for many decades. This was not to suggest that there were not problems in the market. CBOT was infamous, almost from the inception of futures trading, for squeezes, corners in which traders gained control of deliverable supplies of the commodities on which futures were traded, and other manipulative activities on its trading floor that adversely affected farm prices. While members of Congress introduced some 200 bills calling for regulation of the futures exchanges between 1880 and 1920, none passed. Nevertheless, regulation of the commodity futures markets preceded that of the securities markets.

Commodity market–related legislation was enacted before America's entry into World War I, while stock market regulation would not arrive until the 1930s. A Cotton Futures Act was passed in 1914 under Congress's tax powers that established a system for grading cotton. A federal court struck down that statute because it did not originate in the House of Representatives, as required by the Constitution for tax measures.[4] That statute was replaced by the Cotton Futures Act of 1916, which was correctly enacted. Another statute, the Grain Standards Act of 1916, authorized the secretary of agriculture to determine grading and inspection procedures for grain. The Warehouse Act of 1916 authorized the secretary of agriculture to license and inspect warehouse operators that stored agricultural products on which futures trading were often conducted, but this was a voluntary program.

None of this legislation imposed any direct regulation on the commodity exchanges. However, speculation associated with World War I led to a massive study of the grain trade by the Federal Trade Commission that began after the war. Composed of seven volumes, the study, among other things, examined manipulative activities that disrupted markets and pricing.[5] This study led to the passage of the Futures Trading Act of 1921, but the Supreme Court held that this act was unconstitutional because the statute improperly relied on Congress's taxation power.[6] That was but a brief setback. A market manipulation occurred on the day after the Supreme Court announced its decision. This motivated Congress to pass the act again, this time under its Commerce Clause of the Constitution powers. That statute, which was renamed the Grain Futures Act of 1922 (GFA), was upheld by the Supreme Court when challenged.[7]

The GFA limited futures trading to "contract markets" licensed by the federal government, thereby sanctioning an exchange monopoly and establishing its exclusivity over trading in futures contracts for decades to come, actually until Enron started a parallel market in OTC trading. The theory behind that grant of monopoly power was the belief that limiting trading to "contract markets" would promote the dissemination of price information, expand the regulation and monitoring of the marketplace, and eliminate bucket shops. It was thought that by granting "contract market" status exclusively to registered exchanges, they would have an inducement to police themselves in order to protect their licenses.

The GFA authorized the secretary of agriculture to designate a "board of trade" as a "contract market." Once registered, the contract market was required to prevent manipulation and dissemination of false reports that could affect commodity prices. The legislation also established a commission composed of the secretary of agriculture, the secretary of commerce, and the attorney general, who were authorized to suspend or revoke the registration of a contract market if it failed to prevent manipulative activity by its members. Day-to-day administration of the statute was placed in the hands of the Grain Futures Administration, a small bureau located within the Department of Agriculture.

Like stock markets, grain exchanges were named as culprits in the Great Depression. In the case of the commodity markets, depressed grain prices were blamed on speculators' operating on those exchanges. Short sellers were particularly reviled. Therefore, after finishing with the stock markets, Congress turned to futures markets and passed the Commodity Exchange Act of 1936 (CEA).[8] The CEA prohibited commodity price "manipulation," without defining the term, a failure that would cause uncertainty and result in time-consuming and expensive litigation that the government often lost.

The CEA had a number of other flaws. The legislation was limited in its application only to the trading of futures contracts on certain enumerated commodities. As futures trading expanded to other commodities, the CEA was amended from time to time to bring those futures contracts within the reach of the statute. However, those amendments always lagged behind the development of new contracts, allowing speculators trading these contracts to avoid regulation, at least for a time.

The CEA sought to curb speculation by creating position limits that restricted the amount of futures contracts that could be held by any one speculator. Those limits were being revisited in the wake of the run-up in energy prices that occurred during the subprime crisis. The CEA continued to regulate the contract markets by requiring their registration and imposing duties on those exchanges to prevent manipulation. "Futures commission merchants," which are brokerage firms that handle customer orders for futures contracts, were also required to register with the Agriculture Department.

The CEA renewed authorization of the Commodity Exchange Commission. Day-to-day administration of the CEA was carried out once again by the Agriculture Department, through a renamed bureau—the Commodity Exchange Authority. The Commodity Exchange Authority was a little-known agency and a quiet backwater in the Agriculture Department until the 1970s, when commodity prices exploded. That inflation was blamed on futures speculators, which raised the ire of consumers and Congress, a situation that was strongly reminiscent of the commodity price run-up in 2008.

Scandals in the trading of commodity options and concerns over price manipulation involving grain sales to the Soviet Union were added to that mix, making legislation inevitable. The commodity markets had fought off legislation in 1968 that would have given the Commodity Exchange Authority some teeth. Some minor amendments were made in 1968, but none that measurably strengthened the role of the Commodity Exchange Authority. However, the turmoil in the market in the 1970s gave Congress sufficient leverage to pass broad and intrusive regulation over the commodity exchanges.

That legislation, the Commodity Futures Trading Commission Act of 1974, created a new federal regulatory agency, the Commodity Futures Trading Commission (CFTC), which was intended to be the futures industry analogue to the Securities and Exchange Commission (SEC). The CFTC Act expanded the scope of the CEA to include all commodities without enumeration, which swept up even futures contracts on financial instruments. The CFTC was given broad powers, including injunctive authority to stop violations and the ability to impose civil penalties of as much as $100,000 per violation. Additional categories of new registrants were added, including commodity pool operators (now considered hedge funds) and commodity trading advisers.

The contract market monopoly was continued by the 1974 legislation, but the commodity exchanges were required to submit their rules to the CFTC for approval. That requirement proved overly cumbersome, until the CFTC streamlined the process to allow exchange rules to go into effect unless there was some objection by the CFTC. In other words, unlike the securities markets, the contract markets do not have to seek permission to adopt a rule from the CFTC. In theory, the CFTC could object to an exchange rule, and it would then have to be withdrawn by the exchange, but that has never happened.

The Stock Market Crash of 1987

Futures contracts traded on securities led to a great deal of trading by institutions that had previously shunned the commodity markets. A number of new trading strategies were also developed, including "dynamic hedging" and "portfolio insurance," which were trading programs that allowed portfolio managers to protect their portfolios from, or expose them to, market changes without liquidating the assets held in the portfolio. The liquidity of futures contracts and their replication of broad-based indices made them popular with managers who employed the "modern portfolio" theory of diversification. With futures contracts, these managers could quickly change their market exposure without engaging in costly and time-consuming purchases or sales of the securities in their portfolio.

Another new popular addition to financial markets was "program trading," which involved trading on the basis of algorithmic signals generated by computer programs that sought to predict market changes using mathematical models. Those models analyzed massive computerized databases for trends that appeared to replicate themselves over time. Concern was raised that the coupling of these new financial futures with those computerized trading programs might pose a danger to the markets—the "cascade theory." This pro-cyclic concern centered on the fact that, while each computerized trading program had individual variations and nuances, they all generally shared a common feature, namely, in the event of a market decline the computer programs would all generate "sell" signals. That selling would push the market down even further, which would then cause the computer programs to generate more sell signals, in a descending spiral that would continue until the market completely collapsed.

That prophecy was nearly fulfilled in the stock market crash of 1987. During that event, the Dow Jones Industrial Average dropped more in absolute and relative terms than had been the case in the stock market crash of 1929. That freefall in prices paralyzed NYSE because it simply did not have the capacity to handle that unexpected volume and price volatility. NASDAQ market makers also fled the market, leaving their customers no way to avoid the crash in prices. However, the commodity exchanges did continue to function throughout the crisis.

A number of studies were conducted after the stock market crash of 1987, in order to ascertain whether the commodity futures markets should be subject to further regulation. The SEC advocated the adoption of crippling margin requirements that would curb speculation in the futures markets. Instead, President Ronald Reagan created a Presidential Task Force on Market Mechanisms (the Brady Commission), headed by Nicholas Brady, who eventually became treasury secretary. The Brady Commission concluded that the uncertain division of regulatory jurisdiction between the SEC and the CFTC over futures products on securities was a contributing factor in the affair. Some critics sought a merger of those two agencies, but the Brady Commission did not believe that such a merger would create an effective intermarket regulator. Instead, the commission recommended that the Federal Reserve be given the task of promulgating regulations that would cut across the securities and commodity markets. That recommendation was never implemented, but was renewed by the Obama administration in the wake of the subprime crisis. The effort, however, soon bogged down in internecine turf battles among the various financial services regulators.

The Brady Commission made other recommendations, but little was done in any of the areas that it considered. One exception was the adoption of trading collars ("circuit breakers"). This concept was borrowed from similar limitations employed by the futures exchanges during volatile market conditions. Called "price limits" on the commodity exchanges, these rules suspended trading whenever changes in market prices exceeded certain levels. Similarly, the circuit breakers adopted for futures on securities products required the suspension of NYSE trading when prices moved a predefined, and largely arbitrary, amount. The Brady Commission believed that circuit breakers would slow electronic program trading, allow traders to respond more rationally to market events, and thus, provide NYSE with additional time to process trades, which would lead to a more orderly market. Such timeouts from trading would also allow traders to gather funds to meet margin calls and thereby avoid liquidity concerns.

One significant development that followed the stock market crash of 1987 was the creation, by President Reagan, of an interagency task force that was to be responsible for ensuring the coordination of regulation between the stock and futures markets. This group, called the President's Working Group on Financial Markets (PWG) and led by the treasury secretary, was composed of the heads of the Federal Reserve, the SEC, and the CFTC. It was through the PWG that future jurisdictional battles would be fought between the SEC and the CFTC. Among the matters considered by the PWG after its formation was whether regulation should be imposed on OTC derivatives, hedge funds, and private equity. The PWG also explored various policy initiatives involving financial markets.

Forex Fraud

Despite its broad powers, the CFTC was unable to stop a series of scandals in commodity options that arose almost immediately after the formation of that agency. The CEA had prohibited options trading on the enumerated commodities. However, that prohibition had been evaded by trading options on nonenumerated commodities, at least until the SEC stepped in and stopped that activity by claiming that they were securities that had to be registered with it under the federal securities laws. The CFTC Act removed SEC jurisdiction, which was uncertain in any event, and gave the CFTC exclusive jurisdiction over commodity options.

Unfortunately, the CFTC did not have the resources to stop the flood of fly-by-night operators that immediately began selling commodity options to public investors through high-pressure, fraudulent selling operations. The CFTC had to eventually suspend virtually all trading in OTC commodity options in order to stop the boiler room operations that were fleecing unsophisticated customers by promising enormous profits with little risk. The CFTC later allowed options trading on the commodity exchanges, but still faced problems in OTC commodity options market for foreign currency.

A number of fraudulent operators selling foreign currency (forex) derivatives still engaged in widespread fraud through solicitations directed at unsophisticated retail customers. Between 2001 and 2007, some 26,000 investors were defrauded of over $460 million through forex schemes involving OTC derivatives. A provision in the CFTC Act called the Treasury Amendment removed such trading from the jurisdictional reach of the CFTC, unless it was conducted via a "board of trade." The CFTC attempted to avoid the effects of the Treasury Amendment by declaring that any and all OTC forex would be deemed to be traded via a board of trade, which would give it jurisdiction. The only exceptions, according to the CFTC, were the interbank currency market and trading in currency by large institutions, which the CFTC believed were the only legitimate forex markets that should fall within the Treasury amendment. The Supreme Court, however, rejected that interpretation, holding that the Treasury Amendment was not so limited.

The Supreme Court's decision, once again, opened the OTC retail currency market to widespread fraud.[9] Congress responded with further amendments to the CEA in the Commodity Futures Modernization Act of 2000 (CFMA). Those amendments required retail OTC forex contracts to be traded only through regulated futures commission merchants and certain other institutions. However, the Court of Appeals for the Seventh Circuit in Chicago undercut that legislation by creating a loophole for "spot" transactions. Normally, spot transactions involve the actual purchase and sale of the actual commodity. However, the transactions at issue in that case rarely involved delivery and were usually offset in much the same fashion as futures or options traded on an exchange.[10] This ruling allowed the forex firms to continue their fraud.

Congress closed the loophole opened by the appeals court decision through the CFTC Reauthorization Act of 2008, which gave the CFTC regulatory authority over all retail forex transactions offered on a leveraged or margin basis or that the seller or its affiliates financed. The legislation created a new category of registrants, "retail foreign exchange dealers." Those dealers were required to have minimum adjusted net capital of $20 million. This net capital requirement was also applied to futures commission merchants acting as foreign-currency counterparties. The CFTC was given broad regulatory authority over other forex market participants, including commodity pool operators and commodity trading advisers.

Other Over-the-Counter Derivatives

Financial engineering came to the fore during the last three decades of the twentieth century. In addition to financial futures, a wave of new instruments appeared after the CFTC was created, which often contained elements of futures or options. The CFTC was then faced with the issue of whether and how such instruments should be regulated. If CFTC jurisdiction were applied to those instruments, the exchange-trading requirement would have precluded its use because OTC dealers could not act as self-regulators or incur the expense of such regulation. In addition, institutional traders neither wanted nor needed the regulatory protection of the CEA.

A fight over futures-type trading in the Brent oil market for oil recovered from the North Sea resulted in a federal district court ruling that this market was subject to the CEA. That decision would have required this global market to register as a contract market with the CFTC, which had no interest in regulating this institutional market but had no exemptive authority. Market participants in the Brent oil market had neither the desire nor the ability to act as a contract market. As a consequence, the district court's decision threatened to shut down the Brent oil market, at least in the United States. However, Congress allowed the CFTC to exempt the Brent oil market from regulation as a contract market.

Another new contract, the "swap," was immediately popular in the financial markets. A swap involves the exchange of one income stream for another, say periodically swapping fixed interest rates on the nominal amount of a loan for floating rates on that same amount. It, too, was not tradable on a regulated contract market and would have perished if an exchange-trading requirement had been imposed. The popularity of the swap grew as the result of standardization of some terms through documentation created by the International Swap Dealers Association (ISDA, later renamed the International Swaps and Derivative Association). This made it easier to enter into swap transactions. The ISDA, which was created in 1985, expanded to include over 830 institutional members around the world.

The swap market grew rapidly through the use of derivatives dealer firms that arranged the transactions and guaranteed their performance. These swap dealers were heavily capitalized and performed many of the same functions as clearinghouses do for futures.[11] By 1996, the notional amount of financial swaps was estimated to exceed $29 trillion. The growth of swaps expanded even more with the creation of the credit-default swap, an instrument that would play a large role in the subprime crisis.

The CFTC issued a policy statement in 1989 that omitted swap transactions among institutions from its regulatory reach, but there was some uncertainty over whether the CFTC had the power to adopt such an exemption. To provide that certainty, the Futures Trading Practices Act of 1992 authorized the CFTC to exempt swaps, which it did. The CFTC also exempted various OTC energy contracts, in the wake of the Brent oil market decision, and some other hybrid instruments were exempted as well.

Other instruments with hybrid features of options, futures, and securities also posed regulatory issues. For example, bonds appeared that had a fixed interest rate of return with a commodity price kicker. Such bonds provided an additional return if a commodity, such as silver or oil, increased in value by a specified amount. There being no free lunch on Wall Street, the holder of this bond paid for the commodity price kicker by receiving a lower interest rate than would be paid on a comparable instrument without such a feature. The CFTC tried to regulate these and other instruments by ascertaining whether their options or futures elements outweighed their other features. That effort resulted in much confusion and complexity.

Commodity Futures Modernization Act of 2000

Congress directed the Presidential Working Group on Financial Markets to conduct a study of the OTC derivatives market and to make recommendations to Congress on whether it should be regulated. That report, issued in 1999, was followed by the enactment of the Commodity Futures Modernization Act of 2000 (CFMA).[12] The CFMA exempted OTC instruments from regulation where the parties to the transactions were sophisticated counterparties, that is, banks, investment bankers, and other financial institutions, pension funds, large businesses, and high-net-worth individuals. "The primary justifications for recommending exclusion for such transactions were a determination that most OTC financial derivatives (e.g., interest rate swaps) were not susceptible to manipulation and that the counterparties in such transactions do not need the same protections as smaller, unsophisticated market participants who rely on intermediaries to conduct their transactions."[13]

After a change in the leadership of the CFTC, that agency decided to abandon its traditional rules-based regulatory structure in favor of a "principles"-based system, an approach that was popular abroad. Principles-based regulation seeks to regulate by broad directives rather than by micromanagement through a set of lengthy and complex regulations, the model employed by the SEC. The CFMA incorporated a principles-based regulatory scheme within its provisions. The CFMA also created a multitier derivatives market, in which each tier was subject to differing levels of oversight based on the nature of the participants, the commodity traded, and the type of trading.

The most regulated tier was the traditional contract market in which retail traders participated. However, even for that tier, the nature of regulation was changed to a principles-based regimen that allowed the exchanges to have more control over their operations. Those principles set eighteen goals for futures exchanges to meet in carrying out their self-regulatory functions, including requirements that they prevent manipulation of prices and carry out their activities in the most competitive way. Nevertheless, the CFMA left the traditional "designated contract markets" (DCMs) saddled with some cumbersome regulatory requirements, while upstart electronic execution facilities were left virtually unregulated. The DCMs were required to continue to act as self-regulatory bodies in conjunction with the National Futures Association (NFA). The DCMs and the NFA have yet to consolidate their self-regulatory activities, as NYSE and the NASD did when they created the Financial Industry Regulatory Authority (FINRA). However, a Joint Audit Committee was formed by the DCMs and the NFA to coordinate the monitoring and examination of common member futures commission merchants.[14]

Like the CEA, the CFMA sought to keep retail traders confined to DCMs, which could then be subject to CFTC oversight and to the self-regulatory protections of the DCMs. Nevertheless, OTC derivative products extended into consumer markets. For example, NYSEG, an energy provider in upstate New York, was offering an "electricity supply pricing option" that allowed consumers to choose various pricing options for their electricity. Consumers could choose between either a fixed or floating amount payment for electricity, the latter allowing the consumer to bet that monthly prices would fall.

The CFMA separately regulated another market tier that was called "derivatives transaction execution facilities" (DTEFs), which could be either "retail" or "commercial" DTEFs. These operations were to be regulated more lightly than a DCM, but it was not entirely clear how their regulation would differ from that imposed on DCMs. In any event, no trading platforms have yet been created that would fall within this DTEF category.

The CFMA also created an exemption from most regulation for electronic trading facilities used by institutional traders. These facilities were called "exempt commercial markets" (ECMs). ECMs were required to restrict trading through their electronic facilities to principal-to-principal transactions between "eligible commercial entities," comprising large institutional traders, including hedge funds that traded "exempt" commodities: energy products, metals, chemicals, and emission allowances. ECMs became popular quickly and even challenged traditional DCMs for market share.

Foreign exchange presented another source of competition for domestic exchanges. The CFTC approved the trading of a broad range of foreign futures contracts in the United States, much of which occurred on electronic platforms. The CFTC exempted foreign brokers from registration, provided that they limited their client base to persons located outside the United States. These foreign brokers were also required to trade through a U.S. futures commission merchant on an omnibus basis, a form of chaperone requirement. Another breakthrough came when foreign futures exchanges were allowed to place terminals in the United States that could be accessed by U.S. traders. This added another layer of competition to the traditional pit traders on the futures exchanges and fostered a global trading environment.

The subprime crisis raised concerns that the "coupling" of markets around the world, and the role played by derivatives in helping to create a "shadow" banking structure, evidenced a need for more regulation. In response to those concerns, the CFTC announced in October 2008 that it was co-chairing a task force of the International Organization of Securities Commissions (IOSCO) that would study global commodity markets and seek to determine whether additional regulation was needed and what form it should take.

EnronOnline

Enron played a leading role in pushing the commodity markets toward electronic trading. EnronOnline was launched in 1999 as an Internet trading platform for energy products. That trading system was developed by one of Enron's gas traders, Louise Kitchen, who convinced others at Enron to work with her, after hours, to develop the system. Even Jeffrey Skilling, the person in charge of trading activities at Enron, was unaware of its existence until a few weeks before its launch. EnronOnline provided real-time quotes posted by Enron traders for wholesale customers. The system had no human interface in the transactions effected. Rather, Enron acted as a principal in the transactions quoted and executed, which provided Enron with a considerable competitive advantage because no one outside the company was aware of the spreads used by the Enron traders to profit on their transactions.

EnronOnline was awarded the *Financial Times*'s "Boldest Successful Business Investment Decision" award. That trading platform was an almost-instant success and eventually traded over 2,000 different commodity contracts in 15 different currencies. Products traded by Enron included U.S.-delivered natural gas and crude oil, weather derivatives, lumber, Argentine natural gas, and Dutch aluminum. EnronOnline executed 548,000 transactions in 2000, with a total notional amount of $336 billion. Before Enron's demise, EnronOnline traded a total of $880 billion in energy contracts.

At its peak, EnronOnline's daily trading volume reached about $2.8 billion per day. This made it a serious competitor to the $13 billion per day in energy contracts traded on NYMEX, then the leading derivatives exchange for energy products. In 2001, EnronOnline traded nearly a quarter of all energy contracts in the United States and earned $3 billion before Enron collapsed. At that time, EnronOnline was the world's largest online energy trading platform. EnronOnline was quickly copied by other energy firms including Dynegy, which operated DynegyDirect. Other competitors included Mirant, Sempra Energy, Reliant Energy, El Paso, and Williams Cos.

After the collapse of Enron, EnronOnline was purchased by UBS Warburg and renamed UBSWenergy.com. However, the CFTC decided to ignore that sale and the terms of the CFMA. The agency brought an action in the Houston Federal District Court that claimed that EnronOnline was an illegal futures exchange that should have been registered with the CFTC. Alternatively, the CFTC claimed that EnronOnline should have notified the agency that the platform was exempt from registration, which it did not do. Of course, everyone in the industry, except possibly the CFTC, was well aware of the existence of the operations of EnronOnline and knew that it was not registered. The district court entered a consent order of permanent injunction in that case, and the Enron estate agreed to pay a $35 million civil monetary penalty to settle the case, depriving more-deserving Enron creditors of that recovery.[15]

Energy Market Manipulations

Enron's innovative development of electronic trading exposed how traders could abuse such unregulated markets. One of the more infamous chapters in the Enron saga was its "gaming" of the California wholesale electricity market in 2000–2001. Enron was able to take unfair advantage of that market because it had been deregulated in an incredibly inept manner by the California state government. California utilities were bankrupted during that failed experiment in deregulation, while Enron made massive profits by exploiting its flaws. San Francisco and other California cities experienced brownouts and blackouts as the system failed. The state also accumulated a massive deficit as it tried to ease the situation, with political consequences. Governor Gray Davis was recalled by voters and replaced with Arnold Schwarzenegger, a.k.a., the "Terminator," who proved to be a better actor than governor, as his state faced bankruptcy during the subprime crisis.

The new "deregulated" structure in California was so flawed that it practically begged to be manipulated, and the Enron traders were quick to oblige. Enron made $1.3 billion in the California electricity market through transactions it variously dubbed "Fat Boy," "Death Star," "Russian Roulette," "Ping Pong," "Donkey," and "Get Shorty." Outrage soon grew when these transactions were made public after Enron failed. That publicity, of course, also attracted criminal prosecutors. Jeff Richter, the head of Enron's California trading operations, pleaded guilty to obstruction of justice for engaging in gaming transactions. Guilty pleas were also obtained from two other Enron traders, Timothy Belden and John Forney. The three traders were given two years' probation and a small fine, a startling contrast to the sentence that was given to Jeffrey Skilling. That leniency stemmed from the fact that, as a part of his guilty plea, Belden agreed to testify against Ken Lay and Skilling. Belden did so at their trial, where he revealed that the Enron traders knew that the California electricity market was susceptible to abuse and that Belden's traders made nearly $1 billion in profits from its shortcomings.

The Justice Department had less success when it became necessary to prove a case of manipulation. Most embarrassing was the decision by the Justice Department to indict Reliant Energy and four of its traders, accused of manipulating the California electricity market during 2001 by shutting down four of five of Reliant's California generating plants. The prosecutors thought that they had a certain victory because tape recordings of the traders' conversations indicated that they had shut down the plants in order to limit supply, so that they could reap larger profits from their trading in electricity. Attorney General John Ashcroft personally announced the indictment of those defendants with great fanfare. The defendants were charged with violating the CEA's prohibition against commodity price manipulation by false reports, a sort of rumor-mongering prohibition.

A federal district court in California allowed the Reliant case to go forward, even though only one other criminal prosecution had been attempted under that false reports prohibition in the sixty-five-year history of the CEA. However, the district court later issued jury instructions and made an evidentiary ruling that made it very difficult for the government to prove its case, and the Court of Appeals for the Ninth Circuit upheld that evidentiary ruling. This convinced the prosecutors that they should settle the case, which they did by imposing a relatively paltry $22 million fine on Reliant Energy. What was most unusual was their granting the defendants a deferred-prosecution agreement after an indictment, particularly one that included the individual defendants and had such lenient terms.

Energy traders also disrupted the natural gas market, even as the electricity crisis in California mounted. However, Enron was only one of a number of firms engaged in manipulating that market. The Federal Energy Regulatory Commission (FERC) concluded that natural gas prices rose to "extraordinary" levels and so facilitated increased electricity prices. Those increases in natural gas prices were found to have been the "result of dysfunctions in the natural gas market [that] stemmed from efforts to manipulate price indices compiled by trade organizations, including reporting of false data and wash trading."[16] This was a reference to "round-trip" trades in the vernacular of the trade, which involved offsetting purchases and sales by the same traders in order to boost their trading volumes, so that it would appear to other market participants that they were large traders with liquidity. These trades were then reported to industry publications such as *Inside FERC's Gas Market Report,* the *Gas Daily,* and *Natural Gas Intelligence.* The FERC staff found that such "false reporting became epidemic."[17] Traders also used round-trip trades to set artificial prices that could be used to justify charging more favorable prices on actual contracts. FERC brought a number of actions against these traders under its power to regulate natural gas and electricity.

Disruptions in the energy markets also attracted the attention of the CFTC. Although the CFTC prudently let others address the complex issues raised by the California electricity market, it responded to the Enron-era scandals arising from the natural gas market by bringing enforcement actions against several large energy firms. It charged in those cases that the reporting of round-trip trades and false reports to widely read industry publications constituted an attempt at manipulation by false price reports. The CFTC also charged that the false price reports submitted to industry publications constituted an attempt at manipulation of commodity market prices even though no regulated commodity exchange was involved, which took the agency rather far afield from its traditional focus on the futures exchanges.

The commission also significantly expanded the traditional concept of manipulation, using claims of false reports both as a separate charge and as a part of an "attempted" manipulation claim. It adopted this new approach in order to spare itself the burdensome, often impossible, task of proving an actual manipulation, which would require it to show that: (1) the trader had a specific intent to create an artificial price; (2) the trader had the actual ability to influence prices through market power; (3) an artificial price was present; and (4) the trader caused the artificial price.[18] Under the CFTC's novel doctrine of attempted manipulation, it need only prove an overt act (the false report) and manipulative intent. With respect to the latter, according to the CFTC, a false report charge requires only a showing that a report was false and knowingly made.[19]

The CFTC lost the first case that went to trial under its newly created theories.[20] A federal district court judge also threw out a CFTC case claiming false reporting of cattle prices to the Agriculture Department. The motivation for reporting the suspect cattle prices was "suspicious," but proof of an intent to manipulate failed. At this point, the CFTC had not been able to prove even a single case of manipulation in court. The CFTC did convince a jury that Anthony Dizona, a trader for Shell Trading Gas and Power Company, had attempted to manipulate natural gas prices on eight occasions between October 2001 and June 2002 by making false reports to industry trade publications such as *Platts* and *Intelligence Press, Inc.* The jury rejected the false report charges. The CFTC charged that Dizona had acted with five other traders, who settled the charges brought against them, to circulate e-mails instructing one another on how to report prices in a way that would benefit their positions. However, the trial judge set aside the jury verdict, and the Fifth Circuit Court of Appeals affirmed the trial judge's action.

A district court ruled favorably in a case brought by the CFTC against Hunter Shively, a trader at Enron Online. Shively was charged with attempted manipulation after engaging in a massive fifteen-minute buying spree in Henry Hub natural gas spot market contracts through EnronOnline. Shively agreed to cover any losses among traders who assisted that operation. The court noted that, historically, manipulation required a purchase of long futures contracts in excess of deliverable supplies or by the purchase of the entire cash supply, or a combination of both. However, the court concluded that proof of control of the relevant cash market was no longer necessary to prove attempted manipulation.[21] Shively paid $300,000 to the CFTC to settle the case after the judge's decision.

This change in the law by the CFTC was not harmless bureaucratic over-reaching. It put traders in jeopardy from second-guessing by government investigators for any aggressive trading practice. This will, of course, breed timidity, but fearful traders will lead to worse, not better, or more efficient, price discovery—the core goal of the CEA and the fundamental policy support for commodity markets. Nevertheless, this unilateral change in legal standards was a successful strategy, at least from the view of the agency. Between 2002 and 2007, the CFTC filed thirty-nine cases that charged attempted manipulation and false reporting. The agency collected fines totaling over $434 million in settlements. The respondents in those actions included many of the largest energy companies. One of those cases was settled by Sempra Energy for $410 million in April 2010, some ten years later.

This cornucopia of cash could not be ignored by the Justice Department, which brought a joint action with the CFTC against BP America, one of the largest energy companies in the world. The government charged that BP had manipulated the propane market for residential and commercial heating in the Northeast in February 2004 and that it attempted to manipulate that market in April 2003. The joint actions charged that BP and its employees claimed to "control the market at will," allowing BP to dictate prices and reap large trading profits. BP agreed to pay the CFTC $125 million in fines and $53 million in restitution to propane consumers. This was the largest settlement for a manipulation case in the CFTC's history, but it was nothing to brag about. It was simply the result of coercion, through the threat of criminal prosecution by the Justice Department, which would have destroyed BP. The payments demanded by the Justice Department for avoiding a criminal indictment included an additional $100 million in fines and another $25 million into a consumer fraud fund. BP also agreed to establish a compliance and ethics program and to hire an independent corporate "monitor" to oversee its trading activities. Four BP traders were indicted for their role in the activity.[22] As a measure of the flimsiness of the government's case against BP, a federal court subsequently dismissed the indictment brought against the individual BP traders, finding that the government's legal theory was flawed. The government appealed that decision. BP ran into even more serious problems from the massive oil spill in the Gulf of Mexico after an explosion on a drilling rig.

The Justice Department brought several other criminal cases based on the CFTC's new attempted manipulation and false reports theory. In one of those cases, a trader at El Paso, Todd Geiger, pleaded guilty to criminal charges of submitting false information to *Inside FERC Gas Market Report* with respect to El Paso's trading in natural gas. A Merrill Lynch broker, Daniel Gordon, pleaded guilty to criminal charges in connection with some electricity derivative transactions that allowed Enron to book $50 million income in order to meet 1999 earnings targets. Gordon structured the transaction in a way that allowed him to pocket several million dollars for his own use.

Like the CFTC, the Justice Department had only mixed success when its claims were tested in court, as demonstrated by the dismissal of the case against the BP traders. A jury acquitted Duke Energy trader Todd Reid of federal criminal charges that he had engaged in round-trip trading in order to boost his bonus. The jury also acquitted Timothy Kramer, another Duke Energy executive, of several of the same charges. The jury was hung on other charges, but the government announced that it would not retry Kramer on those charges. The government also allowed another Duke trader, Brian Lavielle, to withdraw his guilty plea in connection with this trading, and those charges were then dismissed.

Criminal charges were brought against Michelle Valencia, a trader at Dynegy, for engaging in round-trip trades. She offered to surrender voluntarily for booking, but the prosecutors had her arrested in front of her children and subjected her to the customary perp walk.

The district court hearing the false reports case against Valencia ruled that the false-report prohibition in the CEA was void on account of vagueness insofar as it prohibited false reports without requiring that they be knowingly false or misleading. The district court later amended its opinion to declare the false-reporting requirement only partially unconstitutional. The Court of Appeals for the Fifth Circuit upheld the constitutionality of the provision. However, the government was unable to obtain a conviction from the jury on the false-reporting charges against Valencia and another Dynegy Trader, Greg Singleton. The jury found them guilty of wire fraud, suggesting that existing laws on fraud were adequate to deal with price-reporting problems without bending other statutes to obtain a conviction.[23]

Four El Paso Corporation traders pleaded guilty to making false price reports to trade publications, and the government was able to convict three other El Paso traders after a trial in February 2008. They were given prison sentences that ranged from fourteen years to eleven years and two months. The El Paso Corporation had also been involved in another Enron-era scandal. The company had overstated its oil and natural gas reserves by 35 percent, requiring it to restate five years of earnings and to take a $1.7 billion charge to equity for 2003 and 2004. El Paso and some of its executives settled SEC charges over those problems in 2008. The company was enjoined from further such conduct, and the individual defendants, including its former president, agreed to pay civil penalties that varied from $40,000 to $75,000, totaling a mere $235,000. Royal Dutch Shell, which had engaged in similar misconduct, but in a smaller amount, had earlier paid $150 million in fines to the SEC and British regulators. No reason was given for this disparity in treatment.

FERC Powers

The Energy Policy Act of 2005[24] expanded FERC's power to attack energy price manipulations by essentially adopting the broad anti-manipulation language used in the Securities Exchange Act of 1934, rather than the more-difficult-to-prove language in the Commodity Exchange Act that prohibits commodity price manipulation. An issue arose over whether FERC jurisdiction extended to transactions in the commodity futures markets, where the CFTC had traditionally had exclusive jurisdiction. In October 2005, the CFTC and FERC entered into a memorandum of understanding (MOU) to address their respective roles where futures contracts were involved in suspected energy price manipulation. According to the MOU, each agency agreed to refer to the other potential violations that were within their respective jurisdiction. FERC was also to be given access to information from commodity exchanges, if needed, in connection with its investigations.

What this MOU really meant was double jeopardy in regulatory actions by both FERC and the CFTC. That proved the case in simultaneous actions filed by both the CFTC and FERC against Energy Transfer Partners, charged with violating the anti-manipulation statutory provisions administered by both agencies as a result of its trading in physical natural gas. Why it was necessary to have two government agencies bring actions against the same company, for the same conduct, defies an answer, especially since government agencies are always claiming they do not have adequate resources to carry out their missions.

Despite their MOU, a related high-profile case resulted in a jurisdictional conflict between the CFTC and FERC. In that case, a thirty-two-year-old trader, Brian Hunter, who worked for a large hedge fund, Amaranth Advisors, lost over $6 billion in a one-week period in September 2006 from trading in energy products. Interest in that loss was heightened by the fact that the Amaranth energy trading department was started by several former traders from Enron after its collapse.[25] The energy trading group at Amaranth had some spectacular successes, making large profits from deep out-of-the-money options (options with strike prices far off the existing market) on natural gas that became profitable after Hurricanes Katrina and Rita. The company also gained large profits from natural gas energy swaps in 2005. However, Amaranth switched its outlook in 2006 from bullish to strongly bearish, a change in view that was its undoing. In implementing its strategy, Amaranth was responsible for almost 70 percent of the open interest in the January 2007 NYMEX natural gas futures contract. At one point it was short more than 100,000 natural gas futures contracts. A move of just one cent would cause a loss of $10 million on such a position.

At first, Amaranth's short strategy was successful, resulting in a $1 billion profit in April 2006. However, the market subsequently turned against the company, causing it to suffer large losses. Amaranth's positions then began to attract the attention of regulators. NYMEX forced Amaranth to reduce its positions on that exchange, but Amaranth, using a regulatory arbitrage, simply shifted its positions to the unregulated market on the IntercontinentalExchange (ICE), an electronic exchange located in Atlanta, Georgia. ICE was an ECM that had become a major global marketplace for trading futures and OTC energy derivative contracts. ICE was the creation of Jeffrey Sprecher, who founded it in 2000 as an electronic marketplace for energy derivatives. ICE experienced rapid success and became a substitute for EnronOnline after Enron's collapse. Several large energy companies and financial institutions backed ICE, including Royal Dutch Shell and Goldman Sachs.

ICE, a publicly traded company on NASDAQ, grew rapidly. It acquired the International Petroleum Exchange in London, which was a leading open-outcry market for petroleum products that was then converted into an electronic market. An ICE affiliate, ICE Futures U.S., was a designated contract market under the CEA and, therefore, could also conduct a retail business. ICE used that market for its soft commodity, foreign exchange, and equity index trading. Another affiliate, ICE Futures Europe, was a "Recognized Investment Exchange" regulated by the Financial Services Authority (FSA) in London. ICE markets in London conducted sales and marketing activities and were also regulated by the FSA. ICE Futures Europe traded about half the world's global crude futures. Volume on other foreign commodity exchanges outpaced that in the United States.

ICE acquired the New York Board of Trade (NYBOT) in 2007 for $1.8 billion. NYBOT had earlier acquired the New York Futures Exchange, a failed NYSE venture to enter the futures markets. ICE was then operating the New York Cotton Exchange, the Financial Instruments Exchange (Finex), the Coffee, Sugar, and Cocoa Exchange, and the Winnipeg Commodity Exchange. ICE announced that it was shuttering most of the floor trading on those exchanges in 2008, causing a sharp rise in ICE stock and placing additional pressure on competitors to shut down their old-fashioned trading floors.

ICE operated an electronic trading platform for institutional traders in the United States as an ECM and supposedly exempt from CFTC regulation. However, ICE became a focal point for regulatory concerns as energy prices spiked and the size of Amaranth's trading was revealed. In the end, Amaranth's regulatory arbitrage did not work to its benefit. The market continued to turn against Amaranth, and it closed its positions in September 2006, after suffering massive losses. The CFTC and FERC then brought separate cases against Amaranth and two of its traders, charging energy price manipulation. As the district court in the CFTC action noted, "Hence, Amaranth is being pursued by two federal regulatory agencies in two separate proceedings in two different jurisdictions, based on the same alleged conduct."[26]

Amaranth claimed that the CFTC had exclusive jurisdiction over manipulation claims in the futures markets. However, FERC claimed that its new jurisdictional mandate under the Energy Policy Act of 2005 was not so limited. The district court judge refused to enjoin the FERC action, even though he had some sympathy for the defendant's plight. Another federal district court made a similar ruling in still another duplicative action by the CFTC and FERC.[27] Amaranth later reached a settlement with the FERC staff, but it was rejected as too lenient by FERC. That hurdle was overcome in August 2009, after Amaranth agreed to pay $7.5 million to settle both the FERC and CFTC cases. In what must be a regulatory first, the SEC decided not to sue Amaranth.

More Regulation

The price of oil had reached $70 a barrel on April 17, 2006, and then jumped to $75 a barrel, pushing prices at the pump to over $3 per gallon. This price explosion set off shockwaves throughout the economy and led to cries for a windfall profits tax, a demand that grew after the oil companies reported billions in profits. Congress then sent the Federal Trade Commission (FTC) on a mission to see whether gasoline refiners, large wholesalers, and retailers had engaged in "price gouging." Congress also directed the FTC to investigate whether gasoline prices nationwide were artificially boosted by reductions in refinery capacity or any other form of market manipulation. In a report issued on May 22, 2006, the FTC said it found no instances of illegal market manipulation that led to higher prices, but did find fifteen examples of what initially appeared to be "price gouging" that could be explained by other factors, such as regional or local market trends.

The FTC report also stated that any federal gasoline price-gouging legislation would be unenforceable and could cause more problems for consumers than it would solve. The report further stated that competitive market forces should be allowed to determine the price of gasoline at the pump. Those market forces proved to be upward bound, as the price of crude oil continued to climb well into 2008. That continuing rise caused Congress to hold hearings during the summer of 2008 on proposals to ban speculation in crude oil. The *Wall Street Journal* pointed out in an editorial that the last time that Congress sought to ban speculation in a commodity was in 1958, when it prohibited futures trading on onions. The onion legislation, which was sponsored by then-Representative Gerald Ford (R-MI), had no effect on the wildly fluctuating prices of onions that had aroused congressional ire. Indeed, an economic study concluded that prices were actually more stable before the ban, which still remains in effect.

An interagency task force was formed in 2008 to determine what was driving up crude oil prices. That task force was chaired by the CFTC and included representatives from the Energy, Agriculture, and Treasury Departments, the Federal Reserve, the FTC, and the SEC. On July 22, 2008, the task force released its report, which concluded that increases in oil prices between 2003 and 2008 were largely due to the fundamentals of supply and demand, rather than to speculation. The size of the crude oil futures market was found to have grown significantly during that period, but the interagency task force could find no support for the proposition that speculative activity had systematically driven changes in oil prices.[28] The task force also confirmed the obvious, namely, the reason for the price increases was imbalance between supply and demand.

This did not satisfy members of Congress, who continued to blame unknown speculators for the phenomenal rise in commodity prices. They were given support in July 2009, after the Obama administration's CFTC appointees decided to rewrite history by declaring that the intergovernmental task force study was wrong and that speculators had played a large role in the volatility in the energy markets in 2008. European regulators and the CFTC announced plans for imposing restrictions on speculators in the crude oil market on July 7, 2009, as prices began to rise again. The CFTC did refute a claim by Senator Carl Levin (D-MI) that traders in London on the ICE Futures Europe exchange were having an undue effect on West Texas intermediate oil prices. It determined that NYMEX traders had the greatest influence on prices. Levin had wanted to use that trading as a pretext for regulating the London ICE exchange.

Congress unexpectedly granted the FTC authority to prosecute faulty reporting and market manipulation in the wholesale petroleum market. That was accomplished through provisions in the Energy Act of 2007, signed into law in December of that year.[29] This means that now three agencies are directly charged with attacking manipulative trading in the energy markets: the CFTC, FERC, and the FTC, as well as the Justice Department for criminal prosecutions. The FTC furthered this overlap in regulation by proposing a rule prohibiting manipulation in both futures and the cash market, the former of which had been the domain of the CFTC. It also adopted the same form of anti-manipulation rule as used by FERC and the SEC, rather than that of the CFTC. Not to be outdone, the CFTC asked Congress in 2009 for power to conduct its own criminal prosecutions of violators of the Commodity Exchange Act. That would be unique power, because the Justice Department is currently the only body entrusted with such authority.

Index Traders

The volume of futures trading increased by 500 percent between 1998 and 2008. A part of that increase was attributable to "index" traders, who took long-term passive positions in commodity futures contracts. Index traders using the Goldman Sachs Commodity Index (GSCI), the Dow Jones–AIG Commodity Index (DJ-AIG), and the Deutsche Bank index were estimated to be holding positions valued at over $200 billion. These index traders included pension and endowment funds that sought to obtain exposure from commodity prices as a part of their portfolio diversification strategies through passive investing in the commodity market indexes traded on the futures exchanges.

The CFTC became alarmed with this index trading, but it is unclear why. Indexing is merely diversifying an asset class. Index traders with a long-term view seemed to be simply following a recognized modern portfolio strategy of diversification. That theory posits that a passive portfolio in a diversified group of assets provides a return higher than could be achieved by the best stock, or in this case commodity, picker.

To be sure, index trading was increasing the open interest on the exchanges and required larger contract rollovers as the existing contracts expired, but that process seemed to proceed smoothly.[30] Nevertheless, index trading was viewed with increasing suspicion as commodity prices spiked.

An investigation of index traders by the CFTC in September 2008 found no conclusive evidence of any adverse effects from the trading of long-term commodity index traders, and the CFTC was unable to conclude that those traders had pushed up prices. In fact, it appeared that the index traders had been reducing their positions as prices increased. Nevertheless, a Senate committee charged in June 2009 that index traders was interfering with agricultural price-hedging operations.

Interestingly, a study by the CFTC's chief economist concluded that the degree of correlation between commodity and equity investment returns had not changed materially over the previous fifteen years. Those asset classes had a very low correlation, and the rates of return on passive investments in the two asset classes had become negative in the previous five years.[31] The CFTC also turned its attention to exchange traded funds (ETFs) that allowed small investors to gain exposure to commodity prices, particularly gold. These funds had exploded in popularity with the rise in gold and other commodity prices. However, the CFTC under the Obama administration curbed this trading by imposing speculative limits on the amount of trading that any one ETF could conduct in a commodity. One proposal bandied about in Congress, as a way to curb energy prices, was to increase margin requirements for traders in energy futures on the commodity exchanges. Critics charged that this would push traders into unregulated markets and limit transparency of trading on futures markets.

The Enron Loophole

As is usual whenever scandal occurs, more regulation was added in the wake of the collapse of Amaranth. The CFTC required large traders on commodity futures markets to report their transactions in exempt markets as well as those in the regulated markets. The CFTC also examined whether to regulate swap dealers that were providing nonindependent research to traders utilizing their facilities. Perhaps the CFTC expected a reprise of a financial analyst scandal in the securities industry, but it was, in all events, seeking to regulate the markets exempted by the CFMA in 2000.

The CFTC announced on September 11, 2008, that it was considering a requirement to regulate swap market participants by requiring swap dealers to report their positions. As a condition of maintaining their eligibility for exemption from DCM regulation, swap dealers would be required to report client positions when they reached certain large-trader reporting levels. Under the CFTC proposal, swap dealers would also have to certify that their clients were not exceeding CFTC speculative limits. Pressure from Congress and the press was forcing the CFTC into this more active role. However, the CFTC was hamstrung in expanding its regulatory reach by a relatively small budget. The SEC's budget ballooned to $906 million in 2008, while the CFTC received only $112 million.

In 2007, the president's Corporate Fraud Task Force reported that the government had imposed over $2.3 billion in sanctions for futures-related manipulation and fraud in the prior five years. The CFTC was on the front line of agencies attacking market participants and imposing record-breaking levels of civil penalties in the process. The CFTC collected over $430 million in civil penalties from energy market manipulation cases. However, a 2007 report by the Government Accountability Office (GAO) on derivative trading in the energy markets questioned the CFTC's oversight ability.[32] The CFTC tried to defend itself with an extensive study on trading in the energy markets, and the CFTC asked Congress for more regulatory authority over ECMs.[33] It also expanded its reporting requirements over ECMs.

The ECM exclusion was often referred to as the "Enron loophole," or "Enron exemption," because it was inserted into the CFMA at the last minute through the lobbying efforts of Enron, which sought at the time to protect its popular electronic trading platform, EnronOnline, from regulation. After Enron imploded in scandal, however, this exemption became suspect. The ECM exemption was exploited by ICE to create a viable, unregulated institutional trading market, but the lack of regulation in those markets caused many to find them suspect.

The imposition of additional regulation could also drive these markets offshore. It would take little effort for ICE to move its present ECM institutional trading operations from Atlanta to London or elsewhere in the world. It is an electronic exchange that is not dependent on any particular facility or location. An ECM transfer to London would be subject to regulation there by the FSA, which, at least until the subprime crisis, had a much lighter regulatory touch than U.S. regulators. The CFTC recognized this vulnerability and, in June 2008, asked the FSA to impose speculative position limits on oil traders operating through ICE Futures Europe, where trading was being shifted as regulatory scrutiny increased in the United States.

Responding to pressure from consumer concerns over skyrocketing energy prices, Congress closed the Enron loophole through amendments included in the CFTC Reauthorization Act of 2008 that was enacted as Title XIII of the Food, Conservation, and Energy Act of 2008 (the Farm Bill). That legislation was passed over a presidential veto on May 22, 2008, but, as a result of a clerical error, one of the titles in the bill had been inadvertently omitted in the version vetoed by President George W. Bush. A slightly embarrassed Congress then voted to present a complete version of the legislation to the president, and it was passed once again over his second veto of the legislation on June 18, 2008.

The amendments in the Farm Bill relating to the Enron exemption might be best referred to as the "ICE amendments" because of concerns over trading in energy contracts on that exchange raised by the Amaranth regulatory arbitrage. To no avail, ICE supporters argued that such regulation was not needed. They pointed out that the Amaranth liquidation had been handled smoothly and that nothing in that affair justified additional regulation. The new amendments sought to close the Enron exemption by subjecting ECMs to CFTC position limits, record-keeping requirements, and large-trader reporting requirements, in those instances where the CFTC determined that an ECM was trading a "significant price discovery contract" (SPD). An SPD was defined as a contract traded on an otherwise exempt ECM that has a price linkage to contracts traded on a regulated contract market or that is used as a material price reference for price transactions in the underlying commodity.

The ICE amendments required the CFTC to monitor trading in SPDs. The legislation effectively regulated ECMs trading SPDs in much the same manner as regulated contract markets. The ECM must comply with nine core principles that, among other things, require the ECM to take steps to prevent price manipulation, to provide information to the CFTC upon request, to adopt rules imposing speculative position limits, and to publish daily price and volume information on SPDs. Large traders on an ECM trading SPDs are also required to report their trades to the CFTC. This legislation increased the maximum civil penalty for manipulation violations to $1 million, and the maximum criminal penalty for such violations was raised to ten years in prison.

Despite the ICE amendments, critics of deregulation under the CFMA continued to claim that the Enron loophole had not been completely closed. Specifically, trading on foreign exchanges through electronic terminals in the United States was still exempt from regulation. It was also claimed that the Farm Bill erred in placing the burden on the CFTC to show that a contract met the requirements for SPD designation. In response to such concerns, legislation was introduced in the House, called the Prevent Unfair Manipulation of Prices (PUMP) Act. That legislation, if enacted, would require all U.S. delivered futures energy contracts executed in the United States to be traded on a U.S. contract market regulated by the CFTC. It would also bar OTC swap contracts in energy products.

Washington politicians continued to blame speculators for the rise in commodity and energy prices. Largely led by Democratic members of Congress, they sought all forms of regulation and chastised the CFTC for not halting runaway commodity prices. Senator Joseph Lieberman (D-CT) tried to bar large financial institutions from trading in commodity markets. That seems a bit absurd because the long-held justification for those markets was their use by institutions to price commodities and to hedge their commodity price risks. However, the markets did have one champion. The otherwise extremely liberal senator Richard Durbin (D-IL) sought to stop efforts to curb futures trading—unsurprising considering that his principal constituency is Chicago, where futures trading is one of the larger industries.

Congress held more than forty hearings on skyrocketing crude oil prices in the first six months of 2008. Dozens of bills were introduced to attack speculators. None of this hand-wringing did any good. Corn prices surpassed $7 a bushel on June 11, 2007, a new record. Wheat and soybean prices also jumped after some unprecedented rainstorms destroyed a substantial portion of the crops in the Midwest. On the same day, crude oil prices increased by more than $5 a barrel, but that was not the end of that price increase. About a year later, on July 2, 2008, crude oil prices closed at $143.57, and gasoline prices exceeded $4 a gallon. However, within less than six months from that lofty peak, crude oil would trade for about $100 less a barrel as consumption waned and oil stocks rose.

ECNs in the Commodity Markets

The colorful open-outcry trading in the pits of the Chicago futures exchanges has long dominated the public perception of how those markets operate. Those exchanges are now in the midst of radical changes, however, that will soon make those images obsolete. Exchange trading floors are fast fading into history as the trading of derivative instruments moves to electronic communication networks (ECNs) that match trades by computers through algorithms. As in the stock exchanges, competition from ECNs has forced the futures exchanges to demutualize, consolidate, and reduce the role of their trading floors, while expanding their own electronic execution facilities.

Historically, the commodity futures industry accepted computerization into its clearing processes as quickly as the technology became available. That technology was needed because of the exchanges' requirement that all trades be matched and cleared before the opening of business the next day. However, no thought was given to computerizing the futures exchange trading floor until the adoption of the Commodity Futures Trading Commission Act of 1974.[34] That legislation required the CFTC to study how computers could aid trading in the industry. In 1977 the CFTC held a conference on that topic, and papers presented there were critical of the perceived inefficiencies of the open-outcry trading system on exchange trading floors.

That criticism had no effect on the futures exchanges. Leo Melamed, a senior official at the Chicago Mercantile Exchange (CME) and a leading figure in the industry, published a passionate defense of open-outcry trading in a widely read article published in the *Hofstra Law Review*.[35] Melamed argued that the psychology of the trading pit generated information that contributed to price efficiency and brought liquidity to the market from the trading by locals. This was the oft-cited defense of floor trading that continues even today: the physiological lift from the noise and energy of the trading crowd that inspires traders to take risks. Actually, the time and place advantage of floor traders over that of other traders is its principal attraction.

The futures exchanges' defense of their trading floors came under increasing criticism as volume expanded. Trading pits and rings for popular financial products became overcrowded, and execution times were delayed in times of high volume. Capacity constraints became a pressing issue for market users. John Conheeney, chairman of Merrill Lynch Futures, noted in 1984, "There isn't a person in the industry who wouldn't agree that the system is breaking down, but we don't see any concrete moves toward a solution, which is the most frightening aspect of the problem." Conheeney contended that merely adding more space on the trading floors, as the exchanges were then planning, was not the solution. Nonetheless, he asserted that "black box" computer trading "lacks the vital human element that makes a market work." Like Melamed, he claimed that "'pit psychology,' eye contact and the chemistry between traders, were often as important in determining prices as the market's technical factors and fundamentals of supply and demand."[36]

The futures exchanges continued their ostrich-like approach to automated execution, but demand was growing for extended trading hours. Trading floors were open only for the limited number of hours permitted by the stamina of the floor traders. Worldwide events with effects on the market often occurred after the close of trading, but traders could not respond to those events until the opening of trading the next day. They, therefore, wanted the ability to trade outside regular trading hours. The demand for extended trading hours led to a linkage between the CME and the Singapore International Monetary Exchange (SIMEX) in 1984. That link allowed trades to be opened on the SIMEX in the evening and reciprocally closed on the CME on the next day or at some other time. The SIMEX link was a substitute for computerized execution, but it was limited in the number of commodities covered and was tied to the floor trading operations of CME members.

The International Futures Exchange (Intex) was created in 1984 by a former Merrill Lynch executive as the first computerized commodity exchange. It was based in Bermuda in order to avoid CFTC regulation, particularly it wanted to avoid the delay of seeking contract market status from the CFTC. Intex traded futures on gold and other commodities and cleared its trades through the London International Commodity Clearing House. Although Intex was not particularly successful, it signaled the future.

Electronic Trading Delayed

The demand for after-hours trading continued to grow. In 1987, CBOT began open-outcry trading in evening sessions, but those sessions were sparsely attended. In 1989, the CME announced the development of a computerized trading system called Global Exchange (Globex) that was to be developed by Reuters Holdings. This system matched buy and sell orders on the basis of time and price after the trading pits closed. CBOT responded to Globex with an announcement that it was developing its own computerized trading system, named Aurora, that would compete with Globex and pose no threat to floor traders during normal trading hours. Aurora never really got off the ground, and CBOT joined Globex.

More pressure for electronic trading arrived in 1989, after a massive FBI sting operation on the CME and CBOT exposed widespread fraud and questionable trading activities. As always, the government was overzealous in its prosecutions of the traders involved in the Chicago sting operation. They were arrested in their homes and threatened with long prison sentences if they did not turn on their fellow traders. Many of the indicted traders insisted on a trial, and the government had only mixed success in obtaining convictions from juries, but was able to obtain a number of guilty pleas.

The practices uncovered by the FBI sting were made possible by archaic trading practices on the floor that involved "dual" trading floor brokers and floor traders ("locals") and the lack of an adequate audit trail that shielded those activities. Former senator (and one-time vice presidential candidate) Thomas Eagleton made headlines by resigning from the CME board after charging that the exchange was filled with conflicts of interest. He recommended that the trading floor be replaced with an electronic trading system that would provide a better audit trail.

The Chicago Sting did not, in any event, stop abuses on the commodity exchange trading floors. Robert M. Morgenthau, district attorney for New York County, indicted seven NYMEX traders in 2008. Steven Karvellas, a NYMEX floor trader, pleaded guilty to felony charges. He had been trading against customer orders and engaging in other fraudulent practices that cheated customers. Karvellas had served on the NYMEX board of directors, had been on its executive committee, and had chaired its compliance committee.

Globex's after-hours trading limitation caused it to struggle to obtain a profit, and CBOT withdrew from the venture in 1994 in favor of its own Project A, an electronic system that never worked very well. CBOT opened a new trading floor in 1997 that was supposed to employ the newest technology, but that exchange remained devoted to open-outcry trading in the pits. New innovations were added elsewhere in the industry. Floor brokers adopted "Electronic Clerk" and "Cubs" devices that allowed them to receive orders electronically in the pits, lessening the need for phone clerks and "runners" who had traditionally relayed customer orders into the pits either in writing or by "flashing" orders to the floor broker through hand signals. Those efforts did not succeed in meeting the competition from foreign exchanges that were becoming increasingly all electronic.

Competition from Abroad

CBOT and the CME's worldwide share of futures and options trading was plummeting, dropping from about 75 percent of all futures trading in 1987 to under 50 percent in 1992. Competition from new exchanges abroad was fierce. "The [American] exchanges have been losing ground to the approximately fifty commodity exchanges outside the United States, about half of which have been founded since 1985. Off-exchange deals between banks and other institutional investors are also a rapidly growing part of the derivatives business."[37]

One upstart foreign exchange was the London International Financial Futures Exchange (LIFFE), which began trading in 1982. It initially modeled its trading operations after those in Chicago, utilizing open-outcry pit trading for executing orders. However, the Deutsche Terminbörse, now called Eurex, a joint venture of the Deutsche Börse and the Swiss Stock Exchange, opened a competing all-electronic exchange in 1989. Ironically, futures trading was not legalized in Germany until the 1980s, and then only after U.S. brokers successfully advocated a change in German law that had, theretofore, treated futures contracts as prohibited illegal gambling.[38]

The competition between Eurex and LIFFE over the German Bund futures contract, one of the most heavily traded financial instruments in the world, proved that electronic trading could compete successfully against open-outcry trading on the floor of an exchange, in that case, LIFFE. In early 1997, LIFFE handled about 65 percent of Bund futures trading, but within two years all trading volume had moved to Eurex. LIFFE then dropped its open-outcry trading system and became an all-electronic exchange.

CBOT had joined in the Eurex competition through a joint clearing link with LIFFE, but its participation could not save LIFFE's open-outcry operations. "In France, MATIF, the derivatives exchange that is a unit of the Paris bourse, tried to offer both electronic and open-outcry trading in April 1998. A month later, most trading migrated to computers and the trading floor was shuttered."[39]

The Chicago exchanges only slowly awakened to the threat from electronic competition, but by the end of the twentieth century even Melamed, the most ardent defender of open-outcry trading, was in full retreat. He sounded the tocsin for this pullback in a May 1999 address at an industry conference in New York. Melamed faulted the regulatory structure for the erosion of U.S. market share in futures trading, but he also stated: "If the futures exchanges fail to quickly embrace current technological and competitive demands, . . . then our exchanges may well be doomed."[40] The Chicago exchanges were still sluggish in their response to the electronic threat. They began a desperate effort to link with foreign electronic markets in order to cling to their remaining businesses. The CME announced a link with the MATIF (Marché à Terme International de France) in Paris, which was then combined with SIMEX.

Treasury bond futures were CBOT's highest-volume contract and were among the most actively traded futures contracts in the world. Electronic competitors arrived to challenge CBOT's monopoly in the trading of futures on Treasury obligations. The New York Cotton Exchange, which had merged with the Coffee, Sugar, and Cocoa Exchange to become the New York Board of Trade (NYBOT), entered into a joint venture in 1998 with Cantor Fitzgerald, a New York government securities trader, in the creation of an electronic futures exchange, the Cantor Financial Futures Exchange (CFFE), to compete with CBOT floor traders. Reacting to this threat CBOT quickly announced that it was opening its own electronic market in those contracts. CFFE responded with a completely interactive electronic trading platform, but it was not successful in challenging the CBOT monopoly.

In 2001 BrokerTec Futures Exchange (BrokerTec), an electronic futures market owned by several large Wall Street investment banks, mounted another challenge to CBOT's monopoly in the trading of Treasury futures, but did not compete successfully either. However, this electronic competition led to the creation of a strategic global alliance between Eurex and CBOT. Under that arrangement Eurex's electronic trading platform replaced CBOT's Project A electronic system. However, this strategic global alliance was an uneasy one because a significant amount of volume in Treasury futures contracts moved from open-outcry trading on the CBOT floor to the Eurex electronic trading system.

CBOT was conflicted over the continued role of open-outcry trading. A hotly contested election over the position of CBOT chairman occurred, in which the central issue was the support of the incumbent chairman, Patrick Arbor, of the Eurex alliance, rather than to upgrade Project A to carry out side-by-side electronic and open-outcry trading. The winner of the election was the CBOT's leader of the "Flat Earth Society," David Brennan. After that vote, Eurex advised CBOT that it would scrap their strategic global alliance if Project A were used instead of the Eurex trading platform. The CBOT membership voted and rejected the strategic global alliance with Eurex in January 1999. It was during that month that Eurex displaced CBOT as the world's largest futures exchange in terms of volume of trading.

In May 1999, after another internal power struggle, the CBOT board voted to revive talks with Eurex. The CBOT membership voted on the issue again in June and this time overwhelmingly approved an alliance with Eurex. In another CBOT power struggle that occurred in April 2000, Brennan succeeded in ousting twenty-year veteran CBOT president and CEO Thomas Donovan, who had supported the alliance with Eurex. CBOT then tried to block the success of the electronic trading on the Eurex platform by declaring that fees for electronic trades would be substantially higher than those for trades conducted in the open-outcry pits.

More uncertainty was added to the strategic global alliance with Eurex after Nickolas Neubauer upset Brennan in elections for CBOT chairman in December 2000. Eurex and CBOT continued to have problems in their relationship, and its terms were renegotiated. That too failed to satisfy CBOT, and it subsequently replaced the Eurex electronic trading platform with one developed by Euronext.liffe, an exchange in Europe that operated the LIFFE Connect electronic trading system.

In the meantime, Eurex had become a competitive threat to CBOT. Before the introduction of the Eurex electronic trading platform in August 2000, only about 22 percent of Treasury futures on CBOT were executed electronically. Within a year after introduction of the Eurex electronic trading platform, that percentage increased to 45 percent and eventually reached 80 percent. On January 10, 2003, Eurex announced its intention to launch the United States Futures Exchange (USFE) as a U.S. futures exchange that would compete head-to-head with CBOT's most popular products, futures, and options on futures on Treasury obligations. However, USFE, unable to obtain significant market share from CBOT, responded with an antitrust action against the Chicago exchanges, charging that they had teamed up and acted improperly to prevent USFE from competing successfully.[41]

Competition and Consolidation

FutureCom submitted the first application to the CFTC to be designated as a contract market for Internet-only trading. Several other electronic futures markets appeared, including CBOE Futures Exchange, HedgeStreet, NQLX, and OneChicago. The CME faced competition from a proposed new exchange being formed by several large banks and financial services firms, including Merrill Lynch, JPMorgan Chase, Deutsche Bank, and Bank of America. However, the subprime crisis seems to have delayed, if not derailed, that plan.

The OTC derivative markets continued to expand. The markets witnessed a return of "difference" trades, which are merely bets on changes in the price of a security. They had previously been outlawed under state laws as gambling contracts. One famous case involving such contracts was won by the estate of General George Armstrong Custer, allowing his estate to avoid losses that he had incurred from such trading before his death at the Little Big Horn. More recently, in 2008, a federal district court rejected a similar claim. Crocs, a footwear manufacturer, lost a large sum from trading in "contracts for difference" that are now being traded widely internationally. The district court rejected claims that such contracts were illegal futures contracts. Rather, it held that these were securities that were subject to the federal securities laws.

Innovation continued in the futures industry. The CFTC sought comment on the appropriate regulatory treatment of financial agreements called event, prediction, or information contracts. Such event contracts are based on eventualities and measure such things as the world's population in some future year, the results of political elections, or the outcome of particular entertainment events, say, a horse race or box office receipts. In years past, such contracts were declared to be gambling and barred. However, it was now argued that these events should be the subject of predictive trading.

The CME and CBOT merged their clearing operations in 2003, and both the CME (in 2002) and CBOT (in 2005) demutualized and became public companies. Still, the proportion of open-outcry trades declined between 2000 and 2007, from 90 percent to 22 percent. Recognizing that the end was near for such trading, CBOT and the CME merged the remainder of their operations in 2007.

That merger was nearly spoiled by a competing bid from ICE for CBOT, in the amount of $11.9 billion. The CME raised its bid for CBOT on July 7, 2007, to almost $12 billion. ICE then dropped out of the competition. The combination of the CME and CBOT made it the largest futures exchange in the world.

After their merger, the CME and CBOT announced that they were consolidating their trading floors and would shift several contracts to their electronic trading platform (Globex), including agricultural products, such as the once-popular frozen pork belly futures contract. Resistance on the floor to electronic trading remained. One trader, vowing not "to go down without a fight," declared, "They're going to have to turn the lights out to get us to trade electronically."[42] Their resistance was aided by no less a personage than former Federal Reserve chairman Alan Greenspan. In March 2007, Greenspan asserted at a futures industry conference that the open-outcry system of trading is still "the optimum model" because, while computers are useful, human beings always prefer personal interactions and that, therefore, open-outcry markets will always be around.[43] However, the growth of electronic trading called that claim into question in both the securities and commodity futures industries.

The CME, which bought NYMEX for $9.7 billion in 2007, had to increase the number of shares in its offer to NYMEX after the stock market undercut the value of its initial offer, which was based in part on the price of CME stock. After that acquisition, the CME Group controlled 98 percent of exchange-traded futures in the United States. NYMEX was a leading exchange in the trading of energy contracts. The CME closed its iconic trading floor in 2010 and removed its remaining floor activity to the CBOT premises, where floor trading in the open-outcry pits continued to wither.

Like other open-outcry exchanges, NYMEX had been under assault from the electronic exchanges. Before its merger with the CME, NYMEX had been embroiled in a fight with ICE over the use of NYMEX quotations for trading on ICE. NYMEX lost that fight.[44] ICE countersued NYMEX, claiming that it was violating antitrust laws, but that claim was dismissed. The CME was already handling NYMEX's electronic trades through Globex before their merger, and the merger signaled the death knell for another open-outcry exchange. The combination of CBOT, the CME, and NYMEX made it the largest futures exchange in the world, wresting that title away from Eurex. However, the subprime crisis caused a cooling of the Treasury complex at the CME, and volumes dropped. Eurex was able to beat the CME's volume figures in February 2009.

Futures Market Clearinghouses

The Role of the Clearinghouse

Clearinghouses that settle and guarantee the futures contracts traded on designated contract markets (DCMs) registered with and regulated by the CFTC form a central part of the futures markets. They were not required to be separately registered with the CFTC until 2000, when the CFMA required such registration. The CFMA also required clearinghouses to adopt some "core principles," including Core Principle 18, which prohibits commodity exchanges from taking actions that cause unreasonable restraints of trade or that impose any material anti-competitive burden on trading on a DCM.

The clearinghouse "plays a vital role in assuring the financial integrity of futures transactions." It interposes itself between the buyers and sellers, acting as buyer to every seller and seller to every buyer. As a party to each contract, the clearinghouse guarantees the performance of both parties as it undertakes and serves as a conduit for a transfer of funds from each day's trading activities.[45] Because the clearinghouse is the counterparty on each transaction, the parties can liquidate their contracts by entering into offsetting positions on the exchange floor. They need not contact or deal with each other to liquidate. Rather, their offsetting orders will liquidate their position at the clearinghouse.

Because the clearinghouse is responsible for the performance of each party, concerns over counterparty default risks are alleviated. That protection has proved a critical element in the success of commodity futures trading because traders need not conduct their own credit assessments of the traders opposite their order. Absent the clearinghouse, such an assessment would have to be made in order to assure that the counterparty could perform on the contract. A default by counterparty could be disastrous for a trader, especially where a defaulted position is offsetting a loss in another position.

Clearing firm members are large institutions that carry customer and proprietary positions with the clearinghouse. Those firms must guarantee their proprietary trades and the trades of their customers. They may also have residual liability in the event that another clearing member fails and cannot meet its obligations. The nature of the guarantee may vary from a "good-to-the-last-drop" model to "live another day" clearing fund arrangements. The clearinghouse guarantee is critical to the success of any exchange. Lack of confidence in the clearinghouse, or even unfamiliarity with its operations, may cause traders to trade elsewhere.

The clearinghouse assures its own performance through an "initial" margin deposit deemed sufficient to assure performance and "variation" margin to reflect losses or gains in the position. Margin in the futures industry should not be confused with margin in the securities industry. The latter is regulated by the Federal Reserve under Regulation T, which generally limits the amount of loans that can be made to purchase a marginable stock to 50 percent of the value of the stock being purchased. Margin for commodities futures is not viewed as an extension of credit, as are securities. Rather, it is a good-faith deposit of money, a "performance bond," set by risk assessment systems, such as Standard Portfolio Analysis of Risk (SPAN), to ensure that the customer will perform its obligations.

In the first instance, an "initial" margin is required for each futures contract when it is initially executed. This amount may be expressed as a percentage of the notional value of the futures contract. Initial margin levels are based on an assessment of the potential amount of a change in price for a commodity before a clearing firm is able to liquidate the account of a defaulting customer. The minimum initial margin that must be posted by a customer is set by exchange rules, but clearing firm members may charge above those minimums, when deemed necessary for their own protection. The initial margin for a futures contract is usually only a small portion of the notional amount of a futures contract, usually less than 5 percent.

In addition to an initial margin, "variation" margin payments are required to be paid by contract holders. This is an additional deposit of money required to reflect losses incurred by traders from adverse price changes on their open commodity futures positions. Variation margin requirements are computed through a "mark-to-market" system, in which the market value of the commodity is computed daily to determine whether its value has changed. The purchaser or seller experiencing a loss is required to post an additional amount equivalent to that loss. The party experiencing a gain is credited with an offsetting amount.

The Stock Market Crash of 1987

The amount of funds flowing through the clearing and settlement process on the Chicago futures exchanges during the stock market crash of 1987 was, at the time, extraordinary. The CME collected $1.6 billion in margin payments from its clearing members on October 19, 1987, and another $2.1 billion on October 20. The Options Clearing Corporation collected $2 billion on that day. The clearinghouses were issuing huge intraday margin calls that had to be met immediately and in cash. However, the clearinghouses did not pay out until the following day, which caused a liquidity problem for clearing members. A number of market participants were unable to obtain cash from the banks to meet those margin obligations on time because their banks were reluctant to pay out until they could establish the financial condition of traders. The banks also began limiting credit, which required the Federal Reserve to step in to ensure the clearinghouses that their members' obligations would be met.

The Presidential Task Force on Market Mechanisms (the Brady Commission), created by President Ronald Reagan to study the causes and effects of the crash, recommended that a unified clearing system be created to centralize credit risk from exchange-traded financial derivatives. That recommendation was not followed. In 1990, Congress authorized the SEC to facilitate the establishment of linkages and coordinated facilities for clearance and settlement transactions in securities, options, and futures contracts. The SEC was directed to coordinate with the CFTC and to consult with the Federal Reserve in order to facilitate that process. In 2000, the CFMA directed the CFTC to "facilitate the linking or coordination of derivatives clearing organizations registered under this Act with other regulated clearance facilities for the coordinated settlement of cleared transactions."[46] Nevertheless, clearing remains specific to exchanges in the futures industry.

Over-the-Counter Clearing

The Delta Clearing Corporation was formed in 1990 to clear OTC options on U.S. Treasury securities and later expanded its clearing activities to include repurchase agreements on those securities. The traders in this system were securities dealers, banks, pension funds, and other institutional investors. They communicated their interest in buying or selling to a broker, who entered the bids and offers in the Delta system's computer. Acting as the clearing agency, Delta matched buy and sell orders anonymously. The interposition of Delta between the traders protected their anonymity as well as guaranteed to each that the other would honor the terms of the option traded.

Delta became embroiled in a fight with the Chicago futures exchanges, which viewed Delta as an unwelcome competitor in trading options and futures on U.S. Treasury securities. CBOT claimed that Delta should have registered with the SEC as a national securities exchange, which would have made it impossible for Delta to operate. The Court of Appeals for the Seventh Circuit eventually ruled that the SEC could properly determine that such registration was not required.[47]

Competition Concerns

Historically, commodity exchanges and their members have not competed against each other on pricing or particular products. It is rare for commodity exchanges to trade futures contracts on the same commodity with the same terms, with a few notable exceptions in product competition, such as heating oil between the New York and Chicago exchanges. Silver and gold futures contracts were traded in New York and Chicago until the NYMEX merger with CME, whose operations were then sold to NYSE Euronext.

The commodity futures exchanges inhibited competition from the securities markets by claiming that competing products were futures or commodity options that had to be traded on a futures exchange regulated by the CFTC. That effort was supported by the Court of Appeals for the Seventh Circuit in Chicago.[48] The market-sharing arrangement for derivative products between the securities and commodities industries was made explicit through the so-called Shad-Johnson Accords (named after the chairmen of the SEC and the CFTC who negotiated this pact), enacted into law by Congress in 1982. That legislation divided trading along product lines, leaving the commodity futures exchanges with the exclusive right to trade futures and options on futures on financial commodities.

The CFMA removed the exchange monopoly requirement for most off-exchange institutional trading in 2000, but kept in place the trading monopoly for DCMs where retail customers were involved. The Justice Department has noted that competition has been restricted by the fact that, historically, commodity futures exchanges used separate clearinghouses to clear their trades. This lack of combined or joint clearing operations impeded competition.

Exchanges trading the same product through a unified clearinghouse in the securities industry competed on the basis of execution quality, efficiency, and timing, rather than on counterparty risk concerns or operational issues relating to trading through different clearinghouses. Joint clearing allowed head-to-head competition in products with favorable effects on pricing, execution times, and narrowing of spreads. The Justice Department has also noted that consolidated clearing reduces clearing fees and collateral movements.

Cross-Margining

The SEC and the CFTC have been exploring whether cross-margining should be permitted for commodity options, commodity futures, and securities options. Traders cross-margin by using securities options to secure futures transactions or vice versa, thereby reducing margin requirements for both positions. The SEC was the first to urge that margin requirements be coordinated and suggest that a system of cross-margining between securities options and futures contracts of commodity options would better reflect net risks in the market and would strengthen the integrity of the clearing system. Cross-margining also allows net cash settlements for activity in different markets. This reduces liquidity requirements in times of stress and permits more efficient use of capital.

The CFTC was initially reluctant to allow a complete cross-margining system because of concerns that it could have a domino effect and jeopardize clearing systems in the event of a large market crisis. The failure of one clearinghouse would decouple the protection relied upon by the other clearinghouse through an offsetting position. Nevertheless, the SEC and the CFTC have allowed stock and commodity futures clearinghouses to cross-margin proprietary positions of clearing members and market professionals held at different clearinghouses for similar products. This is a recognition that the offsetting positions reduce risk and, therefore, require less capital. The CFTC initially allowed cross-margining only for proprietary accounts of exchange members. It was reluctant to extend such treatment to customer accounts until it could weigh the effects of such treatment. The SEC and the CFTC later approved nonproprietary cross-margining.

A coordinated effort has been under way for some time among the exchanges to permit broader cross-margining. In December 1991, the SEC approved a proposal to allow the Options Clearing Corporation (OCC) and the CME to cross-margin futures and options positions held by clearing members for market professionals. In approving the cross-margin program for market profession-als, the SEC noted that, even though the stock, stock index options, and stock index futures markets were "integrally related, the clearance and settlement mechanisms associated with these markets are separate and distinct."[49]

The CBOE subsequently expanded cross-margining for broad-based index futures and options. Cross-margining was allowed for self-clearing member organizations and to customers of a clearing member with account equity of at least $5 million. The OCC entered into a cross-margining program with the IntercontinentalExchange's Ice Clear U.S. The National Association of Securities Dealers (NASD) Regulation, before it was folded into the Financial Industry Regulatory Authority (FINRA), adopted rules recognizing certain trading strategies that were eligible for cross-margining. The Government Securities Clearing Corporation also established a cross-margining program. Regulation T, which governs stock margins, presented some barriers to cross-margining. However, that regulation was amended in June 1996, in order to allow financial futures to act as margin for securities options, if such margin is permitted by the rules of self-regulatory organizations.

"Portfolio margining" was introduced and allowed even broader offsets for the positions in a trader's portfolio. The goal of portfolio margining is to set levels of margin that more precisely reflect the actual net risk in the account. As described by the SEC:

> Portfolio margining is a methodology for calculating a customer's margin requirement by 'shocking' a portfolio of financial instruments at different equidistant points along a range representing a potential percentage increase and decrease in the value of the instrument or underlying instrument in the case of a derivative product. For example, the calculation points could be spread equidistantly along a range bounded on one end by a 15% increase in market value of the instrument and at the other end by a 15% decrease in market value. Gains and losses for each instrument in the portfolio are netted at each calculation point along the range to derive a potential portfolio-wide gain or loss for the point. The margin requirement is the amount of the greatest portfolio-wide loss among the calculation points.[50]

Portfolio margining, like cross-margining, is important to traders because it reduces their margin requirements and reduces capital costs associated with the posting of collateral for margining positions. Portfolio margining usually results in lower margin requirements than do Regulation T requirements.

FINRA created a pilot program for the use of portfolio margining on marginable equity securities, equity-based options, and security futures. Portfolio-margining requirements are based on the greatest projected loss from all positions in a security class or product group contained in customer accounts. That calculation is made by using multiple pricing scenarios under a theoretical pricing model. Customers eligible for portfolio marketing must be approved for writing uncovered options. For unlisted derivatives, the customer must have account equity of no less than $5 million. The OCC also allowed futures to be included with lists of broad-based index options, index warrants, and related exchange-traded funds for portfolio margin treatment. In 2008, Congress directed that the SEC and the CFTC jointly adopt a program for portfolio marketing of security futures products.

Custody Arrangements—Futures Commission Merchants

The CFTC requires customer funds and securities to be maintained in specially segregated accounts. The Commodity Exchange Act (CEA) imposed that requirement when it was adopted in 1936 because Congress was concerned over the failure of a Chicago futures commission merchant (FCM) that resulted in a then-staggering $1 million loss of customer margin funds. In order to provide FCM customers with some protection for their funds, the CEA required FCMs to register with the federal government, and those FCMs were required to "treat their customers' money as trust funds."[51] As Senator Bronson Murray, the Senate sponsor of the CEA noted, "Those depositors of margin rank only as general creditors. Surely they thought their margins were regarded as trust funds and would be handled with a reasonable degree of integrity."[52]

This mandatory trust fund status was intended to stop the then-common practice in the industry in which futures "commission merchants receiving margin monies in excess of the amount required by the exchanges to be deposited use these excess margin deposits as their own capital, for any purpose they choose."[53] The segregation requirements adopted by Congress "merely provide that the public's money put up for margin shall in fact be treated as belonging to the customer, and held in trust. Who can object to this?"[54] The Commodity Exchange Act was amended in 1968 to extend its segregation of customer funds requirement to clearinghouses and other depositories for customer funds, such as banks.

Under the CFTC's rules, customer funds must be kept in specially designated segregated accounts. Proprietary funds cannot be commingled with those of customers, but funds of customers may be commingled with one another. FCMs may retain the earnings generated from customer-segregated funds. CFTC regulations created a "legal" list of investments for customer-segregated funds. These included U.S. government Treasury securities, certificates of deposit, commercial paper, corporate notes, including asset-backed obligations, general obligations of a sovereign nation, money market funds, and, somewhat surprisingly, municipal securities. The list of permitted investments was later extended to include repurchase agreements. Like the SEC, the CFTC adopted the use of the credit rating agencies, requiring high credit ratings for permissible investments by nationally recognized statistical rating organizations (NRSROs), which included Moody's, Standard & Poor's, and Fitch.

The segregation requirement remains important today because, unlike the securities industry, customers of insolvent brokerage firms have no insurance from the Securities Investor Protection Corporation (SIPC). Customers of FCMS are protected only by a requirement that their funds be kept in segregated accounts, on which the general creditors of the FCM have no claim. This was no accident. Upon its creation, the CFTC was directed by Congress to conduct a study of whether account insurance, like that from the SIPC, was needed in the futures industry. The CFTC study concluded that the loss ratios for commodity futures accounts were substantially lower than those in government-sponsored insurance programs, perhaps proving the theory of moral hazard for such programs. The CFTC believed that the loss ratio was so low for commodity accounts that it would not be cost-effective to adopt government insurance. In some instances, however, investors have a choice. The CFMA permitted the trading of single stock futures on both securities and futures exchanges. Customers were allowed to opt for segregated fund treatment either under the SEC rule or the CFTC rule. However, funds held in CFTC-regulated accounts would have no SIPC insurance coverage.

The loss history of customer funds from insolvencies of futures commission merchants continues to be good. This is not to suggest, however, that there have been no failures. In the 1980s, three substantial FCMs failed: Incomco, Chicago Discount Commodity Brokers, and Volume Investors. Customers lost several million dollars as a result of those bankruptcies. The losses were caused by the use of customer funds to meet margin calls, for which the FCMs were responsible because of a customer default or other abuses. Between 1976 and 1985, some twenty-four FCMs failed with losses averaging $2 million per year. That seemed to be the low point, but failures occurred periodically thereafter, including the highly publicized demise of the Stotler Funds and Refco, which was a massive failure that occurred in the wake of the Enron scandals.

The largest FCM failure during the subprime crisis was that of Sentinel Management Group, which failed in August 2007. Sentinel was a CFTC-registered futures commission merchant and an investment adviser registered with the SEC. Its business plan was to invest the funds of other FCMs and their customers and to pay interest rates higher than those customers would have received from a money market fund.[55]

CFTC Capital Requirements

The CFTC also uses capital requirements as liquidity measures to ensure that FCMs have sufficient funds on hand to meet customer demands. The CFTC net capital rule was modeled after the rule used by the SEC, but was based on the amount of customer funds held by the FCM in segregation. That figure contains an element of risk, in that the amount of those funds was tied to exchange margin requirements, which were risk-based.

In 2004, the CFTC went a step further by amending its rules to allow FCMs to make a risk assessment compensation for capital purposes that was based directly on the margin levels of positions carried in customer and noncustomer accounts. This computation was already required by exchange rules and had worked smoothly, for the most part, over the years. This program was intended to allow FCMs affiliated with large investment banks to be a part of a consolidated supervised entity, as mandated by a European Union directive. However, unlike the SEC net capital treatment for those entities that allowed internal risk control systems such as "value at risk" (VaR) to measure capital, the CFTC requirement was based on the exchange-set risk parameters for margin requirements. In 2006, the CFTC increased its minimum net capital requirement for certain futures commission merchants from $50,000 to $1 million.

6. The Rise of the Hedge Funds and Private Equity

Hedge Funds

Background

The term "hedge fund" has been variously defined, but, in essence, it is an "investment company" with some characteristics of a mutual fund, in which investor funds are collectively invested by an investment adviser or "manager." Hedge funds generally trace their history back to A.W. Jones, an entity created by Alfred Winslow Jones, William P. Osterberg, and James B. Thomson in 1949. However, one author has identified the stock pool operators of the 1920s as a form of hedge fund. Those pools were groups of speculators who contributed funds to the pool for management by a pool operator, who would then take large speculative positions in publicly traded stocks, often manipulating their prices in the process.[1] In 1929 such pools manipulated more than a hundred stocks listed on the New York Stock Exchange (NYSE). One of the more famous pool operations involved the stock of RCA, which soared to $101 per share in 1929, before dropping to $2 after the stock market crash that year. Banks supplied large sums to finance the operations of these pools. Chase National Bank, for example, placed over $800 million into various pools in 1929.

Investors in the less-notorious hedge fund created by A.W. Jones after World War II were attracted by its leverage, which generated profits that exceeded 1,000 percent during one ten-year period. As its general partner, Jones received 20 percent of those profits, and this became the standard fee for modern hedge fund managers. The A.W. Jones hedge fund operated in relative obscurity until an article published in *Fortune* magazine in 1966 popularized him and the hedge fund concept. The number of hedge funds thereafter grew rapidly. By 1969, there were over 150 hedge funds, holding over $1 billion in customer assets. The number of hedge funds increased to 800 by 1994, with assets of more than $75 billion. As the twenty-first century began, the number of hedge funds expanded to some 6,000, managing about

$600 billion in assets. The number grew in four years to 7,000 hedge funds managing an estimated $850 billion. Assets under management by hedge funds reached an estimated $1.2 trillion in 2006.

About 1,100 new hedge funds were created in 2007; approximately 87 percent of hedge fund assets under management that year were held at funds managing $1 billion or more, and 60 percent were managed by hedge funds holding $5 billion or more. By 2008, hedge funds were managing assets that were valued at $2.65 trillion. However, hedge fund profits were not matching those achieved by Jones's hedge fund. The average return for hedge funds in 2008 was, while not overly impressive, a still healthy 8 percent.

Hedge fund shares usually have no secondary market, although a few hedge funds have gone public. Rather than having a secondary market, hedge funds generally allow investors to have their shares "redeemed" by the hedge fund manager based on the investors' proportional ownership percentage of the hedge fund's net asset value (NAV). This is not dissimilar to mutual fund redemptions. However, unlike mutual funds, hedge funds often require a one-year "lock up" of the investors' funds after an investment is made. After that initial lockup period, hedge fund investors may have their funds redeemed upon giving proper notice. Such redemptions are usually limited to a monthly, quarterly, or semiannual redemption. The hedge fund manager might also have the authority to restrict redemptions in case of liquidity concerns.

A distinctive feature of hedge funds is their management structure. Mutual funds must comply with detailed requirements of the Securities and Exchange Commission (SEC) for independent directors on their boards, and shareholders must explicitly approve certain actions. In contrast, domestic hedge funds are usually structured as limited partnerships to achieve maximum separation of ownership and management. In the typical arrangement, the general partner manages the fund (or several funds) for an annual fixed fee (usually 2 percent of funds under management) and a portion of the gross profits from the fund (usually 20 percent). The limited partners are passive investors and generally take no part in management activities.

Hedge funds typically trade through a clearing firm that carries the trades of the hedge fund with exchange clearinghouses. Hedge funds may use more than one clearing firm in order to shield their trading strategies from the market. In such cases, orders may be separately entered with each clearing firm for execution. The Government Accountability Office (GAO) issued a report in February 2008 that criticized the use of multiple brokers by hedge funds because this meant that no one broker had access to the complete holdings of the hedge fund, impeding credit decisions. These arrangements were also sometimes used to conceal trading losses.

Another popular clearing arrangement for hedge funds involves a "prime broker." A prime broker clears and carries the trades of customers executed by other brokers at the customer's direction. The hedge fund's trading is concealed from the market under a prime broker arrangement by sending orders for execution to brokers at other firms. The executing broker may be independent of the prime broker, but will "give up" the trade it executes to the prime broker.

The customer maintains its funds and securities in an account maintained by the prime broker. The prime broker is responsible for ensuring that the hedge fund meets exchange margin requirements. The prime broker provides financing and clearing for the customer's securities and other transactions wherever they are executed. This arrangement frees the hedge fund from the need to maintain funds at numerous broker-dealers.

The prime brokerage business is lucrative for clearing firms, and they do whatever they can to attract that business. UBS and Bear Stearns were even accused of operating hedge fund "hotels" in several cities, which provided office space and administrative services to hedge funds. UBS had more than 400,000 square feet of its space devoted to its hedge fund hotel promotions. This raised the eyebrows of regulators, who began an investigation to determine whether the prime brokers were using that arrangement as leverage to charge higher fees and commissions.[2]

The NAV computation on which hedge fund investor profits are based also determines the amount of the hedge fund manager's fees. To ensure their integrity, hedge funds often employ an "administrator" to verify the hedge fund manager's computations. Hedge fund administrators, usually a bank or other financial institution, act as a watchdog over the hedge fund manager by tracking trading results and periodically verifying the hedge fund's NAV. This independent third-party verification is important to investors because it determines whether the NAV figure is accurate.

Hedge funds like to portray themselves as "alternative asset" managers. Alternative assets are investments not found in the typical portfolio, which historically were limited to stocks and bonds. They include derivatives and investment strategies that might, for example, include seeking profits from disparities in the pricing of different classes of assets, interest rate yield plays, and foreign currency fluctuations. The NAV computation may not be difficult where the hedge fund manager is trading assets that are easily valued by referencing exchange prices, a process called "mark-to-market." However, many alternative assets may be difficult to value because no readily identifiable market exists on which to price these assets. In such case, the hedge fund tries to price those assets at their "fair value."

Fair-value accounting assets without a ready market became a controversial practice because the numbers could sometimes be manipulated. Some hedge fund managers used "side pocket" accounts to hold illiquid or hard-to-value assets. Those accounts were also used to place assets in which not all investors in the hedge fund have an interest. The use of such accounts also raised problems in computing NAV and were vulnerable to abuse.

A hallmark of many hedge funds is the complexity of their trading strategies. Hedge fund managers used "quants" with advanced degrees in mathematics, physics, and even nuclear science to formulate algorithmic trading strate-gies. One infamous hedge fund, Long-Term Capital Management (LTCM), employed twenty-five economists with PhDs, two of whom had received the Nobel Memorial Prize in economic science. That brain power did not prevent the collapse of LTCM, and its failure did not discourage hedge funds from continuing the development of complex mathematical trading strategies that sought to analyze market prices and historical trading patterns in order to then generate trading signals. Some of these algorithmic programs sought to discover market inefficiencies or deficiencies that could be exploited by the hedge fund manager through leveraged positions. These trading strategies were implemented through proprietary computer-based programs that were tested and backtested using many variables. These programs could generate thousands of orders every trading day. Such "high-frequency" trading, which accounted for some 70 percent of equity trading in 2009, was widely used in the commodity markets.

Hedge fund trading strategies include directional trading, relative value trad-ing, carry trades, and volatility trading. Directional trading involves forecasting future price movements in a particular asset. This is simply the fairly classic effort to forecast market movements. Relative value trading comprises efforts to identify relative mispricing between two or more instruments. Volatility trading refers to trading activities based on forecasted changes in the level of volatility in a particular investment. Carry trades are transactions that obtain financing advantages. For example, in the money markets, a carry trade could involve borrowing short-term funds and relending those funds on a long-term basis at a higher interest rate.

Secrecy is a hallmark of hedge funds, which are intensely private groups that closely guard their trading activities. This concealment is deemed necessary because a hedge fund provides profits only through its propriety trading strate-gies. If others know those strategies, they can be copied or traded against, and their benefits would be lost. The need for secrecy in trading commodity futures and options is recognized by statute. Although the Commodity Futures Trad-ing Commission (CFTC) has access to trading in regulated futures contracts by large traders, such as hedge funds, that agency "may not publish data and information that would separately disclose the business transactions or market positions of any person and trade secrets or names of customers" except as specifically authorized by Congress.[3] The sensitivity of such information is further evidenced by the fact that it is a felony under federal law for CFTC members, their employees, or employees of contract markets to trade on such information or to disclose it to others for trading.[4]

Hedge funds are high-risk, highly leveraged investment pools. Some hedge fund managers became legends as a result of their successes. George Soros, an egocentric, extremely left-wing billionaire, was able to derail efforts to bring England into the eurozone by shorting its currency in 1992 and realizing profits of some $2 billion in the process. Owners of the Citadel Investment Group and Paulson & Company made billions of dollars in a single year from their investments. The highly leveraged trading of some hedge funds, however, did result in some huge losses very quickly. Tiger Management, for instance, lost $2 billion in a single day in the 1990s. Several hedge funds experienced large losses when bond prices dropped abruptly in 1994.

Especially serious were the losses that occurred at LTCM, which lost 90 percent of its $4.8 billion in capital in September 1998, as a result of its trading positions that took a battering during a financial crisis in Russia.[5] The failure of LTCM raised concerns at the Federal Reserve that it might present systemic dangers, and a rescue was arranged by the Federal Reserve Bank of New York. The rescue itself was carried out by several large investment banks, which invested their own funds to save LTCM. They recovered their investments, but the investors in the fund at the time of its collapse suffered losses. UBS, the giant Swiss bank, lost $700 million and senior managers were forced to resign. During the subprime crisis it would be front and center with massive losses.

Russian debt losses caused other problems. Eduardo Masferrer, chairman of Miami-based Hamilton Bancorp, was sentenced to thirty years in prison for failing to recognize on his bank's books the fact that Russian investments had lost much of their value and the debts from them were mounting. Prosecutors said the scheme benefited Masferrer because it bolstered the price of the bank's stock and boosted his bonus.

Amaranth Advisors' loss of over $6 billion in a single week in energy trading during 2006 also raised eyebrows. Further large losses surfaced during the subprime crisis at hedge funds operated by Bear Stearns, Citigroup, Goldman Sachs, and others, a reflection of the fact that the popularity of hedge funds led the large investment banks to enter that market by operating their own hedge funds.

Mutual Fund Scandals

New York attorney general Eliot Spitzer in September 2003 charged Edward J. Stern and a hedge fund he managed, Canary Capital Partners, with improper market timing and late trading in shares of the Strong Mutual Fund complex. Canary Capital Partners was required to pay $40 million to settle this problem, part of which was to be used for restitution to mutual fund investors. Stern also agreed not to trade in mutual funds or manage any public investment funds for ten years. Spitzer brought several other suits against mutual funds, and others, for allowing or engaging in market timing and late trading, resulting in more publicity and extraordinarily large fines.

The charges filed by Spitzer ignited controversy because it was not entirely clear why a state attorney general was seeking to regulate mutual funds that were under the regulatory control of the SEC. Indeed, "because of perceived inefficiencies inherent in dual state and federal securities registration schemes,

Congress had passed the National Securities Markets Improvement Act of 1996 (NSMIA),[6] primarily to preempt state 'Blue Sky' laws that required issuers to register many securities with state authorities prior to marketing in the states."[7] That legislation specifically exempted from state regulation shares of investment companies registered with the SEC. However, the NSMIA provided that the states would retain jurisdiction to investigate fraud. Spitzer was using that loophole by claiming fraud in his prosecutions for late trading or market timing. That took some effrontery given that his fraud claims were premised largely on the SEC's forward-pricing rule for mutual funds that was adopted under the Investment Company Act of 1940, which was for the SEC to enforce, rather than Spitzer.

Spitzer created more controversy when he began regulating mutual funds by requiring them to reduce their fees as a part of their settlements in the market timing and late trading cases. Those fees had previously been regulated by the National Association of Securities Dealers (NASD) under the oversight of the SEC, as mandated by Congress. Spitzer simply ignored that congressional mandate and created his own public utility regulatory program governed solely by his personal views on what constituted appropriate fees. Further criticism was directed at Spitzer for criminalizing what were common business practices.

The fact that market timing was occurring in mutual funds was widely known before Spitzer's charges were filed. Spitzer admitted as much when he cited, in his complaint against Canary Capital Partners, a study published a year earlier at Stanford University, which complained that mutual funds were losing billions to market timers. Another article published almost three years earlier made a similar complaint. In 1998, David Dubofsky, a professor of finance at Virginia Commonwealth University, published a paper on market timing and notified the SEC of his findings. Dubofsky began following market-timing practices after a student alerted to him to such trading after the stock market crash of 1987.

Another weakness in Spitzer's crusade was that no court had ruled on the validity of his claims. The only proceeding to contest his charges was a criminal trial brought against Theodore Charles Sihpol III, an employee of Banc of America Securities. Sihpol was in charge of the most extensive of Canary Capital's late-trading and market-timing relationships and arranged a $300 million line of credit for Canary Capital to use in such trading. The evidence against Sihpol was rather dramatic. He created an electronic trading platform that allowed Canary Capital Partners to trade late. Tape recordings also revealed that Sihpol was time-stamping order tickets in advance, in order to conceal that the late trades had been entered after the 4:00 P.M. cutoff for calculating the mutual funds' NAV. Nevertheless, Sihpol's criminal trial resulted in a verdict of not guilty on twenty-nine counts and a hung jury (11–1 in favor of acquittal) on the four remaining counts. Spitzer initially announced that Sihpol would be retried on the charges on which the jury was hung, but backed off after receiving much criticism, and those criminal charges were dropped.

So was there fraud involved in these practices? Spitzer's civil suit against Canary Capital Partners charged that the late trader was defrauding long-term mutual fund shareholders by "diluting" their holdings because the late-trading arbitrageur's profits came "dollar for dollar" from the mutual fund. Those profits "would otherwise have gone completely to the fund's buy and hold investors."[8] Spitzer noted that late trading was exploiting the SEC's forward-pricing rule for mutual fund purchases and redemptions and charged that such conduct was fraudulent and violated New York's Martin Act. Spitzer's press release accompanying the Canary Capital Partners complaint stated: "Allowing late trading is like allowing betting on a horse race after the horses have crossed the finish line," and market timing trading "is like a casino saying that it prohibits loaded dice, but then allowing favored gamblers to use loaded dice, in return for a piece of the action."[9]

Late trading involves the entry of a purchase or redemption of a mutual fund share after 4:00 P.M., the time at which the NAV is computed for the forward pricing of orders received earlier in the day. The late trader is using the mutual fund as a hedge to lock in price disparities that occur in the one- or two-hour window used for late trading. Just how are the holdings of other owners of the mutual fund diluted? If the price increase in the alternate market carries over to the close of trading on the following day, there seems, on its face, to be no harm and, hence, no foul because the long-term mutual fund investors will enjoy the same profit as the late trader. If prices go up or down between the NAV computations on succeeding trading days, the status of the late trader and the mutual fund's long-term investors remains the same. However, the late trader paid cash on the day when he bought the mutual funds at their 4:00 P.M. NAV. That cash may not be invested in time to capture the fluctuation in value, which means that the other mutual fund holders will have to bear the cost of that fluctuation.

Market timing is more problematic as a basis for claiming fraud. This was not a new problem for the mutual fund industry, although the angle of attack had changed. Prior to the adoption of the Investment Company Act of 1940 a two-price system for mutual fund shares existed that created an active secondary market in those shares that was sometimes abused. Most funds computed their NAVs daily on the basis of the fund's portfolio value at the close of exchange trading, and that figure established the sales price that would go into effect at a specified hour on the following day. During this interim period, two prices were known: the present day's trading price of the mutual fund shares based on the portfolio value established the previous day; and the following day's price, which was based on the NAV computed at the close of exchange trading on the present day. Anyone aware of both prices could engage in "riskless trading" during this interim period.

Most investors could not take advantage of that situation because of sales loads, but insiders were able to purchase shares without paying the load and could purchase shares for immediate redemption at the appreciated value. It was claimed that this diluted the equity of the existing shareholders. "The existing shareholders' equity interests were diluted because the incoming investors bought into the fund at less than the actual value of the shares at the time of purchase."[10]

The Investment Company Act of 1940 was employed to prevent those and other trading abuses by authorizing the NASD and the SEC to regulate the distribution and trading in mutual fund shares. They both adopted rules that were thought to have ended riskless trading in mutual fund shares. The SEC was thought to have further sealed the fate of such trading in 1968, when it enacted its "forward-pricing" rule,[11] which required redemptions and purchases to be priced after receipt of the order from the customer—"generally using the closing price for the stocks that were set at the end of that trading day."[12]

There were other concerns with using mutual funds for quick, in-and-out trading (market timing). The SEC had long sought to prevent mutual fund salesmen from recommending market timing in mutual funds to retail customers because sales loads and time and place disadvantages made such trading unsuitable for them. However, the SEC did not view market-timing transactions in mutual funds by professional traders as a matter of concern because professionals could look after themselves and the investors whose money they were managing. Further, the restriction on buying and selling mutual fund shares at their NAV was a practical barrier to market timing, even by professional traders. Nevertheless, during the 1980s, some fifty money managers specialized in market-timing mutual funds for even small investors in amounts as low as $2,000. These market timers charged fees of 2 percent or more on assets under management, in addition to any mutual fund sales loads.

Money Magazine conducted a study in 1988 of the five-year performance of market timing by mutual fund money managers.[13] It found that clients of J.D. Reynolds experienced compound returns of more than 20 percent. Most market-timing managers were not that successful, but two-thirds of those managers did better than the Lipper mutual fund average. They were particularly successful in preserving investor capital during stock market downturns. However, these early market timers were not overnight arbitrageurs like those involved in the Spitzer-generated scandals. For example, J.D. Reynolds engaged in less than four market-timing transactions per year because the goal of the market timers in the 1980s was to move investment funds between equity and fixed income funds, in anticipation of changes between those two markets.

These market timers were not popular with mutual fund sponsors because "when market-timing money managers move millions of dollars at a time in or out of funds, as they often do, they force mutual fund managers to buy or sell large blocks of stock at inopportune moments. Hence, fund organizations view timers as disruptive."[14] Several no-load mutual funds (a mutual fund that does not charge an investment management fee) sought to discourage market timers by limiting the number of switches that an investor could make. Undaunted, the market timers moved to load funds, which charged management fees and were less likely to impose such restrictions because of the incentive of those fees.

Market timers became more active during the 1990s and again aroused the ire of the mutual funds that had to deal with their liquidations. Some mutual funds imposed redemption fees on traders engaged in market timing in order to discourage such activity. Those fees had been allowed by the SEC, up to 2 percent, since 1979. The number of funds imposing such fees increased substantially in the 1990s, when the market run-up was encouraging day trading and other speculative trading. Some mutual funds threatened to suspend the redemption privileges of traders engaged in market timing.

"Fair-value pricing" was also used to discourage market timers in international funds that presented arbitrage opportunities because foreign markets might still be open when NAV was computed. Fair-value pricing sought to set a fair price on foreign holdings at the close of trading in the United States, in order to reduce those arbitrage opportunities. These attempts at curbing market timing were described in mutual fund prospectuses. To an outside reviewer of those disclosures, it appeared that the mutual funds were opposed to market timers because they were disruptive and harmful to the funds. However, those objections were dropped for the hedge funds.

According to Spitzer's complaint against Canary Capital Partners, market timing in that case was made possible by the fact that some mutual funds used stale prices to compute the NAV. Spitzer did concede that market "timing is not entirely risk free . . . for example, the timer has to keep his or her money in the target fund for a least a day, so he or she may enjoy additional gains or incur losses, depending on the market."[15] Nevertheless, Spitzer charged that the activity diluted the holdings of other mutual fund owners and imposed transaction costs on them. He also focused on the fact that mutual fund prospectuses warned that market timers were unwelcome and that their redemption privileges could be suspended. He claimed that this misled other investors into believing that such trading was prohibited.

Actually, market timing seemed less like illegal activity and more like mutual fund inefficiency, given that the mutual funds could use fair-value pricing to prevent the 4:00 P.M. NAV from being stale. Some mutual funds did use fair-value pricing in their international funds in order to prevent traders from arbitraging their funds. However, critics claimed that such pricing was arbitrary and resulted in differing values on the same assets because of varying methodologies in making the valuations. The SEC has vacillated over the years on whether to require fair-value pricing, which only confused the situation.

Fair-value pricing posed other problems. Garrett Van Wagoner, a popular mutual funds manager, was charged by the SEC with improperly using fair-value pricing to improve his funds' performance. He was forced to step down from a management role in order for him to focus on portfolio selection. That was an unfortunate choice for the mutual fund shareholders because his investment performance in 2007 was abysmal. A subsequent SEC inquiry into fair-value pricing resulted in industry comments, which asserted that fair-value pricing alone would not prevent market timing.

In addition to redemption fees, some mutual funds had "market-timing police" to detect and prevent such trading. However, redemption fees and policing were waived for large hedge fund traders. There was an incentive for such waivers. The hedge funds engaging in market timing increased the amount of funds under management by many millions of dollars, which resulted in higher fees to mutual fund sponsors because NAV was the basis for their compensation. The hedge funds also provided the liquidity needed for market timing in the form of "sticky assets," which were substantial long-term commitments of capital to the mutual fund. Those sticky assets were to be used to meet the increased costs of market-timing liquidations and could be used to hedge against the deleterious effects of such trading on the mutual fund. However, those sticky assets were "typically long-term investments made not in the mutual fund in which the trading activity was permitted, but in one of the fund manager's financial vehicles (e.g., a bond fund or a hedge fund run by the manager) that assured a steady flow of fees to the manager."[16]

The SEC's Response

The SEC's reputation had been badly blemished by the accounting scandals at Enron, WorldCom, and elsewhere. Despite its pervasive and intrusive regulations, and its reputation for being an aggressive regulator, the SEC had failed to prevent or detect those problems. The agency had literally read about those scandals in the press before becoming involved. Spitzer added to the SEC's growing aura of incompetence with his spectacular charges against the financial analysts that were also regulated by the SEC and by shedding light on the late-trading and market-timing scandals. He even began taunting the SEC and other federal agencies, saying that they had been so "beaten down" and "neutered" that they had been "rendered incapable of fulfilling their fundamental mandate" and "sapped of the desire to regulate."[17]

The SEC did much to confirm Spitzer's charges. It had watched its vaunted full disclosure system crumble from the pervasive accounting manipulations of the Enron era. The subprime crisis would also catch the SEC flatfooted. The large investment banks under its regulatory umbrella all failed or were turned into banks after being bailed out by the government, including Lehman Brothers, Bear Stearns, Merrill Lynch, Goldman Sachs, and Morgan Stanley. The discovery of the largest fraud ever, in the form of a giant Ponzi scheme by Bernard Madoff, added further embarrassment. He too was under the regulation of the SEC, and the SEC had missed numerous opportunities over several years to uncover his fraud. It was only after Madoff ran out of money and confessed his crime that his scheme came to light.

In an effort to regain some credibility after Spitzer's charges, the SEC filed its own suits for late trading and market timing, often in tandem with Spitzer.

Even under pressure from Spitzer, the SEC's charges on market timing were somewhat hesitant. The SEC thus conceded that market timing was not "illegal per se" but argued that it could damage a mutual fund because (a) it could dilute the value of their shares if the market timer were exploiting pricing inefficiencies, (b) it could disrupt the management of the mutual fund's investment portfolio, and (c) it could cause the targeted mutual fund to incur costs that would be borne by other shareholders to accommodate the market timer's frequent buying and selling of shares.[18]

The SEC was more emphatic about late trading, charging that it defrauded innocent mutual fund shareholders by diluting their shares and by giving the late trader an advantage unavailable to other shareholders. However, the SEC's claims against market timers and late traders encountered some resistance in the courts. In one case, a federal district court dismissed the SEC's fraud claims involving Canary Capital's late trading and market timing because improper intent had not been properly alleged. The court stated:

> The market timing agreement with Canary, standing alone, could not be considered per se a fraudulent device intended to defraud investors. The SEC does not allege, nor could it, that market timing practices are per se illegal, since many individual and institutional investors, as part of not uncommon investment strategies, continue to attempt to time markets with varying degrees of success.[19]

In another action, a federal district court dismissed SEC charges against two senior executives at Columbia Funds Distributors. Those executives had allowed market timing in mutual funds that were being sold under prospectuses stating that such trading was barred by the mutual fund. The court said that "market timing arrangements are not the kind of sham transactions which have been held to qualify as schemes to defraud."[20] The SEC subsequently amended its complaint to charge that investors were misled by fund prospectuses, which claimed that the funds were hostile to market timing. However, a survey by the Investment Company Institute found that most investors did not read their mutual fund prospectuses and those who did were focused on other issues.

In still another case, a federal district court dismissed aiding and abetting charges brought by the SEC over market timing. However, that court and two other district courts allowed fraud claims against defendants who had used subterfuges and deceptive devices to avoid mutual fund restrictions on such activity. Motions to dismiss class-action and derivative suits have been denied in cases in which the defendants were charged with violations in connection with late trading and market timing. Nevertheless, several aspects of those claims were dismissed. In still another action, a district court dismissed most charges against two individuals working for an investment adviser of a mutual fund who had allowed a hedge fund to market-time in exchange for sticky assets.

The SEC did achieve success in a case brought against Scott Gann, a broker employed by Southwest Securities, who was charged with market timing on behalf of two hedge funds. The Court of Appeals for the Fifth Circuit upheld a finding that Gann had used multiple registration and account numbers to avoid mutual fund market-timing restrictions. However, the appeals court stated that market timing was not in and of itself illegal. The Court of Appeals for the Fourth Circuit also reinstated market-timing charges against Janus Capital Management, charges that had earlier been dismissed by a district court. Janus was charged with falsely stating that market timing was not permitted in its mutual funds. Separately, NYSE arbitrators entered a $14 million award against Merrill Lynch for firing three brokers who had engaged in late trading.

Despite their lack of success in court, the SEC and Spitzer were able to obtain settlements totaling over $4.25 billion in penalties, disgorgement, and reduced mutual fund fees by the end of 2005, and the number of cases grew. For example, Bear Stearns agreed in March 2006 to pay $250 million to NYSE and the SEC to settle charges of late trading in its mutual funds. Morgan Stanley agreed to pay the SEC $17 million in January 2008 to settle market-timing charges for trading that occurred between 2001 and 2003. Hartford Financial Services Group agreed to pay $115 million to settle market-timing charges brought by attorneys general in New York, Connecticut, and Illinois.

The SEC also proposed regulations that its staff thought would prevent market timing and late trading. That effort was less than successful. One regulatory fix proposed by the SEC was the adoption of a rule requiring a "hard close" of mutual funds that would prevent the filling of any purchase or redemption requests after 4:00 P.M. Orders received after that time would have to be filled at the next day's NAV. That approach proved too complex. Another proposal requiring mandatory redemption fees also stalled, and the SEC adopted a rule that "allowed," but did not require, a 2 percent redemption fee. Even this approach was too complex, and the SEC staff examined the rule for amendment. Other rules were adopted that, among other things, required mutual funds to disclose the effects of market timing.

The Investment Company Act of 1940 constituted perhaps the deepest intrusion by regulation into corporate governance procedures. It required that at least 40 percent of investment company boards of directors be made up of independent outside directors. In 2001 the SEC expanded this requirement for outside directors to a majority. The SEC added that requirement through the back door by requiring such representation before investment companies could become eligible for exemptions from SEC rules on conflicts of interest. Among other things, those exemptions permit mutual funds with majority outside directors to purchase securities in an initial public offering (IPO) in which an affiliated broker-dealer is acting as an underwriter; permit the use of fund assets to pay distribution expenses; allow securities transactions between a fund and another client of the fund's adviser; and permit funds to issue multiple classes of voting stock. The SEC also used its exemption authority to create other governance requirements, including how mutual fund board meetings are to be conducted.

After the late-trading scandals, the SEC sought to expand its intrusion into mutual fund corporate governance. A particularly controversial rule adopted by the SEC required the chairman of mutual fund boards to be independent from the chief executive officer (CEO) and increased the majority requirement for outside directors to 75 percent. Those outside directors would have to meet in separate sessions, at least quarterly, and be allowed to have their own staff. Although there was no evidence that such a corporate governance structure was more efficient or provided greater shareholder protection, the SEC had long pursued efforts to increase participation by outside directors in public corporations as a check on management excesses.

This has also been a popular cause for corporate reformists over the past quarter-century. Their efforts stepped up after the Enron scandal, leading NYSE and NASDAQ to require that at least a majority of the boards of directors of their listed companies be composed of outside directors and that nominating and compensating committees be composed entirely of such outsiders. However, audit committees at public companies had been required since 1977 to be composed entirely of outside directors, though that requirement did nothing to check the audit-based scandals at Enron and elsewhere that arose after the market downturn in 2000.

No empirical evidence supported requirements for majority outside director boards. Professors Sanjai Bhagat and Bernard Black reviewed the results of 112 empirical studies of various aspects of corporate governance from the 1980s and 1990s. They concluded that "studies of overall firm performance have found no convincing evidence that firms with majority independent boards perform better than firms without such boards." Indeed, firms with a majority of inside directors performed about as well as firms with a majority of independent directors. Bhagat and Black also found that "firms with supermajority-independent boards [those with only one or two inside directors] might even perform worse, on average, than other firms."[21]

Anecdotal evidence also suggests that increasing the number of outside directors added nothing to good governance. In fact, many countries allow investment companies to operate without any board of directors. A corporate trustee under defined trading strategies manages those investment companies. The trustee is paid a single management fee for its services. A similar proposal was advanced by Stephen K. West in 1980 for use in the United States and more recently by Peter Wallison of the American Enterprise Institute and Bob Litan at the Brookings Institution.[22]

The boards of directors at Enron, WorldCom, and other centers of scandal consisted of high percentages of prominent outside directors who were unable to do anything to prevent the problems at those companies. In addition, shareholders do not select most outside directors. Rather, their nomination comes from the CEO to the nominating committee, who often chooses them because they are prestigious figures, golfing buddies, or have some other social or business relationship with that officer.

Adding more outside directors to mutual fund boards as a way of stopping future scandals in that industry had an even shakier foundation. The requirement for a majority of outside directors that was already in place did nothing to prevent the late-trading or market-timing scandals. A study by Fidelity mutual funds submitted in response to the SEC's request for comment on its then-proposed 75 percent outside director requirement actually showed empirical evidence that increasing the number of independent board members did not increase returns. That study was given short shrift by the SEC, which gave similar treatment to legislation passed by Congress in response to the agency's then-proposed requirement for splitting the role of chairman and CEO at mutual funds. In a highly unusual move, Congress required the SEC to justify such a requirement, but it did not do so. Instead, it passed the independent chairman and 75 percent outside director rule by a 3–2 vote that was along party lines.

The SEC mutual fund governance rule was promptly challenged by the U.S. Chamber of Commerce and was set aside by the Court of Appeals for the District of Columbia. The court concluded that the SEC had the authority to adopt such a proposal but that the commission had not adequately considered its costs or available alternatives.[23] The SEC shrugged off that ruling by readopting the same rule only a week after it was set aside, without even awaiting the mandate of the appeals court. The repassage of the rule was approved over the dissenting votes of two Republican commissioners, one of whom apologized to the appeals court for the majority's high-handed approach.

The new rule was challenged and was once again set aside by the appeals court.[24] The court held that the SEC should have sought public comment before adopting the rule so quickly after the court's prior ruling. More embarrassment followed for the SEC when a 2006 Harvard Business School study concluded that mutual funds still wrongly priced their mutual fund assets. The study found that, while most mutual funds calculated NAV by using the closing price on the day of the pricing, they applied that value to the shares held on the previous day. That could result in substantial differences in pricing, depending on market conditions.

In all events, the intrusive regulation mandated by the Investment Company Act of 1940 failed completely in preventing the late-trading and market-timing scandals. Hampered by that regulation, mutual fund performance was less than impressive. Market studies found that mutual funds, overall, lagged behind the market. Depending on the study, the lag in performance ranged from severe to moderate. Some 6.5 percent of equity funds were also closed or merged each year in order to boost mutual fund trading records.

In 2010, the SEC, in a continuing effort to regain the ground taken by Spitzer, announced proposed rules to regulate the fees charged by mutual fund distributors. These so-called 12b-1 fees would be capped at 0.25 percent of assets under management in the fund, and additional disclosures would be required as to the purpose of the fees.

Regulating Hedge Funds

Before the market-timing and late-trading scandals, the SEC had not sought to regulate the operations of hedge funds, except that solicitations of investments were subject to the provisions of the Securities Act of 1933. However, an exemption from such registration existed for securities being offered to qualified investors, that is, wealthy individuals or large financial institutions. The SEC intended that only these persons and institutions could invest in hedge funds, believing that they could understand and absorb the risks associated with these highly leveraged investment vehicles. However, small investors were attracted by the high rates of return experienced by some hedge funds. They sought a back-door entry to the hedge funds. They were able to do this by purchasing shares of registered mutual funds that invested in hedge funds. In addition, "wrap accounts" that were managed by investment advisers could be pooled to make an investment in a hedge fund. The SEC expressed concern with this "retailization" of hedge fund investments.

Even though exempt, hedge fund investors are provided with a "private offering memorandum" that operated much like a prospectus for a public company. It described the operations of the hedge fund, provided background on the hedge fund manager, and gave other information about principals in the company. The private offering memorandum also described, in general terms, the types of trading strategies that might be used by the hedge fund manager, disclosed risks and potential conflicts of interest, and set forth other material information.

Initially, hedge funds were able to avoid regulation under the Investment Company Act of 1940 through a provision that exempted investment companies with less than a hundred investors. That exemption applied regardless of the amount of money under management, provided that the company did not make a public offering of its securities. The National Securities Markets Improvement Act of 1996 expanded this exemption, allowing hedge funds to act without registration as an investment company if their investors were "qualified purchasers"—that is, large, sophisticated investors—without limitation as to the number of persons. A "qualified" investor would include someone who had $5 million in investments.

The initial treatment of hedge funds in the futures industry was markedly different under the CFTC. Many hedge funds traded commodity futures contracts regulated by the CFTC, which initially asserted that such activity required those funds to register with the CFTC as commodity pool operators (CPOs) and commodity trading advisers (CTAs) under the Commodity Exchange Act of 1936 (CEA). However, in 1992, the CFTC provided an exemption from most regulatory requirements for commodity pools (the commodity futures industry equivalent to a mutual fund) that were offered only to highly accredited investors, a designation that applied to most of those investing in hedge funds.

Similar relief was not given for CTA registration. The CEA contains an exemption from CTA registration for CTAs with fewer than fifteen clients.

This raised the question of whether a hedge fund or other entity with its own customers is the CTA client or whether the CFTC should also count the number of clients of the hedge fund or other entity. The Court of Appeals for the Ninth Circuit, in an early challenge on that issue, upheld the CFTC's look-through position in which it counted the number of shareholders or investors in the investment fund for purposes of measuring whether the fifteen-person registration threshold had been reached..[25] At about the same time, the Court of Appeals for the Second Circuit made a similar ruling with respect to investment advisers under the Investment Advisers Act of 1940, holding that a general partner of a limited partnership was an adviser to the limited partners, rather than to the limited partnership as an entity.[26] However, in 1985, the SEC adopted a rule that treated each limited partnership, trust, or corporation as a single client, even though the limited partnership, trust, or corporation might have a large number of clients who were depending on the adviser's counsel.

The CFTC's look-through position swept up a lot of hedge funds as CTAs even though those entities advised only wealthy and sophisticated clients. "By regulating commodity pools of all shapes and sizes and treating investment funds as the sum of their individual investors, the CFTC became, by default, the only active regulator of any portion of the hedge fund marketplace."[27] The CFTC began to rethink its regulatory role after the enactment of the Commodity Futures Modernization Act of 2000 (CFMA).[28] That statute was a statutory reflection of a CFTC decision to deregulate the commodity markets conducting transactions in which only wealthy and sophisticated investors are involved. The CFTC was, therefore, receptive to a petition from the Managed Funds Association, a trade association for hedge funds, which sought a "sophisticated investor exemption" from registration as a CTA for advisers working only with wealthy and sophisticated clients.[29] That exemption, adopted by the CFTC on August 8, 2003, was designed to conform to the SEC position on not looking through entities to count clients for purposes of registration as an adviser.

One commentator predicted that, as a result of that and other changes made to CFTC rules,

> the CFTC's regulatory role in the managed futures markets will shrink to a fraction of its former size and this development may well presage a new regulatory map in which the . . . [SEC] exercises regulatory oversight over the hedge fund marketplace, including commodity pools and trading advisors previously regulated by the CFTC.[30]

Indeed, that process was already under way at the SEC, where the staff was considering whether regulation of hedge funds was needed as a result of their involvement in the market timing and late trading at the mutual funds. Not surprisingly, the SEC staff study concluded that regulatory control over the hedge funds was needed, including their registration as investment advisers.

THE RISE OF THE HEDGE FUNDS AND PRIVATE EQUITY   243

The SEC staff was also seeking corporate governance reforms in its settlements with hedge funds involved in the late-trading and market-timing cases.

Some sixteen months after the CFTC adopted the SEC's approach on looking through entities to count clients, the SEC changed its position. It adopted the old CFTC view and began looking through hedge funds to count the number of clients in order to require the registration of hedge funds as investment advisers. The SEC commissioners took that action after another highly partisan vote of 3–2. The rule required hedge fund advisers to register with the SEC as investment advisers by February 1, 2006. Predictably, that requirement became the basis for more regulation after every new hedge fund scandal. As it was, under the new rule, registered hedge funds became subject to SEC audits, were required to maintain specified books and records, and had to hire a compliance officer and establish a compliance program. Those hedge funds were also required to disclose the amount of money under management.

The hedge fund investment adviser registration requirement was challenged in the Court of Appeals for the District of Columbia. That court concluded that the SEC had acted arbitrarily in defining clients to include hedge fund participants. The court stated that the fact that "the Commission wanted a hook on which to hang more comprehensive regulation of hedge funds may be understandable. But the Commission may not accomplish its objective by a manipulation of meaning."[31] The SEC did, however, adopt an antifraud rule for hedge fund advisers, which is probably all that was ever needed for these sophisticated operations. Its staff sent a letter to a number of hedge funds in August 2007 seeking information about potential misuse of inside information out of concern over information leaks from subprime brokers, how the hedge funds were valuing their portfolios, and other matters. Following the SEC's lead, the California Department of Corporations announced a proposal to require hedge funds to register with it. However, that proposal was withdrawn in May 2008.

After the abortive attempt by the SEC to regulate hedge funds, the President's Working Group on Financial Markets (PWG) reexamined the issue of hedge fund regulation. The PWG concluded, "Private pools of capital bring significant benefits to the financial markets"; "market discipline," not additional regulation, it said, was sufficient to protect against abuses by hedge funds.[32] Chairman of the Federal Reserve Ben S. Bernanke also stated with respect to hedge funds that:

> Their rapid growth is one of the most important developments in U.S. financial markets in the past decade or so. Hedge funds vary widely in their investment strategies and in the types of risks they take. Overall, however, most economists agree that the rise of hedge funds has been a positive development for investors and for financial markets. They have stimulated an extraordinary amount of financial innovation in recent years; and, using many of these new financial tools, they have greatly enhanced the liquidity, efficiency, and risk-sharing capabilities of our financial system.[33]

The PWG did recommend several best practices for investors in hedge funds, their managers, and their counterparties.

A GAO report issued in February 2008 concluded that creditors, counterparties, and other market participants demonstrated discipline in their dealings with hedge funds. The effect of that discipline was limiting the leverage and risk incurred by hedge funds, an approach that had been recommended by the PWG. Two months later, in April 2008, the Treasury Department released two reports by advisory committees appointed by the treasury secretary concerning the operation of hedge funds and responsibility of hedge fund investors. The first report that focused on hedge fund operations recommended that hedge funds make more disclosures on the valuation of their holdings and that hedge funds provide investors with audited financial statements. The second report focused on the role of hedge fund investors and, among other things, provided guidelines for fiduciaries planning to invest in hedge funds. One of the advisory groups sought more disclosures on hard-to-value assets, which were referred to as "level-two" assets.

Those reports seemed to indicate that the government had abandoned its efforts to regulate hedge funds and would defer to self-regulation by fund managers. That view was premature. The subprime crisis revealed a number of problems and massive hedge fund frauds that renewed demands for SEC regulation of hedge funds.

Hedge Funds Expand

Hedge Funds Go Public

Traditionally, hedge funds were organized as nonpublic companies, which shielded them from public scrutiny. There was also a regulatory concern as to whether a public offering by a hedge fund would make it an investment company subject to the Investment Company Act of 1940, which would effectively put it out of business. However, the SEC ruled that the statute did not apply. In February 2007, after receiving that regulatory green light, Fortress Investment Group became the first hedge fund to become a publicly traded company. Its five owners valued their stake in the firm at more than $10 billion, but its stock price suffered from turmoil in the credit markets and had fallen by year's end. Fortress granted a $300 million stock award to one of its star traders, Adam Levinson, in 2008. However, it experienced severe investment losses as the subprime crisis mounted. The price of Fortress stock dropped by 25 percent on December 3, 2008, after it suspended withdrawals from its largest hedge fund. Fortress lost 95 percent of its stock value between its IPO and January 2009.

Fortress was involved in a bizarre fraud scheme engineered at the New York law firm of Dreier, which came to light in December 2008. The founder and owner of that prominent law firm was Marc Dreier, a Harvard Law School graduate. He was arrested in Canada at a meeting at the Toronto Teachers Pension Plan, where he was pretending to be an attorney for that pension fund in order to obtain funds from Fortress through the sale of counterfeit notes. Having been released on bail in Canada, he returned to New York but was thereupon arrested as he was already under investigation in the United States. Dreier was charged with selling counterfeit notes purportedly issued by a real estate investment firm, Solow Realty, a Dreier client. The bogus notes were sold to hedge funds and other institutional investors. Dreier was charged with bilking $700 million through his schemes, which included $38 million taken from a bankruptcy account. An accomplice, Kosta Kovachev, was also arrested.

Dreier had been living large on this fraud. He owned a $15 million yacht, two homes on Long Island, and a posh Manhattan apartment. He decorated his law firm's office with $30 million in artwork and paid some secretaries a salary of $200,000. After the Justice Department issued its usual superseding indictment that increased his possible jail time to 145 years, Dreier pleaded guilty to criminal money-laundering charges and was sentenced to twenty years in prison. A former SEC enforcement attorney also pleaded guilty to criminal charges for assisting Dreier in carrying out his fraudulent scheme.

Another hedge fund, Och-Ziff Capital Management, went public with much fanfare in 2007, but its stock price suffered, falling from a high of $26.75 to a low of $3.13 in 2008. Man Group (later renamed MF Global) became the largest public hedge fund company in the world after it went public in the summer of 2007. The IPO was not a hot issue. After concerns were raised over hedge fund exposure to the housing market decline and the subprime crisis, its stock price quickly dropped by some 20 percent. Nevertheless, the company continued to grow. In June 2008, MF Global held $78.5 billion in assets, and it was able to raise some $4 billion in a two-month period in 2008. The subprime crisis, and the lukewarm reception given to hedge fund IPOs by investors, discouraged their additional public offerings.

Hedge Fund Abuses

The SEC noted in 2004 that the growth in hedge funds was accompanied by a substantial and troubling increase in the number of hedge fund fraud enforcement cases. In the previous five years, the SEC brought fifty-one cases involving charges that hedge fund advisers have defrauded hedge fund investors or others of over $1.1 billion.[34] However, the amount of losses cited by the SEC from hedge fund fraud was only a small portion of the $870 billion managed by over 7,000 hedge funds in the United States. Hedge fund fraud affected only about .001 percent of investor funds held in hedge funds.[35] Nonetheless, when fraud struck, it was often on a large scale, as demonstrated by the market-timing and late-trading scandals involving the hedge funds' misuse of mutual fund closing valuations. Even worse were instances of common theft and cover-ups of large losses.

Bayou Securities, a hedge fund that had $450 million under management, was found to be missing $400 million of those funds after its founder, Samuel Israel III, announced that he was retiring at age forty-six in order to spend more time with his family. After those losses were exposed, he was arrested and charged with fraud. Israel and his chief financial officer (CFO), Daniel Marino, pleaded guilty to criminal charges of fraud and were both sentenced to twenty years in prison. James G. Marquez was sentenced to just over four years in prison and ordered to pay $6.26 million in restitution for his role in the Bayou fraud. The draconian sentences now being routinely handed out by judges for financial crimes were having an effect on the violators. Just before he was supposed to report to prison, Israel went missing. His car was found parked next to a bridge, and a suicide message was scrawled in the dust on the car: "suicide is painless," referring to the theme song of the film and, later, television series "M*A*S*H." However, prosecutors were skeptical that Israel had actually committed suicide because no body was found in the river under the bridge. A massive manhunt began. Israel's "most wanted" poster advised that he could be armed and dangerous. Israel's girlfriend, Debra Ryan, was arrested and charged with aiding and abetting his flight, for which she was later sentenced to probation. In reality, he had been hiding in an RV campground in Massachusetts and surrendered a few weeks later. Israel was sentenced to twenty years in prison. The Bayou investors were able to recover $20.6 million from Goldman Sachs in an arbitration proceeding. Goldman Sachs was Bayou's prime broker, and the investors charged that Goldman had ignored warning signs of fraud.

Some other hedge fund fraudsters also tried to flee but were captured. Angelo Haligiannis, the architect of a $27 million hedge fund fraud, cut off his ankle bracelet while under home confinement (in his parents' home) and fled while awaiting sentencing, but was arrested months later on a Greek island and extradited to the United States. Kirk Wright defrauded investors in his Atlanta-based hedge fund, International Management Associates, out of $150 million before fleeing. He was captured in Miami, Florida, but committed suicide while being held in an Atlanta jail. Kirk was facing up to 710 years in prison and fines of up to $16 million. The SEC had already obtained a judgment of $20 million against him. Among Wright's victims were several athletes in the National Football League (NFL) who lost a total of more than $20 million. Those players sued the NFL and their players union, claiming that they had endorsed Wright as a sound investment adviser.

The CFTC charged another hedge fund, Tradewinds International II, with overstating the value of its assets. The hedge fund claimed assets of over $18 million whereas the actual amount was $1.1 million, and purported to have gains of 12 percent when it was actually experiencing losses. The fund's manager, Charles L. Harris, used hedge fund monies to buy luxury cars and a house in Florida. Harris sent his investors a DVD of his confessing to improper trading while fleeing authorities in his yacht. He was later caught.

Michael Berger concealed some $350 million in trading losses from investors in Manhattan Investment Fund, a hedge fund that he managed. Berger fled the country and was on the lam for five years before Austrian police arrested him. Berger's hedge fund had used Bear Stearns as its prime broker. A federal district court held that Bear Stearns was on inquiry notice of Berger's fraud before his exposure and flight, which could expose it to liability under the bankruptcy laws. A senior executive at Bear Stearns heard information at a cocktail party that differed from his understanding of how the hedge fund was operated. However, the district court noted that Bear Stearns did begin to investigate after receiving that information, and such actions could constitute a show of good faith.[36]

The federal district court later rejected the decision of its magistrate that would have required Bear Stearns to pay $125.1 million for its role in the clearing for that hedge fund.[37] A class-action suit by investors in the Manhattan Investment Fund against Bear Stearns was also dismissed. The suit charged that Bear Stearns had not followed margin rules for the hedge fund's trades, but a federal judge ruled that that activity was not the proximate cause of the investors' losses. Rather, they were the victims of Berger's Ponzi scheme.

The Man Group provided clearing services to non-proprietary hedge funds. One such fund was Philadelphia Alternative Asset Management Co. (PAAMCO), a hedge fund based in the Cayman Islands that recruited mostly U.S. investors. Paul Eustace, the manager of PAAMCO, was indicted for concealing some $200 million in losses from those investors. Eustace had previously served for seven years as the president of Trout Trading, one of the largest and most respected hedge funds in the commodity futures industry with over $1 billion under management. He had reported large profits from PAAMCO investments, which attracted additional investors and allowed him to claim large performance fees, when in fact he had lost most of their funds. Eustace was able to conceal his trading losses through an account that he maintained at Man Financial but did not report to the hedge fund's administrator, UBS Fund Services (Cayman).[38]

Eustace was indicted for this fraud. Prosecutors charged that he had spent hedge fund fees on gifts and breast enhancement surgery for a girlfriend. He was ordered by a federal court to pay $300 million in restitution and fines to the CFTC. In December 2007, MF Global agreed to pay $77 million to the CFTC and investors to settle charges that it had failed to supervise Eustace's activities. It was unclear why the CFTC thought that Man Financial was obligated to supervise an independent hedge fund that was separately registered with the CFTC. The CFTC, nonetheless, was taking an expanded view of its supervisory requirements, which normally extend only to the supervision of a firm's own employees.

Hedge fund fraud continued. Howard Schneider, the founder of Gateway Capital, a hedge fund, was sentenced to eight years in prison in April 2008, after he pleaded guilty to using millions of dollars in investor funds for personal expenses and to further his gold coin collection. Michael Lauer, a hedge fund manager, was indicted for defrauding customers of more than $200 million through his Lancer Group hedge fund. He faced up to twenty years in prison if convicted. A hedge fund managed by Ritchie Capital Management was forced into bankruptcy. The manager of that hedge fund had previously raised controversy by trying to move assets into "side pocket" accounts, which were used for storing hard-to-value assets but also limiting the ability of investors to redeem their interests in the hedge fund. These hedge fund frauds would pale in comparison to the Bernie Madoff and Stanford hedge fund Ponzi schemes that emerged during the subprime crisis.

Commodity pools that traded through Refco faced some difficulties after that large futures commission merchant failed just two months after its IPO. That failure followed the revelation that Refco had hidden $430 million in obligations from its auditors. Refco acted as a clearing firm for several large hedge funds and commodity pools. A commodity pool sponsored by celebrity commodity trader James B. Rogers had $362 million on deposit with Refco, and Refco's bankruptcy put those funds at risk. Refco's CEO, Philip R. Bennett, and its CFO, Robert Trotsen, pleaded guilty to criminal charges for their role in this scheme. Just before the end of each SEC-required quarterly financial reporting period, Bennett and Trosten moved the losses from Refco's books to those of another company that they controlled. Having pleaded guilty, Bennett could have faced a prison term as long as 300 years. The district court judge had little sympathy for Bennett, noting that in the "post-Enron era" it was no longer unusual for older executives to begin a sentence in which "their residence in prison is possibly the last residence they're ever going to have."[39] In the end, he was sentenced to a relatively merciful sixteen years in prison. Another former Refco CEO, Tone Grant, a decorated Marine Corps veteran, was convicted in a jury trial for his role in carrying out the scheme and received a sentence of ten years in prison.

Refco's former executive vice president, Santo Maggio, entered into a plea bargain with prosecutors and agreed to testify against other Refco executives in order to reduce his own sentence as well as disgorge $23 million. In an unusual action against outside lawyers, prosecutors indicted Joseph P. Collins, a partner in the law firm of Mayer Brown and a former Air Force captain, who was outside counsel to Refco and a well-regarded derivatives lawyer. The SEC also brought charges against Collins, which he settled. After Collins refused to plead guilty, the government obtained a superseding indictment adding charges that could result in imprisonment of up to eighty-five years. A jury convicted him in July 2009 of fraud and conspiracy, but it deadlocked on nine other counts. Collins was sentenced to seven years, but was appealing his conviction. Class action lawsuits against Collins and his law firm were dismissed because they had made no false statements to investors, a condition for liability under the federal securities laws recently imposed by the Supreme Court.

The Rise of Private Equity

Some History

Concentrations of private capital pools for industrial development were rare in America before the Revolution. Capital concentrations for industrial development were inhibited by restrictions imposed by the British Crown on the issuance of corporate charters. As a consequence, until after the Revolution publicly owned companies could not develop and private businessmen could only operate singly, in partnerships, or through joint ventures.

Those entrepreneurs comprised many of our founding fathers, whose largest speculations involved the land companies that owned vast tracts of property through grants of "patents" from the Crown. Such companies included the Ohio Company, in which George Washington participated and that claimed ownership of some 200,000 acres of land; the Loyal Company, in which Thomas Jefferson's father participated; the Indiana Company, which counted Thomas Paine as an investor; and the Susquehanna Company, which Benjamin Franklin joined. Other land companies were the James River Company, the Cape Fear Company, the Pennsylvania Land Company, the Transylvania Company, the Holland Land Company, the North America Land Company, and the Virginia Yazoo Company.

Shipping was another favorite endeavor, in which groups of investors would commission a ship and crew for whaling and fishing or trading missions. One of the more ambitious of those projects was the development of the China trade. That effort was delayed by the Revolution, so it was not until 1784 that the American ship *Empress of China* reached Canton (now called Guangzhou). The investors in that ship included Robert Morris, the "financier" of the Continental Army. That enterprise demonstrated a weakness in these groups. They had no structured management system and their frequent quarrels over how the business was to be carried out caused their business to suffer.[40] However, the China trade proceeded and laid the groundwork for the great wealth of John Jacob Astor, whose ships carried Hawaiian sandalwood and other goods to China and returned with tea, turning a profit of $100,000 in a single voyage.

After the Revolutionary War, the states began issuing charters to commercial enterprises, which operated as joint-stock companies that often sold shares to the public through subscriptions. Those shares were then traded in the markets, and gave rise to NYSE, the Philadelphia Stock Exchange, and the curb market. Private equity did not disappear, but the center of finance shifted to large public companies, which included banks, insurance companies, canal companies, railroads, and, later, great industrial enterprises.

The public companies began a process of consolidation in the last quarter of the nineteenth century, changing a localized economic structure into a national one. The combinations covered railroads, the oil business (Standard

Oil), and, later, steel (US Steel). Those "trusts" were attacked as monopolies as their giant size fostered abuses. The Sherman Antitrust Act was passed in 1890 to combat the growth of these massive enterprises, with little effect. Large banks and investment bankers, like J.P. Morgan, took positions in large public and privately owned companies. One of the more highly publicized such investments was Morgan's purchase of Carnegie Steel for $480 million in 1901. These private investments were generally called merchant banking, a practice widely used abroad, and had been in use since merchant banks were created in Italy during the Middle Ages.

By the 1930s, public companies dominated commerce in the United States, and it was then that Adolf Berle made his famous attack on the management of those companies, charging that they were being operated for the benefit of their managers, rather than their owners.[41] The public companies were also targeted for reform by the federal securities laws in the 1930s, placing them under the control of the SEC in 1934. The commercial banks were taken out of the merchant and investment banking businesses by the Glass-Steagall Act in 1933. Commercial banks were not permitted to reenter that business until the Gramm-Leach-Bliley Act repealed that legislation in 1999, and even then restrictions were imposed. This left merchant banking in the hands of the investment bankers and private investing pools in what became known as private equity.

Private equity was overlooked in the scrutiny of Congress when it enacted the federal securities laws. Congress focused instead on abuses in publicly traded stocks. For the most part, private companies were exempted from the registration requirements of the Securities Act of 1933. The sale of their shares in secondary transactions also was not included in regulation under the Securities Exchange Act of 1934, as long as the sales were privately negotiated transactions that involved only wealthy individuals or large institutions. As a result, private equity remained private, and their operations and financial affairs had little transparency. They were also able to avoid the intensive scrutiny given to the management of public companies by the SEC, class-action litigants, roving prosecutors, corporate reformers, and the press. The price of that privacy, however, was that they were denied access to an important source of permanent capital, the public shareholder.

Venture Capitalists

Private equity takes many forms, from the mom-and-pop store to the giant private equity firms that rose in prominence before the credit crunch in 2007. The smaller-scale precursors of the large private equity firms were the "venture capitalists" (VCs), or "angels," as they were sometimes called. These investors often made "incubator" or microloans to small start-ups with a potential for success through a new product or market. The VCs often funded start-up companies that had no other source of capital or that had exhausted their credit lines. One famous early example of venture capital funding was the capital support provided to Alexander Graham Bell in 1874 for his work on the telephone by a Boston attorney, Gardiner Greene Hubbard, and a Massachusetts leather merchant, Thomas Sanders. They also provided funding to start Bell Telephone.

Venture capital as a specialty faced some early setbacks. In 1926, Lincoln Filene, a Boston department store owner, formed the New England Council (NEC) to explore ways to attract new business to New England, which was suffering from a decline in textile industry. NEC pursued this effort for many years, but it had little apparent effect on introducing capital to new businesses. In 1941, the New England Industrial Development Corporation (NEIDC) was formed, with a business plan to make a report on new businesses, for which it charged a fee. If the business looked promising, a preferred stock investment would be made. However, most new firms did not have the funds to pay for the investigation. Another entity, called New Enterprises, formed before World War II, provided an engineering survey and a confidential report on perspective new firms. Participants in this enterprise could then invest their own funds if they so desired. Few such investments were made.[42]

Wealthy families sometimes provided venture capital through professional money managers. The model for such investments was the Bessemer Trust, created by Henry Phipps in 1907 with funding of $50 million for investment in private companies. Phipps had been a partner in Carnegie Steel. In 1974, the Bessemer Trust was opened to other wealthy families and had over $50 billion under management as the twenty-first century began.

The Rockefellers also engaged in venture capital projects, some of which turned out to be quite lucrative. They helped start Eastern Air Lines and Douglas Aircraft and made large profits from investments in Intel and Apple Computer. The Whitney family invested $500,000 in Storage Technology and made $50 million.

The first of the modern venture capital firms was American Research and Development (ARD), started in 1946 by a brain trust composed of the president of the Massachusetts Institute of Technology, the president of the Federal Reserve Bank of Boston, and a Harvard Business School professor. ARD sought to exploit technologies developed during World War II. One of its successes was the High Voltage Engineering Company, in which ARD invested $200,000 in 1947 and sold through a public offering in 1955 for $1.8 million. In another investment, ARD purchased 77 percent of the Digital Equipment Company in 1957 for $70,000. That stake was valued at $355 million fourteen years later. Another venture capitalist was J.H. Whitney, who also started his operations in 1946. He was best known for the success of his investment in the Minute Maid orange juice company.

Congress gave the venture capital business a boost in 1958 when it authorized the Small Business Administration to charter small business investment companies (SBICs), which were allowed to borrow funds from the government that they could then use to provide financing for start-up companies. Within ten years, some 700 SBICs were providing the majority of risk capital for start-up firms in the United States. Several of the firms financed by SBICs made IPOs in the 1960s. This set the model for future venture capital financing: supply start-up capital and reap a large reward through a subsequent public offering. However, a stock market collapse at the end of the 1960s slowed venture capital financing to a trickle.

Restrictions imposed by the government for its SBIC loans also undercut interest in this method of venture capital financing. By 1978 the number of SBICs had fallen to 250. In their place, completely private venture capitalist firms began to emerge, including the angels and incubator organizations that provided small amounts of seed capital to start-up ventures and a small number of investment banking firms that sought large returns from start-ups. Typically, after that legislation, venture capital was funneled to VC funds controlled by managers. The institutional investors in these funds were passive participants, usually limited partners. Such funds were typically blind pools, in which investors were told only generally about the venture capitalist investment strategy, for example, Internet firms rather than the particular companies.[43]

Venture capital investors were given another boost in 1978 when capital gains taxes were reduced from 49.5 percent to 28 percent. The enactment of the Employee Retirement Income Security Act (ERISA) of 1979 was another shot in the arm for private equity development. That legislation loosened the investment standards for fiduciaries, allowing them to invest in more risky assets as a part of their total mix of investments. This brought large sums of money into the venture capital world, particularly from pension funds seeking to diversify their portfolios.

The results were impressive. By the end of the 1980s, some 1.3 million new businesses were starting up each year. Before 1980, large corporations created the majority of new jobs in America, but in the 1990s, Fortune 500 companies lost 4 million jobs. In contrast, companies with fewer than a hundred employees created 16 million new jobs during the same period.

The VCs used investor funds as well as their own to fund much of the growth of the dot.com companies in the 1990s that sought to exploit the Internet. Those companies were often funded by the VCs, which took an equity stake in the new venture and then cashed out, along with their owners, through public offerings. The venture capital funds usually obtained capital commitments from large investors with time horizons of up to ten years for the investment. The venture capitalist would call on those commitments on an as-needed basis as opportunities appeared.

These modern VC firms actually trace their history to the early 1960s, when Arthur Rock, an investment banker at Hayden Stone in New York, moved to California, where he started two venture capital funds in Silicon Valley. His investments included Apple Computer, Teledyne, and Intel. Others followed Rock's business model. A $1.5 million investment in Apple by Venrock Associates grew to be valued at $100 million. New Court Securities and other VCs invested $25 million in Federal Express. That stake grew to be valued at $1.2 billion. Those successes led to an industry of venture capitalists, even though about half of all VC investments had to be written off as losses.

This business was largely concentrated on the West Coast, where 48 percent of all investment dollars were being raised in the 1990s. That compared with only 20 percent in the Northeast, the traditional source of capital-raising efforts.

One of the most successful dot.com VCs was Kleiner, Perkins, Caufield, & Byers in San Francisco. It was started in 1972 by Eugene Kleiner, one of the founders of Fairchild Semiconductor, and Tom Perkins, a former Hewlett-Packard executive. Al Gore and Colin Powell were added to the firm in later years to give it political muscle. Kleiner Perkins started in 1972 with an initial investment fund of $8 million, which grew to almost $300 million within ten years. A $1.5 million investment in Tandem Computers by Kleiner Perkins grew to be worth $220 million. One success was an investment in a company called Genentech, which provided a 200 percent return on Kleiner Perkins's investment in two years. Other investments included Netscape, Google, and Amazon.com. In March 2008, Kleiner Perkins announced the creation of a $100 million iFund that would fund add-on applications for the Apple iPhone and iPod.

Other well-known venture capital firms were the HARM group, or the "Four Horseman" as they were sometimes called, a group of investment banking firms that included Hambrecht & Quist (acquired by Chase Manhattan Bank in 1999 for $1.4 billion); Alexander Brown and Sons (acquired by Bankers Trust in 1997 and later by Deutsche Bank); Robertson Stephens (acquired by Bank of America and later sold to FleetBoston); and Montgomery Securities (bought by NationsBank in 1997 for $1.4 billion and thereafter morphed into Bank of America Securities and Thomas Weisel Partners, which was spun out of that group).

The amount of venture capital grew from about $3 billion in the 1970s to over $30 billion at the end of the 1980s, at which time some 650 VCs were raising funds. Between 1972 and 1992, VCs brought nearly a thousand firms to their IPOs, which were often popular "hot issues" that traded up rapidly over their initial offering price. [44] Some of the opening-day price run-ups in these IPOs were incredible. The boom in Internet stocks was said to have begun in August 1995 with Netscape's IPO, which was priced at $28 and immediately rose to $75, before closing on its first day of trading at $58 on volume of over 13 million shares. More than 250 Internet-related IPOs were made in 1999, and they averaged an 84 percent increase in price on their first day of trading. The price of VA Linux rose from $30 to $300 on its first day of trading; Priceline .com opened at $16 and closed at $69, then went to $162 per share; Red Hat saw its stock jump $50 in the first hour of trading; Scient experienced a price rise of $123; and Amazon.com's stock jumped 30 percent on its first day of trading and tripled in price within three months. EBay went public at $18 and was trading at $240 per share within three months.

The collapse of the stock market in 2000 virtually stopped the process of VC IPO transactions. Venture capital did not disappear after the market crash, but focus shifted from the dot.com companies to more established and larger firms, which required more capital and gave rise to the private equity groups.

Private Equity

"Private equity," in many ways, is at the opposite end of the spectrum from the venture capitalists. The VCs bring firms to the public market and make them public companies, while private equity often acquires public companies and takes them private for long-term restructuring before they are resold (often in a public offering).[45] Private equity emerged from the shadows in the 1980s in the form of some spectacular takeover battles aimed at public companies. During that period a great deal of merger activity occurred, as well as "corporate raiding" by the likes of the English businessman Sir James Goldsmith, Carl Icahn, Rupert Murdoch, T. Boone Pickens Jr., the Bass brothers, Irwin Jacobs ("Irv the liquidator"), Saul Steinberg, and Ronald Perelman. In many instances, one public company would take over another public company. However, a new phenomenon also emerged in the form of "leveraged buyouts" (LBOs), in which public companies were purchased by their own management, often with the assistance of a private equity firm or by a corporate raider, and then taken private.

These buyouts were funded by massive debt obtained from banks and through "junk bonds" that paid high interest rates because of their higher likelihood of default. These "high-yield" securities as a funding device were the special dominion of Michael Milken at Drexel Burnham Lambert. Milken provided the parties seeking to take over a public company with a letter in which he would state that he was "highly confident" that funds needed for a leveraged buyout could be raised through a junk-bond offering. He was as good as his word in fulfilling that promise, raising billions of dollars in multiple offerings. As described below, Milken became ensnarled in one of Wall Street's biggest scandals and Drexel Burnham was so badly crippled that it thereafter failed.

One of the more famous private equity LBOs involved Wesray, a company formed by former Treasury Secretary William Simon. In 1982 his firm bought Gibson Greetings for $80 million, of which $79 million was borrowed. Simon sold the company sixteen months later for $290 million, earning a personal profit of $66 million. An even more famous private equity firm was Kohlberg Kravis Roberts (KKR), created in 1976 by three individuals who had been working at Bear Stearns, with initial capital of $120,000. It was not long before KKR was acquiring firms worth billions of dollars through LBOs funded in large measure by junk bonds, many of which were underwritten by Drexel

Burnham. KKR also raised funds from investors, including wealthy individuals, as well as insurance companies. KKR made its first LBO of a publicly held company in 1979. By 1992, KKR had engaged in thirty-eight buyouts valued at over $60 billion.

A public company that became a "target" of an acquisition by a corporate raider frequently found that the announcement of the bid would set off a competitive battle, in which other companies or groups vied with one another with tender offers at ever-increasing prices, sometimes reaching astronomical levels. One of the these fights involved RJR Nabisco, headed by F. Ross Johnson, a colorful figure who treated RJR Nabisco as his personal fiefdom. Johnson used company funds to create a veritable air force of his own, consisting of about a dozen jets, including two Gulfstream G4s that cost $21 million each. He also created a "Taj Mahal" of corporate jet hangers that cost $12 million to build and another $700,000 to fill with furniture and artwork, to accommodate the RJR Nabisco aircraft fleet. Company directors were urged to use the jets for business or pleasure because, in Johnson's words, "I know if I'm there for them they'll be there for me." Johnson's new headquarters for the company, located in Atlanta, included a $100,000 lacquered Chinese screen, a set of antique chairs costing $30,000, and a $50,000 Persian rug for his office. Johnson lavished corporate funds on celebrities. Among others, O.J. Simpson was paid $250,000 for no-show celebrity appearances.

Johnson set off the takeover war at RJR Nabisco after he announced in October 1988 that he and other executives at the company would conduct a $17 billion LBO of the company at $75 per share, a $20 premium over its market price. Johnson had rebuffed a request by KKR to allow it to join his management group in this effort. KKR then decided to compete with Johnson and made its own tender offer of $90 per share for as much as 87 percent of the company's stock, with the rest of the stock to be purchased later. A special committee of the board of directors was formed to auction off the company, and a date was set for the submission of offers. Johnson increased his bid to $100 per share, and KKR responded with a $94 bid.

Another entrant, First Boston, submitted a third bid that was innovative, somewhat complex, and valued at between $98 and $110 per share. The special committee then decided to continue the bidding process. This time, KKR raised its bid to $106 per share, while the Johnson group only raised its bid by one dollar, to $101 per share. First Boston also raised its bid, but its conditions were deemed too uncertain to ensure such a payment.

The special committee selected the KKR bid, but Johnson demanded another opportunity to bid and raised his bid to what he claimed was $108 per share, and then to $112 per share. However, the value of the bid was not completely certain because it included the issuance of some securities that were difficult to value. The investment bankers advising the special committee valued the Johnson offer at a lower $109 per share. KKR also increased its bid to $108, and then to $109, but the investment bankers valued it at $108.50 because it too contained some securities that were uncertain in value. This led the investment bankers to conclude that both bids were substantially equivalent in value. After some study, the special committee accepted the KKR bid.

This epic battle got the attention of the press, as did Johnson's colorful lifestyle. His excesses became legend after he received a $53 million golden parachute as a consolation prize for his defeat in the takeover battle. That fight and Johnson's escapades became the subject of a popular book and a movie called *Barbarians at the Gate*. It would also hold the record for the largest private equity transaction until 2006, when KKR purchased HCA, a hospital company that had been created by the family of Senator Bill Frist. Although the RJR takeover garnered KKR a lot of publicity, it was not particularly profitable, and it took six years for KKR to earn back the investment.

The acquisition boom in the 1980s was derailed by a series of insider-trading scandals featuring the likes of Ivan Boesky and Dennis Levine, two well-known investment bankers on Wall Street who were at the epicenter of those scandals. Boesky, in an effort to reduce his prison sentence, turned on Michael Milken and, after being subjected to some strong-arm tactics by prosecutors, Milken pleaded guilty, was sentenced to a then-staggering ten years in prison, and fined $600 million, which he paid. Milken's sentence was later reduced to three years. His company, Drexel Burnham Lambert, was also indicted, pleaded guilty to felony charges, and paid a fine of $650 million as a result of Milken's conduct. That so weakened the firm that it eventually became bankrupt. At the time of its demise, Drexel Burnham had some $3 billion in debt outstanding. The company was brought down by a liquidity crisis after it could no longer fund its short-term operations in the commercial paper market, a fate that would befall other investment banks during the subprime crisis.

Private Equity Renewed

Private equity continued its growth, but quietly, until its profile was raised as managers of public companies sought ways to escape the heavy costs imposed by the enactment of the Sarbanes-Oxley Corporate Reform Act of 2002. The costs imposed on public companies by that statute and the ever-increasing harassment of management by prosecutors, class-action plaintiffs, and labor union pension funds made life at a public company miserable for executive officers. Private equity did not have to face those challenges, and private equity managers could pay themselves as much as they desired without worrying about criticism from the press and shareholder attacks. In light of Sarbanes-Oxley and costly and ill-thought-out SEC regulations, "who in their right mind would want to sit on a corporate board these days?"[46] However, private equity also had its critics. Warren Buffett once famously compared them to "porn shop operators." He believed that private equity stripped capital from their acquisitions and saddled them with strangling debt in order to gain leverage.[47]

That criticism did not stop the growth of private equity. Between 2003 and 2006, about 25 percent of takeovers of public companies were by private equity. The value of companies going private trebled between 2004 and 2006. More than 2,100 private equity buyouts were consummated in the first ten months of 2006, at a total price of $583 billion, an increase of $138 billion from the year before. The total buyouts of public companies in 2006 reached $709.8 billion by year's end. The total value of private equity investments reached $1.3 trillion in 2007.

Private equity raised more than $300 billion in equity commitments in 2007, "a nineteen percent increase over the prior year when $255 billion was raised, and an amount which will likely sustain well over a trillion dollars in new corporate acquisitions."[48] In 2006 more funds flowed into private equity than equity mutual funds. Even public companies were raising funds in the private equity market. Private equity and hedge funds provided about $27.7 billion in financing to public companies in 2006 through PIPEs (private investments in public equities).

Between 2006 and 2007, nine of the ten largest acquisitions in history were announced. The deals had steadily increased in size. Bain and Blackstone agreed to acquire Michaels Stores for $6 billion in July 2006. HCA went private in 2006 at a price of $21.3 billion plus the assumption of $11.7 billion in debt. A takeover battle began in January 2007 over Equity Office Properties Trust, for which the Blackstone Group bid $20 billion. A consortium of other investors made a competing bid, but the Blackstone Group prevailed with a bid of $23 billion. Blackstone also wanted to buy Pinnacle Foods, and it acquired the Hilton Hotels chain for $20 billion in July 2007. In May 2007, a private equity group agreed to purchase Clear Channel Communications for $19 billion. In still another huge private equity buyout, Ontario Teachers Pension Plan, Providence Equity Partners, and Madison Dearborn Partners acquired BCE for $32.6 billion in July 2007. In still another mega-acquisition, KKR and the Texas Pacific Group sought to acquire TXU for $32 billion.

Private equity pools in 2006 included the Blackstone Group, with $71 billion under management; the Carlyle Group, with $47 billion; Bain Capital, $40 billion; Kohlberg Kravis Roberts, $30 billion; Texas Pacific Group, $30 billion; and Cerberus Capital Management, $24 billion.[49] These private equity pools attracted investors in the form of hedge funds and pension funds seeking alternative investments outside the public exchanges. This burgeoning alternative market gave rise to the development of private equity electronic exchanges by several broker-dealers, which is where pieces of private equity could be bought and sold. That effort was eventually abandoned in favor of using the NASDAQ Portal system for such trading, which operates under SEC Rule 144A, which allows institutions to trade in unregistered securities.

On August 8, 2007, the Blackstone Group closed off all further investment in the world's largest private equity fund after nearly $22 billion was raised. Private equity firms gathered over $35 billion from Asian investors to create buyout funds. KKR created a $4 billion Asian fund, and the Texas Pacific Group (TPG) raised $4.2 billion for an Asian investment fund. CVC Capital Partners sought $5 billion as an Asian investment base. It appeared that the public markets and SEC regulation were becoming a thing of the past for sophisticated investors. General Electric entered the private equity business through GE Capital, which focused on the middle market of acquiring companies valued at less than $1 billion. GE thought that this middle market would present more opportunities for making investments that would provide robust returns. However, Apollo Advisors also entered this market by creating a closed-end mutual fund totaling $938 million that would lend money to companies with revenues of $50 million to $500 million.

The effect of the privatization process was straining the traditional markets. The value of stocks delisted from NYSE and NASDAQ reached nearly $50 billion in 2006. The value of IPOs in 2006 was less than half that of the stock values for public companies going private. In 2007, 926 public companies went private. Venture capital funds traditionally "used the IPO market as their exit strategy. . . . Today, however, nearly 90 percent of those venture-capital-backed start-ups are sold to strategic buyers in private transactions."[50]

Leveraged Loans

Investor funds were not the only source of funding by private equity. In fact, they were highly leveraged as a result of their borrowing. Initially, that borrowing occurred through the junk-bond market and conventional bank loans. Those funding sources evolved into the leveraged loan market that developed through the sale of portions of syndicated loans made by banks. The leveraged loan market then expanded to other financial institutions, including mutual funds, as funding sources for less-than-investment-grade borrowers. This approach was attractive to borrowers because they could avoid the "tedious SEC disclosure process" and attendant costs and risks.[51]

A lead bank would arrange for the underwriting of the loan to a private equity group in leveraged loan transactions that were sold in pieces to institutional lenders. Banks participating in the leveraged loan syndicate would initially provide funds for the leveraged loan. After the loan was closed, the participating banks would sell their loan portions to investors or keep a portion on their own books. Thus, instead of holding on to the loans until maturity, the banks could sell them off as just another asset, a process called "originate-to-distribute." This led to the development of a secondary market in leveraged loans that was attractive to institutional investors because of the higher yields paid by these below-investment-grade borrowers. Such loans were usually made at floating rates at a specified spread over LIBOR (London Interbank Offered Rate).

The value of leveraged loans was triple the amount raised through junk-bond offerings in 2005. The growth of the leveraged loan market allowed private equity to invest $365 billion worldwide in 2006. This was three times the amount in-vested in the previous year, itself a 200 percent increase over the amount invested in 2003.

The leveraged loan market exploded in 2006, with new issues totaling nearly $500 billion in value, a 58 percent increase over 2005. The amount of lever-aged loans held in institutional portfolios jumped by nearly $150 billion in 2006. "The market absorbed this vast expansion with hardly a speed bump."[52] Further leverage was added to the market through "second lien" loans that paid higher spreads than the typical leveraged loan, but that were subordinated to the claims of other lenders in the event of bankruptcy. The leveraged loan market boomed again in 2007 until the credit crunch shut it down. In the first quarter of 2007, $183 billion was raised through leveraged loans. By midyear, outstanding leveraged loans totaled almost $500 billion, of which about half were below investment grade.

Citigroup underwrote $114 billion in leveraged loans for private equity bor-rowers in 2007, earning fees of about $850 million. Bank of America Securities was the underwriter of $145 billion in leveraged loans in 2007, but was exceeded by JPMorgan Chase, which underwrote $217 billion in such offerings. By then private equity groups had become prime bank customers, accounting for about 18 percent of bank revenue from investment banking activities. Leveraged loans were not made only to private equity groups. In January 2006, Georgia Pacific was able to borrow $11 billion through a leveraged loan syndication.

The leveraged loan market was badly damaged by the credit crunch in 2007 and then by the subprime crisis in 2008. The top ten leveraged loan underwrit-ers had almost $200 billion in exposure from those loans on their own books and were forced to write off a portion of those loans, compounding their dis-tress from subprime lending. However, things could have been much worse for the investment banks. In 1995, commercial banks held over 70 percent of syndicated loans, but by 2007, they held only 13 percent of their successor, leveraged loans. Hedge funds and other institutional investors had taken large positions in leveraged loans but dumped those investments at steep discounts in order to raise cash in 2008.

As a result, vulture investors seeking distressed debt began purchasing those investments with a view toward making large profits after the market stabilized and valuations became more realistic. Participants in the distressed debt market included some opportunistic investors like Carl Icahn and Wilbur Ross, but mutual funds began entering the market. Ironically, private equity groups were themselves buying distressed leveraged loans on the theory that large profits could be made after the economic situation stabilized.

CDOs

The leveraged loan market was able to expand even further through the use of collateralized debt obligations (CDOs). The CDO, a structured finance arrangement in which leveraged loans or other debt obligations, such as residential mortgages, are packaged into a pool, is said to have been invented by Drexel Burnham Lambert in 1987 for the Imperial Savings Association, which failed during the savings and loan crisis in the 1980s. A CDO is created by an underwriter, who pools loans into a special-purpose entity, receiving a fee for that service and additional fees for servicing the CDO by passing on loan payments. Ownership interests in the pool are sold to investors, who then receive the payment streams from the leveraged loans or other assets that form part of the CDO. The collateral in most CDOs remained in the pool until its liquidation, in much the same manner as a unit investment trust. CDOs could also be managed, which meant that the managers could actively trade the assets in the pool. The nature of CDOs could vary: Some contained diversified pieces of leveraged loans. This concept was also applied to mortgages, the vehicles at the center of the subprime crisis.

The leveraged loan market helped fund the massive increase in private equity debt through CDOs, which securitized some $90 billion of leveraged U.S. loans in 2006, nearly double the amount of the previous year. Many of these leveraged loans were "covenant lite," which meant that they had few covenants for the protection of the holder of the debt. Another development was the creation of "synthetic CDOs," which gave the investor the same risk exposure as a CDO but without any ownership interest in an underlying loan. This was done through credit-default swaps, which could be funded or unfunded.

The CDO was structured like its predecessor, the collateralized mortgage obligation, which allowed investors to choose among various tranches with payment streams that had varying returns, maturities, and risk. They were made more marketable by the rating agencies, which gave a credit rating to the various payment streams, from investment grade and below. A triple-A rating (AAA) could be obtained by senior tranches, which had to be paid before other tranches. This meant that the lower tranches would absorb the credit risk, or so it was thought. Mezzanine tranches, which were rated AA to BB, were subordinate to the senior tranches and were superior to the equity tranches that were not rated and so carried the most risk in the event of default on the loans being securitized. Some CDOs were rated on the basis of their cash flow from the underlying assets, while others were valued on a mark-to-market basis for the underlying assets. The latter valuation method resulted in large write-offs during the subprime crisis because market valuations were often either unavailable or set at fire-sale prices.

A risk model developed by David Li, the Gaussian Copula model, did for CDOs what Black-Scholes did for options: It allowed them to be valued using mathematical formulas. Li's computerized model weighed the likelihood of a default by the companies whose leveraged loan debt was part of a CDO. His model was based on the "broken heart" concept familiar to actuaries—individuals die faster than they otherwise would after the death of a spouse. The

CDO model used risk assessments for each leveraged loan in the CDO and then correlated those risk assessments to determine the likelihood of defaults that would affect the lowest tranches in the CDO. Unfortunately, this model was deeply flawed. Like other risk models that failed during the subprime crisis, Li's model failed to factor in the occurrence of a hundred-year financial storm, like the one experienced during the subprime crisis. As a consequence, these models failed to predict the effects of a broad market downturn on CDOs.

Private Equity and Hedge Funds

Hedge funds and private equity have never established a bright-line distinction. Their investment time lines generally distinguished the two investment mediums, with hedge funds tending toward short-term trading and private equity tending toward a long-term management role. Nevertheless, private equity groups often owned or controlled their own hedge funds, as well as provided others with investment advice on acquisitions. For example, Blackstone Group announced in January 2008 that it was acquiring a hedge fund, GSO Capital Partners, for $930 million. At the time, the Blackstone Group viewed itself as a global alternative-asset manager for private equity funds, real estate funds, funds-of-funds that were created to invest in other hedge funds, mezzanine funds (hedge funds that invest in mezzanine debt that might include credit enhancements such as warrants or other equity linked securities), senior debt vehicles, hedge funds, and closed-end mutual funds. Hedge funds were also crossing the traditional lines with private equity. Hedge funds were generally passive investors that did not seek to take over public companies, which was the core of the private equity business model. However, hedge funds began to venture into the private equity arena. A consortium of hedge funds led by Och-Ziff and Perry Capital took over the Peacock Group, a private equity investor, in 2005, through a transaction valued at over $400 million.

Another general distinction between private equity and hedge funds was that hedge funds were viewed as passive investors that did not seek to participate in management. In contrast, private equity did seek participation in and control of management of the companies they took over. In recent years, however, a number of hedge funds have become activist investors. Among those engaging in this activity through hedge funds were some old corporate raiders. Ronald Perelman wanted to acquire Morgan Stanley. Kirk Kerkorian, who was then the largest investor in General Motors, unsuccessfully targeted that company for reform. He expressed that criticism through a representative he controlled who sat on the GM board. Kerkorian later tried, unsuccessfully, to buy Chrysler.

Carl Icahn sat on the boards of eight public companies in 2008, as a part of his campaign against corporate mismanagement. Among others, Icahn attacked Motorola's management and floated a proposal to split up its operations. As a result of Icahn's attacks, Motorola divided itself into two companies.

However, the firm continued to have problems, and its credit rating was cut to junk status in December 2008.

Icahn also waged a battle with the managers at Yahoo!, who, he believed, had too casually shunned Microsoft's takeover offers. Microsoft had been pursuing the Internet company but, after much negotiation, withdrew its offer. It offered $33 a share, but Yahoo! wanted $37. As a result, Microsoft was left stranded in its effort to compete with Google in providing Web-based services. Microsoft resumed its quest for Yahoo!, but this time the proposal was for a joint venture for Internet advertising. Microsoft finally threw in the towel after Yahoo! entered into a joint venture with Google, which later fell through. Several stockholders criticized Yahoo!'s management for frustrating Microsoft, and, as a result, losing a great opportunity to sell the company's stock at a substantial premium over the existing market price. Icahn was among those pressuring the Yahoo! board to resume negotiations with Microsoft. As a compromise, those managers agreed to allow Icahn to serve on the Yahoo! board. In retrospect, the decision to turn down the Microsoft offer was a major blunder. By December 2008, Yahoo!'s stock had fallen to $11 a share, about a third of what had been offered by Microsoft. Yahoo! CEO Jerry Yang resigned in November 2008 as a result of criticism of his handling of this situation. Finally, in July 2009, Microsoft and Yahoo! reached agreement on a joint venture.

Icahn also attacked the management at Blockbuster in 2005. After a proxy fight, he was elected to its board and began taking over the management of the company. Icahn was rebuffed in an attempt to effect a merger with the Lear Corporation. Its shareholders refused to approve the deal, but Icahn walked away with a $25 million termination fee—a good thing given that Lear declared bankruptcy in July 2009, as result of the subprime crisis. Icahn also went after ImClone, a company that had been at the center of a major insider trading scandal featuring the house and garden doyenne Martha Stewart and was able to have himself elected as chairman. In 2008, Icahn and the management of ImClone resisted a takeover offer from Bristol-Myers-Squib that would have netted him a profit of $309 million. Eli Lilly entered the competition in October 2008 and won by agreeing to pay $6.5 billion for ImClone.

Icahn faced some big losses during the subprime crisis. His hedge fund's investment in Blogen, a pharmaceutical company, showed a loss of $275 million in August 2008. Icahn experienced a loss of $126 million in WCI Communities, a real estate builder in Florida that was bankrupt. After such experiences, activist investors like Icahn, William Ackman, and Christopher Hohn pulled back from their strategy of attacking management for gain.

The continuing decline in the market in 2008 pushed more hedge funds into activist roles. One such fund was Bulldog Investors, which sought board representation and questioned company strategies. Jana Partners was another hedge fund that sought to influence management through its holdings. It hired former senior business executives to act as consultants and advisers in such activities.

CSX, one of the largest providers of long-distance transport, was under attack by two hedge funds called Children's Investment Fund Management, one of which was based in the United Kingdom, and the other in the Cayman Islands (TCI). The hedge funds were seeking to elect five of their nominees to the twelve-member board of CSX, and they wanted to amend the bylaws to allow shareholders with 15 percent of the company stock to call a special meeting of the shareholders at any time for any purpose. However, instead of actually buying CSX stock to wage that fight, TCI used large positions in cash-settled total return swaps on CSX stock to conduct this campaign. Those swaps gave TCI all the indicia of the stock of CSX through an exchange of payments rather than transfer of actual ownership. Although CSX could not vote the shares, their swap counterparty would vote as directed by TCI.

CSX brought suit against TCI, charging that it was violating an SEC rule that required persons, acting individually or collectively, to file a disclosure form identifying themselves and stating the purpose of their acquisitions, as well as the source of their funding, after they obtained beneficial owner-ship of 5 percent of a company's equity stock. TCI countered that it was not the beneficial owner of the stock, even though the swap counterparties had purchased it as a hedge and would willingly deliver it on demand. A federal district court held that this arrangement made TCI the beneficial owner of the stock, making TCI subject to the SEC rule. However, the judge declined to enjoin the hedge funds from voting the stock of CSX that they might obtain or control through their swaps. The Court of Appeals for the Ninth Circuit affirmed that decision.[53]

A vote on the TCI board nominees was held on June 25, 2008. CSX claimed that the vote was so close that it would take a month to count the votes and to declare who had been elected. TCI eventually won its seats on the CSX board, and TCI paid CSX $10 million to settle claims that it had improperly made short-term profits from its inside position. CSX continued to face challenges that required sound management to resolve. As the subprime crisis worsened, freight volume carried by rail had declined across the country. The famous Greenbrier Resort in West Virginia, which was owned by CSX, declared bank-ruptcy. Such luxury resorts had experienced steep drops in occupancy rates as a result of the deteriorating economy. It was also hurt by attacks in the press, and from the government, on corporations that spent large sums of money to host events and outings at luxury resorts. Moreover, TCI lost 43 percent of its net asset value in 2008.

Private Equity and Privacy

Private equity groups were intensely private. They historically sought to prevent any public or government scrutiny of their activities, which made them nimbler and exposed them to less regulatory cost. Investors in private equity funds were required to sign agreements, under which they pledged not to disclose information about their investment or the operations of the private equity fund. Those agreements usually contained boilerplate language that allowed investor disclosure when required by law. Using that loophole, at the behest of a newspaper, the attorney general of Texas ordered the University of Texas Investment Management Company to disclose information about its private equity investments, including internal rates of return—the net return earned by the group from inception to the last calculation date—something most private equity groups did not want made public. The internal rate of return is calculated as an annualized compounded rate of return, using cash flows and annual valuations.

Other efforts to obtain disclosure involved the use of state Freedom of Information Act statutes, which allow members of the public to request disclosure of a broad range of government records maintained by state entities. The University of Michigan responded to one such request by disclosing its private equity investments and their internal rates of return. One of the private equity groups in which it had invested, Sequoia Fund, then promptly expelled the university from its investment program. That hurt, and Michigan changed its Freedom of Information statute to protect such information from disclosure. Courts in California also ordered disclosures of private equity internal rates of return. The University of California was the subject of one such request, and it too was expelled from the Sequoia Fund. Other prestigious private equity groups also banned state institutions from their offerings in order to avoid disclosures about their operations and returns.[54]

Union Objections

Labor unions attacked private equity because those investors often strongly fought unionization efforts at the factories that they purchased. However, the unions did not have the same leverage in private equity that they enjoyed in public companies, where management could be harassed through the proxy process, in the newspapers, or through class-action litigation under the federal securities laws. In addition, private equity was focused on the long term. It could withstand a union strike if it reduced long-term costs. Management at public companies did not have that advantage because it focused entirely on quarterly earnings, which could be harmed disastrously by a strike. Nevertheless, labor opposition was formidable. Among those opposing private equity was the Union Network International, a global federation of over 900 unions with more than 15 million members.

Labor unions advocated various social programs that they believed private equity should support. Andy Stern, the head of the Service Employees International Union (SEIU), a renegade union that broke from the AFL-CIO in 2005, led this political action movement. The SEIU became embroiled in a controversy after it was revealed in the press that Illinois governor Rod Blagojevich had been negotiating with the union to sell the appointment for the Senate seat left open by Barack Obama's election as president. The union had contributed $1.8 million to Blagojevich's campaigns, making it his largest contributor.

David Rubenstein, cofounder of the Carlyle Group, was interrupted by a group of SEIU members while addressing the Wharton Private Equity Forum on the effects of the subprime crisis on private equity. The SEIU demanded that the Carlyle Group improve conditions at a nursing home that it had just purchased. However, Rubenstein was able to finish his talk, though it was not uplifting. He disclosed that, in January 2008, some $100 billion in already announced private equity transactions were dropped and another $100 billion in transactions were renegotiated. In another protest, SEIU members carted wheel barrels loaded with cash from the IRS to Carlyle's headquarters, and then dumped it around a Carlyle "fat cat tycoon" effigy. Stern also organized a global day of action against KKR for its alleged destructive effects on the businesses it acquired and to ensure respect for trade union rights and equitable tax treatment.

Stern continued his attacks on private equity with an op-ed piece in the *Wall Street Journal* on August 4, 2009, that charged private equity with causing the subprime crisis (no explanation of how they did that). He advocated that private equity be restricted from buying failing banks because the private equity groups might do something sinister.[55] The Federal Deposit Insurance Corporation (FDIC) had previously announced that it planned to propose rules that would govern private equity efforts to take over struggling banks. However, when published on July 2, 2009, the proposed rules sought to make such acquisitions even more difficult because of concerns by Sheila Bair, the FDIC chair, who believed that private equity purchases raised "red flags." Among other things, the proposed rules would have required private equity groups taking over a bank to maintain Tier 1 capital at a level about three times that of other banks, which would reduce leverage and returns.

Critics charged that the FDIC proposal would cut off a valuable source of capital needed to save taxpayer funds, pointedly noting that fifty-two banks had failed in the first six months of 2009. Those critics included several state pension funds, including ones in New York that had invested in private equity. The FDIC met to reconsider those restrictions on August 26, 2009, and agreed to drop the enhanced capital requirement, but did require private equity groups to keep an acquired bank for at least three years. By then eighty-one banks had failed since the beginning of the year, at a cost to the government of $19.3 billion.

The Carlyle Group had other problems. Its energy trading company, SemGroup, experienced large losses in March 2008, and it was under investigation in New York for possible improper payments to obtain the business of the New York state pension fund. That investigation followed the indictment of two aides of former New York State comptroller Alan G. Hevesi for receiving millions of dollars in exchange for steering business from the $105 billion New York Common Retirement Fund, which Hevesi controlled.

Hevesi had resigned and pleaded guilty to criminal charges for using state employees as personal servants, and later to charges for the pension fund payments. The Carlyle Group then announced that it would no longer use placement agents to find money from pension funds. The Carlyle Group also entered into a settlement agreement with New York attorney general Andrew Cuomo, in which it agreed to pay the state $20 million. It also agreed to adopt the Public Pension Fund Code of Conduct, which prohibits money managers from doing business with a public pension fund for two years after making a political contribution to an official associated with the fund, such as Hevesi. (See page 270 for more on the Carlyle Group.)

Riverstone Holdings, another private equity group that was acting as a placement agent for pension fund investments, agreed to pay $30 million to settle similar charges. Cuomo's investigation expanded to include the Quadrangle Group, a private equity fund that was cofounded by Steven Rattner, who was the Obama administration's czar for dealing with the auto industry's application for a bailout in 2009. Rattner denied any wrongdoing and was defended by President Obama, but then resigned on July 13, 2009, after only six months on the job.

Four other investment firms agreed to pay $4.5 million to settle with Cuomo over such payments and agreed to subscribe to his code of conduct. After this scandal, New York announced that it would no longer allow the use of private placement agents to solicit money from its government pension funds. It was also considering the creation of an independent board to oversee state pension fund investments, taking that role away from the state comptroller.

Private Goes Public

Direct access to investment by small investors in private equity was generally unavailable, because private equity did not want to submit to the full disclosure regime of the SEC, with all its attendant problems. Exchange-traded funds (ETFs), which invested in private equity, were listed on exchanges and operated in much the same way as mutual funds. The assets in ETFs grew about 45 percent in 2007, increasing to $608 billion from $420 billion the year before, which the number of ETFs more than doubled. Smaller investors could also access private equity through other pooled investments. A new trading platform was created in February 2009 for investments in private equity and hedge funds. The platform initially listed some $500 million of such stakes. The purpose of the platform was to provide liquidity for these investments.

In a surprising turnaround, large private equity funds, as well as some hedge funds, considered making public offerings of their own shares in 2007. Those private equity groups and hedge funds sought more permanent capital that could not be withdrawn by its investors through redemption demands that could come at inconvenient times. Public equity usually had a minimum investment period, but would still allow investor redemptions after a stated notice period.

This meant that investor funds could be withdrawn in the event of an economic downturn or if concerns were raised over the private equity's or hedge fund's investment program. In contrast, shareholders in a public company could sell their shares to someone else, but they could not demand that the corporation return their capital. Some critics questioned whether the sudden interest by private equity and hedge funds in going public was really motivated by a desire for permanent capital. Rather, they charged that the private equity group participants were actually seeking to cash in on their investments through a public offering, making themselves billionaires in the process.

The Blackstone Group was able to go public before the credit crunch in 2007. It presented itself to potential investors as a leading global alternative asset manager and a provider of financial advisory services. Blackstone also acted as a merger adviser, which, of course, led to charges of inside trading. The SEC charged Ramesh Chakrapani, a Blackstone investment banker, with perpetrating an inside-trading scheme involving a takeover of Albertsons by Supervalu, CVS Caremark, and Cerberus Capital Management, the private equity firm, that resulted in profits of more than $3.6 million. However, in December 2009, prosecutors and the SEC dismissed all charges against Chakrapani because it claimed a key witness would be unavailable to testify, but retained their ability to refile in the future.

The Blackstone Group began its private equity business in 1987. By 2007, it managed five general private equity funds and a specialized media and communications–related investment fund, becoming the largest fund of its kind. At the time of its IPO, on June 21, 2007, the Blackstone Group had fifty-seven senior managing directors and employed 335 investment professionals at its headquarters in New York and in offices around the world. The Blackstone IPO sold a 12 percent stake in the firm to the public for $4.1 billion, which valued it at around $33 billion in the sixth-largest IPO in history. The Blackstone offering proudly noted that it had no golden parachutes for its executives. Its IPO offering documents also stated that the company was focused on long-term strategies and would not attempt to manage by quarterly earnings reports, as was the case for other public companies.

Investors in the Blackstone IPO were given only limited voting rights. They had no right to elect the Blackstone general partner or its directors. Rather, those positions would be filled by the Blackstone founders. In addition, the Blackstone partnership agreement eliminated any fiduciary duties that might be owed by its general partner to the IPO investors, and investors were required to waive conflicts of interests on the part of the general partner—Blackstone Group Management. Its corporate private equity business had grown from $7.6 billion in 2001 to $31 billion in March 2007. That business generated pretax income of over $1 billion in 2006, and the group had an annualized internal rate of return, since its inception in 1987, of 30.8 percent. The Blackstone Group made over $6 billion in a five-year period. It was also managing a $78.7 billion portfolio in June 2007, up from $14 billion in 2000, an increase of over 39 percent.

The founders of Blackstone were Stephen A. Schwarzman and Peter G. Peterson. Schwarzman began his career at Lehman Brothers, where he worked in the mergers and acquisitions department from 1977 to 1984. Schwarzman's prominence in investment circles during the private equity boom had earned him the title "the new king of Wall Street" by *Fortune* magazine. Peterson had served as chairman of the Federal Reserve Bank of New York from 2000 to 2004. He had previously served as chairman and CEO of Lehman Brothers, CEO at Bell & Howell, and secretary of commerce under President Richard M. Nixon. Schwartzman and Peterson controlled Blackstone Group Management. Among other things, they were given the right to elect and remove its directors.

Blackstone warned off investors with a short-term focus. It also stated its belief that the best way to align shareholder and management interests was through the investment of a significant amount of the managers' own capital and by providing managers with carried interest as compensation. Blackstone managers were not historically given a salary or bonus. Rather, they were compensated by the increased value of their ownership interest in the businesses that they managed.

As a result of SEC disclosure requirements, Blackstone reported that Schwartzman had made $400 million in 2006. Schwartzman and Peterson also took home $2.3 billion from the Blackstone IPO, which was oversubscribed sevenfold. They cashed out just in time, because the credit crunch that began in July 2007 would severely affect private equity in general, and Blackstone in particular. Wealth does bring envy. David Blitzer, an executive at the Blackstone Group, was the target of a shakedown by one of his relatives and a lawyer. They were seeking a multimillion-dollar payment in exchange for an agreement to stop harassing him.

The Blackstone Group went public at $31 per share, and its share price rose 13 percent on the first day of trading. However, the Blackstone stock languished afterward and fell by 25 percent between the IPO and year-end 2007. By January 8, 2008, its share price had dropped to $18. Although Blackstone Group had a disappointing performance in 2007, Schwartzman was paid $350 million for his efforts, a reduction of $50 million from the previous year. He agreed to limit his compensation to an annual salary of $350,000 after the IPO, but he owned a significant portion of the carried interest earned from the firm's investment funds. Peterson was paid $171.5 million in 2007, a reduction of almost $40 million from the year before.

There was more bad news. Although the Blackstone Group had reported a profit of $1.13 billion in the first quarter of 2007, it posted a $251 million loss in the first quarter of 2008, having just completed its first year as a public company. Blackstone also had a large loss in the second quarter of 2008. Its revenues declined because of lower performance fees. In the third quarter of 2008, the firm reported a loss of $500 million and began to mark down its assets. Bad news continued with the announcement of another loss in the fourth quarter of 2008. Among other problems, Blackstone's $26 billion investment in Hilton properties was in trouble, as a result of a rapid decline in hotel stays and because real estate property values had dropped. Blackstone had invested $6 billion of its own money in that deal, and it borrowed the rest from banks and other institutional investors. Between its IPO and January 2009, Blackstone's stock price dropped by 85 percent.

KKR

KKR was another private equity group seeking permanent public capital. Still led by Henry Kravis and George Roberts as of 2010, KKR claimed several private equity titles, including the first LBO over $1 billion, as well as several of the largest LBOs worldwide, and the first buyout of a public company by tender offer. It had only some 400 employees, including 139 investment professionals operating out of offices in New York, Menlo Park, CA, San Francisco, London, Paris, Hong Kong, and Tokyo.

KKR sponsored and managed funds that made investments worldwide in private equity and debt transactions on behalf of third-party investors. The firm also managed substantial investments in public equity. Since its inception, KKR had created sixteen private equity funds and raised $60 billion in capital and capital commitments from investors. The amount of assets under management at KKR grew from $18.3 billion in 2002 to $53.4 billion in 2007, representing a compounded annual growth rate of 28.7 percent.

KKR created a publicly traded private equity fund in May 2006, called KKR Private Equity Investors (KPE), which allowed public market investors, including institutions and qualified individuals, to own a liquid investment in KKR's private equity investment strategies. The fund was traded on Euronext Amsterdam. It was a backdoor way of raising capital and allowing public investment without public shareholder involvement in corporate management issues. The KPE portfolio consisted of limited partner interests in five KKR private equity funds, co-investments in thirteen companies, and equity investments. The remainder of KPE's portfolio was invested in opportunistic, short-term investments. The shares of KPE were issued at $25 apiece and the offering raised $5 billion, but those shares traded at under $20 at the end of 2007 and had fallen to under $3 per share by December 2008. KPE marked down its assets by 32 percent at the close of the fourth quarter in 2008, and its share price continued to plunge, dropping to $2.25 at the end of February 2009.

Another publicly traded KKR fund was KKR Financial Holdings, a real estate investment trust that invested in residential and commercial real estate loans, asset-backed securities, and equities. All those assets were badly depleted by the subprime crisis. The shares of KKR Financial Holdings dropped by 95 percent during 2008. Its stock traded at $1.39 in December 2008, after having earlier fallen to .57 per share, compared with $30 per share in 2007. KKR Financial Holdings lost $1.2 billion in the fourth quarter of 2008.

KKR had announced in July 2007 that it planned to make its own IPO. The American Federation of Labor–Congress of Industrial Organizations (AFL-CIO) petitioned the SEC to stop KKR and other private equity groups from going public by requiring them to register as investment companies under the Investment Company Act of 1940. That statute imposes limitations on fees and requires corporate governance structures that would have been completely unacceptable to private equity groups. The SEC did not take such action, which was unneeded in any event because the credit crunch that broke out in mid-2007 derailed the KKR IPO, and private equity then pulled back from such offerings.

In July 2008 KKR announced that it was renewing its plan to make a public offering in order to bail out KPE. The offering was expected to value KKR at around $15 billion. However, in November 2008 KKR decided to delay its IPO until 2009, due to unsettled market conditions. KKR also reduced the valuation of its assets by substantial amounts. KKR reported a loss of $1.2 billion for 2008, as a result of asset write-downs. Although KKR was delayed in listing on NYSE, it refused to give up on its dream of going public, announcing in June 2009 that it was arranging a listing on the Euronext Amsterdam exchange through a merger with KPE. KKR did not realize its dream of listing on the NYSE until July 2010, under an arrangement in which Euronext Amsterdam shares would be swapped for NYSE shares. The firm was then valued at $6.4 billion, down from $26 billion in 2007. George Roberts and Henry Kravis' combined holdings in KKR were then valued at $1.65 billion. Each received annual salaries of $250,000, $17.8 million in profit sharing, a $4.1 million investment in company funds, plus $400,000 in personal expenses for such things as cars, drivers, and personal administrators. The KKR listing on the NYSE traded down 2.9 percent on its first day of trading.

The Carlyle Group

Louis Gerstner, a former CEO of IBM, headed the Carlyle Group, a successful and prestigious private equity group. Former presidents George H.W. Bush and his son, George W. Bush, served on the Carlyle board, and former British prime minister John Major was previously associated with it. The Carlyle Group experienced some early success. Its cofounder, David Rubenstein, was able to pay $21.3 million in December 2007 for a copy of the Magna Carta, which was some 700 years old. He placed it on permanent loan to the National Archives.

The Carlyle Group came to be viewed as a printing press for money, but it faced some uncertainty as the subprime crisis mounted. One of its hedge funds, Carlyle Capital, an affiliate of the Carlyle Group that was listed and traded on Euronex Amsterdam, experienced a rapid meltdown in March 2008. That $22 billion hedge fund had invested in high-quality residential mortgages with a leveraged position of thirty-to-one. The lenders, who had funded that leverage, panicked, however, as residential housing markets collapsed around the world. They demanded more margin than the Carlyle hedge fund could supply. The price of Carlyle Capital stock dropped by 93 percent in three days. A $500 million rescue effort by the Carlyle Group failed.

In addition, the firm had purchased Hawaiian Telecom Communications in 2005 for $1.6 billion, but that company filed for bankruptcy on December 1, 2008. The Carlyle Group announced on December 3, 2008, that it was laying off 10 percent of its staff. Three other hedge funds announced that they were in trouble on the same day that the Carlyle Group hedge fund collapsed.

Asset Managers

Other significant players in the investment field are the asset management firms that manage portfolios for institutional investors. Their predecessors were said to be the trustees hired by ship captains to invest and protect their monies while they were at sea. Asset managers included firms like Putnam Investments, founded in 1937 by George Putnam, the great-grandson of a Massachusetts judge who in 1830 established the "prudent man" rule as the standard for trustee investments. That standard prohibited trustees from making speculative investments on behalf of the beneficiaries of the trust. That rule has been superseded by the more liberal standard of "modern portfolio theory," which encourages diversification of portfolios, even into speculative investments and alternate asset categories, creating the need for diversified management of portfolios.

Putnam Investments was acquired in 1970 by Marsh & McLennan and then sold in 2007 to a Canadian insurance company. Its activities include the provision of investment advice to individual and institutional investors, retirement plans, and more than seventy mutual funds. The firm had over $106 billion under management in 2008, divided almost equally between mutual funds and institutional investors. Putnam was caught up in the market-timing scandals and made news during the subprime crisis when it closed its Putnam Prime Money Market Fund on September 18, 2008, during a run on money market accounts. That money market fund serviced professional investors and held $12.3 billion in assets before its liquidation.

Another asset manager, Fidelity Investments, was founded in 1930. Boston lawyer Edward C. Johnson II, who assumed control of the firm in 1943, built it into a powerhouse. His son Ned succeeded him in 1972. Fidelity provided a wide range of investment services for institutional and individual investors, including wealth management, life insurance and annuities, securities execution and clearance, and even discount brokerage. The firm sponsored more than 300 mutual funds, including the world's largest, the Magellan Fund. The Magellan Fund, managed by Peter Lynch, was hard hit by the stock market crash of 1987 and again by the global monetary crisis in 1994. Fidelity recovered from each of those crises, and it had $1.59 trillion under management in 2007. However, that figure declined by over 20 percent in the subprime crisis. The Magellan Fund experienced a nearly 50 percent decline in value in 2008. As its profits dropped, Fidelity announced that it was laying off 3,000 employees.

Literally thousands of other money managers existed of every description. One of the largest was UBS, a Swiss company with $2.45 trillion under management in 2007. State Street Global Advisors in Boston managed $1.75 trillion. Other managers of more than $1.7 trillion were the AXA Group, based in Paris, and Allianz in Munich. One well-known global investment management firm is PIMCO, with almost $100 billion in assets under management when the subprime crisis began and more than a thousand employees around the world in 2008. PIMCO was founded in 1971 in Newport Beach, California, as a subsidiary of the Pacific Life Insurance Company. It was used to manage accounts for institutional clients of that insurer before it was sold to Allianz, a German financial services firm. PIMCO was a leader in mortgage-backed securities and emerging market bonds and also offered "portable Alpha," which seeks returns higher than those available from diversified trading programs, and "absolute return strategies," which seek a desired return whatever the direction of the markets or market conditions. PIMCO's client base included multinational corporations, wealthy investors, and even central banks. It also operated mutual funds in the United States and Europe.

Most large investment banks had departments devoted to asset management. Merrill Lynch, for example, operated a Global Wealth Management group that was divided into two divisions, Americas Wealth Management (AWM) and Global Investment & Wealth Management (GIWM). These units provided global banking services and advice on investment and wealth management, and retirement planning. AWM serviced wealthy clients (those with investable assets of $1 million or more) for nearly 17,000 Merrill Lynch stockbrokers, in 750 offices around the world, before the firm collapsed during the subprime crisis and was taken over by Bank of America.

The GIWM division serviced wealthy investors outside the United States. It operated hedge funds as an alternative investment medium and provided access to the First Republic Bank, owned by the Merrill Lynch Bank & Trust. First Republic provided global private banking services, real estate lending, and trust services.

GIWM also worked with BlackRock, which Laurence D. Fink and others started in 1989 and which became one of the world's largest publicly traded investment management firms. Fink was previously a managing director at First Boston, where he headed their mortgage department and was a leader in the development of mortgage-backed securities. Fink initially made large profits for First Boston but lost over $100 million in a market downturn in 1987. That and other problems led to a bailout of First Boston by Credit Suisse, which took over control of First Boston. At BlackRock, he would play a prominent role during the subprime crisis as a collateral manager for distressed assets, including those that caused the failure of Bear Stearns.

At the time of its acquisition by PNC Bank in 1998, BlackRock was a fixed income manager of $25 billion. PNC wanted to use the acquisition to consolidate its asset management operations into one entity. Products offered to BlackRock clients included fixed income instruments, money market funds, equities, alternative asset programs, and real estate strategies.

BlackRock made a public offering in 1999, but PNC Financial Services Group retained a 34 percent ownership interest in the firm. Merrill Lynch owned approximately 49 percent of BlackRock, having sold its Merrill Lynch Investment Management Group to BlackRock in 2006, for $9.8 billion in BlackRock shares. The remaining shares were held by employees and public shareholders. The Merrill Lynch Investment Management Group, which included Merrill's $540 billion mutual fund complex, was known for its fixed income and risk management products.

The subprime crisis resulted in a drastic restructuring of Merrill Lynch's controlling position in the BlackRock stock. After suffering massive losses from subprime investments Merrill Lynch was taken over by the Bank of America in a government-brokered arrangement. Under their stockholder agreement, BlackRock was authorized to reduce Merrill Lynch's voting rights in the event of a change in Merrill's ownership, which it did, after the Bank of America acquisition. Merrill's voting rights were reduced to 4.9 percent. PNC's voting rights were increased to 47 percent, but it was required to defer to the votes of BlackRock's independent board members. Bank of America retained Merrill Lynch's equity ownership, but mostly in nonvoting shares.

Among its products, BlackRock offered access to the Quellos Group, an investment adviser and hedge fund manager that catered to the rich and powerful, including former president Bill Clinton and Secretary of State Hillary Clinton. BlackRock acquired Quellos in 2007 for $1.7 billion. That acquisition created some embarrassment after Jeffrey L. Greenstein, the Quellos CEO, was indicted by the Justice Department for promoting tax shelters that created billions of dollars in tax losses and generated massive fees.

BlackRock was at the center of the subprime crisis as an emergency asset manager for the private sector and the federal government. At the conclusion of the subprime crisis, BlackRock was managing or monitoring some $12 trillion in assets, including toxic assets taken over by the government in the bailouts of the American International Group and Bear Stearns. It was also monitoring the balance sheets of Fannie Mae and Freddie Mac after they were taken over by the government.

Its role in those sometimes-conflicting positions came under scrutiny and was the subject of lead stories in both the *Wall Street Journal* and the *New York Times* on May 19, 2009.[56] Although BlackRock performed better than most during the subprime crisis, its fourth-quarter 2008 profits fell 84 percent over the previous year. Its first-quarter 2009 profits declined a further 56 percent from the prior year. In reporting that result, Larry Fink stated, "Obviously asset management businesses are experiencing probably the worst headwinds that they've ever experienced in modern times."[57]

Those problems did not deter BlackRock from continuing its growth. In June 2009 BlackRock paid $13 billion for Barclays Global Investors (BGI), owned by the British Barclays bank, which was selling assets in order to avoid nationalization after suffering massive losses in the subprime crisis. Based in San Francisco, BGI managed $1.8 trillion in assets. The sale raised some eyebrows because it entitled executives at the bank to payouts totaling $630.3 million, of which the bank's CEO, Robert E. Diamond, Jr., received $36.5 million. BlackRock caused further excitement when it announced in September 2009 that it planned to create a global trading platform against all asset classes. Among other things, this would allow the matching of orders of BlackRock customers internally, allowing them to avoid paying the bid-ask spread required in other markets.

Investment banks, like Merrill Lynch, had jumped into asset management as a way of broadening their client base and revenue streams. However, independent money managers were able to compete effectively for that business by offering lower fees and no-load mutual funds. The result was a pullback by some investment banks. Citigroup sold its asset management division and mutual funds to Legg Mason in 2005. American Express spun off its mutual fund operations in 2005. Morgan Stanley tried to sell its asset management business to BlackRock, but that deal fell through. Nonetheless, as of 2009 BlackRock had $1.37 trillion under management.

Taxes

One study found that private equity firms made more in profits from fees charged to their investors than from the deals that they put together. Whatever their source, the profits generated by private equity and hedge funds for their managers, as always, inspired resentment and envy. Those feelings were accompanied by outrage after the press began to report on the tax advantages enjoyed by those managers. The Blackstone Group came under fire for claiming that its managers, rather than its new public shareholders, should have the benefit of tax deductions from write-downs of goodwill of as much as $90 million for fifteen years.

Private equity and hedge firm managers also profited from their deals through "carried interest," a term used for profit constituting the manager's 20 percent cut of profits made from the resale of a previously acquired company or other asset. Carried interest was not taxable until it was withdrawn from the hedge fund or private equity firm. Even then, it was taxed at the capital gains rate of 15 percent, rather than the higher earned income maximum of 35 percent. Although carried interest was being taxed at the same tax rate applied to qualified dividends of public companies, this tax advantage was the subject of much criticism as the private equity groups raised their profile during their buyout binge.

Another tax device popular with private equity were "dividend recaps," which involved acquiring a company with low leverage on its balance sheet and then leveraging it to the hilt through borrowing. The cash from that leveraging was then paid out to the private equity firm as a dividend, which became carried interest and increased the private equity fund's internal rate of return, as well as allowed it to regain its purchase costs. An example of such a transaction was the acquisition of Hertz from the Ford Motor Company in December 2005, by a private equity group composed of the Carlyle Group, Merrill Lynch Global Private Equity, and Clayton, Dubilier, & Rice. Within six months, the private equity managers declared a dividend recap of $1 billion, which was about half its purchase price. That dividend was funded by bank loans.

Simmons Bedding Company, which was sold seven times in twenty years by private equity groups, paid hundreds of millions of dollars in dividends to Thomas H. Lee Partners, which purchased it in 2003. Before declaring bankruptcy in 2009 the firm held $1.3 billion in debt on its balance sheet. Moody's Investors Services warned private equity purchasers that it would negatively consider private equity groups that took out excessive dividend recaps.

Barack Obama, during his 2008 presidential campaign, demanded an overall increase in the tax rate for capital gains on the ground that managers of hedge funds and private equity groups were taxed at a rate that was lower than the income tax rate on the salaries of the secretaries for those managers. After the election, the new president included a provision in his initial budget that would make carried interest taxable as ordinary income. Democrats in Congress, led by Representative Sander Levin from Michigan, also promoted the taxation of carried interest at ordinary income rates. However, private equity groups and hedge funds mounted an intense lobbying effort and beat back that legislation, at least for a time. Various private equity groups also announced the formation of their own trade organization and support for legislation to preempt federal regulation of their operations. That effort was promptly met by a threat from the antitrust division of the Justice Department, which claimed that some of the private equity groups appeared to be colluding in their acquisitions.

Other government pension funds, including those in Texas and California (CalPERS), were advocating a set of principles for private equity that would cap their fees, require more transparency and shareholder control. One private equity group hired counsel to determine if this joint action by the unions constituted a violation of the antitrust laws. The public pension plans had another beef with private equity. State and municipal pension funds were among the largest investors in private equity. Those pension plans paid private equity fees of some $17 billion in the first decade of this century while sustaining large losses during the subprime crisis.

The Credit Crunch and Private Equity

A study by Ludovic Phallppou and Oliver Gottschalg in 2008 concluded that the performance of private equity funds was overstated and that a large part of their performance was driven by inflated accounting valuations. The study found that, for 1980 to 2003, the average net of return for private equity funds was 3 percent a year below that of the S&P 500's performance. When adjusted for risk, that underperformance rose to 6 percent per year, net of fees that were estimated at an additional 6 percent on average per year.[58]

Nevertheless, Henry Kravis was able to claim in May 2007 that the country was in a "golden era" of buyouts. Between 2006 and 2007, private equity groups purchased companies valued at $1.4 trillion. Major deals included the acquisition of ServiceMaster for $4.7 billion. KKR made a $7.1 billion purchase of U.S. Food Service, which was at the center of an Enron-era scandal, from Royal Ahold. Alltel was acquired for $27.5 billion by TPG Capital and Goldman Sachs. Goldman had taken a huge bet on private equity acquisitions and was reported to have $20 billion in leveraged loan exposure. In another deal, First Data, a credit card processor, was acquired by KKR for $29 billion, and it in turn bought TXU, later renamed Energy Futures Holding, for $37 billion. Dollar General was purchased for $6.9 billion. The credit crunch that began in the summer of 2007 and the subprime crisis that followed ended that golden age.

Sovereign Wealth Funds

Another institutional supplier of equity was sovereign wealth funds (SWFs), which are capital pools formed by governments. The International Monetary Fund (IMF) has identified five classes of sovereign wealth funds: (1) commodity price stabilization funds; (2) funds that convert nonrenewable assets into diversified financial assets, for example, selling oil and investing the proceeds in U.S. corporate stock; (3) funds that invest to increase the returns on their country's reserves; (4) funds that help fund projects for development; and (5) pension funds.

Oil-producing and -exporting countries, such as those in the Middle East, and countries with large export surpluses, such as China, were among the most high-profile SWFs. Those countries had hundreds of billions of dollars available for investment from their trade surpluses. China's SWF, for example, had about $300 billion in assets, but only $9.6 billion was invested in U.S. stocks. The Government of Singapore Investment Corporation had over $100 billion under management in 2008. The Korean Investment Corporation had $30 billion in assets in 2008 under management. The staggering amounts of capital in the SWFs of oil-producing countries grew rapidly as oil prices sailed upward past $140 per barrel in 2008, before retreating sharply.

The Kuwait Investment Authority (KIA), which had about $260 billion under management in 2007, was created in 1953 as a hedge against the possibility that the country would some day run out of oil to pump. Every year, the government of Kuwait contributes 10 percent of its oil revenues to the KIA. The Abu Dhabi fund, estimated to hold over $875 billion in 2007 in assets, became a model for other oil-producing countries.[59] Saudi Arabia announced in December 2007 that it would expand its SWF activities to become the largest in the world, surpassing even the one in Abu Dhabi. Other SWFs included the Iranian Oil Stabilization Fund, the Qatar Investment Authority, the Libyan Investment Authority, Azerbaijan State Oil, and several in the United Arab Emirates (UAE).

As the twenty-first century began, more than fifty SWFs were operated in over thirty-five countries, including Australia, Botswana, Brazil, Ireland, Japan, India, New Zealand, Norway, Venezuela, and Vietnam. Such funds could even be found in the United States, such as the Alaska Permanent Fund, which held almost $40 billion of oil revenue in trust for Alaskans in 2007, and the Wyoming Mineral Trust Fund, which held, in trust for the citizens of that state, a more modest $4 billion in severance fees for mineral extraction.

In 2007, SWFs exceeded hedge funds in size, and the amount of their investments grew rapidly. From $1.9 trillion in SWF investments in 2007, the amount was expected to pass $8 trillion in the next five years. However, the Persian Gulf SWFs lost an estimated 15 percent of their value in the first eleven months of 2008, as a result of market downturns and reduced asset values. A drop of over $100 per barrel in crude oil prices in the second half of 2008 put a damper on their growth. The SWFs also took a beating from their investments in U.S. financial service firms. However, China announced in September 2009 that its SWF was planning to invest in U.S. real estate.

David Rubenstein, of the Carlyle Group, noted in November 2007 that the larger private equity firms were in competition with SWFs, corporate investors, and smaller private equity funds, all of which challenged the role of the larger private equity groups. This challenge grew as the subprime crisis worsened. After being turned away by banks on prior leveraged loan commitments, private equity groups were even forced to turn to the SWFs in order to raise capital for their acquisitions.

SWFs invested in stock exchanges around the world, including OMX, the Norse-Baltic stock exchange, which then purchased a stake in NASDAQ and bought NASDAQ's position in the London Stock Exchange. They also became an alternative source of equity for financial service firms whose capital was depleted by subprime-related write-offs. In 2006 and 2007, SWF investments in financial services firms reached $47 billion, including a $5 billion investment by the China Investment Corporation in Morgan Stanley[60] and a $7.5 billion investment in Citigroup by Abu Dhabi, which joined a Saudi Arabian prince as the largest shareholders in that bank.[61] The Singapore SWF made a $5 billion investment in Merrill Lynch in December 2007.[62] The Government of Singapore Investment Corporation also purchased stakes in Citigroup and UBS, as the subprime problems at those banks began to emerge. Those investments were ill-timed, as the stock prices of those and other financial service firms plunged during the stock market panic of 2008. The head of the Government of Singapore Investment Corporation remarked in March 2009 that his fund had invested too early in Citigroup and UBS. At that point, Citigroup stock traded at under $1, down from $57 only a year earlier. However, that was the bottom of the market, and in September 2009 the Singapore SWF was able to sell half its stake in Citigroup, making a profit of $1.6 billion.

The Chinese government vetoed a planned multibillion-dollar investment by the China Development Bank in Citigroup just before its disclosure of additional massive losses from subprime lending in January 2008. Instead, the Chinese SWF invested $20 billion in the China Development Bank, which faced losses on its balance sheet. The Chinese SWF investment program also included purchases of equity interests in three large Australian banks hurt in the subprime crisis. In June 2005, the Chinese SWF announced that it was investing $500 million in BlackRock to purchase undervalued assets. Jianyin Investments, owned by the Chinese government, spent $3 billion to buy 5 percent of Blackstone's public offering, an investment that fared poorly.

Other high-profile SWF investments included the Abu Dhabi SWF's acquisition of the Chrysler building for $800 million. Dow Chemical entered into a $15.3 billion joint venture with Kuwait's state oil company, which sought to rebuild Dow's faltering commodity chemical business by purchasing Rohm and Haas, a specialty chemical maker. However, after crude oil prices fell and questions about the deal were raised in its parliament, the Kuwaiti government announced in December 2008 that it was withdrawing from that joint venture. This caused a 20 percent drop in Dow's stock and a downgrade in its credit rating.[63]

Another SWF suffered losses in the subprime crisis. Temasek Holdings, a Singapore SWF, announced that its portfolio had lost more than 50 percent of its value in the eight months ending November 2008, representing a loss of $40 billion. The Texas Pacific Group (TPG), a global asset investment firm, offered a portion of itself for sale to the KIA and two California pension funds in 2009. However, the two sides could not agree on a price because TPG wanted to use a valuation based on much higher asset levels for 2007. SWFs, like the KIA, had been burned on other investments and now took a more cautious approach. Also participating in those discussions were the California Public Employees' Retirement System (CalPERS), which sought a piece of TPG. TPG disclosed in May 2009 that it had considered 140 LBO proposals and rejected all of them. The firm also announced in February 2009 that it was returning 25 percent of the $6 billion it had raised to invest in distressed financial companies. Such investments were becoming a popular target for private equity groups, such as Carlyle and Christopher Flowers.

National Security Concerns

The size of the SWF investments began to raise concern that they might seek to control or to influence the management of large financial institutions, which could then be used as leverage for political reasons. Andy Stern, the head of the SEIU unsuccessfully sought legislation in California that would have prevented CalPERS and other California state pension funds from investing with SWFs. He claimed that his legislation was a measure to punish countries with human rights violations. Actually, this was a convoluted effort by Stern to punish the Carlyle Group, which had invested with various SWFs. As described above, Stern was seeking that punishment because the Carlyle Group owned a nursing home chain, ManorCare, that was resisting SEIU's efforts to organize employees.

A backdrop to those concerns was the controversy resulting from an effort in 2006 by Dubai Ports World, which was owned by the Dubai government in the UAE, to take over management of container operations in several U.S. ports. Concern was raised that Middle Eastern extremists might use such operations to infiltrate those ports and to carry out terrorist operations. The Bush administration had approved the deal, but it became a major political controversy, with even some Republicans opposing the contract. Legislation was introduced attacking the deal, but President Bush threatened to exercise his first veto. The controversy was resolved after the company announced that it was selling its port management operations in the United States to a U.S. company, American International Group (AIG), which became a center of the subprime crisis in 2008. However, the UAE did not give up on its interest in U.S. ports. Abu Dhabi sought to invest in port facilities in Charleston, South Carolina, in anticipation of the widening of the Panama Canal, which would increase traffic to that port.

In order to provide reassurance that SWF investments in failing U.S. financial service firms were not a threat, Fed chairman Bernanke, in an address in Chicago on May 15, 2008, asserted that investments by SWFs in banks had been a good thing. He noted that their capital took a long-term perspective and that the SWFs were investing for financial, not political, reasons. As further assurance, the Abu Dhabi and the Singapore SWFs agreed with Treasury Secretary Henry Paulson that they would not use their funds for "geopolitical goals." Rather, their investments would be strictly commercial.

The Federal Reserve Bank of San Francisco floated a proposal for easing concerns over investments by SWFs by limiting their investments to broad equity market indexes, rather than individual companies. The Treasury Department adopted regulations in April 2008 that would provide for greater scrutiny of sovereign wealth fund investments in a public company's stock, including investments of under 10 percent.

SWFs were also criticized for their lack of transparency. The IMF asked them to provide greater transparency in order to ease concerns that they might pose a security threat through their acquisitions in other countries. The IMF published a set of best practices for SWFs. The European Commission announced in December 2007 that it did not believe that additional legislation was needed to regulate investments by SWFs. Nevertheless, the commission desired greater transparency with respect to such investments. The Singapore

SWF promised broader disclosure as 2008 began, but was vague as to what disclosures it would make. It subsequently issued a report in 2008 that disclosed that it was shifting its investment focus to alternative assets and emerging market economies. The fund did not disclose the size of its portfolio except to declare, as it had done for almost a decade, that it had over $100 billion under management.

Terrorism and other geopolitical concerns were not the only reasons countries began to question the role of SWFs. Temasek Holdings, the Singapore SWF, caused a great deal of political turmoil in Thailand after Temasek bought a controlling stake in the largest telecommunications company in that country in 2006. Rioting in the streets broke out over acquisition of the company, the Shin Corporation, owned by the Shinawatra family. The Thai prime minister, Taksin Shinawatra, was deposed in a military coup in part over public perceptions of corruption, a perceived conflict of interest by the prime minister, and the fact that the sale was not subject to capital gains tax.

7. The Mortgage Market

Mortgages

Some History

The mortgage concept is an ancient one. "Private financing of homes first began in China more than 5000 years ago."[1] Loans that were collateralized by mortgages on real property were also made as early as the fifth century B.C.E. in Athens. In the Middle East, "antichretic" loans, which allowed the lender to take possession of the rents of a property in exchange for the loan, were used for real estate.[2] Historians have also discovered that the law of ancient Attica recognized loans that involved a pledge of property, without the lender's taking possession. Such arrangements required the erection of a pillar or tablet on the property that inscribed the creditor's name and the amount of the debt.[3]

In England, references to mortgages have been found as far back as 1190. Liens on real estate were also bought and sold in the twelfth century, laying the groundwork for the modern mortgage market. Early mortgages in England took various forms. Leaseholds were used as "gages" to secure loans in France and England in the Middle Ages. As described by Glanville in his treatise on English law, a *vif gage* (living pledge) was a loan in which the income from the leasehold was used by the lender, who took possession of the property to pay down the loan as well as interest. Another form of gage, the *mort gage* (dead pledge), which became the most popular gage device, was one in which the creditor kept the rents and profits from the land until the debt was paid in full.[4] The land was said to be "dead" under a *mort gage* because the land gave no return to the owner: It was as if the land were dead.[5]

These forms of mortgages were replaced in thirteenth-century England by the Bractonian mortgage, which required a borrower to transfer legal possession of an estate to the lender for a specified number of years. The borrower could recover the property after the debt was paid. That form of mortgage was followed in the fifteenth century by the Littleton gage, wherein the borrower conveyed an ownership interest in the property to the lender with a reversionary right upon repayment of the debt.[6] By the fifteenth century, English mortgages typically transferred the title to the property to the lender but with the debtor in possession. If the loan were not repaid on "law" day, the lender would take possession.[7] The modern residential mortgage evolved from those instruments. Although they now take many forms, mortgages today have characteristics in common with a loan secured by residential property owned by the borrower on which interest, in some form, is paid.

Mortgage Lenders

Modern mortgage lenders trace their history to the development of "friendly" societies in the 1600s in the British Midlands. These were cooperatives in which members made regular contributions to a common fund, which was used to extend loans when members experienced hardships, such as a fire that destroyed their home. These friendly societies became a part of an evangelical movement that promoted a spirit of helping one's fellow man, which accorded with the goals of friendly societies. Parliament passed legislation in 1793 that required friendly societies to register with the government.[8]

Spinning off from the friendly society movement were building societies that first appeared in Birmingham in 1781. Participants in those organizations subscribed to shares paid for over time in installments. After enough subscriptions had been received to make a loan, a lottery for the loan was held among the participants. The winner was granted the loan, which had to be repaid with interest. The winner was also required to continue to make his subscription payments. Failure to make subscription payments resulted in fines.[9]

Colonial America had no real banking community that could issue mortgages. However, in 1716, Massachusetts authorities authorized the issuance of bills of credit totaling £150,000. Those bills could be used to purchase real estate. They had a tenure of ten years, at an interest rate of 5 percent. "Loan banks" and "loan offices" began to appear in South Carolina and Massachusetts in the latter part of the seventeenth century. These bodies were based on an idea promoted by William Potter, who published a book in England in 1650 called *The Key to Wealth*. It described a scheme in which a loan office would issue a specified "maximum amount in loan office bills on real estate security."[10]

The loan office concept spread throughout the colonies. In 1723, New Jersey issued "bank" currency that could be used as mortgages on real estate and silver plate. That scheme has been described as follows:

> The New Jersey law of 1723 called for the printing of £40,000 of legal-tender money of denominations ranging from one shilling to three pounds. . . . Loans were to be made in amounts of not less than £12 6/ or more than £100. Loan offices were set up in each county and allotted a quota, based on the county's population. Borrowers had to give as security a mortgage on land or houses at least double the value of the

loan. The interest rate of five per cent, a saving over the current rate of eight per cent, was calculated to make it easy for poor people to borrow. A moratorium was laid on all debts for four months, until March 25, 1724, to allow time for the new money to get into circulation. The borrower was expected to pay back one-twelfth of the principal and interest annually. If he failed to make his payments on time, that failure was considered as judgment against him. If he did not pay within the succeeding thirty days of grace, foreclosure took place. If the money still could not be collected, the county was obliged to stand the loss.[11]

Pennsylvania created a general loan office in 1723 that was authorized to issue bills of credit to residents in the colony in exchange for a mortgage on their property equal to the amount of the bills of credit that they received. Benjamin Franklin printed an issue of Pennsylvania notes that was secured by land, calling those notes "coined land." Rhode Island also created a loan office for real estate purchases. The New London Society United for Trade and Commerce was founded around 1730 in Connecticut for the purpose of issuing bills secured by loans on real estate. However, the legislature stepped in to prohibit that activity over concerns that the bills would become a form of private currency.

The Massachusetts Land Bank, which included Samuel Adams as one of its subscribers, was created in 1739 for the purpose of making loans on produce, manufactured goods, and real estate. Members of the bank could mortgage their land to it but were subject to assessments ranging from £14 to £166. Those who failed to pay had their land sold by the bank. In 1741, the English government directed that the issuance of notes by land banks in the colonies be stopped. Another effort was made in 1765 by the Virginia House of Burgesses to create a loan office, but the crown rejected that proposal.

Residential Mortgage Providers

As a result of restrictions by the crown, the development of mortgage-lending institutions in the colonies had to await the Revolution. After that success, they were free to borrow from developments in the mother country. In an effort to create a mortgage market, English theorists proposed the creation of communal groups that would pool their funds, which could then be lent to participants. In 1797 Jeremy Bentham advanced the concept of a "frugality bank," an effort to encourage savings by the poor. From that proposal sprang the concept of a mutual "savings bank" in which depositors were paid interest on their funds. Those deposits were lent out, and the interest received on those loans was used to pay the interest due the depositors, less expenses. Priscilla Wakefield, an early social reformer, founded the first of these institutions, the Tottenham Benefit Bank, in 1804.[12]

The Reverend Henry Duncan fathered another of these institutions in 1810 at Rockwell, Scotland. Other savings banks followed, and the concept soon spread to America. A savings bank movement began in the United States in 1816, in New York, Boston, and Philadelphia. These mutual societies had deposits initially set at one cent, later rising to five cents, and still later to ten cents. They were particularly popular with immigrants in the northeastern states. The saving banks were usually limited in the investment of depositor funds to real estate mortgages and highly secure bonds. By 1840 savings banks had almost 80,000 depositors, a number that increased to 250,000 by 1850. Deposits increased from $7 million in 1835 to $43 million in 1850. In 1860, savings banks held deposits totaling $150 million, which were available for mortgage loans. By the end of the nineteenth century, savings bank deposits accounted for about a third of all banking-related deposits.

Building and loan societies (B&Ls), which began to appear in America in the first half of the nineteenth century, were a variation on the savings bank model. B&Ls were popular as a safe place for workingmen to deposit their wages and obtain loans. The first B&L was Oxford Provident, founded in 1831 in Frankford, Pennsylvania. Participants in that organization made monthly payments up to $500, at which point they were eligible for loans that could be used to purchase a home. Fines and forfeitures were imposed if the required monthly payments were not made. Funds contributed by the participants were pooled. The Bowery Savings Bank was created in 1834, and the Brooklyn Building and Mutual Loan Association began operations in 1836. Their depositors owned these organizations. Many B&Ls, especially in larger cities, were identified by the ethnic groups that lived in the areas that they served, such as the Czechs, Poles, and Italians.

Another form of communal loan society was the "permanent loan association," the first of which was founded in 1843 in Charleston, South Carolina. Participants in these associations maintained separate accounts and could make any level of savings deposits. Their deposits were pooled, and loans were made at the discretion of the institution's directors. In another variation called the "Dayton Plan," participants received dividends from the association. Then came the "permanent capital" institutions that issued stock like a regular corporation in order to raise funds for lending. State commercial banks also made residential mortgage loans. However, the national banks created by the National Banking Act of 1864 were prohibited from lending on real estate.

In 1890, more than 900 B&Ls were in Philadelphia, and large numbers of such institutions had opened in other large cities. At the same time, almost half of all American families owned their homes. In 1900, over 5,000 B&Ls operated in the United States, most of which had assets of less than $90,000. B&Ls were subject to state regulations, the first of which appeared around the time of the Civil War. Regulation spread and was universal by 1900, but was by no means consistent in scope or application. In 1875, New York required thrifts to file annual reports. In 1887, that state subjected its thrifts to annual examinations, and some states imposed lending restrictions, such as limiting them to first mortgages.

The residential mortgage market in the United States was usually a local one. However, mortgages were marketed broadly in the eastern United States by railroad owners that were selling their vast land grants to settlers moving west after the Civil War. The terms of these mortgages varied. For example, Burlington Northern offered a ten-year "long credit" at 6 percent interest. The borrower paid interest only for the first two years of the loan. The Union Pacific offered a similar eleven-year mortgage at 7 percent, with a down payment of only 10 percent. Interest had to be paid only in the first three years. Those mortgages helped touch off a land boom in the West from 1884 to 1887 that was accompanied by a wave of migration from the East. However, that boom went bust in 1888, as many enterprising pioneers then returned to their former homes, and land prices collapsed.[13]

A B&L mania broke out in the 1880s, with the formation of over 5,000 new B&Ls in that decade. By the 1890s some B&Ls operated on a national basis. At one point those "nationals" held assets totaling $140 million and had branches in every state. However, most of those nationals failed during an economic crisis in that decade, resulting in more state legislation, even in states that had not previously regulated thrifts. There was also an effort to introduce European-style mortgage market trading in the United States. Those European markets have been described as follows: "By the mid-1800s mortgage-backed bonds that were issued by mutually owned institutions (*Landschaften*), privately-owned, joint-stock mortgage banks and a national monopoly bank (*the Credit Foncier*) traded in Germany and France at yields as low as government securities and in markets as thick and deep."[14] Those European markets allowed only well-secured mortgages to back the mortgage bonds.

In the United States, the U.S. Mortgage Company was created by J.P. Morgan and others to sell high-yield mortgage-backed bonds in Europe during the 1870s. The Equitable insurance company organized the Mercantile Trust for originating and selling mortgages. Both companies failed during the downturn in 1873 because of the poor quality of the mortgages that they were selling. More failures occurred in the 1890s, with the creation of mortgage companies that brokered and serviced farm loans for foreign investors. Those mortgage companies also sold debentures that were backed by mortgages placed in trust accounts.

One such firm was the J.B. Watkins Land Mortgage Company in Kansas, which placed the mortgages that it originated in trust with the Farmers Loan & Trust Company in New York. Debentures were then sold that were collateralized by the mortgages held in trust, a process used in the twenty-first century to securitize subprime mortgages. Only seven of the seventy-four companies licensed for such business survived the 1890s, largely due to the poor quality of the mortgages placed in trust.[15]

Efforts were also under way in England in the 1890s to create credit insurance that would protect against loan defaults. That too would be a process used to sell subprime mortgages, which caused much concern during the subprime crisis.

Twentieth-Century Mortgage Markets

In 1904, New York authorized property title insurance companies to insure mortgage payments. This laid the groundwork for a private mortgage insurance business that originated, insured, sold, and then serviced mortgages on both residential and commercial properties. "By 1913 some of these companies also placed mortgage loans in trust, insured the payments on these loans, and sold participation certificates in these mortgages."[16] These "certificated mortgages" could cover a single large commercial mortgage, a form of syndication, or a group of small residential loans and could be packaged in much the same way as modern securitizations.

In 1913, national banks in particular areas were allowed to make farm loans, and that authority was expanded in 1916. Legislation was passed in 1918 to encourage residential housing in industrial areas, in order to support the war effort. A Housing Corporation was created in the Labor Department, but it built only about 6,000 homes before World War I ended. A building program for shipyard workers managed by the Emergency Fleet Corporation produced another 9,000 homes. An effort to create a national mortgage credit bank after the conclusion of World War I failed. That proposal was a response to the housing shortage that occurred after servicemen began returning home.

At a White House conference, the United States League of Local Building and Loan Associations proposed an alternative to that scheme, which would have created a thrift banking system comparable to that of the Federal Reserve that would provide reserve funding. This was the precursor of the federal home loan banking system, but the idea gained no traction in the 1920s because of a recovery in the mortgage market.[17] However, the then-Commerce Secretary Herbert Hoover liked the idea and thought it could be used to promote second mortgages. He would remember that experience when he became president and was faced with the Great Depression. The Brookings Institution also made a recommendation in 1929 to create a central mortgage bank that would buy mortgages across the nation, pool them, and sell interests in the pools to investors.[18]

The trend of local mortgage markets continued through the 1920s. During that decade, savings banks and B&Ls in their various forms were increasingly referred to generically as savings and loan associations (S&Ls) and later as "thrifts." Insurance companies made residential loans and were a significant part of the market by that time. Commercial banks also offered mortgages. Real estate loans issued by commercial banks increased from $1.4 billion in 1923 to $4.5 billion in 1929. Still, individuals were lenders for some 40 percent of residential real estate mortgages. The residential market was also marked by the fact that only 41 percent of homes were owner occupied and less than half of those owner-occupied homes were mortgaged, normally with debt-to-value ratios of 50 percent.[19]

Other actors appeared on the scene in the 1920s. Mortgage brokers originated more loans from consumers than conventional lenders. Mortgage companies began to operate and accounted for some 5 percent of all home mortgage loans by 1929. These institutions raised funds for lending from sales of their stock or through the sale of mortgage-backed securities, a precursor of the modern mortgage market. The mortgage companies also dealt in second mortgages that were highly profitable because of the higher interest rate charged on those loans. However, these mortgage companies were not well capitalized, and most of them failed during the Great Depression, a cycle that would be repeated during the subprime crisis.[20]

Before the Great Depression, most home mortgage loans were for relatively short terms, from six to eleven years for mortgages issued by S&Ls, six to eight years for mortgages issued by insurance companies, and three to five years for mortgages issued by commercial banks.[21] Another distinguishing feature of this loan market was the fact that mortgages were almost always held until maturity or payoff by the institution that originated the loan. Most of the mortgages issued by non-S&Ls were not amortized over the life of the loan but, instead, required a large balloon payment upon maturity.[22] Nevertheless, after the mortgage was obtained, the homeowner could expect that, at maturity, it could be rolled over into a new mortgage.

As noted, most mortgage lending was local before the Great Depression. Lending institutions did not have access to national or even regional capital markets. They were, for the most part, entirely dependent upon local sources for funds, resulting in uneven and unstable flows of funds for mortgage financing.[23] Because of the lack of a national market, interest rates varied from 5 to 9 percent. Rising home prices and increasing incomes, nevertheless, made this mortgage system workable during the 1920s. Residential mortgage lending grew rapidly. During that decade, the number of residential mortgages exceeded the number of farm mortgages for the first time. Assets of the S&Ls quadrupled between 1914 and 1926, growth that was aided by various promotions, including a program endorsed by the Treasury Department called National Thrift Week. That public service campaign urged citizens to save money, and the thrifts provided a ready mechanism for that task.

Herbert Hoover, as commerce secretary, promoted a Better Homes Week extolling the virtues of homeownership. He noted, "The finance of home-building, especially for second mortgages, is the most backward segment of our whole credit system. It is easier to borrow 85 percent on an automobile and repay it on the installment plan than to buy a house on that basis—and generally the house requires a higher interest rate."[24] Hoover persuaded Julius Rosenwald at Sears, Roebuck, which sold prepackaged homes for assembly, to issue second mortgages at 6 percent interest. Commercial banks had been charging 15 percent for such loans, which made them prohibitively expensive. The banks then reduced their charges, which resulted in an expansion of the second mortgage market.

Some S&Ls issued first and second mortgages under the "Philadelphia Plan," which involved a first nonamortizing mortgage from a commercial bank or insurance company for 50 percent of the home's value. The S&L issued a second amortizing mortgage for 30 percent of the property value. This meant that the homeowner would have to make a down payment of only 20 percent and to pay interest only on the first loan until its maturity.[25] Later, some S&Ls made both the first and second mortgages. Such arrangements would be taken to the extreme during the subprime crisis, when "piggyback" second mortgages allowed down payments of zero.

Housing starts quintupled between 1917 and 1925, when they reached 950,000 before starting to decline.[26] Housing prices also increased substantially during the 1920s, before receding during the Great Depression. The Florida real estate market experienced a famous boom before crashing in 1926 after a hurricane, a situation parodied by the Marx Brothers in the musical *Cocoanuts*. Speculation was also rampant in real estate in North Carolina and California. Lending standards were lowered as the stock market boom expanded in the 1920s, a pattern that would repeat itself in the twenty-first century. During the 1920s, loan-to-value ratios increased. Many homeowners took out second mortgages at high interest rates, and credit risk assessments were especially lax. Foreclosure rates began to increase in 1925.

As was the case in the run-up to the subprime crisis, real estate lending was aided by low interest rates, a fact that fueled the stock market boom as well as the real estate market. However, both of those markets suffered a blow when the Federal Reserve increased interest rates in 1928 in order to curb speculation. That mistake would be repeated in the run-up that led to the subprime crisis.

At the end of 1928, over 12,000 thrifts held assets totaling more than $8 billion. Over 1,700 of those institutions would fail in the 1930s. Nevertheless, the failure rate for S&Ls was low in comparison to that of commercial banks during the Great Depression.[27] The downturn did expose some fraud in the operations of the S&Ls. Seventeen Philadelphia thrifts that had interlocking boards of directors were closed after it was discovered that company officers had approved loans on overvalued properties and received kickbacks from developers.

Real Estate Bonds

In the 1920s real estate bonds issued by investment banking firms funded commercial real estate developments. Initially, these real estate bonds covered only specific property, but later they were expanded to include several properties under mortgage. One program allowed investors to obtain a real estate bond for $1,000 that entitled them to participate in 122 different mortgages. The issuer of the bonds often agreed to repurchase the bonds at a discount in order to provide liquidity and make the bonds more attractive to investors. Problems appeared in 1926, when a real estate bond in Florida defaulted during the market downturn there. The New York attorney general warned in 1927 that some real estate bond firms were overvaluing properties. The industry then developed a code of conduct that the bond houses agreed to follow.[28] Such codes of conduct became popular with the New York attorney general Andrew Cuomo during the subprime crisis.

Beginning in 1906, mortgages were pooled and placed in trust, and interests in that trust in the form of collateral trust certificates were sold to investors, giving them an undivided share of the pool. The investment banking firms issuing real estate bonds initially guaranteed them, but dropped that protection in later offerings. Thereafter, the only security was the property underlying the bonds. However, some insurance companies separately provided guarantees on real estate bonds for both principal and interest, in whole or in part. The business of guaranteeing mortgages was an outgrowth of the title insurance business. A statute in New York authorized mortgage guarantees in 1904.

The mortgage guarantee business began to boom during World War I. The number of mortgage guarantee companies in New York quintupled in the 1920s "and the volume of outstanding mortgage loan insurance grew from $.5 to nearly $3 billion; $.8 billion of this total was written on certificated mortgages."[29] The Bond & Mortgage Guarantee Company guaranteed mortgages sold to investors by the Title Guarantee & Trust Company. It guaranteed more than $2 billion in mortgages sold to savings banks and other investors. This was the precursor of the monoline insurance companies that would be at the center of the subprime crisis in 2007.

Mortgage guarantee companies in the 1920s were regulated by the New York State Department of Insurance, which halted further mortgage guarantees in 1933 as those companies began defaulting. The New York insurance department took over control of eighteen companies engaged in the business of guaranteeing and selling mortgages and mortgage certificates. The Moreland Act of 1907 authorized the New York governor to appoint a "Moreland commissioner" to investigate a broad range of activities. Such a commissioner was appointed in 1934 by New York governor Herbert H. Lehman to investigate the collapse of the mortgage bond and mortgage guarantee market in that state. Ironically, Lehman was the son of one of the founders of the Lehman Brothers investment banking firm, which would be destroyed by the mortgage-backed bonds that were at the center of the subprime crisis. The Moreland commissioner found that, as of December 31, 1933, more than $800 million in outstanding mortgage certificates was held by 212,874 investors and covered 9,435 issues, most of which were in default.[30]

The Moreland commissioner found that mortgage bonds were often backed, in whole or in part, by vacant land that produced no income. The commissioner also found that appraisals were often out of date and based on prices that had sharply declined. In some instances, appraisal figures were arrived at by simply multiplying the amount of the loan by 150 percent, the statutory minimum, without any inspection of the property. Many properties on which mortgage bonds were sold in 1932 and 1933 were already in default when they were sold to investors.[31]

The commercial real estate bond market had also become a viable mechanism for investors to make investments in commercial real estate mortgages. However, a few problems arose. Some commercial real estate bonds were issued on the basis of inflated appraisals, and problems associated with the property under mortgage often were not disclosed. Several real estate bond houses failed in 1926. An exchange created to trade these securities, the New York Real Estate Securities Exchange, ran into some especially bad luck. Its trading floor opened on October 21, 1929, just in time to face one of the worst financial crises in American history. The exchange did not survive.

In 1934 the House of Representatives appointed a select committee to investigate real estate bondholders' reorganizations, following a protest by 10,000 defaulted bondholders in Chicago. With Representative from Illinois Adolf J. Sabath as its chairman, the select committee held hearings in Detroit, New York, Chicago, and Milwaukee. It found that some $10 billion in real estate bonds were outstanding and that $8 billion were in default, affecting about 9 million investors, many of modest means. The leading issuers of those bonds were George M. Forman, Greenebaum Sons Investment, American Bond & Mortgage, Central Trust, S.W. Straus, H.O. Stone, and Lackner Butz.

The select committee was concerned with abuses by "protective committees" formed ostensibly to protect the interests of defaulted mortgage bond owners but fraught with abuse through excessive fees and expenses. More than 10,000 protective committees were formed between 1929 and 1933.

These protective committees had a fairly typical pattern. After a default on a mortgage bond, a self-appointed bondholders protective committee was formed, and investors were asked to deposit their bonds with the protective committee. The deposited bonds were then used by the committee as collateral for a loan, the proceeds of which were used to buy the defaulted property, which was then put into a trust. The bondholders were given trust certificates representing their interest in the property. The property was then managed by the protective committee, which was paid a fee of around 4 to 5 percent of the gross annual revenue from the property, plus expenses. The Sabath investigation led to legislation that was incorporated in the Chandler Act in 1938, which gave the Securities and Exchange Commission (SEC) an oversight role in corporate reorganizations.[32] The Chandler Act was repealed in 1978.

The Great Depression

The Great Depression resulted in an almost complete collapse of the banking system. By the end of February 1933, it was common to see depositors standing "in long queues with satchels and paper bags to take gold and currency away from the banks to store in mattresses and old shoeboxes. It seemed safer to put your life's savings in the attic than to trust the greatest financial institutions in the country."[33] Such sights would not be witnessed again until the subprime crisis in 2007 touched off a similar bank run in England.

The New Deal took several steps to address those problems, beginning with a bank holiday declared immediately after Franklin Roosevelt was sworn in as president.

Legislation was passed that strengthened the hand of the Federal Reserve, but it failed to restore liquidity to the banking system, an error that would not be repeated during the subprime crisis. The New Deal also enacted the Glass-Steagall Act, separating the roles of the commercial banks from those of investment banks. The artificial boundary lines created by the Glass-Steagall Act hobbled banks for decades, until they began avoiding many of its restrictions starting in the 1970s, and escaped its reach entirely after that act was repealed in 1999. That repeal has been blamed by some critics as laying the groundwork for the subprime crisis, but the connection they claim is uncertain.

Congress was also interested in the mortgage-lending activities of national banks. It enacted the McFadden Act in 1927, which allowed residential mortgage loans to be made by national banks, whose mortgage activity thereafter expanded "dramatically." That activity raised concerns in Congress that "an immense overexpansion of real-estate values [had been] set in motion" and that many banks were "hopelessly embarrassed by their real-estate commitments and by the fact that rents and selling values [had] so seriously shrunk." To address those concerns, a provision was included in the Banking Act of 1933[34] requiring Federal Reserve banks to ascertain whether banks were unduly using depositor's funds in "'speculative carrying of or trading in . . . real estate.'"[35] That power did nothing to prevent the subprime crisis.

Another New Deal legacy is the Federal Deposit Insurance Corporation (FDIC), which provided federally sponsored insurance for depositor accounts at commercial banks. Lydia Lobsiger received the first federal deposit payout on July 5, 1934, after the failure of the Fond du Lac State Bank in East Peoria, Illinois. Initially, FDIC coverage was capped at $2,500 per account holder, but it was increased to $100,000 in 1980 and to $250,000 during the subprime crisis in 2008. The FDIC was funded by premiums charged to member banks. Its insurance fund totaled more than $45 billion in 2008, when it covered more than $5 trillion in deposits.

The FDIC was effective in stopping bank runs. Nearly 70 percent of the 18,000 banks closed during the bank holiday declared by Roosevelt upon his inauguration were reopened within a few weeks, and depositors returned some $1 billion in funds to the banking system.[36] The Federal Reserve objected to the reopening of the Bank of America, with its 410 branches in California, but Treasury Secretary William Woodin ordered its reopening anyway.[37] That bank had already proved to be a survivor. Its predecessor, the Bank of Italy, reopened quickly after the 1906 San Francisco earthquake despite the destruction of its headquarters. But the Bank of America faltered during the subprime crisis.

Although the FDIC restored depositor confidence in the banking system, it also created a "moral hazard" for taxpayers. Because the federal government stood behind the deposits held by banks, shareholders lost any incentive to monitor the creditworthiness of their banks. That moral hazard would come home to roost during the subprime crisis, when massive government bailouts were required. Blame for those failures was placed, by some critics, on the failure of the banks to manage risks, because they believed the government would rescue them if they encountered problems because of excess leverage. Since depositors had no need to monitor the safety of their deposits, management was allowed to proceed unchecked by depositor oversight.

In 1932, some 20,000 farm mortgages were foreclosed monthly, creating such hardship to the point of creating concern that the farmers might revolt. Boisterous protests occurred in several states, including Iowa, Ohio, Illinois, Oklahoma, Minnesota, Mississippi, and Kansas. Some farm communities organized to stop foreclosure sales. Friends agreed to bid on foreclosed properties at low-enough levels ("penny auctions") that the property could then be returned to its owners.

Several government programs were created to deal with those farm problems.[38] The Frazier-Lemke Act of 1934 required appraisals of foreclosed farms in bankruptcy proceedings. The farmer could then seek to have the mortgage holder sell the property to him at its appraised value under a new six-year mortgage with annual payments set at 2.5 percent of the principal for the first five years, after which the rate doubled, to 5 percent. Annual interest at a rate of 1 percent was required to be paid on all unpaid balances. If the mortgage holder refused such an arrangement, the bankruptcy court was required to stay all proceedings for five years, with the farmer retaining possession of the farm during that period, provided that he paid a reasonable rent. However, the Supreme Court held that the legislation was unconstitutional.[39] The farm crisis was then attacked through creating crop subsidies.

Residential Markets

The building trades were especially hard-hit as residential and commercial construction ground to a halt. By 1933, more than 2 million men were out of work in the construction industry. Housing starts dropped by 90 percent from the highs reached in the 1920s. Residential mortgage foreclosures skyrocketed as lenders began demanding payment of the short-term mortgages issued at the end of the 1920s, which were coming due as the depression worsened. Rather than rolling those mortgages over into new ones, as was customary and expected by homeowners, the lenders began widespread foreclosures. By 1933, more than 500,000 home mortgages had been foreclosed. At one point, mortgages were foreclosed at a rate of 1,000 per day. However, those foreclosures provided little relief to lenders because the properties, once taken over, were usually worth only a fraction of the debt that they secured. "In the conditions then prevailing, many of them could not be sold at any price."[40]

Unemployment mounted, reaching nearly 25 percent in 1933. Construction was at a standstill. The automobile industry lost about half its workforce, and pay was cut nearly in half for those not laid off. Many unemployed homeowners could not meet their mortgage payment commitments. Homeowners engaged in desperate efforts to save their homes, using up all their savings, borrowing from relatives, and realizing the cash value of their insurance policies. Those sources of payment soon dried up as the Great Depression deepened. One study of twenty-two cities found that almost 45 percent of all owner-occupied homes with a first mortgage were in default as 1934 began. Homes in those cities with second and third mortgages had a default rate of more than 54 percent. Overall, half of all mortgages were in default. The highest rate of default was on loans made at the end of the 1920s, suggesting that loan standards had deteriorated.

"By 1933 the mortgage market had effectively ceased to function. Between 1929 and 1933 the stock of mortgage loans declined fifteen percent and housing construction dropped eighty percent."[41] The governors of several states issued proclamations calling on banks and courts handling foreclosure proceedings to hold those proceedings in abeyance. Several states already had legislation on their books that prohibited the judicial sale of foreclosed properties in an amount less than two-thirds (or some other percentage) of the appraised value of the property. Other state statutes allowed foreclosed homeowners to regain their property within a specified period, sometimes as long as one year, after refinancing.[42]

Several states enacted additional statutes during the Great Depression that sought to provide homeowner relief. Most popular was legislation adopted in twenty-eight states that imposed a moratorium on judicial foreclosure proceedings for a defined period. In other state statutes, the redemption period in which homeowners could regain property that had been foreclosed was extended. Another set of statutes prohibited large deficiency judgments in foreclosure proceedings by setting a "fair market value" on the foreclosed property, which would set the maximum amount of any deficiency.[43]

The problems in the residential real estate market were blamed on a number of factors. Real estate values were said to be unstable, as a result of population movements and speculation, and homeowners were saddled with debts that they could not service, often taking on second and even third mortgages. The use of short-term, unamortized mortgages effectively meant that most homeowners would be facing a balloon payment that they could not meet. They were dependent on refinancing through another mortgage, which was not available when the mortgage market broke down. Many homeowners had even borrowed the down payment on their home, a practice that would recur during the subprime crisis.

As would also be the case in the subprime crisis, many loans had been extended to consumers who could not afford them.

> [T]he attempt, fostered largely by financially interested groups on
> sentimental or emotional grounds, to extend homeownership to classes
> unable to afford it on the available terms and to sell others more
> expensive properties than they could afford, which has resulted in the
> assumption by many of debt charges far beyond their capacity to bear
> and thus swelled the volume of foreclosures, increased the fluctuations
> in real estate values, and destroyed the home-ownership aspirations of
> others with adequate financial resources to undertake it.[44]

"People in the cities had been continually urged, especially during the
boom years, to buy houses."[45] Property appraisals were often unreliable,
which undercut the value of the collateral held by the bank. Banks had also
funded longer-term residential real estate mortgages with short-term funds,
which posed a threat of losses if short-term rates increased. All these problems
resurfaced during the subprime crisis.

The Rise of the GSEs

Presidents Herbert Hoover and Franklin Roosevelt introduced several government-sponsored enterprises (GSEs) (at the time called "public business
enterprises") in an effort to restart the financial system. Those GSEs were
not successful and would be at the center of two future financial crises, one
involving the savings and loan associations in the 1980s and the other the
subprime crisis that began in 2007.

The GSE was not a new concept. The U.S. government previously held
a majority (62.5 percent) of the stock in the Bank of North America, a bank
created near the end of the Revolution as a means to manage the country's
finances so that the war effort could be sustained. The federal government
also held a 20 percent stock ownership interest in the two Banks of the United
States, one of which operated between 1791 and 1811, until its charter was
not renewed by Congress, and the other between 1816 and 1833, when it was
destroyed by President Andrew Jackson after an epic clash with his opponents
in Congress.

The federal government had also acted as a joint venture/entrepreneur in
various projects, such as the railroads, the post office, and later the Panama
Canal. During World War I, the federal government assumed control over large
portions of the economy through various GSEs, including the War Finance
Corporation, the Food Administration, the Grain Corporation, and the United
States Housing Corporation. They were eliminated after the end of the war, but
the concept of using a GSE to address financial and other business problems
was by then firmly fixed in government policy.[46]

The federal government also intervened in the mortgage market in 1916
through the creation of the Farm Credit System, which created the federal land
banks and cooperatives. That system was tasked with the job of encouraging

greater flows of credit for farm mortgage loans. The program was broadened in 1923, with the creation of the federal intermediate credit banks and production credit associations, which provided loans for farmers to allow them to pay operating expenses before their harvests.[47]

Federal Home Loan Bank Board

President Hoover's flirtation with GSEs as economic saviors began with a White House conference in 1931 on "Home Building and Home Ownership" attended by more than 3,700 people. The conference called for a system of mortgage credit that would better protect homeowners and lenders. It recommended the development of better homes at lower cost through improved technology, and it advocated the renovation of older homes. That sounded pretty much like pabulum, but housing renovation would be incorporated in the New Deal programs of Hoover's successor, Franklin Roosevelt.

President Hoover rejected a proposal that the thrifts become members of the Federal Reserve system. Instead, he sought legislation from Congress that would create a federal home loan bank system, which would act as a central bank for the mortgage market. This proposal was modeled after the federal land-grant system and advanced by the National Association of Real Estate Boards at the Conference on Home Building and Home Ownership. During his 1928 election campaign Hoover also advocated the creation of a home loan discount bank.

The Federal Home Loan Bank Act of 1932 created the Federal Home Loan Bank Board (FHLBB), which consisted of five members appointed by the president with the advice and the consent of the Senate. This legislation authorized the FHLBB to advance funds to thrifts participating in the system. The advances were to be made through twelve newly created federal home loan banks (FHLBs), which would operate as regional banking centers. Those banks were to be owned by local lending institutions authorized to subscribe to their stock. The FHLBs were governed by twelve-member boards of directors, four of whom were appointed by the FHLBB and the remainder elected by member institutions. A Federal Savings and Loan Advisory Council was created, which consisted of one representative from each of the FHLBs and which was to act as an advisory body to the FHLBB.

State S&Ls could join the FHLB system on a voluntary basis, but many state S&Ls were reluctant to do so. In 1936, only about one-third of state S&Ls were members, but that attitude changed over the following years. In 1941, about 90 percent of all S&L assets were in the FHLB system. Federally chartered S&Ls were authorized by legislation passed in 1933 and were required to be members of the FHLB system. Such charters initially proved unpopular because their charter requirements were more restrictive than those in most states. Only about 10 percent of the state thrifts had switched to a federal charter by 1936. In that year, the FHLBB revised its charter restrictions to place these institutions on a level equivalent to that of the state S&Ls, a move that increased their popularity. By 1938, almost 4,000 S&Ls, and even several insurance companies, had joined the FHLB system. In 1945 about 24 percent of S&Ls held federal charters.

Federal S&Ls had another advantage. Unlike commercial banks, they could open branches in remote locations. By the 1960s, more than 20 percent of all S&Ls had at least one branch. Because they were not-for-profit organizations, the S&Ls were also exempt from most taxes until 1952. However, even so, there were numerous exemptions, and most S&Ls avoided paying taxes until the laws were tightened in the 1960s, when they had to pay taxes on 50 percent of their earnings.

The FHLBs provided loans to their member S&Ls, which were otherwise generally limited to local deposits as sources of funds for loans. Those advances could be secured by first mortgages on residences held by the S&L receiving the loan from the FHLBB. In addition, the Treasury Department was authorized to purchase up to $100,000 of the preferred shares of member S&Ls, but that authority was rarely used. The FHLBB was also authorized to raise funds through issuing its own debentures.

Within a few months of its creation, the FHLBB made nearly $100 million in loans to members. It advanced almost $450 million to its members between 1932 and 1938, with the peak outstanding amount reaching $200 million. However, those lending operations were said to be merely "a small tea kettle full of hot water to pour on the iceberg of frozen home loans."[48]

Reconstruction Finance Corporation

President Hoover tried to deal with the Great Depression through some additional limited governmental intervention, in the form of the Reconstruction Finance Corporation (RFC), created by the Emergency Relief and Construction Act of 1932. The role of this GSE was to provide emergency funding to banks and other businesses in the private sector. However, in signing that legislation, Hoover stated that RFC was not intended to be used to aid large banks or industries, only smaller banks and financial institutions.

Building a Mortgage Market

Roosevelt Acts

President Hoover had opposed the idea of using the government to issue mortgages directly to homeowners without having a bank act as an intermediary. The FHLBB was, nevertheless, authorized by Congress to make direct loans, but its heart was not in assuming such a role. The FHLBB, in any event, could only make direct loans at 60 to 70 percent of loan value, which was unrealistic given the wide extent of poverty across the country. Of more than forty thousand direct loan requests received by the FHLBB in early 1933, only three were approved. President Roosevelt sought more forceful action when he entered office. He believed that the United States was a "nation of homeowners"[49] and that the home mortgage market was the "backbone of the American financial system."[50] That backbone was badly broken. In 1933, residential foreclosures reached a record 250,000, and housing starts were down 90 percent from the high reached in 1925. The values of residential homes declined by some 27 percent from 1930 to 1933.

Roosevelt included the thrifts and the FHLBs in the bank holiday he declared upon assuming office. The FHLBs were allowed to reopen quickly thereafter and made loans to several members that helped them survive the crisis. Roosevelt created an emergency council to address the breakdown of the mortgage market. This National Emergency Council recommended the creation of long-term federally insured mortgages and the creation of associations to purchase those mortgages. The New Deal programs that grew out of those recommendations

> were designed to address four major concerns of housing lenders, then and now: default risk, the chance that the borrower will not make some or all of the scheduled payments; high transaction costs associated with originating, servicing, and selling the mortgage; liquidity risk, the holding of long-term non-marketable assets when funding sources may be of short-term maturity and unpredictable availability; and interest rate risk, the uncertainty over the ultimate rate of return on a mortgage relative to alternative investments with different cash-flow characteristics.[51]

Home Owner's Loan Corporation

In an effort to strengthen the mortgage market, the Home Owners Loan Act of 1933 created the Home Owner's Loan Corporation (HOLC), which was directed by members of the FHLBB. HOLC was funded by a $200 million subscription from the Treasury Department through funds obtained from the RFC. It was authorized to issue its own bonds, backed by a government guarantee. Initially, that guarantee was only for interest, not principal, payments, but in 1934 it was extended to include principal payments as well, in order to make the HOLC bonds more marketable. The value of the bonds eventually authorized for issuance totaled $4.75 billion.

HOLC exchanged its bonds for residential mortgages in an amount not to exceed 80 percent of the value of the property. If the lender did not want to accept the bonds, HOLC was authorized to pay some cash, up to 40 percent of the value of the property. Properties eligible for HOLC mortgage relief could not be valued at more than $20,000. HOLC was also authorized to advance funds to homeowners who had already lost their homes in foreclosure proceedings, so that these homes might be recovered. Purchases of defaulted mortgages injected new funds into the S&Ls, providing liquidity and allowing them to make new loans and continue operating. Between 1933 and 1936, after which its lending authority lapsed, HOLC took over more than a million home loans, exchanging $2.7 billion of its bonds for those mortgages.

HOLC's mission was to stop the massive foreclosures occurring on home mortgages. It hoped to achieve that goal by replacing defaulted or troubled mortgages with new mortgages on terms that the homeowners could meet. Purchasing the troubled mortgages from banks and then issuing new mortgages to the homeowners on lenient terms (fifteen-year maturities at a 5 percent interest rate) accomplished this. HOLC converted the prevalent short-term mortgages into long-term loans that were amortized over the life of the mortgage. HOLC loans were for a period of fifteen years at 4 percent interest. This allowed the homeowners to reduce dependence on short-term refinancing and shielded them from a requirement that they make a large balloon payment only a few years after taking out the loan. Homeowners were able to remain in their homes and build up equity over the years. This loan structure became the model for the "conventional" mortgages that exist today.

HOLC eventually purchased about 20 percent of all home mortgages during the Great Depression. The number of loans applied for totaled about 1.9 million, with a value of $6.1 billion, which was about half the outstanding residential real estate debt. Despite the lenient terms for the new loans, 20 percent of the mortgages purchased by HOLC fell into default. It ended up owning some 200,000 houses, which were sold over several years. At one point, HOLC held an inventory of more than 100,000 homes. HOLC's eleven regional offices were located in large cities across the nation, augmented by some 450 state and local offices with some 20,000 employees. HOLC used some 3,000 contract management brokers to attract renters, to collect rents, and to perform necessary maintenance and repairs to make the foreclosed houses sellable. Those brokers were paid a percentage fee or on a per-unit basis.

The outbreak of war in Europe in 1939 eventually started the engine of economic recovery and recharged the residential housing market. Housing shortages were even experienced in many urban areas as the war progressed. This change in circumstances allowed HOLC to dispose of its foreclosed properties. When HOLC was disbanded in 1951, it was even able to return $14 million to the Treasury as surplus. Nevertheless, HOLC critics charged that the HOLC lending program did more to help lenders than borrowers.[52]

Federal Housing Authority

Notwithstanding HOLC's efforts, the housing market remained in critical condition during the 1930s. In December 1933 President Roosevelt appointed a committee to consider what further action was needed to deal with the crisis, consisting of Frank C. Walker, a New York businessman, John H. Fahey, chairman of the FHLBB, W. Averell Harriman, who was then a special assistant administrator of the National Recovery Administration (NRA), and Henry I. Harriman, president of the U.S. Chamber of Commerce. The committee delegated much of its work to Winfield W. Riefler, an economist who was the chairman of the Central Statistical Board. He conceived the idea of government insurance that would guarantee payment of principal and interest on residential mortgages. This would alleviate concern over the default risk on home mortgages and allow them to be bought and sold in a liquid secondary market. It would also allow the creation of a national market for mortgages.

This recommendation led to the adoption of the National Housing Act of 1934, which provided for such insurance. (That legislation was drafted by Frank Watson, who was recommended to the president by Thomas S. Corcoran, a member of the Roosevelt "brain trust," and a contributor to the drafting of the federal securities laws. Corcoran later became a somewhat infamous lobbyist in Washington.) This novel legislation was sped through Congress in about a month.

The Federal Housing Administration (FHA) was created by the National Housing Act of 1934 as a new independent federal agency,[53] with James Moffett, formerly a senior vice president at the Standard Oil Company, appointed as the first federal housing administrator in June 1934. Moffett declared that the FHA would be managed as a sound, conservative business. Among his recruits was Roger Steffan, a vice president of the National City Bank in New York. The FHA insured private lenders against losses from borrowers who defaulted on mortgages for initial home purchases, construction, and renovation. That insurance could be obtained for dwellings with one to four housing units.

Initially, the FHA made money available for repairs and new construction in order to revive the construction industry, acting as a "pump priming" device. Under that program, lending institutions were insured against losses of as much as 20 percent of their renovation loans. No collateral was required, but repair and construction loans were limited to a maximum of $2,000 and could have maturities of no more than five years. That program was initially slated to last only about eighteen months,[54] but it is still with us and played a key role in the housing market during the subprime crisis.

A "Better Housing Campaign," which was launched on August 9, 1934, promoted the FHA lending program. It was accompanied by massive publicity generated by the FHA like the bond drives during World War II. Newspapers were flooded with advertisements and editorials, and volunteers made more than 3 million door-to-door calls on the public. The FHA was also promoted through a weekly radio program hosted by "The Master Builder," H.R. Baukhage, a popular RCA network newscaster.[55]

By the end of 1934, more than 4,000 financial institutions participating in this program had made some 73,000 home improvement loans. Home improvement loans were then made at a rate of about $400,000 per day. It was estimated that homeowners spent an additional $5 on home improvement from their own funds for each $1 borrowed under the program. These renovations helped reduce unemployment in the housing construction industry. The Better Housing Campaign was estimated to have generated more than $210 million in expenditures on home improvements, employing 750,000 people in the process.

It was thought that an FHA insurance program would reduce the cost of mortgages by replacing short-term, high-interest first mortgages of the past, which were often combined with expensive second mortgages and multiple fees. Insured mortgages were required to have loan-to-value ratios of 80 percent and maturities of up to twenty years. The loans were to be amortized through monthly payments and could not exceed $16,000, with interest rates of no more than 5 to 6 percent.

FHA-insured loans were required to be "economically sound," which led to the creation of an underwriting manual that became the FHA "Bible." In order to be economically sound, the lender had to have a reasonable expectation that the borrower would repay the loan through regular installments of interest and principal. FHA officials monitored loans and counseled borrowers on whether they could afford particular loans. Another requirement for an economically sound mortgage was that the loan be secured by a dwelling, the value of which would reasonably protect the gradually diminishing principal (by amortization) of the mortgage with a fair margin of safety. One matter of concern in meeting this last criterion was the professionalism of appraisers. The American Institute of Real Estate Appraisers was created in 1926 to create an accreditation program for appraisers; however, it failed to address appraisal practices. The United States League of Local Building and Loan Associations corrected that in 1931 through the creation of an appraisal division that adopted a standardized appraisal form and uniform appraisal practices.

In the event of a default, the FHA was required to pay the lender the amount of the outstanding balance on the mortgage. Those payments were to be made in the form of long-term interest-bearing debentures guaranteed by the United States. These FHA debentures paid 3 percent interest and had a maturity of three years. This arrangement gave the FHA some breathing room to dispose of the properties before actually having to pay the lender cash to cover the mortgage default.

Based on a scheme borrowed from the mutual life insurance companies, the FHA program was thus designed to pay for itself. In addition to principal and interest, mortgage payments for FHA-insured mortgages included a small mortgage insurance premium that the holder of the mortgage paid annually to the FHA. It was thought that these premiums would make the FHA self-sufficient and, as in the case of mutual life insurance, possibly provide dividends to the borrowers.

The FHA was authorized to insure mortgages with lower down payments and higher payment-to-income ratios than had been available in a private market. However, FHA lending guidelines excluded risky neighborhoods where those with the lowest incomes lived. The exclusion of those neighborhoods from this government-backed lending program was thought to have contributed to the decline of the cities and the isolation of racial minorities in virtual ghettos. Reverse discrimination was also employed. Neighborhoods where wealthy families tended to reside were also excluded from the FHA program in the 1930s, in the apparent belief that such neighborhoods did not need assistance. The FHA's role changed in the 1980s to target mostly low-income family loans,[56] but reverse discrimination remained, in the form of caps on the amount of the mortgages insured by the FHA.

The Guaranty Trust Company of New York became the first approved FHA lender on November 3, 1934. On December 21 of that year, the Newark office of the FHA issued its first loan commitment for a house to be built with FHA financing. The owners of that house were Mr. and Mrs. Warren H. Newkirk, who borrowed $4,800. When the couple paid off that loan in 1948, they received a dividend of $400 from the FHA under its mutual mortgage insurance dividend program.

By the end of 1935, the FHA made home improvement loans at a rate of almost 1,000 per day. The average amount of these loans was $419, with average maturities of twenty-eight months. Mortgage insurance covered 23,400 mortgages with a total $94 million in value. However, this program did not meet expectations. In its first three years of operation, only about 18 percent of all mortgages were FHA insured. At the end of 1936, however, mortgage insurance premiums and appraisal fees totaled about $500,000 a month. The number of home mortgages insured tripled over the previous year. A secondary market was also developing. In 1936, about $60 million in mortgages had been bought and sold, about 15 percent of the total amount insured.

The National Housing Act of 1934 also created the Federal Savings and Loan Insurance Corporation (FSLIC), as a counterpart to the FDIC coverage available for deposit accounts at commercial banks. However, S&Ls participating in the program faced restrictions that made many of them find it unattractive. Those concerns were alleviated by statutory amendments adopted in 1935. Among other things, the amendments lowered insurance premiums, spurring membership. The Home Mortgage Relief Act of 1935 provided additional funding to reduce stresses on home mortgages.

In February 1935, the FHA insured its first mortgage for low-cost housing, for a project in Arlington, Virginia. Some 15,000 applications were received for the 276 units in that development. The RFC also extended loans for public housing in New York and elsewhere. In addition, the National Industrial Recovery Act of 1933 authorized the Public Works Administration to construct low-cost homes. It was able to build 40,000 units before that legislation was declared unconstitutional. A housing program adopted by Congress in 1937 provided funding to state and municipal authorities for building public housing, funded by subsidized loans, for rental to the poor at low monthly rents.[57]

Reconstruction Finance Corporation—Expansion

The RFC was not as successful in restarting the economy as Hoover had hoped, but Roosevelt continued and expanded its operations after he assumed office. The RFC was given unlimited authority to borrow funds from the Treasury. Congress expanded its powers further to include the purchase of capital stock of banks, insurance companies, and others. During the Great Depression the RFC made more than 15,000 loans to more than 7,300 banks and trust companies, totaling almost $2 billion. The RFC subscribed to the preferred stock of 4,202 banks and trust companies valued at $782 million. It also purchased notes and debentures from another 2,913 bank and trust companies valued at $343 million. An additional $354 million was lent to 432 mortgage companies. About half the funds disbursed to mortgage companies were to firms located in California, New York, and Ohio. Moreover, the RFC lent $140 million to 1,183 B&Ls.

Another RFC program involved direct loans to ailing businesses that did not have access to credit. This program included "participation" loans made in part by both the RFC and a private bank. In some of those loans, the RFC agreed to repurchase the bank's participation amount upon request of the bank, a form of guarantee. In some instances, the RFC purchased the capital stock of companies. The RFC also carried out programs in which it made loans to banks and mortgage companies for immediate relending to specific businesses.

The RFC created a subsidiary in 1935 called the RFC Mortgage Company, which bought and sold mortgages insured by the FHA and, later, traded in mortgages guaranteed by the Veterans Administration. The RFC Mortgage Company also authorized the purchase of $173 million in mortgages on commercial property that were not so guaranteed. Before it was closed in 1947, the RFC Mortgage Company disbursed $419 million in funds.[58] The RFC itself was turned into a war-related agency during World War II and was disbanded in 1957. It reported net income over its life of $333 million.

Fannie Mae

The National Housing Act authorized the FHA to charter national mortgage associations that could buy and sell FHA-insured mortgages. These entities were required to have capital of at least $5 million. The theory behind that authorization was that these institutions would make mortgage funds available throughout the country and reduce interest rates in underserved areas. However, only one such association was ever formed. This lack of interest was due to the fact that these associations were not allowed to make direct loans. They could only purchase or sell loans originated by others.

The RFC created an entity called the National Mortgage Association in 1938. The name of that entity was quickly changed to the Federal National Mortgage Association, now universally referred to as "Fannie Mae." Fannie

Mae operated as a division of the RFC until 1950, when it was transferred to the Housing and Home Finance Agency. The RFC lent $1.3 billion to Fannie Mae while it operated as one of its divisions. Fannie Mae was authorized to buy FHA-guaranteed loans from mortgage lenders. It funded those operations through sales of bonds to the public. This allowed mortgage lenders to originate mortgages that were guaranteed and then sold to the government. The government resold those mortgages to private investors around the country, thereby substantially expanding the ability to raise funds beyond the deposit base of individual S&Ls. After the loans were purchased, the mortgage lender could use the funds received from their sale to make additional mortgages, thereby substantially expanding the mortgage market.

More Programs

A housing act passed in 1937 sought to promote the general welfare of the nation by encouraging employment and rectifying the acute shortage of safe and sanitary homes for families with low incomes. That act had little immediate effect, but set the stage for the massive public housing projects in the future that turned into virtual ghettos. In 1938, Congress eased requirements for FHA-insured loans, raising the maximum loan-to-value ratio to 90 percent and increasing maturities to twenty-five years. The insurance premium was also cut in half. This greatly spurred the growth of FHA-insured mortgages. By 1940, the FHA was receiving sufficient mortgage insurance premiums to become self-sustaining.

The federal government also began promoting programs designed to provide homes for those who could not afford to purchase them. However, all these efforts did not restart the economy or solve the housing crisis. In 1938, more than 10 million workers still remained unemployed, about 16 percent of the labor force. The New Deal programs, many of which still exist, did nothing to end the Great Depression. At least in the case of the federal securities laws, and the punitive taxes imposed by the Roosevelt administration, those programs probably prolonged the depression. The Great Depression ended only after the outbreak of war in Europe. The New Dealers might not be blamed for trying, but their residential mortgage programs also laid the groundwork for the next great financial crisis in 2008, which nearly wrecked the economy, once again.

A government reorganization plan in 1939 created a federal loan agency that was assigned the task of coordinating and supervising the government's various loan programs, including those of the FHA. Wartime legislation was enacted that provided for defense housing mortgage insurance. The requirement of economic soundness was omitted from that legislation as a precondition of the issuance of insurance. A special insurance fund was created to cover losses from those loans. In 1942 the president created a national housing agency, which was given oversight over the FHA and other housing entities in the federal government.

That year, the War Production Board issued its famous "stop construction" order halting all private construction deemed nonessential to the war effort. New housing starts fell by more than 65 percent between 1939 and 1945. Despite the efforts of the Roosevelt administration, homeownership fell to an all-time low of 43.6 percent in 1940. However, there was a silver lining in that cloud, because banks and S&Ls were able to sell off all the property they had acquired in foreclosures, restoring their balance sheets. The president also urged Americans to pay off their mortgages to help curb inflation. To aid that effort, the FHA waived its 1 percent prepayment penalty. The FHA also paid dividends to the homeowners who paid off their mortgages under its mutual mortgage insurance system. Distributions were made to nearly 13,000 borrowers who prepaid their loans in 1944.

Postwar Boom

In 1940, only about 43 percent of housing in the United States was owner occupied, but by 1960, 60 percent was. That growth was spurred by a postwar building boom as well as the conversion of many rental units into owner-occupied ones.[59] The government also expanded its loan subsidy programs in 1944 under the G.I. Bill of Rights. That legislation created the Veterans Administration and provided for long-term, amortizing mortgage loans to veterans with down payments of 20 percent or less. These lenient loan terms allowed a large number of veterans to obtain their own homes. Some 327,000 mortgages were insured under this program. In 1948 Fannie Mae was authorized to purchase these loans, providing further liquidity to lenders.

Between 1935 and 1953, the federal government insured about $30 billion in residential mortgage loans, of which about $24 billion originated between 1946 and 1953, when the net flow of funds into residential mortgages "was markedly larger than the flow into any other sector of the money or capital markets. It amounted to one-third of the total net flow of funds into all types of debt instruments, and was greater than the combined flow into corporate and state and local government securities."[60] About half the mortgages written during that period were conventional mortgages, and the federal government guaranteed the rest. An added encouragement for homeownership was the fact that real estate taxes and interest on a residential mortgage could be deducted from gross income for tax purposes. In contrast, a renter received no such deduction, but had to pay for the cost of living in the home and accumulated no equity as a homeowner does from amortized mortgage payments.

The president appointed Wilson Wyatt, from Kentucky, as the nation's housing expediter in 1946. He was asked to formulate programs and recommend legislation that would break bottlenecks in construction and more quickly allow returning veterans to own their own homes. The Housing Act of 1949, and later the Housing Act of 1968, launched the construction of massive public housing units.[61] The 1949 legislation moved the FHA into the Housing Finance

Agency, together with its Mutual Mortgage Insurance Fund, which was then showing a surplus. The 1949 Housing Act set the goal of "a decent home and a suitable living environment for every American."[62] Later surveys determined that the legislation actually led more housing units to be demolished for slum clearance than were built under its provisions. Even more unfortunately, many of the "projects" that were built became cesspools for crime and ghettos for the impoverished, from which they had no hope of escape. Cabrini-Green, a public housing project developed by the Chicago Housing Authority, became the ugliest symbol of this failure in policy. It was plagued by gang warfare, vandalism, and horrific crime. Even the police were afraid to enter the project, particularly after snipers shooting from buildings in the project in 1970 killed two police officers.

In recent years the drive for such massive housing projects has been replaced by a movement that seeks lower-density housing, made affordable through subsidies. Reformers are also placing political pressure on developers to force them to set aside, at below-market prices, a specified percentage of units in their development projects to lower-income families as a condition of permits to develop the rest of their properties. This movement claims that this requirement is justified because many middle-class workers, such as schoolteachers, firefighters, and police, need a subsidy from developers in order to be able to afford to live near where they work in urban environments.

The 1950s

The Housing Act of 1948 sought to encourage production of private housing in the lower-price and rental ranges. Legislation was also enacted to encourage the use of cost reduction techniques through large-scale construction projects. The result of that effort is best exemplified in the Levittown projects in New York and Pennsylvania. They were developed by the Levitt & Sons construction company, which was founded in 1929 by Abraham Levitt, a real estate lawyer. Levitt brought his sons into the business, and they handled a large construction project during World War II that required the building of 2,350 homes in Norfolk, Virginia. During that project, they developed an assembly-line process for mass-producing homes that was applied to their Levittown projects after the war. More than 17,000 homes were built in the Levittown project on Long Island. At its peak, the company built a house every sixteen minutes. Those houses cost $7,990 and required a down payment of only $90, with payments of $50 per month.

Levittown became a famous symbol of the sameness of suburban American life. Potential buyers could choose from among only five styles of home design, all of them based on the same floor plan, but could select a style and sign a contract for it in short order. The Levittown homes had neither basements nor garages and were built on concrete slabs, with radiant heating coils. Bland or not, they were exceptionally well constructed and popular when first built, and remain so even today. Homes in Levittown that sold for $7,990 when they were first built sold for more than $400,000 in 2007. The Levittown communities were ethnically mixed, but their deeds contained racial covenants that barred ownership by African Americans until the late 1950s.

New housing construction reached a record high in 1950. However, the outbreak of the Korean war in July 1950 resulted in price and credit controls that crimped lending. The Federal Reserve adopted Regulation X, which imposed loan-to-value and loan-to-cost ratios on mortgage loans. By 1951, these restrictions had caused a decline in housing construction, but they were removed in 1953. By 1954, the FHA had repaid to the Treasury Department all the expenses it had been advanced since its inception in 1934. That payment totaled $85.9 million and included interest on the use of the funds supplied by the government.

Scandal struck the FHA in 1954. Several builders of rental housing were able to obtain FHA-guaranteed loans in amounts that substantially exceeded the construction cost of the apartments, allowing them to make millions of dollars in profits, hence the name the "windfall scandals." One developer received $24 million in construction loans for a project that cost $20 million. Representative Wright Patman (D-TX) also found that the FHA had allowed unscrupulous builders to build poorly constructed homes that were sold to the poor at inflated appraisal values. These builders, often operating in inner-city neighborhoods, bought rundown houses, did a "paste-up" job, and resold them to unsuspecting buyers at large markups. In one instance, an old, boarded-up tavern was purchased by a speculator for $8,000, given cosmetic repairs, and resold a few months later for $20,000. Those scandals led President Dwight D. Eisenhower to fire FHA Commissioner Guy T.O. Hollyday.

Congress rechartered Fannie Mae in 1954 to make it a government corporation, with the ultimate goal of turning it into a publicly traded company. The rechartered Fannie Mae was initially to be funded by preferred stock issued to the Treasury and nonvoting common stock sold to institutions selling it mortgages. Those investing institutions were given favorable tax treatment for any losses on that stock and they faced no restrictions in reselling that stock, for which a market soon developed. Fannie Mae was also authorized to tap the capital markets for loans through the issuance of the debentures and short-term notes.

In 1953, the National Association of Real Estate Boards proposed replacing the secondary market offered by Fannie Mae with a private market that would attract investors for the purpose of purchasing mortgage loans from their originators. The industry group proposed the placement of mortgages in a pool that would issue debentures to investors. The proceeds from the debentures would be used to purchase the mortgages from originators. The investors would be paid off from the mortgage payments received from the mortgages placed in the pool. This proposal did not get off the ground but would later be adopted by the GSEs in the form of mortgage-backed securities.

The S&L Crisis

S&L Business Plans

S&Ls created a new mortgage product after World War II called the US Loan Plan, which was a flexible arrangement that allowed homeowners to obtain additional funds for home improvements. This saved the homeowner the cost of refinancing or obtaining a second mortgage. The borrowers could also defer payments on their mortgage after three years. Such deferrals provided homeowners with some flexibility if they were having financial problems, helping them to avoid foreclosure. Over $330 million of these loans were made by 1953.[63] Variations of these mortgages helped fuel the subprime crisis.

During the 1950s the S&L business was an otherwise sleepy, but profitable, affair. Their business plan was mockingly referred to as "3-6-3," which meant that the S&L paid interest on deposits of 3 percent, made loans at 6 percent, and the bankers were on the golf course by three o'clock. Unlike commercial banks, S&Ls were not initially subject to Regulation Q, which limited the amount of interest that banks could pay on deposits. As a result, S&Ls paid interest rates about twice that of commercial banks. This allowed S&Ls to increase their deposits after World War II by over 100 percent, while the banks increased their deposits by only 22 percent. S&Ls avoided rate competition with one another by attracting depositors with "gifts," including some expensive items, such as kitchen appliances. However, in 1956, the FHLB limited the value of these gifts to $2.50. Some competition was introduced through brokered deposits. These funds were acquired by brokers from large investors and deposited among a number of S&Ls in order to keep the investors' funds under FSLIC insurance limits. Deposit brokers shopped for the S&L paying the highest interest rates on deposits, which increased competition for funds and pushed up interest rates. Brokered deposits also created an unstable deposit base because the brokered funds could quickly move to another institution paying a higher rate. In 1959, the FHLB limited brokered deposits to 5 percent of an S&L's assets.

Lending increased in the second half of 1954, and S&Ls rapidly increased their borrowing from the FHLB, which had difficulty in funding those borrowings. The FHLB imposed a moratorium on new borrowing in September 1955, which created a credit crunch. As a result home loans declined. The Federal Reserve also adjusted its Regulation Q to allow banks to be more competitive with S&Ls in attracting deposits. This allowed banks to surpass the S&Ls in attracting deposits through the issuance of certificates of deposit.

The mission of the FHA expanded during the 1950s and 1960s to include relocation of residents and slum clearance projects, and it was directed to encourage the development of cooperatives, condominiums, and even nursing homes. The goal of the Housing Act of 1956 was to assist the elderly. More legislation, in 1957 and 1958, reduced the minimum down payment for FHA

mortgages. The FHA amended its regulations in 1957 to allow mortgage holders to sell securities to the public that were backed by insured mortgages. This
was a turning point for the market in this form of "securitization" that would
dominate the industry at the end of the century and that would become the
focal point of the subprime crisis in this century.

By 1959, the FHA had, since its inception, insured mortgages valued at more
than $53 billion for more than 5 million families. It had provided financing
for 800,000 families in rental and cooperative programs and financed repairs
on 22 million residences. Some 60 percent of American families owned their
own home in 1960. Delinquencies at the time were less than 1 percent of
outstanding mortgages, and mortgages in actual default were less than .006
percent. The FHA had a reserve fund of $700 million.

A private market alternative to the FHA appeared in 1957, when Max Karl,
a real estate attorney in Milwaukee, Wisconsin, created the Mortgage Guaranty Insurance Corporation (MGIC). Unlike FHA loans, MGIC insured only
the top portion of a mortgage, rather than 100 percent, thereby encouraging
low-down-payment mortgage loans to borrowers with a down payment of less
than 20 percent. Karl funded this venture with capital raised from his family
and friends, including his barber, and several S&L executives.

The 1960s

In 1965, a new cabinet-level department was created, the Department of Housing and Urban Development (HUD), whose mission was to increase available housing in the United States. The programs administered by HUD soon
became known for their inefficiencies and even fraud. "The phrase 'FHAing
a neighborhood' came to mean making large numbers of unsound mortgages
in an area, followed by an inevitable round of default, foreclosure, and dete-
rioration of the housing stock."[64]

By that time, S&Ls held more than 25 percent of consumer savings and
provided 46 percent of home mortgages. The Housing Act of 1964 allowed
S&Ls to finance the purchase and development of undeveloped land, a power
denied to commercial banks. S&Ls were also authorized to make education
loans. Their lending territories expanded to include properties within 100
miles of their headquarters and in any large urban area. They were also allowed to create service corporations, in which they could use up to 1 percent
of their assets for investments outside normal thrift activities. However, S&Ls
were still limited in many other activities; for example, they could not offer
variable-rate mortgages.

One phenomenon that became prominent in the 1960s was the development
of holding companies that controlled several S&Ls. They first appeared in 1955,
with the creation of the Great Western Financial Corporation. Congress passed
the Savings and Loan Holding Company Act in 1959 (the Spence Act), which
prohibited holding companies from owning more than one S&L. However, it

grandfathered existing holding companies, which by 1965 numbered about 100, many of them in California.

In 1962, the FHLBB imposed restrictions designed to discourage interest rate competition on deposits by S&Ls. However, those controls did not work. Regulation Q restrictions on commercial banks were eased again in order to allow them to compete with S&Ls for deposits. This change resulted in a rate war in California and Florida. This was stopped by the Interest Rate Control Act of 1966 that allowed Regulation Q limitations to be applied to S&Ls, but with an assurance that S&Ls could pay a slightly higher rate (.25 percentage points more) than commercial banks. The S&Ls then lent that money to borrowers at two to three percentage points above their Regulation Q borrowing ceiling.

In 1955, a moratorium was placed on demutualizations, in which S&Ls converted from mutual societies to stock-issuing corporations after concerns were raised that the conversions were unfairly enriching management at the expense of S&L depositors. One favorite ploy was for management to make large deposits just before a stock conversion, which gave them a larger stock interest upon conversion at little cost. That moratorium was lifted in 1961, but abuses recurred, and it was reimposed in 1963.

The failure of three S&Ls in the mid-1960s resulted in charges to FSLIC of almost $120 million. The insurance fund faced liabilities of an additional $425 million as a result of its exposure to other faltering S&Ls. Concern was raised that FSLIC might be bankrupted. Congress responded by enacting the Financial Institutions Supervision Act of 1966, which was designed to give greater supervisory control to the FHLB in the form of cease-and-desist orders against unsafe and unsound banking practices. These powers were also granted to federal regulators for commercial banks.

In 1968, Fannie Mae was rechartered by Congress to become a privately owned company funded by private investors and was listed on the New York Stock Exchange (NYSE). Fannie Mae's charter required it to "'channel [its] efforts into increasing the availability and affordability of home ownership for low-, moderate-, and middle-income Americans.'"[65] In reaching that goal, Fannie Mae and others would nearly bankrupt the United States during the subprime crisis.

The Government National Mortgage Association (GNMA, also called Ginnie Mae) was created by the Housing and Urban Development Act of 1968. Ginnie Mae, a part of HUD, did not itself originate loans. Rather, it acted as a guarantor of loans originated in the private sector, but with federal involvement from the Federal Housing Authority, the Veterans Administration, and other government-sponsored programs that encouraged broader access to credit by those who otherwise had limited credit opportunities.

With the full faith and credit of the United States behind it, Ginnie Mae guaranteed the timely payment of principal and interest on mortgages that were originated by approved issuers. These issuers were private parties, usually financial institutions that originated or purchased a pool of mortgages, which meant that no federal funds were used in the origination or sale of those mortgages. Federal funds were expended only in the event of a default on a guaranteed mortgage.

Mortgages guaranteed by Fannie Mae were not backed by the full faith and credit of the United States until that organization was nationalized in 2008, during the subprime crisis. Before then, only its own assets backed the Fannie Mae guarantee. However, even though Congress had decreed otherwise, the secondary mortgage market had long assumed that there was an implicit guarantee from the federal government because, if Fannie Mae were allowed to fail, the effects on the economy would be systemic and predictably devastating. That assumption was borne out by the events in the credit markets during the subprime crisis.

Because of the implicit government guarantee, Fannie Mae could issue debt securities at rates only slightly higher than those of the Treasury securities and could do so in virtually unlimited amounts. Fannie Mae used those funds to purchase mortgages from lenders and originators. Those mortgages were then held for investment or were bundled and sold to investors. When they were used for investment, Fannie Mae borrowed the money to buy the mortgages at a low price because of its implicit government guarantee and then profited from the spread on the mortgages purchased. When they were securitized, Fannie Mae guaranteed the performance of the mortgages in the pool, including timely principal and interest payments. Fannie Mae had other advantages. Its earnings were exempt from state and local income taxes, and it had a $2.25 billion line of credit from the Treasury that was never tapped before its failure and nationalization during the subprime crisis. Fannie Mae was also eligible for unlimited investments from federally insured banks and thrifts.

A credit crunch occurred in 1966 that curbed mortgage lending and sharply reduced housing starts. The credit situation seemed to have improved in 1967, but another credit crunch hit in 1968. In 1969, interest rates reached historic levels, further reducing mortgage lending.[66] The Emergency Home Finance Act of 1970 was passed to ease this slowdown. Among other things, the legislation allowed Fannie Mae, for the first time, to purchase conventional mortgages, which were originated by banks without a government guarantee. The act also created the Federal Home Loan Mortgage Corporation (Freddie Mac) for the purpose of providing a mechanism for the purchase of mortgage loans from savings institutions. It, too, was allowed to purchase conventional mortgages and guarantee them, but not with an explicit guarantee from the federal government. However, it also had an implicit government guarantee, and it failed during the subprime crisis as well.

Studies

The Blue Ribbon Commission on Money and Credit, formed by the Committee for Economic Development in 1957 submitted its recommendations to President John F. Kennedy in 1961. Its findings covered broad expanses of the economy and made some recommendations on how to improve the thrift industry, but those recommendations were largely ignored. The Friend Commission Report issued in 1969 also focused on the thrift industry. That commission, headed by Irwin Friend from the Wharton School of Business, made a number of recommendations, including the elimination of Regulation Q.

The Hunt Commission's Report on the President's Commission on Financial Structure and Regulation followed in 1972. That commission was formed by President Richard Nixon to study and to make recommendations for improving the regulation of financial services. Headed by former North Carolina governor Jim Hunt, the commission made a number of recommendations involving thrifts, including the broadening of the services that they could offer. Among other things, the Hunt Commission thought that S&Ls should be allowed to extend construction loans and to invest in equity securities up to 10 percent of their assets. The Hunt Commission also recommended that Regulation Q interest rate ceilings be eliminated. Still another study, this one called "Financial Institutions and the Nation's Economy (FINE)," was undertaken by the House Committee on Banking Currency and Housing in 1975. It too called for elimination of Regulation Q and recommended that a single person should regulate all depository institutions, a recommendation that was well ahead of its time.

More Legislation

Subsidy programs for residential loans were popular with politicians and spread to the states. The Revenue and Expenditure Control Act of 1968 prohibited the use of tax-exempt industrial revenue bonds for most purposes, but did allow their use for residential real estate for family units. Between the 1930s and 1950s, single-family homes dominated residential construction. However, in 1960, apartment housing increased. Single-family homes as a share of residential construction fell from 80.5 percent in 1959 to 55.1 percent in 1973.

The Nixon administration suspended most federally subsidized housing programs in 1973 because of abuses and inadequate screening of participants. Private housing starts peaked in that year and then sharply declined. The 1974 Housing and Community Development Act allowed states to administer some federal housing programs. A somewhat controversial program that began in New York in 1978 involved single-family mortgage revenue bonds (MRBs) that were sold by state and local governments. Proceeds of those loans were used to make subsidized mortgage loans to individual homeowners. These MRB programs spread to other states. Between 1974 and 1990 over a million such loans were extended to households with a value totaling $60 billion. These mortgage loans were offered at below-market rates, which was made possible by the ability of the state and municipal authorities to pay tax-free interest on their bonds, allowing them to pay a lower rate, which was passed on to the homeowners. Some of these programs also allowed reduced down payments. Critics charged that the programs mainly helped the real estate industry and families that could already afford to buy homes. Proponents contended that these loans allowed renters to become homeowners.[67]

S&L Problems

Until inflation reached high levels in the 1970s, S&Ls, as *Newsweek* noted, had "almost a license to print money."[68] That happy situation existed only so long as short-term interest rates did not increase above the Regulation Q deposits ceiling. When that occurred, depositors withdrew deposits and S&Ls would have to obtain funds at higher rates that might exceed the rates paid on the long-term mortgages that they issued. This was the danger of funding long-term assets with short-term liabilities, yet another folly that repeated itself in the subprime crisis.

Inflation in the 1970s had a devastating effect on S&Ls. Regulators fixed the amount of interest that they could charge, but market rates rose above those fixed rates. Mortgage interest rates increased from about 5 percent in the 1960s to 11 percent in 1978. At the same time, housing prices inflated, nearly tripling in the 1970s and requiring ever-larger mortgages at increasing interest rates.

Some new mortgage tools were developed to deal with these problems. The shared appreciation mortgage was a mortgage with a below-market interest rate in exchange for a portion of any increase in the value of the house after it is sold. A new "flexible" mortgage provided for interest-only payments during the first five years of mortgage, and principal and interest payments thereafter. The "graduated-payment" mortgage called for only partial principal and interest payments in the early years and gradually escalated the amount of the monthly payment to allow for amortization over the remaining life of the loan. The theory behind these mortgages was that the homeowner's income would rise while the amount of mortgage remained fixed.

"Step-rate" mortgages had a below-market interest rate that gradually increased over time.[69] "Rollover" mortgages periodically adjusted the interest rate, which was beneficial to the lender but could be costly to the borrower if interest rates increased. More important was the introduction of the "adjustable rate mortgage" (ARM), which adjusted the interest rate on the mortgage periodically to reflect changes in some interest rate index such as LIBOR (London Interbank Offered Rate). However, California was the only state that allowed its S&Ls to make such loans. Federal S&Ls were prohibited from offering ARMs until 1982, when Congress passed the Alternative Mortgage Transactions Parity Act, which attempted to stimulate lending by loosening regulatory restrictions that had previously allowed S&Ls to make only conventional fixed-rate, fixed-term loans.

Home equity lines of credit were permitted as second mortgages on residences. They were attractive to borrowers because interest payments on those lines of credit were tax deductible. Home equity loans rose from around $1 billion in the early 1980s to more than $1 trillion by 2007, when about 25 percent of all homes with first mortgages also had a second mortgage. State S&Ls were authorized to make home equity loans notwithstanding any prohibitions in their own state laws, provided that they complied with federal regulations.

Another innovation was the "reverse mortgage." These mortgages allowed individuals to take out a loan that would pay them either a large lump sum or periodic payments that were secured by the equity in the home. Thus, instead of having the homeowner pay the bank a monthly mortgage payment, the bank would make payments to the homeowner. Of course, the homeowner was spending the equity accumulated in the house.[70] These mortgages became popular with the elderly because they saw it as a good way to remain in their homes while reducing their expenditure on housing. The federal government began guaranteeing reverse mortgages in 1990. Seniors participating in the program could choose to accept a lump sum, draw down the mortgage when needed, like a line of credit, or receive fixed, say monthly, payments. Repayment was not required until the homeowner sold the house or died. The bank issuing the mortgage would then be repaid from the proceeds of the sale of the house. These mortgages remained popular even during the bottom of the subprime crisis. The number of such mortgages increased by 20 percent in March and April 2009 over the same period the previous year. Congress also encouraged these loans by raising the ceiling on their amount from $417,000 to $625,000 in February 2009, while capping fees.

These innovations did not stop the disintermediation (removal) of funds from S&Ls and other depository institutions into higher-paying short-term investments in the 1970s. In earlier years, banks and thrifts were the only available financial intermediaries readily available to many consumers, stockbrokers being viewed as too dangerous or unavailable in smaller cities. The deposit institutions intermediated by taking customer deposits, paying them a set interest rate, and then investing those funds in loans and mortgages with higher interest rates, earning a profit on the spread between the two rates.

That situation changed after Henry B.R. Brown and Bruce R. Bent invented the money market fund and brought their Reserve Fund to market in 1972. A money market fund is simply a mutual fund that accepts customer funds and invests them in short-term money market instruments, such as Treasury bills. The SEC delayed consideration of the Reserve Fund's application to start this mutual fund for months, rejecting the application from Brown and Bent to become a registered mutual fund 144 times before it finally approved. Ironically, the Reserve Fund failed in the midst of the subprime crisis in 2008, an event that set off a national panic by money market investors before being quelled by a government guarantee of performance.

Before the subprime crisis, money market funds "broke the buck"—in which participants in the money market fund received less than a dollar for each dollar they invested—only once. That loss occurred in 1994 at the Bankers Mutual Fund, but investors only lost about $.04 on the dollar. In other instances money market fund sponsors stepped in to cover losses, but overall money market funds had been a remarkably safe investment until the Reserve Fund broke the buck during the subprime crisis.

There is a significant difference between deposit accounts and money market funds. The latter were not insured by either the FSLIC or the FDIC in the event of investment losses in a money market account held with a broker-dealer. This distinction would cause a near-collapse of the money markets during the subprime crisis when the Reserve Fund failed. SIPC coverage was available if the money market account was held at a broker-dealer, and the loss was caused as a result of the broker-dealer's bankruptcy, as opposed to investment losses of securities purchased by the money market fund.

Bank and S&L accounts had no investment risk, only a bankruptcy risk if the money held in the failed institution by a depositor exceeded FDIC or FSLIC limits. Money market funds held with a broker-dealer did have an investment risk. For example, if the issuer of commercial paper held by the money market fund defaulted, investors in the money market fund would share the loss. However, this investment risk was considered minimal because money market funds limited their investments to highly rated, short-term money market instruments.

Initially, withdrawals from the money market funds were subject to minimum deposit requirements and limitations, but within a short time those restrictions were eased. The result was that consumers could obtain money market rates on their idle cash instead of leaving it in their bank or S&L, where they received little interest on passbook and other time deposits, such as certificates of deposit, and no interest on demand deposit accounts, such as a checking account, in which funds were not subject to withdrawal restrictions. Massive amounts of funds fled commercial banks and S&Ls for money market funds in the 1970s.

By 1981, money market funds were the most popular investment in the United States. In 1982, some $230 billion was held in those mutual funds. One example of the dramatic growth of money market funds is the Merrill Lynch Ready Assets Trust started in 1975, which took in $40 billion in a single year. By 1979, some one million Merrill Lynch customers had nearly $70 billion invested in that mutual fund. Merrill Lynch followed that success in 1977 with its Cash Management Account, which allowed clients to withdraw funds by check or debit card and was linked to the customers' brokerage accounts, which could then be used for margin loans.

The thrifts attempted to compete with the money market funds with negotiable order of withdrawal (NOW) accounts, introduced in Massachusetts in 1972 and operated essentially like a money market fund. Congress allowed federal thrifts to offer such accounts in 1973. S&Ls were also allowed to offer four-year certificates of deposit in 1973 that were not subject to Regulation Q interest rate limits. However, those instruments, called "wild cards," touched off a rate war with the banks, and they were ended within a few months.

The wild cards were replaced in 1974 with short-term CDs that paid market rates but were had minimum investments of $100,000. "Money market certificates" were allowed in 1977, with minimum investments of $10,000. They paid interest rates indexed to Treasury bills. In 1978, market rate interest-paying accounts made up about 75 percent of S&L deposits. The amount of passbook savings, which had previously dominated S&L deposits as a source of funds on which interest was paid, dropped to 25 percent of deposits.[71]

The S&L Crisis

In the early 1980s S&Ls struggled to stay solvent. Interest rate competition cut profit margins from a lucrative 25 percent in the 1950s to as low as 7 percent in the 1970s. Billions of dollars were withdrawn from the S&Ls when interest rates rose in the 1970s. Interest rate ceilings prevented the thrifts from competing for funds at market rates, and the net worth of S&Ls fell from $32 billion in 1980 to $3.7 billion in 1982. The one-year period between 1981 and 1982 was the worst for S&Ls since the Great Depression.

Although the thrift industry was composed of more than 3,000 institutions holding about $1 trillion in assets, it was a declining industry. One-third of the thrifts were insolvent or facing severe financial difficulties. Between 1981 and 1982, the FSLIC paid $12 billion to depositors of failed thrifts. The recession that occurred in the early years of the Reagan administration had further adverse effects on S&Ls, resulting in a sharp increase in mortgage foreclosures. Proposals were floated in Congress to provide emergency mortgage assistance that would prevent foreclosure on the homes of troubled borrowers. Those same proposals resurfaced during the subprime crisis in 2008.

The interest rates on short-term deposits and the long-term home mortgages that the S&Ls extended to borrowers were out of sync, which placed intermediaries at risk in the event of a sharp increase in short-term interest rates. Short-term borrowing costs in such an event could exceed the receipts from long-term loans. That scenario became a reality in the early 1980s, when most of the S&Ls' assets were thirty-year fixed-rate residential mortgages yielding less than 9 percent. The mortgages were financed by short-term deposits with rates that increased from about 6.5 percent in 1978 to 11.4 percent in 1982. This resulted in a negative return for S&Ls. To escape that vice, the number of ARMs issued by thrifts increased dramatically in 1984.

The Depository Institutions Deregulation and Monetary Control Act of 1980 provided competitive relief by allowing S&Ls to pay higher interest rates for their deposits. To ensure continued depositor trust, FSLIC coverage for thrift accounts was increased from $40,000 to $100,000. The Depository Institutions Act of 1982 (the Garn–St. Germain Act) tried to further aid S&Ls by allowing them to invest as much as 40 percent of their loans in nonresidential real estate, 30 percent in consumer loans, and up to 30 percent in equity investments. Congress thought that such investments would provide higher returns and help restore profitability to the thrifts. The Garn–St. Germain Act also allowed the thrifts to offer money market deposit accounts with no interest rate limitations. This slowed disintermediation and began to attract deposits back to the thrifts.

The Garn–St. Germain Act encouraged interstate mergers of banks and S&Ls to strengthen the thrifts. The FHLBB also encouraged healthy S&Ls to acquire failing thrifts. The law authorized the FDIC and the FSLIC to prop up troubled S&Ls through government-backed promissory notes called "net-worth certificates." Those agencies agreed to pay off the notes to an S&Ls creditor in the event that it failed. Within a year, $175 million of these notes were issued to rescue fifteen savings banks in the New York area. Congress placed more stress on the mortgage market through the Housing and Community Development Act of 1981, which lowered qualification standards for low-income borrowers who could be insured by the FHA. The result was to increase the percentage of loans with a high loan-to-value ratio. Defaults on those loans nearly bankrupted the FHA's loss reserves in its single-family insurance fund, which had reached $3.4 billion in 1980.

Lifting interest rate controls on lenders also created a troublesome problem. The thrifts lost their ability to pay a higher rate of interest to depositors than could be paid by commercial banks. Thus the thrifts would compete with commercial banks and money market funds for deposits. Deposit brokers assisted S&Ls in their efforts to compete for funds. Large sums obtained from institutional investors by the deposit brokers were broken up into tranches in order to be fully insured by the FSLIC. The brokers then placed the funds with the thrifts paying the highest interest rates. Brokered deposits represented "hot money" because they could be moved quickly as more favorable interest rates became available at another institution. This hot money destabilized the deposit bases of the thrifts.

The FHLBB had limited brokered deposits to 5 percent of an S&L's total deposits before 1980, but that rule was eased to allow expanded use of such deposits. Increased brokered deposits fostered the growth of thrift liabilities, which increased between 1983 and 1986 by 60 percent, or from $674 billion to $1.1 trillion. Those deposits received higher interest rates than were previously available under Regulation Q. That sea change pushed the thrifts toward higher-yielding, riskier investments in order to make a profit. S&Ls could now attract more deposits by paying higher interest rates, but they needed to widen their investment base in order to offset the higher cost of those funds and increase their income. They invested heavily in high-yield junk bonds and in high-risk commercial real estate loans in order to turn a profit.

A lot of lending focused on the "oil patch" states, where many loans went sour after oil prices declined dramatically and crippled the economy in those states. The recession in the oil patch led to widespread unemployment, which then caused increased defaults on residential mortgages. A decline in residential values also caused many homeowners to default on their mortgages and just walk away from homes whose value had fallen below their loan amount. That phenomenon reappeared during the subprime crisis.

Deregulation

Deposit growth increased the pressure on S&Ls to broaden their search for investments that would provide a higher rate of return. In some instances, the thrifts did so through service corporations that allowed them to engage in a wide range of activities outside normal thrift channels. Unitary thrift holding companies were also unrestricted in their investment activities, if they controlled only one savings association, and if the thrift engaged primarily in housing-related activities. State regulators encouraged taking increased risk by loosening restrictions on the investment powers of thrifts. New York State passed legislation in 1984 that, among other things, allowed thrifts chartered by the state to use any and all of their assets for commercial loans and for investment in stocks and bonds. State-chartered thrifts were allowed to invest in real estate development and equipment leasing directly, rather than through subsidiaries, as was required previously. Geographical limitations on lending were removed. Previously, New York S&Ls had been restricted to a 75-mile radius from their headquarters for their lending operations.

Two of the most aggressive states in deregulating thrifts were California and Texas. S&Ls in those states went on a binge after investment restrictions were removed. The Vernon Savings Bank of Texas increased its assets from $82 million to $1.8 billion in a little more than a year. Vernon invested in high-risk real estate projects by using funds obtained through deposit brokers. At first, Vernon was highly profitable, but then losses mounted. Members of its board of directors and management were indicted for fraud. Enormous questionable expenditures were being made on such things as a beach house and personal travel. Don Dixon, one of Vernon's executives, took a two-week culinary tour of France at the S&L's expense and used depositor funds to buy jets and other luxuries. When Vernon was taken over by the government, 96 percent of its loans were in default. Taxpayers were stuck with a bill of $1.3 billion.

The Empire Savings Bank of Texas increased its deposits from $17 million in 1982 to $300 million in 1984, but became the largest failed S&L in Texas history. Charles Knapp's Financial Corporation of America increased its assets from $1.7 billion in 1980 to $5.8 billion in 1982 and then to $10.2 billion in 1983. His firm developed a mortgage trading operation that included mortgage-backed securities. He was highly leveraged, at a thirty-to-one ratio.[72] The Beverly Hills Savings & Loan increased its assets from $600 million in 1981 to $2.8 billion in 1984. Brokered deposits that were invested in high-yield, high-risk investments funded much of this growth.

The S&Ls invested in shopping centers, large malls, resorts, commercial buildings, and other projects. Unfortunately, the thrift managers did not have experience with such investments, and they often misused their customer deposits. Real estate was "flipped" from one S&L to another, and the price of the property increased with each sale. Danny Faulkner, a sixth-grade dropout, bought property in Texas for $3 million that he almost immediately resold for $47 million. His Empire Savings and Loan failed at a cost of some $300 million to taxpayers. Faulkner was convicted of fraud and given a twenty-year sentence, a precursor to what was in store for the Enron-era culprits.

Flipping became a favorite practice of speculators during the subprime crisis. The "go-go" thrifts in the 1980s began investing in a broad range of speculative investments that included oil and drill operations and "windmill farms," which were then in their infancy. Some S&Ls bought worthless assets from their own executives and cronies in what were called "trash-for-cash" deals.

California relaxed its restrictions to allow thrifts to invest in stock and debt instruments of corporations of as much as 25 percent of the thrift's gross capital. No more than 10 percent of the thrift's investments could be made in any one corporation. This opened the door to investments in junk bonds by these thrifts, for which they developed quite an appetite. S&Ls became a favorite dumping ground for junk bonds, many of which were purchased from Drexel Burnham Lambert and Michael Milken, the "junk bond king." At one point about 7 percent of outstanding junk bonds were owned by just a few large S&Ls. Columbia Savings & Loan of Beverly Hills, California, in particular, helped finance various corporate raiders through junk bond purchases with insured deposits of customers. At the end of the 1980s it announced a loss of $591 million.

Problems Grow

Cracks in the S&Ls' profitability continued to widen. In 1984, the FSLIC paid out some $2.5 billion to depositors, as a result of insolvencies at thrifts and other institutions. By then, more than 30 percent of FSLIC-insured institutions were operating at a loss. More than 700 S&Ls became insolvent in 1985. The American Savings & Loan Association in California, controlled by Charles Knapp, had $6.6 billion in mortgage-backed securities in its portfolio in 1984. A large loss on those securities was sustained when interest rates rose.

The Financial Corporation of America (FCA) ran into difficulties during 1984 and 1985. It was the holding company for the American Savings and Loan Association, then the largest thrift institution in the United States. The FCA had grown rapidly, leading the SEC to begin questioning its financial statements and require a restatement of its second-quarter earnings in 1984. That restatement showed a loss of more than $100 million. The FCA posted a third-quarter loss of over $500 million. As these troubles surfaced, institutional investors withdrew $1.4 billion from the S&L. The FCA turned to the FHLBB for assistance, which granted it a total of $3.3 billion within a few months.

On May 9, 1985, a run on deposits at state-insured thrifts in Maryland began after financial troubles surfaced at the Old Court Savings and Loan

Association in Baltimore. Old Court had been making high-risk real estate development loans. In scenes reminiscent of the Great Depression, depositors waited in long lines to withdraw their money. Another depositor run began on Merritt Commercial Savings and Loan Association in Maryland after an announcement that it faced losses from its dealings with Bevill, Bresler, & Schulman, a failed dealer in repurchase agreements (repos). On May 14, 1985, Maryland's governor, Harry Hughes, issued an executive order that limited withdrawals from the deposit accounts of state-insured thrifts to $1,000 a month. In a special session, the state legislature passed a law requiring Maryland's large state-insured thrifts to qualify for federal deposit insurance, which stabilized the situation.

In 1985, the Home State Savings Bank in Cincinnati, Ohio, lost over $500 million as a result of a fraud scheme involving ESM Government Securities in Florida. Home State experienced a run on its deposits, and that panic spread to other institutions. Ohio governor Richard F. Celeste then closed all the state-insured thrifts for three days in order to stop those runs.

The thrift industry, as a whole, continued to suffer. S&Ls lost some $7 billion in 1987. The crisis was exacerbated by the fact that a change in accounting standards had allowed S&Ls to mask the magnitude of their problems. When real estate values collapsed at the end of the 1980s, all the problems that had been building in S&Ls were exposed, and hundreds of them failed. A majority of the distressed thrift associations were in California and the southwest, particularly Texas, where more than 800 banks and S&Ls failed. The FDIC arranged for several mergers, in which regional banks in other states acquired troubled Texas banks. The problems in the oil patch spread elsewhere, to the northeast, Arizona, the mid-Atlantic states, and Florida, turning the problem into a national crisis. Those failures were caused by widespread irresponsible lending and investment activities.

American Diversified Savings Bank, in California, held federally insured assets totaling more than $1.1 billion, of which $800 million was used to make worthless loans. The North American Savings and Loan Association in Santa Ana, California, failed in 1988. The individuals organizing this entity sold properties, through financing provided by the S&L, for $40 million that they bought for $3.65 million. Six of those individuals were indicted after the S&L failed, at a cost of $120 million to the FSLIC. Columbia Savings & Loan in Beverly Hills, California, invested $1.8 billion in risky mortgage-backed securities, and much of that S&L's income was derived from trading gains between 1982 and 1984. Its failure cost the insurance fund an estimated $275 million.

Franklin Savings Association in Ottawa, Kansas, began an expansion program in 1981. In eight years, its deposits grew from $200 million to more than $11 billion. Franklin began acquiring mortgage-backed securities, deep discount securities, repos, loan calls, put options, strips, and junk bonds with deposits it solicited nationwide through brokered deposits. By 1989, Franklin could no longer be described as an S&L but as a securities trading firm. Federal regulators appointed a conservator for this institution after it failed as a result of losses, at which time it had a negative net worth of almost $50 million.

Neil Bush, the son of George H.W. Bush, became known as the "poster boy of bunco banking" because of his association with the Silverado Savings & Loan Association in Colorado, which had engaged in numerous questionable activities and the looting of more than $300 million by insiders. Silverado's downfall cost taxpayers $1 billion. The federal government filed a $200 million lawsuit against Bush, which he settled for $50,000. The abuses by S&L managers became legendary and included paying for prostitutes to entertain customers, private jets, extravagant homes, and expensive art, all paid for with S&L deposits. One S&L executive threw a $148,000 Christmas party for 500 friends. Another S&L employee renovated a house at a cost of over $1 million, on her salary of $48,000.

David Paul controlled the Centrust Savings Bank, which was headquartered in Miami and had more than seventy branches. Centrust bought $1.4 billion in junk bonds from Drexel Burnham and held vast amounts of other unrated bonds. Paul spent $13 million of Centrust funds on a painting and $8 million on a yacht and was accused of using the thrift as his private "piggy bank."

One of the most notorious individuals involved in the S&L scandal was Charles H. Keating, Jr., a once-prominent Cincinnati lawyer. He purchased the Lincoln Savings & Loan Association in Irvine, California, in 1984, with the help of junk bonds provided by Michael Milken. Keating then began using Lincoln's assets to buy more junk bonds and eventually purchased some $800 million of them. He also had Lincoln invest in numerous large-scale real estate projects that failed, including the luxurious Phoenician resort in Scottsdale, Arizona. For his services Keating paid himself and his family $34 million. The failure of the Lincoln Savings & Loan cost taxpayers more than $3 billion.

Keating was convicted of looting the S&L, and he spent almost five years in jail before a federal district court overturned his conviction. He was returned to jail in January 1998 by the appeals court, but was released in February 1998, after the district court set his conviction aside once again. The appeals court, thereafter, refused to reinstate his conviction and reversed a $4.3 billion judgment against him.

Several senators—Alan Cranston (D-CA), Dennis DeConcini (D-AZ), Don Riegle (D-MI), John Glenn (D-OH), and John McCain (R-AZ), dubbed the "Keating Five"—were caught up in this scandal. They had received $1.3 million in campaign contributions from Keating as well as numerous freebies, including vacation trips. In exchange, the senators intervened with regulatory agencies to protect Keating. Two representatives, Jim Wright (D-TX) and Tony Coehlo (D-CA), were also criticized for their efforts to assist other S&Ls in avoiding regulatory requirements.

Blame

The crisis in the thrift institutions was blamed on a number of factors, including poor performance by S&L management, inadequate regulatory supervision, and fraud. Regulators estimated that 40 percent of the thrift failures were due to fraud or insider abuse. A congressional investigation concluded that the accountants for the failed S&Ls often did not adequately audit the financial conditions and the internal control problems of those institutions. The thrift failures were further blamed on the Reagan administration because of its efforts to reduce government regulation. S&Ls were allowed to cover up losses and to engage in a speculative spree through various accounting and regulatory changes that occurred in the 1980s, as a result of calls for "deregulation." The hiring of bank examiners and efforts to regulate the thrifts were frustrated by those opposing regulation.

The government's strategy for dealing with the early stages of the crisis was to change regulatory accounting principles so that struggling S&Ls could continue operating. That change resulted in an overstatement of capital in the industry by $9 billion. The loosening of investment restrictions allowed the thrifts to grow explosively without increasing their capital base. During the height of the S&L crisis, M. Danny Wall, the FHLBB chairman, assured Congress that industry problems were manageable with existing resources. As the magnitude of the crisis became visible to everyone but Wall, he lost his credibility, and some wags were calling him "Danny Off-the-Wall."

The federal government handled the S&L crisis aggressively after its magnitude was finally realized. The FDIC was assigned responsibility for determining which thrifts were insolvent and whether they should be saved or liquidated. Some of the S&L closures were said to be "exciting and dramatic, with features of a police raid."[73] When an institution was taken over, federal officials typically seized the institution and sent bank examiners to S&L branches, wherever they were located.

In one highly publicized action, the Office of Thrift Supervision brought an enforcement case against Kaye, Scholer, Fierman, Hays, & Handler, a large, white-shoe New York law firm. The government claimed that the law firm had made false and misleading statements in documents filed in connection with the firm's representation of Lincoln Savings & Loan, the S&L operated by Charles Keating. The Office of Thrift Supervision wanted $275 million in restitution from Kaye, Scholer, and the law firm's assets were frozen pending resolution of the litigation. This forced the law firm to agree to pay $41 million in fines. The action was controversial because attorneys were not normally held responsible for their clients' conduct.

The government sued several other law and accounting firms in an effort to recover losses caused by the S&L scandal. In settlements of charges brought in connection with their legal advice to thrifts, Jones, Day, Reaves, & Pogue paid $51 million, and Paul, Weiss, Rifkind, Wharton, & Garrison paid about

$40 million. Accounting firms were also the subject of enforcement and class-action lawsuits. In 1992, they were forced to pay $800 million in attorney fees to defend S&L cases. Ernst & Young settled a government action for $400 million, and Arthur Andersen settled with the government for $79 million.

In total, the government recovered about $2.5 billion from lawyers, accountants, and executives of failed S&Ls and other related professionals. The largest contributor to that amount was Drexel Burnham Lambert and Michael Milken, who kicked in $1 billion. However, those amounts covered only a small fraction of the losses sustained by the government during the S&L crisis.

FIRREA

The Competitive Equality Banking Act of 1987 authorized $10.8 billion to bail out the FSLIC, which was facing bankruptcy from the massive amount of claims generated by S&L failures. That legislation created the Financing Corporation (FICO) to raise the necessary funds for the bailout by issuing long-term bonds (FICO bonds). The interest on these bonds was to be paid by FDIC assessments on thrift associations. The thrift industry and the banks paid almost $800 million in annual interest on FICO bonds after their issuance. The amount raised from those bond sales was inadequate as FSLIC was more than $50 billion in debt.

More than a thousand S&Ls closed down in 1988, and another 262 S&Ls in 1989. Congress then passed the Financial Institutions Reform, Recovery, and Enforcement Act (FIRREA), which replaced the FSLIC with the Savings Association Insurance Fund (SAIF). The FDIC was given control over SAIF, which would be used to fund future depositor losses. A separate fund, the Bank Insurance Fund (BIF), was to be used to cover depositor losses at the commercial banks. Supervision of the Federal Home Loan Banks was shifted from the FHLBB to the Federal Housing Finance Board, an independent regulatory agency with a five-member board. Four of those board members are appointed by the president for seven-year terms, and the fifth member is the secretary of housing and urban development.

FIRREA shifted regulatory control over S&Ls from the FHLBB to a new Office of Thrift Supervision in the Treasury Department and reduced their investment powers. Supervisory authority over S&Ls by bank regulators was expanded. Capital requirements for S&Ls were increased, and insurance premiums were raised. The legislation required 70 percent of thrift assets to be held in residential mortgages and mortgage-backed securities, as well as eliminating junk bonds from the 10 percent commercial business loan authority for federally chartered S&Ls. Junk bonds already owned by the S&Ls had to be sold within five years.

This liquidation requirement shrank the junk bond market, leading other financial institutions to reduce their junk bond holdings, which drove down junk bond prices even further. The junk bond market collapsed almost entirely in October 1989, after a proposed buyout of United Airlines failed. Jim Walter Corporation, having been bought out by Kohlberg Kravis Roberts (KKR), went bankrupt shortly afterward, as did the Campeau Corporation and Integrated Resources. Drexel Burnham Lambert was unable to maintain a secondary market in junk bonds, and eventually the decline of the junk bond market, and its resulting difficulties with the government, undermined its credit, causing that firm to fail. In the meantime, scandals continued, and thrifts continued to fail. In 1991, 232 thrifts were liquidated. Another thrift crisis occurred in Rhode Island in 1991, after the Rhode Island Share and Deposit Indemnity Corporation, the private insurer for S&Ls in the state, became bankrupt.

The adoption of FIRREA caused numerous thrifts to convert from mutual ownership to stock companies in order to raise the increased capital requirements required by the legislation. It was later claimed that many insiders had profited from these conversions, to the detriment of the depositors who were the mutual owners. The stock was said to be underpriced in many of these conversions, and managers bought more than their fair share of the underpriced stock. Because of criticisms, federal regulators toughened appraisal standards for conversions.

The Deposit Insurance Funds Act of 1996 imposed a one-time assessment on insured deposits to fill the deposit insurance fund. Some other belated efforts by the government to deal with the S&L crisis encountered difficulties. In April 1999, a federal court judge ruled that because it had engaged in unfair regulatory treatment the federal government was required to pay $908.9 million to Glendale Federal Bank, owned by Golden State Bancorp, which was controlled by Ronald Perelman, the corporate raider. The judgment followed a Supreme Court decision that the government had improperly changed accounting standards retroactively for thrift associations and thus caused them to incur large losses. It was estimated that the Supreme Court's ruling could add another $30 billion to the total cost to the government of the banking crisis.

An irony of the Supreme Court's decision was that several of the plaintiffs seeking damages for such claims were in prison for crimes involving the misuse of S&L funds. Golden State Bancorp did not await collection of the funds from the government in its litigation. It began selling litigation participation certificates that allowed investors to receive a portion of the expected award in these suits. Another S&L was issuing litigation participation certificates that it called "contingent payment rights."

FIRREA appropriated an initial allocation of $50 billion to close down insolvent thrifts and pay off depositors. That proved inadequate, and more was appropriated, a total of $105 billion. Funds were made available to encourage the acquisition of failed thrifts by other institutions, which would be indemnified from losses caused by bad assets. FIRREA created the Resolution Trust Corporation (RTC), a wholly owned government corporation that was assigned the task of managing the liquidation of failed S&Ls. The RTC, which was headed by L. William Seidman, assumed control of almost 700 bankrupt

S&Ls. It quickly became one of the largest managers of financial and real estate properties in the United States.

The RTC sold the assets of failed S&Ls through an army of lawyers, banks, insurance companies, and real estate brokers. By the end of 1990, the RTC had disposed of the assets of more than 340 insolvent S&Ls and received more than $110 billion from those sales. The RTC still managed over $35 billion in assets in 1992. Many sales were made using imaginative techniques, such as securitizations in which large amounts of commercial mortgages were pooled and sold to investors. By 1993, some $14 billion of commercial mortgages had been securitized by the RTC into "Ritzy Maes."

The RTC was generally considered a success, but some critics complained that asset sales were often made at fire-sale prices. However, the RTC was in the midst of a storm during this liquidation process and did as well as could be expected under such conditions. The disaster that followed the S&L de-regulations was said to be "the greatest scandal in the history of American banking," at least until the subprime crisis emerged. By 1992, more than a thousand individuals had been charged with crimes in connection with S&L activities, including Don Dixon and "Fast Eddie" McBirney, and most of them were convicted.

The FHLBB initially estimated that losses on insured deposits at S&Ls would cost the government $15 billion. As more thrifts began to fail, that estimate rose to $200 billion, $500 billion, and then an improbable $1 trillion. It took some five years to complete the liquidation process before a final number was reached, but the estimated total cost to the federal government for failed S&Ls between 1986 and 1995 is now believed to be about $125 billion.

During the S&L crisis, the government closed 1,043 S&Ls, which held more than $500 billion in assets. The number of insured institutions was cut nearly in half during the crisis. Another cost was less apparent. Commercial banks used the S&L crisis to increase their market share of residential mortgages. In 1989 alone, commercial banks increased their market share of mortgage originations to 35 percent, up from about 20 percent in the prior year.

Commercial Banks

Commercial banks also found themselves in crisis. The Penn Square Bank in Oklahoma City failed in 1982, creating large payouts for the FDIC. The Continental Illinois National Bank in Chicago suffered huge losses from the loans it purchased from Penn Square. It also had large amounts of loans outstanding to some major corporations that were in, or faced, bankruptcy, including International Harvester and Braniff Airlines. Continental Illinois was the seventh-largest bank in the United States, with $41 billion in assets. Concluding that Continental Illinois was "too big to fail," the FDIC arranged a $7.5 billion rescue of that bank and waived deposit insurance caps, so no depositors, no matter how big, lost money. The FDIC even protected creditors of the bank's holding company out of concern that, if deposit insurance were not extended to those creditors, systemic panic and failure might follow. This "too big to fail" concept was tested during the subprime crisis, after federal regulators allowed Lehman Brothers to fail.

In 1984, Continental Illinois was nationalized by the government, the first time such action had been taken for a major bank. However, it was not the first time that the government had rescued Continental Illinois. In 1932, the RFC injected $50 million into the bank, in exchange for a class of preferred stock, which was retired in 1939. That was the model for the bank bailouts during the subprime crisis in 2008. The government installed new management at Continental Illinois after its nationalization and eventually sold it to Bank of America, which had its own nationalization concerns during the subprime crisis in 2008. Through this sale, the government was able to recover most of the money it had injected in Continental Illinois.

Between 1985 and 1992, more than 1,200 banks failed. The FDIC was insolvent by 1990 and therefore was required to borrow $70 billion from the federal government to cover depositor claims. The FDIC Improvement Act of 1991 provided additional funding for the FDIC, increasing the line of credit from the Treasury for bank insurance from $5 billion to $30 billion. That statute required risk-based deposit insurance premiums and imposed restrictions on the operations of banks that were not well capitalized.

The Bank of New England Corporation was the nation's third-largest bank when in January 1991 it failed because of defaults on commercial real estate loans. As losses mounted, a run on the bank's deposits began, during which depositors withdrew over $1 billion in just three days. Federal regulators again agreed to insure depositors above the $100,000 cap in order to ease the crisis. The government spent over $2 billion to rescue the Bank of New England, which was later sold to Fleet Bank (itself taken over by Bank of America in 2004).

These failures set off a debate on the proper role of government in the event of a large bank failure. Nationalization, as occurred with Continental Illinois, was generally viewed unfavorably and as a step to be taken only in the most severe circumstances. The FDIC's policy was to avoid a direct takeover. Rather, it preferred to arrange a merger of the failing institution with another larger, healthier bank. In order to encourage that acquisition, the FDIC would agree to take over the bad loans of the failing bank. Experience showed that the value of such bad assets would drop 15 percent as soon as the FDIC took them over, because the market knew they would be liquidated and not managed.

Some FDIC officials were advocating cash infusions into failing banks in order to allow their recovery, but a congressional report warned that this could result in nationalizations of major banks. Representative (later Senator) from New York Charles Schumer contended that experience with the S&Ls indicated such cash infusions would compound losses, because workouts in which assets were sold and debts renegotiated by existing management only resulted in larger losses.[74] These same issues arose during the subprime crisis in 2008.

On July 5, 1991, bank regulators seized the Bank of Credit and Commerce (BCCI) (registered in Luxembourg, but with majority ownership by the emir of Abu Dhabi), the seventh-largest privately owned bank in the world with 1.3 million customers. BCCI turned out to be a giant criminal enterprise of bribery, fraud, and bad loans made to politicians, cronies, and individuals associated with the bank. This disaster was carefully studied by governments around the world because it turned out that—despite the fact that the Basel Committee required supervision of international banking structures on a consolidated basis by the home country regulator—no single country exercised supervisory control over BCCI's worldwide operations. The United States passed the Foreign Bank Supervision Enhancement Act of 1991 in response to that debacle. The concept of consolidated supervised entities spread to large investment banks supervised by the SEC and spelled their doom during the subprime crisis in 2008.

8. A Critical Look at the Reformers

Prosecution Abuses

The New York Attorney General

Eliot Spitzer became a national figure as a result of his prosecutions of Wall Street figures that paved his way to the New York governorship. Of course, Spitzer is not the only New York prosecutor that sought headlines from high-profile investigations for political gain. He was preceded by some giants, including Charles Evans Hughes, Thomas E. Dewey, and Rudolph Giuliani. Spitzer maximized his use of that model, and it worked, putting him in the mansion in Albany with a landslide vote. Yet Spitzer's causes often failed when put to the test of a courtroom. Most visibly, Spitzer lost the contentious fight over Richard Grasso's pay, which should never have been initiated, but that loss came long after Spitzer left the attorney general's office.

Nothing was learned from Spitzer's excesses. As described in the next volume of this financial history, Spitzer's crusades against Wall Street were mimicked during the subprime crisis by his successor, Andrew Cuomo. Like Spitzer, Cuomo has long hungered for the New York governorship and has sought to gain that post using the Spitzer model of high-profile investigations of financial institutions. That model needs some rethinking. The role of the New York attorney general is to enforce the law, not make it, but Spitzer and Cuomo became laws unto themselves, fiercely attacking any business practice that displeased them. They used the vague and uncertain terms of the New York Martin Act as cover for their legislative and political agenda.

Numerous other state officials have tried to copy Spitzer's publicity campaigns through enforcement actions, California, Utah, Massachusetts, and Connecticut being the worst. A legislative audit of the Utah securities division in 2008 found that it had been overly aggressive in pursuing investigations. Division investigators threatened potential targets, telling them that they had no chance of prevailing in any action brought by the division because it would be acting as prosecutor, judge, and jury. Unfortunately, New York has not conducted a similar review of its attorney general's office under Spitzer and Cuomo because they too view themselves as prosecutor, judge, and jury.

Things spun completely out of control on the prosecutorial side after Michael Nifong, a prosecutor in Durham, North Carolina, tried to emulate Spitzer. Nifong sought to assure his reelection as district attorney through a high-profile prosecution of three Duke lacrosse players, unattended by any supporting facts. Like Spitzer, Nifong evidently self-destructed, but not until after irremediable damage had been done to the three players and their team.[1] The players were convicted in the press, and by a large number of Duke faculty members, in the absence of a shred of evidence to support the charges.

What is needed is an inspector general to review the actions of prosecutors like Spitzer, Cuomo, and Nifong for political motivation. That inspector should ask why millions of dollars in state taxpayer funds were spent, for example, to recover Richard Grasso's retirement pay. Certainly, the wealthy members of the New York Stock Exchange could have brought their own lawsuit, if they thought that his pay was inappropriate. The inspector general might also ask why state taxpayer funds were expended to impose state regulation over Wall Street when there is already a federal agency charged with that task, the Securities and Exchange Commission (SEC). If, as Spitzer charged, the SEC is incompetent, then the appropriate remedy is for Congress to fix the SEC.

Spitzer's loose cannon attack on American International Group (AIG) led to a 94 percent drop in earnings at the firm, after it gave up charging fees that were one of its core revenue sources to please Spitzer. AIG also paid $1.6 billion to settle charges brought by Spitzer and the SEC over its accounting practices, bid rigging, and workman's compensation practices. Even more crippling was Spitzer's demand that AIG's senior management be removed, including its CEO, Hank Greenberg, who had built the company into one of the world's largest insurers. The new management turned on Greenberg and sought to develop a new revenue source from the subprime mortgage market. The result was a disaster that bankrupted the company during the subprime crisis and threatened the entire economy, until the federal government committed some $170 billion in taxpayer funds to bail out AIG. Greenberg vindicated himself by not giving into Spitzer or the frivolous lawsuits brought by the Spitzer-empaneled management at AIG, but irremediable damage was done to the company. No state prosecutor should have been given such arbitrary power. Yet Cuomo embarked on the same mission during the subprime crisis by attacking every faltering Wall Street firm and their executives, diverting their attention from dealing with the crisis.

Federal Prosecutors

Unfortunately, state prosecutors are not the only ones to abuse their offices. Federal prosecutors have long used high-profile prosecutions to gain headlines for political advancement. Robert Kennedy was known for his ruthlessness when he was attorney general and later became the senator from New York, even though that was not his political home. Rudolph Giuliani used his prosecutions while U.S. attorney in New York to pave the way for his election as mayor of that city. Giuliani employed some vicious tactics to gain convictions, and several were set aside on appeal, but that did not hamper his political career. Rather, his election as mayor gave the green light to other prosecutors, like Spitzer, to substitute abuse for evidence.

Equally pernicious is the use of criminal prosecutions to make an administration look tough on business, even if it has no evidence of a crime. This requires some creative legal theories, which often do not hold up on appeal. The Enron Task Force's prosecution of Arthur Andersen was particularly misguided. Although much outrage was expressed by the task force, and in the press, over the loss of 5,000 jobs at Enron, little was said about the 28,000 jobs lost at Arthur Andersen as a result of the government's ill-advised prosecution. The reversal of Arthur Andersen's conviction by the Supreme Court came too late to save those jobs, but no prosecutor went to jail for overreaching.

The misguided prosecution of Arthur Andersen imposed other costs. If it had been allowed to carry on its business, investors could have enjoyed a settlement with Arthur Andersen, perhaps a billion dollars or more, but its destruction took that money off the table. Arthur Andersen was also unable to comply with its agreement to pay $217 million to the mostly elderly investors who lost their investments in the Baptist Foundation of Arizona.

It was Michael Chertoff, the assistant U.S. attorney general, who ordered the Arthur Andersen prosecution. It was, perhaps, no coincidence that he had served as a prosecutor in the U.S. Attorney's office under Giuliani and that he participated in the witch-hunt against the Clintons in the Whitewater affair. Apparently, those experiences qualified him for one of the highest career posts in the Justice Department. As it turned out, Chertoff also made considerable political gains from the Arthur Andersen and other Enron-related prosecutions. President George W. Bush appointed Chertoff as secretary of homeland security. Ironically, the reversal of the Arthur Andersen conviction by the Supreme Court came only a few months after Chertoff's confirmation to that post by Congress. As secretary of homeland security, Chertoff's poor judgment once again became apparent during the Hurricane Katrina disaster when his department's disaster relief efforts proved ineffective and more than 1,800 individuals lost their lives.

The Nigerian barge case was another disaster for the Enron Task Force and its victims. In view of the relatively small amount of accounting manipulation at issue in that case, the whole effort seems to have been a colossal waste of time. The SEC could have easily handled it as a civil matter. Despite several setbacks in court, the government continued its pursuit of two of the Merrill Lynch defendants, bending the law to carry out that relentless pursuit, with no positive results in the end. The Enron Broadband Services trial was another fiasco engendered by the Enron Task Force, which again relied on novel and flawed legal theories to carry out their political campaign against corporate executives.

The Skilling and Lay trial gave some semblance of a victory for the Enron Task Force, but it was a badly tainted one. The task force spent two years inventing a crime (the "Dorian Gray" theory that was based on an Oscar Wilde story in which a corrupt man was fine looking in appearance but was corrupt inside) before they could indict. The Supreme Court, however, subsequently reversed that fanciful theory, holding that the "honest services" prohibition in the mail and wire fraud statute applied only to bribes and kickbacks. (Perhaps the Enron Task Force forgot Oscar Wilde's statement "when I was young I thought that money was the most important thing in life; now that I am old I know that it is.") The Skilling and Lay convictions were further sullied by the testimony of Andrew Fastow, which was extorted through the indictment of his wife and a threat to deprive him of his children for many years. The draconian sentence handed out to Skilling was still another example of overreaching by the Enron Task Force.

The coercive tactics employed by the Enron Task Force were, once again, on display in the NatWest Three case. Extraditing those suspects under an antiterror treaty was shameful, particularly when their crime involved fraud in the UK against a UK bank that had filed no complaint. This misguided prosecution further tarnished the United States' reputation abroad and accomplished nothing domestically. The physiological and monetary coercion of those defendants, after they arrived in the United States, was another instance in which the task force failed to cover itself with glory or even common decency.

The Enron Task Force was forced to criminalize ordinary business conduct in order to prove that the Bush administration was tough on corporations that fail and cause job losses or merely experience a drop in stock price. That became a model for prosecutors across the country. Today, any major loss at a public company will engender government investigations and the executives at the company are often immediately blamed for its occurrence and indicted. These Soviet-style prosecutions inevitably involve showy press conferences where the defendants are adjudged guilty before trial. Dawn raids on executive homes, and the shackling of those executives for their "perp" walk, add color and drama. Because their cases are often weak and difficult to prove, prosecutors then seek to coerce guilty pleas. Employees are indicted on multiple counts that will result in life imprisonment, unless the employee pleads guilty to lesser charges and turns on higher-ups. If that fails, more charges are added. Family members are indicted or threatened in order to force a guilty plea from their executive relatives. No tactic is too low for the prosecutors, as seen by its efforts to send target letters and deny immunity to any witnesses that might potentially support the case of a defendant, and to cut off attorney fees that by law and contract were to be paid by the defendant's employer.

Indicted executives have other incentives to plead guilty, even if they are innocent, because, if convicted after a trial, they will automatically receive a lengthy sentence. Federal sentencing guidelines were made more forceful by the Sarbanes-Oxley Corporate Reform Act of 2002, increasing the sentences for executives at public companies. That amendment was not really needed because sentencing guidelines were already based on the amount of money at issue in a financial crime.[2] Because most public companies are dealing in billions of dollars in revenue, any accounting manipulation will weigh heavily in the guidelines. Couple that with judges who seek headlines, and the corporate executive is treated more harshly than murderers and child molesters. That attitude has spread to the state courts. For example, in September 2008, a state court judge in Riverside County, California, sentenced Daniel Heath to 127 years and four months in prison after he was convicted of 522 felony charges in a Ponzi scheme. The fraud was directed at some 1,800 senior citizens and defrauded them of a total of $187 million. That sentence made great headlines, but it was pure grandstanding, as demonstrated by the additional four months. Yet that sentence was bested by the one handed down for Bernard Madoff, who received a sentence of 150 years.

The win-at-all-cost approach at the U.S. Justice Department, and the belief of its attorneys that convictions should be obtained through any means fair or foul, has sullied what was once considered a professional cadre of dedicated public servants. As the Supreme Court has noted,

> The United States Attorney is the representative not of an ordinary party to a controversy, but of a sovereignty whose obligation to govern impartially is as compelling as its obligation to govern at all; and whose interest, therefore, in a criminal prosecution is not that it shall win a case, but that justice shall be done. As such, he is in a peculiar and very definite sense the servant of the law, the twofold aim of which is that guilt shall not escape or innocence suffer. He may prosecute with earnestness and vigor—indeed, he should do so. But, while he may strike hard blows, he is not at liberty to strike foul ones. It is as much his duty to refrain from improper methods calculated to produce a wrongful conviction as it is to use every legitimate means to bring about a just one.

> It is fair to say that the average jury, in a greater or less degree, has confidence that these obligations, which so plainly rest upon the prosecuting attorney, will be faithfully observed.[3]

The Justice Department's refusal to abide by those constraints was again on display in the high-profile criminal case brought against Senator from Alaska Ted Stevens for concealing more than $250,000 in gifts from Veco Corporation, an oil services company. Stevens was convicted, just before a close election for his seat, which he lost by less than 4,000 votes. That conviction almost certainly cost him a Senate seat that he had held since 1968. After the conviction, however, it was revealed that the Justice Department had improperly withheld exculpatory information from Stevens that undermined the credibility of the government's principal witness. Three Justice Department officials were held in contempt over misconduct related to the case. The Justice Department announced that it was dropping the case entirely because of misconduct by its prosecutors, but Stevens did not get his Senate seat back, and he died in a plane crash in 2010.

It is clear that the federal government had learned no lessons from their Enron contretemps. As the Obama administration was taking office, the Justice Department announced that the president's Corporate Fraud Task Force, which had been created to prosecute the Enron-era scandals, was being expanded to include six new agencies that would focus on subprime mortgage and securitization fraud cases. On April 2, 2009, the Justice Department also announced that it was planning to create a joint task force of state and federal prosecutors that would be used to fight white-collar crime. That task force will combine all the abuses of the Enron Task Force and the budding Eliot Spitzers in all the states against corporate executives at failed businesses.

President Barack Obama formalized this effort by signing an executive order on November 17, 2009, creating a new Financial Fraud Enforcement Task Force to replace the Corporate Fraud Task Force established by the Bush administration in 2002, which had a decided lack of success in its criminal trials and appeals. The action by President Obama followed the high-profile loss of a criminal case brought by the Justice Department against two Bear Stearns hedge fund managers after the funds that they managed failed and became a triggering event in the subprime crisis. Undaunted, the FBI announced in June 2010 that it would be employing tactics developed in the war on terror to ferret out financial fraud.

This *in terrorem* approach has had a negative effect on management of public companies. CEO turnover is occurring at an alarming rate. More than 1,100 CEOs gave up their positions in 2006. By 2008, the average tenure of a CEO was just 3.2 years. That turnover is certainly not accidental; those managers are taking their money out and leaving the scene before they become the target of some crusading prosecutor bent on their destruction. The loss of experienced managers requires their replacement with someone less experienced, or incompetent, as occurred at AIG after the ouster of Greenberg by Spitzer. The phenomenon of the "interim CEO" is now becoming a permanent part of the public company community. Concern is raised as to whether these interim CEOs are capable of leading a giant corporation with which they have had no experience.

Justice Department as Regulator

The Justice Department has used its coercive powers to acquire a role as a financial regulator without congressional approval. It is making law by prosecution, rather than by congressional action.[4] These regulatory powers are applied under novel and strained legal theories, such as the "honest services" claim and even, incredibly, an Oscar Wilde story. The department knows that no financial services firm can survive an indictment. So companies targeted by the Justice Department are forced to enter into deferred-prosecution agreements. Under those arrangements, the targeted company (actually its innocent shareholders) must pay a large fine and the company's internal operations are subject to oversight by a "corporate monitor," who is appointed with the approval of prosecutors. Their selections for the corporate monitor position are almost inevitably former government officials, many of whom are former prosecutors, including former attorney general John Ashcroft and the ubiquitous Richard Breeden, the former SEC chairman.

These monitors accomplish nothing, as evidenced by the fact that AIG had a corporate monitor when it entered the subprime business that destroyed the company and threatened the global economy. That corporate monitor was James Cole, partner in the law firm Bryan Cave, who had served in the Justice Department for thirteen years. Cole was the deputy chief of the Criminal Division Public Integrity Section, which tracked government officials gone bad. It is unclear how anyone could have thought that such experience qualified him to act as an overseer of a global insurance company that was entering into a new and complex financial services business.

Rather, the appointment of a corporate monitor is a useful form of patronage for former colleagues, because the companies they are monitoring pay those monitors large sums. Ashcroft was selected as the corporate monitor for Zimmer Holdings, a medical device company accused of paying kickbacks to doctors to use its products. He was selected for that monitoring position by his former subordinate, Chris Christie, the U.S. attorney in New Jersey (and now that state's governor). Ashcroft's lobbying firm was paid at least $29 million for that eighteen-month job. The government also collected $311 million from Zimmer in fines.

After receiving much criticism for this cronyism, the Justice Department announced that, in the future, it was placing the selection of corporate monitors in the hands of a committee. In addition, the selection of a corporate monitor was required to be approved by a senior official at the Justice Department in Washington, DC. This might reduce some abuses, but still begs the question of why the government is involved in the management of public companies or with the selection of monitors of the operations at other companies. That is the job of the company's own board of directors.

Companies subjected to deferred-prosecution agreements in the Enron era were also sometimes forced to make contributions to the favorite charity or alma mater of the U.S. attorney conducting the prosecution. That practice was banned after the Department of Justice received much criticism when Christie required Bristol-Myers-Squibb to endow a chair on business ethics at his alma mater, the Seton Hall University Law School.

Still, this intrusion into corporate management and the punitive fines being borne by innocent shareholders were not enough for the corporate reformers.

In a front-page story, the *New York Times* complained that the Justice Department was too lenient on corporations. As proof, the newspaper noted that the department had entered into fifty deferred-prosecution agreements with public companies between 2005 and 2008.[5] In a separate article, the *New York Times* attacked the SEC, claiming that it was going soft, because it had reduced to $2 million a fine proposed by its staff of $25 million on JPMorgan Chase. The charges involved some esoteric regulatory issues, but the *New York Times* thought a $2 million fine was the equivalent of a "traffic ticket" for a large bank.

Corporate Governance Reforms

Punitive Legislation

A central feature of government responses to financial crises and scandals is the passage by Congress of punitive legislation that imposes unnecessary costs and burdens and accomplishes little. Sarbanes-Oxley has become the poster child for how not to react to a financial crisis. This legislation has cost American businesses billions of dollars without any measurable positive result. It had as its goal the stopping of accounting manipulations at public companies where restatements had become epidemic. Tellingly, despite engendering crippling competitive costs and creating the Public Company Accounting Oversight Board, Sarbanes-Oxley did nothing to diminish the number of accounting restatements. Accounting manipulations went on in public companies, with only a brief pause.

Compensation Issues

The corporate reform effort seeking to curb excess executive compensation has been a colossal failure. Indeed, those efforts themselves were largely responsible for the excesses. Tying corporate pay to stock options in order to align shareholder interests with those of management was a disaster. It led to massive pay packages and considerable accounting manipulation, in order to boost stock process, a game that Enron and WorldCom were engaged in when they collapsed. The backdating scandals that followed those cases only proved that executives will continue to game the system in order to boost their compensation.

The SEC's demand for full disclosure of executive salaries has proved to be another bad idea as well as a counterintuitive one. One of the most closely guarded secrets in the corporate world is the compensation of nonhourly employees. Why is that? It is because disclosure would reveal inequities in pay, which may be brought about by hard work, brilliance, management skills, seniority, strong mentors, or just plain unfairness.

Disclosure will result in a loss of morale as each employee compares his or herself with other employees. Any employee receiving less than someone he or she views as inferior will become disgruntled. Some employees will quit, others will demand more pay, and others will simply lose interest in their jobs. The result will be increases in pay as each employee demands more than that being received by another employee deemed inferior. The only solution for compensation at lower executive levels would then be a stratified compensation structure for those employees, which would provide no incentive for hard work, brilliance, or management skills and undermine the advancement of business.

As it is, at the upper executive level, full disclosure touched off a wave of competition for ever-higher amounts of compensation. The SEC's disclosure requirements only encouraged competition for larger compensation packages, as each successive executive pointed to the larger compensation packages of peers and demanded more for themselves. Certainly, the expansion in the number of executives who must disclose their compensation under the SEC's rule amendments only widened the demands for ever-increasing compensation and prerequisites.

Disclosure had failed in the past, so why does the SEC think it will succeed in the future? The five highest-paid executives at the 1,500 largest publicly owned firms were paid a total of $122 billion between 1999 and 2003. In 2003, those payments were equal to almost 10 percent of the net income earned by those companies. A survey of the compensation for the CEOs at sixty-nine of the largest companies in the United States in 2002 saw a rise of 15 percent in their pay packages. Seventeen chief executive officers saw their restricted stock grants increase by 73 percent.

Options grants did decline in 2003 by almost 50 percent, and a survey of compensation paid to chief executive officers in 2003 saw a decrease in compensation to those officers, down to an average of $8.6 million in payments. However, those payments were still equal to almost 10 percent of those companies' net income. In any event, that decline was only temporary. In 2005, average CEO compensation rose 27 percent over the previous year, reaching $10.5 million. American CEOs were paid 432 times more than the average worker in 2004, up from 142 times the average worker in 1994, and 36 times the average worker in 1976. Those numbers should be compared to compensation in the United Kingdom, where the pay of CEOs was only 98 times that of an average employee in the 1990s, but the British are gaining; as the new century began, that figure rose 2,500 percent in just five years.

The average compensation for a CEO with at least two years of service in that position was $11.2 million in 2007 in the United States, an increase of 5 percent over the previous year. The average pay for CEOs at public companies in 2007 was 180 times more than that of the average worker, a ninetyfold increase over the ratio in 1994. In 2007 CEO median income was $8.8 million per year, while median household income in the United States was $50,000. If further proof is needed that executive compensation was spiraling up, notwithstanding SEC full disclosure, consider the fact that the *Forbes* magazine list of the 400 richest Americans did not include a single millionaire in 2006. They were all billionaires.

The accumulation of wealth in the United States was sometimes startling. The wealthiest 400 taxpayers in the United States received $85.6 billion in income in 2005, an average of about $250 million for each of those taxpayers, up from $173 million in 2004. The wealthiest 1 percent of Americans had income increases between 2003 and 2005 that exceeded the total income of the lowest 20 percent of American taxpayers.[6] More than 5 million households in America had a net worth ranging from $1 million to $10 million in 2007. Overlooked in those statistics was the fact that wealth accumulation was not limited to a few homes. In March 2006, there were more millionaires in America than there were unemployed. In 2006, the 400 wealthiest Americans also paid an average of $45 million in federal income taxes.

The top 5 percent of Americans had a net worth of $1.4 million or more, but 45 percent of those households believed that they needed at least $5 million to be really wealthy. Nevertheless, the old saying that "money cannot buy happiness" was being put to the test. Richard Easterlin, a University of Pennsylvania economist, posited in 1974 that increased wealth did not lead to happiness, which became orthodoxy for the next several decades. However, in 2008, two other University of Pennsylvania economists concluded that increasing wealth did contribute to happiness, even if it did not guarantee it. That being the case, the number of happy people was increasing. In 2007, the number of millionaires (those with $1 million in investable assets, excluding their homes) climbed to 8 million worldwide. The United States had 3.1 million such millionaires, comprising 1 percent of the nation's population, and 460 billionaires. However, the following year millionaires were multiplying abroad five times faster than they were in United States, not a good sign for the U.S. economy.

The subprime crisis created some wealth redistribution. In 2009, economists predicted that the percentage of personal income for the top 1 percent of wealthy households (those making over $400,000) would drop from 23.5 percent of all income in 2007 to under 19 percent by 2010. In addition, median CEO pay decreased by 15 percent in 2008, down to a median of $7.3 million.

Athletes and Entertainers

It is interesting to contrast the many views of compensation packages given to corporate executives with views on the outsize payments made to entertainers and athletes. A small group of athletes, entertainers, and even horses accumulate vast wealth with little resentment in Congress or even the press. The SEC even exempts the pay packages of entertainers from its disclosure requirements. Yet some of the payouts to entertainers are truly astonishing. Shock jock Howard Stern was paid $500 million to bring his lowbrow, smutty talk show to Sirius Satellite Radio. He was given another $82 million in 2006 as a bonus. Right-wing radio commentator Rush Limbaugh received a $400 million compensation package in July 2008 that was to carry him through 2016, providing him with a comfortable income of $50 million per year. Late night talk show hosts David Letterman and Jay Leno received $30 million per year. George Lucas, film producer, was paid an estimated $290 million in a one-year period; actor Mel Gibson, $180 million; David Copperfield, the magician, $57 million; and Madonna garnered a relatively paltry $50 million for whatever she does. Oprah Winfrey made $275 million in both 2007 and 2008, at the height of the subprime crisis. Oprah was worth more than $1 billion, all from sitting on a couch and empathizing with guests for a few minutes a day. On the TV circuit, Kiefer Sutherland was paid $550,000 per episode for his recently concluded show *24*; Charlie Sheen was paid $875,000 per episode for his comedy series *Two and a Half Men*; and three actresses on *Desperate Housewives* were each paid $400,000 per episode. Until his departure in 2010, Simon Cowell was paid $100 million per year to host *American Idol.* NBC paid Conan O'Brien $40 million to leave quietly after ratings for his show dropped. He was then picked up by the TBS network for a reported $10 million per year. Leslie Moonves, CEO of CBS, was paid $43 million in 2009, and Viacom CEO Philippe Dauman was paid $34 million for that year. Where is the anger and resentment over these outsize compensation packages?

What about athletes? The average salary in the National Football League is $1.3 million; in Major League Baseball the average is $2.7 million; and $4.2 million is the comparable figure in the National Basketball Association. As 2007 began, David Beckham, the British soccer star, was paid $250 million to join a Los Angeles team though things did not work out so well. One-year earnings for other athletes included: the golfer Tiger Woods, $120 million before his extramarital sexual liaisons became public knowledge; bicyclist Lance Armstrong, $28 million; tennis star Andre Agassi, $26.2 million; tennis star Serena Williams, $12.7 million; and race car driver Michael Schumacher got a cool $60 million.

Baseball players have also signed some impressive contracts. Pitcher Barry Zito has a seven-year contract valued at $126 million. Another pitcher, Kevin Brown, was paid $105 million under a seven-year contract, but did not do much pitching. How about those Yankees! In 2003, Mark Teixeira, the first baseman, signed an eight-year $180 million contract with the club. Then, in 2008, in the midst of the subprime crisis, contracts worth nearly $500 million were signed in order to boost the team's roster. Earlier, Michelle Wie signed endorsement contracts worth more than $10 million a year when she became a pro-golfer at age 16. It would take 200 years for a worker earning $50,000 per year to match the earnings that young athlete made in a single year. If the time value of money is considered, that time period would be lengthened even more. But Wei's endorsement money was pocket change for LeBron James, who signed endorsement deals worth more than $100 million, having been drafted into the NBA at age eighteen while still in high school. James became a huge success in the NBA and made more headlines when he signed with the Miami Heat in 2010 for an expected package of $96 million over six years. Gilbert Arenas was playing under a $111 million six-year contract for the Washington Wizards before his arrest and suspension from the NBA. Arenas was charged with carrying a firearm into the team locker room where he had an altercation with teammate Jarvis Crittenton, who was also armed.

The heads of not-for-profit organizations were also receiving some remarkably generous compensation packages. Zarin Mehta, the president of the New York Philharmonic, was paid $2.67 million in 2008. Thomas Krens, the director of the Solomon R. Guggenheim Museum, was paid $2.7 million; Peter Gelb, the general manager of the Metropolitan Opera, made $1.35 million; Glen Lowry, the director of the Museum of Modern Art in New York, received $1.32 million; Michael M. Kaiser, president of the John F. Kennedy Center for the Performing Arts in Washington, DC, was paid $1.13 million; Earl A. Powell III, the director of the National Gallery of Art was paid $1.06 million; Richard Levy, president of the Lincoln Center for the Performing Arts, received $1.18 million and Michael Govan, director of the Los Angeles County Museum of Art, was paid $1.06 million, all in 2008.

Let's not forget the horses. Storm Cat received a stud fee of $500,000 for each live born foal in 2002, earning an estimated $21 million that year—nice work if you can get it. A stud fee of $300,000 was charged for Distorted Humor's services in 2008. More than $200,000 was charged for A.P. Indy and King Mambo, and $125,000 per foal produced by Awesome Again. However, the subprime crisis hit the thoroughbred industry pretty hard. The stud fee for Distorted Humor was reported to have been cut in half in 2009. Claiborne Farms announced an across-the-board reduction of its stud fees. That is the farm where Secretariat sired some 600 foals before he was put down in 1989. Secretariat's services as a stud had been syndicated in 1973, for what was then an astonishing $6 million, an amount that would have competed with that of the highest-paid executives in America.

Some dogs did pretty well too. Gail Posner, the daughter of convicted tax evader and corporate raider Victor Posner, willed to her Chihuahua a $3 million trust fund and an $8.3 million mansion in which to reside, as well as a $15,000 Cartier necklace. The "Queen of Mean," Leona Helmsley, the renowned abrasive hotel manager and convicted tax felon, left her foul-tempered dog named "Trouble" $12 million, but a judge reduced that legacy to a mere $2 million. Majel Barrett Roddenberry, the wife of the creator of *Star Trek*, left her dog $4 million, a mansion, and its very own caretaker. Sidney Altman left Samantha, his cocker spaniel, $6 million. Gunther IV, a german shepard, was rumored to have been left an estate of $65 million.

So why is there such a hue and cry over corporate executive pay? If the American public can accept the wealth of successful (and sometimes unsuccessful) athletes, entertainers, and even horses, with little resentment, why the hysteria over the large salaries paid to corporate executives? After all, those executives control resources that employ millions of individuals and shape our economic destiny. Should they not be richly rewarded for those efforts? Sports and entertainment (and horses) are good things, but do they compare in the value added to society by large corporations, which employ millions, and which have provided a standard of living undreamed of in much of the world? So, why not take the same hands-off approach for corporate executives that we do for lottery winners, horses, entertainers, and athletes?

Adding further cynicism to the corporate reformers' crusade against excessive compensation is the fact that most of the populist politicians pushing that platform are themselves multimillionaires. John Edwards, whose presidential campaign failed in 2007, was the loudest of those decrying corporate executive compensation packages. Yet he had a net worth of $54.7 million and earned $3.7 million in 2006. About half his wealth was invested in hedge funds, and he was paid $480,000 annually as a part-time consultant for the Fortress Investment Group hedge fund. Bill and Hillary Clinton disclosed in April 2008 that their combined income for the previous eight years exceeded $109 million, an amount that belies their concern over wealth distribution. If they really believed in wealth distribution, would they not redistribute to the poor that entire fortune and just live on the generous payments they receive for past and present government service? The late Senator Ted Kennedy, a leader of the neopopulists favoring wealth distribution, was a trust fund baby, who never held a full-time, nongovernment job in his life. Kennedy was born to great wealth and remained wealthy beyond the imagination of most Americans, with an estimated $47 million in trust funds plus another $2 million that he received as an advance from the publisher for his memoirs. Kennedy did not distribute that wealth to the poor during his life or upon his death. Rather, it was left to family members who were not in need of any more wealth. Senator John Kerry, the populist Democratic presidential candidate in 2004, had an estimated net worth of $230 million, and he was married to Teresa Heinz Kerry, one of the wealthiest women in America, worth an estimated $1 billion. They, too, are hanging onto their wealth.

Even the relatively young President Barack Obama, a staunch critic of the compensation packages of corporate executives and a leading proponent of wealth redistribution, is a multimillionaire, with an income of $4.2 million in 2007. The president and his wife reported income of $2.7 million in 2008 and paid $855,000 in federal taxes, leaving an after-tax payout of $5,000 per day, not bad for a populist politician. Their taxable rate, however, was only a little over 31 percent, which was well below the 39 percent that the president proposed for other wealthy Americans in 2009. In 2009, the president earned an adjusted gross income of $5.5 million, which was in addition to the $1.4 million he donated to charity after winning the Nobel Prize. Obama's income far outstripped the earnings of prior first year presidents, but so far (other than his Nobel Prize money) he has not redistributed his wealth and agreed to live only on the generous pay given to the leader of the nation.

The *Wall Street Journal* also somewhat gleefully pointed out that Senator from Ohio Howard Metzenbaum, another well-known liberal advocate of wealth distribution causes, changed his domicile to Florida in 2003, before his death in 2008, in order to avoid Ohio estate and income taxes. Florida has no such taxes. That move hardly seems consistent with liberal demands for a redistribution of the wealth.[7]

Scalable Compensation

Nassim Taleb, author of *The Black Swan*, points to the phenomenon of a "scalable" enterprise as the key to accumulating great wealth. Such an enterprise is one in which the participant's presence is not required for each compensation payment.[8] For example, a laborer is paid only for the work he does personally on a particular job site, where he must appear and work to be paid. In contrast, a movie actor is in a scalable business that does not require him or her to appear personally before each moviegoer as a condition of the actor's compensation payment. A laborer can never expect to achieve the wealth of a scalable movie actor. To be sure, a few non-scalable enterprises do generate wealth. For example, the Jockey Club's thoroughbred racing rules require studs to actually cover each mare.

Severe disparities arise even in scalable enterprises. To illustrate, not all movie actors are successful. Indeed, the vast majority of actors live near the poverty line, with a median hourly wage in 2006 of $11.61. The Screen Actors Guild imposes a much higher daily rate, but its 100,000 members still earn, on average, less than $5,000 per year from acting. So should the top fifty or so actors who make the megamillions be required to redistribute their earnings to the less-fortunate mass of other actors? Examples of disparities abound, but to take just one more example—book publishing. More than 172,000 books were published in the United States in 2005 and more than 200,000 in the UK. However, only a handful of those books are successful in generating wealth. J.K. Rowling became richer than the Queen of England from royalties on her *Harry Potter* books, but the vast majority of other authors receive only a pittance in royalties for their efforts. Would it not be fair to require Rowling and her ilk to give up their wealth and pay other authors as a means of equalizing wealth, perhaps on a per-word basis, say, $1 per word for every published author? Shakespeare said, "Brevity is the soul of wit," but under this scheme verbosity could be the source of wealth.

Corporate executives are also in scalable positions, and, as in other professions, their compensation demonstrates great disparity. The vast majority of business managers do not make millions of dollars in bonuses. Most work in small companies, most of which fail. In larger companies, most managers are well paid, but only a small coterie receives the megamillion-dollar packages that cause so much offense. But how are they different from Stephen King in the literary world or Harrison Ford on the big screen?

Results

In any event, the reform movement did not prevent the Enron-era scandals. Indeed, much of the blame for the excesses at Enron and other companies can be traced directly to the corporate governance movement's failed attempt to align the interests of shareholders and management by instituting options-based compensation packages. The reforms that followed the Enron meltdown, in particular the Sarbanes-Oxley Corporate Reform Act of 2002, crippled the U.S. economy and drove financial services, which had once been one of the country's greatest comparative advantages, offshore. In addition, at least until the credit crunch in 2007, many public companies became private corporations by selling themselves to private equity groups, thereby avoiding onerous SEC regulations and harassing litigation from the pension funds.

Union Pension Funds as Reformers

The effort to transfer control from management to shareholders will continue to be the Holy Grail for corporate reformers, led by union pension funds such as the California Public Employees' Retirement System (CalPERS). The union pension funds coordinate their activities through the Council of Institutional Investors in Washington, DC, which represents more than 140 pension funds. The SEC, Congress, and the courts have bought into the agenda of that organization and now seem poised to favor unions over management of public companies, without any apparent regard for the consequences.

The union movement in the United States peaked some years ago and is now in a state of decline, at least in terms of the number of members. Union members comprised about one-third of the total workforce in 1945, but declined to 20 percent in 1983 and then to 12 percent in 2008.

The share of workers in the private sector who are members of unions was only 7.6 percent in 2008. The declining economy during the subprime crisis caused concerns that the labor unions were losing even more bargaining power in negotiations for contracts. In several areas, particularly in the automobile industry, union members were asked to accept reduced wages. The subprime crisis also resulted in a further loss of union membership, which declined by 10 percent in the private sector in 2009. As a result, public union members outnumbered private sector members for the first time.

In the public sector, unions are still popular, because they provide high wages and benefits, shorter working hours, and enhanced job security by drawing on what has been, to date, unlimited taxpayer resources, and they allow early retirement. The proportion of workers unionized in the public sector was 42.2 percent in 2008. Unfortunately, the public union pension funds let their crusade against corporate America divert their attention from their principal job, protecting the assets of the pension fund that they manage. Public union pension funds doubled the share of real estate assets in their portfolios in the decade before the subprime crisis, during which those properties declined sharply in value. CalPERS experienced a decline of 23 percent in the value of its assets at the end of its 2009 fiscal year. It also burdened the California state budget with its generous pension benefits, which allowed state employees to retire at age fifty-five and first responders at age fifty. That distress increased in February 2010 when CalPERS announced that it was cutting its targeted rate of return of 7.75 percent on its portfolio, but was able to exceed that rate in its 2010 fiscal year, posting an 11.4 percent rate of return.

The Government Accountability Office (GAO) found in 2008 that many states did not properly fund their employee pension plans and that a fiscal crisis could be expected in the future. Many of the pension funds examined by the GAO were less than 80 percent funded. It was estimated that state and municipal government pension funds were being underfunded on average by about one-third and that this underfunding totaled over $1 trillion. Other estimates placed the deficit at over $3 trillion because public pension funds were claiming unrealistic expected rates of return on their portfolios to meet their obligations to retirees. New York, for example, was basing its funded status on an estimated return on assets of 8 percent, which did not appear likely.

Actuaries for public pension schemes were also criticized for understating their obligations and the ability of those pension funds to pay retirees. Among the states underfunding their pension plans were Illinois, Kentucky, and Pennsylvania. A Stanford University study concluded that, as of July 2008, the three largest California pension funds (CalPERS, CalSTRS, and the University of California) were underfunded by $500 billion rather than the $55 billion claimed by those pension funds. The Stanford study assumed a 4.14 percent rate of return on pension fund investments instead of the 7.5 percent and above used by the pension funds for their funding assessment. That underfunding was increased by another $100 billion in losses sustained from investments during the subprime crisis. CalPERS reported a loss of 23 percent for its 2009 fiscal year but was able to confound its critics by reporting an 11.4 percent profit for its fiscal year ended June 30, 2007.

Several states were deferring contributions to their pension plans in order to cut their budget deficits. New Jersey's governor was seeking to defer $3 billion of such contributions in order to reduce the state's $11 billion deficit. Illinois increased its retirement age to 67 and capped public pensions at $106,800. Over 50 percent of state pension plans were not receiving their full contributions. Private pension funds were also at risk. Some 93 percent of defined benefit retirement plans of S&P 500 companies were underfunded in 2009. The union pension plans at General Motors and Chrysler were collectively underfunded by $17 billion in 2009.

The SEC sued five former officials in San Diego, California, because of their failure to disclose problems with the city's funding of pension and retiree health-care obligations, which could bankrupt the city. The New York State government pension program also had problems. Alan Hevesi, the state's former comptroller, a crusading corporate reformer and criminal, had used the state's pension fund as a private piggybank to reward friends and advance his political career through "pay-to-play" payments made by hedge funds and others to "placement agents" in order to manage state pension fund assets and fees. A similar scandal brewed in California, at CalPERS, where allegations were made that one of its former board members, Al Villalobos, had been paid some $50 million in fees from money managers employed by the pension fund. CalPERS reported that, in total, private placement agents received $125 million from money managers receiving CalPers funds for investment.

The New York pension funds were roiled by another scandal in 2010 after New York Attorney General Andrew Cuomo announced that his office was investigating pension "spiking." This was a practice by which the income of workers was inflated by overtime or other means in their final years before retirement in order to boost their retirement pay, which is calculated on pay earned in those final years. Cuomo cited an example of a policeman making $74,000 a year who pushed his income in his last year to $200,000 through overtime. This was expected to cost the New York pension fund some $1.2 million. California was also seeking to limit pension spiking. New York residents paid on average $486 in 2007 to maintain the New York pension funds, the highest rate in the country. Some of those pension beneficiaries were receiving over $300,000 per year.

The value of assets in the New York State pension plan fell by 26 percent in the fiscal year ending March 31, 2009. In order to make up for those losses, the New York State comptroller, Thomas P. DiNapoli, sought to increase payroll contributions from 7.5 percent of salaries to 11 percent. The governor of New York, David A. Paterson, announced on June 5, 2009, that he had reached an agreement with the New York State Public Employees Federation (PEF) to sharply reduce benefits for future retiring workers. In exchange, the governor agreed to drop his previously announced layoff of 8,700 public employees and to give existing workers a 3 percent increase in pay. He also agreed to buy out the employment contracts of 4,500 employees for $20,000 each. Among other things, the pension benefit cuts moved the minimum retirement age from fifty-five to sixty-two and increased the period required for vesting from five years to ten. The agreement also required employees to contribute 3 percent of their pay to the state retirement plan for their entire work life, rather than just the first ten years as under the present arrangement. That increased payment, however, would be paid for by the state through the salary increase included in the "reform" package. This agreement did not include New York City workers.

The traditional defined private benefit plans for union employees were also often underfunded. The Pension Benefit Guaranty Corporation (PBGC) announced in February 2008 that it was increasing the risk profile of its portfolio, including investments in equity securities, in order to improve its performance results. At that time, the PBGC had a deficit of $14 billion for shortfalls in pension funds that it insured. Scandal later arose over concerns that the head of the PBGC, Charles E.F. Millard, had improperly awarded management of its new investment strategy to JPMorgan Chase, BlackRock, and Goldman Sachs, after being lavishly entertained by those firms. In any event, the PBGC's deficit tripled between December 2008 and May 2009, growing to $33.5 billion.

The pension fund benefits negotiated by unions had long been a source of their power, but union pension funds increasingly competed with 401(k) retirement plans that were managed by individual employees. Some states were changing to a mixture of 401(k) and defined benefit plans in order to reduce funding liabilities. The Equal Employment Opportunity Commission also ruled in December 2007 that employers could cease to offer health-insurance coverage for employees after they reached age sixty-five, at which point they would qualify for Medicare. This too was a reduction in benefits that had long been enjoyed by union members. Yet, notwithstanding the decline in their membership and relevance, unions remain a powerful force in politics because of their liberal use of member dues for political contributions.[9]

Unions staked everything on a return of the Democrats to the White House and continuing control of Congress in 2008, and they hit the jackpot. The AFL-CIO alone budgeted $53 million to support Democratic campaigns. In all, labor unions contributed more than $300 million to the Obama campaign, and to other Democrats, in order to gain control of the White House, Congress, and perhaps the Supreme Court. Even so, the union agenda met resistance. Wal-Mart and other employers opposed a Democratic plan that sought to allow worker votes on approving the union without secret ballots. The unions wanted to be able simply to obtain signatures of a majority of workers, which would allow the unions to coerce and intimidate workers into agreeing to union representation, but that proposal appeared to be stalled in Congress in 2010, but efforts continued to pass it.

The SEC has also come to the aid of unions by requiring inclusion of union-sponsored social initiatives on the proxy ballots of public companies. One such proposal required shareholders to vote on whether a company should undertake efforts to assure universal health-insurance coverage. The SEC expanded this process under the Obama administration to include "say-on-pay" votes to approval of executive compensation, and it even seeks to allow pension funds to have the opportunity to take over public companies through board of director nominations. Indeed, CalPERS has an inside track in the SEC on these issues, because Kayla Gillan, a former CalPERS general counsel, was hired by the commission to spearhead that effort.

Newspapers as Reformers

Another leader in the corporate governance reform movement has been the press, which is constantly attacking corporate management and advocating corporate reforms that will give more power to shareholders, but that role requires a great deal of hypocrisy on its part. This is because many of the largest newspapers (including the *New York Times,* the *Washington Post,* and, until recently, the *Wall Street Journal*) have traditionally classified their stock, to assure control by the families who own the companies. That classification excludes their public shareholders from having any voice in the decisions of management. If these shareholder advocates actually believe what they preach, why did they exempt themselves from the reforms they seek for public companies?

Newspapers certainly needed better management. Their revenue was decimated by the loss of classified advertising to Web-based sites such as Craigslist. Classified ads had traditionally been the principal source of income for many newspapers before the Internet age. In 2008 the New York Times Company, Tribune Company (publisher of the *Chicago Tribune*), Gannett, and Hearst announced the formation of an online advertising program that would include more than 120 newspapers, but it was unclear how that would restore their prosperity, particularly as they continue to lose circulation at an accelerating pace as readers turn to the Internet for news that provides a wide range of views on events.

The newspaper industry was hit hard by the subprime crisis, which caused a slump in real estate advertising. Newspaper revenue fell by 7 percent in 2007 alone. The *New York Times* announced that its classified advertising declined by 29 percent during the third quarter of 2008. Newspaper circulation also continued to plunge in 2008. The rate of decline nearly doubled during one six-month period in 2008, falling by 4.6 percent. However, *USA Today* and the *Wall Street Journal* did have a small circulation increase during that period. Overall circulation declined another 10 percent between October 2008 and October 2009.

The New York Times Company, which is controlled by the Ochs-Sulzberger family, has been the leading advocate of shareholder control over management, but that newspaper has resisted efforts to reform its governance structure. A Morgan Stanley money manager criticized, and sought reform of, the New York Times Company stock classification arrangement after that newspaper's share price fell by more than 50 percent. The controlling shareholders at that newspaper, in retaliation, pulled all their assets out of Morgan Stanley. Two hedge funds, Firebrand Partners and Harbinger Capital Partners, then increased their stake in the New York Times Company to nearly 15 percent in 2008. They sought four board seats on the thirteen-member board of directors for the newspaper. The New York Times Company eventually allowed the hedge funds to appoint two directors to its board, Scott Galloway and James Kohlberger. However, Harbinger subsequently reduced its interest in the newspaper, and its representative on the Times board, Scott Galloway, announced that he would not stand for reelection in 2010. That board position was then eliminated. David Cohen, a cousin of Arthur Sulzberger, the Times publisher, also announced his retirement from the Times board in 2010. Cohen was replaced by Carolyn Greenspon, a forty-one-year-old psychotherapist, whose only newspaper and business qualification was that she was a fifth-generation member of the Ochs-Sulzberger family.

The stock classification schemes imposed by the newspapers are claimed to be necessary to preserve their editorial integrity. However, this is unrelated to attracting readers, and the *New York Times,* like most print media, is now in a desperate struggle to survive. The newspaper finally appeared to have awoken to its peril after the hedge fund attacks, and it began cutting costs. The *Times* shocked its staff by announcing a reduction of 100 jobs in the newsroom, a move that had been resisted for some time. The newspaper predicted that those and other cost reductions would save more than $230 million by 2009. However, revenues continued to decline, and the newspaper was forced to cut its quarterly dividend by 74 percent in November 2008. That dividend was the principal source of income for the Ochs-Sulzberger family, providing them with about $25 million annually before the dividend cut.

In December 2008, the New York Times Company disclosed that it was borrowing $225 million, using its Manhattan headquarters as collateral, which it later converted into a sale leaseback deal, a bit of financial engineering that provided it with needed working capital. The newspaper had some $1 billion in debt coming due over the next few years, and it was in desperate need of cash. The company was negotiating with a Mexican billionaire, Carlos Slim, for him to inject the company with $250 million. The company also announced that it was seeking to sell its interest in the Boston Red Sox. That announcement came after the paper's fourth-quarter 2008 earnings dropped by 48 percent. The company suspended its dividend entirely on February 19, 2008. It also announced pay cuts for staff and threatened to sell or close the *Boston Globe,* which it owned, unless that paper slashed its costs. The situation worsened with a loss of $74.5 million in the first quarter of 2009, but showed a short-lived turnaround with a small profit of $23.3 million in the second quarter. The company had another loss in the third quarter and announced the layoff of a further 100 employees in the newsroom. Nonunion employees were told that the company would no longer contribute to their pensions. Instead, those employees would be given reduced-cost 401(k) contributions. In addition, the New York Times News Service was moved to a nonunion facility in Florida to save costs.

Were the crusading executives at the *New York Times* being well paid while the wheels were coming off their newspaper? According to SEC filings, New York Times Company CEO and president Janet L. Robinson received total compensation of more than $14 million between 2006 and 2008, including a raise of $1.4 million in 2008 as the company was teetering on insolvency. The firm's general manager, Scott Heekin-Canedy, was paid almost $6 million during that period. The vice chairman, Michael Golden, received nearly $5 million. At the crusading *Boston Globe*, publisher P. Steven Ainsley received over $4 million for two years of work, during 2007 and 2008. To be sure, Arthur Sulzberger, Jr., chairman of the board and publisher of the *New York Times,* had his compensation cut nearly in half between 2006 and 2008, from $4.3 million per year to $2.4 million, but he still made over $10 million in that three-year period. This placed him well above the federal poverty guideline of $22,000 annual income for a family of four and still well above the figure for annual median family income of $50,000. Sulzberger's pay package even exceeded that of the highest-paid schoolteachers, who top out at about $76,000 per year. Assuming he was working full-time, Sulzberger earned about $2,000 per hour, well in excess of the minimum wage of $7.25 per hour. Family control over the newspaper also assured nepotism opportunities. Sulzberger's son, A.G. Sulzberger, is a *Times* reporter. The senior Sulzberger's nephew, Sam Dolnick, was hired as a reporter for the newspaper late in 2009, even as layoffs were being considered for 100 employees in the newsroom, including several reporters. Sulzberger's son also survived the layoffs. Another Sulzberger nephew, David Perpich, was hired in March 2010 to become an executive director for the *New York Times* online service.

The *Wall Street Journal* also came under attack. The Bancroft family, which had controlled Dow Jones and published the *Wall Street Journal* for more than a hundred years, found itself the target of a $5.3 billion hostile takeover attempt by Rupert Murdoch's News Corporation in May 2007. After many months of hand wringing, the family agreed to sell control to Murdoch. Present at the meeting where the shareholders voted to sell the company was Evelyn Y. Davis, the corporate gadfly, who, for decades, had challenged management at thousands of shareholders meetings. As in most business transactions involving public companies, there was a bit of insider trading. David Li, a Dow Jones board member, and two people that he tipped on the News Corporation bid, agreed to pay $24 million to settle insider-trading charges with the SEC. The defendants had made $8 million in profit from their trades.

In order to induce the Bancroft family to sell, Murdoch agreed to create a special committee to oversee the *Wall Street Journal*'s editorial page and to ensure its continued editorial integrity and independence. Nonetheless, several executives at Dow Jones were quickly replaced by Murdoch, including the publisher, L. Gordon Crovitz. The *Wall Street Journal* also introduced a new liberal columnist, Thomas Frank, to its editorial pages on April 21, 2008. This was an apparent effort to mimic the FOXNews cable channel's "fair and balanced" approach. Apparently, this new editorial effort also copied the approach taken by the "Hannity & Colmes" program on FOXNews, in which the liberal commentator is presented as something of an idiot. To that end, Thomas's first editorial charged: "The landmark political fact of our time is the replacement of our middle-class republic by a plutocracy." Frank then makes a somewhat bizarre offer to dump all his prior writings into Lake Michigan if it would "help restore the land of relative equality I was born in."[10] Frank also wanted political candidates to redistribute the wealth but,

unfortunately for the reader, he does not identify any of these dreaded pluto-
crats and does not describe how they pose such a dire threat to America. For
example, what threat is being posed to the Republic by the likes of Warren
Buffett and Bill Gates?

This new lineup on editorial content and some cosmetic changes to the
newspaper's format did not restore the circulation of the *Wall Street Journal*.
News Corporation was hit hard by the market decline during the subprime
crisis. It lost some $80 billion in market capitalization by December 2008,
its stock price tumbling from $21.43 to under $9.31 during the year. The firm
announced a fourth-quarter loss of $6.4 billion in 2008.

The Tribune Company also underwent a metamorphosis. Founded in Chicago in 1847, the *Chicago Tribune* became a national presence in newspapers
and radio during the twentieth century. Control of the newspaper was kept in
the family of Joseph Medill and passed to Robert R. McCormick, a conservative publisher who was a thorn in the side of the administration of Franklin
D. Roosevelt. The Tribune Company conducted an initial public offering and
became a public company in 1983. In 2000, it merged with Times Mirror, in
an $8.3 billion transaction, making it a media giant. Sam Zell, a Chicago-based
investor, took the company private in December 2007, through a leveraged
buyout costing $8.2 billion, leaving the company $12.8 billion in debt.

Zell next tried to apply some rationality to the business practices of its various units, including the ultraliberal *Los Angeles Times*, which was experiencing
declining revenues. The effort was not well received at that newspaper. When
ordered to make staff cutbacks, the editors balked and were replaced (on more
than one occasion), giving rise to a great deal of adverse publicity about the
already beleaguered newspaper. Within a few months, Zell had laid off some
400 employees, but he was facing an uphill battle because of the enormous
debt load carried by the company and continued declining revenues.

Another large cut in newsroom employees at the *Los Angeles Times* was
announced in July 2008, and the publisher, David Hiller, resigned. After those
cuts, the newspaper employed about half the number of people it had only
ten years earlier. However, that cost cutting was not enough, and the Tribune
Company filed for bankruptcy in December 2008. It tried to liquidate some
assets, including Wrigley Field, where the Chicago Cubs play, an effort
touched by scandal after Illinois governor Rod Blagojevich was arrested and
charged with trying to coerce the *Chicago Tribune* into firing editors critical
of his administration in exchange for the state's assistance with the sale of
that baseball stadium.

The premier competitor of the *New York Times*, the *Washington Post*, was
another family-controlled newspaper and television empire that was in a
state of decline. The paper is best known for its investigative reporting. The
Washington Post Company's print media and local television revenues had
been the historical leaders for the company, but were now falling. The firm's
managers then sought to diversify into such things as Kaplan, an educational

enterprise. Management focused its attention on that business and downplayed the declining newspaper and television operations. However, its share price nonetheless dropped by 42 percent between 2004 and 2008.

In a desperate effort to increase revenue, Charles Pelton, an executive at the company, sent advertisements to lobbyists and trade group representatives promoting meetings with the *Washington Post* publisher, Katharine Weymouth, and with *Washington Post* editors and reporters, as well as invited government officials. Attendees were to be charged a fee starting at $25,000 per person. This program set off a furor in the press in July 2009, when its existence became known. It was viewed as crass influence peddling. The program was quickly canceled in response to that criticism, and Pelton resigned. Some time thereafter, the Washington Post company sold its once popular *Newsweek* magazine for $1 and assumption of $70 million in liabilities.

The Washington Post Company is controlled by the Graham family, which owns its A shares. Holders of those shares are entitled to elect a majority of the board of directors of the company, thereby keeping it under family control. In 2008 the family sought to have its cake and eat it too, by cashing out some of their ownership interest and keeping control at the same time. A majority of family members thus voted to convert 25 percent of their A shares to an equal number of B shares, which could be sold in the public market in order to raise funds for various family obligations. However, the public shareholders of the newspaper were advised that this conversion would have no impact on control of the company.

Conclusion

The Enron scandal is now deeply embedded in the collective psyche of our society. The subject of numerous books and television shows, it was even the focus of a musical that was a hit in London in 2009, nearly eight years after the scandal, complete with a Jeffrey Skilling perp walk, though it came and went very quickly when it was mounted on Broadway in 2010. The Enron-era scandals, indeed, made great theater but should have occasioned a searching examination of the flaws in the financial system that encouraged executives to engage in such massive accounting manipulations. No such study was ever conducted. Instead, the government responded with knee-jerk legislation and ill-thought-out prosecutions that made headlines when filed yet ultimately accomplished nothing. Long prison sentences substituted for a thoughtful approach to the correction of the flaws in the regulatory system that allowed, in fact encouraged, accounting manipulation.

Corporate reformers went into full cry and demanded corporate reforms that had not worked in the past and that will be just as ineffectual in the future. For example, more independent directors add little or nothing to the mix. To be sure, a few independent directors add balance and dispassionate judgment to a board. However, a supermajority of directors add nothing, except by chance, and can be easily manipulated by management because management controls information flows. The same can be said for splitting the role of the chairman and CEO, and, certainly, adding board members selected by labor unions will not improve corporate efficiency.

Ironically, the root of the Enron-era corporate scandals lies in the corporate reformers' insistence that the interests of shareholders and corporate management be aligned through stock option grants. That reform, coupled with the Securities and Exchange Commission's (SEC's) requirement for quarterly financial reports, placed irresistible pressure on management to meet analysts' profit expectations each quarter. If those expectations were not met, the price of the company's stock would plunge, and the executives would not gain the millions of dollars they anticipated from their option grants. SEC rules also restricted analysts' ability to ferret out the true conditions of companies. SEC

Regulation FD did not allow them to separately interview executives or to conduct their own investigations. Instead, analysts were left with company-prepared quarterly reports and company press conferences. This led the analysts to abandon analysis and become shills for their firm's underwriting department.

The SEC full disclosure system failed to prevent or detect the Enron-era scandals. That agency had to stand by helplessly as New York attorney general Eliot Spitzer rose to fame by running roughshod over Wall Street and by thumbing his nose at the SEC. The SEC tried to respond with unnecessary and controversial regulations, setting the number of directors on mutual fund boards and requiring hedge funds to register. The commission was badly embarrassed when an appellate court threw out both reforms. The SEC's full disclosure requirements for executive compensation also backfired. Rather than curbing excesses, those requirements only encouraged ever-rising levels of compensation.

The SEC learned nothing from these experiences. It failed, once again, in the run-up to the subprime crisis, to detect any problems or dangers presented by subprime investments to the firms that it regulates. The agency was completely impotent during the crisis itself, as the large investment banks failed one after the other. After each setback, the SEC responded with a flurry of enforcement actions as a means of shoring up its faltering reputation. They accomplished nothing, except to impose a large fine on corporations, a fine drawn from the corporate treasury and thus only harms shareholders.

The SEC full disclosure model is fatally flawed and needs reform. Such reform would include ending the class-action lawsuits based on the federal securities laws that provide benefits only to the lawyers filing them and to union pension funds that act as lead plaintiffs. The financial system has changed dramatically since the SEC was created in 1934. Hedge funds, private equity, sovereign wealth funds, venture capitalists, and electronic trading have created a marketplace that does not fit the model that the SEC was created to regulate.

In the 1930s individual investors drove the market, but today they play no such role. This change should have turned the SEC into a financial services regulator—that did not happen. Instead, the SEC continues to view itself simply as a law enforcement agency that brings cases based on newspaper reports or flashy insider-trading cases, actions that have done nothing to reduce the amount of inside trading. The flaws in the SEC regulatory model became even more apparent during the subprime crisis, an event that the next volume in this financial history explores in detail.

Notes

Chapter 1

1. Arthur Andersen was not the only one sanctioned in that affair. James Koenig, the chief financial officer of Waste Management, was ordered by a federal court in 2007 to pay $1.6 billion as a penalty for his role in the massive accounting fraud at that company. Waste Management's chief financial officer agreed to pay over $4 million to settle charges relating to his role in that company's accounting manipulations. However, an appeals court set aside a jury verdict against Bruce Snyder, Waste Management's chief accounting officer, in a case brought by the SEC. The court ruled that the jury had not been properly instructed on his reliance on a review conducted by Arthur Andersen of the documents he filed with the SEC that were false.

2. *Arthur Andersen LLP v. United States,* 544 U.S. 696 (2005).

3. *United States v. Brown,* 459 F.3d 509 (5th Cir. 2006).

4. Holman W. Jenkins, Jr., "Rethinking the Corporate Crime Spree," *Wall Street Journal,* August 19, 2009, p. A13.

5. *United States v. Brown,* 459 F.3d 509 (5th Cir. 2006).

6. *United States v. Brown,* No. 08-20038 (5th Cir. 2009).

7. *Yeager v. United States,* 129 S. Ct. 2360 (2009).

8. *United States v. Howard,* 2008 U.S. App. LEXIS 3100 (5th Cir. February 12, 2008).

9. Martin Wolf, "Judicial Torture and the NatWest 3," *Financial Times,* November 30, 2007, p. 11.

10. Alexei Barrionuevo and Kurt Eichenwald, "The Enron Case That Almost Wasn't," *New York Times,* June 4, 2006, sec. 3, p. 1.

11. This was not a new tactic utilized by federal prosecutors. During the Whitewater investigation involving President Bill Clinton and his wife Hillary, the special prosecutor, Kenneth Starr, imprisoned Susan McDougal, the former wife and business partner of Jim McDougal, who was at the center of the controversy. McDougal eventually agreed to cooperate with prosecutors after being convicted, but his wife refused to testify against the Clintons. Starr then had Mrs. McDougal imprisoned for twenty-one months. That prison time included one seven-week stint where she was under a twenty-three-hour-a-day lockdown and was held in a soundproof Plexiglas cell. The American Civil Liberties Union charged that McDougal was held under barbaric conditions in order to force her to testify against the Clintons, but she refused to break and was given a full pardon by Bill Clinton just before he left office. Sean Wilentz, *The Age of Reagan,* p. 378.

12. In *United States v. McElhaney,* 469 F.3d 382 (5th Cir. 2006), the Court of Appeals for the Fifth Circuit, which includes Texas, held that the government could coerce a defendant by threatening to prosecute his wife if he did not enter a guilty plea.

13. Greg Farrell, "The Enron Whistle-Blower Who Wasn't," *USA Today,* October 12, 2007.

14. *United States v. Skilling,* 2006 U.S. Dist. LEXIS 42664 (S.D. Tex. 2006).

15. Kurt Eichenwald and Alexei Barrionuevo, "Tough Justice for Executives in Enron Era," *New York Times,* May 27, 2006, p. A1.

16. *United States v. Skilling,* 06-20885, Opening Brief of Appellant (5th Cir. September 14, 2007).

17. Ibid.

18. *In re Enron Corp.,* 2003 U.S. Dist. LEXIS 7632 (S.D. Texas).

19. The author has acted as an expert witness for ECRC in those proceedings.

20. *Regents of the University of California v. Credit Suisse First Boston (USA) Inc.,* 482 F.3d 372 (5th Cir. 2007).

21. *Stoneridge Investment Partners LLC v. Scientific–Atlanta, Inc.,* 2008 U.S. LEXIS 1091 (2008).

22. Kristen Hays, "Law Firm Seeks $688 Million for Enron Work," *Houston Chronicle,* January 8, 2008, p. B1.

23. *United States v. Olis,* 429 F.3d 540 (5th Cir. 2005).

Chapter 2

1. Daniel Fischel, *Payback.*

2. *New England Healthcare Employees Pension Fund v. Woodruff,* 2008 U.S. App. LEXIS 954 (10th Cir. 2008).

3. *United States v. Ebbers*, 458 F.3d 110 (2d Cir. 2006).

4. Letter from John Conyers, Jr., et al. to Alberto R. Gonzales.

5. *United States v. Forbes*, 249 Fed. Appx. 233 (2d cir. 2007).

6. *SEC v. Johnson*, Civ. No. 05-36 (D.D.C. December 5, 2007).

7. *United States v. Stringer*, 408 F. Supp.2d 1083 (D. Ore. 2006).

8. *United States v. Stringer*, 2008 WL 901563 (9th Cir. 2008).

9. Conrad Black, *A Life in Full.*

10. Ibid., p. 995.

11. Jerry W. Markham, "How the Feds Stacked the Deck Against Enron," *Chicago Sun Times*, May 7, 2006, p. B1. See also Eichenwald and Barrionuevo, "Tough Justice for Executives in Enron Era."

12. *United States v. Stein*, 435 F. Supp.2d 330 (SDNY 2006). See also *United States v. Stein,* 440 F. Supp.2d 315 (SDNY 2006).

13. Patricia Beard, *Blue Blood and Mutiny*, p. 150.

14. Susanne Craig, "Goldman's Trading Tips Reward Its Biggest Clients," *Wall Street Journal,* August 24, 2009, p. A1.

15. *United States v. Quattrone*, 441 F.3d 153 (2d Cir. 2006).

Chapter 3

1. The discussion on executive compensation in this book is based in part on a paper that was presented by the author at the University of Maryland law school at a conference sponsored by that school's *Journal of Business and Technology Law,* and subsequently published by that journal as "Excessive Executive Compensation—Why Bother?" (2008), p. 1001.

2. 107 Pub. L. 204, 116 Stat. 745 (2002).

3. Susan Scholz, *The Changing Nature and Consequences of Public Company Financial Restatements.*

4. *SEC v. Yuen,* 401 F.3d 1031 (9th Cir. 2005).

5. Lewis D. Lowenfels and Alan R. Bromberg, "SEC Actions Against Lawyers Post Sarbanes-Oxley," pp. 1739, 1743.

6. "Capital Flight," *Wall Street Journal,* December 2–3, 2006, p. A8.

7. Roberta S. Karmel, "Regulation by Exemption," pp. 681, 689.

8. Peter J. Wallison, "Capital Punishment."

9. Committee on Capital Markets Regulation, "The Competitive Position of the U.S. Public Equity Markets."

10. U.S. Chamber of Commerce, Commission on the Regulation of U.S. Capital Markets in the 21st Century, "Report and Recommendations," p. 11.

11. Financial Services Roundtable, "The Blueprint for U.S. Financial Competitiveness."

12. *Interim Report of the Committee on Capital Markets Regulation.*

13. Deborah Solomon, "Treasury's Paulson Warns of the Costs of Rules Overlap," *Wall Street Journal,* November 21, 2006, p. A2.

14. Charles E. Schumer and Michael R. Bloomberg, "To Save New York, Learn from London," *Wall Street Journal,* November 1, 2006, p. A18.

15. Michael R. Bloomberg and Senator Charles E. Schumer, "Sustaining New York's and the US Global Financial Services Leadership," p. i.

16. "Schapiro Vows to 'Reinvigorate' Enforcement at SEC If Confirmed," p. 77.

17. David Cannadine, *Mellon,* p. 127. These ostentatious displays of wealth gave rise to the term "conspicuous consumption" (Thorstein Velben, *The Theory of the Leisure Class*).

18. Robert L. Beisner, *Dean Acheson,* p. 16.

19. Adolf A. Berle, Jr., and Gardiner C. Means, *The Modern Corporation and Private Property.*

20. Ibid.

21. George T. Washington, "The Corporation Executive's Living Wage," pp. 733, 734.

22. *Rogers v. Hill,* 289 U.S. 582 (1933).

23. *Heller v. Boylan,* 29 N.Y.S.2d 653, 669 (Sup.), *aff'd,* 32 N.Y.S. 2d 131 (App. Div. 1st Dept. 1941).

24. Washington, "The Corporation Executive's Living Wage," pp. 733, 758–59.

25. *Brehm v. Eisner,* 2006 Del. LEXIS 307 (Del. 2006).

26. For a detailed description of this affair see Charles Gasparino, *King of the Club.*

27. Cannadine, *Mellon,* p. 318.

28. Jim Powell, *FDR's Folly,* pp. 83–84.

29. James W. Ely, *The Guardian of Every Other Right,* p. 138.

30. Herbert S. Parmet, *George Bush,* p. 69.

31. James A. Baker III and Steve Fiffer, *Work Hard, Study . . . and Keep Out of Politics!* p. 173.

32. Ibid., p. 189.

33. Conrad Black, *Franklin Delano Roosevelt,* p. 393.

34. David M. Kennedy, *Freedom from Fear,* p. 85 n3.

35. Cannadine, *Mellon,* p. 515.

36. Louis Brandeis, *Other People's Money and How the Bankers Use It,* p. 92.

37. Pub. L. No. 73-22, 48 Stat. 74.

38. Pub. L. No. 73-290, 48 Stat. 881.

39. Masters, *Spoiling for a Fight,* p. 182.

40. Lucian Arye Bebchuk and Yaniv Grinstein, "The Growth of Executive Pay," p. 283.

41. Joann S. Lublin and Scott Thurm, "Behind Soaring Executive Pay, Decades of Failed Restraints," *Wall Street Journal,* October 12, 2006, p. A1.

42. Sue Morgan et al., *Executive Compensation Disclosure Handbook.*

43. "Who Makes What," *TV Guide,* August 10–23, 2009, p. 26.

44. Floyd Norris, "S.E.C. Change Reporting Rule on Bosses' Pay," *New York Times,* December 27, 2006, p. A1; idem, "Does S.E.C. Know What It Is Doing?" *New York Times,* December 29, 2006, p. C1.

45. Eric Dash, "Compensation Experts Offer Ways to Help Curb Executive Salaries," *New York Times,* December 30, 2006, p. B1.

46. Pub. L. No. 103-66, 107 Stat. 312 (1993), codified at 26 U.S.C. §162(m).

47. Lublin and Thurm, "Behind Soaring Executive Pay, Decades of Failed Restraints."

48. 57 Fed. Reg. 29582 & n. 32 (July 2, 1992).

49. Eric Dash, "Congress Is Urged to Hold Off Acting on Options and Pay," *New York Times,* September 7, 2006, p. C3.

50. Francesco Guerrera, "Welch Condemns Share Price Focus," *Financial Times,* March 13, 2009.

51. Serena Ng, "Tracking the Numbers—Street Sleuth—Filing Footnote," *Wall Street Journal,* May 15, 2006, p. C1.

52. *United States v. Lake,* 472 F.3d 1247, 1259 (10th Cir. 2007).

53. "Loose Talk, What Stars Said This Week," *US Magazine,* June 8, 2009, p. 14.

54. Jesse Drucker and Mark Maremont, "CEOs of Bailed-Out Banks Flew to Resorts on Firm Jets," *Wall Street Journal,* June 19, 2009, p. A1.

55. Joann S. Lublin, "A Quiet Response to 'Say-on-Pay' Measures," *Wall Street Journal,* May 18, 2009, p. B6.

56. *American Federation of State, County & Municipal Employees, Employees Pension Plan v. American International Group, Inc.,* 462 F.3d 121 (2d Cir. 2006).

57. Kara Scannell, "Policy Makers Work to Give Shareholders More Boardroom Clout," *Wall Street Journal,* March 26, 2009, p. B4.

58. Robert D. Hershey, Jr., "A Little Industry with a Lot of Sway on Proxy Votes," *New York Times,* June 18, 2006, sec. 3, p. 6.

59. *Stoneridge Investment Partners, LLC v. Scientific-Atlanta Inc.*

60. Joe Nocera, "Serving Time But Lacking Remorse," *New York Times,* June 7, 2008, p. C1.

61. Niall Ferguson, *The Ascent of Money,* p. 180.

62. Steve Stecklow, "Fraud by Trial Lawyers Taints Claims in Pesticide Lawsuits," *Wall Street Journal,* August 19, 2009, p. 1.

Chapter 4

1. M. Van Smith, "The Commodity Futures Commission and the Return of the Bucketeers," p. 13 n26.

2. United States House of Representatives, Report of the Committee Appointed Pursuant to House Resolutions 429 and 504 to Investigate the Concentration of Control of Money and Credit, H.R. Rep. No. 1593, 62d Cong., 3d sess. 37 (1913).

3. W.C. Van Antwerp, *The Stock Exchange from Within,* p. 149.

4. Dale A. Osterle, "Regulation NMS," pp. 613, 640.

5. 70 Fed Reg. 37496 (June 29, 2005).

6. William McChesney Martin, *The Securities Markets,* 3.

7. This discussion of the changes in the stock and commodity markets brought about by advances in information technology and competition is drawn from Markham and Harty, "For Whom the Bell Tolls: The Demise of Exchange Trading Floors and the Growth of ECNs," *Journal of Corporate Law* (reprinted by permission).

8. Office of Technology Assessment, U.S. Congress, "Electronic Bulls and Bears," U.S. Securities Market and Information Technology (September 1990), p. 136.

9. Arthur Levitt, "The Future of Our Markets," pp. 1, 5.

10. Tabb Group, "US Equity Market Structure."

11. *In re Miklas,* Comm. Fut. L. Rep. (CCH) ¶30,818 (CFTC 2008).

12. Charles D. Ellis, *The Partnership,* p. 651.

13. Gasparino, *King of the Club,* p. 96.

14. *Financial Planning Association v. SEC,* 482 F.3d 481 (D.C. Cir. 2007).

15. *Goldstein v. SEC,* 451 F.3d 873 (D.C. Cir. 2006).

16. *United States v. American Stock Exchange, LLC,* 2000 WL 33400154 (D.D.C. September 11, 2000). See also *In re Certain Activities of Options Exchanges,* 2000 WL 1277616 (SEC 2000) (parallel charges by SEC).

17. 69 Fed. Reg. 6124, 6126 (February 9, 1004).

18. U.S. Congress, Office of Technology Assessment, "Electronic Bulls and Bears," p. 107.

19. Securities and Exchange Commission, "Special Study of the Securities Markets," H.R. Doc. No. 95, pt. 1 (1963), p. 427.

20. Securities and Exchange Commission, "Study of Unsafe and Unsound Practices of Brokers and Dealers," H.R. Doc. No. 92-231, 92d Cong., 2d sess. (1971), p. 165.

21. Ibid., p. 13.

22. "Electronic Bulls and Bears."

23. *Report of the Presidential Task Force on Market Mechanisms,* January 12, 1988, p. 69.

24. BIS, "Cross-Border Securities Settlements.

25. BIS, "Delivery Versus Payment in Securities Settlement Systems."

26. BIS, "Cross-Border Securities Settlements."

27. Clearstream International, "Cross-Border Equity Trading, Clearing & Settlement in Europe."

28. BIS, "Recommendations for Central Counterparties, Consultative Report."

29. Giovannini Group, *Cross-Border Clearing and Settlement Arrangements in the European Union*, p. 9.

30. European Union Directive 98/26/EC of the European Parliament and of the European Council on a settlement finality in payment and securities settlement systems (May 19, 1998).

31. Hurd Baruch, *Wall Street Security Risk.*

32. 17 C.F.R. 15c3-3.

33. Giovannini Group, *Cross-Border Clearing and Settlement Arrangements in the European Union*, p. 9.

34. BIS, "Collateral in Wholesale Financial Markets," p. 2.

35. Robert F. Bruner and Sean D. Carr, *The Panic of 1907,* p. 107.

36. *American Bank & Trust Co. v. Federal Reserve Bank of Atlanta,* 262 U.S. 643 (1923).

37. BIS, Committee on Payment and Settlement Systems, "Progress in Reducing Foreign Exchange Settlement Risk."

38. BIS, Committee on Payment and Settlement Systems. "Core Principles for Systemically Important Payment Systems."

39. BIS, Committee on Payment and Settlement Systems, "New Developments in Large-Value Payment Systems."

40. Payments Risk Committee, "Global Payment Liquidity."

41. BIS, Committee on Payment and Settlement Systems, "Cross-border Collateral Arrangements."

42. Kara Scannell, "Judge Rules for Pasternak in SEC's Fraud Case," *Wall Street Journal,* June 13, 2008, p. C2.

43. *First National Bank of Bellaire v Comptroller of the Currency,* 697 F.2d 674 (5th Cir. 1983).

44. International Lending Supervision Act of 1983, 12 U.S.C. §3907.

45. Lissa L. Broome and Jerry W. Markham, *Regulation of Banking Financial Service Activities,* p. 521.

46. Basel Committee on Banking Regulations and Supervisory Practices, "International Convergence of Capital Measurement and Capital Standards."

47. Joe Nocera, "The Story That I Have to Tell," *New York Times Magazine,* January 4, 2009, p. 26.

48. L. Gordon Crovitz, "Bad News Is Better Than No News," *Wall Street Journal,* January 26, 2009, p. A13.

49. Steven L. Molinari and Nelson Kibler, "Broker-Dealers' Financial Responsibility Under the Uniform Net Capital Rule," p. 1.

50. Securities and Exchange Commission, "Report of the Special Study of the Securities Markets," H.R. Doc. No. 95, 88th Cong., 1st sess. (1963), pp. 84–85, 92.

51. Securities and Exchange Commission, Securities Exchange Act Release No. 34-54255 (July 31, 2006).

52. Vikram Pandit, "Toward a Transparent Financial System," *Wall Street Journal,* June 27, 2008, p. A11.

53. Morton Keller, *The Life Insurance Enterprise,* p. 32.

54. Leslie Scism, "Life Insurers Enjoy Relaxed Disclosure Rules," *Wall Street Journal,* February 17, 2008, p. C2.

55. U.S. Congress, Temporary National Economic Committee, "Investigation of Concentration of Economic Power," 76th Cong., 3d sess., Monograph No. 28, p. 7.

56. *United States v. South-Eastern Underwriters Ass'n,* 322 U.S. 533 (1944).

57. 59 Stat. 33 (1945).

58. Lissa Broome and Jerry W. Markham, "Banking and Insurance: Before and After the Gramm-Leach-Bliley Act," p. 723.

Chapter 5

1. Parts of the discussion in this chapter on the development of electronic trading are drawn from Markham and Harty, "For Whom the Bell Tolls."

2. *Bd. of Trade v. Christie Grain & Stock Co.,* 198 U.S. 236 (1905), pp. 249–50.

3. *New York Mercantile Exchange, Inc., v. IntercontinentalExchange, Inc.,* Comm. Fut. L. Rep. (CCH) ¶30,597 (2d. Cir. 2007).

4. *Hubbard v. Lowe,* 226 F. 135 (SDNY 1915).

5. Federal Trade Commission, "Report on the Grain Trade."

6. *Hill v. Wallace,* 259 U.S. 44 (1922).

7. *Chicago Board of Trade v. Olsen,* 262 U.S. 839 (1923).

8. 7 U.S.C. §1 et seq.

9. *CFTC v. Dunn,* 519 U.S. 465 (1997).

10. *CFTC v. Zelener,* 373 F.3d 861 (7th Cir. 2004).

11. The author serves on the Board of Directors of one such swaps dealer, Nomura Derivative Products.

12. Pub. L. No. 106-544, 114 Stat. 2763.

13. U.S. Department of the Treasury, *Blueprint for a Modernized Financial Regulatory Structure,* p. 47.

14. Joint Audit Committee Operating Agreement.

15. *CFTC v. Enron Corp.,* Comm. Fut. L. Rep. (CCH) ¶ 29,811 (S.D. Tex. 2004).

16. *In re Western States Wholesale Natural Gas Litigation,* 408 F. Supp.2d 1055, 1057 (D. Nev. 2005), *reversed and remanded on other grounds,* 2007 U.S. App. LEXIS 22760 (9th Cir. 2007).

17. FERC, "Price Manipulation in Western Markets," p. ES-6.

18. Jerry W. Markham, "The Manipulation of Commodity Futures Prices," p. 281.

19. Jerry W. Markham and Lawrence Hunt, "The California Energy Crisist," p. 1.

20. *CFTC v. Delay,* 2006 WL 3359076 (D. Neb. 2006).

21. *CFTC v. Enron Corp.*

22. The author acted as a consultant in this litigation.

23. *United States v. Valencia,* 2006 WL 3716657 (S.D. Tex. 2006).

24. Pub. L. No. 109-58, 119 Stat. 594 (2005).

25. U.S. Congress, Senate Permanent Subcommittee on Investigations of the Committee on Homeland Security and Governmental Affairs, "Excessive Speculation in the Natural Gas Market," 110th Cong. 1st sess. (2007), p. 58

26. *CFTC v. Amaranth Advisors, LLC,* 2007 U.S. Dist. LEXIS 80978 (SDNY 2007).

27. *Hunter v. Federal Energy Regulatory Commission,* Comm. Fut. L. Rep. (CCH) ¶30,744 (D.D.C. 2007).

28. Interagency Task Force on Commodity Markets, "Interim Report on Crude Oil."

29. Pub. L. No. 110-140, 121 Stat. 1492, ¶¶811–815.

30. CFTC Staff Report on Commodity Swap Dealers & Index Traders with Commission Recommendations.

31. CFTC Study, "Commodity and Equities"

32. GAO, "Commodity Futures Trading Commission: Trends in Energy Derivatives Markets Raise Questions About CFTC's Oversight."

33. CFTC, "Market Growth Trader Participation and Pricing in Energy Futures Markets."

34. Pub. L. No. 93-463, 88 Stat. 1389.

35. Leo Melamed, "The Mechanics of a Commodity Futures Exchange," p. 149.

36. H.J. Maidenberg, "Futures/Options; Automation in Trading," *New York Times,* December 10, 1984, p. D4.

37. Barnaby J. Feder, "Chicago's Exchanges Look Toward an Electronic Salvation," *New York Times,* November 29, 1992, sec. 3, p. 5.

38. William P. Rogers and Jerry W. Markham, "The Application of West German Statutes to United States Commodity Futures Contracts."

39. David Barboza, "In Chicago's Trading Pits, This May Be the Final Generation," *New York Times,* August 6, 2000, sec. 3, p. 1.

40. Leo Melamed, "Futures Markets in the Digital Century."

41. The author is an expert witness for Eurex in that action.

42. Niko Koppel, "In Chicago, a Rowdy Trading Scene Grows Quieter," *New York Times,* October 29, 2007, p. A10.

43. Greenspan, remarks delivered before the Futures Industry Annual Conference.

44. *New York Mercantile Exchange, Inc., v. IntercontinentalExchange, Inc.,* Comm. Fut. L. Rep. (CCH) ¶30,597(2d. Cir 2007).

45. *Board of Trade Clearing Corporation v. United States,* 1978 U.S. Dist. LEXIS 20220 (D.D.C. 1978), p. 2.

46. 7 U.S.C. §7a–1(f).

47. *Board of Trade of the City of Chicago v. SEC,* 923 F.2d 1270 (7th Cir. 1991).

48. See *CBOT v. SEC,* 677 F.2d 1137 (7th Cir. 1982), *vacated as moot,* 459 U.S. 1026 (1983), *CME v. SEC,* 883 F.2d 537 (7th Cir. 1989), *cert. denied sub nom.,* and *Investment Company Institute v. SEC,* 496 U.S. 936 (1990).

49. 56 Fed. Reg. 61,458 (1991).

50. 71 Fed. Reg. 40766-67 (July 18, 2006).

51. H.R. Rep. No. 1637, 73d Cong., 2d 6 (1934). See 7 U.S.C. §7d.

52. U.S. Congress, Senate, *Congressional Record,* 74th Cong. 2d Sess. 7858.

53. Ibid., remarks of Senator Murray.

54. Ibid.

55. The author is a consultant in this proceeding.

Chapter 6

1. Liaquat Ahamed, *Lords of Finance,* pp. 311–312.

2. Jenny Anderson, "Bank Leases to Hedge Funds Are Questioned," *New York Times,* January 2, 2007, p. A1.

3. 7 U.S.C. § 12.

4. 7 U.S.C. § 13.

5. Roger Lowenstein, *When Genius Failed.*

6. National Securities Market Improvement Act of 1996, Pub. L. No. 104-290, 110 Stat. 3416.

7. *Dabit v. Merrill Lynch, Pierce, Fenner & Smith Inc.,* 395 F.3d 25 (2d Cir. 2005).

8. Spitzer, Canary Capital Partners Complaint,

9. Office of New York State Attorney General Eliot Spitzer, "State Investigation Reveals Mutual Fund Fraud."

10. *United States v. National Association of Securities Dealers,* 422 U.S. 694 (1975), p. 707.

11. 44 FR 29,644 (May 22, 1979).

12. David Ward, "Protecting Mutual Funds from Market-Timing Profiteers," pp. 585, 589.

13. Jeanne L. Reid, "Choosing Tactics in the War Against Risk," p. 83.

14. Ibid.

15. Spitzer, Canary Capital Partners Complaint.

16. Ibid.

17. Hannah Bergman, "Spitzer: OCC Is Blocking N.Y.'s Probe of Lenders," p. 1.

18. *In re Strong Capital Management,* SEC Investment Advisers Act Release No. 40-26448 (May 20, 2004).

19. *SEC v. Pimco Advisors Fund Management,* LLC, 341 F. Supp.2d 454 (SDNY 2004).

20. *SEC v. Tambone,* 417 F. Supp.2d 127 (D. Mass. 2006).

21. Sanjai Bhagat and Bernard Black, "The Uncertain Relationship Between Board Composition and Firm Performance," pp. 921, 923, 946.

22. Peter J. Wallison and Robert E. Litan, *Competitive Equity.*

23. *U.S. Chamber of Commerce v. SEC,* 412 F.3d 133 (D.C. Cir. 2005).

24. *U.S. Chamber of Commerce v. SEC,* 443 F.3d 890 (D.C. Cir. 2006).

25. *CFTC v. Savage,* 611 F.2d 2d 270 (9th Cir. 1979).

26. *Abrahamson v. Fleschner,* 568 F.2d 862 (2d Cir. 1977).

27. Susan C. Ervin, "Letting Go," pp. 1, 3.

28. Pub. L. No. 106-544, 114 Stat. 2763.

29. Ibid.

30. Ibid., p. 1.

31. *Goldstein v. SEC*, 451 F.3d 873 (D.C. Cir. 2006).

32. Agreement Among PWG and U.S. Agency Principals on Principles and Guidelines Regarding Private Pools of Capital, p. 1.

33. Bernanke, "Financial Regulation and the Invisible Hand."

34. 69 Fed. Reg. 72054, 56 (December 10, 2004).

35. Jerry W. Markham, "Mutual Fund Scandals," pp. 67, 120.

36. *In re Manhattan Investment Ltd.*, 2007 WL 4440360 (SDNY 2007).

37. *Gredd v. Bear Stearns Securities Corp.* (SDNY December 17, 2007).

38. The author was an expert witness for Man Financial in litigation involving this matter.

39. "Refco's Ex-Chief Pleads Guilty to Fraud and Conspiracy," *New York Times*, February 16, 2008, p. B2.

40. Robert Morris, *The Papers of Robert Morris*, vol. 8, pp. 857–865.

41. Berle and Means, *The Modern Corporation and Private Property*.

42. David Hsu, "Organizing Venture Capital."

43. Ronald J. Gilson, "Engineering a Venture Capital Market," p. 1067.

44. Paul A. Gompers, "The Rise and Fall of Venture Capital."

45. See, generally, Guy Fraser-Sampson, *Private Equity as an Asset Class.*

46. Michael S. Malone, "The Pump and Dump Economy," *Wall Street Journal*, December 21, 2006, p. A16.

47. Hedi N. Moore, "Buffett Versus Private Equity," *Wall Street Journal*, March 3, 2009, p. C3.

48. Steven M. Davidoff, "Black Market Capital," pp. 172, 176.

49. Charles Duhigg, "Can Private Equity Build a Public Face?" *New York Times*, December 24, 2006, sec 3, pp. 1, 4.

50. "Capital Flight," p. A8. See also Kit Roane, "The New Face of Capitalism," *U.S. News and World Report*, December 4, 2006, p. 49 (describing the private equity buying binge).

51. Standard & Poor's Web site, www.standardandpoors.com/home/en/us.

52. Ibid.

53. *CSX Corp. v. The Children's Investment Fund Management* (UK) LLP, 2008 U.S. Dist. LEXIS 46039 (SDNY 2008).

54. Steven E. Hurdle, Jr., "A Blow to Public Investing," p. 239.

55. Andy Stern, "Private Equity and the Banks," *Wall Street Journal*, August 4, 2009, p. A13.

56. Liz Rappaport and Susanne Craig, "BlackRock Wears Multiple Hats," *Wall Street Journal*, May 19, 2009, p. B1; Eric Lipton and Michael J. de la Merced, "Wall St. Firm Draws Scrutiny as U.S. Adviser," *New York Times*, May 19, 2009, p. A1.

57. Michael J. de la Merced, "Profit Falls at BlackRock on Downturn in Real Estate," *New York Times*, April 22, 2009, p. B4.

58. Ludovic Phalippou and Oliver Gottschalg, "The Performance of Private Equity Funds."

59. "Sovereign Impunity," *Wall Street Journal*, December 1–2, 2007, p. A12.

60. Bob Davis, "Wanted: SWFs' Money Sans Politics," *Wall Street Journal*, December 20, 2007, p. C1.

61. Steven R. Weisman, "Oil Producers See the World and Buy It Up," *New York Times*, November 28, 2007, p. A1.

62. Eric Dash, "Merrill Lynch Sells a $5 Billion Stake to a Singapore Firm," *New York Times*, December 25, 2007, p. C1.

63. Keith Johnson, "Dow Chemical Takes Credit Hit as Kuwait Deal Unravels," *Wall Street Journal*, December 30, 2008, p. B1.

Chapter 7

Parts of this chapter are drawn from Jerry Markham, "Glass-Steagall v. Gramm-Leach-Bliley."

1. David L. Mason, *From Buildings and Loans to Bail-Outs*, p. 12.

2. Robert C. Ellickson, "Ancient Land Law," p. 321.

3. "The Story of Mortgage Law," p. 1.

4. Morris G. Shanker, "Will Mortgage Law Survive?" p. 69.

5. Ann M. Burkart, "Lenders and Land," p. 249.

6. Berman, "Once a Mortgage, Always a Mortgage-B," p. 76.

7. Peter M. Carrozzo, "Marketing the American Mortgage," p. 765.

8. Mason, *From Buildings and Loans to Bail-Outs,* p. 13.

9. Ibid., p. 14.

10. Donald L. Kemmerer, "The Colonial Loan Office System in New Jersey," p. 867.

11. Donald L. Kemmerer, "A History of Paper Money in Colonial New Jersey 1668–1775."

12. Mason, *From Buildings and Loans to Bail-Outs,* p. 15.

13. James Grant, *Mr. Market Miscalculates,* pp. 147–153.

14. Kenneth Snowden, "What Can History Tell Us About the Crisis in Mortgage Securitizations?" p. 16.

15. Ibid.

16. Ibid., p. 18.

17. Mason, *From Buildings and Loans to Bail-Outs,* pp. 76–77.

18. Kenneth H. Snowden, "The Anatomy of a Residential Mortgage Crisis," pp. 16–17.

19. Ibid., p. 8.

20. Mason, *From Buildings and Loans to Bail-Outs*, p. 65.

21. Leo Grebler et al., *Capital Formation and Residential Real Estate,* p. 233.

22. Barry P. Bosworth et al., *The Economics of Federal Credit Programs,* pp. 47–48.

23. E.S. Wallace, "Survey of Federal Legislation Affecting Private Home Financing Since 1932," pp. 481, 482.

24. Fred Wright, "The Effect of New Deal Real Estate Residential Finance and Foreclosure Policies Made in Response to the Real Estate Conditions of the Great Depression," pp. 231, 236.

25. Snowden, "The Anatomy of a Residential Mortgage Crisis," p. 12.

26. Charles P. Kindleberger, *The World in Depression,* p. 60.

27. Mason, *From Buildings and Loans to Bail-Outs,* p. 67.

28. Snowden, "The Anatomy of a Residential Mortgage Crisis," p. 16.

29. Snowden, "What Can History Tell Us About the Crisis in Mortgage Securitizations?" p. 18.

30. Report of the Moreland Commissioner, p. 3.

31. Saperstein, "Real Estate Bond Issues of the Future."

32. Final Report of the Select Committee to Investigate Bondholder Reorganizations, pp. 521–523.

33. William E. Leuchtenburg, *Franklin D. Roosevelt and the New Deal,* p. 39.

34. 12 U.S.C. §301.

35. John A. Deangelis, "Riches Do Not Last Forever," pp. 777, 783.

36. James Stuart Olson, *Herbert Hoover and the Reconstruction Finance Corporation,* p. 114.

37. Frank Freidel, *Franklin D. Roosevelt*, p. 95.

38. Murray R. Benedict, *Farm Policies of the United States*.

39. *Louisville Joint Stock Land Bank v. Radford,* 295 U.S. 555 (1935).

40. Federal Housing Administration, *The FHA Story in Summary*, p. 1.

41. Bosworth et al., *The Economics of Federal Credit Programs*, p. 48.

42. Robert H. Skilton, "Developments in Mortgage Law and Practice," p. 315.

43. J. Douglas Poteat, "State Legislative Relief for the Mortgage Debtor During the Depression."

44. Wallace, "Survey of Federal Legislation Affecting Private Home Financing Since 1932," pp. 481-482.

45. Thomas S. Stone, "Mortgage Moratoria."

46. David Lilienthal and Robert H. Marquis, "The Conduct of Business Enterprises by the Federal Government." The federal government expanded the use of the GST even more during World War II, with most of the economy operating under one or the other such enterprises, such as the Export-Import Bank.

47. Thomas H. Stanton, "Federal Supervision of Safety and Soundness of Government-Sponsored Enterprises."

48. Wallace, "Survey of Federal Legislation Affecting Private Home Financing Since 1932," pp. 481, 488.

49. Franklin D. Roosevelt, Letter to the Board of Directors of the United States Savings and Loan League. November 10, 1942.

50. Fred Wright, "The Effect of New Deal Real Estate Residential Finance and Foreclosure Policies Made in Response to the Real Estate Conditions of the Great Depression," pp. 231, 236.

51. Bosworth et al., *The Economics of Federal Credit Programs*, pp. 48–49.

52. Robert S. McElvaine, *Great Depression,* p. 162.

53. Public Law No. 73-479.

54. Federal Housing Administration, *The FHA Story*, p. 5.

55. Ibid., pp. 8–9.

56. Kerry D. Vandell, "FHA Restructuring Proposals: Alternatives and Implications."

57. David Listokin, "Federal Housing Policy and Preservation."

58. Reconstruction Finance Corporation, *Final Report of the Reconstruction Finance Corp.*

59. Alvin E. Coons and Bert T. Glaxe, *Housing Market Analysis and the Growth of Home Ownership,* p. 3.

60. Saul B. Klaman, *The Postwar Residential Mortgage Market,* p. 5.

61. Joseph L. Stevens, *Impact of Federal Legislation and Programs on Private Land in Urban and Metropolitan Development,* pp. 9–10.

62. Public Law No. 83-560 (1949).

63. Mason, *From Buildings and Loans to Bail-Outs,* pp. 133–134.

64. Anthony Pennington and Anthony M. Yezer, "The Federal Housing Administration and the New Millennium."

65. Jason T. Strickland, "The Proposed Revelatory Changes to Fannie Mae and Freddie Mac," pp. 267, 270.

66. Richard W. Bartke, "Fannie Mae and the Secondary Mortgage Market."

67. Danny W. Durning, *Mortgage Revenues Bonds, Housing Markets, Home Buyers and Public Policy,* p. 1.

68. Rachel G. Bratt et al., *Critical Perspectives on Housing,* p. 71.

69. Mason, *From Buildings and Loans to Bail-Outs,* p. 189.

70. Walter J. Woerheide, *The Savings and Loan Industry,* pp. 76–81.

71. Mason, *From Buildings and Loans to Bail-Outs,* pp. 190–191.

72. Ned Eichler, *The Thrift Debacle,* p. 112.

73 Kathleen Day, *S&L Hell.*

74. Kenneth H. Bacon, "As Deposit Insurance Dwindles, FDIC Wonders If It Should Start Running the Banks It Seizes," *Wall Street Journal,* December 31, 1990, p. 30.

Chapter 8

1. Stuart Taylor, Jr., and K.C. Johnson, *Until Proven Innocent.*

2. Paul N. Monnin and Joseph Burby, "Off the Chart."

3. *Berger v. United States,* 295 U.S. (1935), 78, 88.

4. This has long been a problem at the SEC. See Karmel, *Regulation by Prosecution.*

5. Eric Lichtblau, "In Justice Shift, Corporate Deals Replace Trials," *New York Times,* April 9, 2008, p. A1.

6. "Taxes and Income," *Wall Street Journal,* December 17, 2007, p. A20.

7. Karl Marx's theory that "societal deviations in terms of the distribution of wealth for example, must be minimized," proved to be a very bad idea that only led to the suffering and death of millions in the Soviet Union. Lennard J. Davis, "Constructing Normalcy."

8. Nassim Nicholas Taleb, *The Black Swan,* p. 28.

9. *Abood v. Detroit Board of Education,* 431 U.S. 209 (1977).

10. Thomas Frank, "Obama's Touch of Class," *Wall Street Journal,* April 21, 2008, p. A17.

Selected Bibliography

A Note on Sources

The *Wall Street Journal,* the *New York Times,* and the *Financial Times* (London) are the principal sources for market events, statistics, reports of indictments, prison sentences, and other contemporaneous events described in text. Numerous government, corporate, and other Web sites also provided a treasure trove of information. Space prevents citation to the thousands of articles and Web sites used as sources, but they are readily accessible by searching on LEXIS-NEXIS or Google.com. The following selected bibliography contains some of the other sources consulted.

Abood v. Detroit Board of Education, 431 U.S. 209 (1977).

Abrahamson v. Fleschner, 568 F.2d 862 (2d Cir. 1977).

Adams, James Ring. *The Big Fix: Inside the S&L Scandal: How an Unholy Alliance of Politics and Money Destroyed America's Banking System.* New York: John Wiley & Sons,1990.

Agreement Among PWG and U.S. Agency Principals on Principles and Guidelines Regarding Private Pools of Capital (February 22, 2007).

Ahamed, Liaquat. *Lord of Finance: The Bankers Who Broke the World.* New York: Penguin, 2009.

American Bank & Trust Co. v. Federal Reserve Bank of Atlanta, 262 U.S. 643 (1923).

American Federation of State, County & Municipal Employees, Employees Pension Plan v. American International Group, Inc., 462 F.3d 121 (2d Cir. 2006).

Anders, George. *Perfect Enough: Carly Fiorina and the Reinvention of Hewlett-Packard.* New York: Portfolio, 2003.

Anderson, Jenny. "Bank Leases to Hedge Funds Are Questioned." *New York Times,* January 2, 2007.

Arthur Andersen LLP v. United States, 544 U.S. 696 (2005).

Bacon, Kenneth H. "As Deposit Insurance Dwindles, FDIC Wonders If It Should Start Running the Banks It Seizes." *Wall Street Journal,* December 31, 1990.

Baker, James A., III, and Steve Fiffer. *Work Hard, Study . . . and Keep Out of Politics!* New York: G.P. Putnam's Sons, 2006.

Bank for International Settlements (BIS). Committee on the Global Financial System Working Group on Collateral. "Collateral in Wholesale Financial Markets: Recent Trends, Risk Management and Market Dynamics." March 2001.

———. Committee on Payment and Settlement Systems. "Core Principles for Systemically Important Payment Systems." January 2001.

———. Committee on Payment and Settlement Systems and Technical Committee of the International Organization of Securities Commissions. "Recommendations for Central Counterparties, Consultative Report." March 2004.

———. Committee on Payment and Settlement Systems of the Central Banks of the Group of 10 Countries. "Cross-Border Securities Settlements." March 1995.

———. "Cross-Border Collateral Arrangements." January 2006.

———. "Delivery Versus Payment in Securities Settlement Systems." September 1992.

———. "New Developments in Large-Value Payment Systems." May 2005.

———. "Progress in Reducing Foreign Exchange Settlement Risk." May 2008.

Barbash, Tom. *On Top of the World.* New York: HarperCollins, 2003.

Barboza, David. "In Chicago's Trading Pits, This May Be the Final Generation." *New York Times,* August 6, 2000.

Barrionuevo, Alexei, and Kurt Eichenwald. "The Enron Case That Almost Wasn't." *New York Times,* June 4, 2006.

Bartke, Richard W. "Fannie Mae and the Secondary Mortgage Market." *Northwestern University Law Review* 66 (1971):1.

Baruch, Hurd. *Wall Street Security Risk.* Washington, DC: Acropolis Books, 1971.

Basel Committee on Banking Regulations and Supervisory Practices. "International Convergence of Capital Measurement and Capital Standards." 1988.

Bd. of Trade v. Christie Grain & Stock Co., 198 U.S. 236 (1905), pp. 249–50.

Beard, Patricia. *Blue Blood and Mutiny, The Fight for the Soul of Morgan Stanley.* New York: William Morrow, 2007.

Bebchuk, Lucian Arye, and Yaniv Grinstein. "The Growth of Executive Pay." *Oxford Review of Economic Policy* 21 (2005): 283.

Beisner, Robert L. Dean Acheson. *A Life in the Cold War.* New York: Oxford University Press, 2006.

Benedict, Murray R. *Farm Policies of the United States, 1970–1950.* New York: Twentieth Century Fund, 1953.

Berger v. United States, 295 U.S. (1935), pp. 78, 88.

Bergman, Hannah. "Spitzer: OCC Is Blocking N.Y.'s Probe of Lenders." *American Banker,* May 19, 2005.

Berle, Adolf A., Jr., and Gardiner C. Means. *The Modern Corporation and Private Property.* Reprint. New York: Harcourt Brace World, 1968.

Berman, Andrew R. "Once a Mortgage, Always a Mortgage-B the Use (and Misuse of) Mezzanine Loans and a Preferred Equity Investments." *Stanford Journal of Law, Business and Finance* 11 (2005): 76.

Bernanke, Ben S. "Financial Regulation and the Invisible Hand." Remarks delivered at the New York University Law School, New York, April 11, 2007.

Bhagat, Sanjai, and Bernard Black. "The Uncertain Relationship Between Board Composition and Firm Performance." *Business Law* 54 (1999): 921, 923, 946.

Black, Conrad. *Franklin Delano Roosevelt, Champion of Freedom.* New York: PublicAffairs, 2003.

———. *A Life in Full, Richard M. Nixon.* New York: PublicAffairs, 2007.

Bloomberg, Michael R., and Charles E. Schumer. "Sustaining New York's and the US Global Financial Services Leadership." January 2007, available http://apostille.us/news/bloomberg-schumer_report_ny_in_danger_of_losing_status_as_world_financial_center_within_10_years_without_major_shift_in_regulation_and_policy.shtml.

Blustein, Paul. *The Chastening.* New York: PublicAffairs, 2001.

Board of Trade Clearing Corporation v. United States, 1978 U.S. Dist. LEXIS 20220 (D.D.C. 1978), p. 2.

Board of Trade of the City of Chicago v. SEC, 923 F.2d 1270 (7th Cir. 1991).

Bosworth, Barry P., et al. *The Economics of Federal Credit Programs.* Washington, DC: Brookings Institution Press, 1987.

Bower, Tom. *Outrageous Fortune: The Rise and Ruin of Conrad and Lady Black.* New York: HarperCollins, 2006.

Brandeis, Louis. *Other People's Money and How the Bankers Use It.* New York: Fredrick A. Stokes, 1914.

Bratt, Rachel G., et al. *Critical Perspectives on Housing.* Philadelphia: Temple University Press, 1986.

Brehm v. Eisner, 2006 Del. LEXIS 307 (Del. 2006).

Brewster, Mike. *Unaccountable: How the Accounting Profession Forfeited a Public Trust.* Hoboken, NJ: John Wiley and Sons, 2003.

Broome, Lissa L., and Jerry W. Markham. "Banking and Insurance: Before and After the Gramm-Leach-Bliley Act." *Iowa Journal of Corporation Law* 25 (2000): 723.

———. *Regulation of Banking Financial Service Activities, Cases and Materials.* Rochester, MN: West Group, 2008.

Bruner, Robert F., and Sean D. Carr. *The Panic of 1907, Lessons Learned from the Market's Perfect Storm.* New York: John Wiley & Sons, 2007.

Burkart, Ann M. "Lenders and Land." *Missouri Law Review* 64 (1999): 249.

Butkiewicz, James L. "The Impact of a Lender of Last Resort During the Great Depression: The Case of the Reconstruction Finance Corporation." *Exploration in Economic History* 32 (1995): 197–216.

Byron, Christopher. *Martha Inc.* New York: John Wiley and Sons, 2002.

Calavita, Kitty, Henry N. Pontell, and Robert H. Tillman. *Big Money Crime: Fraud and Politics in the Savings and Loan Crisis.* Berkeley: University of California Press, 1997.

Cannadine, David. *Mellon: An American Life.* New York: Vintage Books, 2006.

Carron, Andrew S. *The Plight of the Thrift Institutions.* Washington, DC: Brookings Institution Press, 1982.

Carrozzo, Peter M. "Marketing the American Mortgage: The Emergency Home Finance Act 1970, Standardization and the Secondary Market Revolution." *Real Estate Property Problems & Trial Journal* 39 (2004–2005): 765.

Cassidy, John. *Dot.com: The Greatest Story Ever Sold.* New York: HarperCollins, 2002.

CBOT v. SEC, 677 F.2d 1137 (7th Cir. 1982), *vacated as moot,* 459 U.S. 1026 (1983).

Certain Activities of Options Exchanges, In re, 2000 WL 1277616 (SEC 2000) (parallel charges by SEC).

CFTC. "Commodity and Equities: A Market of One?" December 19, 2007.

———. "Market Growth Trader Participation and Pricing in Energy Futures Markets." Com. Fut. L. Rep. (CCH) ¶30,451 (CFTC 2007).

———. Staff Report on Commodity Swap Dealers and Index Traders with Commission Recommendations. September 2008.

CFTC v. Amaranth Advisors, LLC, 2007 U.S. Dist. LEXIS 80978 (S.D.N.Y. 2007).

CFTC v. Delay, 2006 WL 3359076 (D. Neb. 2006).

CFTC v. Dunn, 519 U.S. 465 (1997).

CFTC v. Enron Corp., Comm. Fut. L. Rep. (CCH) ¶ 29,811 (S.D. Tex. 2004).

CFTC v. Savage, 611 F.2d 2d 270 (9th Cir. 1979).

CFTC v. Zelener, 373 F.3d 861 (7th Cir. 2004).

Chernow, Barbara Ann. *Robert Morris.* New York: Arno Press, 1978.

Chicago Board of Trade. *Commodity Trading Manual.* Chicago, 1982.

Chicago Board of Trade v. Olsen, 262 U.S. 839 (1923).

Clearstream International. "Cross-Border Equity Trading, Clearing & Settlement in Europe." White Paper, 2002.

CME v. SEC, 883 F.2d 537 (7th Cir. 1989), *cert. denied sub nom.*

Cole, Benjamin Mark. *The Pied Pipers of Wall Street.* Princeton: Bloomberg Press, 2001.

Committee on Capital Markets Regulation. "The Competitive Position of the U.S. Public Equity Markets." December 4, 2007.

Coons, Alvin E., and Bert T. Glaxe. *Housing Market Analysis and the Growth of Home Ownership.* Columbus: Ohio State University Press, 1963.

Covington, Howard E., Jr., and Marion A. Ellis. *The Story of NationsBank: Changing the Face of American Banking.* Chapel Hill: University of North Carolina Press, 1993.

Cronin, Mary J., ed. *Banking and Finance on the Internet.* New York: John Wiley and Sons, 1998.

CSX Corp. v. The Children's Investment Fund Management (UK) LLP, 2008 U.S. Dist. LEXIS 46039 (S.D.N.Y. 2008).

Dabit v. Merrill Lynch, Pierce, Fenner & Smith Inc., 395 F.3d 25 (2d Cir. 2005).

Dash, Eric. "Compensation Experts Offer Ways to Help Curb Executive Salaries." *New York Times,* December 30, 2006.

———. "Congress Is Urged to Hold Off Acting on Options and Pay." *New York Times,* September 7, 2006.

———. "Merrill Lynch Sells a $5 Billion Stake to a Singapore Firm." *New York Times,* December 25, 2007.

Davidoff, Steven. "Black Market Capital." *Columbia Business Law Review* (2008): 172, 176.

Davis, Bob. "Wanted: SWFs' Money Sans Politics." *Wall Street Journal,* December 20, 2007.

Davis, Lennard J. "Constructing Normalcy: The Bell Curve, the Novel, and the Invention of the Disabled Body in the Nineteenth Century." *Disability Studies Reader, Second Edition* (2006): 6.

Day, Kathleen. *S&L Hell, the People and the Politics Behind the $1 Trillion Savings and Loan Scandal.* New York: W.W. Norton, 1993.

Deangelis, John A. "Riches Do Not Last Forever: Real Estate Investment by National Banks." *University of Illinois Law Review* (1991): 777.

Dillon, Patrick, and Carl M. Cannon. *Circle of Greed.* New York: Crown Publishing Group, 2010.

Drucker, Jesse, and Mark Maremont. "CEOs of Bailed-Out Banks Flew to Resorts on Firm Jets." *Wall Street Journal,* June 19, 2009.

Duhigg, Charles. "Can Private Equity Build a Public Face?" *New York Times,* December 24, 2006.

Durning, Danny W. *Mortgage Revenues Bonds, Housing Markets, Home Buyers and Public Policy.* Boston: Kluwer Academic, 1992.

Eichenwald, Kurt. *Conspiracy of Fools: A True Story.* New York: Broadway Books, 2005.

Eichler, Ned. *The Thrift Debacle.* Berkeley: University of California Press, 1989.

Elkind, Peter. *Rough Justice: The Rise and Fall of Eliot Spitzer.* New York: Penguin Group, 2010.

Ellickson, Robert C. Mason. "Ancient Land Law: Mesopotamia, Egypt, Israel." *Chicago-Kent Law Review* 71 (1995): 321.

Ellis, Charles D. *The Partnership: The Making of Goldman Sachs.* New York: Penguin, 2008.

Ely, James W., Jr. *The Guardian of Every Other Right, A Constitutional History of Property Rights.* Oxford: Oxford University Press, 2008.

Endlich, Lisa. *Goldman Sachs: The Culture of Success.* New York: Alfred K. Knopf, 1999.

———. *Optical Illusions: Lucent and the Crash of Telecom.* New York: Simon and Schuster, 2004.

Enron Corp., In re, 2003 U.S. Dist. LEXIS 7632 (S.D. Texas).

Ervin, Susan C. "Letting Go: The CFTC Rethinks Managed Futures Regulation." *Futures & Derivatives Law Report* 24 (2004): 1.

Fabritius, M. Manfred, and William Borges. *Saving the Savings and Loan: The U.S. Thrift Industry and the Texas Experience, 1950–1988.* New York: Praeger, 1989.

Fannie Mae. *Housing Matters: Issues in American Housing Policy.* Washington, DC, 2004.

Farrell, Greg. "The Enron Whistle-Blower Who Wasn't." *USA Today,* October 12, 2007.

Federal Housing Administration. *The FHA Story in Summary (1934–1959).* Washington, DC, 1959.

Federal Trade Commission. "Report on the Grain Trade." 1921.

FERC. "Price Manipulation in Western Markets," Staff Report, Doc. No. PA02-2-000. March 26, 2003.

Ferguson, Niall. *The Ascent of Money: A Financial History of the World.* New York: Penguin, 2008.

Final Report of the Select Committee to Investigate Bondholder Reorganizations. Washington, DC: U.S. Government Printing Office, May 16, 1938.

Financial Planning Association v. SEC, 482 F.3d 481 (D.C. Cir. 2007).

Financial Services Roundtable. "The Blueprint for U.S. Financial Competitiveness" (Introductory Message). 2007.

First National Bank of Bellaire v. Comptroller of the Currency, 697 F.2d 674 (5th Cir. 1983).

Fischel, Daniel. *Payback: The Conspiracy to Destroy Michael Milken and His Financial Revolution.* New York: HarperBusiness, 1995.

Flanagan, William G. *Dirty Rotten CEOs: How Business Leaders Are Fleecing America.* New York: Citadel Press, 2004.

Fox, Loren. *Enron: The Rise and Fall.* Hoboken, NJ: John Wiley and Sons, 2003.

Fraser-Sampson, Guy. *Private Equity as an Asset Class.* New York: John Wiley and Sons, 2007.

Freidel, Frank. *Franklin D. Roosevelt, A Rendezvous with Destiny.* Boston: Little, Brown, 1990.

GAO. "Commodity Futures Trading Commission: Trends in Energy Derivatives Markets Raise Questions About CFTC's Oversight." October 19, 2007.

Gasparino, Charles. *Blood on the Street.* New York: Free Press, 2005.

———. *King of the Club: Richard Grasso and the Survival of the New York Stock Exchange.* New York: Collins, 2007.

Giovannini Group. *Cross-Border Clearing and Settlement Arrangements in the European Union.* November 2001.

Gilder, George. *Telecosm.* New York: Free Press, 2000.

Gilson, Ronald J. "Engineering a Venture Capital Market: Lessons Learned from the American Experience." *Stanford Law Review* 55 (2003): 1067.

Goldstein v. SEC, 451 F.3d 873 (D.C. Cir. 2006).

Gompers, Paul A. "The Rise and Fall of Venture Capital." Newcomen Prize Essay. Graduate School of Business, University of Chicago, 1994.

Grant, James. *Mr. Market Miscalculates, The Bubble Years and Beyond.* Mount Jackson, VA: AXIOS Press, 2008.

Grebler, Leo, et al. *Capital Formation and Residential Real Estate, Trends and Prospects.* New York: National Bureau of Economic Research, 1956.

Gredd v. Bear Stearns Securities Corp. (S.D.N.Y. December 17, 2007).

Greenspan, Alan. Remarks delivered before the Futures Industry Annual Conference, Boca Raton, Florida, March 14, 2007, reprinted in *Commodity Futures Law Reporter,* no. 782, March 23, 2007.

Greider, William. *Secrets of the Temple: How the Federal Reserve Runs the Country.* London: Simon and Schuster, 1987.

Guerrera, Francesco. "Welch Condemns Share Price Focus." *Financial Times,* March 13, 2009.

Hamilton, Robert W. "Corporate Governance in America 1950–2000: Major Changes But Uncertain Benefits." *Iowa Journal of Corporate Law* 25 (2000): 349.

Hays, Kristen. "Law Firm Seeks $688 Million for Enron Work; Request to Be Taken Up at February Hearing." *Houston Chronicle,* January 8, 2008.

Hector, Gary. *Breaking the Bank: The Decline of BankAmerica.* Boston: Little, Brown, 1988.

Heller v. Boylan, 29 N.Y.S.2d 653, 669 (Sup.), *aff'd,* 32 N.Y.S.2d 131 (App. Div. 1st Dept. 1941).

Hill v. Wallace, 259 U.S. 44 (1922).

Horn, Frederick F., and Victor W. Farah. *Trading in Commodity Futures.* New York: New York Institute of Finance, 1979.

Hsu, David. "Organizing Venture Capital: The Rise and Demise of American Research & Development Corporation, 1946–1973." Wharton School Working Paper no. 163. December 2004.

Hubbard v. Lowe, 226 F. 135 (S.D.N.Y. 1915).

Hunter v. Federal Energy Regulatory Commission, Comm. Fut. L. Rep. (CCH) ¶30,744 (D.D.C. 2007).

Hurdle, Steven E., Jr. "A Blow to Public Investing: Reforming the System of Private Equity Fund Disclosures." *UCLA Law Review* 53 (2005): 239.

Interagency Task Force on Commodity Markets. "Interim Report on Crude Oil." July 7, 2008.

Interim Report of the Committee on Capital Markets Regulation. November 30, 2006.

Investment Company Institute v. SEC, 496 U.S. 936 (1990).

Jackson, Tim. *Inside Intel: Andy Grove and the Rise of the World's Most Powerful Chip Company.* New York: Dutton, 1997.

Jeter, Lynne W. *Disconnected: Deceit and Betrayal at WorldCom.* Hoboken, NJ: John Wiley and Sons, 2003.

Johnson, Jo, and Martine Orange. *The Man Who Tried to Buy the World: Jean-Marie Messier and Vivendi Universal.* New York: Portfolio, 2003.

Joint Audit Committee Operating Agreement. *Commodity Futures Law Reporter* (CCH) ¶30,908 (September 11, 2008).

Kahaner, Larry. *On the Line.* New York: Warner Books, 1986.

Karmel, Roberta. *Regulation by Prosecution: Securities and Exchange Commission Versus Corporate America.* New York, Simon & Schuster, 1982.

Karmel, Roberta S. "Regulation by Exemption: The Changing Definition of Accredited Investor." *Rutgers Law Journal* 39 (2008): 681.

Keller, Morton. *The Life Insurance Enterprise, 1885–1910.* Cambridge, MA: Belknap Press, 1963.

Kemmerer, Donald L. "The Colonial Loan Office System in New Jersey." *Journal of Political Economy* 47 (December 1939): 867

———. "The Colonial Loan Office System in New Jersey." 74th Proceeding of the New Jersey Historical Society, April 1956.

Kennedy, David M. *Freedom from Fear: The American People in Depression and War, 1929–1945.* New York: Oxford University Press, 1999.

Kindleberger, Charles P. *The World in Depression, 1929–1939.* Berkeley: University of California Press, 1973.

Klaman, Joseph L. *The Postwar Residential Mortgage Market.* Princeton: National Bureau of Economic Research, 1961.

Leuchtenburg, William E. *Franklin D. Roosevelt and the New Deal.* New York: Harper & Row, 1965.

Levitt, Arthur. "The Future of Our Markets: Dynamic Markets, Timeless Principles." *Columbia Business Law Review* 1 (2000):

———. *Take on the Street: What Wall Street and Corporate America Don't Want You to Know.* New York: Pantheon, 2004.

Lichtblau, Eric. "In Justice Shift, Corporate Deals Replace Trials." *New York Times,* April 9, 2008.

Lilienthal, David, and Robert H. Marquis. "The Conduct of Business Enterprises by the Federal Government." *Harvard Law Review* 54 (1941): 545.

Listokin, David. "Federal Housing Policy and Preservation: Historical Evolution, Patterns and Implications." *Housing Policy Debate* 2 (1991): 152.

Long, Robert Emmet, ed. *Banking Scandals: The S&LS and BCCI.* New York: H.W. Wilson, 1993.

"Loose Talk, What Stars Said This Week." *US Magazine,* June 8, 2009.

Louisville Joint Stock Land Bank v. Radford, 295 U.S. 555 (1935).

Lowenfels, Lewis D., and Alan R. Bromberg. "SEC Actions Against Lawyers Post Sarbanes-Oxley: A Reasoned Approach or an Assault Upon the Practicing Bar." *Securities and Regulation Law Report* 41 (2009): 1739.

Lowenstein, Roger. *Buffett: The Making of an American Capitalist.* New York: Random House, 2005.

———. *When Genius Failed: The Rise and Fall of Long-Term Capital Management.* New York: Random House, 2000.

Lowy, Martin. *High Rollers: Inside the Savings and Loan Debacle.* New York: Praeger, 1991.

Lublin, Joann. "A Quiet Response to 'Say-On-Pay' Measures." *Wall Street Journal,* May 18, 2009.

Lublin, Joann, and Scott Thurm. "Behind Soaring Executive Pay, Decades of Failed Restraints." *Wall Street Journal,* October 12, 2006.

Malik, Om. *Broadbandits.* Hoboken, NJ: John Wiley and Sons, 2003.

Mallaby, Sebastian. *The World's Banker.* New York: Penguin, 2004.

Manhattan Investment Ltd., In re, 2007 WL 4440360 (S.D.N.Y. 2007).

Markham, Jerry. "Glass-Steagall v. Gramm-Leach-Bliley—A Test Match on the Bankers." *University of Pennsylvania Law and Business Journal* 4 (2010) 12.

———. "Excessive Executive Compensation—Why Bother?" *Maryland Journal of Business & Technology Law* 2 (2008): 1001.

———. "How the Feds Stacked the Deck Against Enron." *Chicago Sun Times,* May 7, 2006.

———. "The Manipulation of Commodity Futures Prices—The Unprosecutable Crime." *Yale Journal on Regulation* 8 (1991): 281.

———. "Mutual Fund Scandals—A Comparative Analysis of the Role of Corporate Governance in the Regulation of Collective Investments." *Hastings Business Law Journal* 3 (2006): 67.

Markham, Jerry, and Daniel Harty. "For Whom the Bell Tolls: The Demise of Exchange Trading Floors and the Growth of ECNS." *Journal of Corporate Law* 33 (2008) 865.

Markham, Jerry, and Lawrence Hunt. "The California Energy Crisis—Enron's Gaming of Governor Gray's Imperfect Market." *Futures and Derivatives Law Report* 24 (2004): 1.

Marshall, John F., and Michael E. Ellis. *Investment Banking and Brokerage.* New York: McGraw-Hill, 1993.

Marshall, Matt. *The Bank.* London: Random House, 1999.

Martin, Dick. *Tough Calls.* New York: AMACOM, 2005.

Martin, William McChesney, Jr. *The Securities Markets 3.* New York: New York Stock Exchange, 1971.

Mason, Christopher. *The Art of the Steal.* New York: G.P. Putnam's Sons, 2004.

Mason, David L. *From Buildings and Loans to Bail-Outs: A History of the American Savings and Loan Industry, 1831–1995.* Cambridge: Cambridge University Press, 2004.

Mason, Joseph R. "Do Lender of Last Resort Policies Matter? The Effects of Reconstruction Finance Corporation Assistance to Banks During the Great Depression." *Journal of Financial Services Research* 20 (2001): 77–95.

Masters, Brooke A. *Spoiling for a Fight.* New York: Henry Holt, 2006.

Mayer, Martin. *The Greatest-Ever Bank Robbery: The Collapse of the Savings and Loan Industry.* New York: Charles Scribner's Sons, 1990.

McElvaine, Robert S. *Great Depression, America, 1929–1941.* New York: Times Books, 1961.

McGinn, Daniel. *House Lust: America's Obsession with Our Homes.* New York: Doubleday, 2008.

McLean, Bethany, and Peter Elkind. *The Smartest Guys in the Room: The Amazing Rise and Scandalous Fall of Enron.* New York: Portfolio, 2003.

McNish, Jacquie, and Sinclair Stewart. *The Fall of Conrad Black.* New York: Overlook Press, 2004.

Melamed, Leo. "Futures Markets in the Digital Century." Address delivered before the Derivatives and Risk Expo, New York, May 11–12, 1999.

———. "The Mechanics of a Commodity Futures Exchange: A Critique of Automation of the Transaction Process." *Hofstra Law Review* 6 (1977): 149.

Meltzer, Allan H. *The History of the Federal Reserve.* Chicago: University of Chicago Press, 2003.

Michaelson, Adam. *The Foreclosure of America.* New York: Berkley Books, 2009.

Miklas, In re, Comm. Fut. L. Rep. (CCH) ¶30,818 (CFTC 2008).

Molinari, Steven L., and Nelson Kibler. "Broker-Dealers' Financial Responsibility Under the Uniform Net Capital Rule—A Case for Liquidity." *Georgetown Law Review* 72 (1983): 1.

Monnin, Paul N., and Joseph Burby. "Off the Chart: The U.S. Sentencing Guidelines Become Increasingly Irrelevant in the Wake of the Market Meltdown." *Securities Regulation and Law Reporter* 41 (2009): 821.

Morgan, Sue, et al. *Executive Compensation Disclosure Handbook: A Practical Guide to the SEC's New Rules*, Thomson-West 2006.

Morris, Robert. *The Papers of Robert Morris, 1781–1784, Vol. 8.* Pittsburgh: University of Pittsburgh Press, 1995.

Munk, Nina. *Fools Rush In: Steve Case, Jerry Levin and the Unmaking of AOL Time Warner.* New York: HarperCollins, 2004.

New England Healthcare Employees Pension Fund v. Woodruff, 2008 U.S. App. LEXIS 954 (10th Cir. 2008).

New York Mercantile Exchange, Inc., v. IntercontinentalExchange, Inc., Comm. Fut. L. Rep. (CCH) ¶30,597 (2d. Cir. 2007).

Ng, Serena. "Tracking the Numbers—Street Sleuth—Filing Footnote: This Insider Sale Helps Hedge Bets." *Wall Street Journal,* May 15, 2006.

Nocera, Joe. "Serving Time But Lacking Remorse." *New York Times,* June 7, 2008.

———. "The Story That I Have to Tell." *New York Times Magazine,* January 4, 2009.

Office of New York State Attorney General Eliot Spitzer. "State Investigation Reveals Mutual Fund Fraud." Press Release. September 3, 2003.

Olson, James Stuart. *Herbert Hoover and the Reconstruction Finance Corporation, 1931–1933.* Ames: Iowa State University Press, 1977.

Osterle, Dale A. "Regulation NMS: Has the SEC Exceeded Its Congressional Mandate to Facilitate a 'National Market System' in Securities?" *New York Journal of Law and Business* 1 (2005): 613.

Pandit, Vikram. "Toward a Transparent Financial System." *Wall Street Journal,* June 27, 2008.

Parmet, Herbert S. *George Bush, The Life of a Lone Star Yankee.* Piscataway, NJ: Transaction, 2000.

Payments Risk Committee. "Global Payment Liquidity: Private Sector Solutions." New York. October 2005.

Pennington, Anthony, and Anthony M. Yezer. "The Federal Housing Administration and the New Millennium." *Journal of Housing Research* 11 (2000): 357.

Phalippou, Ludovic, and Oliver Gottschalg. "The Performance of Private Equity Funds." University of Amsterdam and HEC Paris, 2007.

Pilzer, Paul Zane, with Robert Deitz. *Other People's Money: The Inside Story of the S&L Mess.* New York: Simon and Schuster, 1989.

Pizzo, Stephen, Mary Fricker, and Paul Muolo. *Inside Job: The Looting of America's Savings and Loans.* New York: McGraw-Hill, 1989.

Poteat, J. Douglas. "State Legislative Relief for the Mortgage Debtor During the Depression." *Law and Contemporary Problems* 5 (1938) 517.

Powell, Jim. *FDR's Folly.* New York: Three Rivers Press, 2003.

Reconstruction Finance Corporation. *Final Report of the Reconstruction Finance Corp.* Washington, DC: Government Printing Office, 1959.

Regents of the University of California v. Credit Suisse First Boston (USA) Inc., 482 F.3d 372 (5th Cir. 2007).

Reid, Jeanne L. "Choosing Tactics in the War Against Risk." *Money* 17 (September 1988): 83.

Report of the Moreland Commissioner. Albany, New York. October 5, 1934.

Report of the Presidential Task Force on Market Mechanisms. January 12, 1988.

Roane, Kit. "The New Face of Capitalism." *U.S. News and World Report,* December 4, 2006.

Rogers v. Hill, 289 U.S. 582 (1933).

Rogers, William P., and Jerry W. Markham. "The Application of West German Statutes to United States Commodity Futures Contracts: An Unnecessary Clash of Policies." *Georgetown Journal of Law and Policy In International Business* 19 (1987): 273–324.

Sampson, Anthony. *The Money Lenders.* London: Hodder and Soughton, 1981.

Schilit, Howard. *Financial Shenanigans.* New York: McGraw-Hill, 2002.

Scholz, Susan. *The Changing Nature and Consequences of Public Company Financial Restatements, 1997–2006.* Washington, DC: Department of the Treasury, 2008.

Schumer, Charles E., and Michael R. Bloomberg. "To Save New York, Learn from London." *Wall Street Journal,* November 1, 2006.

Scism, Leslie. "Life Insurers Enjoy Relaxed Disclosure Rules." *Wall Street Journal,* February 17, 2008.

SEC v. Johnson, Civ. No. 05-36 (D.D.C. December 5, 2007).

SEC v. Pimco Advisors Fund Management, LLC, 341 F. Supp.2d 454 (S.D.N.Y. 2004).

SEC v. Tambone, 417 F. Supp.2d 127 (D. Mass. 2006).

SEC v. Yuen, 401 F.3d 1031 (9th Cir. 2005).

Securities and Exchange Commission. "Report of the Special Study of the Securities Markets." H.R. Doc. No. 95, 88th Cong., 1st sess. (1963).

———. Securities Exchange Act Release No. 34-54255, July 31, 2006.

———. "Special Study of the Securities Markets." H.R. Doc. No. 95, pt. 1 (1963).

———. "Study of Unsafe and Unsound Practices of Brokers and Dealers." H.R. Doc. No. 92-231, 92d Cong., 2d sess. 13 (1971).

Seidman, L. William. *Full Faith and Credit: The Great S&L Debacle and Other Washington Sagas.* New York: Times Books, 1993.

Shanker, Morris G. "Will Mortgage Law Survive?" *Case Western Law Review* 54 (2003): 69.

Skilton, Robert H. "Developments in Mortgage Law and Practice." *Temple University Law Quarterly* 17 (1942–1943): 315.

Smith, Randall. *The Prince of Silicon Valley*. New York: St. Martin's Press, 2009

Smith, Rebecca, and John R. Emshwiller. *24 Days: How Two Wall Street Journal Reporters Uncovered the Lies That Destroyed Faith in Corporate America*. New York: Harper Business, 2003.

Snowden, Kenneth H. "The Anatomy of a Residential Mortgage Crisis: A Look Back to the 1930s." Paper presented at the Panic of 2008 conference, George Washington University Law School, April 3–4, 2009.

———. "What Can History Tell Us About the Crisis in Mortgage Securitizations?" *Financial History Magazine* (Winter 2003).

Solomon, Deborah. "Treasury's Paulson Warns of the Costs of Rules Overlap." *Wall Street Journal,* November 21, 2006.

"Sovereign Impunity." *Wall Street Journal,* December 1–2, 2007.

Spiegal, John, Alan Gart, and Steven Gart. *Banking Redefined*. Chicago: Irwin Professional, 1996.

Squires, Susan E., Cynthia J. Smith, Lorna McDougall, and William R. Yeack. *Inside Arthur Andersen: Shifting Values, Unexpected Consequences*. New York: Prentice Hall, 2003.

Stanton, Thomas H. "Federal Supervision of Safety and Soundness of Government-Sponsored Enterprises." *Administrative Law Journal* 4 (1991): 395.

Stevens, Joseph L. *Impact of Federal Legislation and Programs on Private Land in Urban and Metropolitan Development*. New York: Praeger, 1973.

Stiles, T.J. *The First Tycoon*. New York: Vintage Books, 2009.

Stone, Thomas S. "Mortgage Moratoria." *Wisconsin Law Review* 11 (1935–1936): 203.

Stoneridge Investment Partners LLC v. Scientific–Atlanta, Inc., 2008 U.S. LEXIS 1091 (2008).

"The Story of Mortgage Law." *Harvard Law Review* 4 (1890–1891): 1.

Strickland, Jason T. "The Proposed Revelatory Changes to Fannie Mae and Freddie Mac: An Analysis." *North Carolina Banking Institute* 8 (2004): 267.

Strong Capital Management, In re, SEC Investment Advisers Act Release No. 40-26448 (May 20, 2004).

Stuart, Guy. *Discriminating Risk: The U.S. Mortgage Lending Industry in the Twentieth Century*. Ithaca: Cornell University Press, 2003.

Swan, Edward J., ed. *Derivative Instruments*. London: Graham and Trotman, 1994.

Swartz, Mimi, and Sherron Watkins. *Power Failure: The Inside Story of the Collapse at Enron*. New York: Doubleday, 2003.

Sweeny, James L. *The California Electricity Crisis*. Stanford, CA: Hoover Institution Press, 2002.

Tabb Group. "US Equity Market Structure: Driving Change in Global Financial Markets," www.tabbgroup.com/Page.aspx?MenuID=13&ParentMenuID=2&PageID=8/, March 2008.

Taleb, Nassim Nicholas. *The Black Swan: The Impact of the Highly Improbable*. New York: Random House, 2007.

Tarring, Trevor, and Peter Robbins, ed. *Trading in Metals*. New York: Metal Bulletin, 1983.

Taylor, Stuart, Jr., and K.C. Johnson. *Until Proven Innocent: Political Correctness and the Shameful Injustices of the Duke Lacrosse Rape Case*. New York: St. Martin's Press, 2007.

Toffler, Barbara Ley, and Jennifer Reingold. *Final Accounting*. New York: Broadway Books, 2003.

Truell, Peter, and Larry Gurwin. *False Profits*. Boston: Houghton Mifflin, 1992.

United States House of Representatives. Report of the Committee Appointed Pursuant to House Resolutions 429 and 504 to Investigate the Concentration of Control of Money and Credit, H.R. Rep. No. 1593, 62d Cong., 3d sess. 37 (1913).

United States League of Savings Associations. *'74 Savings & Loan Fact Book*. Chicago: United States League of Savings Associations, 1974.

United States Senate. *Congressional Record,* 74th Cong., 2d sess. 7858 (May 25, 1936).

U.S. Chamber of Commerce. Commission on the Regulation of U.S. Capital Markets in the 21st Century. "Report and Recommendations." March 2007.

U.S. Chamber of Commerce v. SEC, 412 F.3d 133 (D.C. Cir. 2005).

U.S. Chamber of Commerce v. SEC, 443 F.3d 890 (D.C. Cir. 2006).

U.S. Congress. Office of Technology Assessment. "Electronic Bulls and Bears." U.S. Securities Market and Information Technology. September 1990.

————. Senate Permanent Subcommittee on Investigations of the Committee on Homeland Security and Governmental Affairs. "Excessive Speculation in the Natural Gas Market." 110th Cong., 1st sess., 2007.

————. Temporary National Economic Committee. "Investigation of Concentration of Economic Power." 76th Cong., 3d sess., Monograph no. 28. Washington, DC: GPO, 1940.

U.S. Department of the Treasury. *Blueprint for a Modernized Financial Regulatory Structure.* March 2008.

United States v. American Stock Exchange, LLC, 2000 WL 33400154 (D.D.C. September 11, 2000).

United States v. Brown, 459 F.3d 509 (5th Cir. 2006).

United States v. Brown, No. 08-20038 (5th Cir. 2009).

United States v. Ebbers, 458 F.3d 110 (2d Cir. 2006).

United States v. Forbes, 249 Fed. Appx. 233 (2d cir. 2007).

United States v. Howard, 2008 U.S. App. LEXIS 3100 (5th Cir. February 12, 2008).

United States v. Lake, 472 F.3d 1247, 1259 (10th Cir. 2007).

United States v. McElhaney, 469 F.3d 382 (5th Cir. 2006).

United States v. National Association of Securities Dealers, 422 U.S. 694 (1975), p. 707.

United States v. Olis, 429 F.3d 540 (5th Cir. 2005).

United States v. Quattrone, 441 F.3d 153 (2d Cir. 2006).

United States v. Skilling, 2006 U.S. Dist. LEXIS 42664 (S.D. Tex. 2006).

United States v. Skilling, 06-20885, Opening Brief of Appellant (5th Cir. September 14, 2007).

United States v. South-Eastern Underwriters Ass'n, 322 U.S. 533 (1944).

United States v. Stein, 435 F. Supp.2d 330 (S.D.N.Y. 2006).

United States v. Stein, 440 F. Supp.2d 315 (S.D.N.Y. 2006).

United States v. Stringer, 408 F. Supp.2d 1083 (D. Ore. 2006).

United States v. Stringer, F.3d (9th Cir. 2008).

United States v. Valencia, 2006 WL 3716657 (S.D. Tex. 2006).

Van Antwerp, W.C. *The Stock Exchange from Within.* London: Effingham Wilson, 1913.

Vandell, Kerry D. "FHA Restructuring Proposals: Alternatives and Implications." *Housing Policy Debate* 6 (1995): 299.

Van Smith, M. "The Commodity Futures Commission and the Return of the Bucketeers: A Lesson in Regulatory Failure." *Notre Dame Law Review* 57 (1981): 7.

Ver Steeg, Clarence L. *Robert Morris: Revolutionary Financier.* New York: Octagon Books, 1976.

Wallace, E.S. "Survey of Federal Legislation Affecting Private Home Financing Since 1932." *Law and Contemporary Problems* 5 (1938): 481.

Wallison, Peter J. "Capital Punishment." *Wall Street Journal,* November 4, 2006.

Wallison, Peter J., and Robert E. Litan. *Competitive Equity, A Better Way to Organize Mutual Funds.* Washington, DC: AEI Press, 2007.

Ward, David. "Protecting Mutual Funds from Market-Timing Profiteers: Forward Pricing International Fund Shares." *Hastings Law Journal 56* (2005): 585.

Washington, George T. "The Corporation Executive's Living Wage." *Harvard Law Review* 54 (1941): 733.

Weisman, Steven R. "Oil Producers See the World and Buy It Up." *New York Times,* November 28, 2007.

Western States Wholesale Natural Gas Litigation, In re, 408 F. Supp.2d 1055, 1057 (D. Nev. 2005), *reversed and remanded on other grounds,* 2007 U.S. App. LEXIS 22760 (9th Cir. 2007).

White, Lawrence J. *The S&L Debacle: Public Policy Lessons for Bank and Thrift Regulation.* New York: Oxford University Press, 1991.

"Who Makes What?" *TV Guide,* August 10–23, 2009.

Wilentz, Sean. *The Age of Reagan: A History, 1974–2008.* New York: HarperCollins, 2009.

Woerheide, Walter J. *The Savings and Loan Industry, Current Problems and Possible Solutions.* Westport, CT: Quorum Books, 1984.

Wolf, Martin. "Judicial Torture and the NatWest 3." *Financial Times,* November 30, 2007.

Wright, Fred. "The Effect of New Deal Real Estate Residential Finance and Foreclosure Policies Made in Response to the Real Estate Conditions of the Great Depression." *Alabama Law Review* 57 (2005): 231.

Yeager v. United States, 129 S. Ct. 2360 (2009).

Zaloom, Caitlin. *Out of the Pits.* Chicago: University of Chicago Press, 2006.

Zweig, Phillip L. *Belly Up: The Collapse of Penn Square Bank.* New York: Crown, 1985.

Name Index

Storage Technology, 251
Storm Cat, 338
Stotler Funds, 225
Strike System, 147
Strong Mutual Fund, 231
Strum, Donald, 66
Sullivan, Scott, 44-46
Sult, John R., 24
Sulzberger, A.G., 347
Sulzberger, Arthur, 346
Sulzberger, Arthur, Jr., 347
Sun-Times Media, 59
Sunbeam, 7
Super-DOT, 144
SuperMontage, 146, 149
Supervalu, 267
Susquehanna Company, 249
Sutherland, Kiefer, 337
S.W. Straus, 290
Swartz, Mark, 52
Swiss Stock Exchange, 215

T

Take-Two Interactive Software, 65, 111
Taleb, Nassim, 149, 180, 340
Tandem Computers, 253
Tarbell, Ida, 85
Targus Group International, 65
Task Force on Payment System Principles
    and Practices, 173
TCI, 263
Technical Committee of the International
    Organization of Securities Commissions
    (IOSCO), 166–167, 174, 199
Teitelbaum, Herbert, 74
Teixeira, Mark, 337
Teledyne, 252
Telerate, 146
Temasek Holdings, 278, 280
Temple, Nancy, 8–9
Texas Pacific Group (TPG), 257–258, 278
Thain, John, 151–152
Thomas H. Lee Partners, 275
Thomas Weisel Partners, 253
Thompson, Larry D., 6–7, 61
Thomson, James B., 227
Thomson, Todd, 114
Thornton, Grant, 57, 83
TIAA-CREF, 79
Tiger Management, 179, 231
Time, 94
Times Mirror, 348
Timothy Plan, 118
Title Guarantee & Trust Company, 289
TONTO System, 147
Tops, 56

Torkelsen, John, 133–134
Tokyo Stock Exchange, 152
Toronto Stock Exchange, 148
Toronto Teachers Pension Plan, 245
Toronto-Dominion Bank, 34
Tottenham Benefit Bank, 283
Toyota Motor Co., 129
TPG Capital, 276
TRACE, 149
Tradewinds International II, 246
Trading System, 147
Transylvania Company, 249
Treacy, James J., 111
Tribune Company, 345, 348
Trinkle, Tina, 11
Trotsen, Robert, 248
Trout Trading, 247
Tullos, Nancy, 110
Turquoise, 147
TXU, 257, 276
Tyco International, 51–53, 113, 129, 133

U

U2, 114
UBS, 34, 56, 63–64, 154, 174, 229, 272,
    277, 278
UBS Fund Service, 247
UBS Warburg, 200
UBSWenergy.com, 200
Unicredit, 57
Union for Textile and Hospitality Industry
    Workers, 123
Union Network International, 264
Union Pacific, 285
United Airlines, 323
United Brotherhood of Carpenters and
    Joiners of America, 122
United States Futures Exchange (USFE),
    217
United States Housing Corporation, 294
United States League of Local Building and
    Loan Associations, 286, 300
United Technologies, 103, 113
UnitedHealth Group, 106, 108
University of Texas Investment Management
    Company, 264
U.S. Chamber of Commerce, 81, 123, 240,
    299
U.S. Food Service, 276
U.S. Mortgage Company, 285
U.S. Steel, 87

V

VA Linux, 253
Valdez, 128

Subject Index

About the Author

Jerry W. Markham is a professor of law at Florida International University at Miami, where he teaches corporate and international business law. He was previously a partner in the international law firm of Rogers & Wells (now Clifford Chance), chief counsel for the Division of Enforcement of the U.S. Commodity Futures Trading Commission, secretary and counsel for the Chicago Board Options Exchange, and attorney in the Office of General Counsel at the U.S. Securities and Exchange Commission. Markham taught as an adjunct professor of law at the Georgetown Law School in Washington, DC, and was a professor of law at the University of North Carolina at Chapel Hill before moving to Florida. He holds law degrees from Georgetown and the University of Kentucky. Markham is the author of the three-volume series *A Financial History of the United States,* published by M.E. Sharpe and selected as a *Choice* Outstanding Academic Title for 2002. He also wrote a follow-on volume to that history covering the Enron-era scandals. Markham is the author and coauthor of several other books and articles on finance-related matters.